When Our Eyes No Longer See

Realism, Science, and Ecology in Japanese Literary Modernism

Harvard East Asian Monographs 296

When Our Eyes No Longer See

Realism, Science, and Ecology in Japanese Literary Modernism

Gregory Golley

Published by the Harvard University Asia Center
and distributed by Harvard University Press
Cambridge (Massachusetts) and London, 2008

Printed in the United States of America

The Harvard University Asia Center publishes a monograph series and, in coordination with the Fairbank Center for Chinese Studies, the Korea Institute, the Reischauer Institute of Japanese Studies, and other faculties and institutes, administers research projects designed to further scholarly understanding of China, Japan, Vietnam, Korea, and other Asian countries. The Center also sponsors projects addressing multidisciplinary and regional issues in Asia.

Library of Congress Cataloging-in-Publication Data

Golley, Gregory, 1964–
When our eyes no longer see : realism, science, and ecology in Japanese literary modernism / Gregory Golly.
p. cm. -- (Harvard East Asian monographs ; 296)
Includes bibliographical references and index.
ISBN 978-0-674-02794-7 (cloth : alk. paper)
1. Japanese literature--20th century--History and criticism. 2. Modernism (Literature)--Japan. I. Title.
PL726.55 G58 2008
895.6'112–dc22

2007043144

Index by Aiko Kojima

♾ Printed on acid-free paper

Last figure below indicates year of this printing

18 17 16 15 14 13 12 11 10 09 08

To my parents

Acknowledgments

Many people and institutions helped me write this book. Parts of Chapters 1 and 2 rely on research I undertook while writing my dissertation at UCLA. I thank the members of my dissertation committee—Michael Bourdaghs, Henry Em, Theodore Huters, and Herman Ooms—for their help and support during that time. I owe a special thanks to my dissertation advisor, Leslie Pincus, whose friendship and kindness have been constant over the years. I am especially indebted as well to Herman Ooms for the guidance he gave me during my time at UCLA. Professor Ooms always showed equal patience toward all of his students. I came to understand this as a disciplined and principled professional stance, which I have tried to emulate.

I learned how to read literature from Komori Yōichi who served as my advisor while I studied as a research student at the University of Tokyo, supported by a fellowship from Japan's Ministry of Education (Monbushō). Over a thousand cigarettes (his) and several hundred cups of coffee, Professor Komori guided me through the modern masterpieces of Japanese literature, demonstrating with his attention to detail together with the breadth of his ethical imagination how literary scholarship might concern itself with the struggle for social justice. His example instilled in me the belief that teachers of literature too must work to improve the world.

The bulk of the research for this book was undertaken with the support of a generous fellowship from the Japan Society for the Promotion of Science between 2002 and 2003. I thank Mita Munesuke for sponsoring me during that research year in Tokyo and for reading through several of the manuscript chapters in their most primitive stages. I also want to thank Satō Tsukasa and Fusako for opening their home to me during my many trips to Morioka that same year while I was researching Miyazawa Kenji.

I owe thanks to Norma Field for her intellectual companionship during my time at the University of Chicago, for reading and rereading the entire manuscript, for offering advice and encouragement, but mostly for continuing against all odds to care about ideas as if they were living and breathing entities—which they are, as I came to find out. I thank Julia Adeney Thomas for her advice about improving the work, and for her infectious enthusiasm. Kevin Doak and Tom Gunning wrote on my behalf at crucial points in the process. Michael Raine spent many evenings discussing with me movies (he calls them "films") and the meaning of modernity. Bill Sibley provided a standard of wit and erudition that I could only hope weakly to imitate. Takeshi Oka, astrophysicist at the University of Chicago, kindly checked through my discussions of relativity and quantum mechanics. Peter Galison generously read and commented upon parts of the manuscript's penultimate draft. Carol Hennessy always dropped everything to help me out whenever I was in an administrative jam. Environmental attorney and teacher Rodger Field, a great friend and wise counselor, provided the basics for my first crash course in environmental ethics. He is teaching me still.

I could not have completed this book without the support of the Franke Institute for the Humanities at the University of Chicago, which gave me time away from teaching to write during the 2005–2006 academic year. I thank my colleagues at the Franke Institute for their interest in my work, but I owe a special thanks to Jim Chandler's incisive red pen, which scrawled its way through many of the manuscript's pages with the characteristic acumen of its owner.

A number of graduate and undergraduate students helped me work out the ideas contained in this book in the course of classes and seminars. They include Nick Albertson, Xavier Bensky, Emily Chung, Mika Endo, Shawn Fetty, Alisa Freedman, Matthew Jong, Jae-Yon Lee, Miho Matsugu, Chris Oakes, Madeleine Schmidt, Amanda Seaman, George Sipos, Robert Stolz, Mamiko Suzuki, Katy Tanaka, Dennis Yee, Ryan Yokota, Mike Yong, and Yijiang Zhang. Aiko Kojima compiled the index and provided invaluable assistance in preparing the manuscript for publication.

I continue to be astonished by and grateful for the patience and care displayed by the two anonymous readers for the Harvard University Asia Center, whose advice and comments have surely improved this book. To William M. Hammell, editor, I offer my thanks for seeing value in this project when it still wore the dumb, pleading look of an unpublished manuscript, and for all his intelligent help along the way. I must also acknowledge an indefinable debt to Steve Anderson, Kenny Bender, and Donald Nagai for thirty-odd years of friendship without which this book somehow could not have been written. My sisters, Elisa Pirrone and Cindy Mecate, helped too, along with their families, with frequent gifts of food and beer—and a lifetime of tolerance for my apparently esoteric interests.

Things that go without saying need finally to be said aloud. So I offer my love and thanks to my parents, Richard and Helen Golley, to whom I dedicate this book. Their greatest gift to me has been to admire my struggles even more than my successes—a wise and courageous response to the conditions of life.

Finally, I thank my wife, Maia, who read every sentence in the manuscript in its early and late stages, holding firm to the belief that nothing worthwhile is ever achieved without risk. In essence, this book is a confession of my love for her.

Contents

PART II: EARTH, STARS

Reference Matter

When Our Eyes No Longer See

Realism, Science, and Ecology in Japanese Literary Modernism

Prologue

To be *sensuous*, that is, to be an object of sense, to be a *sensuous* object, and thus to have sensuous objects outside oneself—objects of one's sensuousness. To be sensuous is to *suffer*.

—Karl Marx, *Economic and Philosophic Manuscripts of 1844*

There is a way of knowing the world that reaches beyond the limits of the human body. I will call this mode of perception realism. By this, I do not refer to a particular literary convention or artistic style, but to a belief system: a faith in the real existence of an insensible world and in the possibility of depicting a human connection to it. It is this faith—or the hope of such a faith—that has united some of the most ambitiously experimental writers of the industrialized world under the banner of aesthetic modernism.

To say that human beings perceive the world not only with their bodies but also with their minds, with their imaginations, is merely to repeat an age-old insight. To outline a specific moment in the history of this relationship, however—between mind and body, sensation and knowledge, perception and reality—requires an encounter with one of the central problems of modernity, a problem suffused with political and ethical significance.

Realism envisions a world external to human experience, but it also implies the human capacity to know and depict that world, to engage with it. As developments in early twentieth-century industry and science transformed the meaning of "observation" and "objectivity," modern writers and poets struggled to capture what they too came to see as an evolving network of relations joining human beings to each other, to non-human beings, and to the things of this world. This book portrays an extraordinary moment in the history of this realist mode of perception and the life it lived in Japanese literature from the late 1910s to the mid-1930s—or from late Taishō (1912–26) to early Shōwa (1926–89). Widely acknowledged as Japan's most prolific and creative period of literary modernism, these years are also characterized by an aesthetic *shift outward*, when authors turned from the claustrophobic and egocentric concerns of the "I-novel" (*watakushi shōsetsu*) to face the political and ethical demands of the world outside. At their creative peak, despite profound ideological differences, Japanese modernists seem to have shared an aspiration to depict *accurately* and *objectively* an external universe which was seen as indistinguishably natural and historical: a strangely "ecological" world of objective material forces and events that both *defined* and *exceeded* the sensory parameters of the human body, the limits of human language, the laws of social conflict.

For very good reasons, scholars who have studied modernist literature from this period in Japan have taken the elements of "uncertainty," "disintegration," and "fragmentation" identifiable with these texts as signals of alienation and a general concern with the "unreal."[1] The characterization of aesthetic modernism as a version of anti-realism, directed toward linguistic and sensory surfaces and away from objective reality, accounts for the emphasis scholars have put on subjective fracture and the phantasmal in these works. Indeed, no one could reasonably deny these responses their rightful place in the spectrum of the modern experience. For the most stylistically and thematically daring authors of the period, however, the dissociative trauma of sensory and cultural *breakdown*—embodied in the twin notions of subjective and representational crisis—is only half the story. From the photographic and cinematic obsessions of Tanizaki Jun'ichirō (1886–1965) to the shocking and disjunctive portraits of the imperial economy as conceived by Yokomitsu Riichi (1898–1947), to the tender depictions of astrophysical phenomena and human-wildlife relations in the children's stories of Miyazawa Kenji (1896–1933), these authors' works manage to balance a chaos of sense experience against the imagined contours of an objective totality—a reality that exists beyond the senses yet is no less *real* for that—in a way that readers still find compelling today.

It may be useful here to suspend the colloquial value of the word "breakdown," with its implications of psychic and cultural collapse, and consider the term the way a chemist might: as a method of analysis, a means of comprehension. For the physical scientist, the purpose of breaking down an object or process is not to deny its real connection to the world, but to understand it.[2] In important ways, the everyday instruments and technical systems informing the lives and works of the authors in this study offered new insights into social and natural relationships precisely by fragmenting the world and reassembling it as a meaningful abstraction. It is no accident that the modern revolution in theoretical physics, which these same technologies both enabled and embodied, relied increasingly on abstraction and non-mimetic models to make "visible" bizarre and contradictory laws at work in the cosmic and subatomic realms. In a certain sense, the competing descriptions of the atom that filled the pages of physics journals in the early years of the twentieth century had their everyday equivalents in the selective and diagrammatic "world pictures" presented on the front pages of any number of national newspapers—a phenomenon made possible, not incidentally, by the telegraph's practical mastery of the electron. For the modern reader, no less than for the theoretical physicist, abstraction had become an essential tool for grasping, depicting, and "seeing" the world.

Against this backdrop of technical transformation and scientific discovery, I will approach aesthetic modernism in Japan not as a moment of representational or subjective collapse—not, in other words, as the death knell of the referential impulse—but rather as a singular and anomalous moment of *perceptual and referential expansion.* Each work treated in this study explores in its own register the consequences of what amounts to an enlarged definition of observation, a notion of perception uncontained by the limits of immediate corporal experience, though imbued with its textures and codes. It is precisely this fusion of the visual with the visionary that allows these works to assemble in their pages an image of objectivity that focuses not upon distinct objects and individuals, but upon the *relations between them.* The most innovative experimental and popular narratives produced during this period in Japan may be said to have aspired commonly to this "higher" form of objectivity, making use of abstraction not as a means of establishing distance but as a way of depicting *involvement* and *mutual transformation.* In this fundamental sense, and across the political spectrum, the masterworks of Japanese high modernism are united by a species of realism that could be called dialectical: a literary version of what Friedrich Engels described as the "science of interconnection."[3]

What does it mean to say that Japanese literary modernists engaged with the world "dialectically"? In his classic *All That Is Solid Melts Into Air,* when Marshall Berman speaks of modern environments and experiences as forming a "unity of disunity," he makes clear that what he is describing is not really a unity at all, but a "maelstrom of perpetual disintegration and renewal, of struggle and contradiction, of ambiguity and anguish," a world in which "all that is solid melts into air," to invoke the phrase from Marx's *Communist Manifesto* made famous by Berman.[4] Indeed, by underscoring the poetry of Marx's observation—and by adopting this descriptive phrase about the social processes of modernization as the title and refrain of his project—Berman focuses the reader's attention upon the sense of accelerated instability these words express, transforming their frantic tone into the signature of aesthetic modernism itself. It is not surprising, then, that in Berman's analysis, Marx's contribution to modernism ends up amounting to the contours of a rhetorical style: a literary "voice" that displays not only a "breathless pace," but also a "readiness to turn on itself" in order to "express and to grasp a world where everything is pregnant with its contrary. . . ."[5]

In spite of an obvious debt to Berman's work, this book will proceed along a different point of sail.[6] Berman's emphasis on voice, while useful, invites the conclusion that, because nothing in the descriptive content of the modernist text is stable, nothing it refers to is "real" except for its own discursive surface and the chaotic sensory response it portrays. It is this focus on voice, for instance, that allows for the unsettling, and ultimately misleading, connection Berman draws between Karl Marx and Friedrich Nietzsche. The two great minds, he tells us, share a "similar voice and feeling for modern life" expressed through an "ironic and dialectical" engagement with modern history.[7] Still, we must ask ourselves how significant this stylistically "dialectic" connection can be when it is precisely Nietzsche's spellbound absorption in his own modernist voice that leads him finally to deny—as a metaphysical figment of the "popular mind"—the very idea of the historical or ethical "subject."[8] Reflecting the sensory literalism of his age (and anticipating the postmodern skepticism of our own), Nietzsche's anti-metaphysical stance resists the "subject" as part of a general denial of anything at all purported to exist *beneath the surface of things*. There is "no such substratum," he would tentatively conclude in his *On the Genealogy of Morals*, "there is no 'being' behind doing, effecting, becoming; 'the doer' is merely a fiction added to the deed. . . ."[9] In the same passage, Nietzsche clarifies the anti-realist implications his position holds for modern science, taking it upon himself to deny the existence of the atom itself as science's version of "that little changeling, the 'subject,'" an assertion that echoes unexpectedly the positivism of his famous contemporary in physics, Ernst Mach (1828–1916).[10]

For Marx himself, however, and for the most important authors of Japan's age of high modernism, that which I am calling dialectical thinking never implies a world of pure surfaces with no underlying reality—with no "doer" behind the deed—but envisions instead a universe in which no "doer" can exist independently of social and material relations. This book will proceed from the proposition that Marx's great contribution to a later aesthetic modernism is not to be found in the breathless inflection of a literary voice, but in the far-reaching horizon of an epistemological and ontological conviction. What is modernist about Marx—and what is "Marxist" about Japan's most important literary modernists—is a revolutionary form of relational realism that implies an underlying belief not only in humanity's *objective* and *interdependent* existence in an eternally evolving network of material relations, but also in the human capacity to *know* this reality, to appreciate its history, and to determine "objectively" a position within it. Realism in this sense overcomes the limits of the human body not by effacing those limits, but precisely by recognizing in their peculiar shape evidence of communication with a larger, interconnecting cosmos.

It is in this context that human sensuousness takes on a crucial, if contradictory, significance. The senses proved to Marx—in contrast to the skepticism they provoked for positivists like Mach and moral relativists like Nietzsche—not only the real existence of an objective world external to human experience, but the material and objective inclusion of the human body itself in that world. "To be *sensuous*," Marx wrote, in his *Economic and Philosophic Manuscripts of 1844*, "that is, to be an object of sense, to be a *sensuous* object, and thus to have sensuous objects outside oneself—objects of one's sensuousness." Being an "object" in a world shared by other objects becomes, for Marx, an essential part of the *human* experience. "A being which is not itself an object for some third being has no being for its *object*; i.e., it is not objectively related." Objectivity emerges in these early writings as an epistemological stance, as a sensory experience, but also as the hallmark of existence: "An unobjective being is a *nullity*—an *un-being*."[11] So when Marx finally and enigmatically concludes that "to be sensuous is to suffer," the term "suffer" must be understood with its full range of meanings, including as Robert C. Tucker advises, "in the sense of 'to undergo'—to be the object of another's action."[12]

To be sensuous is to suffer. In essential ways, the works that form the core of this study explore the meaning that this statement acquires at a time when the senses themselves undergo enormous and sudden enlargement through transformations in science and industry. New social and geopolitical relations forged and made visible by modern technology cannot be separated wholly from newly recognizable *natural* relations revealed by the concept of the "energy field," associated with mid-nineteenth-century experiments in electromagnetism. The discovery of x-rays in 1895, of natural radioactivity in 1896, and of the electron in 1897 would only intensify the perceptual and metaphysical challenges already inherent, for instance, in the earlier invention of photography, forcing a generation of scientists in the 1920s and 30s—in a remarkable parallel with their literary contemporaries—to develop what physicist Sakata Shōichi called a "new cognition of nature" based on its "dialectical structure," according to which no object is final or indivisible, and there is always something *beyond*.[13] Thus, the "*forming* of the five senses," in Marx's memorable phrase, understood as a "labour of the entire history of the world down to the present," must include the historical *expansion* of those senses beyond their organic limits.[14]

The link between the new reality revealed by modern physics and the reality a generation of novelists and poets began to describe is too fundamental to be treated using the language of influence. Scientists and poets seem rather to have been jointly discovering, as it were, a new observational grammar inseparable from modernity itself. By highlighting this parallel, however, I am not attempting to "heal" the social divide that exists (and existed) between science and letters in modern Japan, or to correct what Joseph Murphy calls a "comic dissymmetry" between the two disciplines in contemporary debate.[15] The significance of this homology lies rather in its capacity to reveal a historical aspiration common to science and literature during these years: the impulse to *accommodate* but also to *push beyond* the sensory immediacy of reality. To be sensuous is to suffer, which means to undergo the effects of a world of perpetual disintegration, where "all that is solid melts into air." In another sense, however, it means to recognize material disintegration for what it is: to see natural and human history as a relationship of solid to air, to acknowledge as real the process of melting itself and to reclaim this process as an object of representation and belief.

Few places in the industrialized world saw the scope of this literary ambition pursued with the expansiveness it was afforded in Japan during the late Taishō and early Shōwa years. For the self-described members of Japan's aesthetic avant-garde—but also, in essential ways, for the leftist authors they opposed—it was this realist impulse that led prose fiction away from the self-involved minutiae of Taishō fiction and toward the outward-reaching, cartographic logic of high modernism: what I call the language of non-mimetic referentiality. The modernist text in Japan struggled to depict fragmentation and cataclysm, but also to penetrate the surface of these experiences, to reach toward the invisible boundary of some elusive totality, the varied contours of which will be the subject of this book. Competing forms of narrative emerged that focused on navigating the space of sociality itself—defined by class relations, by national or ethnic conflict, but also by the interconnections between human and nonhuman species, between living beings and inorganic processes. This turn outward—at least in its non-ecological sense—has been noted in Seiji Lippit's *Topographies of Japanese Modernism*, an exhaustive study that stands as a necessary precursor to my own. Much of what follows began as an effort to carry forward certain problems raised by Lippit's work and contained especially in the explicit rationale of its periodization. Although *Topographies of Japanese Modernism* treats works from roughly the same decades examined in this study, it is a sign of our fundamental difference in approach that Lippit chooses Kobayashi Hideo's (1902–83) elegiac essay, "Kokyō o ushinatta bungaku" ("Literature of the Lost Home"; 1933) as representative of the spirit of the modernism we both set out to study.[16] For me, Kobayashi's essay, with its emphasis on the anxiety of cultural homelessness and on the gap that stands between the concreteness of reality and the abstraction of art, marks the *end* of the period in Japan I am calling the era of high modernism. The world-weary skepticism of Kobayashi's essays from the early 1930s—especially regarding modern literature's capacity to represent nature as a "concrete and actual" thing[17]—might be more usefully characterized as a recapitulation of the anti-realism expressed so vividly two decades earlier by that great figure of Meiji (1868–1912) literature, Natsume Sōseki (1867–1916). The introductory chapter will begin, therefore, with a 1911 lecture by Sōseki and end with a 1933 essay by Kobayashi in order precisely to highlight the fragile uniqueness of certain texts that came *in between.*

At stake in arguing for this distinction among modernisms is the logic of inevitability that often colors discussions of Japanese literature's eventual and well-documented turn to the reactionary ideology of cultural self-defense in the 1930s. There are many reasons to characterize the artistic and intellectual history of this period as a story of profound moral failure. Indeed, it is impossible to speak of Japanese modernism without addressing the problems of nationalism, imperialism, ethnic and racial oppression, and the other related incarnations of tyranny associated with the rise of Japanese militarism. Aesthetic modernism fed these trends, to be sure. And yet there is something to be gained by remembering that this is not *all* it did. There may be another legacy to appreciate, another ethical vision hidden beneath the very struggle itself—however short-lived—to make an accurate accounting of the world, to formulate the material laws of art and empire, to trace the contours of the non-human universe.

If there is a consistency to modernism's agonizing political ambivalence—its tentative flirtations with both socialist revolution and an emergent fascism—the content of this consistency can be reduced to an earnest, if confused, aspiration toward an integrative ideal. And yet the consistency of this aspiration is deceiving. I began this book convinced that Japanese modernism led inevitably and logically to Japanese fascism because of its very concern with totality itself. I now believe that Japanese fascism represents the replacement of one modernist vision of totality with another: a moment at which identity and difference cease to be understood in terms of *interconnection* and *mutual transformation*, becoming instead a problem of *assimilation* and *exclusion*. This book will present the former, dialectical version of "totality" as the most valuable ethical and political legacy of aesthetic modernism, a legacy that survives today in the fundamental concepts of contemporary ecological discourse. It is unaccountably rare for scholars to observe that the central ideas of contemporary environmental ethics and of "deep ecology" found poetic and narrative expression in Japan of the 1920s. So while Chapters 1 and 2 take up the fiction of Tanizaki Jun'ichirō and Yokomitsu Riichi—widely studied figures of a thoroughly urbanized image of Japanese modernism—the last half of this book focuses on the ecological vision of Miyazawa Kenji, a pioneer in experimental narrative and verse whose themes of human-wildlife relations have been largely ignored in English language scholarship.

Despite the common association of Japanese modernism with the gritty textures and exhilarating pace of city life, the most creative works from this period portray far more than merely the experience *per se* of industrialized, urban life. More precisely, these works absorbed the structure of industrialized environments as the logic of nature itself. Modern industrial conditions are directly visible in Yokomitsu Riichi's exploratory move "out onto the streets" and "onto the fluidity of city space" that Seiji Lippit describes,[18] but these same conditions also, more furtively, inform Miyazawa Kenji's poetic migration toward the open fields and forests of Tōhoku, into the stars, and beyond the edge of the cultivated world. To study Japanese modernism is to appreciate an era when the "*social* reality of nature," to turn once again to Marx, and the "*natural science about man*" had become "identical terms."[19] It is a sign of the latently ecological grammar of this equation that the very idea of materialism in Marx's work, as John Bellamy Foster has observed, suggests "both an *ontological* and an *epistemological* category."[20] In the pages that follow, the term "high modernism" will designate the poetic encounter with precisely this enigmatic image of nature: the struggle of literature to make visible a historical and material reality that both *envelops* and *stands outside* our senses, to picture with accuracy a world our eyes could never see.

INTRODUCTION
The Things of This World

What we call the things of this world are the things that humans like us have seen. We cannot begin to know whether this is all there is.

—Terada Torahiko, "Butsurigaku to kankaku," 1917

There must be something behind things, which is deeply hidden.

—Albert Einstein, *Autobiographical Notes*, 1947

In 1911, Natsume Sōseki, one of the founding figures of modern Japanese literature, delivered a lecture in Wakayama entitled "Gendai Nihon no kaika" (The civilization of modern Japan).[1] Widely studied as a classic statement on the meaning of Japanese modernity, the text of this address finds its way into classrooms and seminars today not only as a rhetorical masterpiece, but also as an important cultural document. Born a year before the founding of the Meiji state, Sōseki himself is often seen as both a keen observer and a beleaguered product of modernization, and this duality permeates the adjectives that typically attach themselves to the facts of his life: his *traumatic* break from the Chinese classics, his *lonely* research trip to London, his *neurotic* tenure as a lecturer at Tokyo Imperial University, and his *scandalous* decision to leave that position to become a professional writer. "All of you and myself," he told his audience on that August afternoon, "as Japanese, born into modernity . . . clearly share an intimate and unbreakable bond with these three words: 'modern,' 'Japan,' and 'civilization.'"[2] To our eyes, Sōseki's famous essay both describes and embodies the hidden violence, the contradictions, and the sense of psychic trauma that we have come to associate with the modern experience. At the same time, no example better illustrates the radical division that separates Sōseki's time from what succeeded it: the era of high modernism.

The key to Sōseki's statement is to be found in its digressions. Despite his stated goal of offering a definition of "modern Japanese civilization," the author spends the first quarter of his address convincing his audience of the pitfalls built into the very process of definition itself. Strictly speaking, this is not a digression at all, but a critical assertion central to the larger meaning of his address. Most definitions, Sōseki tells his audience, however convenient, function by "freezing" or "rigidifying" the phenomenon in question, by removing it from the process of endless transformation that characterizes objects "in the real world [*genjitsu yo no naka*] . . . as if placing a living thing into a coffin."[3] With this macabre image, Sōseki registers a deep suspicion of the processes of abstraction and isolation at the heart of the most advanced—especially scientific—modes of knowledge of the twentieth century.

After comparing scholarly definitions to the metaphysical figments of geometry—a discipline, he reminds us, that can only render a circle in terms of a mental ideal of roundness utterly disconnected from the constant transformations of "existing round objects in the real world"—Sōseki then asks his listeners to consider another, quintessentially modern example: a photograph of a moving train. Such a photograph, he argues, may unmistakably depict a train, but because its image "lacks movement, the one thing that is essential to a train, we must admit that it is so different from a real train as to be beyond comparison with it." Knowledge produced by scholarly "explanations" and "definitions," he finally concludes, is often like the image of the train in this photograph, or like a fossilized specimen of a fly in amber: "clearly visible, but dead. . . ."[4]

Delivered just five years before the author's own death, "Gendai Nihon no kaika" unveils the contours of a crisis concerning the most basic questions of perception and objectivity. It was this crisis that would give rise, in the following decades, to the outwardly expansive, enormously creative visions of the natural and social world characteristic of Japanese literary modernism. Sōseki's own response to these questions, however, would remain rooted in a positivistic obsession with *unmediated sensory experience*, fundamentally at odds with those later movements. In the following segments of his lecture, Sōseki gradually replaces what he sees as an insidious impulse toward deadening abstraction with an alternative response that takes change or "motion" into account on its own terms.

It soon becomes clear, though, that Sōseki's commitment to direct observation of concrete reality has drawn his attention away from the external *object* of observation and focused it upon the psycho-neurological dynamics of observation itself—a shift similar to that which characterized nineteenth-century positivist science as well. In effect, the perceptual faculties and their operations come to *replace* what the author repeatedly refers to as "the real world." In this sense, Sōseki may be said to represent the "essential modern ontology," as described by Samuel Hynes in an essay on Joseph Conrad: "reality is consciousness."[5] It should not be surprising then that Sōseki's solution to the problem of "the real world" relies so heavily upon a theory of consciousness inherited from nineteenth-century Western psychology.[6] Strongly influenced by the work of William James, Sōseki places under grave doubt the entire question of whether it is possible to objectively know reality, taking pains to explain to his (probably puzzled) audience exactly how their minds perceive stimuli: not as a series of fixed units but as a progression of flowing waves of "infinite number."[7]

There is indeed something puzzling, not to say disturbing, about Sōseki's oblique approach to the subject of modern Japanese civilization. By the year this speech was delivered, the Japanese government was irreversibly committed to a campaign of colonization in Asia—with the 1910 annexation of Korea as its most recent acquisition—and in the midst of an oppressive crackdown at home. Sōseki delivered several lectures that year as part of a series sponsored by his employer, the Asahi Shinbun. His disquisitions on consciousness were usually preceded by lectures with such titles as "Conditions in French Annam," "The Manchurian Problem," and "Interests of the World Powers in China."[8] Only seven months before Sōseki's address on modern civilization, the reactionary Katsura cabinet had executed twelve leftist activists charged falsely with attempting to assassinate the emperor.[9] If there was at this time a "special urgency to the theme of freedom," as Jay Rubin suggests in the foreword to his translation of this and other essays, what could it mean for Sōseki to have spent so much time discussing the complexities of human perception and cognition?[10]

To confront this question is to confront the crucial distinction between the merely modern and what I am calling the *modernist* vision of reality. For Sōseki and many of his contemporaries, the effort to understand how the human mind "moves" did indeed constitute one of the modern world's most urgent problems.[11] This is not to suggest that Sōseki denied material history, but rather that it was the *subjective experience* of that history which concerned him most. The search for concrete reality always led Sōseki back to the same thing: the psychology of perception. Apparently indifferent to the fate of colonized people in Asia, and certainly steering clear of openly critical statements about a government administration he had no reason to admire, Sōseki saw the greatest crimes of the modern Japanese state manifested in the alienating and disorienting effects its institutions and technologies had wrought upon the individual and collective psyche of its people. Even his most direct critique of industrial capitalism, which he perceived as originating in (and imposed by) the West, focused on these narrow parameters of cognition. Defining civilization as a kind of self-regulating, vitalistic economy of "human energy" (*ningen katsuryoku*),[12] Sōseki warned that a modernizing process imposed from the outside could force Japan's balance of human energy out of its "natural" or "internal" rhythms, causing a sort of collective "nervous breakdown."[13] What this author feared most about modern Japanese civilization, in other words, was not the blood spilled in its name, nor the innocents confined behind its prison walls, but the capacity it showed to disrupt natural mental rhythms.

For Sōseki, to define modern civilization less subjectively than this—that is, as an external or objective "reality" existing beyond the cognitive patterns of immediate experience—would be merely to mimic the disjunctive logic of modernization itself, akin to attempting to capture the essence of a moving train with a photograph. Profoundly antimetaphysical in spirit, Sōseki's essay portrays abstract speculation—"explanations" (*setsumei*) or "definitions" (*teigi*)—as well as all mediating instrumentation as implicated in a broadly fragmenting modernizing process, a process that functions precisely by hindering meaningful access to the textures of direct sensation. After considering the author's discussion of train photography at the beginning of the essay, we are left with the impression that the only sort of "representation" adequate to the phenomenon of a moving train is *an actual moving train*, which is to say, *the subjective content of a direct encounter with an actual train.* Photography, for Sōseki, like the divisive methods of mathematical abstraction, functions by uprooting consciousness from the flow of time and direct experience, from the very basis of the "real."

At first, Sōseki's keen recognition of the gap between the photograph and its objective referent tempts us to place this essay in line with a modernistic self-consciousness about sign systems and the processes of signification. Indeed, Sōseki seems to have laid the groundwork for a belief-system that would soon displace his own. Presciently recognizing photography's ability to disjoin the object from its image and to circulate freely, he treats the mechanically reproduced photograph in much the same way later thinkers would treat language: as a signifying system distinct from, though not wholly unconnected to, the world of objects it depicts. Far from anticipating the dialectical relationship that a succeeding generation of modernists in Japan would propose between material sign-systems and material reality, however, Sōseki remained committed instead to capturing the sensory content of "direct" experience. So while his portrayal of modernity as a crisis of perception might suggest an affinity with later classics of high modernism, Sōseki's own subjectivist response to this crisis underscores an essential barrier separating himself from the most creative literary movements that would emerge after his death. Rather than signaling the inauguration of an aesthetic revolution, Sōseki's essay exemplifies the moribund posture of a positivistic skepticism driven by a quest for empirical truth that was reaching the limits of its own logic.

In a sense, Sōseki's obsession with the literal content of perception expresses the disengaged posture demanded by the institution of literature itself since the early decades of Meiji. In a recent essay on the beginnings of modern prose theory in Japan, literary historian Atsuko Ueda warns readers against taking as a call to realism Tsubouchi Shōyō's (1859–1935) early insistence that modern prose narrative break from its didactic tradition and describe the world "just as it is" (*ari no mama*).[14] Driven neither by an idea of political engagement nor by the sort of documentary impulse associated with later forms of "social realism," Shōyō's doctrine—famously put forth in his foundational work

Shōsetsu shinzui (The essence of the novel, 1885–86)—represents instead what Ueda describes as a reactionary ideology of political and ethical "neutrality": the modern notion of literary autonomy. With Shōyō's canonical treatise, political "disinterestedness" is established as one of the central principles of the truly *aesthetic* response.[15]

In significant ways, Sōseki's distillation of historical reality to the sensory textures of interior experience carries this logic forward in the form of a sort of "perceptual autonomy." Sōseki's best-known prose narratives—staples of the modern literary canon—explore the full possibilities of this version of subjectivism. Astutely and unforgettably descriptive, the defining passages of Sōseki's classic works are symphonies of sense impressions. Scenes and events are fraught with shadow or shot through with light and color; comprehension is rendered as a quality of visibility.[16] It is not the acquisition of Taiwan or the war with Russia that takes center stage, but the composition of the moon against the branches of an evergreen framed by a bedroom window, the sound of a camellia blossom falling to the floor. All the external processes and relations that a later generation of writers would take as their aesthetic "objects"—the defining structures of ethnic and class conflict, mechanized war, and global empire—gather toward those famous moments of epiphany in Sōseki's fiction where they are reduced to the signals of corporal perception. Reality is consciousness.

What separates Natsume Sōseki from the authors whose work will be the subject of this book, in other words, is an essential pessimism about the individual's ability to know, or literature's capacity to depict, the historical contours of an *extrasensory* reality. The most representative works of high modernism in Japan all stand in creative opposition to this extreme version of sensory literalism. This assertion may at first seem unremarkable. As early as 1958, H. Stuart Hughes famously described literary modernism as part of a broader "revolt against positivism."[17] But when we consider the deep connection between Sōseki's own "positivist" disposition and the self-referential subjectivism that is usually attributed to modernism itself, we are faced with an apparent paradox.

Modernist writers and poets all over the industrial world have long been applauded for their reflexive instincts, for what Raymond Williams describes as their "denaturalizing of language, their break with the allegedly prior view that language is either clear, transparent glass or a mirror."[18] It is doubtless this linguistic opacity that has led scholars such as Dorothy Ross (echoing Hughes) to identify modernist movements in literature and philosophy with a "turn away from objective reality to a fractured subjectivity."[19] Literary historians in Japan have typically shared this view, often reading prominent Japanese modernist texts as defined by non-referential, prototypically "semiotic" concerns.[20] If we accept this interpretation of the modernist text as essentially self-referential, and if we further understand positivism not as a form of naïve realism, but rather as it was understood in nineteenth-century science and philosophy—as a bulwark against the metaphysics of realism itself—then aesthetic modernism and positivism would appear to stand in a position of mutual affinity.

In fact, the general characterization of aesthetic modernism as a species of subjectivism attentive to the surfaces of language and sensation at the expense of objective reality accounts for precisely the connection Jonathan Crary makes between nineteenth-century modernist art and the physiological model of vision associated with positivist science in his classic study *Techniques of the Observer.* Fifteen years after its publication, Crary's work remains indispensable for its clear insights into how nineteenth-century visual instruments and popular optical devices (including but not limited to photography) came to embody a "visual 'nihilism'" at the forefront of "empirical studies of subjective vision, a vision that encompasses an autonomous perception severed from any external referent."[21] As nineteenth-century science moved away from "the mechanics of light and optical transmissions," turning instead to "an interrogation of the physiological makeup of the human subject," the distinction between understanding the observer and understanding the object observed began to fall away.[22]

Considering the sort of naïve realism that the term "positivism" often connotes for humanists today—a "fashionable term," in Peter Allan Dale's words, "for an unfashionable way of thinking"—it is important to remind ourselves of its essentially anti-realist inflection.[23] With roots in Enlightenment-era empirical trends associated with Locke, Hume, and others, positivism began as a radical rejection of the pseudo-knowledge of theology and metaphysics. By the end of the nineteenth century, however, precisely through its equation of knowledge with the "experience of the senses," this strain of radical empiricism—exemplified by the ideas of physicist and philosopher Ernst Mach—found itself in the curious position of denying the verifiability of just about everything.[24] In a limited (and ironic) sense, Mach's empirical purism shared with phenomenology's *critique* of scientific empiricism a central concern with documenting consciousness.[25] Although Crary goes on to describe this anti-realist posture as a "precondition for modernist painting in the later nineteenth century," the validity of this historical connection should not obscure for us the realist substratum that would eventually come to underlie aesthetic modernism in its later, twentieth-century forms.[26]

The pages that follow will show how Japanese fiction in the 1920s and 30s broke from nineteenth-century notions of subjectivist vision, how modernism really did "revolt against positivism," but precisely as an expression of its realist aspirations. Crucially, this realism was no mere return to some earlier "decorporalized" vision of reality that simply sundered "the act of seeing from the physical body of the observer," a stance Crary identifies with seventeenth- and eighteenth-century science and philosophy.[27] For Japanese modernists of the 1920s, external reality was understood neither as some metaphysical entity severed from the body nor as an illusory figment of the body's organic senses, but rather as an evolving set of *relationships* between the body and a surrounding universe: a space of interconnection. Experimental writers in the decades following Sōseki's death penetrated the boundaries of an outdated scientific positivism by committing themselves to an enormously expansive and dialectical language of objective accuracy, a *relational* form of realism. In Japan, in other words, modernism's "fractured subjectivity" came to serve the interests of a *higher objectivity*.

What unites the works gathered together here as modernist—and, paradoxically, what accounts for their conflicting ideological valences—is their common realist belief in the independent existence of the social and natural object of perception and in the hope of achieving its adequate depiction. The authors of Japan's modernist movement took issue with the *limits* of positivism's objectivity, not its excesses. To be sure, the works that will be examined in this book all stand emphatically at odds with the thematic and stylistic conventions of *literary* realism; but none of these works opposes realism as an ontological or epistemological disposition. The modernist rejection of literary realism, in other words, amounted to the embrace of scientific realism in the literary realm: an expanded realism driven by the hope of a more comprehensive, more profound, more accurate account of objective and social reality.

Not coincidentally, a similar ambition animated the most daring claims and discoveries emerging from the scientific community during these years, claims which themselves provoked powerful internal resistance. If modernism really *was* a revolt against positivism, this revolt must be understood not as part of a broad humanistic rejection of science's authority (the way H. Stuart Hughes meant it),[28] but rather as the literary expression of a rupture that was occurring at the time *within science itself.* In fact, the reconceptualization of "accuracy" that will occupy the center of this study shares all the complexities and perceptual contradictions associated with those radical shifts in theory and instrumentation that defined late nineteenth- and early twentieth-century science—especially physics.

The first requirement for approaching Japanese modernism as a poetic encounter with a global perceptual crisis is to break from the theme of "national culture" that has characterized much of the recent scholarship on modern Japanese literature. Implicitly or explicitly, native loss is often taken as the central fact (however ideological) of Japanese modernity. Even Karatani Kōjin, whose groundbreaking work provides the framework for many of the most recent studies of Japanese modernism, often runs the risk of recapitulating the nativist complaint he sets out to analyze: the notion of an ineffable indigenous tradition displaced by an alien culture. While seeming to focus on a "semiotic" rupture at the heart of modernity, Karatani ultimately views this rupture as a clash of cultural unities, interpreting instances of modernist critique in Japan as the resurgence of a submerged *native* epistemology against a dominant *Western* one. In the aesthetics of Kuki Shūzō (1888–1941), for example, or in the "I-novel" narrative form of the Taishō period, Karatani sees evidence of momentary returns to an imperfectly suppressed mode of thought that held sway in premodern times, when Japanese literature, presumably untainted by the metaphysical dichotomies of the European Enlightenment, lacked "either interiority or objectivity," offering instead a "pure play of language."[29] For Karatani, modern consciousness, forged at the very end of the nineteenth century, provided only a partial barrier to this earlier though no less monolithic cultural mode, "which in some senses had already transcended the modern."[30] In his most famous book, *Origins of Modern Japanese Literature*, Karatani presents the formalist detachment of Natsume Sōseki's psycho-neurological excursus in *Bungakuron* (A theory of literature, 1906) as a leading example of this natively postmodern sensibility.[31]

Without dismissing the importance of the image of Western intrusion in early twentieth-century Japanese representations of modernity, and without disregarding the semiotic consequences of imported notions about language and knowledge, this book will focus instead upon the *sensory* dimensions of an epistemological dislocation whose somatic and psychic effects carried very few definite references to an "originating" tradition. I treat the culture of modernity not as a product of the West, but as a product of industrialization, and the brief watershed moment of literary modernism as both a bodily symptom and a cognitive exploration of discoveries and inventions associated with science and industry. Only by considering modernization in its most concrete terms is it possible to clarify what is truly local about the Japanese incarnation of aesthetic modernism. A more literally material history needs to be considered, then, when reading Sōseki's essay—a history that both accommodates and exceeds the cultural codes implied by Karatani's discursive analysis.

In his lifetime, Sōseki had witnessed the legendary birth and expansion of Japanese industrialization. By the end of the Meiji period (1912), Japan had more than 32,000 factories containing among them some 5,400 steam engines, and even more importantly, over 2,700 electrically powered machines.[32] Although these numbers would be dwarfed in the next fifteen years by an enormous increase in Japan's industrial capacity—with consumption of electricity rising from under 300,000 kilowatt-hours in 1914 to over 1.5 million annually in 1925—by the year Sōseki delivered his speech on civilization, the groundwork for Japan's power and communications network was well established.[33] Significantly, the infrastructure of Japan's industrial and commercial base relied more and more on the interactions of electrons across metal cables and wires. Sōseki's generation, for example, saw the construction not only of a nationwide railway system, but of a national telegraph network essential to the operation of that system.[34] They also saw the establishment of a more limited telephone network that strengthened both the commercial economy and the policing powers of a newly centralized state.[35] By the year of Sōseki's lecture, it was electricity that illuminated public buildings, transmitted international news stories, moved streetcars full of people to and from their places of work. The importance of this fact cannot be overstated.

Electromagnetic energy must be accorded its place in the history of modern Japanese literature. Not simply because it was a central (and *literal*) driving force of industrialization, but because its very existence catalyzed an unprecedented epistemological crisis that would haunt the pages of early twentieth-century fiction and define the rise of modernism in the following decades. The link between the notion of "energy" (already implied by nineteenth-century light bulbs and telegraph poles) and modernist fiction of Japan's 1920s and 30s is far more decisive than the relationship typically (though not incorrectly) drawn between modernism's stylistic experiments and the immediate perceptual effects of cinema, phonograph recordings, and other mass techniques characteristic of later decades. As early as the late nineteenth century, for instance, the compressive inflection of the daily newspaper's front page reflected the international network of telegraph links that made it possible. Japanese readers could encounter, in a single page of headlines, culturally and geographically disparate news events joined together by the simple, if surreal, fact that they all happened on the same day. As one Meiji textbook intoned: "The newspaper, where events of the city, events from the countryside, even events from foreign countries a thousand miles away can be understood at a glance. Ah, the handy newspaper!"[36] Even the daily newspaper of late Meiji must be understood as an *electromagnetic* phenomenon.

From its beginnings, the concept of electromagnetic energy and the early inventions from which it grew demanded a new way of *knowing* and *depicting* the universe. The concrete effects of electricity implied the existence of entities outside the realm of natural *or even assisted* human detection, a reality expressible only by means of metaphors and "models."[37] At the heart of the modernization project, it seems, operated the most elusive powers of the universe. The suspicions that early Meiji subjects expressed toward telegraphy, for example—directed, significantly, at the *wires themselves*—suggests an occult dimension popularly recognized in this mysterious technology at the same time that it reveals a lucid understanding, as Yoshimi Shun'ya has argued, of the real political threat that telegraphic instrumentality posed to local autonomy.[38] The electron reached into the bedrock of the modern world, making its effects felt at every social stratum and across enormous geographies. While peasants vandalized telegraph poles in the Japanese countryside, the theory of electromagnetism was taxing the imaginative limits of scientists and philosophers at universities all over the world. Even by the year that Sōseki delivered his speech on civilization, although electric current had come to be employed quite effectively to move information, freight, and human bodies across the landscape of a growing capitalist economy, the literal existence of electrons and other subatomic particles—as well as the exact ontological status of energy and energy fields—remained a matter of heated debate among the leading scientists of Europe and Japan.

Electromagnetic theory was born in the mid-nineteenth century, around the same time as the Meiji state itself. Its appearance in the physical sciences marked a major transformation from what had been a focus on mechanics to the "study of energy and its transformations."[39] The physics of energy emerged simultaneously with the controversial notion of the "field," spawning a sudden flurry of theories that were, in Norton Wise's words, "essentially mathematical, without definite reference to physical models."[40] Crucially, the first step that physics took toward its twentieth-century position at the forefront of knowledge was also the occasion of its own perceptual and ontological crisis. Scientists could not agree whether energy was to be taken as an "effect" of physical entities, as an entity unto itself, or merely as a theoretical fiction—something to be described and measured without reference to its physical "cause." Electromagnetic theory forced positivist science toward its most radical logical achievement: an unprecedented focus on the subjective boundaries of knowledge itself.

On the one hand, nineteenth-century physics evinced such an extreme impulse toward objectivity that it gave rise, through a kind of dialectical reversal, to what science historian Theodore M. Porter describes as the "death of the object." A new emphasis on "description" (of empirical data) replaced older efforts at "explanation," revealing, in Porter's words, a "disinclination of many late-nineteenth century physicists to believe they could gain access to independently existing objects."[41]

Rather than attempt to capture the true nature of subatomic phenomena, the argument goes, physicists came to rely increasingly on descriptive "models."

Although Porter characterizes the use of models in physics as a "concession" to positivism's anti-realist tendencies, it is equally important to recognize models for their foundational role in generating a new species of realism, a renewed hope in accurate (if not mimetic) representation. Austrian physicist Ludwig Boltzmann credited James Clerk Maxwell (1831–79), famous for his work in electrodynamics, with first understanding the importance of models in physics. For Maxwell, he wrote, models were not "true representations," but rather "means by which phenomena could be reproduced, bearing a certain similarity *to those actually existing*" (italics mine).[42] Models, in other words, released science from the strictures of mimetic representation without destroying its faith in the object of representation itself. Although they may have been stylistically "unrealistic," theoretical models in physics represented a historic victory for the *ontological* realism that would later come to dominate twentieth-century science. It was typical of Maxwell's style, as Porter himself admits, "to reason by way of fictions in order to reach, in the end, a likely physical truth."[43] In the end, electromagnetic theory demanded a realism capable of operating beyond the realm of sensory verification, and models provided the grammar for that new style of thinking. "Electrical field theory," Porter writes, "arguably the most consequential theoretical shift in the nineteenth century physics, began as nothing more than a working out of models."[44]

So electrical field theory was engaged in a *realist* enterprise from the beginning: a struggle to know and represent not only objects in space, but also the continuous fields of energy pervading and defining the space *between* those objects.[45] For some, the concept of the energy field resuscitated the most dubious and metaphysical dimensions of Newtonian gravity: the magic of "action at a distance." Although there may have been no empirical doubts in the minds of Japanese engineers when a pressure-pipe burst in Hitachi's newly constructed 10,000-horsepower hydroelectric turbine in 1915, or when a high-voltage circuit breaker exploded that same year at the massive Inawashiro power plant in Fukushima, the *fact* of electricity demanded a new and paradoxical way of acknowledging the material universe.[46] Behind these explosions operated the greatest mysteries and philosophical problems of the age.

Michael Faraday (1791–1867), the inventor of the electric motor who first guided physics away from mechanical notions of "force" and toward the idea of "fields of energy," embodied the contradictions of the new scientific realism.[47] Faraday's famous "lines of force," a phrase used to explain electrical and magnetic polarization, foreshadowed the controversial break from positivism that would characterize twentieth-century physics, though Faraday himself only became a realist about his own lines of force in 1852, when he was over 60 years old. At first, he described the idea as a mere intellectual convenience without physical significance. Long after he invented the motor, however, Faraday reported a change in his own thinking. "I cannot conceive of curved lines of force," he wrote, "without the condition of physical existence in that intermediate space."[48] Science historian Ian Hacking describes this as a watershed moment in modern science. For Hacking, no materialist who followed a strict definition of "concrete reality" as consisting of substantial, countable entities could regard lines of force as real. "Faraday, tinged with immaterialism, and something of a causalist, made just that step," Hacking observes. "It was a fundamental move in the history of science. Next came Maxwell's electrodynamics that still envelops us."[49]

But what can it mean to be enveloped by electrodynamics? This strangely compelling image evokes the almost occult power attained by scientific language during the era of Japanese modernism itself, when a world permeated by energy fields demanded a species of poetry capable of "picturing" the invisible.

The Revolt against Positivism

In 1911, the very year that Natsume Sōseki was puzzling over questions of perception and reality with his audience in Wakayama, one of Japan's leading physicists, Nagaoka Hantarō (1865–1950), was publishing his account of a "revolution" taking place in European physics.[50] Few in Japan were in a better position to understand this revolution. Nagaoka's earlier "Saturn" model of the atom had helped shape the successful nuclear model that Ernest Rutherford would introduce that year.[51] By the last decade of the nineteenth century, with the introduction of electron theory, representations of electromagnetic energy—a strange and revolutionary concept in its own right—had begun to show signs of incompleteness. Faraday and Maxwell's notion of continuous fields of energy had now to be reconciled with elusive subatomic "particles" of electricity called electrons. With Rutherford's 1911 discovery of the atomic nucleus, neither classical mechanics nor the "magic" of Maxwell's electrodynamics could explain how the atom held itself together.[52] Contradictions mounted, and faced with these contradictions physicists found themselves confronting the same questions of perception and reality that seemed to trouble Sōseki. By the time Nagaoka wrote his article, the electrodynamic revolution had given rise to two distinct but equally radical propositions: that the flow of time itself changes according to physical conditions, and that light exists as a wave and as a particle at the same time. The two theories that ultimately emerged from these discoveries—relativity and quantum theory—would famously revolutionize the material picture of the world in the twentieth century.[53]

Registering the recent emergence of these two new theoretical trends, Nagaoka identified some of this revolution's key figures (Max Planck, Hendrik Lorentz, Albert Einstein, and Hermann Minkowski) as well as its central stakes: the most elementary units of nature, "time, space, mass."[54] In the same year, another Japanese physicist, Kuwaki Ayao (1878–1945), a student in Berlin of the pioneering quantum theorist Max Planck and an acquaintance of the young Einstein, published a translation of Planck's work on the "new physics" as well as an essay on Einstein's 1905 special theory of relativity.[55] With the introduction to Japan of what cultural historian Kaneko Tsutomu calls the "two pillars of modern physics [relativity and quantum theory], the attention and admiration of the world both inside and outside science was captivated by theoretical physics."[56] Not without reason, the non-scientific community in Japan would eventually come to focus its attention upon the wistfully sagacious image of Albert Einstein, broadly accepted as the incarnation and originating genius of this revolution.[57] And although Einstein's theories would not enter the *popular* imagination in Japan until the 1920s (the most creative decade for aesthetic modernism), as early as 1912, when the philosopher Tanabe Hajime published in *Tetsugaku zasshi* (Journal of philosophy) the article "Sōtaisei no mondai" (The problem of relativity), the crisis of knowledge and perception revolutionizing physics had entered the realm of general philosophical discussion.[58]

It was not merely its decisiveness in transforming the discipline of physics that attracted intellectuals and general readers to this revolution. Nor was it simply the esoteric novelty the new physics represented. These theories were recognizably "revolutionary" precisely because of the everyday significance of their content. Beginning with Einstein's "miraculous year" of 1905, when the young patent clerk accomplished his first foray into relativity theory (special relativity) and laid the foundations of quantum theory (his hypothesis of "light quanta"), a new picture of the physical world had begun to emerge centered upon a notion of objectivity that was both earthly in its consequences and spectacularly avant-garde in its style. According to relativity and quantum theory, what it meant to *be an object* and what it meant to *objectively observe* another object had been altered in ways that defied intuition, yet also somehow rang true to the daily experiences of modern life. If relativity theory recast "objective knowledge" as a curiously local affair, quantum theory (especially as it matured in the 1920s) seemed to abandon the hope of ever measuring or defining an object with any *certainty* at all. Famously divergent in their pictures of reality, relativity and quantum mechanics would nonetheless play parallel roles in generating a species of realism that was relational in structure and dialectical in spirit: a style of reasoning peculiarly adequate to the modern world.

It is fitting that in the same year Natsume Sōseki denied photography's adequacy to the reality of a moving train—warning against allowing the mere traces of visual instruments to stand in for direct perception—Charles Wilson published his epoch-making photographs recording the "tracks" of alpha rays, produced in his newly invented cloud chamber.[59] Modern life and modern science developed inseparably, and both relied increasingly upon new techniques for detecting and depicting a world beyond appearances. Over the next decades, as mechanically reproduced images multiplied and as electrical power systems and communication networks spread, theoretical physics would depart not only from Newtonian notions of "absolute" time and space, but also from the very possibility of observing or describing an object or event in any *final* sense. In Japan, the aesthetic manifestations of these radical perspectives would not blossom until the 1920s—after Einstein introduced his broader general theory of relativity in 1915 and especially after his widely publicized visit to Japan in 1922. But by the year Nagaoka wrote his essay, it was already clear to Japanese intellectuals that the physical sciences were in the midst of a full-scale epistemological and ontological crisis. If the field of physics was undergoing a paradigm shift in the classic sense of Thomas Kuhn's definition, the most visible sign of this shift was the desperation with which "normal science" was giving way to philosophy.[60]

In 1947, quantum physicist Sakata Shōichi (1911–70) would look back at these years as an extraordinary period of confusion and doubt. At the end of the nineteenth century, Sakata writes, when all the classical theories stood on the brink of collapse, many physicists in Europe, such as Ernst Mach and Henri Poincaré (1854–1912), turned to the most extreme sort of positivist skepticism in order to inoculate themselves against cognitive chaos, accepting in principle nothing but the raw "facts of experience" (*keikenteki jijitsu*).[61] And although traditional realists like Ludwig Boltzmann and Max Planck stepped up to oppose this view, neither camp seemed capable of solving what had come to be clearly recognizable as a "crisis of physics" (*butsurigaku no kiki*).[62] In Japan, too, by the early years of the twentieth century, the physical sciences had become so fraught with contradiction that many resorted to precisely this form of empirical purism. From this positivist perspective, Sakata tells his readers, science ceases to reflect or refer to "objective nature" and comes to be viewed instead as "merely a product of human consciousness" whose function it is to "record [human] experience faithfully rather than to explain the essence (*honshitsu*) of nature."[63] Even when mediated by technology, the data of positivist science is necessarily reduced to the organic experience of *reading the instruments themselves.* What science presents as the "laws of nature," wrote physicist Kikuchi Seishi (1902–74) in upholding this approach, "should be thought of as descriptions of relations among readings of various gauges attached to instruments used in experiments." To infer anything beyond these narrow descriptive limits, Kikuchi continued, represents a profoundly naïve and wholly unscientific category of realism.[64]

But what exactly is "naïve" about the realism Kikuchi criticizes? For Sakata Shōichi, what Kikuchi dismisses as "naïve realism" (*soboku jitsuzairon*)—the inference of a reality beyond bodily experience—is only described as such because of the *practical* assumptions associated with "daily life" that this belief reflects.[65] In fact, Sakata goes on to argue, this supposedly naïve faith in a material world independent of direct human perception represents a disposition betrayed by Kikuchi himself in his highly accomplished experimental work on the "diffraction of electrons" and the "scattering of neutrons." What Kikuchi calls "naïve realism," in other words, might be described more precisely as a belief in the possibility of *engagement* with the world, a realism rooted in *involvement*: the logic of experimentation. "If we may call this practical, then human life has been practical from the very beginning," Sakata observes. "But in order to engage in this sort of practice, we must acknowledge that nature (the external world) exists independently of our consciousness, that it is projected into consciousness through our senses." Though it might be dismissed as naïve, Sakata finally concludes, what such a conviction really represents is "the stance of materialism."[66]

By an apparent contradiction, "the stance of materialism" offends the radical empiricist precisely by its appeal to the imagination. Compare Kikuchi's sober and constrictive reality—the "relations among readings of various gauges"—to the one Albert Einstein dared to conceptualize as a five-year-old when he first encountered the needle of a magnetic compass. "That this needle behaved in such a definite way," Einstein recalled in his 1947 autobiography, "did not at all fit into the kind of occurrences that could find a place in my unconscious conceptual world (actions connected with touching or contact)." To the child Einstein, the quivering indications of the compass needle demanded more than merely to be read or recorded; the instrument itself appeared to his eyes as an object of mystery calling out for interpretation. "There must be something behind things," he concluded, "which is deeply hidden."[67] Deeply hidden, yet real enough to guide and protect generations of navigators on the open sea. To the pragmatic mind of a nineteenth-century mariner, few things could make more sense than the "reality" of magnetic north.

For Sakata Shōichi too, it is no ivory-tower idealism, but a thoroughly "practical point of view" (*jissen no tachiba*) that allows humanity to "overcome the limits of our senses and to expose the essential relations that lie behind phenomena. . . ."[68] According to Sakata, it would be the dialectics of Friedrich Engels and V. I. Lenin that finally enabled a key group of renowned quantum physicists in Japan to overcome in practice "the epistemology of positivism."[69] Lenin's sustained critique of Machist empiricism in his *Materialism and Empirio-Criticism* (1908; translated as *Yuibutsuron to keiken hihanron* in 1909) together with Engels' earlier, though posthumously published *Dialectics of Nature* (1925; translated as *Shizen benshōhō* in 1929) formed the foundation of a broadly subversive approach to quantum mechanics pioneered during the early Shōwa years.[70] Developed by physicist Taketani Mitsuo (1911–2000), and associated most notably with Yukawa Hideki's (1907–81) Nobel Prize–winning work on "meson theory," this dialectical methodology, known as the "three stage theory" (*sandankairon*), presented a picture of the natural universe as a complex of mutually dependent and interconnected "strata [*kaisō*] . . . ceaselessly coming into being and passing away."[71]

Published in the openly resistant popular front journal *Sekai bunka* in 1936, Taketani's groundbreaking essay presented a challenge to the irrationalism dominating the scientific and philosophical work of his reactionary colleagues at Kyoto Imperial University. In the context of rising militarism, even this apparently esoteric thesis on subatomic structure carried profound political consequences. Seduced by mystical trends of the time, many scientists had come to understand the contradictions of subatomic physics as proof of the limitations of reason itself, lending the authority of their own anti-realist views to the cause of fascism.[72] Against this trend, Taketani conceived of the subatomic realm as a constellation of evolving relations, what he identified as "the dialectics of antagonism and unification, essence and appearance, part and whole, necessity and chance." Moreover, he told his readers, these distinct fields of opposition and interaction must themselves be perceived as "mutually and intimately connected with one another."[73]

Working alongside leftist intellectuals like Nakai Masakazu, Taketani would publish two major pieces on his dialectical approach under the pen name Tani Kazuo before being arrested in 1938 and jailed for eight months.[74] It is a sign of the enormous breadth and outward thrust of Taketani's realism that the author himself conceived of his quantum manifesto as a logical contribution to the "resistance against Japanese militarism" just as the state was preparing to invade the Chinese continent.[75] Professing faith in a reality behind appearances, Taketani's natural dialectics envisioned a substratum of evolving relations whose very depiction requires a kind of involvement. Even while underscoring the inseparability of understanding and engagement, however, Taketani made clear from the beginning that knowledge (*ninshiki*) "is in no way an arbitrary construct of the subject."[76] And this may be the most "subversive" dimension of his approach. Crucially, for Taketani, as for Engels, the external world *responds to* human consciousness without being *reducible to* it.

Neither positivist nor realist in the traditional sense, Taketani's methodology followed Engels' departure from the idea of "eternal and indivisible" elementary particles, presenting instead a reality that defies all final definitions.[77] "There is no need to despair if an electron is both a 'wave' and a 'particle' at the same time," Sakata explains, summarizing Taketani's position, "for this only serves to predict that behind these phenomena, a more fundamental relationship will be discovered that unifies the opposing ideas of 'wave nature' and 'particle nature.'"[78]

Ultimately, for Sakata, the extraordinary accomplishments of twentieth-century physics, far from representing the figments of some deluded metaphysic, suggest instead the *practical* overcoming of a paradoxically "blind" faith in the truth of sensory literalism. "The reason why physicists could and did discover the atom and reveal its structure," he concludes, "is not because they observed nature just as it is (*aru ga mama*)." Rather, these achievements were "based on the success of human practice."[79] Indeed, two years after the United States' nuclear attack on Hiroshima and Nagasaki, the *real* consequences of humanity's practical engagement with subatomic phenomena could no longer be sanely dismissed. If electric lights and radio signals had failed to convince turn-of-the-century positivists of the existence of atoms and electrons—"Have you seen one?" was Ernst Mach's notorious rebuttal—after August 6th 1945, it could not have been more patently absurd to doubt the everyday reality of the sub-visible world.

In the early years of the twentieth century, however, the future of realism as a scientific enterprise was far from certain. Michio Kaku attributes Boltzmann's 1906 suicide in part to the "incessant ridicule he received for advancing atomic theory."[80] Between 1909 and 1910, quantum theorist Max Planck engaged Ernst Mach in an urgent public debate over the necessity of realist strategies in theoretical physics, illustrating the authority and vitality positivism still retained in the early years of the century. Meanwhile, the exact relationship between Albert Einstein's celebrated general theory of relativity and Mach's positivism would remain unsettled for several years. Ultimately, Einstein—who played a founding role in every aspect of the "new physics"—would openly criticize Mach's philosophy as an unnecessary constraint on science, and this criticism carried broad, if poorly understood, cultural significance throughout the industrialized world. If Einstein's theories of relativity can be described as the expression of a personal "pilgrimage," in Gerald Holton's words, "from a philosophy of science in which sensationism and empiricism were at the center, to one in which the basis was a rational realism," the era of literary modernism in Japan—enigmatically linked and artistically indebted to Einstein's famous theories—must also be acknowledged as essentially realist in orientation.[81] At the same time, this was no simple revival: both quantum theory and relativity clearly signaled the end of realism, too, *in its classic sense*, so Einstein's pilgrimage was not without its complications.

In 1922, literary critic Tsuji Jun (1884–1944) declared "Professor Einstein, who denies the absolute," to be "a dadaist."[82] His words reveal not only the avant-garde status that Einstein had acquired by late Taishō, but also an underlying confusion about relativity theory itself, which may indeed have contributed to the theory's "revolutionary" reputation. The year that Tsuji wrote these lines, Einstein had reached a peak of popularity in Japan. His lecture tour there in the late autumn and winter of 1922 had made him an instant superstar whose photographed image—standing on a train platform in Nagoya or at a garden in Kyoto, among Japanese scientists at Tokyo Station or on the cover of the journal *Kaizō* (the tour's sponsor)—always seemed to convey at once the ideal of the gentle science-philosopher, the purveyor of radical wisdom, and the modern genius. Although Einstein's Japanese tour included only seven speeches (about five hours of total talking, after calculating for breaks), his presentations provoked a far-reaching popular response.[83] The attendant "relativity boom" saw at least 23 books on the subject of Einstein's theory published between 1921 and 1922 alone, including a translation of Einstein's own explanation for the general reader, and several easy-to-read versions by physicist, poet, and science journalist Ishiwara Jun (1881–1947).[84]

Not surprisingly, this explosion of explanatory texts never exactly clarified for non-specialists the basics of a theory that defied so fundamentally an older, intuitive picture of the world. Although the cryptic nature of relativity may have been part of its appeal, few had any doubts about the connotations of the term "relativity" itself. As Tsuji Jun's words suggest, many mistook relativity theory for nothing other than the scientific proclamation of the victory of *relativism* over the dictatorial rule of "the absolute": the final authoritative triumph of *subjectivism*. It was a confusion that had its roots in the scientific community itself.

At first, for instance, relativity theory was viewed by many scientists in Europe and Japan, including its earliest Japanese promoter Kuwaki Ayao (and, for a time, even by Einstein) as a *tour de force* in the sort of radical empiricism championed by Ernst Mach.[85] It was, after all, a deep skepticism toward non-empirical "explanations" that had inspired Mach's own prophetic criticisms of the time-honored constructs of Newton's mechanics, including what he called the "conceptual monstrosity of absolute space"—a monstrosity because it was "purely a thought thing which cannot be pointed to in experience."[86] This sort of iconoclasm had inspired the young Einstein, who deeply admired Mach's ideas from early on. In its final form, Einstein's relativity theory challenged Newtonian physics with an audacity remindful of Mach's own work. According to Newton's conception of the universe, time was "absolute"—flowing evenly and universally, independent of motion or mass, equal everywhere in the cosmos and for every frame of reference. An hour was an hour no matter where you were going or how fast you were going there. The same held true for space. Newtonian space was a kind of transcendentally fixed "empty stage" on which events occurred. Stable and homogeneous, it too was "absolute." But Einstein would finally and famously depart from these classical conceptions, conceiving of time and space as mutable and inter-related, joined together as a unified object he called "space-time." According to his 1915 theory of general relativity, it is nothing other than the local and ceaselessly evolving contortions of space-time, determined by the uneven distribution of mass and energy, that we experience as "gravity."

The universe that Einstein envisioned—a universe that was celebrated and puzzled over by Japan's poets and intellectuals throughout the 1920s—acquired the revolutionary quality physicists now refer to as "background independence" because it contained nothing fixed or absolute against which to measure objects or events. "In contrast," writes quantum physicist Lee Smolin to clarify this point, "a theory such as Newtonian mechanics or electromagnetism is *background dependent* because it assumes that there exists a fixed, unchanging background that provides the ultimate answer to all questions about where and when" (italics in original).[87] The implications of relativity—that neither events in time nor objects in space can be measured or experienced independently of their conditions of observation—seemed at first to fulfill the anti-realist project that Mach spent his career promoting. In fact, however, as Smolin makes clear, Einstein's discovery that the objective world was "observer dependent" in no way endangered the *reality* of the objective world; it simply meant that "objectivity" had ceased to mean "knowable by all."[88]

To suggest that there is no preferred viewing point from which two events can be said to be "really simultaneous," for example, does not signal the end of objective measurement, but the beginning of a *new category of measurement* that takes into account several viewpoints at once, in the manner of a Cubist painting.[89] Albert Einstein thus personifies the modernist moment in Japan not simply for his popularly recognized questioning of a universal frame of reference, but also—and perhaps more importantly—for his more subtly accomplished *preservation* of the boundaries of objective certainty. Lewis Feuer has observed that the word "relativity" in many ways amounts to a "misnomer" for the logical content of a theory aimed at "a higher absolutism, a more general objectivity of natural law, rather than a relativism or subjectivity."[90] But this apparent contradiction is exactly what made Einstein's famous theory so fertile for Japanese poets and writers in the 1920s. Relativity's accommodation of local viewpoints, when combined with this abiding image of a higher totality, calls up a singular picture of the world that is both finite and limitless: a quintessentially *modern* cosmos determined by the experiential boundaries of the observer even as it far exceeds those boundaries.

If the "whole of science is nothing more than a refinement of everyday thinking," as Einstein wrote in 1936, relativity theory may in some fundamental way be taken as a documentary artifact of the transmutation of everyday life itself.[91] It is in this sense that the image of relativity resonated so profoundly with interwar culture in Japan, carrying such far-reaching consequences for literary depictions of society and the natural world.

In the end, Einstein's theory represented not a fulfillment of, but a *radical departure from* the subjectivism extolled by Ernst Mach, whose positivist doubts about the object world were so corrosive that they extended to virtually all "hypothetical" entities such as atoms and electrons and, if pressed, would dismiss "space-time" itself as another metaphysical figment. Writing also in 1936, quantum realist Taketani Mitsuo praised relativity theory as the final abandonment of all "hidden parameters" (*kakusareta parametā*) that lacked truly "objective meaning": a profoundly materialistic vision of the world in which only "relative motion" retains any significance. "For the first time," Taketani wrote, "time, space, matter, and movement were grasped in terms of their intimate dialectical interconnection."[92] But neither the materialism at the heart of Einstein's conceptual system nor the far-reaching consequences of its dialectical grammar were immediately understood. Into the early years of the twentieth century, positivism continued to color the language of science, retaining the rhetorical authority of its unyielding skepticism. And the underlying logic of this skepticism was Sōseki's subjectivist ontology: the equation of reality with consciousness. Impressionistic to the core, Mach's philosophy of science survived into the twentieth century as the last great expression of a nineteenth-century obsession with observability: "Colors, space, tones, etc." he wrote in his day book. "These are the only realities. Others do not exist."[93]

Science and Sensibility

In Japan, the growing inadequacy of this nineteenth-century standard of observation created a flurry of theoretical denials, proclamations, and responses that will strike anyone studying avant-garde literature of the 1920s as prophetic. After 1911, the words "sensation" or "perception" (*kankaku*) and "knowledge" (*ninshiki*) suddenly occupied the center of debate in the world of Japanese physics and philosophy. Kuwaki Ayao, credited with first introducing relativity to Japan, published two essays in 1912 that focused on this very problem: "Setsumei to kisai" (Explanation and description) and "Butsurigakujō no ninshiki no mondai" (The problem of knowledge in the physical sciences).[94] In the latter essay, inspired by the Mach-Planck debate that Kuwaki witnessed while studying in Berlin, the author sides unequivocally with Mach's positivism—what he calls the view of the "epistemologists" (*ninshikironsha*)—against Planck's "realism" (*jissairon*).[95] Knowledge in the physical sciences, he proclaimed with Machist finality, "is abstracted from a complex of colors, sounds, temperatures, and shapes." Steadfastly committed to a factual universe bounded by sense impressions, Kuwaki dismisses his own mentor's insistence on a scientific "emancipation from the senses" as the expression of an illusory metaphysical aspiration: a benighted hope in the possibility of knowledge unmoored from the limits of "individuality" (*kosei*), one's "historical epoch" (*jidai*) and "ethnicity" (*minzoku*).[96]

Three years later, in an essay entitled "Bungeijō no byōsharon to kagaku" (Science and the theory of description in literature, 1915), Kuwaki would extend his criticism to the literary realm, denouncing as misguided the efforts of Japan's prevailing school of literary Naturalism (*shizenshugi*) to "remove the shadow of the author" from the text and to achieve a "purely objective description."[97] In remarks suggestive of the true breadth of science's perceptual crisis, Kuwaki underscores the inevitability of subjectivism in both literature and science, inadvertently identifying a sort of latent positivism at the heart of early Taishō literature: the logical link between the "objectivity" of literary Naturalism and what would later be called the "I-novel" (*watakushi shōsetsu*). It is worth noting that Kuwaki takes issue in this essay not with Naturalism's descriptive methods, but with its ideology of "objectivism" (*kyakkanron*), invoking a now-familiar photographic analogy to highlight the illusory nature of Japanese literature's "objective" self-image. "Even with a mechanical photograph [*kikaiteki na shashin*]," Kuwaki observed, "we can recognize differences between the photo and its object based on discrepancies in the lens and the light. . . ."[98] Judging from Kuwaki's tone, there would seem to be no point at all in attempting an "accurate" or "objective" literary representation. Like Natsume Sōseki the novelist, Kuwaki Ayao the physicist sees the human mind as hopelessly alienated from the object world, with all intervening instrumentation serving only to deepen this condition.

It is a sign of an approaching shift, however—and a premonition of what would emerge as the logic of literary modernism's *outward turn*—that in this same essay, Kuwaki also begins to compromise subtly with a realist image of science. Citing Henri Poincaré, Kuwaki concedes that, although we have no way of knowing, for example, if the color red is experienced the same way by any two people, we *can* know with absolute certainty the measurable difference *between* colors: what we call red and what we call blue.[99] And it is toward this refuge of quantifiable relations—where language ceases to refer mimetically to particular objects and becomes instead the abstract rendering of relationships—that Kuwaki finally turns to find the faint promise of scientific objectivity. Following the sort of thinking that Einstein would eventually exemplify, Kuwaki entertains the possibility of an objective reality "in which a number of eternal absolutes and relative values coexist peacefully": a reality that can be represented, but only *as an abstract model.* From this view, he remarks, science functions "not so much through description (*byōsha*) as through symbolization (*shōchō*)."[100]

In important ways, Kuwaki's concession to realism in this essay (presented almost as an afterthought) is rooted in an implicit recognition of a reformulated link between science and sensibility: a wholly transformed idea of what it means to "observe." To acknowledge empirically verifiable distinctions among light frequencies is to depart from the "physiological" model of observation that Jonathan Crary identifies with nineteenth-century science: to embrace an abstract terrain occupied by pure energy.[101] When color is replaced with wave frequencies, the human body can no longer serve as the final point of reference. Similarly, in 1918 when Albert Einstein defended relativity as a "fact of experience" in a letter to a friend, he also inadvertently revealed the breadth of this transformation.[102] By that year, in the wake of the First World War, modern experience had become so saturated with technology—not only movie cameras, telephones and radios, but cloud chambers, Geiger counters, and x-ray machines—that experiential fact (which, for Einstein, included the constant velocity of light) could no longer reasonably adhere to the limits of Mach's "colors, space, and tones." The effects of this material shift upon the political and ethical imagination of aesthetic modernism cannot be overstated. In moving away from the corporal boundaries of the human sensorium, modern science and modern culture were extending the boundaries of the knowable universe itself.

If there is a single figure in Japan whose work confronted directly the implications of this sensory enlargement, it was Natsume Sōseki's own former pupil, physicist and popular essayist Terada Torahiko (1878–1935). No one seems to have thought more deeply about the meaning of the human senses, or to have considered more openly the consequent effect of their historical transformation on the shape of scientific knowledge. Although Terada suffered professionally during his lifetime for pursuing non-conventional research interests—as well as for dividing his time equally between his laboratory and his writing desk—it is precisely by occupying the border between disciplinary demands of the scientific community and general appeal, between esoteric distinctions and everyday relevance, that his work achieved its historical and scientific insights. Indeed, Terada's quirky (often experimentally untenable) investigations into everyday phenomena have recently come under serious reevaluation in the context of complexity theory.[103] In light of Terada's ultimate retreat to such low-budget and inglorious topics as the physics of ink stains, of falling camellia flowers (an homage to Sōseki), and of color patterns on the fur of domestic cats, it is all the more significant that his first research project after returning from study in Europe in 1911 dealt with the subject of x-rays. As a research topic, x-ray crystallography placed Terada's early work on what Joseph Murphy calls the "international cutting edge of physics" at a time when the best minds in the field had turned their attention to "domains outside the possibility of human experience."[104] So Terada knew what was at stake when he later withdrew to the realm of housecats and camellia blossoms.

Like many of his contemporaries, Terada had entered science guided by an abiding faith in the data of his own senses. He thus felt profoundly challenged—even personally offended—by the discoveries of the new physics. Never fully extricating his own language from its Machist roots, Terada maintained an extraordinarily complex relationship to human sensation throughout his life. While conceding the necessity of mathematical abstraction and analysis, Terada also understood the remarkable capacity that raw sensation continued to have for grasping patterns, laws, and relations. It was this insight that drove Terada's eccentric forays into what he called the "physics of form" (*katachi no butsurigaku*): explorations of such disparate phenomena as fracture patterns, electric sparks, and the flow of charcoal calligraphy ink. "When phenomena share the same form," Terada wrote, "then surely as phenomena they are governed by the same laws. To disregard formal similarity as mere surface agreement is to misunderstand the true meaning of the word 'form.'"[105]

Terada's famous student, Nakaya Ukichirō (1900–62), who was later recognized internationally for his research on ice and snow, praised

Terada's efforts to reconnect the methods of an increasingly abstract discipline with the poetry of the senses, to hold up a "physics of wholeness" (*sōgō no butsurigaku*) against the modern trend toward ever finer levels of mathematical analysis.[106] Terada once considered supplementing a mathematical model of a complex energy wave by printing the wave's contours on a motion picture soundtrack, then playing it back as sound so that the observer could "hear the shape" of the wave as a series of changes in pitch. This broadly communicative impulse represents Terada's defense against a cerebral trend in science similar to what T. S. Eliot vilified as a "dissociation of sensibility" in modern poetics. For Terada, physicists labored under the same holistic obligations that Eliot identified in 1921 with the "metaphysical poets" of England's seventeenth century: to allow others to "feel their thought as immediately as the odour of a rose." Eliot himself deeply admired this capacity to fuse ideas with sensory experience and presented this image as the model for his own generation of modernists:

> A thought to Donne was an experience; it modified his sensibility. When a poet's mind is perfectly equipped for its work, it is constantly amalgamating disparate experience; the ordinary man's experience is chaotic, irregular, fragmentary. The latter falls in love, or reads Spinoza, and these two experiences have nothing to do with each other, or with the noise of the typewriter or the smell of cooking; in the mind of the poet these experiences are always forming new wholes.[107]

At the heart of Eliot's famous essay is an appeal to that peculiar image of realism that would eventually define modernist aesthetics in Japan: a poetry of "wholeness" that neither ignores nor merely reflects sensory experience but *reorders* it, recasts it as the very substance of thought and the link to an outside reality. Although Terada, for his part, would eventually admit that science faces an obligation to disengage itself from the limitations of the senses, he never stopped reminding his readers and colleagues that science was also *inconceivable without them.* And this may have been Terada's greatest insight: that reading an abstract model of an invisible wave of energy itself amounted to a sensual experience.

In 1917, the year before Einstein declared relativity a "fact of experience," Terada published an eloquent meditation on the meaning that sensible experience had acquired in the world of physics. He begins his essay "Butsurigaku to kankaku" (Physics and perception)[108] by asking his readers to imagine a science that might be produced by a society of people born blind and deaf. His point is simple: any system of knowledge that could emerge from these somatic circumstances—that is, any science built entirely around tactile, gustatory, and olfactory information—would be nearly impossible for humans with visual and aural endowments to imagine. And so it is with science in general, including modern physics. The capacities of our bodies determine the possibilities and limitations of our knowledge. And yet it is precisely by highlighting the link between sensation and knowledge that Terada recognizes the logic that demands severing this connection. "Although our five senses are the only things we have to detect directly the phenomena of the outside world, to acknowledge its existence, these senses are extraordinarily crude, and are never consistent between individuals."[109] As inconceivable as the idea might be of a science that makes no reference to bodily sensation, it is no less absurd to imagine a science that refers to *nothing but* the data of sensory experience. "In order to establish universal knowledge about the material world," Terada finally and reluctantly observes, "we must first immediately abandon subjective standards—the standards of our direct perceptions—and move toward standards of the material world itself outside of ourselves. This is the principle of the 'non-humanistic view of nature' (*hi-ningenteki shizenkan*) that pervades modern physics."[110] It is for this reason, he explains with a mixture of resignation and regret, that science today finds itself speaking oxymoronically of "inaudible sounds" (*kikoenai oto*), treating radio waves, light waves, and heat from the sun as a single category of energy.

With an elegiac wistfulness, Terada's essay concedes the rising legitimacy of a new perceptual regime. In the rarefied stratum addressed by the new physics, the human body could no longer occupy a central position. "The problem of visible light has been turned over to the territory of biology," Terada tells his readers. "In physics we think only of non-human electromagnetic waves."[111] For many of his contemporaries, it was both disturbing and exhilarating that the most basic of the sciences—the foundation of all others—could no longer speak simply of colors, space, and tones. At the heart of the new physics operated a strange new world-picture, traceable to the first stirrings of electrodynamics and identifiable with modernity itself. And this image does indeed still seem to envelop us today, when our eyes no longer see the forces and processes that surround and define us. By 1920, when the special and general theories of relativity had become popularly identified as the most exciting and daring ideas in science, Terada would mournfully suggest in a letter to Kuwaki that Einstein's greatest glory had amounted to an "insult to humanity": the revelation of the essential "incompetence of our five senses."[112] Sōseki's plea to abandon abstract definitions, mathematical constructs, and mechanical images in favor of direct sensory encounters—his metaphorical promotion of eyes over cameras—had been finally and irreversibly overturned.

Art and Accuracy

In a sense, the rupture was too profound to be commonly remembered. Within a generation, no recognizable conflict existed between science's abstract methods and its claim to material knowledge. In Japan today, as in the West, the old dichotomy between empiricism and rationalism has virtually dissolved. But for a time, the displacement of purely organic notions of observation by an expanded model of perception that both accommodates and overcomes the limits of the observer's body provided endless inspiration for experimental writers and poets. For these writers, modern science and the technical world it created meant not an indictment of the five senses, but an emancipation from them: the opening of a vast, unexplored terrain of objectivity reality.

Even before the Great Kantō Earthquake of 1923 transformed Tokyo into a fully modernized world capital by destroying much of it one September morning (killing over 100,000 people and burning over 500,000 buildings),[113] literary celebrations of modern life assigned special meaning to the city as a staging area for the most fundamental kind of material and sensory reorganization. "The city is the motor," wrote Hirato Renkichi in his 1921 leaflet, "Nihon miraiha sengen undō" (The Japanese futurist manifesto movement). "At its heart, the 'dynamo electric.'"[114] Although we can only speculate about the ideological trajectory this admirer of F. T. Marinetti might have followed had he not died the next year at 29, Hirato Renkichi's invocation of chemistry, electrodynamics, and of vaguely Einsteinian imagery in this early artifact—captured by its repeated references to "light and heat," to "dynamos," to "time and space," and to "velocity"—establishes the materialist ambitions of Japan's literary avant-garde. "All divine attributes have been taken over by human hands," Hirato wrote. "Today, the engine of God is the engine of the city, and partakes in the activities of humanity's millions."[115] Almost every sentence of this document seems to anticipate Paul Virilio's 1997 equation of "new technologies" with the "three traditional characteristics of the Divine: ubiquity, instantaneity, and immediacy."[116] Although Virilio refers here to a much later technological revolution, the logic of his thinking echoes the poetics of Hirato Renkichi. "The rule of God now exists in the organic connections of all our lives," Hirato observed with the familiar grandiosity of Japan's early generation of modernists. For Hirato, the powers of the divine had come to reside in "the impulsive candor of the machine, in its light, its heat, its ceaseless rhythms."[117]

If Hirato Renkichi saw the elemental powers of the universe manifested in the workings of the city's infrastructure, the 1923 earthquake impressed upon its witnesses the *historical* consequences of these material interconnections. Unlike the Great War, a well-established benchmark for the inauguration of high modernism in Europe, the Great Kantō Earthquake has always presented scholars of Japan with the difficulty of using a *natural* disaster to mark a *cultural* shift. In a certain sense, however, nothing could be more appropriate. For it is precisely a reformulation of the link between "natural" and "human" history that animates the outward turn characteristic of Japanese high modernism. In some ways, the earthquake only punctuated a growing interest in the materiality of social dynamics that had been brewing for years. The industrial boom that accompanied World War I and the much-cited expansion of the urban work force underscored widening gaps between a new salaried middle class and an impoverished class of factory workers who were especially vulnerable to inflation and economic shifts. Before the earthquake, Japan had witnessed the rice riots of 1918, the growth of labor unions, and the increased visibility of anarchist and socialist movements. The year in which Hirato Renkichi wrote and distributed his "Futurist Manifesto" leaflet also marked the appearance of the foundational journal of the Japanese proletarian movement, *Tane maku hito* (February 1921). This is no mere coincidence. Beneath the surface of these antithetical literary events operates a deeper logic common to both: the emergence of a new grammar of seeing that appeals in some essential way to the "scientific," that places human history squarely in the larger context of material—even *natural*—relations.

On the morning of September 1st, 1923, nothing could have been clearer: the disasters of history were both natural and human. In the immediate aftermath of the earthquake, mobs of wandering vigilantes and police notoriously massacred resident Koreans amid rumors of poisoned wells; prominent radicals, including Ōsugi Sakae (1885–1923) and Itō Noe (1895–1923) were arrested and killed.[118] A strange new ecology had been exposed: a surprisingly material barrier standing between moral chaos and collective dignity. For leftist critic Hirabayashi Hatsunosuke (1892–1931), the earthquake underscored the civilizing power of "social existence" (*shakai seikatsu*)—the importance of human organization and interconnectedness. "Japan is, needless to say, a civilized nation," he wrote in 1924. "But for several days after the earthquake of September 1st, Tokyo, Yokohama, and the other affected areas were temporarily isolated from other regions. Due to supply shortages brought about by the fire, the people in these regions were temporarily reduced to the living conditions of primitive peoples."[119]

The earthquake is remembered by historians, though, not just for what it destroyed, but for what emerged in its wake. In the next few years, Tokyo dedicated itself to the business of installing, replacing, and improving the machinery of modern life, and by the mid-1920s, all the technologies of communication, transportation, and popular entertainment that might be associated with Hirabayashi's "social existence" had reached a crescendo of expansiveness and efficiency. Life in modern Tokyo had become suffused with the convenience and immediacy of mass culture: not only cafés, cabarets, and movie houses, but also radio broadcasts, private telephone networks, and a newly powerful mass press—the famously affordable "one-yen books" (*enpon*) and journals like *Kingu* with their huge circulation numbers.[120] Neither the self-consciously experimental schools of aesthetic modernism nor those movements identifying themselves as politically revolutionary are conceivable apart from these conditions. As literary historian William Gardner reminds us, when avant-garde poet Hagiwara Kyōjirō (1899–1938) proclaimed the destruction of traditional poetic and literary forms in a 1925 sketch for the experimental *MAVO* journal, what he saw replacing them was an "electric-radio advertising tower" (*denki rajio no kōkokutō*).[121]

Not surprisingly, the machinery of this modern world was both a common subject of literature and a source of its insights. For Japanese writers of the 1920s, there was something profound to be learned from the technologies of the modern city, something that bespoke the most basic laws of material history. Modern technology was where capitalist exchange converged with revolutionary possibility; switchboard signals carried stock quotations *or* news of a strike. At another level, the mysterious power of generators and transformers channeling a wilderness of electromagnetic energy, like the "controlled explosions" of the internal combustion engine, seemed to mirror what was—or might soon be—happening on factory floors and in the streets. Behind every system of control lurked the specter of chaos. Almost overnight, the technical systems driving modern entertainment, modern business, and modern science had fused with the sensory apparatus of the modern artist. The "imaginative proximity of social revolution," to cite Perry Anderson's unforgettable phrase,[122] was also an imagined proximity to a newly recognizable "natural" world of dynamic instability and mutual interaction, a *literally material* cosmos with both subatomic and global dimensions. Whether pursuing the interests of political revolution or embracing the poetics of profit and empire, authors found in the machines of the modern world a new way of seeing beyond the body's limits: a form of objectivity that Hirato Renkichi might have called "divine."

In 1930, the avant-gardist-turned-proletarian author Kataoka Teppei (1894–1944) published a short story in the leftist journal *Senki* (Battle flag) that demonstrates the material logic of this outward turn. "Tsūshin kōshu" (The linesmen) begins with a brief but indelible portrait of the modern world's communications industry:

> In the sky, below the earth, even at the ocean's floor: consider the wires that stretch across the planet like a spider's web.
>
> Telegraph wires. Telephone wires.
>
> Countless wires above our heads, below our feet, stretched taut all around us.
>
> Capitalists all over the world, without moving an inch, are joined together by the wires of telegraphs, telephones. . . .[123]

If the front page of any Meiji newspaper furtively suggests (by the expansiveness of its content) the enormous reach of electromagnetic technology, this literary depiction strips that technology to its essentials: a "spider's web" of wires and cables, carrying the nerve signals of international capital. Telling of the laborers who repair and maintain this network—who are awakened at three in the morning for an "emergency muster" (*hijō shōshū*), who trudge through miles of suburban snow drifts to inspect lines, who climb poles in the blackness of an icy wind "growling in the wires"—the story places the miracle of this newfangled convenience in stark relief against the physical exertion and discomfort of the laborers who support it. Although alternating between two characters, the story is really told from the perspective of *the repair itself* as it is undertaken against the perversely old-fashioned enemy of a winter storm. What is unique about the story's two featured linesmen—who by necessity of the story's form and purpose are both "types"—is neither "character" nor "personality," but rather *what they hear* and the *singular position from which they hear it.* And this peculiar narrative approach emerges inseparably from the technology it portrays.

The story begins with a confusion of voice signals that one linesman, implausibly named Tokimoto (written with ideographs meaning "time source"), overhears as he is testing a line on the night of the storm:

> "Hello. Hello," he called. He could hear faint voices in conversation coming from what seemed to be a cross-connection in the city.
>
> "A finger. A finger," a distant voice leaked out.
>
> "A finger. A pinkie, an index finger. . . ."
>
> Damn. This is a strange conversation. A strange thing to be selling. Tokimoto's curiosity was aroused. Pressing the receiver close to his ear, he held his breath.
>
> "About how much can you buy it for, a finger? . . ."
>
> This time it was another voice that sounded clearly in his ear.
>
> "Maybe . . ." The voice once again became distant. "An impressive thing . . . cut with a knife . . . lecture. . . ."
>
> He could only hear fragments.
>
> Again, a clear voice came on the line: "About a hundred yen charged as expenses to the Culture Club and—no, we better not over the phone. Could you come over?"
>
> "Right. I'll bring him with me. . . ."
>
> And that was all Tokimoto heard.
>
> He wanted to hear more, but it was useless. What sort of connection could there be between a finger and a Culture Club?
>
> He suddenly remembered the task at hand. And when he did, the hand he was holding the receiver with turned immediately cold. The groaning of the wires swinging in the wind assaulted his ears with a sudden violence.

But the connection between the Culture Club and the finger bothered him. Which Culture Club? There could not be any connection between the finger and their own Communication Repairman's Culture Club.[124]

Appropriately for a telephone repairman, Tokimoto is obsessed with connections. Bad connections, clear connections, cross connections, connections made in conversation, business connections. Connections are his trade, and from his position on the "test pole," Tokimoto is exposed to a peculiar perspective on the business life of Tokyo. In an important sense, it is these connections that are at stake when the system falters, and the point is driven home later when the narrative offers another sketch, a telegraphic montage of the network, only this time instead of the wires themselves, it is the content of the signals they carry:

"Five hundred tons of coal. Provide market quote. Urgent."

"Shipment of 20,000 bags of rice arriving from Saigon on the 20th."

"Will sell 3,000 shares of Tokyo stock."

"Postal stock down 20 points."[125]

And sharing the wires with the data of profit and exchange, the oppressive chatter of ceaseless police activity: "XX *maru* arriving in port tomorrow. Search thoroughly. Party member disguised as businessman on board."[126]

This is what the linesmen of Kataoka's story hear when they tap into the network: an aural pastiche of "free exchange" and police intimidation—an abstract portrait of the Japanese state itself. So when it is determined that the storm has caused a major breakdown in the system, team members dispatched to locate and repair the problem—led by a linesman named Soroku—carry in their heads a strange constellation of social, economic, and physical laws. On the one hand, Soroku and his crew are on the look out for "crossed wires, short circuits, broken lines. . . ." "When the snow collected on the wires," the narrative carefully informs its readers, "the electricity would flow to the earth, rendering communication impossible. That was a short circuit."[127] On the other hand, their technical virtuosity provides the linesmen opportunities to glimpse the historical dimensions of this material reality, provoking discussions of revolt. In a limited and paradoxical sense, despite their low wages and long hours, the workers of Kataoka's story are masters of the modern world. They know the laws of electricity, which, if properly engaged, could serve the interests of the proletariat as efficiently as it serves the state and its capitalists, just as they know in their bodies the injustice of the class system that traps them. The reader imagines each linesman assembling in his head the enormity of Japan's capitalist empire from the platform of a test pole, hearing the voice of an increasingly draconian police state bound to protect it.

The telephone system becomes in this story both an *object* and a metaphorical *means* of engagement with history. After their introduction to Japan in 1877, telephones had first been deployed (in the manner of telegraphy) as a means of centralization and administrative control. It was government and police organizations that first established telephone systems for use in prisons, mines, and in agricultural fields where prison labor was used.[128] By the mid-1920s, however, banks, hotels, restaurants, delivery services, stock brokerages, and newspapers had equipped themselves with telephones.[129] The installation of the first direct dial phones in Tokyo in 1926 marked the full-scale entry of telephone technology into the realm of private profit and exchange.[130] Like the electric light and telegraph businesses before it, the telephone industry organized itself around the ontologically dubious processes of generating, distributing, controlling, and exchanging the flow of electrical current.

Subatomically, the phone signal was no different from the telegraph signal. But the transmitted voice of the private telephone conversation brought the paradoxes of electromagnetic energy to a new level of corporal intensity. Unlike the coded telegraph message, the telephone signal could actually extend the human voice itself, releasing it from the bounds of vocal physiology, allowing a kind of ghostly contact over unheard-of distances. Talking on the phone (and listening in from a "test pole") could take on the character of an out-of-body experience. By the mid-1920s, an expanding network of wires and relays had created a new category of intimacy between individuals, but also between the individual and the larger economic and political universe. The telephone conversation created an intimacy of *abstraction*. It could only be achieved by a process of disjunction, quantification, and magnification: only by translating a voice into waves of electrical energy that traveled at velocities approaching light speed across miles of cable to the ear of the listener. In 1929, when Hirabayashi Hatsunosuke observed how literary form changes to contain "new ways of life," it was the high speed associated with the physics of energy—"the distribution of motive power, especially electricity"—that he identified as the central fact of his own generation's formal experiments.[131] In Kataoka's story, where proletarian technicians tap into the hardware of this vast network, telephone technology makes clear the revolutionary value of a modernist mode of "objectivity." The linesmen know the world in a way that is both *rooted in* and *freed from* the limits of local perception.

In the final scene of this piece, when the telephone workers are treated to a ghastly spectacle at their Culture Club meeting of a "repentant" communist who severs his own finger with a knife to demonstrate his newfound loyalty to "his majesty" the emperor, Tokimoto witnesses the scene with an objectivity peculiar to this modernist mode. Finally making sense of the exchange he had overheard days earlier, he realizes that what he had "observed" over the phone lines was an individual being bought and sold for the purposes of political intimidation. Tokimoto evinces an insider's knowledge here that partakes in neither neutrality nor transcendence, but in what might be identified, in Einsteinian terms, as "observer dependence." His insights are clearly the unique product of his observational position, characterized by the clarity of his outrage: the hallmark of any truly *objective* politics. In the world of Kataoka's story, political objectivity suggests a form of truth that is neither *knowable by all* nor *entirely knowable by any*. "Objectivity does not mean judging from nowhere," Marxist critic Terry Eagleton has recently reminded us. "On the contrary, you can only know how the situation is if you are in a position to know."[132] If Eagleton's comments are meant to revive for twenty-first-century readers the hope of political engagement against the skepticism of postmodern theory—which has tirelessly, if tediously, dismissed the notion of objectivity altogether—his view is rooted squarely in the modernist tradition, and remindful of early twentieth-century physics. "Only by standing at a certain angle to reality can it be illuminated for you. . . . Objectivity and partisanship are allies, not rivals."[133]

From his earliest writings, Kataoka Teppei concerned himself with overthrowing the old standards of subjectivism associated with I-novel "realism" in order to achieve a higher form of referential accuracy. As if taking up the challenge of Natsume Sōseki's skepticism, Kataoka's initial impulse aimed at the most literal depiction of sensory data possible, free from the emotional and cognitive constructs that writers had typically engaged to assemble a meaningful narrative. When Yokomitsu Riichi's (1898–1947) experimental short story "Atama narabi ni hara" (Heads and bellies) appeared in the inaugural issue of the modernist journal *Bungei jidai* (Literary age) in 1924, Kataoka wrote in defense of its tersely cinematic grammar and counterintuitive imagery.[134] In particular, he applauded the effectiveness of its abbreviated depiction of a speeding express train in the story's opening sentences, focusing on the author's attention to the data of sensation itself. "In order to represent the condition of a material object such as a train," Kataoka proclaimed, "nothing other than sensationist expression (*kankakuteki hyōgen*) is likely to be as animated or as effective."[135] It is important to note that Kataoka invokes sensation here not to uphold some Machist view that presents *human subjectivity* as reality's final reference point, but rather to introduce a philosophy of *human objectivity*. Kataoka understands sensory signals not as the substance of reality itself, but as the mechanism of material interconnection between the author and reality. For Kataoka, the author himself must be recognized in some sense as a material object. "The most direct practical power source (*dengen*) that mediates between the author's existence and the material object," he wrote, "and which gives this existence life, is sensation."[136]

Two things are clear from Kataoka's comments. First, that early Japanese modernists understood the basic data of any literary text to be sensation. Second, that these same modernists understood the goal of literature to be referential accuracy. By an apparent contradiction, the very focus on perception characteristic of Japanese modernism had the effect not of binding literary narrative to the limitations of the body, but of freeing it from those limits. Perceptual data was embraced, but *in an abstracted form*. Kataoka would retain this stance even after turning in 1927 to proletarian concerns. To "see" the capitalist system could mean *to listen to fragments of unrelated conversations through a handheld receiver across miles of copper wire*. The empire was both "visible" and representable, then, but only as a non-mimetic model, a diagrammatic construct. Like the mathematical models of Maxwellian electrodynamics, Kataoka's portrait of the Japanese state refers to an entity whose formal complexity defies direct experience, but whose *real existence* would never be questioned by the workers whose labor sustains it. The communicative power embedded in this referential logic—in the basic assumption that a moving train could indeed be represented accurately and objectively—infuses Japanese modernism's outward turn, its sudden impulse to confront the most spectral processes of the historical and natural world. Against Sōseki's famous doubts, abstraction was no longer an enemy to literature, but the very foundation of its greatest ambitions. Indeed, for those writers who began their careers associated with what would come to be called the New Sensationist school (Shin kankakuha)—organized, during its brief existence, around the journal *Bungei jidai*—accurate reference to the object world would be viewed as possible *only through abstraction*: through the creative assembly of what might otherwise be experienced as sensory confusion.

If Ezra Pound's quintessential proclamation that "bad art" can be defined simply as "inaccurate art"[137] captures the spirit of Japanese modernism in the 1920s, the emergence of this aesthetic of accuracy, with its focus on the complexities of an evolving material world, signaled the collapse of the autonomous authority of the individual subject. In fact, the disintegration of authorial subjectivity associated with this period has taken on the status of a truism. Any student of Japanese modernism knows that the 1920s witnessed the downfall of an ideal of subjective coherence and continuity that had defined the most influential texts of the Taishō period. Neither is it a discovery that this shift occurred simultaneously with new demands upon literature for political and social engagement, a trend felt most famously (if not most productively) by Akutagawa Ryūnosuke (1892–1927), whose suicide in 1927 stands as a defining moment in Japanese literary history. It is less often remembered, however, that the trauma Seiji Lippitt describes as a "crisis of subjectivity" surrounding Akutagawa's death was experienced by many writers at the time as an opportunity for an *expansion of objectivity*.[138] And this was just as true for dedicated experimentalists such as Yokomitsu Riichi, who resisted the pull of openly Marxist literature, as it was for writers like Kataoka, who joined the ranks of Japan's leftist literature movement just after Akutagawa's highly publicized overdose of sleeping pills.[139]

In a sense, the birth of Japanese modernism amounted to the discovery of a new world. Like the cosmos of relativity and the subatomic realm of the electron, the world that poets and fiction writers uncovered in the 1920s was both a "fact of experience" and a theoretical construct. Inseparable from industrialization, modern reality in Japan was at once an entity viewed with instruments and a universe built from models. And this is where Japanese modernism and the new physics share their deepest affinity. Science historian Peter Galison has explored the relation of industrialization to the birth of relativity in his book *Einstein's Clocks, Poincaré's Maps*, a useful companion piece for any student of avant-garde aesthetics. Focusing on the obsession with metric precision and simultaneity manifested in the effort by industrial nations to electrically coordinate public and commercial clocks in the late nineteenth and early twentieth centuries, Galison describes his subject as both "lofty abstraction and industrial concreteness."[140] Living in Bern during the early twentieth century, the young Einstein was "not only surrounded by the technology of coordinated clocks," Galison observes, "he was also in one of the great centers for the invention, production, and patenting of this burgeoning technology."[141] Indeed, for Galison, the 1905 publication of Einstein's historic paper on special relativity cannot be understood apart from the technical environment of industrial Europe, where two of Einstein's central intellectual concerns daily converged: electromagnetism and philosophic time. "In 1904–05," Galison writes, "clock-coordinating cables were thick on the ground and under the seas. Synchronized timepieces were everywhere."[142]

It seems far from coincidental, then, that Einstein and his senior contemporary, mathematician and mining engineer Henri Poincaré, began independently to ask a previously unheard-of question: What does it mean to say that two events are "simultaneous"?[143] Although the two great minds would arrive at opposing conclusions—for Poincaré simultaneity was a mere convention based on imperfect sensory data, while for Einstein simultaneity was real even if observer dependent—Galison's study suggests that the seemingly esoteric logic of their inquiries grew out of the experience of daily life in the industrialized city, where "physics, engineering, philosophy, colonialism, and commerce collided." As Kataoka's story suggested at a different social register, to labor in the industrial world meant to encounter at once the concrete substance of everyday machinery and the abstract mysteries of the universe. "At every moment," Galison writes, "synchronizing clocks was both practical and ideal: gutta-percha insulator over ironclad copper wire *and* cosmic time."[144]

A critical feature shared by Poincaré and Einstein in their approach to physical phenomena—ranging from airflow through mineshafts to the dynamics of time and motion—was the diagrammatic grammar of their descriptions. Because both of these thinkers confronted problems that were mathematical and physical at the same time, even their most abstract solutions remained at bottom referential "portraits": cartographic renderings of elusive processes and systems. Indeed, the language of the diagram seems peculiarly adequate to industrial life itself, with its vast communications networks and strange new instruments of detection. It is a sign of its surprisingly general applicability that the four-dimensional geometry invented by Hermann Minkowski (1864–1909) to represent Einsteinian space-time owed something to Poincaré's earlier non-Euclidean illustrations, or that these same four-dimensional renderings helped to guide the development of Cubism, an art for which abstraction betrayed enormous referential ambitions.[145] The jarring appearance of Cubist painting reflected not a willful self-absorption, but a new standard of accuracy in portraying the natural and built environment. In the hands of the Cubists, the diagram reached its apogee: an aesthetic object that was also an explanation.

The diagram emerges as a central image of Japanese literature too during its modernist moment. All the novels and stories examined in this study are united by a common diagrammatic aspiration: not to "reflect" the world so much as to "map" it, to picture it as a network of relations. This is no mere affectation of style. The diagrammatic inflection of Japanese literary modernism in the 1920s reaches far beyond the boundaries of some avant-garde cult of difficulty, beyond the sometimes impenetrable proclamations of New Sensationist authors and the responses they elicited from their rivals on the left. This modernist posture is recognizable even in popular novels and stories associated with the era's thriving and newly powerful sphere of mass literature (*taishū bungaku*).

For Tanizaki Jun'ichirō (1886–1965), one of the most recognizable today of these highly paid popular authors of the 1920s and 30s, the casting of pivotal narrative scenes in the image of a diagram would become a uniquely fertile creative strategy.[146] In the years when daily life in Japan's cosmopolitan centers had become permeated with freely circulating photographic and cinematic images, this author entertained and scandalized his audience by exploring the erotic and aesthetic potential of these technologies: engaging an ocular relation to the world that was non-mimetic, yet profoundly and attentively (often pornographically) referential. Precisely by absorbing the visual logic of techniques associated with mass culture (especially advertising and film), Tanizaki's prose managed to "expose" social relations underlying the very institutions his work sets out to celebrate—and from which his career clearly benefited. To read Tanizaki's work from the 1920s is to ask one of the central questions facing historians of popular culture: What does it mean finally to *unveil* social inequities and *embody* them at the same time?

Tanizaki's work is suffused with optical instruments, electrified by the "image of the image." But because he absorbed the diagrammatic (rather than merely reflective) dimensions of this newly ubiquitous visual technology, it is the relational logic of his realism that animates Tanizaki's greatest literary achievements. His fiction and essays seem especially attuned to the photograph's double capacity to document the object world and to record a singular observational relationship to it at the same time. Almost thirty years ago, Susan Sontag described photographs as "evidence not only of what's there but of what an individual sees, not just a record but an evaluation of the world." Undiminished today in their status as objective artifacts, photographs nevertheless continue to remind us that "nobody takes the same picture of the same thing."[147] If mimesis, in the classic Socratic definition, stands for an effacement of this observational relationship, "for those cases in which the poet attempts to create the illusion that it is not he who is speaking," it was Tanizaki's unique achievement to highlight the *non-mimetic* potential of photography and cinema as part of a narrative effect.[148] This is especially true with the author's earlier fiction from the late Taishō and early Shōwa years in which photography and cinema often serve a key function in the story itself.

In Tanizaki's famous 1924 novel *Chijin no ai* (*Naomi*), for instance—the subject of Chapter 1 of this book—the protagonist and narrator, Jōji, cultivates a sexual relationship with his young lover, Naomi, that revolves closely around the very abstracting processes that Sōseki condemned thirteen years earlier.[149] Using a portable camera and private darkroom, Jōji documents Naomi's physical transformation from an impoverished young café waitress into the seamy facsimile of a Hollywood starlet, eventually assembling a photo-journal that chronicles this metamorphosis by diagramming the changing contours of her body. I say "diagramming" because the form this photo-diary ultimately takes departs almost wholly from any pretenses of mimetic representation. Described with great care, Jōji's photo-montage embraces the power of a new observational relationship, a new category of "objective" knowledge. For Tanizaki, this knowledge is both erotic and aesthetic. But it is also, in important ways, "scientific," evincing a form of precision that *refers to its object without imitating it.*

It is the peculiar yield of what I am calling "non-mimetic referentiality" that Naomi's flesh can only be portrayed in terms of its ceaselessly evolving relationship to Jōji's observing eyes—or, more precisely, to his instruments of observation. Clearly avoiding a naturalistic portrait of Naomi's "character," the narrative also turns away from any truly naturalistic depictions of her physique. Readers are not given a picture of Naomi's visible body, in other words, but a feverishly accurate pornographic map: a diagram of those invisible but real relations that form the basis of Jōji's own aesthetic and erotic aspirations. Like the atomic models of the day, Tanizaki's novel sacrifices naturalism for accuracy, focusing on a "reality not of things seen," as Gertrude Stein said of Picasso, "but of things that exist."[150]

If science "describes nature as exposed to our methods of questioning," as Werner Heisenberg wrote, then Jōji describes Naomi's body as it is exposed to the interrogations of a photographic camera.[151] At first, Tanizaki's novel might seem suggestive merely of free-floating fantasy, and we may be tempted to understand the scenes it depicts simply as scandalous variations on Sōseki's earlier observation that photographic images are so profoundly disjoined from reality "as to be beyond comparison with it." Jonathan Crary's characterization of photography as one of numerous technical instantiations of a nineteenth-century obsession with the "physiological status of the observer and of vision" might encourage such a conclusion. By recognizing a discursive connection between the era's popular optical devices and "empirical studies of subjective vision," Crary's powerful argument tempts us to understand photography as inherently (because originally) "bound up in *non-veridical* theories of vision that effectively annihilate a real world."[152] When reading Tanizaki's fiction and essays from the late Taishō and early Shōwa years, however, it becomes impossible not to recognize that the same instrumentality that stood for a subjectivist paradigm in the nineteenth century, might easily serve the interests of a new "objectivism" in the twentieth. It is the argument of Chapter 1 of this book, in fact, that in Tanizaki's literary universe, the well-noted capacity of the photographic image to "circulate and proliferate,"[153] to abstract itself from the fabric of space and time, far from severing its link to the real world, actually enhances its documentary connection to it.

But what exactly does Tanizaki's fiction "document"? Scholars have long invoked Tanizaki's *Naomi* to substantiate discussions of gender, race, and the geo-cultural dynamics of national identity (surface "talking points" the story openly invites), but this well-known and widely translated novel is also an explication of art itself and the social relations that make it possible in the modern world. Even more fundamentally, it is a story about *observation* as a relational act.

Language and the Politics of Realism

Tanizaki's work anticipates the world we live in today, but it also represents a long endangered disposition. The realist substratum that distinguishes Japanese modernism from what preceded it also marks its distinction from our own postmodern present. To identify Japanese modernism as a realist deviation from a positivist past is thus both to distinguish it from the present and to unveil surprising commonalities between late twentieth-century poststructuralist theory and late nineteenth-century empiricism. It is only an apparent paradox that Karatani Kōjin, in his influential *Origins of Modern Japanese Literature*, finds echoes of his own Foucauldian imagination in Natsume Sōseki's radically empiricist disquisition, "Bungakuron" (A theory of literature, 1906), with its relativizing discussions of form.[154] In fact, there would seem to be a natural affinity between Karatani's tendency to view history in terms of discursive constructs or "semiotic configurations" and Sōseki's notion of reality as a subjective figment, a *sensory* effect.[155]

Ostensibly, Sōseki's essay sets out to explore the "psychological origins of literature" as well as the "social factors" behind its development, but it is the anti-realist logic of his approach that determines its claustrophobic structure. Sōseki's "consciousness charts" and his notorious reduction of literary content to the formula {F+f} ("impressions/concepts" plus "accompanying emotions") originate from an apparent belief that neither literature nor the senses can refer to anything but themselves: the ironic culmination of a positivist's obsession with empirical verifiability.[156]

By describing Sōseki's essay as a "flower that bloomed out of season," Karatani overlooks much of what was inevitable about this text.[157] In important ways, Sōseki's insights were perfectly attuned to the mimetic worldview of late Meiji literature. It is an effect of mimesis itself, for instance, that when the consciousness of the "speaking author" becomes the focal point of a work, the "objective world" must disappear. The very subjectivism that journalist Nakamura Murao (1886–1949) would condemn in 1924 as emblematic of late Meiji and early Taishō literature's failure to engage in "authentic" mimetic realism only underscores the inward dimension that Sōseki had already intuited as inherent to the mimetic point of view.[158] Though peculiar in literary history to what would later be designated as Japan's I-novel form—what Nakamura called "state-of-mind novels" (*shinkyō shōsetsu*), associated most famously with Tayama Katai's 1907 "Futon" (The quilt)—this compulsive attention to the details of subjective perception is not unconnected to a broader epistemological crisis recognizable across the industrial world and registered in much of Sōseki's work. As I have already suggested, the metaphysics of classical Enlightenment-era realism, which Karatani treats as a cognate for "the West" (which serves, in turn, as a cognate, for "the modern") was in a state of crisis even as it was being introduced to Japan in the 1890s. Natsume Sōseki does not deviate from this historical moment; he *embodies* it.

In a peculiar way, so does Karatani. It is the central insight of *Origins of Modern Japanese Literature* that before there could be any mimetic tension between the objective world and the writing subject, a clear distinction between the two first had to be "discovered," which is to say *constituted* through signification. The "world outside," according to Karatani's famous thesis, amounts to nothing more than a discursive effect, the product of an ideology of writing that emphasized neutral and transparent representation. The emergence in the late nineteenth century of a vernacular writing style (*kōgo*)—associated with pedagogical, literary and bureaucratic movements organized loosely around the term *genbun itchi* (literally, "the unification of speaking and writing")—signaled for Karatani a departure from the "figural" emphasis of Sino-Japanese literary script (*kanbun* and *bungo*) and a fateful transition toward a modern, unproblematically referential view of writing. Within the space of a generation, written language had come to be understood, above all, as a tool for *expressing* interior states or for *representing* external reality. For Karatani, this shift not only explains the emergence of naturalism as the dominant style of narrative, but also, more generally, stands for a moment of profound native loss: when a supposed pre-modern genius for understanding writing as a play of signifiers gave way to the benighted dichotomies of the European Enlightenment.[159]

Within the strictures of Karatani's argument, to speak of a newly visible objective world—what he calls the "discovery of landscape"—is to speak of the "illusion" of reference itself. Not surprisingly, Karatani has much to say about perception, but the word for him has nothing at all to do with the organs of the body or its material surroundings. "I am not here talking about a matter of vision," he writes of the historical emergence in Japan of naturalistic writing techniques and the sudden capacity of late nineteenth-century writers and artists to "see" an external world. "This inversion, which transforms our mode of perception, does not take place either inside of us or outside of us, but is an inversion of a semiotic configuration."[160] The external world that Sōseki understood as a function of the cerebrum, Karatani sees as a function of the sign. For this postmodern scholar and celebrity, the "perceptual" transformations of history take place exclusively in the realm of signification, which is portrayed as curiously without location: neither "inside of us" nor "outside of us." If this assertion exemplifies the anti-realism of postmodernism's reflexive inclination, it is crucial to distinguish that stance from the linguistic opacity associated with high modernism. In fact, the realist impulse at the heart of Japanese modernism's experimental revolt in the 1920s might best be understood by looking at the relationship modernist writers themselves envisioned between language and perception.[161]

In 1941, when Yokomitsu Riichi looked back on the history of his own experimental New Sensationist school, it was science, technology, and human perception that remained the protagonists of the modernist epoch. He described a time right after the destruction of the Great Kantō Earthquake in 1923:

> Before our eyes, the great city had become a vast unbelievable wasteland. And in its expanses, a fleeting specter called the "automobile" began to roam; soon

that vocal deformity called "radio" appeared, and a bird-shaped device known as the "airplane" began to cross the skies. These were all the concrete expressions of modern science as it came to life in our country after the earthquake. For those human beings whose youth saw the cutting edge of modern science take shape in this wasteland, their senses had, in some sense, no choice but to undergo transformation.[162]

Remindful of the material and relational principles that would become the hallmark of his fiction, Yokomitsu's retrospective essay describes what he and his fellow artists experienced as changes *to* their senses occurring inseparably from transformations unfolding *before* their senses—literally "the great city we saw" (*me ni suru daitokai*). Concretized in new machines for moving and communicating, the empirical facts of modernization seemed to demand a new way of sensing the world: a new relationship of human experience to external reality.

It was critic Chiba Kameo (1878–1935) who first called Yokomitsu's self-consciously experimental literary movement "New Sensationism," thereby marking a fateful division between Japan's literary avant-garde and its Proletarian Literature movement.[163] The moniker was happily adopted by the writers it described. Although scholars in the last 25 years have focused on the linguistic rather than the sensory dimension of New Sensationist texts, it is important (though by no means conclusive) to remember that the New Sensationists themselves understood their work precisely in terms of sensation. In fact, it is probably even more accurate to say that authors associated with this group and with the broader modernist movement to which it gave rise understood "reality" as a matter neither of the senses nor of signs alone, but rather as a problem of their dialectical interconnection.

In 1924, Kawabata Yasunari (1899–1972) published what is perhaps the most lucid attempt by a New Sensationist writer to theorize the movement at the moment of its birth. Crucially, Kawabata approaches the subject of the group's stylistic "newness" from the standpoint of "epistemology" (*ninshikiron*).[164] "Without a new language (*hyōgen*)," he wrote, "there can be no new content. And without new modes of perceiving (*kankaku*), there can be no new language."[165] Struggling to settle what he sees as a general confusion about the work of his most famous colleague, Yokomitsu Riichi, Kawabata gropes for a way to make sense of a style that is fundamentally referential, but far outside the conventional bounds of realism. "There are those who say Yokomitsu's style is 'naturalist,'" he wrote, "that his language is objective. This is clearly a mistake. If this is objectivism, it is a new objectivism, an objectivism in which subject and object are unified." Acknowledging the "Cubist" dimension of Yokomitsu's approach, Kawabata recognizes that the "feeling" (*kimochi*) contained in the author's work not only requires "new sensation" to be grasped, but actively "makes new our senses" (*kankaku o atarashiku suru*).[166]

The most memorable idea of this essay, however—the notion of a stylistic "unification of subject and object"[167]—is also its most misleading. Dismissing Japan's reigning school of literary naturalism as a form of "old fashioned objectivism" marked by its treatment of the subject and the object as separate entities, Kawabata finds unexpected commonalities between a burgeoning literary avant-garde and ancient East Asian mystical traditions. For Kawabata, New Sensationism (exemplified by Yokomitsu's style) reflects a "way of thinking" that, if carried through, would culminate in a "unity of self and other, a unity of nature, and a single world in which the boundaries of everything in heaven and earth disappear and all is harmonized as a single spirit."[168] The ideological danger of such an assertion—the same lyrical attraction to "mysticism" (*shinpishugi*) that Miyamoto Yuriko (1899–1951) would later criticize in Kawabata's work as a reflection of fascism[169]—is compounded, in this case, by analytical inaccuracy. For Yokomitsu Riichi, literary language was rooted not in the mysticism of spiritual unity but in the materialism of physical interconnection.

"Literature," Yokomitsu would write in 1928, "is that object (*buttai*) through which individuals represent with written signs the movement of matter (*busshitsu no undō*)."[170] And "content," in turn, is the "energy" (*enerugī*) that arises between the reader and written forms (*moji no keishiki*)."[171] Describing printed characters on the page as "solid objects with volume" (*yōseki o motta buttai*) capable of depicting the very material world to which they themselves belong, Yokomitsu understood textual language as both *literally material* and *radically referential*: embedded in the very network of relations it functions to portray.[172] Following the convolutions of this Einsteinian logic, Yokomitsu would ultimately produce a "materialist theory of literature" (*yuibutsuronteki bungakuron*) that revolved around an unexpectedly ecological insight: that being *connected* to the object world is not the same as being *one with it.*

Indeed, the very notion of objective reference loses all meaning when subject and object are no longer differentiated. So it is not a vision of oneness that animates Yokomitsu's theory of literature, but an image of intimacy—of *common involvement* in a network of relations. And it is this image that captures the peculiar form of realism at the heart of Japanese modernism. The poetics of New Sensationism, Yokomitsu explained, function by allowing the movement of language to "fuse" with the movements of the object world, forming together "a kind of progressive realism" (*shinpoteki na isshu no shajitsu*).[173] This notion of progressive realism infiltrates Yokomitsu's most successful works from the 1920s: an idea of language that was also a theory of matter and corporal perception. In his most important fiction from these years, Yokomitsu consistently depicts the human body as a sort of "material object" embedded in a field of political, economic, and physical relations. Human experience, from this perspective, is first and foremost an objective fact of a material universe. For Yokomitsu Riichi no less than for Karl Marx, to exist in the world meant "to be an object of sense, to be a *sensuous* object, and thus to have sensuous objects outside oneself—objects of one's sensuousness."[174] Although he opposed Marxism as a political ideology throughout his life, the essence of Yokomitsu's early materialism echoes the earliest insights of Marx himself. "That man's physical and spiritual life is linked to nature," Marx had written in 1844, "means simply that nature is linked to itself, for man is a part of nature."[175]

Yokomitsu's notorious turn in the 1930s to an ideology of cultural and racial nationalism signals the final displacement of this vision of material *interconnection* with a more plodding image of spiritual and ethnic *unity* immersed in the familiar logic of cultural relativism and self-reference. To understand this shift as a failure and not a fulfillment of the logic of high modernism is to break the spell of a common conceptual narrative. This narrative originates in many different sources, but is most memorably articulated in a passage from Fredric Jameson's book *Postmodernism, or, The Cultural Logic of Late Capitalism.* I owe a great deal to this passage; in many ways, the book I write now is a culmination of my departure from the ideas it contains:

> Once upon a time [Jameson wrote] at the dawn of capitalism and middle-class society, there emerged something called the sign, which seemed to entertain unproblematical relations with its referent. This initial heyday of the sign—the moment of literal or referential language or of the unproblematical claims of so-called scientific discourse—came into being because of the corrosive dissolution of older forms of magical language by a force which I will call that of reification, a force whose logic is one of ruthless separation and disjunction, of specialization and rationalization, of a Taylorizing division of labor in all realms. Unfortunately, that force—which brought traditional reference into being—continued unremittingly, being the very logic of capital itself. Thus, the first moment of decoding, or of realism cannot long endure; by a dialectical reversal it then itself in turn becomes the object of the corrosive force of reification, which enters the realm of language to disjoin the sign from the referent. Such a disjunction does not completely abolish the referent, or the objective world, or reality, which will still continue to entertain a feeble existence on the horizon like a shrunken star or red dwarf. But its great distance from the sign now allows the latter to enter a moment of autonomy, of a relatively free-floating Utopian existence, as over against its former objects. This autonomy of culture, this semiautonomy of language, is the moment of modernism, and of a realm of the aesthetic which redoubles the world without being altogether of it, thereby winning a certain negative or critical power, but also a certain otherworldly futility. Yet the force of reification, which was responsible for this new moment, does not stop there either: in another stage, heightened, a kind of reversal of quantity into quality, reification penetrates the sign itself and disjoins the signifier from the signified. Now reference and reality disappear altogether, and even meaning—the signified—is problematized. We are left with that pure and random play of signifiers that we call postmodernism. . . .[176]

The power of the story Jameson tells resides in the elegance of its linear structure. The sign—linked essentially here to capitalism itself—moves dialectically from its original heyday as the transparent tool of "scientific discourse" to its own final dissected humiliation in the contemporary moment of surfaces and "random play"—a progression, in other words, from *reference* to *signification.* Understood as an ensemble of signifier (the sound-image) and signified (the concept represented by the sound-image), the sign gradually loses its legitimate kinship with the extra-linguistic universe until finally, by a syllogistic leap, the external and internal universe itself (of pine-trees and revolutions, heartbreak and fear) ceases to exist. Within this framework, modernism serves necessarily as the halfway point between the benighted metaphysics of the Enlightenment and the reflexive insights of postmodernism: an ambiguous position in which objective reality remains, but only as a crepuscular vestige. Jameson is not alone in characterizing modernism as a sort of "missing link" in the evolution of postmodernism. In his summary of European modernism for *The Cambridge Companion to Modernism*, Michael Bell conceals his own version of this evolutionary approach behind an alimentary metaphor: "The change from Modernism to postmodernism," he tells us, "is not a difference in metaphysic so much as a different stage in the digestion of the same metaphysic."[177]

In recent decades, Japanese scholars too have come to interpret the texts of Japan's modernist moment as prototypically postmodern. Komori Yōichi's analysis of *Naomi*, for example describes Jōji as a man charmed by empty signifiers, an "interpreter of signs" who carries out his erotic fantasies in a world without content or referentiality;[178] Maeda Ai celebrated Japan's 1920s as an "age of surfaces";[179] and Karatani Kōjin has asserted that Akutagawa Ryūnosuke understood his own narrative style "as what we might call postmodern . . . as a kind of deconstruction of the late nineteenth-century Western novel."[180] But reading the texts of Japanese modernism as nothing more than embryonic expressions of contemporary pieties and taboos amounts to a proleptic misstep that can only obscure the significance of this brief efflorescence of literary creativity.

Modernism was a crisis of *perception* before it was a crisis of representation. When viewed within the history of empiricism—a history of the senses, not of the sign—this short-lived movement emerges as a resuscitation of an object world that had already come close to extinction in the late nineteenth century. Profoundly referential in ambition and deeply materialist in its logic, Japanese literature's experimental enterprise of the 1920s must be recognized not as the hesitant gesture toward some incipient (or, as in Karatani's argument, imperfectly submerged) ethos of reflexivity, but as a historic bulwark against it. It was precisely its referential inflection, for example, that made the language of the new physics so attractive to Yokomitsu Riichi. Indeed, the recurrence of words like "matter," "energy," and "movement" in Yokomitsu's theoretical proclamations highlights the importance of twentieth-century physics to this author. Like many of his avant-garde colleagues, Yokomitsu felt the impact of Albert Einstein's 1922 lecture tour of Japan and of the popular explanatory articles by Ishiwara Jun. This author regarded his own theory of form (*keishikiron*) as the culmination of an effort to achieve in the literary realm a vision of material interconnection that had already been accomplished by Einstein in the physical sciences: "the restoration of time and space to a single dimension."[181] Far from representing the surface semiotics that leading literary scholars find in it today, Yokomitsu's "formalism" constituted the framework of an outward-looking poetics of precision: a literature of accuracy.

From this perspective, it makes sense that the very history which never found its way into Sōseki's discussion of modern civilization—Japan's expanding empire in Asia—became the subject of Yokomitsu's greatest full-length experimental novel, *Shanghai* (*Shanhai*, 1928–32), the focus of Chapter 2 of this book.[182] A sprawling portrait of the citywide riots of May 30, 1925, this work famously tested the applicability of the author's theory of "materialist" literature. In surprising ways, his disjunctive and diagrammatic style was ideally suited for documenting the global events of modern history. Yokomitsu's journalistic compulsion—his attraction to the world of actual places and events—suggests a subterranean kinship with those openly radical works being produced at this time by his literary opponents on the left. (What better subject for Proletarian Literature than an urban revolt in the heart of colonized Asia?)

Even at its most "materialist," however, *Shanghai*'s excavation of the underlying laws of empire—of social conflict, racial oppression, and capitalist exchange—betrays the hazardous equanimity of a purely descriptive impulse, an essential tolerance of the violence it sets out to depict. It is part of the novel's dark reputation that its exposure of the brutal workings of capitalism cannot cancel out its equally materialist "explanations" of racial hierarchy and national identity. When all of human history is conceived in terms of material laws—and therefore, in a sense, as "natural"—there is always a danger of misunderstanding those laws as "inevitable." Even during the years when it was relatively safe to do so, Yokomitsu never sympathized with the politics of resistance, and this probably cannot be explained without reference to his fatal misconception of nature as normative. In predictable (if irrational) ways, Yokomitsu's "scientific" approach became the basis of an underlying complacency about social injustice and military violence. Over the four years *Shanghai* was serialized, a divide deepened between the author's formalist theories and his narrative practice. His original view of "objectivity" as a category of material involvement (theorized in his essays on language) finally expressed itself in the form of a studied indifference: an ethical conviction in its own right. This author's instincts were descriptive to the core, and *Shanghai* shows us how easily such a descriptive stance can become a prescriptive one.

If Yokomitsu's greatest contribution to Japanese literature was epistemological, what then was the politics of this epistemology? By asking this question, we skirt the edges of a dangerous fallacy, identified by John Guillory as part of the "spontaneous philosophy" at work behind most critical attacks on scientific realism in contemporary theory: the "assumption that epistemological positions have a *necessary* relation to political positions."[183] For critics in the humanities today, Guillory argues, scientific realism has become uncritically equated with a reactionary "normative complacency" based on science's supposed denial of its own social dimensions, or the social dimensions of the "natural" world it presumably takes as a given.[184] Since "nature" assumes numerous forms in the natural sciences, as Guillory points out, it cannot be generally condemned as that which "underlies the naturalization of all cultural practices."[185] A critique of science's "complicity in certain oppressive social practices," in other words, "is not the same as a critique that extends to the status of scientific truth generally."[186]

To say that epistemology harbors no specific political content, however, is not to suggest that it has no connection with politics at all. Indeed, it is the underlying premise of the present book that realist epistemology constitutes an essential—if not sufficient—component of meaningful political critique in the modern age. Realism in literature may not guarantee the emergence of radical politics, but its absence guarantees against it. Starting from this belief, the final section of this book outlines what I see as a crucial link between Japanese modernism's relational realism and the most important ethical revolution of the twentieth century: the rise of environmental criticism and the birth of ecology.

The Things of This World

In his 1933 essay "Kokyō o ushinatta bungaku," when critic Kobayashi Hideo (1902–83) confessed a growing skepticism about his own habit of going into the mountains to be inspired by "nature's beauty" (*shizenbi*), his criticism was aimed not only at the artificiality of a specific leisure activity, but at the abstract logic of modernism itself. "I have come to doubt the existence of anything fixed or real behind the emotion I feel when encountering nature's beauty," he writes near the beginning of this essay. "When you look carefully at it, being intoxicated by the beauty of a mountain is really quite similar to being intoxicated by the beauty of an abstract idea."[187] Reviving the complaint of Sōseki's 1911 lecture on modern civilization, Kobayashi presents his own cosmopolitan incapacity for simple and direct encounters with the world as evidence of a general "homelessness" pervading modern (urban) life and literature in 1930s Japan. "It is a fact," he would famously conclude, "that we are a generation of youths who have lost their innocence, embracing a literature that has lost its home."[188]

But what does "home" really mean in this work, and how is it linked to this opening image of "nature"? In the most general—if circular—sense, home for Kobayashi refers to *that which has been lost to modernity*. More precisely, Kobayashi's titular image of the lost home or "native place" (*kokyō*) functions throughout the essay to suggest an endangered relationship to *certainty* and *stability* combined with some receding quality of *singularity* that the term "nature" is meant to signify. Home is where natural encounters with the concrete, the "actual" or "the real" (*genjitsu*) are still possible.

Predictably, no modern city qualifies as such a place. When he tells his readers "my life has been extraordinarily lacking in concrete substance (*gutaisei*)," Kobayashi blames the frenetic pace of modern Tokyo, his own birthplace.[189] "In retrospect, I can say that from the time I was young, my mind has been tormented by all the endless and various changes occurring too fast; there was never time to cultivate any powerful memories attached to concrete things."[190] It is the city's ceaseless metamorphosis that unsettles this author, eroding the sense of continuity he understands as the essence of reality itself. "I do have memories," he writes, "but they lack actuality [*genjitsuteki na naiyo ga nai*]."[191] If actuality here means certainty and stability, it also points—more crucially—to an image of uniqueness that Kobayashi associates with the countryside as well. Urban experience pales, he argues, next to the overpowering sense of "native place" that memories of a particular mountain road might inspire. Describing Tokyo-born individuals as "human abstractions" (*chūshōjin*), no different from urban-dwellers anywhere in the industrial world, Kobayashi would seem to stand unequivocally opposed to the homogenizing forces of modernization. "To meditate upon these human abstractions no doubt amounts to a kind of literature, but it is a literature that lacks a foundation in reality (*jisshitsu aru urazuke ga nai*)."[192] Against the inimitable and presumably abiding contours of provincial geography, Kobayashi contrasts the insubstantiality of his own urban identity: "I simply cannot grasp what 'born in Tokyo' means."[193]

By the end of the essay, however, this image of regional authenticity has been transfigured by a rhetorical shift in emphasis from local to national identity. Through a familiar totalizing gesture, Kobayashi finally presents "singularity" as the endangered feature of Japan itself: a paradoxically homogenized and nation-bound image of cultural unity. It is no longer the city-dweller's estrangement from the rural particularities of a mountain road that concerns the author, but modern Japan's growing indistinctiveness from other industrialized states. In the end, home stands for the "uniqueness" of Japanese culture as a whole, the loss of which signals impending defeat in a cultural war with the West. To be homeless means to have been deprived of "all signs of our nation's character, all signs of its individuality."[194]

If "actuality" means *stability*, *certainty*, and *continuity* in this essay, and "singularity" means the uncritical acceptance of a *homogeneous state-centered cultural totality opposed to "the West,"* it is hard to imagine a biological or physical model that might match this author's idea of "nature." More interested in denying dynamic processes than in depicting them, Kobayashi's essay evinces a profound suspicion toward the abstract idiom that natural scientists were pioneering in the early twentieth century in order precisely to grasp and depict unstable organic and inorganic systems. Indeed, it is the specter of the "abstract idea" itself that haunts this author, whose rhetoric holds abstraction responsible somehow for the very loss he eulogizes. A year before publishing "Literature of the Lost Home," Kobayashi made clear this position in an essay entitled "Gendai bungaku no fuan" (The anxiety of modern literature, 1932), a telling attack on the notion of "modern beauty" (*kindaibi*). Casting doubt upon the "deceptions of modern science that allow us to circle the globe in an instant," Kobayashi describes the modern, technological world as a dreamscape constructed from "all the numberless absurd images that dreams require"[195]:

The miracle of the machine materialized by science was, of course, anticipated by the miracle of the theory that underlies it. With our knowledge of celestial orbits, we were able to recognize the resemblance between planetary movements and the movements of electrons. The idea of maximum entropy has given us detailed insights into the death of our own bodies. Beams of light, previously thought to simply overcome darkness, have been transformed into a plain substance with weight. We now understand not only that light surrounds us even on a dark night, but that it permeates and constitutes our very spirits. Once the atom was understood to be unstable, time and space, as pure concepts, lost all meaning. . . . Nothing remains fixed or certain. There has probably been no other time in human history when the words "new facts" have carried such great significance. To our eyes, exhausted by the search for new facts, the color of things multiplies, their outlines blur. Nothing remains fixed or certain.[196]

Echoing the central insight that Marshall Berman traces to Karl Marx and Friedrich Engels, Kobayashi attributes to science what the Communist Manifesto identified with the bourgeois order: an end to all "fixed, fast-frozen relations."[197] For Kobayashi, though, little good could come from such an all-pervasive instability. Depicted more as a creation of modern science than a discovery, the uncertainties of the subatomic realm are related, through an abrupt shift of imagery in the very next passage, to the anxieties provoked by the experience of the city streets:

We go into the streets full of anxiety. There is nothing there, however, that can be called with any certainty "the city" or "society." Oddly, everything that is necessary for a city and for a society is right before our eyes: railway stations, post offices, buildings, factories. But we have no belief in the mechanism behind it all, the strings that make it all work.[198]

Kobayashi describes here a crisis of faith, a fading willingness to *believe* in the invisible forces and institutions that animate the industrial city—mechanisms the author correctly recognizes as inseparable from all the "new facts" about electrons, light energy, time, and space. When viewed against his later lament over modern Japan's alienation from nature, Kobayashi's suspicion toward abstract scientific language strikes an ironic chord. For it was these very "abstractions" that had enabled the emergence of early ecological models in the 1920s and 30s, that would define the concept of the "ecosystem" in 1935 (with its emphasis on energy flow and nutrient exchange), and that would later be the cognitive premise of all environmental ethics.[199] Unexpectedly, the same technical conditions that Kobayashi blames for humanity's estrangement from "nature" animated the modern world's growing understanding of evolutionary interdependence and ecological interconnection—the emergence after 1920 of what is sometimes called the New Ecology. Like the physics of energy fields, ecology was a realist enterprise, reliant upon a deep grammar that might easily have been dismissed as another version of "action at a distance." Ecology implies a belief-system peculiar to the modern world: a faith in the verifiable existence of "something behind things, which is deeply hidden." A historical kinship thus adheres between the science of electromagnetic exchange—the "strings" that make Kobayashi's city function—and New Ecology's burgeoning recognition of the hidden mechanisms joining the forest to the farmer, the hunter to the bear. According to environmental historian J. Baird Callicott, for example, Arthur George Tansley's 1935 ecosystem model "was expressly designed to be the 'field theory' of modern biology."[200]

When Kobayashi wrote his essays, biological science was fundamentally changing its thinking about inter-specific relations. The natural world, no longer viewed by biologists as a stable collection of distinct entities, was increasingly depicted in terms of co-evolution, of ceaselessly interacting wild and cultivated systems. As the biology of evolution joined insights with the chemistry of soil science and geology, the lines between the organic and inorganic began to blur. Kobayashi's anxieties about the subatomic world together with his romanticized image of "nature"—as something that exists "out there," stable and distinct from the city, untouched somehow by modern history—reveal a homocentric belief-system resistant to these newly visible realities. Like Sōseki several decades before him, Kobayashi sees natural science's abstract tendencies—as well as its instruments of detection and calibration—not as new means of engaging with the outside world, but as further evidence of our alienation from it: harbingers of a rising regime of the unreal. In a certain sense, therefore, Kobayashi's concern about modern Japan's estrangement from nature merely expresses the impulse to revive an earlier subjectivism. Behind the author's fear that humanity had disengaged from nature lies the more significant belief that humanity *can* disengage from nature. "Nature and humanity no longer confront each other," he would observe in a final recapitulation of Sōseki's earlier skepticism. "The machine has come between them."[201]

Precisely for its attention to themes of alienation and cultural dislocation, Seiji Lippit presents Kobayashi's later essay, "Kokyō o ushinatta bungaku," as a distillation of Japan's modernist era.[202] Considering Kobayashi's nervously atavistic evaluation of modernity's conditions and inflections, however—exemplified by his tendency to equate the "abstract" with the "unreal"—this work might more usefully serve to mark the *end* of Japanese modernism's most radical phase. This is hardly a forced interpretation. In certain obvious ways, Kobayashi's essay announces the termination of a literary epoch and the inauguration of another. Not three months before its publication, interrogators at Tsukiji Police station had beaten to death novelist Kobayashi Takiji (1903–33), the most prominent figure in the Proletarian Literature movement, signaling the virtual collapse of organized revolutionary literature in Japan.[203] The next few years would witness the flourishing of a broadly elegiac moment known as "the period of cultural renaissance" (*bungei fukkō*), a deeply romantic intellectual trend galvanized by the idea of cultural return and organized increasingly around the concept of *minzoku* (ethnic people).[204]

After 1933, literature's critical energies would be increasingly brought to bear against modernity itself—viewed unequivocally now as identical with a hostile West. Ideas about cultural salvation continued to organize themselves around competing concepts of "the real" or "the actual" (*genjitsu*), but these concepts lost the breadth of modernism's earlier relational vision. "Throughout the 1930s," writes Harry Harootunian, capturing the general outlines of this struggle, "a variety of differing outlooks contested the meaning of what constituted the actual (*genjitsu*), usually in an effort to lay claim to defining daily life, and either located it outside of contemporary phenomenal life, as in the writings of Kuki Shūzō or Nishitani, or tried to reunite it with the lived reality of daily life, like Tosaka Jun and the aesthetician Nakai Masakazu."[205] As this sentence suggests, what disappears from view during these years is high modernism's incipiently "ecological" or "Einsteinian" capacity to understand the actual as rooted in "the lived reality of daily life," yet somehow mysteriously *beyond it at the same time.*

Nineteen thirty-three was a year of loss. The year Kobayashi Hideo stylishly lamented literature's "lost home" and Kobayashi Takiji gasped his last painful breaths in police custody was also the year Miyazawa Kenji (1896–1933), one of Japan's great ecological visionaries, died of a lung infection in his native town of Hanamaki. For this experimental poet and children's writer, the language of abstraction amounted to a sacred idiom of *connection* with the actual world, not a sign of its degradation. A teacher of chemistry and soil science at an agricultural college in the remote and impoverished Tōhoku region of Japan's rural northeast, Kenji's fascination with the physics of energy, together with his early exposure to Darwin's theory of evolution by natural selection, formed the basis of a poetic departure from a human-centered world.[206] Kenji's poems and nature-tales—the subject of Chapters 3, 4, and 5 of this book—draw their ethical force from the author's willingness to assess the ethical content of a cherished Buddhist cosmology against the material insights that new scientific theories provided about humanity's relative position in the world: what deep ecology founder Arne Næss might call the "total view."[207]

From the strange chemistry and galactic imagery of his enormously (if posthumously) popular "Ginga tetsudō no yoru" (Night of the Milky Way railroad, 1923–33), to the unsettling tales of human-wildlife relations in his collection *Chūmon no ōi ryōriten* (The restaurant of many orders, 1924), to his tender portrait of predation in the story "Nametokoyama no kuma" (The bears of Nametokoyama), Miyazawa Kenji's works carry aesthetic modernism's relational realism to its most radical conclusions. Early in his life, Kenji absorbed the fact of human materiality as a far-reaching ethical conviction, candidly portraying—even in his most "quaint" children's fiction—humanity's interdependent relationship with the nonhuman and non-living world. In a dialect ranging from the technical language of science to the deceptively simple idiom of the folk tale, this author seems to have spent the bulk of his artistic career exploring the moral and political consequences implied by the simple organic fact of material interaction: what Marx called "metabolic relations."[208]

Indeed, Kenji's poetic treatment of human materiality might easily be related to the ecology that John Bellamy Foster has identified with Karl Marx himself in his recent book, *Marx's Ecology: Materialism and*

Nature. Structuring his argument around the work of Marx and Charles Darwin, what he calls "the two greatest materialists of the nineteenth century," Foster defies various anti-science strains running through contemporary Green theory by arguing that "the development of both materialism and science promoted—indeed made possible—ecological ways of thinking."[209] Well-crafted and penetrating in its analysis, Foster's work recognizes Marx's departure from philosophical "ideals" as crucial to the deep structure of any environmental program. If ecology requires us to understand "how spiritual conceptions, including our spiritual connections to the earth, are related to our material, earthly conditions," as Foster suggests, it is the centrality of science in Kenji's work rather than the author's much-studied Buddhist piety that determines the true foundation of its ecological content.[210] At bottom, Kenji's greatest "environmental" insights are less concerned with suffering as a universal condition of existence than as a local, historical problem. Many of his best-loved children's tales—including those examined in the final two chapters of this book—take as their subject the collapse of those very material relations with nonhuman life that make humanity's historical existence possible: the departure from what environmentalists today call "sustainability."

Apart from a brief stay in Tokyo, Kenji lived most of his life in the rural setting of his native Iwate Prefecture, a biographical fact that resists the standard equation of "Japanese modernism" with "urban Japan." Although his poems and stories betray a life-long interest in the technologies of modern life—with their famous images of trains and electric power stations, of telescopes and telegraph lines—Kenji applied the material insights embodied in these technologies to an ideal of totality far more complex than those images of national unity or class solidarity typically associated with literature from this period.

In Miyazawa Kenji's fiction, "social totality" meant the natural universe itself and all it involved: wild sparrows perched atop power line poles, molecules of galactic gas swirling in the vacuum of space, the warm beating heart of a deer. Through Kenji's work, contemporary ecology is revealed as one of the living legacies of aesthetic modernism's Neo-Copernican instincts. The revolt from positivism emerges here as inseparable from one of the most powerful ethical impulses of the modern age: to imagine and to cherish *as real* a world that may live and die unseen by humans. Affected, like many of his urban contemporaries, by the allurement of Einstein's theory of relativity—especially as it was explained in Charles Steinmetz's published lectures and non-Euclidean illustrations—and profoundly inspired by the evolutionary theories of early twentieth-century biologist Oka Asajirō (1868–1944), Kenji combines the insights of theoretical physics and biology with unprecedented ingenuity. "I believe that the main lesson of relativity and quantum theory," physicist Lee Smolin wrote in 2001, "is that the world is nothing but an evolving network of relationships."[211] It was the peculiar genius of Miyazawa Kenji, some seventy years earlier, to explore the poetic and *moral* significance of this material lesson.

Animated throughout by a vision of interconnection, Kenji's work is careful to avoid the sentimentality of natural "harmony." Despite his much-studied public commitment to the saving wisdom of Nichiren Buddhism, Kenji's poems and stories intuitively resist the grand unities of an uncritical mysticism, focusing instead upon mutual dependence and conflict between species, between living organisms and inorganic processes, between the cultivated and the wild things of this world. Here is modernism's dialectical insight applied to the natural world itself: *connected* but not *one*. Kenji's work reflects an ethical sensibility rooted in modernist aesthetics, though by no means guaranteed by it: an attraction to the "dark mystery" that Stephen Spender recognized in another, entirely different sort of writer from the same period. On D. H. Lawrence, Spender writes: "He had a sense that the distinctions between outer and inner are sacred: that whilst the inner life should meet the outer, the outer world should not become the inner world of the writer. To him the idea of the separateness of perceiving from what is perceived, of man from nature and from other men, is sacred."[212]

And so it is in Kenji's poetic world. A gap remains between the perceiving subject and the object, the depiction and the depicted, between human experience and the vastness of the non-human world. What is sacred is the mystery of the gap itself, and the imaginative capacity to see beyond it to the other side.

PART I

Art, Empire

ONE

Erotic Science: Realism and Aesthetics in the Fiction of Tanizaki Jun'ichirō

I never feel like writing or reading anything realistic, anything that takes as its material reality just the way it appears.

—Tanizaki Jun'ichirō, "Jōzetsuroku," 1927

Why do we read Tanizaki? Not surprisingly, the answer largely depends upon who the "we" is in that sentence. Memorialized through decades of cinema treatments and television plays, this author's venerable and provocative body of work has been a source of required reading in "national literature" (*kokubungaku*) courses for generations in Japan. At the same time, Tanizaki Jun'ichirō stands as one of the few canonized authors of his own generation whose novels can just as easily be found on the shelves of mainstream bookstores in Europe and the Americas. This dissemination has carried consequences far beyond monetary profit. Inevitably, once modern Japanese fiction entered the contradictory arena of "world literature"—receiving critical attention from such luminaries as Jorge Luis Borges and John Updike[1]—these works began to be taken as somehow representative: instances of an aesthetic vision that was, above all, *Japanese.*

In his prologue to the 1959 Spanish translation of Akutagawa Ryūnosuke's *Kappa* (1927), Borges describes "a certain restrained sorrow, a certain preference for the visual, a certain lightness of stroke" which strike him as "essentially Japanese."[2] For years, this was a pattern perpetuated by marketing strategies, by the state-oriented logic of international literary prizes, by academic discourse, and by Japanese writers themselves. The ethnic essentialism reflected in the Nobel committee's rationale for awarding Kawabata Yasunari the literature prize in 1968—"for his narrative mastery, which with great sensibility expresses the essence of the Japanese mind"—was matched only by the self-mystifying gestures of Kawabata's acceptance speech, "Utsukushii Nihon no watakushi" ("Japan, the Beautiful and Myself").[3] For decades after World War II, translations of Japanese fiction carried this curious burden. Readers in the West expected to learn something profound about Japan by reading Kawabata, Akutagawa, or Tanizaki in a way that far outstripped their expectations to learn about Ireland by reading Joyce, or to penetrate the mysteries of the "French mind" by reading Proust.[4]

If there is anything to be gained from working in an economy that describes itself as "global," it is the hope that this essentializing myth of national sensibility might finally be dispelled from popular consciousness. Although for most academics "global" culture refers in practice to nothing more than a circumscribed terrain of websites, institutions, hotels, and airport waiting areas, it was the *idea* of the global—and the new relationship to national traditions it implied—that allowed Ōe Kenzaburō to deliver his critical response to Kawabata's nativist meditation in his own 1994 Nobel acceptance speech, "Aimai na Nihon no watakushi" ("Japan, the Ambiguous, and Myself").[5] Scholars will always read works of literature at some level as cultural documents, but the parameters of the word "culture" have come to be recognized as at once far too wide-ranging and far too local to be meaningfully coincident with the category "Japanese."

The reader may object that Tanizaki's work is very often openly *about* being Japanese. Some of the author's most famous fiction revolves around an image of native identity *emancipated* by the exhilaration of Western culture, *endangered* by its seductions, or *revived* through a rediscovery of "native" sensibilities. Tanizaki's 1924 classic *Naomi*, the subject of this chapter, famously (if ironically) celebrates the thrills and dangers of Westernization as part of its erotic appeal. Far more fundamental than the specific image of national culture this novel conveys, however, is the deep grammar that drives its rhetoric: a subterranean logic that it shares with those later works whose content it would seem otherwise to oppose. Tanizaki's later nativist allegory *Tade kuu mushi* (*Some Prefer Nettles*, 1928–29) and his classically atavistic essay, "In'ei raisan" ("In Praise of Shadows," 1933)—both associated with a broader cultural "return to Japan" (*Nihon e no kaiki*)[6]—echo the celebratory *Naomi* by presenting aesthetics as the quintessential terrain of geopolitical conflict. It is a conceit common to each of these works that the specter of Euro-American hegemony may be embraced or resisted exactly here: where the senses meet the material world.

Indeed, much of Tanizaki's writing presents culture itself as nothing other than a way of imagining a sensory connection to the world, and the historical instability of this relationship amounts to the most consistent object of his own realism. Consider the following sentences from "In'ei raisan":

> Suppose, for example, we had developed our own physics and chemistry. Is it not likely that the technologies and industries based upon them would have developed differently, that all the various gadgets, medicines and industrial products would have emerged in forms more suitable to our national character? Indeed, it seems probable that even the basic principles of physics and chemistry would be understood in a way quite distinct from the Western view we are taught today, that the nature and function of light and electricity and even the atom would have disclosed themselves to us in completely different forms.[7]

Here is the target of Tanizaki's realism stripped to its essentials: not "reality just the way it appears," but reality as it has been "disclosed" (*rotei shite ita*) through the interrogations of culture. Crucially, even in his most defensive moments, Tanizaki never portrays the external universe as purely a "cultural construct." He does not deny the objective reality of light energy, electricity, or atoms, but merely reminds his readers that our *picture* of these basic elements emerges out of a deeply cultural engagement with the object world. Electromagnetic energy and atoms are presented as historical artifacts of a dialectical relationship: local instances of a more general interplay between the observer and the observed. Largely ignorant (by his own admission) of scientific matters, Tanizaki brilliantly intuits here the transformation of "objectivity" engendered by subatomic physics itself, centered around the insight that there can be no *final* description of the world.

From the beginning years of his career, Tanizaki explored the aesthetic possibilities of this principle of uncertainty. Many of his works from the 1910s and early 20s concern themselves directly, in style and in theme, with the optical paradoxes and referential mysteries of a burgeoning movie industry. Indeed, the relational and realist instincts that characterize "In'ei raisan"—with its emphasis on the unseen, on a vision of "depth" (*fukami*) both constituted and obscured by "shadows" (*in'ei*)[8]—probably cannot be separated from this early flirtation with cinema. Neither can it be understood apart from Japan's own expanding power grid, the permeating noise of its radio broadcasts, and the flashy international commerce in photographic imagery that Tanizaki famously studied and absorbed in order finally to "reject" in the name of Japanese tradition. When examined in its most concrete terms, Tanizaki's work tells us far more about what it means to be modern than about what it means to be Japanese. More precisely, it shows "modern" and "Japanese" to be inseparable categories of experience.

Tanizaki's *Naomi* stands as the fullest expression of this modernist disposition. Self-consciously absorbed in mechanized optics and infused with the shadowy chemistry of photography, this novel both exposes and exploits the social iniquities underlying a sensibility peculiar to industrial capitalism. By remaking aesthetic value in the image of a graphic advertisement, *Naomi* reveals the modern art object—and, inseparably, the modern object of male erotic desire—to be built upon a set of deceptions that nevertheless reflect real social relations. If science "describes nature as exposed to our methods of questioning," as Werner Heisenberg wrote, then Tanizaki's method of questioning in *Naomi* is prurient, his means photographic.[9] Tracing the allurements of its male protagonist and narrator in an idiom that is at once scientific and commercial, this novel offers an engrossing and textured description of modern fantasy even as it diagrams its material conditions of possibility. In the end, it is neither Western nor Japanese *beauty* so much as it is a modern ideal of *glamour* that Tanizaki's novel engages and unveils.

Here, then, is at least one reason we read Tanizaki in industrial countries today: to glimpse the terrible edifice of pleasure and happiness that his characters pursue. As art gives way to pornography in this story, *Naomi* generates an aesthetic ideal that is socially inclusive and unapologetically reliant upon male domination at the same time. The narrator's explicit treatment of his wife's body as an aesthetic and erotic object leads finally to the creation of a kind of "high pornography"—and the reader is left to fathom the meaning of a novel that lays bare the social iniquities underlying its own popular appeal.

Surface and Depth

There is already something faintly pornographic about the opening lines of *Naomi*:

> I am going to try to write down the facts about our marriage just as they stand, as honestly and openly as possible. It would seem to be a relationship unlike any other. This will serve as a valuable record of events I myself do not want to forget. At the same time, my account will no doubt provide useful reference for the reader as well. Especially as Japan has grown more and more international and as natives and foreigners increasingly interact, a variety of ideas and ideologies have entered the mix. Men—and women too, of course—have become much more open and cosmopolitan. In such an age, it is reasonable to expect that others will soon begin to form relationships like ours, the sort of relationship unheard of until now.[10]

Addressing readers with the lurid solicitude of an unimpeachable historical document, this opening paragraph offers at once the promise of shameless candor, the prospect of private matters exposed in a public forum, and the first hints of non-conventional sexual content. Evoking the ponderous rhetoric of Naturalism (*shizenshugi*), the reigning school of late Meiji and early Taishō fiction, *Naomi*'s first-person narrator commits himself from the beginning to linguistic transparency and strict factuality—to writing down "the facts . . . just as they stand" (*ari no mama no jijitsu*)—suggesting a didactic, almost scientific purpose to his testimony. Reminiscent of the parodic gestures of eighteenth-century *gesaku*, the "frivolous works" of the Tokugawa period that habitually couched their own scandalous content in the moralizing rhetoric of Confucianism, this opening passage suggests a ludicrous enormity of purpose, a commitment to truth and cultural legitimacy underlying what would seem otherwise to be a gossipy record of deviant sexuality, a testimonial to the fetish of "the West," and a tribute to popular fashion.

There is something polemical as well at work behind the comedic solemnity of these opening lines. By assuming the posture of the confession, Tanizaki's narrative alludes self-consciously to the I-novel form, by then the dominant style of serious prose fiction in Japan. Mimicking the form's dual preoccupation with personal testimony and documentary truth, *Naomi* would seem to claim for itself the trappings of high seriousness. In a preface to this work, written when serial publication was about to resume after a five-month interruption, Tanizaki openly described *Naomi* to his readers as "a kind of 'I-novel.'"[11] The deadpan audacity of this self-definition carries all the complexity of the author's characteristic irony. Although the term "I-novel" (*watakushi shōsetsu* or *shishōsetsu*) itself had only entered the critical lexicon around the time *Naomi* first made its appearance, the type of narrative it described had its roots in Meiji and was closely tied to the rise of literary Naturalism. Originally referring to a limited range of highly personal, autobiographical texts, the designation "I-novel" quickly came to signify the confessional spirit of a broader literary movement, typically identified with Tayama Katai's (1871–1930) inaugural psycho-sexual classic "Futon" (The quilt, 1907) and often understood to have reached stylistic perfection with the works of Shiga Naoya (1883–1971).[12]

Accepted by many readers and critics of the 1920s as a form of nonfiction, the I-novel's commitment to unmediated documentation revolved around the ideal of the "true confession."[13] And it was through this confessional mechanism that the philosophic grandeur of "truth" and the social exclusivity of "high art" finally merged. In a certain practical sense, this convergence was a *literal* effect of the I-novel's idiosyncratic style. The confessional narrative spoke so "truthfully" that its inward content could only seem relevant to a small group of male writers and critics: the cognoscenti of Taishō literature known as the *bundan.* Soon, the I-novel's formal dedication to linguistic transparency—developed in the service of unmediated renderings of interior experience—would be codified as the language itself of high literature, dedicated to the claustrophobic activities of the *bundan*, and associated with what would come to be called "pure literature" (*junbungaku*).[14]

By the time the "confessional" opening lines of *Naomi* appeared in the entertainment pages of the *Ōsaka asahi shinbun* in March of 1924, serious literature in Japan had come to define itself explicitly *against* the sort of fictionalized narrative that Tanizaki's novel clearly exemplified. *Naomi*'s distinction from standard I-novel narrative was further underscored by its open appeal to a burgeoning, commercially lucrative, and socially expansive reading public: the new species of reader-consumer that constituted Japan's now thriving market in "mass literature" (*taishū bungaku*). Against this trend, Japanese producers of "pure" literature held up limited readership as evidence of their own authenticity, eventually equating artistic legitimacy with commercial irrelevance. By late Taishō, following a pattern familiar throughout the industrial world, serious literature in Japan had absorbed the perverse evaluative grammar that Pierre Bourdieu has identified with the "anti-economy" of modern cultural production: not a dissolution of economic logic, but an *inversion* of it, according to which commercial failure becomes synonymous with artistic success.[15]

Beyond its implicit rejection of the social privilege symbolized by this inverted economy, the plot-driven, fantastic structure of Tanizaki's novel carried implications that can only be described as epistemological. A tale of marriage and betrayal in cosmopolitan Tokyo, this novel tells the story of Kawai Jōji, a mild-mannered, low-level engineer at an electrical company whose erotic obsession with an adolescent café waitress, Naomi, expresses itself in an attempt to mold her into an embodiment of modern life. After taking her into his home, Jōji undertakes to "train" Naomi in the ways of Tokyo's cosmopolitan culture, which had come to represent a new kind of individual freedom and sophistication for Japan's urban masses—a freedom in which Jōji himself seems capable only of timidly and vicariously participating. Jōji's efforts backfire when, as spiritual *education* gives way to empty *consumption*, Naomi develops into a treacherous vamp who ruthlessly deceives her benefactor and leads him to near financial ruin, eventually flowering into a notorious voluptuary amid the dance halls and cafés of Tokyo.

This Pygmalian nightmare, the Frankenstein version of the era's ubiquitous fantasy of the "modern girl" (*modan gāru*), offers its own benefits to Jōji, however, whose masochistic desire to be dominated by a heartless, "Westernized" female becomes the subtext of the narrative, undercutting its most obvious gestures of social critique with an ever-present, if submerged, element of erotic exhilaration.[16] It soon becomes clear that Jōji—whose name consists of the ideographs for the verbs "to yield" (*yuzuru*) and "to pacify" (*osameru*)—dominates Naomi, paradoxically, by his willingness to be dominated, confronting the "truth" of his own life only through a twisted and willful logic of self-deception.

"You often hear about a 'woman deceiving a man,'" Jōji tells his readers early in the narrative. "But in my experience, it never really begins with the woman 'deceiving' the man. In the beginning, it is rather a case of the man allowing himself the joy of 'being deceived.'"[17] Jōji's tendency to approach reality by way of fiction finally emerges as one of the central themes of the novel. This famously pitiful protagonist discovers love and beauty through a series of intensely ocular—often technically mediated—encounters with everyday material existence, but the epiphanies produced by these encounters can never be separated from some collusive act of deception. Adding to the commercial logic implied by its own mass production and distribution, the surface deceptions at the heart of *Naomi*'s style and theme allow this novel to absorb as part of its aesthetic identity all the ambiguities and contradictions associated with mass culture itself.

The scandal of *Naomi* consists not merely in the popular appeal of its erotic content, in other words, but in the relationship that content unveils between language and reality, truth and deception, surface and depth. And this was precisely what set it apart from the typical I-novel. "Lately, by some perverse habit," Tanizaki would notoriously declare several years later, "either in my own writing or when reading someone else's work, I cannot seem to get interested in anything that is not a lie."[18] Uttered in the context of a famous 1927 debate with Akutagawa over the role of structure and plot in Japanese fiction, this may be the most enigmatic plea for realism in the history of Japanese literature.[19] "This is largely why I never sit down to read the various pieces that appear every month in the magazines," Tanizaki told readers of the journal *Kaizō*. "After glancing at the first five or six lines, I realize 'Aha! He's writing about himself,' and at that point I lose all interest."[20] Tanizaki went on to clarify, though, that it was not factuality per se that offended him about these I-novel narratives, but the tedious prospect of its straightforward exposition: "A factual narrative is certainly fine," he explained, "it is just that in recent years, I have developed a sensibility that prefers the twisted (*hinekure*) to the candid, the corrupt over the innocent: stories constructed with the greatest possible artifice (*saiku*)."[21] Tanizaki would tolerate a true story, in other words, as long as it *read like a lie.* This author's fictional ideal is "realist," then, in the profoundest sense of this term: focused not upon the actual data of a writer's experience, but upon the relationship between the story's truth and the "deceptions" required by the telling of it.

But it was Tanizaki's recognition of "artistic value" inherent to this dissembling "narrative appeal" (*suji no omoshirosa*)—described as a kind of "architectural beauty"—that provoked a response from Akutagawa Ryūnosuke.[22] Although Karatani Kōjin has described Akutagawa's resistance to Tanizaki's celebration of plot as a prototypically "postmodern" recognition of the I-novel as "a kind of deconstruction of the late nineteenth-century Western novel," the central stakes of the public dispute that followed, ostensibly over structure, cannot be understood apart from the class codes permeating the language used by the two authors.[23] "There is an expression 'a narrative so interesting even a layman can understand,'" Tanizaki wrote, now speaking directly to Akutagawa. "This seems appropriate enough, considering that novels are meant to be read by a large number of readers."[24] The statement incited Akutagawa, who responded with a counter-ideal he called the "plotless novel"—literally, the "novel without a plotlike plot" (*hanashi rashii hanashi no nai shōsetsu*). Comparing the structural simplicity of the plotless novel to Cézanne's reliance upon color over "design," Akutagawa emphasized its proximity to poetry, countering Tanizaki's quirky celebration of the sprawling narrative entertainments of the late Tokugawa period (1600–1867) with an evasive, though unmistakable, re-inscription of social exclusivity: "I will say it for the third time," Akutagawa wrote. "I do not think the 'plotless novel' is the *best* kind of novel. But from the standpoint of 'purity'—of a work that has no popular interest—this is the *purist* form of fiction."[25]

For his own part, Akutagawa did not deny the role of "interest" (*kyōmi*) itself in the narrative arts, but made a telling distinction between the sort of "vulgar interest" (*tsūzokuteki kyōmi*) that might be aroused, to borrow his own example, by a street fight between a driver and rickshaw puller, and what he called the "higher interest" of the plotless novel.[26] It was precisely this vertical social framework implied by Akutagawa's notion of "higher interest" that Tanizaki openly rejected. Tanizaki's celebration of lies, his promotion of baroque plot-lines and twisted narratives, cannot be separated, then, from this larger defense of the novel as a popular art. "For members of the *bundan* today," he wrote later in the debate, "an 'interesting story' means a 'popular story,' and 'popular' equals 'low class.' Because of this trend in thinking, there are really very few novels that are both high class and popular."[27] Tanizaki's ideal of an art form that could be both authentic and accessible, and the connections he saw between the "truth" of this species of art and deception itself, permeates *Naomi*. In one way or another, Tanizaki's cryptically "confessional" relationship to fiction and mendacity has remained for generations the object of fascination and suspicion, as well as the focal point in a number of competing interpretations.

In the midst of this so-called plot debate (*shōsetsu no purotto ronsō*), for example, fellow modernist and sometimes friend Satō Haruo (1892–1964) would describe Tanizaki as "half genius, half swindler."[28] Appearing just three years after *Naomi*'s enormous popular success, Satō's exaggerated assessment of Tanizaki's literary persona captures the complexity of that novel's scandalous reputation, establishing a critical pattern that would persist for the next several decades. Citing the author's self-proclaimed fascination with "lies," his inability to resist the allure of plot and the "appeal of the superficial" (*gaimenteki no omoshirosa*) over either philosophical conviction or psychological characterization, Satō finally proclaims the author's work to be without content or "ideas" (at least without ideas that could "take root in the ground of the intellect"), to be infused, in other words, with a kind of terrible depthlessness.[29]

With remarkable acumen, however, Satō also identifies this depthlessness as the source of a unique energy galvanizing Tanizaki's work. *Naomi* itself succeeds, Satō argues, "precisely because it makes no attempt to enter into the interiority" of its characters, generating its meaning instead through the material surfaces it portrays.[30] In this context, the novel's confessional voice becomes itself the substance of a far-reaching parody. Resisting the I-novel's "expressive" posture—with its mimetic implications of an autonomous interior subject—*Naomi* draws the content of its own confession from the material surfaces of an external world littered with film stars, cafés, dance halls, and movie titles. By weaving the erotic life of its lower-middle-class narrator into the very fabric of Tokyo's burgeoning mass culture of the 1920s, *Naomi* finally presents itself, in Satō's reading, as a "novel of manners" (*fūzoku shōsetsu*): both a critique and an artifact of the conditions of its own existence.[31]

The laudatory inflection of Satō's provocative observations would be overshadowed in subsequent years, however, by the implication of ideological superficiality. Despite the subtle approbation of Satō's argument, it was the specter of frivolity associated with his notion of a "writer without ideas" (*shisō no nai sakka*) that would reemerge throughout the postwar years as the central problem of Tanizaki criticism: the image from which scholars attempted to deliver him (by restoring "depth" to his work), or by means of which they explained his artistic and ideological failures. In his influential 1952 study, for example, Nakamura Mitsuo explained the suddenness of Tanizaki's turn to traditional themes in the late 1920s as a function of a certain kind of "shallowness"(*senpakusa*) or "vulgarity" (*hizokusa*) in his appreciation of the culture of the West.[32] A year later, critic Itō Sei would reject the very notion of Tanizaki as a "writer without ideas" by identifying the central problem or "idea" in his work as "the existence of the self based on carnal conditions," suggesting a parallel with Jean-Paul Sartre and Albert Camus, the leading existentialists of postwar Europe.[33]

In 1979, more than fifty years after Satō's essay appeared in *Kaizō*, Maeda Ai published in the journal *Gendai shisō* a brief, impressionistic account of Tokyo in the 1920s that signaled a curious (though by now familiar) reversal. "Japan's 1920s," Maeda wrote, "was a season of popular culture, an age of surfaces. The masses, who had never doubted the virtue of knowing their place during Meiji, allowed their oppressed desires to rise to the social surface of popular fashion."[34] In a few laconic paragraphs of analysis, focusing upon advertisements, fashions, and technical developments of late Taishō, Maeda inverted the evaluative pattern that had dominated postwar criticism, recognizing a positive, even emancipatory, dimension to the appearance of popular desire on the "social surface"—literally "social epidermis" (*shakaiteki hifu*)—of commodity culture. With the repetition of terms like "surface," "polished bare skin," "skin without depth," and "social epidermis," in its first five sentences, this piece presages a generation of Japanese historians and literary critics who would seize upon "depthlessness" itself as the most salient indicator of modernism's radical break from the fetters of Meiji-era humanism. Maeda's pithy collection of images and commentary quietly demonstrated what was then a new willingness to find in the brittle pages of popular magazines and catalogues from the 1920s an exhilarating sensuality liberated from the seriousness of Meiji, unmoored from the oppressive weight of depth and meaning: from *content itself.*

To guard against the most egregious kind of proleptic misstep, however, Maeda's celebration of surfaces must be distinguished from Satō's own invocation of depthlessness in his 1927 essay on Tanizaki. In fact, the 1920s in Japan were not precisely the "age of surfaces" that Maeda's commentary suggests. When Tanizaki published the first installments of *Naomi*, Japan's most influential thinkers and writers (radicals and reactionaries alike) had not, after all, wholly disabused themselves of the "metaphysical pieties" of depth and meaning that Maeda's postmodern sensibility seems implicitly to dismiss. As the rise of dance halls, movie houses, and commercial radio broadcasts compounded the effects of mass education and print capitalism, adding a dubious veneer to what Minami Hiroshi refers to as the "industrialization of culture," these effects elicited a number of variously ambivalent responses.[35] And throughout the 1920s, it was often precisely the values of "depth" and "meaning" that modernist intellectuals sought to resuscitate or to protect against the specter of modern life itself, even as they embraced the ideological possibilities of mass culture.

Marxist poet Nakano Shigeharu (1902–79), for example, saw in Japan's age of mechanical reproduction a powerful means of waging revolution matched by an equally potent capacity to absorb revolutionary content and meaning into the homogenizing regime of the commodity—what he called "Jintan" culture after a popular breath mint.[36] Similarly, in a series of essays collected in the 1930 book *Modansō to modansō* (Modern stratum, modern form), cultural critic Ōya Sōichi (1900–70) acknowledged the emancipatory significance of "modern life" (*modan raifu*) at the same time that he detected in it the superficiality of an epicurean decadence, expressed as a neurotic quest for "sensory stimulation" (*shigeki*) over "ideals" (*risō*), "morality" (*dōtoku*), or "deep emotion" (*kangeki*).[37] Modernity was failing in its obligations to civilization, Ōya suggested in a characteristically homonymous moment of insight, by replacing the values of "truth" (*shin*) and "depth" (*shin*) with a consumerist obsession with "the new" (*shin*).[38]

Meanwhile, leftist critic Nakai Masakazu's 1929 ruminations on "machine aesthetics" would present the fragmenting processes of "mechanization" (*kikaika*)—which he associated with the increasing isolation of autonomous artistic fields and academic disciplines—as inseparable from the unifying processes of "massification" (*taishūka*).[39] Crucially, this tension was not presented merely as a contest between the futility of fragmentation and the inauthenticity of sameness. In the most hopeful passages of Nakai's dense and erudite analysis, the machine functions as the metaphorical and material foundation of alternative forms of cognition and social organization in the modern world: the locus of an "organizational sense" (*soshikikan*), which itself promised to serve as a "new protoplasm of pleasure" (*kaikan no atarashiki hitotsu no genkeishitsu*).[40] Still, it is the sign of a more general atmosphere of doubt that Nakai recognized behind machine civilization's social and sensory unities a newly insidious species of cognitive disjunction and social isolation he called "mental mechanization" (*seishinteki kikaika*).[41]

Against this backdrop of ambivalence, what could it mean for Tanizaki to have published a novel so thoroughly and unequivocally imbued with the textures and techniques of mass culture? And what can it mean today to call such a novel "modernist"? On the one hand, to accept *Naomi* as a classic of high modernism throws into doubt the applicability of Andreas Huyssen's identification of the modernist text with an "anxiety of contamination by its other: an increasingly consuming and engulfing mass culture."[42] On the other hand, the driving force of Tanizaki's narrative would be lost if it were simply taken as an uncritical celebration of that culture: an expression of those "oppressed desires" referred to in Maeda's essay. There is, after all, a profound gap that remains between the content of Tanizaki's novel and the commodity culture it depicts. This gap is everything. The structural parallels that Franco Moretti has observed between Lautréamont's "umbrella and a sewing machine meeting on an anatomical table" and the surreal logic of the first department store windows lead to a crucial question: not so much who was imitating whom, but *to what end*?[43]

However thoroughly Tanizaki absorbed the language of department store slogans, graphic advertisements, and Hollywood publicity photos—what Miriam Bratu Hansen might call the "vernacular" of the modernist moment[44]—there is an essential distinction that qualifies Tanizaki's work as "modernist" while Moretti's department store window remains simply modern. Characterized neither by the convoluted fastidiousness of a submerged elitism, nor by the tedious enthusiasms of an uncritical embrace, *Naomi* can be most usefully described as a realist exploration of the relational substratum underlying mass experience itself. Tanizaki's inimitable flair for storytelling grows precisely out of this realist sensibility, this capacity to attend neither to mere surfaces nor to hidden realities alone, but to the *relationship between them.* If the array of visions and ideas associated with modernism can be united by their common "aim to make men and women the subjects as well as objects of modernization," as Marshall Berman has argued,[45] Tanizaki's novel locates the key to this aspiration in the ability to see real social relations at work behind that new species of pleasure that would seem to be only expressible in the "vernacular" of mass production and mass consumption—leaving to the reader's imagination the specter of "mass annihilation," which Miriam Hansen wisely includes in her own reassessment of modernism.[46]

In fact, it is far from accidental that *Naomi* began serialization just six months after the Great Kanto Earthquake had crushed or burned to death 106,000 human inhabitants of Tokyo and its suburbs.[47] In many ways a preview of the "modernist" incendiary destruction American bombers would deliver two decades later, Tokyo's earthquake of 1923 is notably missing from the content of Tanizaki's novel, which purports to "document" an eight-year period from 1916 to 1924.[48] Yet the earthquake suffuses this text in a number of different ways.

By destroying the communications infrastructure critical to Tokyo's rising culture industry, this epoch-making disaster—the inaugural event of Japan's modernist era—had awakened in the minds of Japan's citizenry a newly universalized, newly transportable notion of "culture" itself.[49] Minami Hiroshi's study *Taishō bunka* (Taishō culture, 1965) contains what still stands as a classic examination of this relationship between the city's destruction in 1923 and the sudden recognition of culture as mobile, material, and universally exchangeable.[50] On the one hand, the earthquake broadened the geographical horizons of art and entertainment by highlighting alternative centers of "Japanese culture"—such as Osaka—that rose up to compete with the beleaguered capital. As writers and artists fled the disaster area to take up residence in new cities, the very image of culture became uprooted in a way that was essentially modern, and Minami takes Tanizaki's own move to the Kansai region (where he wrote *Naomi*) as a case in point.[51] Meanwhile, censure from the international community after the massacre of resident Koreans in the weeks following the earthquake awakened among Japan's citizens what Minami calls a "consciousness of national dishonor" (*kokujoku ishiki*) inseparable from a newly immediate sense of membership in a "world culture."[52]

But this recasting of culture was social as well as geographical. After 1923, mass marketing and mass journalism, which had been developing steadily since the early Taishō years, suddenly exploded in a frenzied effort to compensate for losses sustained by earthquake-damaged commerce and industry. By 1925, newspapers like the *Ōsaka asahi shinbun* were increasing the number of pages devoted to arts and entertainment (at the expense of political and economic news) in order to compete with circulation giants such as the recently launched journal *Kingu*, as well as with regular radio programming which had begun that same year.[53] An incarnation of "culture" (*bunka*) now emerged that presented itself alongside food, shelter, and other daily necessities as universally available for purchase. Inevitably, a new image of the public came into view as well: what Minami calls the "masses as consumers."[54] It was this quintessentially modern species of cultural consumer that made up the audience of Tanizaki's novel.

For decades, this specter of culture-as-commodity, which defined *Naomi*'s original readership and infiltrated its narrative, has marked this work as insubstantial and amnesic. Yamada Yūsaku, for instance, has described this novel as ahistorical and flat: a pastiche of external simulacra assembled to form an erotic "fairy tale world." Though filled with markers of contemporary culture—the names of film stars, cafés, dance halls, movie titles, etc.—the text remains, in Yamada's view, eerily *detached* from those substantive historical events, domestic or international, that framed the years of its composition. For Yamada, *Naomi*'s consumerist logic conceals its own vacuity behind a curtain of empty signs, a "flood of words."[55] In important ways, though, it is precisely through this immersion in the language of the commodity and the publicity image that the novel approaches its most significant "historical content": the looming transfiguration of culture that permeated its own moment of production. From behind Yamada's "flood of words," a crucial set of relations emerges—between word and referent, high and low, appearance and reality. And this constellation of relationships finally stands as the work's true object of depiction.

Pornographic Realism

Certainly, the novel invites us to think about signs. To explain his original attraction to the undemonstrative young Naomi, a teenage café waitress (*jokyū*) working in one of Asakusa's dubious entertainment quarters, Jōji begins with language itself—in particular, the written script. It is not the young girl's face or body that attracts his attention at first, but the name "Naomi":

Everyone called her "Nao-chan." When I asked about it, I learned her real name was Naomi, written with three Chinese characters. This name "Na-o-mi" really sparked my curiosity. A lovely name. If you wrote it in Roman script—NAOMI—it seemed like it belonged to a Westerner. And that's when I began to notice her more and more. The strange thing is, the moment I learned she had such a cosmopolitan name, her face started to take on a very intelligent, Western look. I began to think, "What a shame it is for her to be working in a place like this."[56]

Initially seduced by her name, Jōji begins his fateful manipulation of the adolescent Naomi by experimenting with the writing of "Naomi" itself. First liberating it from its cumbrous Chinese characters—heavy with the dark weight of history and officialdom—he starts by investing the name with the exotic value afforded by the Western alphabet. Signaling the central role that ethnic ambiguity will play throughout the story, the narrator finally settles on using *katakana*—the native syllabary reserved for transliterating foreign words and names—explaining his decision parenthetically in terms of capturing the right "feel." "In fact," he goes on to say, "Naomi's face did bear some resemblance to the cinema star Mary Pickford; there really was something Western about her."[57]

The writing of names in this passage is fraught with causal mysteries. Once "Naomi" is rendered in *katakana*, the name seems to enter a different order of meaning, acquiring a destiny infused with the enchantment of a Hollywood star whose own "imported" name it now formally resembles. Moreover, when juxtaposed with the transliterated "Mary Pickford," the name "Naomi" begins to imply a *physical* appearance remindful of the cinema star's, an image that would have been easily imagined by Tanizaki's readers. Naomi in *katakana* evokes the picture of a face that is not only Western in its features, but detachable and reproducible, available for exchange and consumption. Even a human face, this passage seems to suggest, is subject to the transformative powers of packaging.

Literary historian Komori Yōichi has suggested that this passage presents the sign itself, disjoined from the referent, as the focal point of Jōji's erotic desire.[58] From this view, signs may be taken literally to constitute the world they "name." But these sentences also call to mind a more ambitious position outlined by Tanizaki himself in a 1917 essay entitled "Shi to moji to" (Poetry and script).[59] In this brief meditation on the nature of the written word and its role in art, Tanizaki privileges neither sign nor referent, but rather conflates the two in a deliberate relational overlap. "For the poet," he writes, "the written word is a jewel. And like the luminescence of a jewel, it has a radiance, a color and a scent."[60] Defending himself against those who would criticize the many "Chinese compounds" (*kanbun no jukugo*) that appear in his own prose, who would describe these difficult characters as "eyesores" (*mezawari*) or as linguistic anachronisms "hardly suitable for Japanese of the modern age," Tanizaki offers a telling rhetorical rebuke: "If [these critics maintain that] the function of the written word goes no further than to represent or to elaborate upon fixed ideas (*ittei no shisō*), then I must concede."[61] For Tanizaki, however, the mystery of written script emerges precisely from its capacity to move *beyond* the realm of representing "fixed ideas," to reach toward and to participate in the world of the senses.

Revealing an early skepticism toward literary Naturalism's mimetic disposition, Tanizaki locates the true poetic power of Japanese writing in the "sensuality" of its ideographic script (*kanji*). Of all forms of notation, he tells his readers, *kanji* is the most "sensual" (*kannōteki*).[62] And it is this *sensuousness* that Tanizaki champions for continued "use" (*riyō*) and "application" (*katsuyō*). "To neglect *kanji*'s decorative and visual methods would be like throwing away a jewel and replacing it with rubble."[63] Sentences such as this may tempt us at first to see Tanizaki's clear resistance to the ideology of transparency associated with the *genbun itchi* language reform movement[64] as a dismissal of meaning and reference altogether. Highlighting this author's sensitivity to the written character's "figural effect," for example, Thomas LaMarre takes Tanizaki's essay to be a kind of *inversion* of the idea of representation itself, according to which the "poetic or artistic impact of writing . . . arises from the combination or assemblage of figures, not from their meaning or signification."[65] According to this reading, "it matters less what a poem means than how it makes sense, so to speak."[66] And yet it may be even more useful to acknowledge that the general effect of this essay is not to *devalue* the capacity of written words to "represent" and to "elaborate upon" fixed ideas, but to suggest that this is not *all* they do. It is not that "what a poem means" matters *less* to this author than "how it makes sense," but that these two dimensions have come to be viewed as patently inseparable.

Far from denying language's representational or signifying function, Tanizaki's essay seems rather to *expand* upon it. The reader is confronted with the unforgettable image of sensual signification, of a written language capable of representing an idea and constituting a feeling at the same time. Indeed, Tanizaki's casual rendering of "written script" (*moji*) as an object in its own right that nonetheless retains its referential and signifying capacity anticipates Yokomitsu Riichi's own more rigorous "materialist" theory of language published a decade later.[67] By proclaiming that Chinese characters should not be disjoined from the substance of their own "visual and decorative" materiality, Tanizaki seems to be complicating rather than eradicating the link between sign and referent, between word and significance. Meaning remains: both *on* the surface and *behind* it. By attributing to *kanji* the capacity to refer to an object and to *evoke* it at the same time, this essay prefigures a notion of referential accuracy that would infuse Tanizaki's later work, carrying implications far beyond the sensual specificities of Chinese script.

In important ways, Naomi's non-ideographic name retains the sensual dimension referred to in "Shi to moji to" through its association with Hollywood culture. When Sergei Eisenstein recognized affinities between the Japanese ideograph and the filmic image—an analogy repeated later by Yokomitsu Riichi and Kawabata Yasunari, and echoed indirectly by Abel Gance who compared the cinema to Egyptian hieroglyphs[68]—he might have had this very image of non-mimetic reference in mind.[69] Early filmmakers and authors seem to have understood the movie image as charged with the same contradictions captured in Tanizaki's depiction of Japanese poetic script: a sign that is capable of representing the world even while it remains what Alexandra Keller calls a "representation of itself."[70] It is not that the "cosmopolitan" (*haikara*) connotations of Naomi's name *constitute* her "intelligent" and "Western" appearance, as Komori's reading seems to suggest, but rather that her name and her face reveal themselves to be inextricably and *dialectically* bound, joined by a bond of "sensuousness." Whether appearing as ideographs on the page or as the syllabic indicators of mass-produced images, words in *Naomi* become objects of sense—sensuous objects—even as they refer to the world around them. In this unapologetically epicurean novel, language attains a kind of opalescence unique to the moment of modernism and central as well to the photographic logic of Tanizaki's poetic world.

Nagai Kafū (1879–1959) may have been the first to recognize the complex role of signs and sensuousness in Tanizaki's work when he wrote the 1911 review that helped launch the younger writer's career.[71] Accounting for the peculiar effectiveness of Tanizaki's early story, "Shisei" (Tattoo, 1910), Kafū famously described a "mysterious beauty born of carnal fear" (*nikutaiteki kyōfu kara shōzuru shinpi yūgen*) combined with a thoroughly urbane sensibility and a "perfection of style" (*bunshō no kanzen naru koto*).[72] The strange relationship portrayed between art and reality in "Tattoo"—in which a terrifying black widow spider is inscribed by the protagonist onto the skin of a female captive who then begins to embody the nightmarish figure that decorates her flesh—initiates a thematic tension between image and object that would recur throughout Tanizaki's creative life.[73] Crucially, it is not the reflexive logic of *signification* that intrigues this author, but the outward-looking dynamics of *reference*. As Nagai Kafū seems obliquely to have recognized, the interplay of flesh and writing in this story—the bizarre fusion of *sign* and *referent*—constitutes its most effective challenge to literary Naturalism.[74] And it is precisely this focus upon the ironies and contradictions of referentiality that marks Tanizaki as one of the founding authors of modernism's outward turn.

Film and photography have everything to do with the relational inflection of Tanizaki's realism. On the one hand, the importance to the author of Hollywood cinema during the time he was writing *Naomi* has been commonly noted in biographical studies. Even the novel's Japanese title—*Chijin no ai* (literally "Love of a fool")—seems to allude to a 1920 Fox Film Corporation film entitled *A World of Folly*, distributed in Japan under the title *Chijin no yume* (Dream of a fool).[75] It has also been generally acknowledged that Tanizaki modeled the character of Naomi after his sister-in-law, Seiko, who played (under the stage name Hayama Michiko) one of the leading roles in a Japanese film entitled *Amachua kurabu* (The amateur club), based on a scenario written by Tanizaki himself.[76] These details are both intriguing and illuminating. But the recurrent invocation of Mary Pickford as a point of reference in this narrative reflects far more than the protagonist's (or the author's) starstruck fixation upon Hollywood and the West. Jōji compares Naomi's face to Mary Pickford's not only because she is a beautiful and well-known Westerner, but because her face occupies the shadowy terrain of the movie image itself.

In one sense, Mary Pickford is not the name of a person but the name of a fantasy: a disembodied face projected on movie screens or printed on publicity posters, immediately available and, in some ways, already "possessed" or "consumed" by the imaginations of Japanese movie viewers. On the other hand, this circulating image fulfils the erotic requirement of an undeniable connection to a *real person* whose flesh has been recorded and exposed by the mediating apparatus of cinema. In *Naomi*, the pornographic potential of this double logic—the intoxicating freedom of fantasy in conjunction with the realist ontology of the obscene[77]—reaches comical extremes when, after Jōji and Naomi have become a couple (though still only platonically involved, with Jōji playing an avuncular role in Naomi's "education"), Jōji "discovers" her body for the first time while they vacation at the beach at Kamakura:

> Although Naomi and I had been living together, up to then I had not yet had a chance to find out what sort of figure she had—to see the shape of her naked flesh, to say it frankly. Now, I found out for certain. When she first made her appearance on the beach at Yuigahama, wearing the dark green bathing cap and swimsuit we had bought the night before on the Ginza, honestly, I was overjoyed by the proportion of her limbs. Yes, I was completely overjoyed. Why? Because I had been speculating from the beginning about the contours of Naomi's body based on the way her kimono fit her, and I had been right.
>
> Without thinking, my heart cried out: "Naomi! Naomi! My Mary Pickford! What symmetry your figure has! How supple your arms! How straight and lean are your legs, like a boy's!" And I could not help being reminded of Mack Sennett's lively "bathing beauties" that I knew so well from the movies.[78]

The careful portrait of Naomi's body that follows this passage carries out the pornographic promise implied by the novel's opening paragraph. Despite Jōji's disclaimers about the "unpleasant" task of disclosing the physical details of the woman who would later become his wife, some of the most erotic intonations (and suggestive puns) color his language here.[79] From his description of Naomi's "brief torso curving like the letter 'S' to an extraordinarily slim waist, where it swelled to the full roundness of feminine buttocks," to the "long and slender triangle" created by the line from her hips to her ankles when she stood "with her thighs together with no space between her legs," Jōji's somatic diagram combines the textures of realism with the miraculous geometry of fantasy.[80] And this is exactly what makes this scene so alluring. With its fragmentary cinematic "close-ups"—focusing with implausible intensity upon Naomi's torso, hips, waist, ankles, etc.—Jōji's description evokes the erotic thrill of "accurate" exposure without succumbing to the fetters of everyday visible experience. In a sense, this passage mimics the pornographic logic of cinema and photography itself: the capacity to fulfill the voyeur's demand for ontological realism as well as the dreamer's requirement of transcendence.

If the "ontological conditions of the cinema reveal it as inherently pornographic," as Stanley Cavell has observed, these conditions betray a similar combination of indexical reference and sensory emancipation.[81] Indeed, it is partly the disjunctive proclivities of photographic objectivity—its capacity to *overcome* the boundaries of perceptual experience—that draws it innately to pornography. "The objective nature of photography," André Bazin once observed, "confers on it a quality of credibility absent from all other picture making." But the core of this verisimilitude cannot be separated from a fundamental "deception," which inadvertently presents itself when Bazin goes on to say: "The photographic image is the object itself, the object freed from the conditions of time and space that govern it."[82] What Bazin sees captured in the photograph, in other words, is finally *not* "the object itself" at all, but rather "the object freed from the conditions of time and space that govern it," which is to say, an *abstraction*. Disjoined from the flow of time and the conditions of space, the photographed object is freed from the limits of organic experience: not an equivalent, but a *model* of reality.[83]

Bazin's point is well taken, though, for even if the photograph is not "the object itself," it may still be said to stand as *evidence* of the object. The continuing forensic authority of photography today supports this assertion. While scholars have long rejected the uncritical characterization of photography as a "realist" apparatus in the classic sense of the word, warning against overvaluing its "apparent similarities with older types of images, such as perspectival paintings or drawings,"[84] it is difficult to deny photography's referential powers, which seem to account in part for its epoch-making significance in the history of visual representation. "Photographs furnish evidence," Susan Sontag once declared, savoring the wonder of this common-sense observation: "A photograph passes for incontrovertible proof that a given thing happened."[85] So if the photograph is to be understood historically as "a central element not only in a new commodity economy but in the reshaping of an entire territory on which signs and images, each effectively severed from a referent, circulate and proliferate," as Jonathan Crary has argued, how do we reconcile this image of disjunction and dissemination with the photograph's undiminished documentary authority?[86] In fact, it is one of the remarkable and recurring insights of Tanizaki's fiction that the mobility of the camera, together with the reproducibility and promiscuity of the images it records, far from dismantling photography's referential function, actually *enhance* its documentary connection with the world. Photography's capacity to capture what escapes visible experience, and then to replicate and distribute that image, reaches to the core of its realist ontology and utility. There are very good reasons, after all, as Julia Adeney Thomas once remarked, that no one ever presents an oil painting as proof of spousal infidelity.[87]

In the end, it is not simply the visual style of Jōji's language that makes this passage photographic, but the referential authority implied by his depiction. Productive of non-mimetic "deceptions" but also insistent upon truth, Jōji's photographic portrait of Naomi in this scene establishes the parameters of the novel's *pornographic* ambition as well, combining the intoxication of fantasy ("Naomi! Naomi! My Mary Pickford!") with the credibility of documentation: "But if I don't speak honestly, the story will lose its effect, and the whole point (*igi*) behind keeping a record of my marriage will be lost."[88] It is characteristic of Jōji's pornographic relationship with the world that his first direct encounter with

Naomi's *actual* naked flesh is punctuated by his request that she imitate a pose taken by the swimmer Annette Kellerman who had just appeared, as Jōji informs his reader, in the fantastically entitled film *Neptune's Daughter*. "Naomi! Naomi! Do Kellerman for me!"[89]

Between 1920 and 1921, Tanizaki worked with director Thomas (Kisaburō) Kurihara as a "literary consultant" (*bungei komon*) for Taishō Katsudō Shashin film studios, writing and adapting silent film scenarios.[90] This experience would inform the author's work at various levels for the rest of his life. But the logistics of film production and distribution—as well as the optics of exposure and the chemistry of development—so profoundly shaped Tanizaki's literary disposition that the role of cinema and photography in defining his worldview far exceeds the parameters typically implied by the term "influence." As a child Tanizaki had witnessed the birth and flourishing of the Japanese film industry, and the social and epistemological possibilities suggested by this epoch-making form of mass entertainment seem to have infiltrated his poetic and erotic sensibilities from the beginning.[91]

Even before he worked in the film industry, Tanizaki explored what might be called cinema's natively pornographic disposition. The moving picture's innate capacity to fuse the visual with the visionary, the social breadth of its appeal, and the global reach of its commercial distribution combined to underscore for Tanizaki both the radical potential and the uniquely obscene relationship cinema held with its objects of depiction. In his much-studied essay "Katsudō shashin no genzai to shōrai" (The present and future of cinema, 1917), Tanizaki describes the aesthetic promise of film as a function of unprecedented *social* and *perceptual* advantages. While the affordability and wide-ranging circulation of the movie performance suggested to him that cinema would eventually overtake the increasingly restrictive sphere of the "aristocratic arts," it was the mysterious agility of cinema's realism that constituted, for Tanizaki, the core of its artistic power. "That a film seems real (*shajitsu rashii*) no matter what the subject," Tanizaki tells his readers, "stands as evidence of its superiority over stage performance for depicting either realistic or fantastic (*mugenteki na*) stories."[92] And yet, as Tanizaki goes on to explain, film's ability to make both actual and hallucinatory narrative objects "seem real" is tied to the paradoxical deceptiveness of its *referential* function.

Equally suited to the actual and the illusory, the power of cinema's "realism," in Tanizaki's assessment, arises out of an aesthetic flexibility which itself cannot be separated from the anti-naturalist disposition of the cinematic apparatus. The movie's capacity to enlarge and isolate the "details" (*deiteiru*) of a scene, to project with "extreme precision" the most "minute features of [an actor's] face and body," to offer up what he calls a "purification of nature" (*shizen no jōka*) by disjoining sound from image, clearly suggests to Tanizaki the opening of fresh and exciting aesthetic horizons.[93] Cinema lies to us, in other words, by showing us the world with a precision that defies visible experience. When its faithfulness is no longer to the senses but to the object world itself, referential fidelity becomes its own kind of "special effect."

At the same time, however, the author reminds his readers that these very powers of accuracy placed new *restrictions* on the range of legitimate artistry. After lauding the movie camera's optical precision, Tanizaki goes on to note the consequent obsolescence of traditional stage techniques of deception and camouflage. In the age of cinema, he tells his readers, "[a] beautiful actress must play the part of a beautiful woman; an old man must play the part of an old man."[94] If the rise of film meant the end of hairpieces and female impersonators (*oyama* or *onnagata*), it also meant the beginning of a fundamentally voyeuristic (and innately pornographic) relationship between the observing apparatus and the object observed. After the rise of cinema, Ayako Kano tells us, when "clothing, movement, and distance" could no longer disguise the biological maleness of the *onnagata*, the conventions of stage performance ceased to define the feminine ideal. On the movie screen, it was the actress's *body* that became "the privileged sign of womanhood."[95]

This is precisely the insight that haunts Tanizaki's essay. Even as he celebrates the new sense of archival permanence (*eikyū fuhen*) that film has afforded the dramatic arts, the author furtively recognizes the enormous threat it posed to the individual actor's autonomy. What does it mean, for example, when Tanizaki tells his readers that "[in] the West, there are occasions when, in order to film a scene of drunkenness, the actors are made to drink real alcohol"?[96] Regardless of its factuality, such a statement suggests, among other things, that for Tanizaki, film's capacity to create believable fantasy is bound up inextricably with its documentary authority. At the movies, believability emerges from the recognition that, in front of the camera lens, a human being is first and foremost an objective presence. In the end, Tanizaki's much-noted fixation upon cinema's relation to "fantasy" cannot be understood apart from this recognition of its referential function. And although Tanizaki's essay remains wholly celebratory, it is clear from other texts that he recognized unprecedented dangers associated with the objectifying power of this rapidly evolving technology. Consider, for example, the opening passage of one of this author's strangest works, the story "Jinmenso" (The boil with a human face, 1918):

> Recently, on several occasions, Utagawa Yurie had heard rumors about a certain incredibly strange film, a mystery drama in which she herself had played the leading role. Having premiered at some not very famous cinema houses around Shinjuku and Shibuya, the film was now making the rounds on the outskirts of Tokyo. It seemed to be one of the pictures she had made while taking on various roles as a contract actress for Globe Studios in Los Angeles during her time in America. According to those who had seen it, the "Globe" insignia appears at the end of the film, and the cast includes several Caucasians in addition to the Japanese characters. The Japanese title was *Obsession*, but the English title meant something like *The Boil with a Human Face*. At five reels, the film was relatively long and was reported to be a very fine work of extraordinary artistry—both melancholy and weird.
>
> Of course, this was not the first time that one of Yurie's films shot in America had been shown at movie houses in Japan. Even before returning from the States, Yurie's image occasionally appeared among the five or six films that Globe Studios exported to Japan. Ranking alongside Western starlets, Yurie was by no means inferior. Japanese film connoisseurs soon took note of her full, sleek figure and of her beauty that tempered the erotic allure of the West with the trim simplicity of the East. Her film image was unusually vivacious for a Japanese woman and she happily took on even fairly adventurous roles. Equipped with both courage and physical agility, she specialized in playing female robbers, evil women, female detectives, and vamps, or any roles that required nimble or shrewd action. There was one film in particular called *Warrior's Daughter* that was once screened at the Shikishima Theater in Asakusa. It told the story of a young Japanese woman named Kikuko commissioned to investigate the military secrets of a certain foreign nation. In the story, Kikuko becomes a spy who travels all over the Eurasian continent disguised as a geisha, as an aristocratic lady, as a circus stunt rider, and so forth. The brilliant artistry displayed by Yurie, who played the part of Kikuko, caused quite a stir for a while among film viewers in Asakusa Park. Having won such enormous

popularity among Japanese viewers with that film, Yurie was invited to return last year, after four or five years in America, by Tokyo's Nittō Film Studios, who offered her a lucrative contract with a salary of unprecedented size.

But Yurie seemed to have no memory of ever having performed in a drama called *The Boil with a Human Face.* Even after hearing a detailed explanation of the film's content and its individual scenes from someone who had seen it, she herself could not recall when she might have made such a work.[97]

Taking as its "setting" cinema's international network of production and distribution, this tale encompasses an entirely modern web of cultural and economic relations, stretching from the distant sound stages of "Globe Studios" in Los Angeles (a thinly veiled stand-in for Universal Studios) to the lonely movie houses of Tokyo's outskirts. A set of portentous juxtapositions defines the opening paragraphs of Tanizaki's story: the continental vistas of an epic spy drama meet the glitzy theaters of Asakusa Park; a movie starlet's lucrative contract is offered in contrast to the unsettling detachment of her own circulating and fragmented image. Understandably disturbed by receiving starring credit in a film she had no memory of making, Utagawa Yurie is further unnerved by the bizarre content of the movie itself.

The film in question, she learns, tells the story of a high-priced Japanese courtesan named Ayame (reportedly played by Yurie herself) who rejects an impoverished suitor—a wandering beggar whose haunting *shakuhachi* music had enchanted her before the man's repulsive appearance broke the spell. Ayame eventually escapes the beggar's stubborn affection by stowing away with the help of an American sailor on a ship bound for the United States. To accomplish her escape, the sailor enlists the help of the beggar himself who is promised in return a single night with Ayame. When Ayame denies him this, the beggar commits suicide in a fit of bitter rage. At the moment of this character's death, Yurie learns, the film reveals to the audience that a boil has appeared on the woman's knee, a strange abscess that seems to resemble the face of the rejected *shakuhachi* player. After arriving in San Francisco, Ayame's effort to hide the ghastly lesion on her knee leads to her American lover's accidental death, and soon she is "possessed" by the human-faced boil, which seems indeed to be alive. Through unseen powers, this mysterious pustule directs Ayame through the machinations of a new life as a dangerous vamp who murders numerous men to collect their money. Thus does the boil—with its animated, castigating glare—carry out its revenge upon Ayame, leading to her fall into madness and, finally, her suicide.

The remainder of Tanizaki's detective story narrates the details of the young starlet's investigation into the production and commercial circulation of this weird movie called *Obsession.* Through her inquiries, Yurie confronts the far-reaching implications of cinematic postproduction, which indeed constitutes the thematic core of this work. Because the content of any movie is often shot out of sequence, the narrative explains, "there are many examples of film actors not knowing the plots of the dramas in which they themselves have performed."[98] Moreover, any number of "tricks" (*torikku*) of editing and superimposition may have been employed to implant the beggar's face into the image of Yurie's knee. "It is as if she were part of a giant machine," the narrative remarks, "an operative made from a single gear-wheel or a spring."[99] Each step that Yurie takes toward discovering the origins of this film brings her closer to a much greater mystery: the enormous complexity of the cinematic apparatus itself. Characteristically, Tanizaki captures the extravagance of this mystery by investing it with occult dimensions. Yurie finally learns that the film in which she herself "performs" the starring role is not only ultimately untraceable—having changed ownership innumerable times and having floated around Asia and the colonies for years—but that it has, since entering the Japanese market, acquired a reputation as "cursed." Technicians working with the film have come to fear it, reaching a closely guarded conclusion that solitary viewings of *Obsession*—in an editing room or in a private screening—invariably drive the viewer insane.

First published in the alternative journal *Shin shōsetsu*, the narrative of "Jinmenso" revolves explicitly around a haunting resonance between the content of the film-within-the-story and the unmooring of Yurie's own professional and personal identity. In this long-neglected work, Tanizaki has crafted a modernist allegory centered upon the capacity of film to create what the author's Italian contemporary Luigi Pirandello (1867–1936) once described as the film actor's "exile . . . from his own person." As early as 1902, Pirandello recognized a "vague unease" emerging out of the movie actor's encounter with his own image: "an inexplicable void, stemming from the fact that his body has lost its substance, that he has been volatilized, stripped of his reality, his life, his voice, the noises he makes when moving about, and has been turned into a mute image that flickers for a moment on the screen, then vanishes into silence. . . ."[100] In Tanizaki's 1918 story, the crisis engendered by this experience is invested with supernatural overtones. Walter Benjamin (1892–1940)—who cited Pirandello in his famous essay, "The Work of Art in the Age of Its Technological Reproducibility" (1936)—would later see the darkest dimensions of the cinema bound up with its capacity to make the actor's image "detachable" and "transportable."[101] If Benjamin understood the Hollywood movie as a distillation and refinement of the processes of advanced capitalism, identifying popular cinema's "cult of the movie star" with the "putrid magic of its own commodity character," Tanizaki's story casts this "putrid magic" as the pornographic specter haunting Yurie and the entire arena of commodity culture itself.[102]

Crucially, it is not only the detachable nature of the photographic image that constitutes its pornographic substratum in this tale, but also its documentary tie to an original "bodily source": what Tom Gunning has described as photography's capacity for "gaining purchase on a fugitive physicality."[103] To describe a photographic image as pornographic, then, is to underscore not only its easy availability, but also its integration into a larger code of ontological authenticity. If Yurie is haunted by her own commercial image, it is not merely because this facsimile of herself is invested with its own autonomous biography, but because this circulating and multiplying image continues to hold a stubborn connection to her actual existence. Far from some free-floating Saussurean sign that "broods on itself," in Terry Eagleton's words, "in grand isolation from anything as lowly as a referent," Yurie's filmic image—with its "sleek figure" and "erotic allure"—remains profoundly referential, drawing its pornographic authority in part from its foundational tie to Yurie's real and historical presence.[104] In the end, this story unveils the obscene consequences of cinema simply by reminding its readers that the movie image retains an indexical link with its original "object" (Yurie herself) even as it gives itself over to disintegration, multiplication, circulation, and manipulation.

It is important to clarify here that to call Tanizaki's story an instance of "pornographic realism" is not to identify the story itself as pornography. Neither do I mean to define pornographic photography as innately "modernist" in the sense that I use the term in this book. Applied to "Jinmenso," the term is meant simply to identify as this story's true object of depiction the pornographic inflection of modernity's social and technical conditions. Having been photographed, and having been edited into this strangely perverse film, Yurie enters the terrain of a wholly modern category of vulnerability. Toward the end of this bizarre story, a technician remarks: "How strange it must be when an actor sees her own image appearing in a film, moving around alone on the screen. Surely, it must seem that the image on the screen is the true, living self while the self who looks on, lingering in the darkness, becomes the shadow."[105] These few lines anticipate the specter that would haunt Tanizaki's full-length novel, *Naomi*, six years later—the image of human existence rendered as a commodity. Through a strategy perfected in the later novel, this early work deploys modernity's technological "vernacular" in order precisely to *critique* it and the material processes it represents. In important ways, it is this paradoxical object that finally emerges as Tanizaki's most enduring literary subject: the historical conditions of his own aesthetic vision.

Truth in Advertising

Scholars have struggled for decades to make sense of the centrality of the commodity form in Tanizaki's *Naomi*. The overarching and permeating presence of late Taishō consumerism in this work finds its most succinct expression in the word *haikara*, an adjective recurring with notable frequency throughout the text. Ostensibly a transliteration of the English term "high collar"—which, though seemingly resonant with social connotations, signifies nothing in English beyond what it literally says—the Japanese *haikara* had gained currency in Tanizaki's time as a cognate for "Western-style" or "fashionable."[106] Appearing interchangeably or in conjunction with words for "chic," "progressive," or "international," this term is variously rendered in Anthony Chambers's translation as "sophisticated," "up-to-date," or simply "modern." As this range of meanings suggests, *haikara* refers in this novel not only to the fashions and external accoutrements of modern life, but also to the less tangible internal dispositions harbored by the story's cast members: a vaguely progressive "philosophy of life," an emancipated mode of consciousness.

Naomi describes as *haikara*, for example, the impractical, Western-style home she and Jōji decide to rent together. Delighted by the building's staginess, by its absurd gestures toward Western design and construction, Naomi invokes this term to signal her enthusiastic approval. "My goodness, how modern!" (*Maa haikara da koto!*) she announces, seeming to rejoice in the structure's spurious entablatures. "This is the kind of house I want!"[107] Here, *haikara* denotes an emphatically superficial charm, the flimsiness and inutility befitting a movie set. But the very shoddiness of the building's architecture seems also to symbolize the narrator's own wistful hope for social emancipation:

> I suppose it was what we would call today a "culture home" [*bunka jūtaku*] though this was before those had become popular. It seemed that more than half the structure consisted of a steeply sloped, red slate roof. The white walls of its exterior reminded me of a matchbox; rectangular glass windows had been cut out of them here and there. Facing the front porch, there was not so much a "garden" as a tiny bit of open space. On first impression, it had the look of a place it would be more fun to paint a picture of than to live in. But this is to be expected since the house was originally built by an artist who lived there with one of his models after marrying her. . . . I guess Naomi, with her childlike ideas, probably felt intrigued by the building's eccentric design—which was like an illustration from a book of fairy tales—despite the impractical layout of its rooms. Certainly, it was a good place for a carefree young couple to live and play without all the conventional fuss of establishing a household.[108]

In many ways the architectural equivalent of what Satō Haruo described as Tanizaki's own "recklessly gaudy" literary style, this matchbox home—or "fairy-tale house" (*otogibanashi no ie*)—eventually becomes the staging area for Jōji's fantasy life.[109] As with the author's prose, however, the ludicrous superficiality of *haikara* simultaneously alludes to a deeper, more dangerous narrative. The inanity of the "culture home," with its fairy-tale façade, also represents the couple's revolt from the social conventions of "establishing a household" and the scandalous priority they assign to sexual "play." Elsewhere, Jōji uses the word *haikara* to describe his own critical disposition toward the institution of marriage in post-Meiji Japan: his aspiration to replace the ceremonial formalities, class restrictions, and family complications of "maintaining a household" (*setai o motsu*) with the social freedom of the "simple life" (*shimpuru raifu*). "When it came to marriage," he tells the reader in the opening chapter, "I held fairly advanced and sophisticated (*haikara*) opinions."[110] Signifying, on the one hand, the stupefying pleasures of commodity culture, *haikara* also manages to suggest the faint outlines of dissent. The challenge for critical readers today is to clarify the nature of the relationship envisioned in this novel between ideological subversion and this peculiar manifestation of the commodity form.

Ken Ito's landmark study of Tanizaki's career traces the links between Jōji's fantasy life in *Naomi* and the displacement during Taishō of the state-centered public aspirations of Meiji—captured in the term "civilization" (*bunmei*)—by the inward values of individual self-cultivation associated with the term "culture" (*bunka*).[111] By the early 1920s, the logic of privatization that drove the shift from *bunmei* to *bunka*, reflecting, in H. D. Harootunian's words, "the development and triumph of that concept of private interest and atomized individuality which is at the heart of the liberal political and social creed," had begun to reverberate throughout the more thoroughly atomizing and alienating space of the mass market.[112] In *Naomi*, the humanistic ideal of "culture"—which had provided a rhetorical justification for the turn inward and rejection of politics characteristic of bourgeois intellectual and literary activity during Taishō—is openly replaced by a more broadly accessible version of sensual emancipation: what Ken Ito calls "low *bunka*."[113] For Taishō's growing stratum of middle-class consumers, individual improvement and liberation from the strictures of tradition had come to be linked with certain mass-produced commodities to which the term *bunka* was attached: the *bunka nabe* ("culture pot"), for example, or the *bunka konro* ("culture gas burner"). In the imaginations of many of Tanizaki's readers, a truly "cultured" life might culminate in exactly the sort of *bunka jūtaku* ("culture home") that Jōji and Naomi decide to inhabit.[114] Through this peculiar incarnation of culture—culture distilled through the operation of the market—capitalism began to carry out its most essential and familiar operation: the translation of human fulfillment into the language of material possession.

In certain obvious ways, *Naomi* merely replicates this transfiguration, capturing the sheer exhilaration of unprecedented material abundance, mobility, and multiplicity as it might have been experienced by Japan's new middle class. Clearly, this aspect of the novel contributed to its popularity. Enjoying huge success with the expanding (and younger) readership of the *Ōsaka asahi shinbun*, *Naomi* seemed to breath life into the newly-minted concept of the "modern girl," the "glittering, decadent, middle-class consumer," in Miriam Silverberg's classic description, "who, through her clothing, smoking, and drinking, flaunts tradition in the urban playgrounds of the late 1920s."[115] For its part, Tanizaki's novel spawned its own related word, "Naomi-ism" (*Naomizumu*), to add to the lexicon of modern life. Drained of all critical meaning through popular usage, the term "Naomi-ism" came to express what Nomura Shōgo describes as the "longing" and "aspirations" of a generation of youth.[116]

Meanwhile, the novel's lurid content—likely another reason for its popularity—also elicited a powerful backlash from older readers who saw the work as a threat to public morals. Mounting disapprobation from this more conservative readership, together with intensifying pressure from censorship authorities, led to the discontinuation of the novel's serialization in June of 1924. With a tenacity that surprised his contemporaries, however, Tanizaki announced his intention to find another publisher as quickly as possible, and *Naomi* resumed publication that November in the journal *Josei*, a Kansai-based women's magazine that was enjoying swelling circulation numbers after the earthquake had savagely undermined its Tokyo competitors.[117]

A promotional publication for a cosmetic company that had remade itself into an "art" journal directed at upper-class women, *Josei* embodied the dual affiliation of commodity culture and high art that Tanizaki's novel explored.[118] In a sense, *Naomi*'s reemergence in this journal becomes inseparable from the author's own gestures toward self-parody. It is partly *Josei*'s popular and presumably female readership that affords Tanizaki's prefatory invocation of the "I-novel" its ironic thrust. Scholars have long acknowledged the gendered inflection of the vertical social axis running through late Taishō and early Shōwa debates on mass literature. Predictably, for established artists struggling to protect the sanctity of "pure literature," women took on all the common freight of "inauthenticity" associated, more generally, with mass culture. In Japan, as in the West, "the masses knocking at the gate" of authentic tradition, in Andreas Huyssen's words, "were also women, knocking at the gate of a male-dominated culture."[119] Against this backdrop, Tanizaki's revolt against the boundaries of high culture must be understood as both a reassessment and a reassertion of a generally vilified notion of female readership.

The image of the "modern girl" itself, as it emerged through the critical commentary and commercial imagery of the 1920s mass press, echoes the ideological ambiguity of Tanizaki's irony, acknowledging women as key agents in the social transformations of modernity even as it relegated them to the trivializing terrain of fashion and middle-class consumerism.[120] Miriam Silverberg's essay, "The Modern Girl as Militant," foregrounds the distinction between a journalistically constructed image and the militant dimensions of actual women's history that the very term "modern girl" often functioned to obfuscate and to neutralize. In fact, Silverberg tells us, the militancy of Japanese women of the 1920s expressed itself not only through daring new fashions, but also "through labor in new arenas, and through political activity that consciously challenged social, economic, and political structures and relationships."[121] But even as these developments culminated in official debate over revising the family provisions of the Meiji Civil Code, commercial advertising and popular journalism continued to define the modern girl as a lightly enigmatic figure defined by casual freedom and decadence, whose fierce autonomy expressed itself largely through sexual frankness, consumer appetite, and boldness of style.[122]

In a series of essays published between 1928 and 1930, for example, Ōya Sōichi—oscillating characteristically between admiration and disapproval—would describe the modern girl as both hedonistic and intelligent, sophisticated yet primitive, fearlessly independent yet economically parasitic.[123] For Ōya, in fact, the modern girl's flighty reputation seemed to symbolize the problematic status of radical politics as a whole in the context of the "lifestyle philosophy" he called "modernism" (*modanizumu*),[124] reducible itself, in his words, to a "philosophy of consumption."[125] The modern girl represented what Ōya called elsewhere, the "consumer vanguard" (*shōhiteki zen'ei*) of the modern world.[126] To be modern meant to live in the eternal present of exchange and acquisition, to be keenly sensitive to the uniformly shallow, at-tuned to the unbroken brilliance and glitter of a "perfected Epicureanism."[127] Crucially, however, the modern girl of this depiction emerges not only as a seasoned consumer negotiating the shiny surfaces of mass consumption, but also as the very *image of consumption*.[128] To be a modern girl meant much more, in other words, than merely to occupy a world defined by commodities; it meant to *embody* the commodity form itself.

Tanizaki's novel pursues the consequences of this popular discourse with ominous precision. As her character "matures" in the early parts of the narrative, Naomi blossoms into a shamelessly voracious consumer whose appetite for new clothes, Western-style dancing, and culinary delicacies forces Jōji, at one point, to press for a frantic loan from his aging mother. At the same time, though, this increasingly seductive young woman remains for Jōji—and for the reader as well (who knows her, after all, only through Jōji's eyes)—the *object* of a depraved and pornographic obsession, an optical commodity in a photographically inflected web of consumption. Naomi is not only the Taishō consumer *par excellence*, but (to Jōji's eyes) the ultimate "consumer item."

Although associated with willful acts of expenditure, Naomi's "commodity character" finds its most vivid manifestation through a seemingly limitless series of corporal transmutations. Receptive to Jōji's cinematic fantasies, Naomi proves endlessly skilled at Hollywood poses. At first, this play-acting remains a private, indoor game, and Jōji describes Naomi's costumes as "no more than a variety of containers [*utsuwa*] or packages [*iremono*] into which I put her in order to gaze at her in our room."[129] Surrounding herself with "props" and wrapping herself in an array of dazzling costumes, she shocks and pleases Jōji by contriving increasingly bold violations of gender, class, and cultural convention. "Probably her most expensive and extravagant outfit for wearing indoors," Jōji tells us, "was a three-piece velvet suit, inspired by a costume she had seen a man wear in an American movie."[130] From the beginning, then, Naomi's image is far less ambiguous than it might at first appear. Although she will become the subject of her own narrative of rebellion—faintly resonant with suggestions of an emancipated feminine agency—Naomi nevertheless remains, first and foremost, the object of Jōji's erotic obsessions, his target of trivialization. Jōji depicts his lover as dangerous, but only because she is empty, superficial, without content or depth: in any case, "frighteningly *haikara*" (*osoroshiku haikara*).[131] It is not Naomi's character that drives this novel, in other words, but the image of *haikara* itself, an image most succinctly captured in the ideal of *glamour*.

By taking the conditions of glamour as its true narrative object, this novel distinguishes itself from what it might otherwise have become: a literal imitation of capitalist conditions, a mere reflection of modernity's consumerist vernacular. In fact, there is an undertow at work in *Naomi* that continually—if subliminally—reminds its reader that commodity culture is less about the acquisition of objects than it is about the imagining of social relations. The energy generated by the young couple's shopping sprees in the department stores and entertainment areas of Tokyo confers its emancipating effects less upon Naomi (a mere mannequin upon whom to hang "organdy, Georgette, cotton voile," etc.) than upon Jōji himself, who feels a sudden surge of social mobility. Through Naomi's gaudy charm, Jōji hopes to appropriate the aura of "respectability" (*erai*) and "excellence" (*rippa*) he associates with the term *haikara*.[132] What Jōji expects from the young café waitress he has sponsored and cultivated—what he demands for his money, in other words—is "a modern, sophisticated (*haikara*) woman I could take out anywhere without feeling ashamed."[133] And it is precisely this dream of social ascension, manifested through a peculiarly modern quest for scandalous enviability, that dominates this novel. If glamour is nothing other than "the state of being envied," as art historian John Berger has suggested, Tanizaki's novel may be usefully characterized as a realist portrait of glamour itself.[134] Parading Naomi before a shocked public in one of her ethnically ambiguous outfits, Jōji revels in the whispers elicited by the sight of the "glittering fabric" enfolding her:

> "I wonder who *she* is?"
> "An actress?"
> "A Eurasian?"[135]

It is Naomi's unique gift in this story to allow Jōji to imagine himself being envied. Her much-noted capacity to transcend fixed boundaries of class, gender, and even ethnicity—through cheap fabric and popular cosmetics—provides him an imagined escape from the rigors of conventionality. "We would never have been mistaken for master and servant," Jōji tells his readers, recounting the first few weeks of their decidedly non-Confucian courtship, "or brother or sister, or man and wife, or friends."[136] Judging from such statements, Jōji's dream of social ascension might at first be mistaken for a general revolt from social distinctions altogether. But it soon becomes clear that the traditional code of domination has simply been replaced by another: a narrative of "emancipation" that casts Jōji as the liberated (male) consumer and Naomi as the (female) consumed.

It is essential to this novel's lasting significance that Jōji's quest for glamour always culminates in moments of openly exploitative and profoundly pornographic epiphany. The structure of these epiphanies reveals itself most obviously through his method of documentation: a diary and photo album he begins to keep in Naomi's sixteenth year. This journal, the primary source material for Jōji's "confessional" narrative, documents Naomi's progress toward physical maturity, but it also constructs from its own images and observations a narrative of erotic promise that borrows its language from the era's burgeoning field of graphic advertisement: "'Naomi's Development' was the title I gave my diary. Needless to say, I only recorded matters concerning Naomi. Soon I bought a camera, and the pictures I took of her face—which was looking more and more like Mary Pickford's—in different light and from various angles, I pasted here and there between entries."[137]

Alternately prurient and "scientific"—meticulously matching dates and times with physical change—Jōji's journal pays special attention to the surface textures and coloration of Naomi's flesh. Remindful of the "depthless skin" that Maeda Ai identified as the salient feature of a 1925 cosmetics advertisement, Jōji's diary entries focus on tan lines and skin tones as they strike his eyes—and later his camera lens—during Naomi's evening bath.[138] "Her sunburn from the beach still hasn't faded," he writes. "She is white only where her bathing suit covered her, everywhere else is deeply tanned. I am dark too, but Naomi is so perfectly white that the contrast is sharper; naked, she looks as if she is still wearing her suit." Or, in another entry: "Her sunburned skin has gradually stopped peeling. It is even glossier than before, even more extraordinarily beautiful."[139]

Although it begins as a record of physical development, Jōji's photo diary comes to serve later as a catalogue of fantasies—of facial expressions and costumes, and of the Hollywood personae Naomi has learned to imitate. Tabulating photographs taken in "different light and from various angles," Jōji begins to treat his collection of images as if they were part of a magazine layout, assembling an elaborate pastiche that, when it is described later in the story, bespeaks the ephemeral charm of the commercial advertisement:

> There were pictures of all the various costumes and getups she liked to wear at the time, filling almost every inch of space: strange ones, lively ones, extravagant ones, humorous ones. On one page, there was a photograph of her wearing a man's velvet suit. On the next page, she stood as if she were a statue, with her body wrapped in a thin cotton voile. Next, her figure appeared in a glittering satin kimono and jacket, with a narrow sash tied just beneath her bust and a ribbon for a neckpiece. And then there were all the various poses and impersonations of cinema stars: Mary Pickford's smile, Gloria Swanson's gaze, Pola Negri's rage, Bebe Daniels' wit. . . .[140]

At one level, these passages simply embrace—or "document" in a mimetic sense—the exhilarating provocations of the increasingly visual language of commercial advertisement in late Taishō. Proliferating with particular intensity after the earthquake, advertisements of mass consumer goods (especially cosmetics and pharmaceuticals) increased six times between 1912 and 1926, enabling the very publishing explosion that underwrote *Naomi*'s success. Although the advertising business had its roots in Meiji—Mannensha was founded in 1890 (Meiji 23), for example, and Nihon Kōkoku (later Dentsū) began in 1901 (Meiji 34)—the second and third decades of the twentieth century witnessed an emergent emphasis on visual design and "aesthetic" technique.[141] During the 1920s and 30s, the photographs of Kanamaru Shigene and Suzuki Hachirō—who together formed Kinreisha, one of the earliest commercial photography agencies in Japan—were using light and shadow manipulation, visual fragmentation, extreme close-ups and other compositional techniques borrowed from the German avant-garde photography movement to promote products from companies like Karupis, Kao, Morinaga, and Pilot fountain pens.[142]

In Kinreisha's early commercial work, the object for sale sometimes dominates the frame, as with the cluster of glasses filled with Calpis soda pictured in one promotional image. In others, the product remains conspicuously absent except as a name superimposed over a more generalized object of attraction. An ad for the nutritional supplement Asupara ekisu ("Asparagus Extract"), for example, simply shows the product's name floating over a close-up of a woman's bare legs, exposed to the hemline of a short, Western-style skirt.[143] While these portraits of comfort and health may present themselves as openly erotic or superficially materialistic, it is important to remember that their true "object" of depiction finally amounts to a vision of social advantage presented as a *promise*. The promise of the commercial advertisement, in other words, as John Berger reminds us, "is not of pleasure, but of happiness: happiness as judged from the outside by others."[144] It is no surprise then that, while obviously concerned with fixed objects, material commodities, and the sensory immediacy of human flesh, commercial art in late Taishō often violates (as it does today) the parameters of conventional realism in order to capture better the contours of the *relational* reality it ultimately aspires to depict.

If it is the function of advertising to portray social iniquity in the language of human fulfillment—of happiness—the narrator of *Naomi*, by absorbing the poetics of advertising in order to "package" the image of his own wife, seems clearly to imitate the logic of capitalism. Indeed, at certain key moments in this novel, advertising and its techniques become so profoundly intertwined with the substance of Jōji's own "confession" that the voice of *Naomi*'s "I-novel" narrator cannot be separated from another historic development defining the conditions of this novel's production: the recent appearance on the market of an affordable portable camera. Just as the photo image was beginning to penetrate every corner of Taishō Japan's commodity culture, the personal camera itself was becoming a popular novelty device among the middle and working classes of Tokyo. George Eastman's relatively inexpensive No. 2 Folding Autographic Brownie camera was first introduced to Japan during World War I, and after the war, journals dedicated to amateur photography (like *Kamera*, established in 1921) began to appear together with companies dedicated to the manufacturing of film and photo equipment, like Nihon Kōgaku Kōgyō (Nikon, established in 1917) and Dai Nihon Seruroido (a commercial ancestor of today's Fuji Film, established in 1919).[145] At the very moment *Naomi* was being serialized, the camera was leaving the portrait gallery and the studios of art photographers and entering the private lives of mass consumers, where it was used to document, to preserve, to circulate, and otherwise to "consume" the experience of everyday life.

By inventing a narrator who engages with the world through a private camera lens, Tanizaki not only explores the social consequences of this technological shift, but presents his readers with an entirely new form of "confessional" literature. Through the mediation of photographic exposure, development, and display, Jōji's confessional voice is ultimately displaced by an instrumental process that does not tell the story so much as it lays bare the conditions of the story's telling. In contrast to the graphic advertisement's emphatically superficial allurements, *Naomi*'s photographic passages invite the reader to dwell upon the relationship itself between these surface features and the promise of happiness they imply. Far from a mere reflection of consumer capitalism, in other words, Tanizaki's novel deploys the furtive dynamics of advertising's own form of relational realism in order finally to unmask the material and social conditions underlying the very vision of beauty and desire that capitalism requires us to pursue.

Erotic Science

The narrator's relationship with Naomi follows a well-known trajectory. Having cast her as the star of his own masochistic fantasy, Jōji is both enraged and captivated by Naomi's resistance to refinement and by her increasingly belligerent indiscretions and betrayals. When he finally abandons the dream of a truly "cultivated" wife, Jōji gives in wholly to the seamy seductions of vulgarity itself:

> I realized then that my hopes of her someday becoming a respectable wife were a complete fantasy. When all is said and done, there is no disputing bad breeding, and it is perfectly fitting that a girl from Senzoku should become a café waitress. It makes no sense to provide her with an education unbefitting her station. I quietly resigned myself to this. At the same time, though, just as I gave up on the dream of Naomi's refinement, I grew more and more powerfully attracted to her body. Yes, I say "body" because it was the beauty of her skin, her teeth, her lips, her hair, her eyes—the beauty of her entire form—that attracted me. There was nothing spiritual about it.[146]

Giving up the dream of cultivating Naomi's "respectability," Jōji finds himself confronting the raw erotic power of her "body" or "flesh" (*nikutai*). More precisely, he is forced to make sense of the attraction he feels toward the very taint of baseness her flesh seems to carry. Throughout the novel, allusions to Naomi's origins in the "squalid [*gomigomi shita*] back streets of Senzoku" suggest the stain of some original defilement, the shadowy mark of an innate status or condition that cannot be erased.[147] Evoking the uncertainties of itinerant labor and the desperate humiliations of street-level prostitution (associated with *jokyū* or "café waitresses"), Naomi's native Tokyo neighborhood of Senzoku represents historically what Isoda Kōichi describes as the "side of defeat" throughout the struggles of Japan's twentieth century: from the relatively high ratio of foot soldiers its population would contribute during the Pacific War to the great number of air raid casualties it would later sustain.[148] Famously portrayed in Higuchi Ichiyō's (1872–96) story *Takekurabe* (Child's play, 1895–96) as home to an urban population left behind by the modernizing projects of Meiji, this neighborhood would have also been marked by its association with the so-called *burakumin* outcaste group and by the echoes of ritual impurity suggested by its butcheries.[149]

It is impossible to overestimate the narrative consequences of Naomi's birth in Senzoku, for the blatant race-thinking that suffuses this novel's language—most memorably displayed in what Ken Ito calls the "outrageous racial slapstick" of Jōji's first terrifying and clumsy dance lessons with his Russian dance instructor—extends to the entire social spectrum it represents.[150] Thus, the somatic manifestation of Naomi's *ethnic* ambiguity—she seems to look "yellow one day, white the next"—serves at the same time as an outward marker of her dubious *class* origins. "Hers was a 'whiteness' different from the shadowless luminescence of high-noon," Jōji tells his readers in one of his many meditations upon the color of Naomi's skin. "It was a 'whiteness' wrapped in rags, amid soiled, filthy, unsightly blankets, which drew me to it all the more."[151] The commonness of Naomi's magnetism—the innate vulgarity of her beauty—becomes, by the end of the novel, the central focus of Jōji's obsession. And unveiling the allure of a beauty poised on the verge of a terrifying corruption becomes the ultimate goal of this novel's photographic form of confession.

In *The History of Sexuality*, Michel Foucault identifies the confession as a central feature in a number of modern disciplines and discourses—including medicine, law, psychoanalysis, and pornography. Organizing these modern (and, for Foucault, uniquely European) forms of truth production around a discursive mode he calls the *scientia sexualis*, Foucault famously distinguishes this mode from the externalized pleasures characteristic of the ancient or non-Western tradition of *ars erotica*. In contrast with *ars erotica*, he argues, *scientia sexualis* does not describe the surfaces of the sexual act itself, but focuses instead upon "reconstructing, in and around the act, the thoughts that recapitulated it, the obsessions that accompanied it, the images, desires, modulations, and quality of the pleasure that animated it."[152] Defined by confession, erotic desire becomes, for Foucault, a subjective feature in an economy of knowledge.

Notably, this is necessarily a *male* economy. Despite discontinuities from one tradition to the next, as Linda Williams has observed in her discussion of Foucault's distinction, "the fact remains that the pleasure of women is alien and other to both systems."[153] Although Williams convincingly identifies pornographic cinema with the *scientia sexualis* tradition, her work nevertheless raises a question with uniquely modernist overtones: What can it really mean to "confess" with photographs? In Tanizaki's novel, the photographic mode of confession becomes the occasion of an unforgettable narrative crescendo when, in an uncharacteristic moment of pride and outrage at her infidelity, Jōji forces Naomi to leave his house. At this critical juncture, he is left with nothing but his visual record, and the images preserved therein reveal a talismanic power far exceeding the usual boundaries of the autoerotic:

> I pulled out the album from the bottom of the bookshelf and began to leaf through the pages one after the other. Since these were the sort of photographs that could never be shown to a stranger, I had done all the developing and printing myself. I guess I had not rinsed them completely, though, because now they were freckled with tiny spots. Some had really aged and seemed as faint and indistinct as some antique image. But this only strengthened their nostalgic hold on me, and I felt as if I were searching through some distant dream of youth—ten or twenty years past. . . .
>
> As I looked through the diary, there were photographs of every kind. The way I had taken them had become gradually more detailed and precise, with enlargements of certain parts: the shape of her nose, of her eye, her lips, her finger, the curve of her arm, her shoulder, the contours of her backbone, the line of her leg, her wrist, her ankle, elbow, kneecap, even the sole of her foot. Each part was treated as if it were a Greek statue or an image of Buddha from Nara. At this point, Naomi's body had become a work of art, appearing more perfect to my eyes than a real Buddhist image from Nara. As I looked on in profound silence, I even felt a kind of religious inspiration well up within me. Why on earth had I taken such detailed photographs? Had I predicted that they would one day serve as this sad memorial?[154]

Referring neither solely to the subcutaneous truth of the *scientia sexualis* nor to the mere surface descriptions of the *ars erotica*, Jōji's photo album depicts the relation itself between the depth of his desire and the surface of Naomi's skin, between a fragment of her flesh and the provocation of an almost "religious inspiration" (*shūkyōteki na kangeki*): the entire material and "spiritual" structure, in other words, that conjoins what Ōya Sōichi might call "sensory stimulation" and "deep emotion." It is a strange objectivity, an objectivity rooted in photography, that enables this non-mimetic yet profoundly referential portrait: a kind of *scientia erotica.* Finally departing almost completely from the bounds of "naturalistic" representation, Jōji's photo montage penetrates Naomi's physicality in ways that would have been impossible with the unaided eye. With its close-ups and surreal juxtapositions, the narrator's graphic memory book employs the tricks and accidents of photography together with its ancillary processes—development, cropping, assembly—in order finally to release Jōji from the limits of his own body. And this may be the fundamental irony of the novel's eroticism. For the very apparatus that emancipates the narrator from his organic senses produces an artifact that—like Terada Torahiko's filmic models of energy waves[155]—becomes itself the object of a deeply sensual experience.

In important ways, Jōji's photo diary evinces a form of realism reminiscent of Maxwell's mathematical models of the electromagnetic field. Both unnaturalistic and precise, referential yet necessarily abstract, the photo-images of *Naomi* seem to embody the dialectical aspirations of modernism itself, the effort to render reality in terms of observational relationships. Indeed, the accuracy of Jōji's photo collage functions precisely by refusing to reveal its object (Naomi's body) in any final form. The only totality is the photo album itself, presented as a kind of "field of vision" without any fixed viewing point. Jōji's photo diary seems thus to reunite the colloquial meaning of the word "obscene" with Jonathan Crary's literalistic definition, which describes a shattering of classic realism's "*scenic* relationship between viewer and object."[156] Eventually, this inorganic—what Terada would call "non-human"—sensibility permeates Jōji's most intimate cognitive processes. After his relationship with Naomi has collapsed, even his memories take on the structure of the photographic montage. Toward the end of the novel, when Jōji remembers Naomi, he recalls not his direct encounters with her, but rather the disjunctive and fragmented content of his infinitely more "accurate" memory book:

> I began to remember the most detailed parts of Naomi's body even more precisely and tenaciously than before. . . . They floated before my eyes more clearly than when they were actually shown to me in reality; when I followed the outline of her lips or leg, my daydream would expand and gradually parts of her that I had never seen in reality came magically into view like images developed from a photographic negative. . . . Like "close-ups" in a movie, each individual part of her became vividly enlarged. . . . In their ability to arouse me, these images were no different from the real thing. Apart from existing beyond the touch of my hand, these images were even more alive than reality.[157]

It is essential to emphasize here the importance of "the real thing" (*honmono*) in Tanizaki's narrative. Jōji's memory has absorbed the language of photography not merely for its suitability in constructing free-floating fantasies, but for its strangely objective disposition, for its non-mimetic capacity to *refer* to the world. The narrator's mental processes imitate the photography of his memory book, in other words, precisely because of the outward expansiveness of its documentary authority. Despite its unnatural magnifications, manipulations of perspective, and jarring juxtapositions, Jōji's photographic portrait of Naomi maintains an undiminished existential identity with its object. It is the actual existence of Naomi's body, after all, that makes his memory book erotically meaningful. What has been severed here is not the link between the observer and the referent, but the link between the observer and the limitations of his own physiology. Decades ago, Susan Sontag keenly identified photography as a technology of assemblage and equivalence that is inadvertently and "natively" surreal.[158] But even the openly surreal grammar of Jōji's collage suggests nothing to contradict its claim to referential precision or its "objective" veracity.

I am not speaking, then, of what Peter Galison calls the "mechanical objectivity" of science during the mid-nineteenth century, an objectivity centered on the notion of a "machine ideal" that casts photography in the role of a "neutral and transparent" instrument capable of registering an event without intervening.[159] For Jōji, the camera is in no way an impartial "stand in" for his own eyes. Echoing the openly experimental works of his modernist contemporaries, Tanizaki's novel registers obliquely the importance of a new form of "scientific" objectivity, an observational disposition that by the early twentieth century, as Galison's work makes clear, has turned its energies away from the literalism of sensory imitation and toward the interpretive labor of the diagram.[160] Observational technology had given rise at this time to a new practical belief in the sciences that "the picture we construct from the world," in Galison's words, "need not correspond in form to something one has seen—or even could see were one somewhere else (or even were one to be much bigger or smaller than our given human size)."[161] Tanizaki's fiction explored the aesthetic and erotic promise of this radical form of accuracy, this higher objectivity.

Early on, critic Hashizume Ken (1900–64) described Tanizaki's fiction as part of a thoroughgoing pursuit of "realism," loosely identifying this author as a "celebrant of modern science."[162] When Hirabayashi Hatsunosuke objected to this characterization in a 1926 article, the content of his objection signaled not only a lingering confusion about basic terminology, but also a growing recognition among writers and critics of a transformation occurring in literature around the very notion of "realism" itself and of a parallel shift happening in the sciences—especially physics. Responding to Hashizume's original essay in *Shin shōsetsu*, Hirabayashi felt compelled to remind readers of Tanizaki's apparent indifference to the naturalistic rendering of unmediated sensory experience—the common understanding of realism. At the same time, though, Hirabayashi acknowledged a similar indifference on the part of modern science: "it is an open question," he observed, "whether science—at least modern science—is in accord with realism." Objecting not to Hashizume's invocation of modern science itself, in other words, but to his identification of modern science with "realism," Hirabayashi correctly observes the emergence of a new relationship with reality in twentieth-century science, describing this change as an abandonment of the "real" (*riaru*) in favor of "truth" (*shinri*).[163]

If we accept Hirabayashi's definition of the "real" as a cognate for organic experience, it is difficult to object to what he sees as Tanizaki's anti-realism or indeed to his observations about the anti-realism of modern science. From this perspective, when Hirabayashi asks his readers, "does the concept of the fourth dimension have any relevance to the real?" the implied answer is beyond debate.[164] Gripped by ever increasing levels of abstraction and technical mediation, neither the mathematical models associated with Einstein's relativity nor the disjunctive renderings of Tanizaki's fiction could possibly be contained by Hirabayashi's concept of realism. It is not that Tanizaki avoids looking at the world, Hirabayashi concedes, but that he simply avoids looking at it *with his eyes alone.* "Instead of looking at the world with a naked eye," he writes, "he looks at it through a microscope or a telescope, and sometimes a kaleidoscope."[165]

It is exactly these sorts of instrumental interventions that enable the feverish accuracy of Tanizaki's picture of Naomi. But this aspiration to transcend the limits of the senses defined Tanizaki's aesthetics from the beginning. In the essay "Katsudō shashin no genzai to shōrai," Tanizaki had already explored the meaning of this very species of accuracy, which he saw embodied in the cinematic close-up. "The human face," he writes, "however ugly, is something that can give a person the sensation, if he stares closely at it, that it is somehow concealing a certain mysterious or sacred form of eternal beauty. For me, whenever I look at a movie close-up of a human face, I feel this sensation with particular depth. By some nameless magic, I am suddenly made aware of those details of face and body that I would ordinarily overlook."[166] But then, as Joel Snyder has asked in relation to high-speed photography, "what can it possibly mean to say that a picture that shows us something unseeable—something that can only be shown by means of a technical process—is nonetheless accurate?"[167]

It means, for one thing, that the universe has ceased to be understood as empty space filled with discrete objects, describable from some absolute perspective, and has come to be viewed instead as a *field of relations* whose accurate depiction stands largely outside the human sensorium. "I am an eye," wrote Soviet film director Dziga Vertov in 1923, the year before *Naomi* was published. "A mechanical eye. I, the machine, show you a world the way only I can see it. . . . Freed from the boundaries of time and space, I coordinate any and all points of the universe, wherever I want them to be. . . . Thus I explain in a new way the world unknown to you."[168] The mobility of the movie camera embodies, in this sense, what Arthur I. Miller describes as physicist Hermann Minkowski's "ultimate dream": "to fill up space with points in a space-time."[169] The photographic camera too, no less than the movie camera, confirms Einstein's most famous insight by revealing the visible itself as something fugitive, as infinite in form as the number of possible observational positions. "The camera," John Berger observes with his signature concision, "demonstrated that there was no centre."[170] From this perspective, Jōji's photographic portrait of Naomi—like the cinematic close-up he lauded in his earlier essay—can no longer be understood as a diminished "copy" of a distinct and separate "original," but rather as the *unique dialectical effect* of an observational relationship: a kind of cartographic depiction, a non-Euclidean rendering of details and angles, surfaces and textures. And just as a map would never be confused with the place it represents, Jōji's photo album could never be taken as a final rendering or equivalent of its object. In the end, the picture this narrator offers of Naomi might best be understood as a *diagram* of a set of relationships—both an enlargement (that brings up close what is too small to see naturally) and a miniature, a compression of space.

In a textbook on microscopy intended for biologists, *Optical Methods in Biology*, E. M. Slayter uses this same cartographic metaphor to address the problem of the scientist's belief in the magnified image of a specimen. It may be true, she tells us, that the microscopist operates on the assumption that the enlarged image is "the same as" the object itself. "But what is actually implied," she asks, "by the statement that 'the image is the same as the object'?"[171] Without questioning the factuality of the magnified image, Slayter reminds her readers that the image is really an "optical effect." Moreover, she continues, with microscopes that use ultraviolet light, x-rays, or electrons, the image produced by the instrument—no longer even an *optical* effect, strictly speaking—loses all semblance of mimetic veracity. The magnified image, Slayter concludes, is not "the same as" the object to which it refers, but must be viewed rather as "*a map of the interactions between the specimen and the imaging radiation.*"[172]

Indeed, the content of any photograph could be understood in this way, as representing a unique combination of relationships registered between the instrument and its object, between the observer and its image. In Tanizaki's novel, the nature of the relationship between Jōji and Naomi—the observer and the observed—is clearly defined by relations of both social and sexual dominance. "To photograph," according to Susan Sontag's classic description, "is to appropriate the thing photographed. It means putting oneself into a certain relation to the world that feels like knowledge—and, therefore, like power."[173] So despite all the convolutions of his own masochism, the carnal excitement Jōji "confesses" to his readers amounts to the excitement of social advantage, the thrill of domination. And this is exactly what is "diagrammed" through the commercial grammar of his photographic portraits. Even Naomi's most profound betrayals never exceed the boundaries of this commercial or pornographic framework; for Jōji, discovering his wife's infidelity simply means he has been stuck with faulty merchandise. It is no accident that, as Naomi's extramarital treacheries become bolder, Jōji's language mimics even more transparently the semantics of the market. After finally confirming the infidelity he always suspected, Jōji tells his readers that Naomi's "value" (*neuchi*) had decreased by "more than half," that his proprietary "rights" (*kenri*) to the flesh of the woman he had "cultivated" (*saibai*)—his natural claim to "remuneration" (*hōshū*) for his labors—had been plundered.[174]

It is a short distance between Jōji's fantasy of Naomi as a "commodity" and the rarefied language of art. Scholars have long noted Marx's own debt to the aesthetic lexicon in his early discussions of the commodity form. For Marx, in Terry Eagleton's description, the commodity becomes "a kind of grisly caricature of the authentic artefact, at once reified to a grossly particular object and virulently anti-material in form, densely corporeal and elusively spectral at the same time."[175] In this light, Jōji's rendering of his wife's body into a work of art runs parallel to the novel's ironic, "consumerist" disposition toward I-novel narration. Just as Jōji satisfies both his prurient instincts and his cultural aspirations by equating the body of his uncultured wife with a Greek statue or a Buddhist icon from Nara, *Naomi* satirizes the conventions of high art by introducing a new vision of beauty that translates the social exclusivity of "pure literature" into a broadly inclusive ideology of glamour. In this way, the novel manages to attack the *class* hierarchy surrounding traditional aesthetics without diminishing its *gendered* inflection. Despite its presumably feminine readership, Tanizaki's novel accomplishes this peculiar "radicalization" by transforming instances of feminine "vulgarity" into occasions of aesthetic and erotic experience that could be seen as authentic and yet broadly available to (male) consumers of mass culture: a kind of *high pornography*.

When Jōji finally accepts Naomi's betrayals as an unavoidable feature of their marriage, the story of his resignation is told in the language of the sublime. In a crucially overwhelming encounter, an estranged Naomi shows up at Jōji's house having adopted a newly convincing Western persona. Naomi is so fundamentally altered, in fact, that she appears to Jōji at first as another woman altogether. "This strange and mysterious young girl—she did not seem to be Naomi at all, but Naomi's spirit somehow transfigured into an apparition of ideal beauty."[176] But by now, the reader knows exactly what that "somehow" is. Indeed, it is the "somehow" (*nanika no sayō de*) of this sentence that constitutes the core of the narrative. In the end, *Naomi* tells us far less about this "apparition of ideal beauty" than it does about the conditions that make it possible: about the relationship it implies between Naomi and Jōji's own observing eyes.

TWO

A Dark Ecology: Yokomitsu Riichi's Universe

Literature is that object through which individuals represent with written signs the movement of matter.

—Yokomitsu Riichi, "Yuibutsuronteki bungakuron ni tsuite," 1928

In the opening scene of Yokomitsu Riichi's *Shanghai* (1928–32), the novel's protagonist, Sanki, meets a group of exhausted Russian prostitutes resting on a bench as he walks along the embankment of Shanghai's Huangpu River. One of the women—displaced, presumably, by the recent Bolshevik Revolution—engages Sanki in a laconic, world-weary exchange. He casually rebuffs her advances with a half-hearted show of sympathy:

"You look like you're out of money."
"Money?"
"Yeah."
"I've got no cash and no country."
"That's a shame."
"Yes."[1]

The sense of dislocation initiated by this dialogue only deepens with the knowledge that the words are uttered, according to the narrative, not in the Japanese of the novel's readership, but *in English*, the linguistic currency of foreign residents of Shanghai and the native language of *neither* character. Although it is "reported" to us in Japanese, the suggestion that this first conversation of the novel occurs between aliens in a mutually foreign idiom resonates, in essential ways, with Yokomitsu's entire literary project of the 1920s. In cosmopolitan and colonial Shanghai, English is the language both of exile and of international trade. It is, on the one hand, a language of strangeness and distance, which makes evident the alien status of nearly all residents of this city of immigrants—Chinese and non-Chinese alike. And yet, for the non-native speakers obliged to use it, English also makes available, by its very strangeness, a whole new set of relations with "native traditions" and "foreign cultures," as well as with class and racial identity. By historical accident, this language of exchange and exploitation serves also as a code of interdependence remindful, in unexpected ways, of Engels' "science of interconnections."[2]

For those occupying, policing, or managing this urban Mecca of Japan's interwar empire, the English language may well have induced a chronic state of semiotic shock reminiscent of those very techniques that Yokomitsu Riichi and other members of his "New Sensationist school" (Shin kankakuha) deployed as the centerpiece of their stylistic experiments.[3] To speak in a foreign language is to confront the arbitrariness of *any* language, to abandon all intuitive or naturalistic relations with meaning. In this sense, the "English" conversation between Sanki and the Russian prostitute presents the specter of estrangement not only as a fact of existence in the foreign settlements of Shanghai, but also, more obliquely, as a fundamental feature of signification. And yet, the ultimate vision of this experimental work reaches far beyond its author's well-documented insights about sign systems. Throughout Yokomitsu's novel, the disjunctive operations of language are ceaselessly engaged to enable new discoveries about *the world itself*. Indeed, it is precisely through the "foreignness" of its own narrative language that this novel makes visible those material relations, previously hidden from view, that shape the enormously complex, peculiarly modern external reality it depicts.

Underpinning *Shanghai*'s opening images of cultural exile and linguistic dispossession, in other words, is an even more remarkable dimension of *sensory* dislocation, linked to newly visible *material* instabilities. The dialogue between Sanki and the Russian women, for whom the illusion of a stable national identity has disintegrated, is preceded by the novel's opening description of the river port as seen from "the Bund" (the embankment of the Huangpu River where it borders the International Settlement). While the lines of this passage carry a certain visual solidity on the page—an effect of the thick columns of Chinese characters, linked together with minimal inflection—the solidity of the material world to which they refer dissolves as normal categories of perception bleed together:

> When the tide came in, the river swelled and reversed course. Waves at the necks of motorboats, swarming with their lights off. A line of rudders. A mountain of cargo that had been hauled out and stacked. The black legs of the wharf, bound in chains. The weather station signal-flag climbed its tower, indicating calm winds. The customhouse spire smoked in the evening mist. Atop barrels stacked on the pier, a group of coolies sweated.[4]

The Shanghai riverfront in 1925, where the most powerful imperialist nations on earth converged, is portrayed here as a space where the tide of the ocean joins the perspiration of laborers, where machines and human bodies merge. With its characteristically elliptical syntax and haiku-style noun-endings, this novel's opening passage presents an oddly declarative landscape in which motorboats have "necks," and the "legs" of the wharf are "bound," ominously, in chains. If it is an essential technique of art to "make objects 'unfamiliar,'" as Victor Shklovsky (1893–1984) famously argued in 1917, Yokomitsu's prose style may at first seem perfectly attuned to this Russian Formalist's idea of resisting perceptual "habitualization."[5] And yet, the documentary impulse that animates Yokomitsu's sprawling avant-garde novel cannot be contained within the limits of Shklovsky's notion of defamiliarization (*ostranenie*).[6]

"The purpose of art," Shklovsky wrote, "is to impart the sensation of things as they are perceived and not as they are known."[7] In 1920s Japan, on the other hand, it was precisely this positivist opposition between the thing *perceived* and the thing *known* that Yokomitsu and others associated with the New Sensationist journal *Bungei jidai* worked so creatively to overcome. If "the process of perception is an aesthetic end in itself," as Shklovsky maintained, then to perceive the machines of the Huangpu riverfront as swarming or struggling organisms, almost indistinguishable from the sweating bodies of laboring "coolies," amounts to a *defiance* of the known world, not a *depiction* of it. "*Art is a way of experiencing the artfulness of an object,*" Shklovsky would emphatically proclaim, "*the object is not important.*"[8] For Yokomitsu Riichi, though, nothing was more important than the object: analyzing it, depicting it, knowing it. At the height of his creativity in the late 1920s, in fact, this author would produce his most insightful portraits of colonial reality by capturing the very relationship that Shklovsky denied: between the literal data of perception and the "algebraic" economy of an abstract system of knowledge.[9] The realist logic of Yokomitsu's aesthetic vision would finally emerge—in practice and in theory—as a kind of poetic science, driven by this peculiar aspiration toward a relational (and profoundly referential) form of accuracy.

The vision of materiality suggested in *Shanghai*'s opening passage foreshadows what will serve as a constant refrain for this novel, and as the central heuristic paradigm used to explain the dynamics of the city-wide labor strike and riot of 1925, the historical subject of the work. Against the social and economic inflection of classic Marxist "materialism" (*yuibutsuron*), as it was interpreted by his contemporaries, Yokomitsu introduced an almost perversely literal materialist model that focused on the bio-substance of human flesh and its relation to external matter, energy, and "velocity"—the irreducible elements of modern physics. For this author, the forces of nature and the machines of civilization converge upon the human body itself, which becomes in *Shanghai* and in the theoretical essays surrounding its production, the conduit through which international capitalism and imperialism must operate. This novel envisions a universe in which human identity, oppression, and emancipation are determined by a dark ecology of circulation and exchange: a weird combination of physics, biology, and commerce epitomized by the city of Shanghai in 1925, poised on the brink of riot and revolution.

To invoke the term "ecology" here is not as far-fetched as it may at first appear. Yokomitsu's penetrating materialist vision not only reflects the fashionableness and authoritative stature of theoretical physics, openly echoed in the novel's language, but also anticipates the focus on material systems that would define Arthur George Tansley's (1871–1955) concept of the ecosystem and the related emergence, in the 1930s, of what would come to be called the New Ecology. For Tansley, writing in 1935, "the more fundamental conception is, as it seems to me, the whole system (in the sense of physics), including not only the organism-complex, but also the whole complex of physical factors forming what we call the environment of the biome—the habitat factors in the widest sense."[10] The New Ecology, Donald Worster reminds us, "brought a model of the environment based on both thermodynamics and modern economics," a model structured around the "study of energy flow."[11] If Tansley's ecosystem model can be understood to be "the 'field theory' of modern biology," as J. Baird Callicott has suggested, then Yokomitsu Riichi's novel might be understood as applying a homologous category of systems logic to the city of Shanghai itself.[12]

By pointing to the urban and colonial "ecology" that emerges through the details of Yokomitsu's novel, I mean to suggest consequences far more real than metaphorical. But this in no way displaces the irony of applying the ecological model to this context. In contrast with the bio-centric concerns the term "ecology" typically connotes, the relationship diagrammed in this novel between individual human life and the in-organic forces surrounding it functions not in the interest of breaking through the ideology of the modern state, but of *justifying its existence.* The human body as it is depicted in this novel serves as an "object" in an entirely new sense of the word: a means of tracking what might best be described as a geopolitical "field of forces." It is here, in the very substance of the body—specifically, its points of articulation with the constantly shifting material world it inhabits—where consciousness of nation and race emerge and the driving forces of class relations find expression. Even more crucially, it is only by confronting this somatic "objectivity" that the *characters in the text* and the *readers of the text* can transcend these historical forces—in order precisely to explain them.[13]

Yokomitsu articulated these materialist principles most vividly in a series of essays on language and form published in the context of the "formalist literature debate" (*keishiki shugi bungaku ronsō*) of 1928, the year that *Shanghai* began serialization. Initially sparked by an internal struggle over "artistic massification" (*geijutsu taishūka*) within the ranks of Japan's artistic left, this exchange pitted Yokomitsu's avant-garde code of materialism against the historical dialectics associated with the powerful Proletarian Literature movement, concerned ostensibly with class struggle above all else. What began as an intramural effort to conceptualize a species of narrative that could be both politically engaged and authentically "artistic" finally distilled itself, through this larger conflict, into a fundamental struggle over the relationship of form to content, matter to consciousness, art to reality. Despite glaring ideological differences, it is the aspiration to revive literature's *realist* authority—to replace the delusions of "idealism" with a renovated vision of aesthetic "objectivity"—that reveals itself in this debate as the most salient common feature shared by Japan's literary left and the (by then, somewhat beleaguered) New Sensationist school represented by Yokomitsu. Prefiguring a similar conflict over expressionism that took place a decade later in Germany between Ernst Bloch and Georg Lukács, the content of Japan's "formalist debate" makes clear that the institutional anxiety Seiji Lippit has linked to a modernist "crisis of subjectivity" might just as easily be understood as a crisis of *objectivity*.[14]

For Yokomitsu, science and its newest theories (loosely interpreted, to be sure) played a central role in his own objective vision. From the beginning, this author borrowed heavily from the scientific lexicon to lend authority to his stylistic experiments. By 1928, though, the technical terminology of physics and the relational grammar associated specifically with Albert Einstein's general theory of relativity had become unexpectedly central to defending his "theory of literary materialism." Few members of Japan's literary and artistic community in the 1920s remained untouched by the iconoclastic reputation of Einstein's theory, especially as it had been interpreted and explained by physicist and poet Ishiwara Jun. For Yokomitsu Riichi, however, the paradoxical structure of these theories reached to the very core of his understanding of history and aesthetics. Encoded in the "scientific" vocabulary of his critical essays and in the narrative strategies of *Shanghai*—in important ways, the practical expression of the author's position in the "formalism" debate—a fundamentally Einsteinian realism emerges, aimed at describing with accuracy humanity's inextricable involvement in a constantly evolving network of material and historical relations. Remindful of the optical syntax of Tanizaki's *Naomi*, *Shanghai* represents the culmination of Yokomitsu's effort to generate a uniquely referential, "non-Euclidean" narrative form, capable of accommodating but also of reaching beyond the sensory data of individual experience. Although the contours of Yokomitsu's realism clearly touch upon the openly ecological vision of his contemporary, Miyazawa Kenji (whose first posthumous three-volume anthology would be co-edited by Yokomitsu himself in 1934),[15] Yokomitsu's own disposition would take as its ultimate stakes not humanity's place in nature, but Japan's place in a "natural" system of geopolitical conflict.

Indeed, the unbridgeable gap dividing the fiction of Yokomitsu Riichi and Miyazawa Kenji has everything to do with these authors' disparate notions about what constitutes the "natural world." Each writer's distinctive way of engaging Einstein's theory of relativity as a narrative device and as an ideological metaphor displays the far-reaching consequences of this essential difference. On the one hand, the two authors' literary responses to relativity theory shared deep, structural commonalities. The image that Einstein's theory implied of material and temporal interconnection clearly formed the basis of this shared response. Both Yokomitsu and Miyazawa Kenji, moreover, understood as the foundation of relativity's critical potential the referential paradoxes exemplified by its mathematical and geometrical descriptions: the capacity to stand "outside" a system of relations even while acknowledging that system as inescapable. The gap that separates Yokomitsu from Kenji amounts, rather, to the ideological distance between each author's distinct interpretation of what literally constitutes the "system of relations"—the essential elements to which the "natural world" can be reduced.

In contrast with the dialectical interactions between human culture and wild systems emphasized in Kenji's fiction and poetry—the subject of the last half of this book—*Shanghai* treats all of human culture as a metaphorical wilderness, not *connected to* but *indistinguishable from* the larger world of material nature. Degenerating at times into a kind of ecological parody, this novel presents capitalism itself as a version of cosmic law, depicting as "natural" a historical and thoroughly human universe in which cultural unities compete within an international system of exchange. Yokomitsu's ultimate faith in national identity as the irreducible "given" of this cosmos finally transforms his most penetrating insights into expressions of cultural self-defense. By the final installments of the novel, the protagonist's resignation to his own Japanese identity becomes his only means of surviving the blind material forces of modernity. Indeed, Yokomitsu's much-noted shift from "materialism" (*yuibutsuron*) to "spiritualism" (*yuishinron*)—associated with what the author himself described as his "period of submission to the national language" (*kokugo e no fukujū jidai*)[16]—is already implied in this novel's most important, epiphanic passages. By defying his own relational vision of "materialism," the author of *Shanghai* binds himself finally to this nativist impulse, departing from the truly ecological grammar of interconnection and moving decisively toward the fascist logic of assimilation and exclusion.

When Was Shanghai?

In November of 1928, six months after returning from a 30-day sojourn in Shanghai, Yokomitsu Riichi published, in the journal *Kaizō*, the first installment of the first full-length novel of his career. The inaugural segment of this work took the title "Furo to ginkō" (Baths and banks), suggesting with this bizarre juxtaposition both the smoldering humor and the imaginative breadth of his project. It would be followed later by installments with equally provocative titles such as "Ashi to seigi" (Feet and justice, March 1929) and "Hakidame no gimon" (The question of garbage dumps, June 1929).[17] The full-length, revised edition would be published as a book in 1932, under its final title, and though it was to be revised again in 1935 when Shomotsu Tenbōsha publishers presented the "definitive version"—with some of the more vivid details concerning the anti-Japanese dimensions of the May 30 Incident expurgated from the text—it is 1932 that marks, most decisively, the date of its completion.[18]

When Yokomitsu visited Shanghai, it had been three years since the citywide riots of May 30, 1925. Nevertheless, by his own account, Yokomitsu intended to explore through this novel the broader meaning of this incident, which—though it had paralyzed the city and called into question the future of British and Japanese power in the region—had remained, for the most part, unexamined by his contemporaries. More than the drive to create a "fine work of art," he wrote in the preface to the 1932 book, he felt rather a "childlike" (*kodomoppoi*) desire to know "this wretched East Asia in which I myself live."[19]

In many ways, the city of Shanghai was the modernist literary subject *par excellence* of the 1920s, situated as it was at the center of East Asian imperialist competition, where the world's great economic and military powers converged. For Japanese writers of the 1920s, Shanghai was where the workings of empire mingled with the appetites of capitalist consumption and sexual desire. Here, the narratives of racial, class, and national struggle played themselves out not only at the desks of colonial administrators and bank managers, but also in dancehalls and bathhouses, or on the streets and factory floors. A major focus of Japan's business and trade interests in China during the 1920s and 30s—in contrast with Manchuria, where mining and railway construction prevailed—Shanghai's population had grown from 500,000 in 1895 to 3 million by 1920. As one of the port cities to undergo large-scale industrialization after the Treaty of Shimonoseki in 1895, Shanghai became the fourth largest treaty port in the world and the center of Japanese investment in China's cotton industry, with Japanese control of this industry increasing dramatically after World War I.[20]

Although its relationship with China until 1931 was defined not by colonial possession but by participation in the "unequal treaty system," Japan's presence in the International Settlement (*sokai*) of Shanghai constituted an important component of what has been termed its "informal empire" in East Asia.[21] Some scholars have argued that because this informal occupation of China was less stable or secure than "formal" instances of colonization, popular and political opinion in early twentieth-century Japan came to view China as the core of a far-reaching geopolitical problem, the resolution of which, in Peter Duus's words, "carried the temptation of further expansion."[22] Viewed as both a strategic and economic foothold in Asia, inseparable from Japan's own national destiny, China cast its shadow across Japanese intellectual and artistic culture in the 1920s in a way that Japan's colonial possessions did not. Although the formal colonies produced important food crops for the nation—Korea, for example, served as Japan's granary—only China could provide the raw materials and the vast populations of potential consumers that might enable Japan's development into a major industrial power. The *idea* of China, with all of its dangers and promise, loomed so large in popular and official imagination, according to Duus, that to remove the "China problem" from Japan's domestic political history during this period "is to render it incomprehensible."[23] Japanese critics and politicians who recognized the Chinese continent as the threatening and threatened frontier in a story of imperial greatness, created from its image the mythical landscape of their own desperate spiritual struggle. "A civil war or collapse in China may not have any direct effect on other nations," Ishii Kikujirō told the United States Secretary of State Robert Lansing in 1917, "but to Japan it will be a matter of life and death."[24] If China had become a cognate for an elusive kind of geopolitical opportunity—the ambiguous symbol of a greatness that was in perpetual danger of dissolution—the city of Shanghai itself had come to represent a distillation of these anxieties and ambitions.

By the time Yokomitsu published his first installment of *Shanghai*, this cosmopolitan center, where the typical Japanese resident was a business man or a banker (as opposed to the official or the railway employee of Manchuria),[25] had long since blossomed into a major center of Japanese foreign enterprise. But it had also become an important locus for increasingly powerful Chinese nationalist movements. The partial reunification of China under the Kuomintang during the 1920s had put the unequal treaty system—embodied in the International Settlement at Shanghai—most emphatically in danger. Shanghai had become the site at which Japan's "life and death" struggle to subjugate China crystallized both in actuality and in popular and literary consciousness. Between 1918 and 1932, walkouts and labor unrest had become a constant concern: the four cotton mills in Shanghai owned by Japanese companies were struck 118 times.[26] These incidents spurred increasingly violent measures of control. For Yokomitsu's audience, then, Shanghai had come to signify not only a location in space, but a *moment in history* when the forces of national and class conflict were conspiring to undermine the story of Japan's imperial destiny.

As the subject for a novel, the city of Shanghai thus offered the historical and revolutionary significance required of leftist literary subjects together with the exotic allure that the thriving colony held for the imperialist imagination. In late Taishō and early Shōwa Japan, Shanghai seems to have been an irresistible destination on intellectual and literary travel itineraries as well as a seductive subject for fiction and poetry. The same year that Yokomitsu's novel began serialization, the young poet Kondō Azuma was publishing in the new journal *Shi to shiron* (Poetry and poetic theory) his own fragmented, cinematic images of Shanghai based on his experience visiting the city as the manager of his college hockey team.[27] But he and Yokomitsu had been preceded by Kaneko Mitsuharu, Tanizaki Jun'ichirō, and Akutagawa Ryūnosuke, among many others, both in visiting and writing about this international colony.

While many writers used the occasion of their Shanghai journey to pay homage to such indigenous cultural figures as the hugely influential Chinese writer Lu Xun, Shanghai was also treated as one of the more exhilarating stops on a "tour of the colonies," a place to witness and to celebrate Japan's own entry into the hierarchy of world powers.[28] It surely must have been an ambiguous experience for Japanese travelers, however, to visit this city where the recognition of Japan's status as an imperial power coexisted with the less "advantageous" effects of global inequity. Despite the great number of Japanese nationals in Shanghai—by 1915, Japanese residents formed the largest foreign group in the city—the British retained administrative control of the International Settlement.[29] The very logic of global racism that Japanese state policy attempted to exploit, as exemplified by the "Okuma doctrine," turned continuously against its own representatives. Japanese residents of all classes typically enjoyed a lower standard of living than their British counterparts and this peculiar imbalance reached even to the most elite levels. Only the Japanese consul-general, for example, was permitted to join the British Shanghai Club.[30] Shanghai thus represented imperial success at the same time that it symbolized a subtle but unmistakable dishonor, the place where the ugly privileges of empire were most stingingly denied.[31]

For Yokomitsu's readership, the May 30 Incident of 1925 exemplified the volatility of Japan's empire and the tenuousness of its historical destiny. On May 15, Gu Zhenghong, a cotton worker and activist, was killed by a Japanese factory foreman during a melee at a Japanese-owned textile plant in Shanghai.[32] The martyred worker became a catalyst for a general protest against foreign powers in China, with thousands of workers attending his memorial service. On May 30, British police fired on the throngs of students and workers who had joined together in a massive demonstration, killing ten and wounding fifty. The demonstration turned into a citywide strike of unprecedented scale. The subsequent breakdown of order and the virtual halting of vital city services (more than 200 enterprises and over 200,000 workers participated in the strike) constitute the climactic subject matter of the final chapters of Yokomitsu's novel. By reducing the international metropolis to the most elemental levels of organic survival, the strike provided the perfect subject for demonstrating Yokomitsu's materialist vision. Significantly, however, it is not the crippled Shanghai but the thriving Shanghai that dominates this novel's narrative. Rather than the revolutionary city, it is the unapologetically capitalist and colonial city—the city of racial hierarchy, of sensual indulgence, and of economic exchange—that functions most effectively to define Yokomitsu's universe.

In Yokomitsu's novel, then, Shanghai serves not only as the volatile locus of class and ethnic tension, but also as a uniquely voluptuous territory of irrepressible, if sometimes seamy, allure. At the time of his journey there, the Hongkou district north of Suzhou Creek was imbued with a thoroughly Japanese identity, complete with Japanese department stores, hospitals, a library, and even a Japanese cemetery.[33] But despite these homey comforts, the Japanese settlement remained surrounded by the more darkly seductive attractions and the encroaching dangers of the International Concessions. A place of profit for great banking and shipping interests, prewar Shanghai was also a landscape of nightclubs and brothels, beggars and opium addicts. Yokomitsu's portrait of the city suggests a vital energy that is held always in tension with an undertow of decay: the brutal energy of capitalist exchange and bodily pleasure undercut by the torpor of disease and poverty. During these decades, as the novel strains to make clear, there was a cosmopolitan tolerance to the city's economy that somehow bordered on the obscene: visitors from Western countries referred to Shanghai as the "whore of the Orient," as a city willing to supply anything for a price (including, according to some observers, heroine on room service).[34] But Shanghai's was a sublime species of decadence that repelled visitors at the same time that it inspired in them a kind of awe. "Even blindfolded," writes Harriet Sergeant, "you would have recognized Shanghai by the sheer, almost hysterical energy of the place."[35]

For many literary observers, the vitality of Shanghai was inseparable from the inimitable cultural chaos of its ethnic mix. No description of the city seemed complete without mention of the Sikh policeman, the Eurasian, the rickshaw coolie, or the ubiquitous Russian prostitute. There were newspapers from every capital and films in a variety of languages. For Yokomitsu's contemporaries, Shanghai was not merely a foreign city, but a city of foreigners—a symbol of *foreignness itself.* "In the evening," writes Sergeant, "an invitation to a formal English dinner party might be followed by a visit to a nightclub to watch a Japanese dancer who called herself a Filipino [*sic*] princess undulate to the music of a German Jewish band."[36] Shanghai's raw energy gave many the impression of untamable natural forces. "So much life," wrote Aldous Huxley in 1926, describing a crowded Shanghai street, "so carefully canalised, so strongly flowing—the spectacle of it inspires something like terror."[37] But barely contained beneath the city's seductive vitality, there remained always the specter of a terrifying chaos that seemed to strain at its edges, threatening either violent explosion or else the festering dissolution of an apocalyptic decay. For some, the radiant pulsations of the city's crowded boulevards and alleyways housed an undercurrent of disease, giving the impression that the very pavement of its sidewalks, in Kaneko Mitsuharu's description, "squished with the pain, the blood, and the pus one finds beneath a dried scab."[38]

It was this tension between vitality and decay, between stability and dissolution—what Maeda Ai identifies as the dynamic of "flow" (*nagare*) and "stagnation" (*yodomi*)[39]—that Yokomitsu attempted to explain in his own depiction of the city. Shanghai becomes, for this author, not only the occasion for a discussion of labor politics and a foray into literary exoticism, but the historical object around which to construct a grandly conceived ontological system. It has been suggested by many critics, including Maeda Ai and Shimamura Teru, that Shanghai served as a symbol of East Asian modernity itself, in all its contradictions: an open text available for endless manipulation.[40] Yokomitsu, for his part, wrote to an editor at Kaizōsha that he intended to describe that "wondrous city" that had become "East Asia's garbage can."[41] After his brief visit there, the International Concessions area of Shanghai remained for Yokomitsu a haunting image to which his thoughts incessantly returned, a kind of "ancestral home of problems" (*mondai no kokyō*).[42] As such, it came to suggest the mystery of colonial modernity, holding within its secret streets and brothels, within its thriving shops and factories, the meaning of empire and of capitalism in its advanced form. Through the candor of its sensuality and through the contradictory energy of its chaotic exuberance, Yokomitsu's Shanghai seemed to expose the hidden workings of an enigmatic historical process by which human flesh had come to be embedded in a system of rationalized exchange. In this colonial city, his novel suggests, the human body is revealed in its essential form: an infinitely divisible substance reducible to a commodity, to a machine of labor, or to an object defined by racial and national identity.

Urged by an editor at Kaizōsha to write a travelogue along the lines of Akutagawa's "Shina yūki" (Travels in China, 1925), Yokomitsu finally decided to transcend the limits of that genre and to confront in one enormous novel what Kuritsubo Yoshiki describes as "the basic problem of what controls human beings" in history.[43] With this ambitious goal at its core, Yokomitsu's *Shanghai* project stretched to the limits the stylistic techniques pioneered by the New Sensationist movement—for which, in 1928, Yokomitsu still served as the unofficial spokesperson, despite its diminishing ranks. The novel outlines the sexual adventures and economic struggles of a group of Japanese expatriates. This includes Sanki, the protagonist, a mid-level bank employee who is described in the opening pages as the residual embodiment of a medieval morality, a kind of Don Quixote amid the glossy seductions of modernity. Sanki's anachronistic ethic is challenged when he is drawn into the drama of rebellion as a general strike spreads throughout the city after the shooting death of a Chinese worker. The shooting takes place at the Japanese textile company where Sanki (after losing his bank job in the midst of a scandal) has come to be employed, forcing him to confront his own romantic attraction to a beautiful revolutionary, Fang Qiu-lan, who works on the factory floor.

The ideological conflict of this culminating episode—and, indeed, of every subplot in the novel—is portrayed as an instantiation of the mechanical and biological determining factors of human behavior. From class conflict to sexual desire, *Shanghai* pictures history in these grimly ecological terms, as inseparable from an immense, bio-material network of matter and energy, of geopolitical "velocity" and time.

A Dark Ecology

Yokomitsu's ontological vision announces itself most forcefully in the novel's early descriptions of the city's fetid back alleyways:

> A neighborhood of crumbling brick. In its narrow streets, a Chinese throng dressed in long black sleeves swelled, then stagnated like stylish seaweed at the bottom of the ocean. Beggars crouched on the gravel road. In the shop-window above their heads hung the egg sacs of fish and the bodies of gutted carp, dripping with blood. Next door, mangos and bananas overflowed in piles

onto the sidewalk from a fruit stand. Next to the fruit stand was a hog butcher. Innumerable pigs with their hides removed, hanging by their hooves, formed a flesh-colored cave, a kind of gloomy hollow. From the recesses of this wall of tightly packed pig, the white face of a wall clock shone through like an eye.[44]

The gratuitous precision of this passage both repels and informs the reader, suggesting an almost cannibalistic violence underlying what is, at another level, a simple market scene. It is no coincidence that the most vivid item for sale here is flesh itself: the anthropoid bodies of skinned pigs hanging from their feet, so numerous they resemble a geographic feature. Through its characteristically bizarre juxtapositions, the prose of this passage nearly erases the distance that stands between living flesh and dead meat, between animal and object, human and nonhuman. Inert matter bleeds (even literally in this scene) into the realm of human commerce, which, in turn, takes on the appearance of a natural phenomenon. Indeed, there is little variation between the oceanic vocabulary used to describe the thronging consumers on the street and the "flesh-colored cave" formed by the butchered carcasses displayed as commodities in the open stall. From the flowing crowds—whose movements are compared to the undulations of a kelp bed—to crouching beggars and the dripping bodies of fish, the limpid and telegraphic details of this passage suggest the contours of an overarching, autophagous economy. Even as it sweeps from images of abundance and vitality to the ragged edges of squalor and degradation, Yokomitsu's prose never strays from the "materialistic" grammar of cosmic indifference.

Nowhere are the consequences of this gloomy ontology more explicit than in the story of Osugi, a young employee in a Chinese-style "Turkish bath" (*toruko buro*) who attracts Sanki's attention early in the novel. When Sanki's romantic aspirations are thwarted by Oryū, the female proprietor of the bathhouse who fires Osugi in a jealous rage, Sanki's love interest is left homeless and vulnerable, lingering outside his boarding house awaiting his return. As she waits, she looks pensively into a filthy canal (*dobu*) that traverses the back alley neighborhood of the Japanese residential area. The procession of refuse that floats through Osugi's field of vision underscores the urgency of her situation. Described in careful detail, the image of the canal suggests a sluggish and scatological variation on the theme of circulation and exchange captured in the opening description of the riverfront. The confluence depicted here of flesh and matter offers a grim parody on the sensory shock and material proliferation of modernity, unveiling the final ignominious phase of the chaotic process of production and consumption: the story of decay, of exhaustion, and, finally, of disposal.

Capturing the enormity of Shanghai in the stagnant currents of a sewage ditch, Yokomitsu invents in this series of scenes a poetics of decay that mixes the images of consumption with the language of hydraulics, the syntax of *haiku* with the idiom of biology, creating, in the end, a full-scale garbage dump aesthetic that will serve an important function throughout the novel:

> Leaning against the stucco railing, Osugi pressed one hand to her forehead. Next to her, a gaslight, leaning to one side, stood amid the spat-out husks of chewed sugarcane and pork bones. Perhaps she would not move until the gaslight went out and the window to Sanki's room opened. On the surface of the canal where she was looking, even while she looked, black foaming garbage slowly gathered together to form a little island. In the middle of the island, the yellow carcass of a chicken joined the swollen corpse of a cat at the neck; a chamber pot showed its belly; shoes and vegetable greens clumped moistly together and did not move.[45]

Placing decaying bodies alongside the more inert substance of urban refuse, this passage suggests the same radical species of confluence and disorder established in the earlier market scene. A chicken's "yellow carcass" meets the "swollen corpse of a cat," but also a discarded chamber pot, a pair of old shoes. Through the native surrealism of a garbage ditch, Yokomitsu manages to express an overarching vision of the modern world. If the author viewed Shanghai itself as "East Asia's garbage can," then the sewage canal behind Sanki's apartment house constitutes a distillation of that image: the garbage can's garbage can. The rotting tissue of dead bodies and the material decay of discarded commodities echoes Osugi's fate as well. In the next episode of Osugi's story, this canal will serve not only as a narrative *symbol* of her predicament, but as the mechanism of her decision making: a tool she uses for thinking. Before Sanki returns, a friend named Kōya, who is visiting on business from Singapore (but who has spent most of his time looking for a wife to take back with him), shows up to let Osugi into the room. Kōya is drunk and his carnal appetites have been dangerously inflamed by an evening of debauchery.

The rape occurs that night in a dark confusion. And when Osugi wakes up the next morning to see both Sanki and Kōya sleeping there, she cannot determine which of the two men is responsible. Here, the specter of Shanghai's somatic economy begins to emerge in full view. Unemployed and with nowhere to stay, Osugi finds herself profoundly, almost "objectively," altered by the experience. The fact of her violation has undermined her identity not by insulting or shaming her in any absolute sense, but by devaluing her flesh in the economy of the International Settlement. Already in a dubious position as a bathhouse employee, Osugi now finds herself on the threshold of the same dark lostness that envelops the Russian prostitutes of the opening scene. Looking at the two men sleeping before her, she wonders which of the two, when he wakes up, she should ask for protection: which one owes her "compensation," in other words, for her evening's "services." By depicting Osugi's rape as merely a carnal transaction—by translating the last crumbling ramparts of human dignity into the idiom of relational values—Yokomitsu's narrative lays bare, but also *legitimates* what historian Gayle Rubin might describe as Shanghai's "political economy of sex."[46]

Indeed, it hardly needs explaining that the novel's thematic evocation of objectified female bodies—especially through the recurring image of the prostitute—perpetuates the very somatic economy it means to describe. But there is a documentary dimension to this voyeuristic fixation as well. In fact, Japanese prostitution flourished in a variety of forms in colonial Shanghai, from bar hostesses (*shakufu*) to employees of fancier restaurants and teahouses. While contemporary Japanese travel guides hint that the most daring sexual entertainments were to be found in other parts of the International Settlement, Japanese residents rarely left the Hongkou district, and it is clear that part of the "colonial" experience included, paradoxically, the freedom to enjoy Japanese prostitution.[47] Especially on North Sichuan Road (known as "Mystery Street"), the Hongkou district was filled with brothels. Some of the prostitutes who worked on North Sichuan Road doubled as maidservants or waitresses, while others depended on street hawkers and rickshaw drivers to solicit business.[48] For Yokomitsu, this lowest level of prostitution exemplified the material logic of Shanghai's modern cosmos.

While Osugi ponders her future, she looks down from the window of Sanki's room onto the same filthy ditch of the previous scene. Once again, on the surface of the ditch, Osugi sees the eclectic fragments of industry and commerce moving slowly by in a peristaltic process of urban discharge:

> On the canal she was looking at the night before, a cargo boat loaded with coal was stopped with its black sail unfurled. On its stationary rudder and on the iron pipes jutting out from the path, straw shoes and socks and fruit rinds were caught, unmoving. The froth of bubbles that foamed up, clumping together like mud, illuminated on one side by the morning sun, flowed slowly through the center of the narrow back alley.
>
> When Osugi looked at those bubbles, it seemed that her own body, flung over the rail, had become an article for sale casually hanging there. If she went away from here, it was unclear where she should go. Soon, rubbish was thrown from several windows here and there toward the ditch. Each time the garbage fluttered up, a flock of chickens spread and flapped their wings and jumped over the back wall.[49]

Through the exterior signals of the "landscape" before her, Osugi begins unconsciously to recognize her position in the city's metabolism, to understand her own body as hovering on the shadow-line between being "an article for sale" or a piece of garbage for disposal. Later in the novel, when she finally resigns herself to prostitution, Osugi once again feels the irresistible force of the canal's material presence, experiencing an almost mystical union: "When Osugi looked at the moon," the narrative tells us, "she became like the moon. When she looked at the canal, she became like the canal." It is during this ironically lyrical crescendo that she suddenly remembers a friend who "rents a room" and "takes guests." And it is at this moment too that Osugi begins most sharply to feel the "emptiness of her stomach."[50]

Osugi's decision to become a prostitute encapsulates the essential insight generated by this ambitious, experimental novel. If human destiny is determined by the needs, desires, and vulnerabilities of the physical body, then, for Yokomitsu, the whole of reality can only be pictured from within the laws that satisfy those needs, incite those desires, exploit those vulnerabilities: the laws of capitalism itself. At the height of the institutional vitality of proletarian literature in Japan, this beleaguered modernist ventured to suggest that even the most belligerently revolutionary text has its roots in the deep structure of capitalism. In 1928, the year *Shanghai* first appeared in serial publication, Yokomitsu struggled to clarify this insight, distinguishing his own self-consciously "internal" approach to the problem of capitalism from the transcendentally antagonistic "idealism" (*risō shugi*) of "communist literature."[51] In the essay "Shin kankakuha to conminizumu bungaku" (The New Sensationist school and communist literature), Yokomitsu attempts to redefine the politics of literature's central challenge, urging writers to distance themselves from the delusions of (leftist) ideology and to take a grander, more "scientific" view.

Regardless of a writer's politics, he told his readers, "it is essential to admit that the reality [*genjitsu*] of our nation is capitalist." Leftist literature would remain deluded, he went on to suggest, until it came to terms with the magnitude of this fact. "The problem concerning literature today is not whether this capitalist structure is in decline," he wrote. "Our problem, rather, amounts to whether literature should be used as a weapon for destroying capitalism, or whether literature should regard the opposition between Marxism and capitalism as part of a single reality."[52] Clearly advocating the latter position, Yokomitsu presented this "higher" objectivity as the hallmark of the "scientific" approach offered by New Sensationism. "Imagine a situation in which all of literature had become Communist," he writes. "In such a case, literature would lose the specific character of its scientific power." Indeed, this entire essay may be summarized as a call to recognize the *realist* potential of "literature's proclivity for scientific composure."[53] For Yokomitsu, it is only through the "spirit of materialist observation" (*yuibutsuronteki na kansatsu seishin*) embodied in the New Sensationist style that literature can comprehend the expansive hegemony of capitalism. "The next new literature to appear," he wrote, "will be born out of the New Sensationist school and not out of socialist literature. This is because our society exists within the single great power of capitalism. However much you deny it, the fact is that we live a capitalist existence."[54]

The cosmic enormity Yokomitsu attributed to capitalism accounts for the epistemological complexity of his critical essays and the paradoxes of his style. Indeed, the whole of this author's creative career seems to revolve, in one way or another, around the problem of imagining a species of literature capable of representing the very conditions that define it: the challenge implied by Theodor Adorno's assertion that "total unfreedom can be recognized but not represented."[55] Yokomitsu's belief that capitalism as a "single great power" (*ichidai seiryoku*) subsumed all other political and moral positions amounted to the most productive and most dangerous of his theoretical insights. Critic Itō Sei would later observe that in Yokomitsu's works, and in particular the novel *Shanghai*, "human beings rise or fall based on the movement of combinations of people and people, or of people and labor, unrelated to good intentions or efforts."[56] The economy portrayed in *Shanghai* is thus revealed not only as morally impenetrable, but as physically inescapable: an unbounded network centered upon the human body itself.

From Fang Qiu-lan, the revolutionary leader whose physical beauty seduces followers of a proletariat-led Chinese nationalism, to Miyako, whose body becomes the focus of "international competition" in the dancehalls of Shanghai, every important character and scene in this novel obeys, at some level, the somatic logic of this totalizing structure. Revealed in its most ghastly manifestation through the minor character Yamaguchi, who makes extra money collecting corpses to sell for medical use, Yokomitsu's universe conflates the logic of capitalism with the materialism of science, the historical enigma of class and race with the biological drives of human lust. "With one cadaver," Yamaguchi boasts cheerfully in an early passage, "I can maintain seven living Russian mistresses. Seven! I'm talking Russian aristocrats!"[57] In the world of *Shanghai*, every body has its place in the system, and it is only through the relative movement of these bodies that the shape of that system can ever come into view.

Mapping the Empire

In 1988, Komori Yōichi observed: "Among Yokomitsu Riichi's works, there is no novel as inundated with the word 'body,' or with words referring to body-parts and their movements, as *Shanghai*."[58] In fact, when Komori wrote these words, the meaning of this novel's peculiarly somatic worldview had already been addressed by such luminaries as Kamei Hideo and Shinoda Kōichirō.[59] But it was Komori himself who first understood the centrality of the human body in *Shanghai* as an expression of the author's interest in Einstein's theory of relativity. Komori's classic *Kōzō to shite no katari* (Narrative as structure, 1988) devotes a chapter to outlining the impact of relativity theory (as it was popularly understood in 1920s Japan) upon Yokomitsu's aesthetic vision. But because Einstein's influence is made most explicit in Yokomitsu's essays on language and form—which themselves betray the impact of Ferdinand de Saussure's *Cours de Linguistique Générale* (translated as *Gengogaku genron* in 1928)[60]—it is perhaps no surprise that Komori presents relativity theory not as the basis of a radical realism, but as the framework for a fundamentally non-referential theory of signification. For Komori, if the bodies and flesh that "inundate" the narrative of *Shanghai* are to be understood as "objects" (*mono*), they are "objects that have been made into signifiers" (*kigōka sareta mono*) moving through a field of "symbolic exchange" (*shōchō kōkan*).[61]

Although the structural dynamics of language clearly fascinated Yokomitsu, his portrait of Shanghai would seem to reach far beyond the discursive contestations of "symbolic exchange." The realist consequences of Yokomitsu's aesthetic are most clearly displayed in his description of the citywide strike of the May 30 Incident. But the "Einsteinian" logic of this realism also permeates the narrative language of an earlier episode, when Sanki is dismissed from his job at the bank after unsuccessfully challenging his corrupt supervisor. Unemployed and adrift in the city, Sanki finds himself face to face with expatriation in its most naked terms. Meeting Osugi by chance on the street, the two make their way through the crumbling landscape of butcher shops, beggars, and opium addicts that serves as the visual refrain for the first half of the novel. Joined now in despair, they stop at a café where, waiting for their food, Sanki's thoughts turn to the nature of Shanghai itself, its relation to his "home country," and his own place in the imperial system. Knowing that there would be no work for him back in Japan, he considers the nature of imperial power and the means through which it extends itself in space, dominating and controlling the world even without the benefit of formal annexation:

> With the exception of Russians, an individual's flesh, however idle or jobless, even if that person is just wandering aimlessly, functions as an expression of patriotism to the extent that it occupies space. Sanki smiled when he thought about it. In fact, if he were in Japan, it is certainly true that he would only decrease the Japanese food supply. But as long as he was in Shanghai, the space occupied by his flesh would flow continuously as Japanese territory.
>
> *My body is territory. This body of mine and Osugi's body too.*[62]

If colonial power extends *through the bodies of the colonists*, Sanki reasons, then his physical existence alone could be construed as a service to his nation. According to this logic, all the various "races" (*jinshu*) represented in Shanghai can be seen as "tentacle suckers for their home countries, sucking up excess terrain."[63] Sanki's meditation focuses explicitly upon the role of human flesh (*nikutai*) in the dynamics of empire, suggesting a theory of nationalism that claims to tell as much about the laws of nature as it does about the vicissitudes of history. The key concepts that emerge in this passage—"flesh," "flow" (*nagare*), and "Japanese territory" (*Nihon no ryōdo*)—run parallel to analogous concepts central to relativity physics—matter, time, and space—and are assembled together not as separate and distinct categories, but as functionally interdependent phenomena that form a kind of geopolitical continuum. National space is neither inert nor empty, from this view, but rather "flows" through the medium of human flesh. On the other hand, individual identity and consciousness—suggested by what Sanki calls the "expression of patriotism" (*aikokushin no araware*)—are no less bound to the human body and its place in the system of state-centered capitalism. In the world of this novel, human bodies do not exist neutrally in "empty" space or time, but constitute in and of themselves a kind of national gravitational field. At the far edges of the empire, in other words, the nation-state exists *in* and *through* the human body. "*My body is territory. This body of mine and Osugi's body too.*"

It is crucial to recognize the degree to which this image of corporal "territory" refers to a *literal* reality for Yokomitsu, not a metaphorical one. Compare this passage to a related discussion in the critical essay "Yuibutsuronteki bungakuron ni tsuite" (On the theory of materialist literature, 1928), published in the first year of *Shanghai*'s serialization. In a subsection labeled "Genjitsu no sokudo to yuibutsuronteki bungakuron" (On the velocity of reality and the theory of materialist literature), Yokomitsu offers the following enigmatic picture of the relationship between human identity and political changes in the "external world" (*gaikai*):

> The transformations we share are the transformations of a polity that controls our contemporary national territory. In other words, these changes are nothing other than transformations of the external world, received from the political system of national capitalism. . . . That is, the transformations we undergo

together amount to the daily time that inheres in the political system of this Japanese territory. And what I mean by 'daily time' is the velocity of reality of our Japanese nation.[64]

Positing a reality (*genjitsu*) defined, at its deepest levels, by the cosmic elements of the physical universe, but also, inseparably, by the vaulting historical structure of "national capitalism," Yokomitsu ties the political and economic dynamics of the Japanese state to the literal time and space of the "external world": the "velocity of reality of our Japanese nation" (*ware ware Nihonkoku no genjitsu no sokudo*).[65] The author's debt to relativity theory, implied here by the suggestion that a nation-state can be said to have its own "velocity"—which determines, in turn, the "daily time" (*hibi no jikan*) experienced by its occupants—animates some of the most memorable scenes in *Shanghai*, centered precisely upon the specter of the city's financial and commercial activities.

When Sanki and Kōya commute to work in one of the novel's early scenes, the "daily time" of capitalism acquires the physical urgency of a relentless tidal force, as currents of humanity deluge Shanghai's streets and boulevards with a terrifying vitality. Fused together in a massive channel of productive energy, the bodies of commuters and drivers become indistinguishable from one another and from the ubiquitous rickshaws that form with them a great sea of flesh and steel. As in the novel's scenes of decay and stagnation, the "movement of matter" prevails here, becoming the basis for an unsettling kind of sensory dispossession:

From between two buildings, another stream of rickshaws gushed forth. When the currents met at the intersection, the figures of the drivers—now even more tightly packed together—disappeared altogether. Passengers floated chest-high upon the wave, a silent throng, gliding along all at the same speed. Sanki could not even see the group of drivers below who were now propelling the vehicles with even greater force, hidden beneath the crowd.[66]

But the narrative quickly proceeds from this image of hydraulic energy to the larger structure it implies: the totality of the capitalist universe. A few paragraphs later, in a depiction of the financial district, the reader is confronted with a more comprehensive view of this immense, pulsating cosmos:

A swarm of carriages carrying exchange brokers were dashing around. The carriages raced through the streets and alleys, tangling together in a clatter, then lining up in rows, the sound of hooves like a spray of small stones thrown on the pavement. The speed of the Mongolian horses that drove these carriages was driving the New York and London exchange markets. Now and then a carriage wheel would bounce up and the carriage would float up lightly like a yacht. The brokers riding in the carriages were almost all Westerners. They raced around from bank to bank, armed with shrewdness and smiles. Expanding and contracting from moment to moment, their trading margins amounted to the energy source that moved both East and West.[67]

Identifying the kinetics of organic tissue—the "speed of the Mongolian horses"—with the ominous movements of distant exchange markets in New York and London, this scene presents another variation of the novel's somatic theme: the almost incomprehensibly vast interrelated universe in which the velocity of a horse in China cannot be disengaged from the price of gold in London. This is a cosmos governed by the spectral energies of a terrible unity, where the lifeblood of finance capital, in the words of Lenin, "spreads its net over all the countries of the world." By the early twentieth century, the permeation of corporate and imperial interests into the smallest corners of daily life had given rise to a new experience of spatial and temporal interconnection identifiable with what Lenin called the "socialization of production." As he wrote in 1916, "When a big enterprise assumes gigantic proportions . . . when the raw materials are transported to the most suitable place of production, sometimes hundreds or thousands of miles away in a systematic and organized manner; when a single centre directs all the successive stages of work right up to the manufacture of numerous varieties of finished articles; when these products are distributed according to a single plan among tens and hundreds of millions of customers . . . then it becomes evident that we have socialization of production."[68]

Yokomitsu's struggle to theorize an aesthetic adequate to this interlocking universe, capable of *representing it* and *acknowledging its limitlessness* at the same time, accounts for the convoluted epistemology galvanizing the most memorable passages of *Shanghai*. But it was in the critical essays surrounding *Shanghai*'s initial publication, produced in the context of the debate on "formalism," that Yokomitsu openly acknowledged his debt to Einstein. In 1928, a conflict arose within the ranks of the All Japan Proletarian Artists' Alliance (Zen Nihon Musansha Geijutsu Renmei; officially known as Nippona Artista Proleta Federacio in Esperanto, or NAPF) over the relative priority of "artistic" and "political" values in the age of mass literature.[69] For Yokomitsu, the "artistic massification debate" (*geijutsu taishūka ronsō*) was reducible to a theoretical rift over conceptualizing the relationship of form to content, of consciousness to practice, and of individual experience to the larger historical totality. As such, it also represented an opportunity to inject his own radically relational definitions of language, objectivity, and materiality. The "formalist literature debate" ensued as the result of his modernist intervention.

In important ways, Yokomitsu's modernism matured at exactly this moment, when it stood forlorn against the increasingly powerful literary left. By 1928, the New Sensationist journal *Bungei jidai* (Literary age) had already ceased publication, and some of its most prominent contributing members, such as Kataoka Teppei, had already "converted" to the proletarian cause. Stubbornly resisting this shift, Yokomitsu called into questioned the entire framework within which Kurahara Korehito (1902–91), Hirabayashi Hatsunosuke and others presented their arguments, identifying at its base what he called an "obeisance to Kantian idealism."[70] Only by overturning the "metaphysical theory" underlying leftist literary ideology, Yokomitsu told his readers, could the problem behind content and form be properly settled.[71] Challenging the scientific authority that Marxist theory had come to connote, Yokomitsu introduced a permeating and all-encompassing vision of materiality, offering his own idiosyncratic vision of literary "science" as the antidote to the spiritualist values he saw haunting revolutionary literature's deep structure. In the essays that followed, terms like "content" (*naiyō*), "consciousness" (*ishiki*), and "subject" (*shukan*) would be infused, characteristically, with bio-physical value.[72] But it is the paradoxical image of mutual causation, implied by the interdependence he attributed to these phenomena, that make up the core of Yokomitsu's contribution.

"Having restored time and space to a single dimension," Yokomitsu writes in the 1928 essay "Bungei jihyō (1)" (Literary commentary [1]), "the cutting edge of science moves forward, once again, by overturning philosophy."[73] Citing the contemporary article "Ainshutain no shin gakusetsu ni tsuite" (On Einstein's new theory, 1928) by physicist and science journalist Ishiwara Jun, Yokomitsu establishes from the outset of this inaugural essay the magnitude of his own ambition. If Albert Einstein's relativity theory provided a singular disposition from which to "comprehend all material phenomena," as Ishiwara had suggested, Yokomitsu's essay clearly sets out to imply an epistemological affinity with this revolution in theoretical physics. At another level, this essay lays common claim to the anti-metaphysical, profoundly "material" vocabulary of the physical sciences in general. "That is why our theory of form begins, first, by taking written script as objects (*buttai*)," he explains. "So 'form' is the place where these objects become script, and 'content' is the energy (*enerugī*) that arises out of the movement of these objects, which constitute form."[74]

Although Yokomitsu maintains rhetorical agreement with the dialectical language of leftist theory throughout these essays, his emphasis on material interdependence pushes the logic of this rhetoric to its most literal conclusions. Even as Kurahara Korehito argues for the inseparability of content and form, Yokomitsu observes, an idealist substratum persists in the priority he affords "content" as the determining agent in artistic development. To describe artistic progress as "the evolution of past forms determined by new content," Yokomitsu tells his readers, citing Kurahara, is merely to resuscitate the age-old notion that "content determines form."[75] Yokomitsu directs a similar critique against Hirabayashi Hatsunosuke, whose suggestion that the content of a work originates in authorial intention seemed to parallel Kurahara's idealism at another level. "For Hirabayashi," Yokomitsu writes, "content is not a question of what is written, but of what [the author] intended to write."[76] By contrast, Yokomitsu's own theory of "formalism"—offered in response to these leftist versions—posits a paradigm within which a writer's consciousness *cannot exist apart from the form it takes*. For Yokomitsu, that is, the words on the page and the meaning they "contain" constitute a single field of interaction, comprehensible only as a network of relations. In imitation of Einstein's revolutionary picture of space-time, Yokomitsu's theory aimed to restore content and form to a single, continuous dimension. "What is called 'form,'" he writes, clarifying his position, "is nothing other than the rhythmical arrangement of written signs that transmit meaning. Could 'content' be possible without this formal arrangement of written signs?"[77]

The anti-metaphysical vehemence of this position would be adopted later by Nakagawa Yoichi (1897–1994), Yokomitsu's New Sensationist colleague, whose 1930 book *Keishiki shugi geijutsu ron* (A theory of formalist art) echoed Yokomitsu's literalist approach to artistic form. In his discussion of such figures as Anatoly Lunacharsky and Victor Shklovsky, historically associated with the term "formalism," Nakagawa dismisses the notion of treating form as mere "technique" (*gikō*), presenting his own theory as part of an overarching ontological system. "Formalism," he writes in one of the early chapters, "is the claim that nothing exists apart from its form."[78] To substantiate this view, Nakagawa himself turns to the essays of Ishiwara Jun, finding in this physicist's popular explanations of the space-time continuum both the metaphorical idiom for describing his aesthetic theory and the authoritative foundation of a far-reaching belief system. In one chapter—broken into subsections with tellingly non-literary titles such as "What are Atoms and Electrons?" and "On Energy Theory"—Nakagawa cites one of the numerous articles on relativity that Ishiwara had published over the decade in the journal *Shisō*. "Matter cannot exist apart from the space-time continuum," Ishiwara had elegantly explained. "One could even say that our theory of matter no longer requires that any [material] elements be added to the geometry of the space-time continuum. Time and space are not forms that contain matter within them, but are themselves the elements from which matter is constituted."[79]

A former student of Einstein's in Zurich, an accomplished physicist in his own right, and the best-known interpreter of relativity theory for the popular Japanese reading audience of the 1920s, Ishiwara Jun played a crucial role in the "scientific" dimensions of Japan's literary avant-garde.[80] Regarded by some as the originator of the "light molecule theory" that led eventually to the discoveries of Louis de Broglie, Ishiwara's international research career came to a sudden end when he was forced to resign his position at Tōhoku University because of a scandalous love affair with the poet Hara Asao.[81] Turning to popular science writing and poetry, Ishiwara would go on in the late Taishō years to play a key role in the rise of science journalism, a relatively new genre associated with the appearance of a variety of new journals, including *Kagaku* (Science), where Ishiwara served as the editor-in-chief beginning in 1931.[82] Remembered even today as Einstein's interpreter during his 1922 lecture visit to Japan, for modernists like Yokomitsu and Nakagawa, Ishiwara Jun was the simultaneously passionate and coolly competent scientist-poet who gave voice to a new understanding of reality, which, in turn, inspired an entirely new model of literary realism.

When Yokomitsu defined literature as "that object through which individuals represent with written signs the movement of matter," he captured in this deceptively simple, if bizarre, image, the enormity of this realist revolution.[83] If the printed characters of a literary text are to be viewed as "objects" (*buttai*), bound to the very laws and limits they "represent," and if the content conveyed by these objects arises out of the "energy" generated by their formal arrangement, then Yokomitsu's "theory of signs" must also be understood, fundamentally, as a *theory of reality*. Paralleling the observational convolutions of Einstein's relative universe, Yokomitsu's definition of literature posits a text capable of referring to the very world that surrounds and penetrates it. For Yokomitsu, in other words, the basic material element of any literary work—the "written script" (*moji*)—must be understood as an opaque object with curiously retained referential powers: a sign that is also a referent, deeply embedded in the world it depicts. Content, from this perspective, becomes the domain of knowledge *in relation to* sensation. "In accordance with our senses and our knowledge," Yokomitsu would later write in the essay "Moji ni tsuite" (On script, 1929), "we perceive content as an energy that arises from the objective form of the written script, telling us a mountain is a mountain, the sea is the sea."[84] Crucially, the "energy" attributed to the literary text is ultimately defined as a relational effect, generated by interaction between the substance of the text and *the body of the reader*. "Content is the energy that arises between the reader and the formal arrangement of written signs (*moji no keishiki*)," Yokomitsu told his readers, adding: "It is clear that this energy does not transform itself through unified written forms, but through the brains (*zunō*) of the readers."[85]

Invoking the same somatic logic running through *Shanghai*, Yokomitsu presents the human body as the central mediating "object" at the heart of his theory of literary form. "Until we look at a newspaper," he had observed in an earlier article, "the sculptural forms of its printed words remain as nothing but meaningless stones."[86] Placed at the interchange where matter gives rise to the "energy," Yokomitsu's image of the "objective" human body—*connected* to the external world, though not *identical* with it—exposes the ecological structure of his realism.

For decades, scholars have struggled to define the true significance of Yokomitsu's formalism and the theory of language that accompanied it. For Komori Yōichi, these essays serve, above all, as evidence of the early influence in Japan of the linguistic lectures of Ferdinand de Saussure. The newly translated content of Saussure's language theory probably reached Yokomitsu through the work of Nishiwaki Junzaburō (1894–1982) and Toyama Usaburō (1903–80), who both published prototypically "semiotic" essays on poetics in the avant-garde journal *Shi to shiron* in the late 1920s. Komori's work carefully describes the ways in which, under the impact of Saussure's seminal theories, Nishiwaki Junzaburō's surrealist disquisitions served to weaken the link between language and referent for contemporary experimental artists and writers in Japan.[87] In the essays of Toyama Usaburō as well, Komori tells us, "reality as the 'referent' is already bracketed, and language as a signifying system is taken as the subject of discussion." Indeed, for Komori, Yokomitsu's own language theory betrays a similarly anti-referential inflection, concerning itself ultimately with "language as an independent semiotic system" and not with "the 'referent' as physical nature or reality."[88]

And yet, in the end, it may be more accurate to take Yokomitsu's theories at their word. What can it mean, for example, when the author ascribes to his own poetics the aspiration to effect "a more concise fusion of the movement of material phenomena with the movement of written signs"? And how do we explain his characterization of this operation as "a progressive kind of realism" (*shinpoteki na isshu no shajitsu*)?[89] From these statements and from the evidence of their practical expression in the novel *Shanghai*, a radically relational and interlocking vision of referential accuracy begins to emerge. Far from bracketing "physical nature" or placing "reality" beyond the scope of the text, this author's many essays on language and materialism present instead an image of nature that penetrates the operations of the text itself. If written language illuminates the material world by interacting with it—as well as with the body of the reader—then the text can hardly be described as *disjoined* from reality; rather, it must be understood, at least theoretically, as deeply and paradoxically *connected* to it. It is not that nature has been recognized as a figment of sign systems, as Komori argues, but that sign systems themselves have come to be recognized as part of the natural world.

Nowhere is the breadth of this realist disposition more stunningly engaged than in those scenes of riot and revolution in *Shanghai* that are presented as telegraphic messages received and recorded on a company "bulletin board" (*keijiban*). A recurring point of reference in the novel, the bulletin board is first introduced when Sanki finds employment in the trade division at Tōyō-men, a fictional double of the historical textile company, Nagai-men (the notorious flash-point of the citywide walkout in 1925). Sanki's new duties include monitoring economic and political events that concern the cotton trade, and as he assesses the influx of telegrams and phone messages from around the globe, he encounters a terrifyingly unified—and oddly "natural"—geo-economic cosmos:

> On the bulletin board, because of recent storms, the market price of American cotton had gone up. The cotton market at Liverpool was being supported by the Bombay futures market. And the Kutchakhandi and Tejimandi markets were, in turn, supporting the Bombay market. Sanki's most important duty at the trade division was to watch the condition of these two Indian cotton markets. Raw cotton had to be bought somewhere. Solving this resource problem was of the utmost importance to the company's production.[90]

If Sanki's job offers him a unique glimpse at a network of market relations, the vastness of this network can only present itself to him as an abstract model: a diagram of place-names and production numbers. In a certain sense, therefore, it might be said that the events that Sanki monitors in this passage do not occur *in the world*, but only "on the bulletin board" (*keijiban de*). This is true only in a limited sense, however, for there is never any doubt in Sanki's mind (or in the reader's) that the data presented on the board refer to actual conditions: a world of events beyond the reach of immediate visibility, though deeply linked to "the company's production."

The urgency of the bulletin board's documentary authority only intensifies after the shooting death of a Chinese worker in the factory of the company where Sanki is employed. When massive demonstrations crystallize around the body of the martyred laborer, Sanki plots the movement of urban unrest as it sweeps across the city and reverberates throughout the world economy. In this surreally historical passage, Yokomitsu's language captures not only the "total picture" enabled by the conditions of modern technology, but also the sensory experience of living under those conditions. The reader is invited not simply to interpret the content of the messages delivered, in other words, but to experience the immediacy of the delivery system itself.

The body of the slain worker, which had been laid out at union headquarters, was carried with pomp to a local square. Minute by minute, phone calls from observers reached the management offices of Sanki's company. The messages were posted on the bulletin board:
— Over 500 flags at funeral site.
— Over 30 participating organizations. Approximately 10,000 attend funeral.
— Enraged speakers, crowds gather around coffin. Assault on factory this evening at latest.
— Clashes with police. Dozens arrested.
— Student groups attack police to free those arrested.[91]

For nearly two pages, the narrative assembles these truncated and disjunctive declarations, placing information from the funeral site against intelligence reports on leftist activities ("Meeting at the home of Russian Communist Party Secretary Cherkov") and information on world trade ("*Hakata Maru* departs Bombay, 2,800 tons raw cotton").[92] Finally, the reader is given a series of "coded" telegrams from various Japanese commercial organizations:

— Greater Japan Textile Manufacturers Association. Several members sent to Tokyo. Meeting with Foreign Ministry yesterday.
— Japan Industrial Club. Recommends warning. Completed arrangements with Foreign Ministry, Ministry of Commerce and Industry.
— Kyoto Chamber of Commerce. Mutual effort with Osaka Chamber of Commerce. Awaiting report.
— Kobe Chamber of Commerce. Following Foreign Ministry orders, will dispatch emergency measures to local General Trade Association.
— Osaka Chamber of Commerce. Will petition government for aid. Have requested mediators to resolve current problems with regional trade offices.
— Tokyo Chamber of Commerce. Meeting with Foreign Minister. Government decides on resolute measures. Strong protest to Chinese government, and other steps. Chinese government responds: will suppress strike soon.[93]

Yokomitsu's remarkable decision to narrate half of an entire chapter as a series of telegrams reflects the audacity of this novel's stylistic ambition. Though hardly compelling as a narrative technique, the fragmentary appearance of the words on the page must be taken, in a certain sense, as a *demonstration* as well as an *explanation* of the story's content. Part of what this passage presents, in other words, is a picture of modern language itself: detached and depersonalized, yet infused at the same time with panic and urgency. Oddly poetic in its density and economy, compressive in its capacity to speak at once from distant points in space, the telegraphic code that makes up the second half of this chapter might justifiably be understood as forming a *visual portrait* of the modern world. For to *read* sixteen telegrams, assembled on the bulletin board, is also to *look at* them all at once: to confront the immediacy of an interconnected cosmos. In important ways, then, the bulletin board in this passage provides an abstract picture of a larger totality that is also directly and viscerally experienced: "Sanki felt the shudder of his homeland," the narrative observes, "revealed in these telegrams. . . ."[94]

Crucially, it is only through the bulletin board's disjunctive, "semiotic" intervention that the world of the referent—the world of storms, labor unrest, and police violence—*comes into view.* Remindful of Tanizaki's diagrammatic depictions in *Naomi*, Yokomitsu's telegraphic portrait of the May 30 Incident presents a non-mimetic picture that functions by underscoring the relationship between the sensory immediacy of its own language and the larger reality it depicts.

In this sense, Yokomitsu's classic of Japanese modernism demonstrates a long misunderstood realist dynamic at the heart of literary modernism in general. When Georg Lukács presented his famous attack on modernism in his essay "Realism in the Balance" (1938), he would dismiss the various aesthetic movements of Europe's early twentieth century as "frozen in their own immediacy." He wrote: "The modern literary schools of the imperialist era . . . from Naturalism to Surrealism, which have followed each other in such swift succession, all have one feature in common. They all take reality exactly as it manifests itself to the writer and the characters he creates."[95] Lukács told his readers that the critical capacity of literature to "pierce the surface to discover the underlying essence" had been lost amid the frenzy of stylistic experimentation. For Lukács, reviving the realist powers of literature meant disengaging from the temptations of this sensory literalism; it meant "abandoning and transcending the limits of immediacy."[96] But it was exactly this notion of transcendence, and the view it presumably offered of an integrated social reality, that Ernst Bloch resisted in his response to Lukács. Defending the descriptive legitimacy of modernism's "fragmentary, open-ended character,"[97] Bloch's rejection of Lukács's realism revolved around another question altogether: "What if authentic reality is also discontinuity?"[98]

Indeed, this is the very predicament Fredric Jameson describes as characteristic of everyday life under capitalism in its "stage of imperialism" in his essay, "Cognitive Mapping" (1988). In British literature produced during this imperial stage, Jameson tells us, the "truth" of individual experience "no longer coincides with the place in which it takes place," but is bound up instead "with the whole colonial system of the British Empire that determines the very quality of the individual's subjective life." The crisis of modernism, from this perspective, has everything to do with newly recognizable historical limits imposed upon phenomenological experience—a view with which neither Lukács nor Bloch would be likely to disagree. "There comes into being, then," Jameson observes, "a situation in which we can say that if individual experience is authentic, then it cannot be true; and that if a scientific or cognitive model of the same content is true, then it escapes individual experience."[99] The question remains, however, as to a useful aesthetic response to these stipulated historical conditions. Ultimately, Jameson rejects the notion of merely settling for Bloch's "discontinuity" as the equivalent of "authentic reality," calling instead for an aesthetic built around what he terms "cognitive mapping": the capacity to see and to depict the gap itself between the "phenomenological perception and a reality that transcends all individual thinking or experience."[100]

Although Jameson identifies this operation as particularly adequate to *postmodern* conditions, the structure of Yokomitsu's bulletin board passage in *Shanghai* suggests the possibility of conceiving of a *modernist* literary aesthetic built around this very process of "cognitive mapping"—an aesthetic capable, that is, of accommodating the textures of sensory experience even as it reaches beyond them toward some greater, invisible totality. Indeed, this is exactly what Lukács himself seemed to be suggesting when he identified as the essence of literature's realist project the effort to understand the correct dialectical link between "appearance and essence."[101] Ironically, what Lukács finally presented as the basis of his anti-modernist stance might easily be understood as the core of Yokomitsu's *modernism*: the very framework of the novel *Shanghai*. But if Lukács recognized this particular form of realism as essential to the capacity of literature to resist the "reactionary prejudices"[102] of fascist ideology, Yokomitsu's work demonstrates that such an approach might, with equal logic, be engaged to *legitimate* them. The capacity to map "the economy of the whole world" as "an objectively unified totality," to borrow Lukács's language,[103] and to depict the relationship between that cognitive totality and the textures of sensory experience, may indeed constitute a necessary element of any socialist political project. But it is one of the darker lessons revealed in Yokomitsu's novel that the appearance alone of such a disposition in no way guarantees the critical ethic it enables.

The Fourth Person

In *Shanghai*, when Sanki contemplates the dynamics of political revolution—comparing conditions in the city with the chemical properties of a sealed and shaken soda bottle—he becomes, explicitly for a moment, the cartographer of Yokomitsu's colonial universe, holding at once the entire empire in his head: "But the vast whirlpool of East Asia did not look like such an immense image to Sanki. To him, it was like a map folded up in his head. Studying the dry loose ring around the cigar leaves he held between his fingers, he suddenly thought: could reality be, for me, the dried leaves of this cigar, this map in my head?"[104] As the novel approaches its conclusion, and the material inevitability of this "reality" (*genjitsu*) makes itself clear, Sanki's cartographic inclination turns unapologetically to a program of nativist retreat.

With chaos spreading throughout the city, Sanki's mapping proclivities increasingly display themselves through a bizarre, grammatical effect. Sentences in which "Sanki" or "Sanki's body" serve as both the subject and object of the verb begin noticeably to recur, especially during the novel's climactic moments. Signaling the author's growing interest in narrative reflexivity, these passages seem to demonstrate, *avant la lettre*, what Yokomitsu would later introduce in his seminal essay "Junsui shōsetsuron" (A theory of the pure novel, 1935) as the grammatical "fourth person" (*yoninshō*): a narrative strategy centered around the image of the "self that looks at the self" (*jibun o miru jibun*).[105] Openly transcendent, yet simultaneously concerned with the local limits of bodily experience, these reflexive passages evoke, in some essential way, the "Einsteinian" paradoxes of mapping in its most mundane sense.

For to use a map is to discover a local physical truth by means of an imagined transcendence: to consider a specific position from the perspective of a cognitive totality. And it is this peculiarly cartographic image of the "self that looks at the self" that permeates the most ideologically revealing passages of *Shanghai*'s latter episodes:

Sanki had hardly slept the night before. He wandered the streets and alleyways dressed in Chinese clothing. He no longer thought about what might happen on the streets. Only, from time to time, he would measure the position of his own heart as if blankly adjusting the focus on a film. Then suddenly the world around him began to roar, and a streetcar passed through the neighborhood, stained with blood and with its windows broken from rocks. It passed as evidence of street fighting that was taking place nearby. Once again, he became aware of the fact that he himself was Japanese. How many times had he been made aware of the fact that he was Japanese? He suddenly felt the danger of expressing his mother country through his flesh. He felt the mob of monsters with their fangs bared. He thought of the scene of his body flowing from his mother's womb at the same time that he thought of the scenery through which he now walked. His time, which flowed between these two scenes, was none other than the time of the flesh of Japan. And probably it would remain that way from now on. His own mind may attempt to forget his home country, and to freely escape from his flesh. But his flesh could not resist what the exterior world directed against him, the coercive insistence that he was Japanese.[106]

Measuring the "position of his own heart" in the manner of some spectral film projectionist, Sanki observes from a transcendent "fourth person" position the "coercive insistence" of his own somatic destiny. However much "his own mind" (*kare jishin no kokoro*) may try to resist, the narrative suggests, it is the physical inevitability of Sanki's native identity—the "fact" of his "mother country" (*bokoku*) expressing itself "through his flesh" (*nikutai to shite arawashite iru*)—that will determine Sanki's actions in the uprising. These same material factors will also decide the outcome of Sanki's relationship with Fang Qiu-lan, the beautiful revolutionary whose seductive power incites the protagonist's initial and persistent internal conflict over racial, class, and national loyalty. Sanki's out-of-body observations in this scene anticipate the novel's reactionary conclusion by portraying individual action as deeply embedded in the determining structures of some larger, "natural" law. The images that Sanki conjures simultaneously of his own body (*jibun no karada*) emerging from his mother's womb and the image of himself walking through the riot-filled streets of Shanghai, leave little doubt as to the inevitability of Sanki's national allegiance. Native identity is portrayed here as a simple fact of geo-cultural space-time. Sanki's "time," the narrative observes, was identical to the "time of the flesh of Japan" (*Nihon no nikutai no jikan*). Sanki's flesh is unfree, in other words, not because it is the property of Japan, but because it *is* Japan.

Though it would not be theorized until 1935, when Yokomitsu's "Junsui shōsetsuron" would provide philosophical authority to the openly reactionary "cultural renaissance" (*bungei fukkō*) of the 1930s, the reflexivity embodied in the notion of the "fourth person" grammatical position is clearly recognizable in some of the most important scenes of *Shanghai*.[107] Eventually linking this paradoxical narrative strategy directly with the "problem of ethnicity" (*minzoku no mondai*),[108] Yokomitsu seems from the beginning to have intuitively deployed the "self that looks at the self" in the service of a profoundly nativist disposition. In one of the final scenes of the novel, when Sanki, pursued by a roving band of Chinese rebels, is thrown over the railing of a footbridge and into a barge filled with night soil, he finds himself observing once again the movements and positioning of his own body, resigning himself, finally, to the logic of material inevitability:

> Suddenly, Sanki noticed that his body had stopped and was tightly grasping the edge of a piece of wood. But this place. . . . When he extended his legs, he realized he was in the middle of the boat he had been looking down upon. He looked around to see the mushy surface of the night soil soaking his body up to his neck. He was about to raise himself up, but then he thought, once I get out, what will I do then? The heavy atmospheric layer of his own past moved by, passing before him in black blotches. He fell back just as he was, face up in the night soil. When he closed his eyes, he began to feel his head moving freely once again. He followed the motion of his own head, wondering how far it would go. And then, as if measuring his own specific gravity, he felt his body sink completely into the excrement, and grinned.[109]

As if "measuring his own specific gravity" (*jibun no hijū o hakaru ka no yō ni*), Sanki feels his body sinking deeper into the organic discharge of Shanghai itself. The unexpected physical pleasure of this revolting immersion suggests the transcendence of an out-of-body experience. Grammatically distinguishing Sanki's conscious self (*kare*) from the "objective" existence of his own body (*jibun no karada*)—"He followed the motion of his own head, wondering how far it would go"—this passage once again evokes the "fourth person" position of the cognitive cartographer. Suspended in sewage, Sanki experiences a brief moment of clarity: "Ah, but the smell of this fertilizer filling the boat, this is the aroma of my Japanese home. Right now, at home, my mother is probably mending the soles of a pair of tabi, with her rusty glasses around her neck. She would never dream that I had ended up here in this boat. . . . But what about Fang Qiu-lan? Ah, Fang Qiu-lan, please get me out of here."[110]

The moment Sanki envisions Fang Qiu-lan's sultry lips and beautiful face, the spell is broken. Suddenly the stars above him "shine one notch brighter" and he awakens, once again, to the conflicting forces of the larger universe. But it is to Japan—the source of his own material destiny—where his thoughts eventually return. And it is to Osugi's room and not Fang Qiu-lan's that Sanki retreats to wait for the landing of the Japanese army that will save them.

The great strike and historic work stoppage of May 30, 1925, concluded three months after it began when the Japanese government agreed to compensate the family of the martyred Gu Zhenghong and to improve working conditions at Japanese factories. An apparent victory for the Communist labor movement in China, the events of May 30 actually culminated in what Elizabeth J. Perry describes as the "uneasy and fragile alliance" between left-wing labor organizations and the right wing of the Kuomintang.[111] In 1931, political instability resurfaced in Shanghai when anti-Japanese associations (formally disbanded in 1928) launched another citywide boycott in protest of Japan's September invasion of Manchuria.[112] "In meeting after meeting," writes Christian Henriot, "thousands of demonstrators demanded the dispatch of troops to Manchuria, the withdrawal of the Japanese army, or, failing that, a declaration of war, the breaking of economic ties with Japan, and the political reunification of China."[113] Dock workers refused to work, employees of Japanese firms were encouraged to walk out, and, by October 1931, the city was once again in a state of crisis.

By the beginning of the next year, despite efforts at peaceful negotiations by Chinese officials, Japanese marines were marching into Zhabei, one of Shanghai's most heavily populated districts.[114] In many ways, the bloody clash that ensued between the Japanese soldiers and China's

Nineteenth Army consummated the destiny described as inevitable in Yokomitsu's novel. What came to be known in Japan as the Shanghai "Incident" (*jihen*) demonstrated with finality what Yokomitsu might have described as the "material" clash between incompatible cultural "velocities." Foreshadowed by the events of 1925, the Shanghai Incident inaugurated a period of expansion and devastation that would achieve its final culmination on the battlefields of World War II.[115]

Although characterized throughout by a tone of descriptive equanimity, Yokomitsu's vision of the capitalist and imperialist system in *Shanghai* does present to its readers the outlines of a profound and far-reaching ethical conviction. Deceptively bold in style, this novel finally represents what might be termed an ethic of resignation, centered upon the inevitability of an abstract and abstracting violation of individual human sovereignty. "What made Japanese economic penetration truly 'imperialistic,' writes Albert Feuerwerker, "was what it shared with the totality of the Japanese presence in China: an invasion of China's sovereignty that derogated not only the autonomy of an abstract polity, but also, more critically, the autonomy of particular and individual Chinese who apprehended and reacted to the intruding foreign presence."[116] If the "scientific" inflection of Yokomitsu's novel helped to *describe* imperial aggression in these terms, it also served to *sanitize* that aggression and to *neutralize* indigenous resistance to it by placing it in a framework of natural law.

There is surely little need to demonstrate further the ideological dangers posed by placing human history under the rubric of "nature." In a certain sense, as Yokomitsu's fiction makes clear, these dangers are inseparable from Japan's modernist moment. The outward-looking impulse of Japanese modernism's relational realism—the tendency to see human experience as fully explicable only in relation to a larger network of invisible realities—always carries this dark potential to become a "science" of legitimation. I have called Yokomitsu's novel an ecological parody, however, because, for the true ecologist, the point is not to see human history as natural, but rather to understand nature as historical: to see inscribed on the material surfaces of the world traces of a dialectical process centered on what Marx called "the metabolic interaction between man and the earth."[117] It is in this sense alone that Marx continually characterized his own materialism as belonging to "the process of natural history."[118] Similarly, for Yokomitsu's ecologically-minded contemporary, Miyazawa Kenji—the subject of the next three chapters—it is never a question of *equating* human history with natural history, but simply of recognizing their *connection*. Rooted in this essential insight, the fiction and poetry of Miyazawa Kenji, still an understudied figure in Western scholarship, are perfectly situated to reveal to us the most useful ethical and political dimension of the realist disposition in Japanese literary modernism. Kenji's work will therefore take center stage in the second part of this study.

PART II

Earth, Stars

THREE

Things Near and Far Away: Geometry and Ethics in the Stories of Miyazawa Kenji

The space of heaven seems immediately next to my senses.

—Miyazawa Kenji, " Indora no ami"

Thus *society* is the consummated oneness in substance of man with nature—the true resurrection of nature—the naturalism of man and the humanism of nature both brought to fulfillment.

—Karl Marx, *Philosophical and Economic Manuscripts of 1844*

For reading audiences in contemporary Japan, it might be difficult to imagine a category of analysis that could place the seamy eroticism of Tanizaki Jun'ichirō and the grim geopolitical ruminations of Yokomitsu Riichi alongside the world of talking animals and interstellar fantasy found in the children's stories of Miyazawa Kenji. Celebrated today by his native city of Hanamaki as a local genius and promoted by Iwate Prefecture's regional tourist industry as the embodiment of the gentle folk wisdom of Japan's rural northeast, Kenji has risen from the relative obscurity that characterized his life to the ironic summits of posthumous popular appeal.[1] In the process, the author has acquired an image often far removed from the social conflict, ideological crisis, and artistic experimentation that defined the historical moment in which he lived and wrote.

As with all canonized writers, Miyazawa Kenji survives through the mechanisms of literary scholarship and the commercial press, immortalized in the pages of illustrated volumes, several recently updated paperback editions, and an extraordinarily detailed annotated "complete collection" (*zenshū*) of his work that appeared in 1995.[2] But the words and images of Kenji's work have also proliferated and circulated throughout the pastel terrain of greeting card illustrations, calendars, and novelty kitchen utensils: the universal language of the gift shop. Against the neutralizing effects of this ever-broadening field of consumption, however, it is crucial to recognize Kenji's fiction and poetry as rooted in the consciousness of revolution—in the uniquely radical epistemological and political insights of the early decades of the twentieth century. Indeed, no body of work could tell us more about the oppositional grammar of the *realist* disposition I have identified in this study as the defining feature of Japanese literary modernism.

Commonly portrayed as a spiritual eccentric, Kenji's youthful conversion to Nichiren Buddhism (a defection from the Jōdoshinshū sect to which his family belonged) remains for many critics the central fact of his life. For some, the author's lifelong devotion to the *Lotus Sūtra* (*Myōhō renge kyō*) amounts to the final interpretive key to a vast and mysterious body of work. But if Kenji really was a "minor prophet in the Blakeian mold," in the words of Mallory Blake Fromm, "subject to visitations visual and auditory," the poems and tales that contain these prophesies, as Fromm herself admits, often speak the language of chemistry, biology, and physics.[3] However resonant with the *Lotus Sūtra*'s image of universal salvation and cosmic unity, the singularity of Kenji's ethical vision cannot be understood without reference to another set of "sacred" texts: Charles Steinmetz's essays on relativity, for example, or Katayama Masao's chemistry text *Kagaku honron* (Fundamental issues in chemistry, 1915)—a book that was never far from the author's side.[4]

An experienced researcher and teacher, Miyazawa Kenji maintained a broad and imaginative, but rigorously detailed interest in the discoveries of the natural sciences throughout his life. In 1918, as a 23-year-old research student at the Morioka Kōtō Nōrin Gakkō (Morioka School of Agriculture and Forestry)—today the Faculty of Agriculture at Iwate

University—Kenji published a geological survey and topographical map of his native Hienuki County.[5] Covering the fields and mountains of his home on foot and charting the contours of their hidden histories proved to be an experience of both practical and poetic significance. The author, trained in agricultural chemistry, taught himself to navigate the surface and depths of the land, attending not only to its material character but also to the "social" tension between that inorganic world and the living community inhabiting it. The physical trials—he was already suffering from the lung condition that would eventually kill him—together with the abstract cognitive exertions required by this mapping project seem in some profound way to have prefigured Kenji's idiosyncratic notion of *the social*: a set of relations dependent upon but not reducible to the laws of matter and energy.

From the beginning, Kenji's orientation was fiercely local. His poems and stories focus almost exclusively on the culture of Japan's 40th parallel, the universe of Iwate Prefecture. At the same time, however, Iwate's deciduous hardwood and evergreen forests, its animals, its local dialect, its rivers and farms become in Kenji's work the constituent elements of a microcosm in whose tiny details the history of the entire universe is contained.[6] Given the name "Ihatov"—a sort of Esperanto transliteration—Iwate takes on a transcendent existence, the ethnically and nationally ambiguous locus of Kenji's fictional and poetic world. Apart from a few short stays in Tokyo, the author himself lived most of his life in Iwate. But Kenji's confinement to this bio-region cannot be equated with the sort of provincialism that so many of his modernist contemporaries moved to the city to escape. His work reflects both a disciplined attention to local particularities and a (sometimes naively) ambitious universalism that his early geological and geographical activities may indeed have helped to foster. Later teaching chemistry, soil science, and crop production at the Gunritsu Hienuki Nōgakkō (Hienuki County School of Agriculture),[7] Kenji continued to develop and refine a practical understanding of the relationship between molecular phenomena, geological history, and human culture, an understanding that would serve as the core of his literary vision.

Although only a fraction of Kenji's prodigious output would be published during his short life (he died at 37), the peculiarly "scientific" flavor of his vocabulary and perceptual disposition emerged from the beginning as one of this author's most powerful assets. In 1924, soon after Kenji published (at his own expense) the sprawling, experimental poetry collection *Haru to shura: shinshō suketchi* (Spring and Asura: mental sketch, 1924), the critic Tsuji Jun noted the freshness of its sensibility, praising the young poet as a master of "idiosyncrasy."[8] Later that same year, in an article for the journal *Nihonjin shijin* (Japanese poets), Satō Sōnosuke described Kenji with baffled admiration as a poet of "genius" who seemed "not to possess a single word currently in use among other poets today."[9] Miyazawa Kenji, Satō told his readers, "made poetry out of geology, botany, mineralogy, and meteorology," evincing a "cool discernment" (*reitetsu*) unequalled by his contemporaries. Indeed, as Amazawa Taijirō has observed, although Kenji wrote from the critical and commercial margins throughout his life, his poetry seems to have been broadly if "secretly" appreciated by writers and poets all over Japan in the 1920s, admired above all else for its strange observational clarity.[10] But it was his children's stories, with their vengeful forests, their sad and dignified bears, and their heartbroken signal lamps, that reveal the true consequences of Kenji's scientific perspective. However fantastic, these narratives are electrified by the critical power of realism in its most fundamental form, freighted with the ethical weight that accompanies the simple notion that organisms, entities, and processes can and do exist independently of human knowledge and perception.

In the preface to his collection of children's stories *Chūmon no ōi ryōriten* (The restaurant of many orders, 1924), Kenji famously describes the tales he is introducing neither as inventions nor as true depictions, but rather as "received" objects: "I received every one of these stories," he told his readers, "in the forests and fields and on the railroad tracks, from rainbows and moonlight."[11] The author asks his readers to accept the stories of this collection not as fiction, strictly speaking, but rather as faithful recordings of discoveries made under specific conditions of time and place: when walking "through a green oak forest in the evening" or standing "shivering in the November mountain wind."[12] To appreciate the critical scope of Kenji's work, it is essential to take these sentences, in some sense, as literal, if playful, testimony to the consequences of realism. These tales ask us to consider what it means to occupy a world that has experienced (and continues to experience) its own history beyond reference to human subjectivity, but which is nonetheless profoundly connected to humanity. Kenji's fiction—rhetorically, the legacy of light-waves and spectral effects—is built around an exploration of what science philosopher Roy Bhaskar calls "intransitive objects of knowledge."[13]

For Bhaskar—who acknowledges a social dimension to science, but only as one of its "sides"—*intransitive* objects are precisely those entities and mechanisms that are not reducible to social constructs, not mere products of human cognitive history. Light propagation, the process of electrolysis or gravitation, unlike their *transitive* counterparts—theories, paradigms, or methods of inquiry—exist and act in the world independently of human knowledge. They are indeed the very foundation of what Bhaskar calls "the real." As Bhaskar observes almost mystically in his classic book *A Realist Theory of Science*: "We can easily imagine a world similar to ours . . . containing the same intransitive objects of scientific knowledge, but without any science to produce knowledge of them. In such a world, which has occurred and may come again, reality would be unspoken for and yet things would not cease to act and interact in all kinds of ways. . . . The tides would still turn and metals conduct electricity in the way that they do, without a Newton or a [Paul] Drude to produce our knowledge of them."[14] Kenji's fiction, like Bhaskar's philosophy of "transcendental realism," places all of its critical and ethical emphasis on this notion of a reality that is neither *constructed* by humans, nor even necessarily directly *perceived* by them, but which nonetheless exists somehow to be *discovered.*

From this perspective, it is the role of the poet and author to let speak a world as yet "unspoken for." Yet such a disposition suggests far more than the sentimental personifications associated with the most saccharine kind of children's fiction. Rather, Kenji's understanding of art pursues the logical consequences of an observational paradox that operates at the heart of Bhaskar's transcendental realism and indeed, latently, at the heart of modernism itself. The narrative that places human culture in conversation with a nonhuman—even nonliving—world both *reveals* and *transcends* the peculiar boundaries of the human frame of reference. This natively realist insight animates the literary world of Miyazawa Kenji at every level, uniting his poems and stories by a common impulse to locate human culture's relative position in a dark and elusive universe. By allowing the intransitive world to speak—through stories narrated by the wind, for example, as in "Shishi odori no hajimari" (The first deer dance, 1924), or told from the perspective of a geological formation, as in "Oinomori to zarumori, nusutomori" (The hills of Oino, Zaru, and Nusuto, 1924)[15]—Kenji reminds his readers that all stories speak *from somewhere*. If human knowledge is limited by the local parameters of human experience, those parameters begin to dissolve in the very effort to determine humanity's place within a larger totality—an operation comparable to the mariner's indispensable skill of triangulation.[16] To triangulate is to recognize perceptual limits; but it also implies the possibility of surmounting those limits through an act of calculation: an appreciation of relationships. At its foundations, then, much of Kenji's work acquires the hidden structure of navigation. Writing a poem or telling a story (especially a children's story) becomes, for Kenji, inseparable from the art of "getting one's bearings."

The navigator's triangulating operation recognizable in much of Kenji's fiction represents more, in other words, than merely the subtle contours of a narrative theme. In fact, this navigational metaphor serves as the structural framework of a far-reaching ethical vision and the defining feature of what can only be described as Kenji's political program. In 1926, the author assembled a series of telegraphic proclamations intended as notes for several lectures he delivered at the Hanamaki School of Agriculture on the subject of "the art of the farmer" (*nōmin geijutsu*). Collected under the title "Nōmin geijutsu gairon kōyō" (A summary introduction to the art of the farmer), these aphoristic pronouncements constitute a sort of programmatic vision, a manifesto linking Kenji's aesthetic philosophy to a model of social transformation. For readers today, the enigmatic declarations that make up this piece provide critical insight into the historical urgency of a body of work that is too often denied its radical valences.

"Nōmin geijutsu" outlines and describes what Kenji envisioned as an artistic and social revolution emerging out of the farming communities of Tōhoku, the northeastern region of Honshu. Extrapolated from this elliptical document, Kenji's notion of the ideal farmer seems to follow the familiar utopian formula of the self-actualized individual, what writer and Kenji critic Inoue Hisashi describes as a human "polyhedron," living as a "theologist in the morning, a scientist in the evening, and an artist at night."[17] In fact, the very year Kenji put together his notes on this subject, he made every effort to realize this ideal by leaving his teaching position, establishing himself on a small piece of rural property, and founding the artistic and educational cooperative Rasu Chijin Kyōkai (Rasu farmer's association).[18] At a time when "newness" was the justifying feature of any legitimate art movement, and when cities were seen as the laboratories of artistic experimentation and political change, Kenji, with characteristic audacity, removed the center of the avant-garde to the fields and forests of Iwate, where he imagined a group of farmer-artists poised to "create a new beauty" that recognized the unity of "our own intuition" with the "proofs of modern science and the experiments of the truth-seekers."[19] Although the inclusive language in this essay belies its author's own class advantages in pursuing these ideals—Kenji was the son of a wealthy used-clothing dealer and pawn broker[20]—this biographical contradiction does not detract from the temerity of the document's central concept: the notion of a thinking and creative individual who is also poor and a farmer, living far from the center of cosmopolitan modernity. While avoiding specifics, "Nōmin geijutsu" clearly attacks the academic and commercial isolation of art, science, and religion, proposing as a solution a creative rural movement capable of liberating not only the farmers themselves, but the people of the modern cities as well. "Our art," Kenji frankly declared to his implied community of cultivators, "is the foundation of a new culture" (*shinkō bunka no kiso*).[21]

Most striking about the social formulations in this piece, however, are the jarring abstractions by which the texture of local daily experience—the "gray labor" (*hai iro no rōdō*) of the cultivator in the fields—is forcibly joined with the elemental energies and far-flung materials of the cosmos. It is here where Kenji distinguishes himself most clearly from contemporary rural nationalist movements with which he might otherwise be confused.[22] "To live justly and strongly," the author proclaims in a breathtakingly compressive gesture, "means to be aware within ourselves of the Milky Way Galaxy, and to respond to that awareness."[23] For physicist and Kenji scholar Saitō Bun'ichi, this statement represents a radical new line of thinking (*hitotsu no atarashii shisō*) about the galaxy, a way of conceiving the Milky Way not as something remote or isolated from humanity, but rather as "mutually, practically, and subjectively" related to human culture.[24] More generally, this cryptic sentence can also be understood as the manifestation of a new *structure of reasoning.* Here and throughout this essay—sometimes almost imperceptibly—the themes of creative production and social emancipation are transformed somehow into grandly conceived "spatial" problems, expressed in the language of *location.*

Although educated in chemistry, Kenji evinced a particularly avid (if non-specialist) dedication to the latest developments in physics and astronomy. When he urged his listeners to join him to "make from our fields and our lives a great four-dimensional work of art," Kenji was only reiterating what can be seen throughout his poetry and fiction as a curiously persistent dedication to the geometrical formulations of Hermann Minkowski, the mathematician credited with providing the non-Euclidean means of representing Einstein's concept of space-time.[25] Deeply influenced by his reading of Charles Steinmetz's *Four Lectures on Relativity and Space* (1923) with its geometrical explanations and stereoscopic projections, Kenji seems at times to write from the belief that all the great problems of history and philosophy are reducible to the four-dimensional idiom of Einsteinian relativity, the abstract poetics of time and space.[26] Like many of his modernist contemporaries, Kenji proposed a world beyond the purview of any single frame of reference, a world conceivable not as a stable totality, but rather—to borrow the words of physicist Lee Smolin—as an "evolving network of relationships."[27] And although he emphasized the collective dimension of his vision—identifying the "new age" with the process by which the "world becomes an organism of one consciousness"[28]—Kenji's calculated invocation of the geometry of relativity functions precisely, it would seem, to distinguish his own collective logic from the monolithic ideologies of other mass movements of the time, either progressive or reactionary.

Like the surprisingly difficult imagery of his greatest children's stories, the abstract language of Kenji's "Nōmin geijutsu" finally asks his listeners to hold an image of *unity* and an image of infinite *incommensurability* in balance. "We are, to begin with, all shining atoms scattered throughout space," the document states toward its conclusion. "We each, moreover, live separately within our own sensations, within our own separate worlds." But against this fact of disunity, Kenji offers the following laconic observation, not as a resolution but rather as a kind of sacred mystery: "This place is here, a field in the land of Rikuchū, in Japan, in the solar system, in the Milky Way Galaxy. . . ."[29] Shedding the naïve impracticalities of its more abstract demands, "Nōmin geijutsu" finally offers this concrete antidote to the infinitely fragmented vastness of the universe itself: the simple exhortation to *know where you are.* Taken together, all of Kenji's poetry and fiction can be understood as an exploration of the image contained in this single sentence, as a sustained meditation on the dizzying, telescopic, and microscopic mysteries of *place.*

As with the work of Tanizaki and Yokomitsu, it was the technological and ideological web of twentieth-century industrial capitalism that enabled Kenji's poetry and fiction. But unlike the commercial, sexual, and geopolitical relationships diagrammed by these other writers, the subject of Kenji's body of work is never anything less than the *cosmos itself.* In keeping with his revolutionary proclamations, Kenji's stories and poems reveal a tension between the human-centered social totality of industrial capitalism on the one hand, and the "natural" universe independent of human experience on the other: the "intransitive" world that modern science and the very technologies associated with industrial modernity had themselves begun to theorize and to measure. The ethical and political breadth of this tension colors Kenji's work at every level. This author understood, perhaps better than any writer of his time, that the anti-positivist stance of the most progressive trends in the natural sciences carried implications far beyond the disciplinary limits to which these sciences necessarily confined themselves. If rocks and deer and pine trees have their own histories, as well as the chemical processes of distant stars, then these nonhuman entities must become equally the "citizens" of any meaningful social totality, the subjects of any ethical program. Whether "egg-born, womb-born, humidity-born, or born by metamorphosis," in the inimitable words of the *Lotus Sūtra*, the "formed" and the "formless," the "footless" and the "many-footed" all take their place in the assembly.[30]

Though historically and ideologically distinct from today's deep ecology movement, Kenji's work serves to identify scientific realism as the fundamental logic underlying what we now term "environmental ethics."[31] Neither the shape of his pronouncements on art nor the Buddhist inflection of his fictional and poetic world could have been conceived outside the framework of this ontological (and ecological) realism. It was ultimately as a realist that Kenji promoted the saving wisdom of the *Lotus Sūtra*, that he formed his notion of the revolutionary function of art, that he conceived of the dark and beautiful material world depicted in his children's tales.

Kenji's realist stance must be distinguished, then, from what Hubert Dreyfus describes as contemporary culture's "worship of natural science," a deluded faith, Dreyfus tells us, that tends to ignore the clear limits of science's scope "as if what science tells us about the fundamental particles has fundamental importance for all aspects of life."[32] For Kenji, it was not simply what science told us about the fundamental particles that was important, but rather what it told us about our *relationship* to those particles. As the invocation of the "fourth dimension" in the "Nōmin geijutsu" essay (and, indeed, throughout his writings) suggests, the physics of energy and relativity theory provided Kenji with a language that concisely and dispassionately articulated the unique limits of the human sensorium even while presenting the possibility for a cognitive transcendence of those limits: *the redemptive power of imagination itself*. This author was profoundly aware, in other words, of the expanded notion of "observation" at the heart of the newest theories in science. For Kenji, the scientific redefinition of this concept—as part sensation, part calculation, and part intuition—made possible new horizons of knowledge, but also brought with it new responsibilities. It is the fundamental structure of his observational position that amounts to the ethical and political content of Kenji's literary vision.

Nowhere is the importance of this observational position more evident than in Kenji's most famous children's tale, "Ginga tetsudō no yoru" (Night of the Milky Way Railroad), the subject of this chapter. In the lonely expanses of this enigmatic narrative, Kenji's commitment to the "triangulating" function of art expresses itself with elegant candor in its recurring and detailed descriptions of astronomical charts, spatial models, and maps. Indeed, it is the map itself—as an *idea*, as an *aesthetic object*, and as a *practical tool*—that constitutes the central image and defining syntax of this work. The story of a boy, Giovanni, who journeys one evening across the galaxy by an interstellar railroad, accompanying his drowned friend to the threshold of the afterlife, "Ginga tetsudō no yoru" operates by the logic of what I have called elsewhere in this study "ontological realism." This acknowledged (though unfinished) masterpiece renders a "reality not of things seen," as Gertrude Stein said of Picasso's art, "but of things that exist."[33] And like Picasso's Cubist work, the cartographic structure of Kenji's story, as it navigates the planets and constellations of the Milky Way, reveals the anti-positivist valence of its historical conditions, a moment in scientific, technical, and aesthetic history when the link between direct observability and existence had been severed.

If Picasso struggled in the early years of the twentieth century to formulate a method of painting adequate to a new notion of objective reality—finally producing art that was, in Arthur I. Miller's words, "conceptual rather than perceptual"—it is important to remember that the resulting geometrical masterworks of Cubism remain stubbornly referential.[34] The diagrammatic explorations of *Les Demoiselles d'Avignon* (1907) or *A Woman Seated in an Armchair* (1909), despite their "conceptual" dimensions, refer unequivocally to a recognizable object world. Indeed, these works focus their energies wholly upon *depicting* that world, offering new ways of navigating its spaces and surfaces. In important respects, then, Cubism also imitated the non-mimetic but thoroughly referential language of the map, one of the oldest conventions of spatial representation. But "Ginga tetsudō no yoru" takes this cartographic grammar a step further. Allowing the logic of the map to thrive in all of its metaphorical complexity, this work shows its readers how to "chart a position" in what turns out to be an *imaginable*, but never wholly *visible*, ontological and social totality. It is part of this story's prophetic force, in fact, that it imitates so fundamentally the unassuming perceptual ironies built into any map. With the cartographic capacity to place its reader inside a space and outside of it at the same time, this work affords the imagination new legitimacy as an indispensable dimension of "perception." In this story, the imagination becomes an instrument of limitless magnification, whereby even distant phenomena may be understood as part of a beautiful and terrifying web of intimacy, whereby alien entities and processes can be seen to engulf us.

Thus, a paradoxical image of *proximity* becomes the most revolutionary feature of Kenji's famous tale, the governing theme of a literary vision that has only recently emerged as recognizably "political." With its baffling confluence of organic and inorganic phenomena, of the human and the nonhuman, of vastly disparate coordinates in the fabric of space and time, "Ginga tetsudō no yoru" lays bare a "social" world in which all is in a certain sense close at hand, though never reduced to sameness. The world commonly called "natural"—of rain and rivers, of electromagnetic energy, of molecules and meadowlarks—is revealed to be both alien to human experience and intimately a part of it.

You Are Here

In its latest version, "Ginga tetsudō no yoru" begins in a classroom:

> "All right everyone, this faint whiteness here, what some have called a river or compared to a stain left behind after milk is spilled, can anyone tell me what it really is?" The teacher questioned his class, pointing to a hazy white area that looked like a band of flowing silver running from top to bottom of the big astronomical chart hanging on the blackboard.[35]

Written and repeatedly revised over a period of about ten years (between 1923 and 1933), this later—commonly published as the most "complete"—draft of the story announces itself from its famous opening pages as frankly pedagogical.[36] "'If you were to examine it thoroughly [*yoku shiraberu*] with a large telescope,'" the teacher continues, clarifying his unanswered question, 'what, generally, *is* the Milky Way?'"[37]

Although the term "Milky Way" remains in some ways an unsatisfactory translation of the Sino-Japanese *ginga*—literally "silver river"—the image of a flowing liquid body evoked by the galaxy's name in both English and Japanese (in which it is also called *ama no gawa* or *tenga*, "River of Heaven") underscores the problem the teacher means to address in this passage: the rift between appearances and reality. "If we look at this misty white Milky Way with a big telescope," the teacher finally explains, "it will appear as many tiny stars. Right Giovanni?"[38] With this seemingly uncontroversial empirical observation, "Ginga tetsudō no yoru" begins by simultaneously upholding and undermining the legitimacy of vision. From the content of the teacher's lesson, a crucial problem quietly emerges: the question of what it means "to see" in a world that exists largely beyond the bounds of vision. If you want to understand a thing, the teacher seems to be telling his students, then you must look at it, yes. *But not with your eyes alone.*

One of the essential, if forgotten, functions of literature—though generally less forgotten in children's literature—revolves around its unequalled capacity to teach. Although dismissed by most contemporary critics, the pedagogical function of art, as Fredric Jameson has reminded us in the recent past, "seems in various forms to have been an inescapable parameter of any conceivable Marxist aesthetic, if of few others."[39] In its unabashed compulsion to teach its readers, then, Kenji's chosen genre of children's fiction overlaps unexpectedly with important elements of those works associated with Japan's Proletarian Literature movement, which dominated the field during the most productive years of Kenji's career. Many (perhaps the majority) of Kenji's readers are, in fact, adults. But this only makes the generic category more meaningful: a choice defined by form rather than readership. The genre of the children's story allowed this author to address openly, in the form of an "instruction," what was in fact the central concern of *both* politically engaged art and aesthetic modernism: the underlying structure of reality.

Kenji's decision to write children's fiction, in other words, reveals the pedagogical to be an "inescapable parameter" not only of any Marxist aesthetic, but of any conceivable *modernist* aesthetic as well. In spite of its fantastic and seemingly nonpolitical themes, Kenji's children's stories share with Proletarian Literature the didactic structure of an *unveiling*, the salvaging of a truth beyond appearances. "Reality," John Berger writes, "always *lies beyond*, and this is as true for materialists as for idealists, for Plato and for Marx."[40] It is useful to note here that when Berger further describes this reality to be "inimical to those with power," he is talking in this context not about openly political art, but about the painting of Van Gogh. So it makes a converse kind of sense when Jameson reminds us that the cumbrous-sounding pedagogical structure of political art, what he calls art's "cognitive" function after the work of Darko Suvin, can in fact become "in and of itself the immediate source of profound aesthetic delight," inseparably beautiful and subversive.[41] In Kenji's story too, the pedagogical and the aesthetic cannot be disjoined. Indeed, in this opening chapter, "Gogo no jugyō" (The afternoon lesson), all of art's traditional uses—to teach, to move, to delight[42]—seem distilled in the image of the astronomical chart itself.

The focus of the teacher's lesson, the reader's first abstract glimpse at the itinerary of a journey that will take up the bulk of the narrative, the star chart is also the source of keen emotional ambivalence for the story's young protagonist, Giovanni. His Italian-sounding name (rendered, like the names of the story's other characters, in *katakana*, the syllabary reserved for foreign words) highlights the cultural mutability of Kenji's fictional land of "Ihatov," but it also playfully evokes the great astronomers of sixteenth-century Italy. As the teacher suspects, Giovanni knows the answer to his question about the galaxy but simply lacks the confidence to respond. With an absent father—who is either working on a fishing vessel in the north or imprisoned for a crime that remains obscure—Giovanni has had to work after school to support his mother, and his studies have suffered. Now the object of weary taunts from his classmates, Giovanni has come to be almost entirely ostracized by the children of this farming village. Against feelings of shame and self-doubt, however, Giovanni remembers with pleasure reading about the galaxy in a magazine at the home of his best (and one remaining) friend and classmate, Campanella, whose father is a professor.[43] Spurred by the article that day, Giovanni remembers, Campanella had "brought out a large book from his father's library, opened it to a place marked 'Milky Way,' and the two of them had gazed endlessly at the beautiful photograph, an ink-black page filled with white specks."[44]

This memory has special significance to Giovanni not only as a moment of revelation concerning the literal structure of the galaxy, but also as the confirmation of a friendship solidified by this shared discovery. Indeed, in the world of the story, these two aspects of knowledge—what Walter Benjamin opposes as the self-explanatory narrowness of "information" and the transformative wisdom of "experience"—cannot be separated.[45] Fated to share a profound adventure, Giovanni and Campanella have been brought closer together by this technical photograph, united in a new way of seeing and in a shared awareness of a new relationship to the "seen" object. Noticing his friend sorrowfully removing himself from the discussion, Campanella also remains silent in an expression of sympathy and support. Even after the teacher calls on him directly, "Campanella, who had raised his hand so eagerly, just stood there fidgeting, unable to answer."[46] And this too suggests a kind of seeing. Giovanni's best friend—fated to drown in the river that night while saving another child from the current—is identified from this opening passage with the ability to "sense" spheres of experience beyond his own, a perceptual endowment encapsulated in the very name Campanella. Referring obliquely to the seventeenth-century Italian scholar and utopian thinker, Tommaso Campanella (1568–1639), who was imprisoned by church authorities for his prototypical "empirical" philosophy that emphasized "direct knowledge of God through the things of the external world," Campanella's name manages to suggest, anachronistically, an unmistakably modern metaphysic of "perception" that combines sensation, abstract calculation, and imagination.[47]

The opening chapter of this story is infiltrated by vision: the eye of the teacher sensing (*mitsuketa*) Giovanni's suppressed motion to raise his hand; the same eye directing itself to Campanella (*me o Kamupanerura no hō e mukete*), fathoming his silence; Campanella detecting "Giovanni's eyes filled with tears."[48] Throughout this passage, the subtle dynamics of sight underscores the theme of the teacher's lesson: what the eye sees must not be limited to what it merely registers organically. The ethics of "seeing" implied by this opening passage, then, reveals unexpected connections to a newly emergent scientific understanding of empiricism enhanced by instrumentation and calculation. The very term "observation" (*kansoku*), historically associated in both English and Japanese with the study of heavenly bodies, is compounded of the ideographs "to regard" and "to measure" (also "compute" or "estimate"). Before the rise of positivism in the nineteenth century, the concept of observation in science had always implied the use of instruments, what Francis Bacon (1561–1626) called "evoking" devices that "reduce the non-sensible to the sensible; that is, make manifest, things not directly perceptible, by means of others which are."[49] It is no surprise, then, that the venerable science of astronomy functions so naturally in this story as part of the author's modernist meditation upon vision and visibility. But here, this meditation reaches far beyond the simple technical issues of enlargement or optical enhancement.

For Giovanni, the "observed" reality he remembers contained in the astronomical photograph carries the power of a revealed truth. The beautiful black page dotted with pinpoints of light that he and Campanella had studied was, of course, a visual record of data registered by a telescope. But the image assumes such a laconic and mysterious form that it suggests the amplitude of *myth* rather than the narrow transparency of a scientific *explanation*. Magnified beyond recognition, yet, paradoxically, forming a pictorial miniature of its referent, this photo-image of the Milky Way defies the requirements of the category of "information" in Benjamin's terms precisely because it demands interpretation.[50] In this sense, the astronomy book of Giovanni's memory represents the absolute limits of the "machine ideal" of nineteenth-century science, an understanding of visual detection that had revolved around notions of "neutral and transparent" instruments of objective registration.[51] The book of photographs described here, suggestive of any number of stellar atlases in circulation in Japan at the time,[52] attempts to allow the optically magnified images of the galaxy to "speak for their own reality themselves," as the American astronomer Percival Lowell said of his 1905 photographs of the "canals" of Mars.[53] For Giovanni, though, this image of the galaxy generates more mysteries than it clarifies—as did the Mars photos for many. The photograph fails, that is, to inform its observer "neutrally and transparently."

In fact, this could be said of *any* photograph of *any* object. But the special significance of the photograph of the Milky Way in this passage consists in the unexpectedly abstract nature of its image. Inadvertently, the optical grammar of this technical image unveils the expanded horizons of an entirely new (modernist) species of "photographic realism." It is able to do this because the object it depicts is not an object in the usual sense but *the galaxy itself*, the enormity of which has been reduced to a pattern of refracted light, to inscriptions of electromagnetic energy (within a certain range of frequency) recorded onto film over unthinkable distances. The power of this photograph, in other words, lies in the impossibility of what it portrays. It is, one could say, the strangest sort of photograph imaginable: *a picture of the space that surrounds us*. As such, the photograph of Giovanni's memory—like the astronomical chart before him in the classroom—forms a vision of what could never be "seen" in any ordinary sense of the word. Not because what it represents is too small to see but precisely because *it is too large*. It is this enormity that constitutes the paradox of the image, representing both inconceivable *distance* and all-encompassing *proximity*. The galaxy is too far away to see and yet it surrounds us, environs us, permeates the structures and processes of our world. It is where we are.

To "see" the galaxy requires a radical imaginative leap, a cognitive dislocation that animates this story from its very opening sentences. And it soon becomes clear that *dislocating* oneself is essential to the process of *locating* oneself. The consequences of this new way of seeing amount to a new consciousness of place, as the teacher's lesson elegantly illustrates when he analyzes the galaxy from the perspective of the traditional Japanese moniker "River of Heaven":

> So, if you think of this "River of Heaven" as really a river, then each of these little stars is like a grain of sand or gravel at the bottom of that river. And if you think of it as a giant river of milk, this comes even closer to resembling the galaxy. What I mean is that the stars could be seen as corresponding to the delicate globules of oil floating in the milk. You might wonder, then, what would play the role of the water in that river. Well, that would be something called a "vacuum" through which light is propagated at a certain velocity; the sun and the earth are both floating in that vacuum. In other words, you and I are all living in the water of this "River of Heaven." And when we look out in all directions from this water, in the same way that water will appear bluer the deeper it is, the deeper and farther away the "river bottom" of the galaxy is, the more stars will be seen gathered there, and the whiter and hazier it will look.[54]

Both poetic and pedagogical, the teacher's analogy in this famous opening chapter asks the students to conceive of the vacuum (*shinkū*) of outer space not as an inert or empty "container" but rather as a living entity with form and substance, like the flow of a great river. This image of a galactic river—an image that will gain increasingly literal significance as the narrative progresses—suggests more than mere descriptive convenience. By equating the space of the galaxy with the flow of a river, the teacher's lesson translates the incomprehensible conditions of distant space into the terrestrial idiom of streambeds, gravel, and blue water. Indeed, we soon learn that the *actual* river running through the village (an unnamed mythical counterpart to Hanamaki's Kitakami River) will play an important ritual role in the town's "Milky Way Festival" (*ginga matsuri*) to be celebrated that night, a sort of fictional combination of Italian celebrations of St. John the Baptist (not coincidentally, San Giovanni in Italian) and summer solstice rituals in which those celebrations originated.[55] And it is the river too that will take the life of Campanella, revealing the water's baptismal function to be inseparable from its potential hostility to human life. But even before Campanella's drowning, as the children prepare to release lanterns made from snake gourds (*karasu-uri*) into its current in honor of the Milky Way, the river becomes a symbol of enormous concentric complexity, the earth's miniature galaxy mirroring the sky that surrounds and cradles it. It is not that distance has been eliminated here, or been made meaningless, but rather that distant phenomena have been recognized as locally relevant: "In other words, you and I are all living in the water of this 'River of Heaven.'" The intellectual challenge of the teacher's lesson, then, like the theme of the Milky Way Festival and the structure of the narrative itself, centers on an act of *orientation.*

The lesson culminates, in fact, in a *tour de force* in navigational reasoning when the teacher directs the children's attention to another "miniature" of the galaxy, a lens-shaped glass model filled with sand. This intriguing model demands of its beholders (and, by extension, of the story's readers) a supreme effort of imaginative duplicity: the ability to comprehend the structure of the galaxy *from the outside*, while simultaneously seeing oneself—indeed one's whole world—as defined by one's position *on the inside.*

> The teacher pointed to a big, double convex lens filled with shiny grains of sand.
>
> "The Milky Way is shaped exactly like this. Think of each of these shining grains as stars independently shining, just like our own sun. Our sun is just about in the center of this, and the earth is right near it. At night, I want everyone to look all around you while imagining yourself standing in the middle of this lens. This part of the lens is thin, so you will only see a few shining grains, or 'stars.' Over here the glass is thick, so you will see many many shining stars, and those that are far away will appear to you as a hazy light. And that's today's explanation of the Milky Way. Since we're out of time, we will talk about the approximate size of this lens and about the various stars it contains during our next science period. Well, today is the Milky Way Festival, so I want everyone to go outside tonight and take a good look at the sky. . . ."[56]

Kenji lived and wrote at a time when extraordinary discoveries were being made in astronomy, physics, and cosmology. The key problems occupying scientists all over the world in late Taishō included the shape of the galaxy and the sun's position within it. As the above passage suggests, it was believed then that the sun was near the galaxy's center. (Scientists now believe the sun to be about 30,000 light years from the center of the Milky Way.)[57] Astronomers puzzled over mysterious dark spots or "dark nebulae" (*ankoku seiun*) visible in certain parts of the sky. The competing explanations of these dark spots published during these years inspired and fascinated the author.[58] In 1924, around the time that Kenji began writing this story, Edwin Powell Hubble (1889–1958) had determined that the nearest galaxy, Andromeda, and our own were in fact moving away from each other, laying the foundation for the theory of the expanding universe and further compounding the sense of the relative insignificance of the earth and its inhabitants.[59]

But by far the most extraordinary discoveries in astronomy in the early decades of the twentieth century were linked to Einstein's theory of relativity and the four-dimensional worldview it generated. It is worth noting that the careful description of the "double convex lens" model in this passage closely mimics the language used to describe the Milky Way in the eight-volume *Kagaku taikei* (1922), the Japanese translation of A. Thompson's *Scientific Compendium*, and one of the author's known sources on astronomy.[60] In a more important sense, however, the description of this model manifests an epistemological posture shared by the logic of Einstein's theory and Kenji's own ambitious literary vision. Einstein visualized all entities and events as embedded in the geometry of time and space, beyond the grasp of any single frame of reference but not beyond the realm of calculation. This position required, as I have argued earlier, a sort of double-consciousness. On the one hand, relativity theory endeavors to appreciate an event "from within" a constantly shifting network of relationships, to define that event by its unique position in space-time. On the other hand, this theory calculates the uniqueness of an event "from the outside" or from a "higher plane," by means of a *universally valid* set of formulations. It must have been part of its creative allure that relativity subscribed to this unprecedented epistemological intimacy—understanding an event locally (from "close-up")—while maintaining an equally unprecedented standard of objective distance, subjecting that event's particularity to the uncompromising rule of universal law.

As sociologist and Kenji scholar Mita Munesuke has argued, the convex glass model in Kenji's story embodies this Einsteinian "reversibility," envisioning the objective shape of the galaxy from an imaginary position on the outside, but only as a means of comprehending the significance of a specific position on the inside.[61] The model in the classroom only acquires relevance, in other words, when the teacher elicits a cognitive reversal: "At night, I want everyone to look around you while imagining yourself standing in the middle of this lens." From this double point of view—what Cubist painter Jean Metzinger might have called a "mobile perspective"[62]—the galaxy has no "final" shape. It is *both* a hazy river-like fluorescence streaking across the night sky *and* a lens-shaped disc filled with innumerable "grains" of stellar material floating in a vacuum, emitting electromagnetic energy. When Einstein determined the geometry of time and space to "curve" following the distribution of mass and energy, the imaginative effect of this discovery paralleled the intellectual demands of Kenji's double convex lens. "There is no true simultaneity," science historian Arthur I. Miller explains in his discussion of Einstein and Picasso, "just as there is no true shape to an object. Cubism and relativity both require one to pick out from nature particular aspects of it."[63] The afternoon science lesson in "Ginga tetsudō no yoru" echoes this Cubist disposition, focusing ultimately not upon what shape the galaxy "really" is, but upon a *higher* form of precision altogether: an accuracy that awakens a consciousness of *place* rather than generating an illusion of *omniscience*.

The final object of the teacher's lesson on the Milky Way must be understood, then, as navigational. The lens-shaped glass model—suggestive of what the author himself repeatedly referred to as "four-dimensional perception" (*yojigen kankaku*)—serves as a tool for charting a position in a space so immense that it could never really be "seen," but that nevertheless defines us. In this sense, Kenji's beloved children's tale shares with Einstein's relativity theory the deep grammar of cartography. Even the simplest map asks us to transcend the space it represents, to take in the whole (which is to say, to overcome the sensory limits of our bodies) at the same time that it requires us to "picture" ourselves inside that space, enveloped by it. This existential duplicity is captured by the unassuming words attached to most floor-guides found in any American shopping mall: "You Are Here." The Japanese equivalent, *genzaichi*, adds a temporal axis, further emphasizing the surprisingly demanding metaphysics of maps: "You Are Here *Now*." Kenji's story, echoing the Cubist structure of Einstein's theory, aims at exploring the social implications of this "cartographic" form of objectivity.

Society and the Fourth Dimension

In previous chapters, I outlined the collusive (if inadvertent) role that Einstein's ideas played in shaping the deeply reactionary ideology at the heart of Yokomitsu Riichi's fiction. If relativity can be taken as a "higher" form of objectivity, a perfected species of scientific absolutism, how could the grammar of its realism serve in any but an oppressive capacity? Kaneko Tsutomu, the leading scholar of the "relativity boom" of late Taishō, identifies Hermann Minkowski as one of the first to characterize Einstein's physics as productive of "an absolute world."[64] Minkowski's efforts to formulate a four-dimensional geometry adequate to Einstein's view of space-time led him to understand relativity theory as a profoundly conservative form of scientific realism, what Kaneko himself describes as a "divine physics as seen through God's eyes" (*kami no me kara mita kami no butsurigaku*).[65] The paradox has been widely noted. "Einstein's theory of relativity is unique among the great epoch-marking ideas of the world," wrote Herbert Dingle, "in that it caused a revolution by keeping to tradition; its heterodoxy lay in the strictness of its orthodoxy."[66]

The "revolution" to which Dingle refers, of course, is a purely scientific one. There is no inherent politics to Einstein's theory of relativity (nor to any other discovery in the natural sciences), and it serves no useful purpose merely to "equate" in John Guillory's words, "the political and the epistemological."[67] The trick is, rather, to identify and display potential affinities between logical structures and specific ideologies not in the language of causality, but in the language of complement and resonance. Miyazawa Kenji meditated deeply—much more deeply than Yokomitsu, it would seem—upon the details of physics and chemistry; it is the subtle inflections of those details, therefore, that can throw light on the extraordinary social insights of his fiction.

Scholars in science studies who have characterized Einstein's theory as merely another "absolutism" (a term that implicitly opposes it to "relativism," which relativity never claimed to be) have produced predictably narrow assessments of the potential social significance of relativity. Bruno Latour's analysis of Einstein's theory in the journal *Social Studies of Science* devotes most of its critical energy to uncovering the specter of "privilege" operating behind this theory's original challenge: its effort to maintain the universal status of nature's laws in the face of experiments that showed inconsistencies in the Newtonian framework of absolute time and space (the famous Michelson-Morley experiment).[68] Latour insightfully describes the terms of this founding dilemma: "either we maintain absolute space and time and the laws of nature become different in different places; or we maintain the equivalence of the laws of nature, and we 'discard' absolute space and time." Relativity, of course, chose the latter—betraying, in Latour's view, a deceptively conservative disposition. What scandalizes Latour here is Einstein's clear insistence that the laws of nature remain universal. "The question," Latour writes, "is not how to revolutionize our thinking, but how to maintain, to conserve, to stabilize, to rigidify, one thing that appears more important than anything else." For Latour, this conservative epistemology implies an equally conservative politics. The noted physicist's "rejection of some privileges in order to shore up some others," he writes, "throws a rather new light on the usual argument that Einstein is a revolutionary."[69]

Latour's essay announces itself from the beginning as an effort to treat relativity theory—the epitome of "the more formal sciences"—from the point of view that "the content of any science is social through and through."[70] This alone is an extraordinary and path-breaking ambition. But in order to prove Einstein's work as "*explicitly* social," Latour must first reformulate "the concept of society" itself.[71] In Latour's analysis, this apparently means recognizing signification as one of the fundamental constituent elements of society. Even a mathematical formula, the author seems to suggest, is shot through with the social. Accordingly, Latour subjects the theory of relativity (or, more accurately, the English translation of Einstein's semi-popular work, *Relativity: The Special and the General Theory*) to a semiotic analysis, identifying as its key feature the phenomenon of "shifting in" and "shifting out" (the moving between different narrative frames of reference within a text).[72] In the process, he keenly recognizes a sort of modernistic reflexivity as the "peculiarity of Einstein's narrative," its tendency to "focus the reader's attention upon these very operations."[73]

Conceding that relativity did away with the notion of a privileged frame of reference, Latour must reformulate the concept of "privilege" as well, proposing in the end a perversely incontestable definition that equates *social* and *institutional* privilege with the *denial of epistemological* privilege. Latour's understanding of the logic of inequity built into relativity theory necessarily acquires a hybrid quality, both abstractly "semiotic" and curiously personal in nature. Ultimately for Latour, "privilege" in the theory of relativity is equated with the position of "the enunciator" who occupies a "centre of calculation" where information from all other frames of reference is gathered and superimposed. "It is not his [*sic*] privileged point of view that gives a centre any superiority over other locations, but its rejection of any privilege to any local point of view including its own, thus permitting the gathering in one point of all the superimposable traces."[74] The editorial inconsistency of pronoun usage here (of "his" and "its") inadvertently highlights the creative ambiguity of Latour's depiction of "social" advantage in physics, as rooted simultaneously in the flesh and blood of "actors" or "observers" and in the impersonal structures of sign-systems. In the end, though, Latour favors a decisively semiotic reading, and relativity's signature "rejection of privilege" is understood to be merely a clever disguise for a furtively centralizing system of thought. Latour's critical analysis ultimately targets relativity theory's "universalism" and "objectivity"—the usual suspects in the search for the discursive engines of privilege. Social and institutional advantage, in other words, becomes the secondary material effect of an epistemology that places the enunciator (the physicist; in this case, Einstein himself) in a position to "accumulate" the other frames of reference "in the last frame."[75] The physicist's office or laboratory becomes the place where the "'big picture'" is kept: "not given in one frame of reference, but in going from one frame to all others through a network."[76]

It is important to acknowledge, however, that if there is a "big picture" in Einstein's worldview, it represents a very strange sort of universalism, since the number of frames of reference is infinite, and since the only kind of "picture" that can ever be represented is a relative one. Indeed, what made Einstein's theory useful and new was precisely this peculiar form of "absolutism" that belonged to no single frame of reference—not even Latour's "last frame"—but to a universally valid natural law that exists beyond any "centre" of human experience. If there was anything "revolutionary" about relativity, it was the radical thoroughness with which it removed human beings to the role of incidental and imperfect spectators in a vast and self-sufficient reality. Yet it is this very notion of an outside world independent of human society that Latour's argument implicitly denies by refusing to take the referential object of Einstein's theory literally.

In fact, Latour's groundbreaking work in science studies has consistently emphasized "social" reality over objective or "external" reality, a position that has served as a thoughtful and useful corrective to postmodernism's curiously celebratory abandonment of reality altogether.[77] But in denying reality its "outside-ness," Latour's form of realism—what he calls "radical realism"—has abandoned any possible understanding of "society" that extends *beyond* the human community.[78] Paradoxically, then, Latour's effort to identify centers of privilege embedded in Einstein's universalism—his reading of Einstein's formulations as "social through and through"—itself amounts to a plea for privileging human society as the source and center of all that matters.

Why, apart from the challenge of engaging a purely formal theory, did Latour choose to apply his "radical realism" to relativity? Einstein's four-dimensional worldview is built upon an objectivity by which, in Kaneko Tsutomu's words, "humanity is removed from the center" to become itself an object of "differential calculus."[79] It was this Neo-Copernican impulse to overcome the perceptual limits of subjective experience that gave the language of the fourth dimension its life in early twentieth-century science as well as in the arts. For the "revolutionary" dimension of modernism too lies in a certain kind of scientific hyper-orthodoxy, an unprecedented commitment to realism. If classical art "took man as the centre of the universe," Guillaume Apollinaire wrote in a 1913 study of Cubism, "the art of the new painters takes the infinite universe as its ideal."[80] From this perspective, Latour's critique of Einsteinian realism carries its own atavistic logic, marked by a latently positivist compulsion to maintain human consciousness as the defining boundary of the "real." In important ways, then, Latour's radical realism evinces what Roy Bhaskar has called empiricism's "concealed *anthropocentricity*."[81]

At the time of its appearance in the early twentieth century, relativity theory meant much more to modern culture than merely another dialect of elitism. In contrast with Latour's radical realism, which comes closer to Yokomitsu's response to Einstein, Miyazawa Kenji understood the content of new theories in physics and chemistry as *literally* and not metaphorically social. His genius expressed itself most powerfully here, through a seemingly naïve proclivity to take discoveries about the material world at face value. For Kenji, what was "social through and through" was not science itself, but its referent: the historical world of matter and energy, of time and space, of rivers and wind and stars. The "outside-ness" of reality becomes, for Kenji, one of its most important features: the "place" or "dimension" shared by humans and a larger community of objects, beings, and phenomena. "In other words, you and I are living in the water of this 'River of Heaven.'" This author recognized the tiniest event of an obscure country village as both *containing* and *contained by* this vast web of materiality: "Today is the Milky Way Festival, so I want everyone to go outside tonight and take a good look at the sky." A radically material (literally anti-humanist) and de-centering inflection defines Kenji's body of work at every level, revealing itself most openly in his poetic relationship with the new physics.

When understood in this way—as a plea for a more thorough understanding of materialism—Kenji's absorption of Einstein's relativity theory carries political implications far different from what Latour's notion of semiotic elitism might suggest. In fact, the poet's Einsteinian revolt from sensory literalism echoes the materialist vision recognizable in Marx's own theory of dialectics. In many ways a distillation of the most iconoclastic elements of nineteenth-century science, Marx's own epoch-making concept of materialism must be understood, according to John Bellamy Foster, as "both an *ontological* and an *epistemological* category," requiring a stance that is "both realist and relational (that is, dialectical)."[82] In Marx's view, Foster argues later, it was "essential to posit the existence of an objective world and human beings as objective beings, that is, genuine realism and naturalism."[83] Einstein's relativity theory seems to have provided Kenji with a similarly far-reaching vision of relational realism: the conceptual language to describe a material universe that both *exceeds* and *defines* human history.

The materialist dimension of Kenji's scientific language has been overshadowed, however, by what has often been taken as an uncomplicated, metaphysically reactionary religiosity. However fundamental it is, this misreading is understandable. The months when Albert Einstein visited Japan coincided with a relatively blank period for Kenji in terms of creative output. While Einstein delivered his famous lectures in Tokyo, Sendai, Nagoya, Osaka, Kyoto, and Fukuoka, Kenji was nursing, then mourning his sister Toshi, whose death was to become one of the defining events of his life.[84] It was also during this period that Kenji converted to Nichiren Buddhism, a sect whose focus on the redemptive power of the *Lotus Sūtra* would continue to shape the author's ideas and beliefs to the end of his life. This convergence of the personal and the historical—of human loss, of religious conversion, and of scientific discovery—seemed to transform the basis of Kenji's work in the years 1922 and 1923. According to Ono Ryūshō, Kenji had been studying relativity theory for some time before Einstein's famous visit.[85] But it is only after the rise of the "relativity boom" in 1922—that is, the year of his sister's death—that Kenji's poetry came to revolve so explicitly around the concept of the "fourth dimension" and "four-dimensional art."[86] From the final lines of his much-quoted poetic "Introduction" to *Haru to shura*, in which all of the work's "propositions" are described (somewhat cryptically) as "the essence of mind and time/presented from within the fourth dimension,"[87] to the "Nōmin geijutsu" essay with its repeated references to "four-dimensional art," Kenji seems to associate this idea directly with a vision of timelessness. "The great theater of human life itself," he wrote, "traveling along the axis of time, constitutes an immortal work of four-dimensional art."[88]

Critics seem commonly to have interpreted Einsteinian depictions of "different space" in Kenji's poetry and stories as transparent gestures toward a realm of refuge and appeal that had been lost with the downfall of traditional world religious cosmologies.[89] Saitō Bun'ichi even identifies the revolution in physics of the early twentieth century as an important metaphysical boost to the modern career of the *Lotus Sūtra* itself, and especially the significance of the crucial sixteenth chapter of its latter half, "Nyorai-juryō-bon" ("Revelation of the [Eternal] Life of the Tathagata").[90] In this chapter, the Buddha's enlightenment is depicted, by an apparent contradiction, as both historical and eternal—a classic instance of theological timelessness.[91] It is not surprising, therefore, when Ōtsuka Tsuneki finally describes Kenji's "four-dimensional perception" not as a cognate for any scientific disposition, but as an equivalent to the Buddhist concept of *tengen* (or "heavenly eye"), suggesting a supernatural sort of optical omniscience: the power of enlightened beings to penetrate beyond the visible dimensions of the human world.[92]

It is essential to recognize, however, that even after 1926, as Kenji turned away from the psychology of grief and increasingly to problems of social and political engagement—establishing the Rasu Chijin Kyōkai, helping to finance the opening of the Hanamaki office of the Farm Labor Party, and showing intensified interest in the Proletarian Literature movement[93]—his fiction and essays continued to concern themselves with the language of the fourth dimension, with galactic imagery, and with themes of *limitlessness*. Critics like Yoshida Tsukasa who have reduced Kenji's religiosity to an expression of "Lotus Fascism" (based mostly on the author's ambivalent association with the openly nationalistic Kokuchūkai, an organization affiliated with the Nichren sect) have had to ignore the content of Kenji's creative work and much of his political activity to maintain their position.[94] Revising "Ginga tetsudō no yoru" throughout these years, Kenji seems to have operated under the deepening conviction that the most essential historical problems facing humanity carried social and ecological (not national or ethnic) implications. Though sometimes unmistakably "religious" in tone, images of the eternal in Kenji's mature work find their most obvious animating power not in supernatural or occult traditions, but in the unadorned material fact of the universe. If there is a mystical energy to Kenji's fiction, it comes from the author's fascination with the problem of triangulation and the related process of magnification: the scientist's compulsion to "bring up close" things from far away. By measuring (cartographically, so to speak) spatially or socially distant phenomena against a local point of view, this abstract (and profoundly Einsteinian) process of "enlargement" has the effect of embedding all local experience in a vast web of cosmic relationships.

Kenji's telescopic consciousness of space defines the next few short chapters of "Ginga tetsudō no yoru," leading to Giovanni's dreamlike departure on a journey to the far ends of the galaxy. After the astronomy lesson, the story follows Giovanni to his after-school job as a typesetter in a print shop, where the din of the rotary presses, the artificial light, and the closed-in atmosphere contrast sharply with the sunlit world of the other children preparing for the festival outdoors. Critic Komori Yōichi has read this scene as a naked evaluation of capitalism itself, a surgical exploration of the link between labor and commodification. For Komori, Giovanni's painstaking efforts at tweezing and arranging individual bits of script (the size of "millet grains") represents the fragmenting and objectifying process of manufacture. It is the function of the print shop, Komori tells us, to remove the vitality from living language only in order to reanimate its "corpse" as a commodity: as "language that must be purchased with money."[95]

But what can it mean that this critique of capitalism appears here, against the background of an interstellar festival, and just before the protagonist begins his own journey through the galactic immensity of the fourth dimension? Clearly, there is an intended irony to the image of Giovanni working after school in the production of printed material he himself could not afford. Yet a discernable undertow persistently contradicts these more critical dimensions, for it was this very sort of commodity—the astronomy books and magazines of Campanella's father's library—that had inspired Giovanni so profoundly in the previous scene. In a sense, Kenji's grim portrayal of the print shop in this scene can be understood as a glimpse into the social ambiguities of mechanical reproduction and modern science itself. The apparatus of the print shop stands, in important ways, as a cultural echo of the sort of scientific "magnification" embodied in the telescopic photo-image of the galaxy. Just as the astronomical photograph abstracted, disjoined, and reassembled light waves from outer space in order to produce the enlarged image of the Milky Way for the general observer, the print shop breaks apart and reassembles written language to form the sort of mechanically reproducible commodity capable of satisfying what Walter Benjamin calls "*the desire of the present-day masses to 'get closer' to things.*"[96] As with Benjamin's essay, which infuses these words with every available fiber of ambiguity, Kenji's story shows the apparatus that enables us to "get closer" to the larger world as pregnant with *both* visionary (if not auratic) possibilities as well as exploitative dangers.[97] The print shop is Komori's dark and cold "graveyard of words"[98] at the same time that it is the locus of a more hopeful "enlargement" of culture.

Importantly, it is also a site of exchange. Giovanni receives for his labor one "silver coin" with which he then purchases sugar and bread for himself and his mother before returning home. This brief but memorable scene of work and remuneration, where the value of Giovanni's labor equals the mere cost of replacing his metabolic fuel, foreshadows later descriptions of a much broader material and organic economy. It is when the protagonist ventures out again that evening to retrieve a bottle of undelivered milk for his sick mother—inaugurating what will become a recurring thematic connection between ethical imperatives and biological necessity—that his extraordinary encounter with this more literally *material* universe begins.

The chapter entitled "Kentauru matsuri no yoru" (Night of the Centaurus festival) stands as one of Kenji's most masterful variations on the themes of triangulation and magnification. Referring to what is called elsewhere in the story the "Milky Way Festival" (*ginga matsuri*), or simply the "star festival" (*hoshi matsuri*), the impending ritual of the constellation Centaurus saturates this twilight scene as Giovanni makes his way through the streets of town, now painfully aware of his exclusion from the village festivities. We see Giovanni dawdling in the empty streets, playing in the shadows of a streetlamp, fending off unexpected taunts from a particularly cruel child, and finally, with the exquisite aimlessness of childhood, stumbling upon the window of the town's clock shop:

> With his mind racing busily from one thing to another, Giovanni passed through town, which was beautifully decorated with tree branches and all kinds of lights. Inside the clock shop with its bright neon sign, the red stone eyes of an owl moved back and forth with each passing second, and an array of gems covered the top of a thick glass tray the color of the sea. This tray with all its gems was revolving like the stars, and a copper Centaur slowly approached from the other side. In the center of the platter, there was a round black constellation chart decorated with green asparagus leaves.
>
> Forgetting himself, Giovanni gazed deeply into the map of the constellations. Though it was much smaller than the star chart he had seen that afternoon in school, the heavens appeared in the elliptical center of the tray as it revolved, just as they would look according to the time and date. Sure enough, right in the middle, stretching from top to bottom, the Milky Way formed a misty band in the sky. Near its lower end, there appeared something like a faint explosion of steam. Behind the revolving platter, a small telescope on a tripod stood gleaming yellow, and behind everything else, hanging on the wall, was a giant stellar map with all the constellations of the heavens depicted in the strange shapes of animals, snakes, of fish and pitchers. Giovanni wondered if the sky was really filled like this with heroes and scorpions. Thinking how much he would like to walk deep into the sky to find out, he lingered remotely for some time.[99]

There is a surreal compressiveness to this window display that suggests at once the enormity and the baffling intimacy of the author's vision of nature. The terrestrial proximity of "green asparagus leaves" meets the remote chemistry of the heavens represented in the revolving astronomical chart they "decorate"; the figure of an owl and the gems of the earth dissolve into the circular image of the immense surrounding sky, which reflects, in turn, the "color of the sea"; the mythical figures of the human imagination collide suggestively with the more sober diagrams and instruments of empirical observation and spatial calculation—the Centaur shares the stage with the telescope. Kenji's depiction of the clock shop window becomes itself a radiant vision of magnification, an enlargement of a cosmos that is also a miniature, a microcosm. Although one of Kenji's favored reference books on astronomy, Yoshida Genjirō's *Nikugan ni mieru hoshi no kenkyū* (Studies of the stars visible to the naked eye, 1922), emphasized in its title the knowledge available to unenhanced eyesight, here the preeminent symbol of magnification, the telescope, stands as a gleaming reminder of the inadequacy of unaided perception to knowing the earth's own galaxy.[100]

The clocks and maps that crowd this scene in a riot of Einsteinian symbolism imply a diagrammatic realism that refers with hopeful precision to the galaxy from within local time and space. At the same time, though, the abstract geometrical language of these navigational tools becomes itself an aesthetic object. It is as if these glimmering instruments and stellar atlases had been invented in the artistic spirit of high modernism; the *objects of reference* (the stars themselves) and the conceptual *language* used to represent them hold the viewer's attention equally. If the black "constellation chart" (*seiza hayami*) in the middle of this window display is meant to resemble the star chart the author himself used, the metric intricacy of its round revolving frame and oval-shaped center—designed to map the skies from a specific latitude on Earth according to time and date—could easily become an object of wonder in itself.[101] If the reader imagines the stellar map hanging in the background as resembling the one Kenji had hanging in his own classroom in Hanamaki—the *Shinsen kōseizu* (New map of the fixed stars, 1910)—it may be seen as a dizzying, almost baroque complexity of spheres and ellipses, of intersecting lines loaded with obscure meanings.[102] For Giovanni too, the window display is, above all else, supremely beautiful. "Forgetting himself," (*ware o wasurete*) Giovanni "gazed deeply" into the details of the stellar map in the sort of trance that pertains to aesthetic delight. At the same time that he is moved by the chart, however, Giovanni is also *informed* by it, reminded of the structure of the galaxy and of his position within it. Indeed, the word "gaze" (*miiru*), a combination of the characters "to look" and "to enter," suggests the specific demand of the cartographic form. Like any map, the map of the stars before Giovanni invites him to "enter" its space. And this navigational realism is clearly part of the map's *aesthetic* power.

Echoing the concentric consciousness expressed in the "Nōmin geijutsu" essay—"This place is here, a field in the land of Rikuchū, in Japan, in the solar system, in the Milky Way Galaxy. . . ."—the electrified shop window also becomes a microcosm of the village itself on festival night, where, in the following passage, we see the tops of "poplar trees on the edge of town floating high into the starry sky," and hear the song of the children calling for Centaurus to "let fall the dew"; where the "atmosphere" (*kūki*) of the town (suggesting the "vacuum" of space described earlier by Giovanni's teacher) "flowed utterly clear like water through the streets and into the shops," and where "the street lights were wrapped in the green branches of fir and oak" in honor of the stars.[103]

The inclusiveness of these descriptions hints at the outlines of an ethic underlying Kenji's "four-dimensional perception," an ideological position that has pushed the implications of theoretical physics to astonishing new limits. It is not only time and space that have been unified into a single dimension, but things near and far away, the organic and the inorganic, the human and the nonhuman: "The naturalism of man and the humanism of nature," in Marx's words, "both brought to fulfillment." The defining framework of local human society, this story seems to tell us, is the vast and largely undetectable material universe itself. And "charting a position" in that universe amounts to calculating a relationship to the limitless.

By taking the literal content of modern physics as its "social message," Kenji managed to draw out and to enhance the most revolutionary inflection of relativity theory. One of the most important books that Kenji read during these critical years of his writing career (the mid-1920s) was the English version (no Japanese translation existed) of Charles Steinmetz's *Four Lectures on Relativity and Space* (1923). This thin volume, authored by an unassuming socialist exile and electrical engineer living in Schenectady, New York, came into Kenji's unlikely possession probably during a short excursion to Tokyo in 1926, around the time he was adding the crucial "Gogo no jugyō" chapter to his "Ginga tetsudō" manuscript.[104] An unrecognized classic in science writing, Steinmetz's lucid, yet surprisingly demanding "non-specialist" collection of lectures was hardly known in Japan, where an abundance of less rigorous Japanese-language articles and books on the subject of relativity were in circulation.[105] Emphasizing the geometrical dimension of Einstein's theory, Steinmetz's analysis featured lengthy discussions of non-Euclidean space, and the book even included stereoscopic projections. What is most striking about Steinmetz's book, however, is the cartographic logic used to explain Einstein's extraordinary discovery that space "curves" around heavy masses.

Steinmetz begins by listing the most commonplace and intuitive geometric ideas that relativity undermined through its idea that space is neither empty nor homogeneous. If space is viewed not as a flat plane (as in Euclidean geometry) but as the surface of a sphere (as in Einsteinian space), then it follows, the author explains, that "any two lines in a plane intersect each other, that there exist no parallel lines, and that there exists no infinitely distant point on a straight line, but that all the points of a straight line are at finite distance and the total length of a straight line therefore is finite."[106] From this astonishing set of non-Euclidean formulations, Steinmetz works up to a crescendo of cosmic insights, throwing light on Kenji's four-dimensional realism as subtly but utterly distinct from the religious mysticism with which it is often confused. Focusing on the consequences of Eintsein's curved space, Steinmetz's vision of the universe, it soon becomes clear, does not concern itself with the mystery of the infinite, but rather with the mystery of finitude itself—a finitude that has no limits. "By mathematical deduction from relativity theory," he wrote, "we thus derive the conclusion that our three-dimensional universe is not infinite, but finite, though inconceivably large. Although finite, it is limitless, just as the surface of a sphere is a two-dimensional space which is finite but limitless."[107]

It is easy to imagine Miyazawa Kenji, thousands of miles from Schenectady, pondering these paradoxical sentences in his room in Hanamaki. In a significant footnote, Steinmetz clarifies this difficult image of limitless finitude by invoking obliquely the metaphor of map making:

When the relativity theory leads to the conclusion that the extent of our universe is not infinite, but that the volume of the universe is finite, most people will ask, "What is beyond the finite extent of the universe?" and find it most difficult to conceive that there is no "beyond," but that the universe, though finite, has no limits, or, in other words, that a finite volume can be all the universe. Just as for ages it was difficult for man to conceive that the earth on which we live should not be infinite, but finite in area and still have no limit or "edge," and kept asking for an "edge" of the world. We got over this by familiarity and have no difficulty to conceive a surface like that of the earth, which is finite in area but without boundary. Analogous thereto is the universe of the relativity theory—finite in volume, but without limit or boundary.[108]

There is no "beyond" the universe, nothing outside of it. However, Steinmetz goes on to say, we can only understand its "shape" and our relationship to it by stepping outside of it in our minds. Similar (though, of course, not identical) to the cognitive (and realist) leap Giovanni's teacher asked his students to take while studying the convex lens, Steinmetz introduces the notion of an imagined "higher space," the cognitive plane of the cartographer. When standing on the earth's surface, for example, a line may indeed appear straight, but "looking at the 'straight line' of the spherical surface from the outside, from higher space, we see it curved. . . ."[109]

To invoke the image of mapmaking, then, is to invoke a referential—though far from "mimetic"—form of diagrammatic representation that shares more with Cubism's "mobile perspective" than with the Renaissance perspectivism with which it is often associated. But linking Kenji's ethics to a notion of "mapping" the universe involves an ideological danger that cannot be ignored. Whatever its semiotic structure, the practice of cartography has been associated in contemporary criticism with geopolitical crimes of the highest order. Donna Haraway, in a critical analysis of the concept of "genetic mapping," has described a cartographic "fetishism" that has historically misrepresented maps as spaces of "clarity and uncontaminated referentiality" when they are actually "models of worlds crafted through and for specific practices of intervening and ways of life."[110] Considering the link between global conquest and the rise of mapmaking in early modern Europe, this position is a sturdy and well-grounded one. But Haraway's invocation of the sixteenth-century Flemish cartographer Gerardus Mercator, after whom a biotechnology firm has been named, inadvertently highlights a paradox more pertinent to Kenji's children's story.

Maps produced by Mercator, who developed a famous technique of "projecting" the spherical surface of the globe onto a flat page, may indeed have been "geared to navigation on the high seas in a period of intense world exploration by Europeans,"[111] but there is nothing ideologically inevitable about the semiotics of Mercator's projections. Indeed, one of the insights generated by his mathematical achievement (ignored, no doubt, by the forces of empire-building) was a new understanding of the earth's surface as an unbounded series of relationships. Foreshadowing Einstein's own four-dimensional vision of the universe, Mercator's maps had to grapple conceptually with a single unavoidable fact: that the surface of a sphere (the world itself) has no center and no edges.

Space Is Not Empty

Giovanni's journey through the fourth dimension, which occupies four out of this story's nine chapters, can be viewed, then, as a sort of Cubist revelation, the fulfillment of an extraordinary ethical vision whose demands are inseparable from the material structure of time and space itself. Forgetting for the moment about his errand at the dairy, Giovanni leaves the festive atmosphere of town and makes his way to the top of a grassy hill behind the cow pasture where he throws himself down to rest at the base of something called a "weather wheel pole" (*tenkirin no hashira*). Referring indirectly to a local practice in Tōhoku of erecting stone pillars for the purpose of prayer near temples, graves, or at the edge of villages,[112] this "weather wheel pole" also evokes the columnar "support," or *yorishiro*, found in any Shinto shrine. In Japanese shrine architecture, the *yorishiro*—often a stone, a group of stones, a tree, or a pillar—serves as what historian Allan Grapard calls the shrine's "landing site," a "point of contact for the divinity with the earth." The *yorishiro* also unmistakably marks an *axis mundi*, or "cosmic center," common to many of the world's oldest religious traditions.[113] From his position at the weather wheel, Giovanni confronts another microcosmic vision:

> The lights of the town shone through the darkness looking just like a palace at the bottom of the sea. He could hear faintly the singing and whistling and intermittent shouting of the children. The wind cried in the distance; the grass on the hill trembled; and Giovanni's sweat-soaked shirt turned cold. From his position at the edge of town, Giovanni surveyed the darkly expansive plains in the distance.
>
> Out of the darkness the sound of a train arose. He could see the tiny red line of windows on the little train. When Giovanni thought about the many travelers behind those windows peeling apples, laughing, and doing all sorts of things, he felt an indescribable sadness and raised his eyes once more toward the skies.

Ah! And they say that white band in the sky is all stars!

But no matter how long he looked at it, he could not think of that sky as empty and cold the way his teacher had described it that afternoon.[114]

As he slips into a dream, the "weather wheel pole" above him transforms into a kind of triangular signal post, and Giovanni suddenly realizes that he is aboard the train itself, surrounded by a sea of light as brilliant as "the fossilized flame of ten million firefly squid."[115] He is now traveling on the Milky Way Railroad, navigating the heavens.

It is in the details of this well-known scene that Kenji's strange understanding of distance and proximity emerges most forcefully as the driving insight of the story. At first, a palpable sense of space in the classic sense—Giovanni's "objective distance" from the lights of the village, from the singing and whistling of the children, from the travelers on the "little train"—provokes in the protagonist an "indescribable sadness." But soon this very sense of distance, this sense of viewing reality from what Steinmetz called "higher space," proves to be nothing more than a cognitive posture. The train that Giovanni observes from far away one moment becomes the train that *contains* him in the next. The sea of blackness and light "in the distance" (the town below) has now been swallowed by the larger galaxy of stars and nebulae above. In many ways, the remaining episodes of the story serve to demonstrate the truth of Giovanni's premonition revealed to him at this transitional moment, from his imagined position "outside" the world: that the space of the galaxy is not "empty and cold."

Space is not empty. The significance of this startling proposition permeates the details of one of the most popular journey narratives in children's literature. But what could space be if not the emptiness that separates us from each other and from the objects of the world? Even Giovanni's teacher, in describing the Milky Way as a river, hints at the importance of this idea. For him, the "River of Heaven" is not exactly empty but *filled* (so to speak) with "something called a 'vacuum.'"[116] The vacuum, commonly understood as nothingness itself, paradoxically becomes the essential "entity" of the galaxy, comparable to the flow of a river: a kind of fugitive movement or, in the teacher's explanation, a *propagation*. It is where "light is propagated at a certain velocity," where the sun and the earth are "floating." Fascinated with the early twentieth-century downfall of the notion of the ether—the last conceptual stronghold in the struggle to retain a Newtonian image of space[117]—the author found endless inspiration contemplating the new significance of the word "vacuum" (*shinkū*). Recognizing its connotations of "emptiness" (*kyomu*) in the Buddhist sense and simultaneous associations with the latest theories in physics, Kenji found many creative uses for this term, even naming a poem from his *Haru to shura* collection "Shinkū yōbai" (Vacuum solvent).

Understood as the medium, the locus, and the essential condition of the most mysterious forces in the universe, the vacuum is often treated in Kenji's writings as the final element to which all else can be reduced. "A wonderful taxonomy," he wrote in his poem "Gorin tōge" (Gorin Pass, 1924), "All matter reduced to electrons / Electrons to another form of vacuum."[118] Although openly suggestive of a common Buddhist emphasis on the "emptiness" of the material and phenomenal world,[119] it is the scientific inflection of this image that underlies its farthest-reaching significance in Kenji's poetry. This strange materialism prevails in "Ginga tetsudō no yoru" as well, where Giovanni's encounters with the vacuum of outer space may be counted among the most astonishing literary images of Japan's modernist canon.

Giovanni soon finds that he is not alone in this interstellar train car, but that his friend Campanella is there too, looking pale and vaguely distressed. The duration of this journey—the attenuated moment, we eventually learn, of Campanella's death by drowning—becomes for Giovanni a dreamlike exploration of the inorganic (though seemingly alive) structures of the galaxy. From the window, he sees the "shore of the Milky Way shining a pale white light," and "the sky's silver pampas grass . . . undulating in the wind."[120] A characteristic conjunction of galactic phenomena with the homey comforts of earth, this is the first of many depictions of spectral luminescence and wave-like movement. When Giovanni leans out the window to examine what his teacher had described as the "water" of the river of heaven, he confronts an object whose existence can never quite be confirmed by direct perception. "However, when he looked more carefully, he saw that its beautiful water was more transparent than glass or hydrogen, and sometimes, as his eyes seemed to adjust, he saw that it was flowing silently with delicate shining purple waves glittering like a rainbow."[121]

The river of the galaxy—the vacuum of space, the water "in which the earth and sun are floating"—evinces the empirical paradoxes surrounding the earliest studies of energy in physics. When Giovanni and Campanella have an opportunity in the next chapter to run to its beach and, in a poignantly human gesture, "place their hands in its water," the boys find that the "invisible" water of the Milky Way reveals itself only through evidence of its movement. "They could tell for certain that it was flowing by the faint mercury color that floated up as their wrists sank into its water and by the beautiful phosphorescence they could see glimmering as the waves struck their wrists."[122]

In important ways, "Ginga tetsudō no yoru" translates into the language of children's fiction one of the most scientifically and aesthetically revolutionary concepts of the modernist moment: what Cubist painter George Braque described as the "materialisation" of space.[123] Braque's self-proclaimed attempt to transform the space around and behind objects into "tactile space" could easily be taken as the intuitive response of visual art to the post-positivistic scientific engagement with the invisible universe.[124] As with the improbable images of Kenji's work, the counter-perceptual results of Cubism do not imply some perverse species of subjectivism, but rather a *celebration of scientific fact.* Braque, Picasso, and other pioneers of Cubism may be understood, in this (limited) sense, as *painters of knowledge* in the Renaissance tradition, focused with an unprecedented intensity on the "corporeal significance of objects."[125] But what made Cubism revolutionary was its capacity to extend those early modern "tactile values" to include the newly discovered corporeal significance of subatomic reality, of space itself.

"The metaphorical model of Cubism," writes John Berger in his classic essay on the subject, "is the *diagram*: the diagram being a visible, symbolic representation of invisible processes, forces, structures."[126] This diagrammatic disposition, like Kenji's own cartographic approach, implies a new emphasis on relationality and continuity over the traditional notion of discrete objects and empty distances. For the Cubist, it is not the objects themselves but their interaction that matters. "Space is part of the continuity of the events within it," Berger explains. "It is in itself an event, comparable with other events. It is not a mere container. And this is what the few Cubist masterpieces show us."[127] Instinctively responding to a new scientific relationship with the object world, the Cubist painters of Europe discovered independently one of the most significant consequences of Einstein's general relativity. "Space," writes physicist Lee Smolin, explaining Einstein's theory, "is nothing apart from the things that exist; it is only an aspect of the relationships that hold between things." As with the notion of "society" itself—a concept that collapses without individuals to be "members" of it—there can be no space without events, without entities or organisms, without energy or movement. By way of explanation, Smolin asks his readers to consider the idea of a "sentence." Just as there can be no space without objects for it to "contain," he tells us, there is no such thing as an empty sentence. "It is absurd to talk of a sentence with no words in it."[128] From this perspective, space comes to be viewed not as the distance that separates us from the things and beings of the world, but rather as the "syntax" that binds us to them.

If physicists first confronted the paradoxes of space through experiments in light propagation, which problematically proved to be constant in velocity, the properties of light as an aesthetic image played a similar role in the work of Miyazawa Kenji. In "Ginga tetsudō no yoru," the Cubist transformation of space recognizable in its various scenes of magnification—starting with the photograph of the galaxy in the opening chapter—expresses itself most often in the language of light:

> Suddenly, the inside of the train bloomed with a brilliant white light. When he looked, he saw that the water was flowing soundlessly and shapelessly over the glittering riverbed of the Milky Way as if every kind of magnificence—of diamonds or dew on the grass—had been gathered together there. In the middle of the current an island appeared, radiating a hazy blue-white halo of light.[129]

The image, the word, and the very concept of "light" (*hikari*) had undergone major transformations in the early years of the twentieth century. Kenji's early literary influences, poets such as Kitahara Hakushū (1885–1942) and Hagiwara Sakutarō (1886–1942), represent what critic Ōtsuka Tsuneki has identified as the "age of celebrating light" (*kōmyō sangō no jidai*).[130] Hakushū's influential work "Jashūmon" (Heretical faith, 1909), for example, seems to revolve closely around the optical insights of post-impressionism, as encountered in the pages of the Taishō literary journal *Shirakaba*.[131] But much more important than this "trend" (*ryūkō*) in poetic imagery, Ōtsuka suggests, was the discovery that light itself was a form of electromagnetic energy that travels in waves—"soundlessly and shapelessly," as Kenji might say—through vacuums and matter alike.[132] As an ambiguously "visible" manifestation of electromagnetic energy, light in its many forms became for Kenji "the expression of the principal power of the cosmos," to quote the literary scholar Onda Itsuo.[133] Indeed, Kenji was studying chemistry and writing his first poems at a moment in history when the natural sciences had just begun to discover the enormity of their own energy revolution. "With the discovery of electrons," proclaimed the aforementioned Japanese translation of Thompson's *Scientific Compendium*, "many aspects of the ideas we have held up to now have had to change completely. . . . Not only has it been made clear that all matter of any kind is constructed out of this single shared fundamental material . . . but that all matter is merely a manifestation of electrical energy."[134]

For Kenji's generation, moreover, it is likely that electrical energy in its *literal* form, transmitted through wires and cables, was far more persuasive than its theoretical counterpart, which asked to be received and accepted from the pages of books with chapter headings like "Ion no dendōdo oyobi sokudo" (The conductivity and velocity of ions) and "Makkusueru no sokudo bunpairitsu" (Maxwell's law of velocity distribution).[135] By the mid-1920s in Iwate Prefecture, the reality of electrical energy as a binding and motive force in the universe was indeed a material fact of daily life. As I have documented elsewhere, electrons were moving drive-belts in factories, carrying coded messages, and illuminating public spaces even before they were known, precisely, to exist. The first Hanamaki telegraph office was opened in 1882, a decade before an explicit electron theory had emerged from the academies and laboratories of Europe.[136] By 1884, the entire region of Tōhoku had been linked by a telegraph network stretching from Aomori to Shirakawa, and connecting, in turn, to a national network that spanned from Hokkaido to Kyushu.[137]

But the early years of telegraphy pale next to the electrical power revolution of the 1910s and 20s in Japan's rural regions. The exact years of Kenji's youth and early writing career in Iwate Prefecture coincided, in fact, with a massive and irreversible electrification of that region. In 1908 (when Kenji was twelve years old), there were 721 buildings with electric light in the entire prefecture. By 1925 (when he was 29), there were well over 85,000.[138] Out of Iwate's 27 electric companies operating in 1927—including companies in Hanamaki, Morioka, Kamaishi, Tōno, and Miyako—some 23 of those opened during the Taishō period. An expanded network meant an increase in power output as well; the number of generating stations in Iwate *doubled* between 1915 and 1920 alone.[139] By the end of Taishō, electricity was a well-established fact of commercial and private life everywhere in Japan. Electricity communicated messages and illuminated space, but it also moved people and their things: Tōhoku's first electric railway opened in 1915, testifying to the raw strength of electricity and to the increased generating capacity of Japan's rural northeast.[140]

The history of this technological expansion infuses Kenji's writing. "There is no writer in modern Japanese literature," Ōtsuka Tsuneki observes, "who feels or describes 'electric energy' [*denki enerugī*] in all its various forms the way Kenji does."[141] Immersed in Thompson's *Scientific Compendium* and Steinmetz's book on relativity, Kenji came to recognize energy as the realist (which is to say, modernist) subject *par excellence*: an entity that exists beyond direct perception, yet which also defines human experience in some fundamental way. Unexpectedly, then, energy emerges in Kenji's work as the shadowy beginning of a resolution to the very epistemological conflict its discovery in the nineteenth century had occasioned: the opposition between the sensory limitations of positivism and the abstract interventions of realism. Charles Steinmetz, for instance, hints at this resolution almost inadvertently, describing energy as the primal substance of reality precisely because of its link to sensation itself. "All sense perceptions are exclusively energy effects," he wrote. "That is, energy is the only real existing entity, the primary conception, which exists for us because our senses respond to it."[142] Contradicting the basic premise of positivists like Ernst Mach (who considered energy fields mere conceptual conveniences), Steinmetz pronounces energy as real not in spite of its undetectability, but because it is the *only* thing that *is* detectable. "Obviously then," Steinmetz continued, "by carrying the explanation of light and electromagnetic waves back to the energy field—that is, to energy storage in space—we have carried it back as far as possible, to the fundamental or primary conceptions of the human mind, the perceptions of the senses, which give us the entity energy and the form under which the human mind conceives it, that of space and time."[143]

For Kenji, though, the concept of energy acquires an even more grandly unifying function: not merely the key to reconciling positivism with realism, but the ontological link between the human and the nonhuman, the organic and the inorganic, the large and the small. In his poem, "Koiwai nōjō" (Koiwai farm, 1922), Kenji wrote:

> Into the scattering silver atoms of space
> A meadowlark flies
> Darkly, swiftly silver
> Brownian movement in the sky[144]

The characteristic collision of worlds in this memorable verse captures an essential theme that runs through much of Kenji's work. The meadowlark, with its beating heart and alert eyes, encounters the atomic vibrations of space. The molecular atmosphere communes with the flutter of wings, the pulse of warm veins. A technical, though no less beautiful term "Brownian movement" stands out here (even more so in the original since it is written with Roman letters) as part of a brilliant aesthetic and conceptual effect. Pertaining to a specific field of crossdisciplinary study known as "colloid science," which had its heyday between 1910 and 1930, the term evokes an ambitious investigative approach to the natural world in which theories of chemistry and physics were brought to bear upon the fundamental understanding of biological organisms.[145] Brownian movement refers to the vibrations detectable in tiny particles (colloids) in water that result from the bombardment of atoms. Einstein himself had published a paper on this phenomenon early in his career, providing what Michio Kaku calls "the first experimental proof of the existence of atoms."[146] But Kenji probably first read about Brownian movement in his well-worn copy of Katayama Masao's *Kagaku Honron*, a key source of data and inspiration for the author.[147]

Colloid science explored the consequences of the simple yet farreaching hypothesis that we now take for granted: the proposition that everything is made of atoms. "The most important hypothesis in all of biology," writes physicist Richard P. Feynman in his discussion of Brownian movement, "is that *everything that animals do, atoms do.* In other words, *there is nothing that living things do that cannot be understood from the point of view that they are made of atoms acting according to the laws of physics.*"[148] The logic of such a view continued to astound scientists for generations after Kenji's death, inspiring poetic reveries in unexpected places.

Feynman writes, for example, in his textbook on basic physics: "if water . . . can form waves and foam, and make rushing noises and strange patterns as it runs over cement; if all of this, all the life of a stream of water can be nothing but a pile of atoms, *how much more is possible*?"[149] The question seems to address itself directly to Kenji's poem, where the meadowlark—itself a complex of energy and atoms—can no longer be viewed separately from the space that surrounds it.

And this too is a kind of magnification. This fragment of verse presents what amounts to an enlargement or a diagrammatic vision: a portrait of a bird intimately interlocked *and continuous with* the universe that "contains" it. Evoking for some scholars the concentric doctrine of unity associated with the *Kegon Sūtra* known as *jūjū mujin*—a concept of reality reducible to the statement "inside one there are ten; inside ten there is one"[150]—the image of the meadowlark in this poem is no less suggestive of Bhaskar's transcendental realism itself. For Bhaskar, the material world defines human existence even as it enjoys an ontological legitimacy beyond direct human perception. And this is the significance of "Brownian movement" appearing in this poem. The term hints at what Bhaskar has called "the possibility of naturalism," which is to say "the thesis that there is (or can be) an essential unity of method between the natural and the social sciences."[151] If Kenji really did spend his evenings studying the *Lotus Sūtra* alongside Katayama's chemistry textbook, as his younger brother testifies in his biographical sketch, it may indeed have been in search for a language adequate to the grandeur of such a vision of materiality.[152]

Kenji's struggle to articulate this permeating materialism parallels, in surprising ways, Karl Marx's foundational efforts to conceptualize humanity's relationship to "nature." In his landmark study, *Marx's Ecology*, John Bellamy Foster makes clear that Marx's central and famous concept of the alienation of labor, first developed in his *Economic and Philosophical Manuscripts of 1844*, grew out of a more general understanding of the historical "alienation of human beings from nature, from both their own internal nature and external nature."[153] Contradicting several generations of Marxist and environmental criticism, Foster presents the case that Marx's view is not only "deeply, and indeed systematically, ecological," but that "this ecological perspective derived from his materialism"—which is itself traceable to the scientific revolution and, more fundamentally, to Epicurus.[154] According to this view, Marx's entire philosophical framework and the revolutionary politics it entails cannot be separated from a vision of material *interpenetration* that, had he lived later, might have resonated even more closely with Kenji's subatomic and chemical vocabulary. In Marx's words: "Nature is man's *inorganic* body, that is to say, nature in so far as it is not the human body. Man *lives* from nature, i.e. nature is his *body*, and he must maintain a continuing dialogue with it if he is not to die. To say that man's physical and mental life is linked to nature simply means that nature is linked to itself, for man is a part of nature."[155]

In a sense, the only sort of language adequate to such an all-encompassing vision of nature—capable of portraying "nature linked to itself"—is the language of modernism, with its inclination to take *relationships* and not discrete *objects* as its subjects. Cubism is such a language, and so is the four-dimensional geometry of Einstein's realism. Giovanni's and Campanella's journey through the galaxy might also be understood as a narrative version of this relational realism, an allegorical portrait of humanity's encounter with natural forces, entities, and processes: a picture of the space that connects us.

The Ethics of Realism

When they come upon an excavation site along the shore of the galactic river (during a brief stop at "Swan Station"), Giovanni and Campanella approach a bespectacled paleontologist in charge of the dig who explains to them the millennial history of the area known as the "Pliocene shore." The two boys learn that the walnuts they have been gathering along the riverbank are over a million years old, and that beneath them lies a stratum of fossilized shells and the bones of creatures long extinct. "For us," the scientist explains, "this thick and magnificent layer of soil holds all sorts of evidence from 1,200,000 years ago, but to others it might just appear to be a layer of earth, or wind, or water, or empty space. . . ."[156] Echoing what is by now a familiar theme, this passage shows observation and imagination conspiring to unveil a reality beyond appearances. For the paleontologist at work on the River of Heaven and for the two boys gathering walnuts along its shore, space is neither empty nor inert, but marked by traces of geologic time, filled with "evidence" of a living past.

This unlikely image of mapping the "geology" of the galaxy, reminiscent of the geological and topographical activities of Kenji's own student days, represents an unmistakably modernist impulse to see past the surface of the material world, to bring its (otherwise invisible) details "up close," to diagram the layers of its hidden history. This, in itself, constitutes one of the most striking aspects of the author's realism. For to attend to this layered geology means to acknowledge humanity's historical link to a nonhuman realm. In "Ginga tetsudō no yoru," the recognition of an alien world independent of human experience—what physicist Terada Torahiko described as the "nonhumanistic view of nature" revolutionizing physics at the time[157]—opens onto a whole new range of ethical demands. In one way or another, the moral content of this story seems to touch upon this deceptively simple belief: that there exists "a law-governed world," to borrow Roy Bhaskar's words, "independent of man."[158] Dissolving the positivist's injunction to equate existence with perceivability, Bhaskar himself argued that "being experienced or experienceable" should no longer be viewed as "an essential property of the world," but rather as "an accidental property of some things, albeit one which can, in special circumstances, be of great significance for science."[159] But what sort of ethic does such a position imply? Much of Kenji's fiction might be taken as a lengthy reply to this question. For this children's author and teacher, to accept the notion of a world in which we are directly shown only a fragment of what exists (or has existed) is to acknowledge the indispensability of imagination itself: the capacity to envision what cannot be seen, to understand what cannot be experienced, to navigate an ocean too big ever to represent in any *final* sense.

If the fundamental metaphor of "Ginga tetsudō no yoru" is the map, and the "place" it describes is the cosmos, the relationships at the heart of its "law-governed world" follow the logic of the food web: what poet and environmental activist Gary Snyder calls "the scary, beautiful condition of the biosphere."[160] Like Einstein's relative universe, the food web is both scary and beautiful because it is greater than any single point of view or experience. To recognize human culture as embedded in this limitless (but not infinite) network of material interconnection is to shrink human significance and expand human responsibility in the same breath. The most revolutionary dimension of "Ginga tetsudō no yoru," then, moves far beyond the parameters of standard leftist critique, finally addressing the problem of subsistence itself: the taking of life for food. By the end of the tale, it becomes clear that the struggle for existence can be viewed as another manifestation of the web of energy joining the meadowlark with the sky and the sky to the rest of the galaxy. The story's *ethical* content thus emerges inseparably from its author's understanding of the ceaseless unfolding of *material* interactions that connect human culture to the nonhuman, or "natural," world—what Marx himself called "metabolic relations."[161]

In a chapter called "Tori o toru hito" (The bird catcher), Giovanni and Campanella are drawn into a conversation with another passenger, a courteous and raspy old man who makes his living on the River of Heaven catching cranes, geese, herons, and swans. He directs the boys' attention to their cries. To the ears of the children, the cries of the birds resemble "the sound of water boiling between the echo of the train and the wind in the pampas grass."[162] Giovanni addresses the bird catcher:

> "How do you catch a crane?"
>
> "Do you mean a crane or a heron?"
>
> "Heron," Giovanni answered, not really caring which.
>
> "Well, it's easy. A heron is made of congealed sand from the River of Heaven, so they always come back to the river. You just wait by the bank and, at the moment a heron is about to land it always does like this with his feet, and that's when you grab it. And when you do, the heron just stiffens up and dies peacefully. Of course, you know what happens next. We press them."
>
> "You *press* them? Do you mean like specimens?"
>
> "Not specimens. People eat them!"
>
> "How strange," Campanella cocked his head to one side.
>
> "Nothing strange about it at all. See." The man stood up, took a bundle down from the rack and untied it. "Take a look. I just caught these."
>
> "They're really herons!" The two boys cried out involuntarily. There were ten herons lined up like medallions with their snow-white bodies, a little flattened, shining with the light of the Northern Cross itself and their black feet curled up.
>
> "Their eyes are closed." Campanella softly touched the white, crescent moon eyelid of one of the birds.[163]

Against a backdrop of electromagnetic waves and stellar iridescence, this beautiful and disquieting vignette captures the barest outlines of another form of energy exchange: the dynamic of death and nourishment. The birds themselves (whose cries are like "water boiling") behave in this scene almost as pure energy effects, plucked effortlessly from the sky as they return to their source: the gravel beneath the shimmering current of the Milky Way. The bird catcher's prey die promptly and peacefully, and their flesh tastes not of meat, we later learn, but of cake or candy (*okashi*).[164] Bypassing the blood and struggle of the hunt, this passage concentrates instead on the most essential geometry of survival, *diagramming* the fundamental structure of what Gary Snyder calls the "sacramental" economy. "Eating is a sacrament," Snyder writes. "Millions of grains of grass-seed that will become rice or flour, millions of codfish fry that will never, and *must* never, grow to maturity. Innumerable little seeds are sacrifices to the food-chain. A parsnip in the ground is a marvel of living chemistry, making sugars and flavors from earth, air, water." There is a chemistry and a physics to subsistence. But there is an etiquette too. If we do eat meat, Snyder continues, "it is the life, the bounce, the swish, of a great alert being with keen ears and lovely eyes, with foursquare feet and a huge beating heart that we eat, let us not deceive ourselves."[165]

Kenji's bird catcher chapter offers a glimpse into the elegant structure and ethical weight of this daily occurrence, this simple exchange of energy. By distilling the drama of the kill to its material essentials, this passage presents an abstract model of subsistence itself. When the bird catcher disappears suddenly from the train carriage only to reappear on the riverside outside their window, the two boys are able to watch him at work. Together with another passenger, identified simply as "the lighthouse keeper" (who functions in this chapter and the next as an impromptu guide), they look on as the bird catcher harvests herons from an abundant sky:

> "He's over there. A strange sight, isn't it? He must be catching some more birds. I hope some hurry up and land before the train leaves him behind."
>
> No sooner had the lighthouse keeper spoken these words than, out of an empty sky the color of bellflowers, some herons, no different from those the boys had just seen, came fluttering down like falling snow, letting out cries all the while. As they landed, the bird catcher, wearing a look of ecstasy—the look of someone getting just what he ordered—stood with his legs apart at an exact 60-degree angle. Using both hands, he grabbed the herons by the edges of their black feet, which were tucked in for landing, and stuffed them into his cloth bag. For a while, the herons gave off a flickering blue glow like fireflies from inside the bag, but finally they all turned a misty white and closed their

eyes. Far greater in number than these captured birds, however, were those landing safely on the sands of the River of Heaven, uncaught. Just as their feet touched the sand, these birds crumpled and flattened out like melting snow. Before long, they had spread out over the sand and gravel like molten copper from a blast furnace. Although they kept their bird shape for a moment on the sand, after glowing and dimming two or three times, they too became indistinguishable in color from their surroundings.[166]

Visually compressive and enigmatic in tone, this passage could reasonably be taken as a poetic rendering of what would later become the central paradigm of the New Ecology: the process of energy flow and nutrient exchange. Not only the blood of the kill and the messiness of ingestion and excretion, but the final stages of decomposition and molecular breakdown are all condensed in this scene, transfigured into a miraculous image of combustion and liquefaction. There is a dignified sorrow, too, marking this depiction of the hunt, captured somehow—as in the earlier passage—with the closing of the birds' eyes. This scene, together with the rest of the narrative, finally conveys a tender acceptance of these basic conditions of the universe: the dependence of life upon death. As the narrative moves toward its conclusion in the next chapter, taking on the still-wet victims of an ocean liner disaster, it becomes clear to the story's protagonist (and to its reader) that at least some of the passengers riding the Milky Way Railroad are themselves booked through to the afterlife. Supernatural imagery increases as the train moves closer to heaven, but the struggle for existence continues to unfold in the landscape outside—albeit with increasing levels of refinement.

Politely sharing with his fellow passengers some magnificent gold and red apples, the lighthouse keeper explains the conditions of food production at these rarefied existential heights:

Of course we have agriculture in these parts, but there's a promise here that good things will grow pretty much on their own. Farming is not all that hard. You can just about plant whatever kind of seed you want and it will grow up quick all on its own. The rice doesn't have husks, like rice in the Pacific region, and it's about ten times bigger than normal, and smells good too. But where you folks are going, there is no farming at all. And since even apples and cakes don't leave any waste, their delicate fragrance—different for every person—is absorbed through the pores of the skin.[167]

In this variation of the bird catching scene, the lighthouse keeper's apples too are shown to be composed of an ethereal or volatile material. When the fruit is peeled, "even their beautiful skins, carefully removed, evaporated into a soft grey glow before they could fall, twirling in a corkscrew shape, to the floor."[168] In her analysis of this scene, Kenji scholar Sarah M. Strong places this narrative's progression toward "more refined and less agricultural modes of sustenance" squarely in the framework of "the canonically correct hierarchical ordering" of the author's "Buddhistic other-world."[169] Within this classic ethical structure, Strong explains, the apple plays an important role since its consumption incurs no loss of life to animal or plant. Indeed, an ecologist might add that it is precisely by the apple's consumption—and the consequent dispersal of its seeds in feces—that the tree's survival as a species is guaranteed. "For someone seeking escape from the built-in wrongdoing of the food chain," Strong argues, "fruit such as the apple represented a nearly ideal food."[170]

And yet, in acknowledging the Buddhist framework of Kenji's narrative, it is important not to misread the author's mysticism as an expression of disconnection from the material world and its conflicts. In the end, "Ginga tetsudō no yoru" offers its readers not an escape from the food chain, but an abstract picture of it—not a denial of reality, but a model by which to understand it. A distinction must therefore be maintained here between *idealism* and *abstraction*. Much of the critical confusion surrounding this story emerges, in my view, precisely where its poetically rendered *abstractions* are taken as *idealities*. It is true that the narrative does not depict in naturalistic detail the killing of animals, that it generalizes the multitudinous sacrifice represented by grain production. But even here, animals continue to die and corn continues to grow. Consider the image of the Native American, the "Indian" who appears outside the train as it passes through a dreamlike landscape remindful of the American West. The scene is witnessed by the two boys and by the young man from the ocean liner:

> "He's running this way! He's running this way! He must be chasing us!"
>
> "No, he's not chasing the train. He's hunting. Or dancing." The young man spoke with his hands in his pockets, as though he had forgotten where he was.
>
> The Indian did indeed seem to be half-dancing. For one thing, if he had been running his steps would have been more economical in movement, more

earnest. Suddenly the bright white feather [in his hair] seemed to fall forward and the Indian came to a dead stop, nimbly drawing his bow and aiming into the sky. Out of the sky, a crane came tumbling down and into the outstretched arms of the Indian, who had begun to run again to catch it. The Indian then stood there smiling happily. Then the image of the Indian holding the crane and gazing back at the train grew rapidly smaller and more distant. The insulators on the telegraph poles flashed by two times and they were once again in a forest of corn. From the windows on the other side, you could see that the train was running along a very high cliff, and that the river was flowing wide and bright at the bottom of the gorge.[171]

As Strong points out in her perceptive discussion of this passage, "[e]very line of Kenji's description here seems intended to transform the act of hunting into a bloodless ritual."[172] Clearly unconcerned with naturalistic depictions, the narrative offers instead a choreographed *model* of the hunt; the killing of an animal converges with the poetry of dance. No arrow is visibly fired; the beating heart of the crane is never visibly pierced. No blood flows. But the animal does fall from the sky into the arms of the hunter—the kill is consummated. If this scene really does transform the act of hunting into a "bloodless ritual," as Strong suggests, it is useful to remember that the purpose of ritual is not to deny reality, but to explain it, to celebrate it, or otherwise to reveal its sacred dimensions. In fact, the universe of Kenji's story is shot through with the "wrongdoing of the food chain," a feature that in no way diminishes its sacred character. To emphasize the promise of an "other-world" in the story's details is to risk overlooking its relevance to *this* one. For in the end, this cryptic masterpiece makes the most sense as an explanation of everyday conditions. When we consider the historical role in science of seemingly occult "energy fields" and arcane mathematical models in representing the world of the atom, it seems less reckless to suggest that the bizarre imagery of "Ginga tetsudō no yoru" is aimed, in its own register, at revealing the world around us *for what it is*. The story offers neither its reader nor its protagonist a final release from the sin of existence, in other words, only a *purer vision of it*.

There is finally no conflict between Kenji's religiosity and his materialist stance. This tale presents without contradiction an ethereal tapestry of molecular transformation, energy exchange, and nutrient cycles alongside an eclectic array of religious symbols—of crosses, halos, white-robed figures meeting travelers on the way to heaven. It is precisely this surreal logic that allows Kenji's narrative to locate the meaning of death in two seemingly disparate but inseparable conditions: the material fact of energy exchange and the moral fact of sacrifice. Ultimately, "Ginga tetsudō no yoru" asks its readers to see every death, however small, as an *offering* to the galaxy. The theme of sacrifice and its link to the food chain is underscored near the end of the narrative through a Buddhist-style story surrounding the constellation known as Scorpius. When Giovanni and Campanella notice a bright fire-like brilliance on the opposite shore of the Milky Way, "more transparently red than ruby, and more beautiful than lithium," Campanella refers to his galactic map and determines it to be "the fire of Scorpius" (*sasori no hi*).[173] He then relates to Giovanni the details of a story he heard from his father. A scorpion who, after surviving all of its life by killing and eating insects, was one day caught by a weasel. In the struggle to escape, the scorpion fell into a deep well from which he would never be able to escape and in which he would be sure to drown. Suddenly regretting that he was going to die without at least being able to feed the weasel, the scorpion prays that, in his next life, his body will not be lost in vain, but will be of some use to the living. "At that moment, the scorpion's body turned into a beautiful crimson flame lighting up the darkness."[174]

However anthropomorphized in this passage by the allegorical conceit of self-conscious will, the image of a scorpion sacrificing itself to the food chain cannot be dismissed as idealism. Such sacrifices are, in fact, an everyday feature of existence, a moment-by-moment occurrence in the natural world. Every day plants and animals give up their individual lives for the continuance of life in general; this is the fundamental condition of the "sacramental economy." In the world of Kenji's tale, sacrifice is both an austere, material fact of the universe, and a miraculous event: a source, at once, of sadness, of comfort, and of terrifying beauty.

In important ways, Campanella's own death—his literal passage into an enigmatic astronomical phenomenon called the "coal sack" (*sekitan bukuro*), one of the "dark nebulae" or "cracks" (*sakeme*) in the galaxy whose mysteries are discussed in several of the author's astronomy books—parallels both the material death of the heron in the earlier chapter and the ethical death of the scorpion.[175] By dying, Camapanella's body returns to the rudimentary elements of the galaxy; but it also becomes an offering because his death allows another child, whom he saves from drowning, to live.

When Giovanni wakes up from his dream on the hillside, he sees "the Milky Way of his dream hanging, just as before, above the pitch-black southern horizon and the red star of Scorpius twinkling to the right."[176] In the manner of children's tales, the narrative has returned Giovanni safely to earth, to the village, to the hillside on the edge of town. But of course everything is different too, because now *he knows where he is*. Giovanni has taken his bearings, and the reader now sees that this "navigational" act has also been a way of reckoning the value of Campanella's life, of assessing the cost incurred by saving another. When he gazes downstream along the river, watching what he knows to be a hopeless search for his lost companion, Giovanni sees the river fused visibly with the sky above: "Downstream, the river was filled with the enormous reflection of the Milky Way as if there was no water in it at all, but only sky."[177] By conjoining this local site of tragedy—a river in which a boy has drowned—with the vaulting, galactic night enfolding its shores, the image manages to reveal both the littleness of a child's life and the enormity of its significance. Humans are not the center of the universe, this passage seems, unforgettably, to suggest; they simply *belong* to it—together with everything else. And it is the nature of this belonging that constitutes the final mystery of Kenji's story.

So the Cubist logic that serves as the animating vision of "Ginga tetsudō no yoru" moves far beyond the surface textures of aesthetic experimentation or the clever insights of scientific theory. By taking the universe as his subject and by removing humanity from the center of that universe (by removing the center itself), Kenji's work reveals a curious and unexpected connection between Japanese literary modernism and the rudiments of an "ecological" disposition. However stigmatized by theoretical currents in the humanities, the scientific realism that suffuses this famous work—its abiding faith in a material reality external to human consciousness—shares an epistemological heritage with what historian Roderick Frazier Nash calls "arguably the most dramatic expansion of morality in the course of human thought": the historical emergence of "environmental ethics."[178] Indeed, the strange and beautiful descriptions of light and energy, of matter and space in

"Ginga tetsudō no yoru" provide the intellectual context for some of Kenji's more earthbound stories, centered on animals and trees, on the rocks and rivers of Iwate Prefecture. These terrestrial, though no less revolutionary, tales reveal more obvious connections between Kenji's work and what would much later be called "deep ecology," with its characteristic opposition to "speciesism."[179] The next two chapters will focus on examples of this type of story.

FOUR

The Wild and the Cultivated: Kenji, Darwin, and the Rights of Nature

And when humanity has turned to coal
somewhere some invisible geologist
will record them in his notebook.

—Miyazawa Kenji, "Seijika," 1927

It is absurd to talk of one animal being higher than another.

—Charles Darwin, "Notebooks on Transmutation," 1838

When understood in the context of high modernism, the wilderness poems and tales of Miyazawa Kenji yield unexpected insights into the historical amplitude of this aesthetic movement. A legacy of the machine and the metropolis, of movie houses and capitalist exchange, modernism also shares a deep connection with another less predictable facet of industrial capitalism: the relational logic of ecology. The final two chapters of this book will be devoted to appreciating this connection, leading toward an endpoint from which other books might usefully begin.

If Kenji understood the totality of the natural universe as his essential poetic subject—with humans serving as both participants and accidental witnesses—this posture reveals a realist substratum connecting literary modernism with what would eventually emerge in the interwar and postwar periods under the rubric of New Ecology. Kenji's poetic treatment of the natural world might even be said to prefigure what today has come to be called "deep ecology"—a political, ethical, and philosophical movement that may in turn be identified as one of the most important remaining expressions of a modernist sensibility. Anticipating the radical materialism implied by the physics and chemistry of the "ecosystem"[1] concept of the 1930s, with its emphasis on "energy flow" and nutrient exchange in nature, Kenji's poems and tales draw their *ethical* force from what deep ecology founder Arne Næss calls the "total view": an abiding vision of the place of human beings in the world.[2]

The term "ecology" itself was coined by Darwinian biologist Ernst Haeckel (1834–1919) in 1866, but did not enter into common usage in Europe or Japan (where it was translated *seitaigaku*) until the 1890s. Borrowing the root for the word "economy" (the Greek *oikos*, meaning "household"), Haeckel's language stressed the importance of understanding life forms within the concrete particularities of their dwelling places, even while depicting the natural world in general as an enormous system of abstract exchange. "By ecology," he wrote, "we mean the body of knowledge concerning the economy of nature—the investigation of the total relations of the animal both to its inorganic and its organic environment."[3] For self-educated German- and English-speaking readers at the turn of the century, Haeckel's popular books constituted what Anna Bramwell has called a "life-line to political awareness through scientific knowledge . . . on par with Darwin and Karl Marx."[4]

In Japan, too, a translation of Haeckel's book *The Wonders of Life* (*Seimei no fukashigi*, 1904) provided a new diction for Marxist debate concerning the nature of materialism in history. Haeckel's worldview seems to have drawn its power, in fact, from the tension between the material and the ideal that animated much political and philosophical discussion in early twentieth-century Japan. Miyazawa Kenji read this book as a teenager in 1913, and the impact of Haeckel's theories upon his work has been widely acknowledged. Kenji mentions Haeckel by name in the poem "Aomori banka" (Aomori elegy) as well as in the story "Bijiterian taisai" (The grand vegetarian festival). But it is through the deep structure of several extraordinary short stories that the ecological grammar of Kenji's modernism finds its most compelling expression.[5] Kenji's best-known portraits of Iwate Prefecture's natural universe of forests and animals were published in the collection of children's tales *Chūmon no ōi ryōriten* (The restaurant of many orders, 1924).[6]

Each of the nine tales in this collection takes as its subject the drama of those encounters that can only occur in the border country that separates the world of domestic human activity—farming, building, buying, and selling—from the world of untamed nature. In this border terrain, wildcats remind human hunters of their place in the food chain, indignant oak forests hold tribunals against careless woodsmen, and a community of deer invents a curious ritual to mark the initiation of a fragile relationship with encroaching farmers.

The power of these tales—and many others that went unpublished during Kenji's lifetime—can be traced to the author's mastery of the "mobile perspective" that played such an important role in "Ginga tetsudō no yoru." These stories depict with indelible candor unexpected "local" perspectives: the experience of a wild deer stumbling upon a dyed cloth dropped by a human being, of a stone cliff witnessing the beginning of human settlement in a valley, or even of electrical energy flowing through telegraph lines (another example of wild nature in Kenji's world). At the same time, these local perspectives always open onto what an Einsteinian physicist might call a higher objectivity, the "total view" of a network of relations that can be abstractly imagined even if never depicted mimetically: the general shape of the human-forest relationship, for example, or the threat posed by capitalism to the life of an individual bear. The stories discussed in this and the next chapter, in other words, reveal a deep kinship between the realist disposition of modernism's experimental aesthetic and the ethical framework of an emergent ecological consciousness.

Ernst Haeckel did not invent the study of ecology, only the word to describe it. By the mid-nineteenth century, the "ecological" approach to natural science in the West was arguably several generations old.[7] Although the breadth of ecology's scope often pulled the terms of its discussion into the orbit of metaphysics,[8] Haeckel worked hard to bring scientific rigor to investigations into the interdependence of living things and their environment. In an 1869 lecture, Haeckel identified two essential tenets as characteristic of this new discipline. The first was an understanding and belief that all life on earth constitutes a "single economic unit." This *holism*, nothing new as a concept (though perhaps increasingly convincing as an experience), foreshadowed what would become in the twentieth century an alternately troubling and hopeful emphasis on totality: the organicist vision that would help shape *both* the quasi-spiritual ideologies of race and empire as well as the image of world revolution. Haeckel's holistic paradigm, however, possessed an explicitly Darwinian character that, if understood correctly and taken seriously, stood to derail the very logic of ethnic nationalism and geopolitical conquest that it might otherwise enhance. Although his own work would eventually come under the corrupting spell of social Darwinism—ultimately serving the cause of German fascism[9]—Haeckel's original efforts to link ecology and Darwinian evolution established the seeds of a deep resistance to those later ideological strains. By making clear that the study of ecology operated within the framework of Darwin's theory of evolution—placing what Donald Worster calls an "explicitly Darwinian border" around the word itself[10]—Haeckel acknowledged ecology's fundamental *departure from the human-centered view of the world* and its move toward what would today be termed a "biocentric" approach.[11]

In some ways, the polemical nature of the word "biocentrism" limits its usefulness. Through its morphology, *biocentrism* highlights an opposition to *anthropocentrism.* But by sharing a suffix with its "opposite," the term actually contradicts the most radical aspect of what it signifies: a view that acknowledges *no center at all.* The spirit of this radicalism made its first incipient appearance in Darwin's *The Origin of Species by Means of Natural Selection* (1859), which introduced the theory that would eventually be identified with the term "evolution," a comprehensive explanation of speciation that departed decisively from the study of organisms in isolation, emphasizing instead the interrelations of life forms and the material processes that support them. More significantly, by regarding variations *within* a species and variations *between* species as ontologically related, Darwin's theory removed the essentialist underpinnings from the category of species itself, throwing into irrevocable doubt the assumptions of human privilege that colored the most influential approaches to biology of the time.[12]

First introduced to Japan in the 1870s by the American zoologist Edward Morse (1838–1925), who taught for several years at Tokyo Imperial University, evolutionary theory is often remembered by historians of Japan not for its influence as a biological model but rather for its loose association with Herbert Spencer's ideas about social struggle and survival in the theater of human history. Indeed, as Julia Adeney Thomas reminds us, the enormous influence of Spencer's "social Darwinism" in Meiji Japan may qualify it as "the West's greatest intellectual export to Japan in the late nineteenth century."[13] In spite of this undeniable impact, molecular biologist Shibatani Atsuhiro warns against confusing the content of Spencer's social Darwinism with "the original Darwinian version" so crucial to the development of the life sciences in Japan's twentieth century. If early Meiji intellectuals welcomed evolutionary theory with such "notable enthusiasm," Shibatani argues, this was not for its promise as a "biological theory proper," but rather for what Spencer's social formulas promised to those who believed in the "progressive ideology of the modernized world."[14] Popular enthusiasm in Japan for Spencer's *misrepresentation* of Darwin's actual biological paradigm may even suggest that Meiji progressives intuitively recognized something in Darwin's original theory running deeply counter to the modernization program.

Of course, more faithful renditions of Darwin's theory did eventually have a profound if quieter impact in Japan. As a strictly *biological* model, evolution was interpreted, translated, and popularized by scientists like Ishikawa Chiyomatsu (1860–1935) and Oka Asajirō (1868–1944).[15] Oka's *Shinkaron kōwa* (Lectures on evolution, 1904), in fact, inspired passionate interest in the young Miyazawa Kenji when he read it in 1912.[16] Oka's book on evolution and his later *Jinrui no kako genzai oyobi mirai* (The past, present, and future of humanity, 1914), which introduced the thesis of humanity's inevitable extinction, highlighted the ephemerality and relative insignificance of human life, inviting links between Darwinian evolution and the Buddhist concept of "impermanence" (*mujō*).

In an article entitled "Jinrui no seifuku ni taisuru shizen no fukushū" (Nature's retaliation against human conquest), published in the general interest journal *Chūo kōron* in the last year of Meiji (1912), Oka tacitly recognized a conflict between Spencer's notion of a "Darwinian" struggle for social and political dominance on the one hand, and the web of organic and inorganic interdependence that Darwin's theory actually depicted on the other. Acknowledging that "civilization" (*bunmei*) has been predicated from the beginning on the impulse to "conquer nature" (*bunmei towa shizen o seifuku suru koto dearu*), Oka reminded his readers that the natural world follows its own system of "laws" (*rihō*) that transcend immediate human needs. In the context of modern civilization's intensifying agricultural and industrial productivity, he observed, nature has responded with floods, with pestilence and polluted rivers: a quiet and inexorable revenge.[17]

Though the bulk of Oka's article amounts to an excursus on the ecological consequences of progress—a meditation on the principle of "reaping what one sows" (*jigō jitoku*)[18]—the author falls far short of drawing any radical conclusions. Rooted in the ideological soil of late Meiji, Oka Asajirō concludes his essay by neutralizing his own most salient insights, landing ultimately on the side of homocentric progress. "Even if we ease up on our research and rest in our efforts to conquer nature," he finally warns, "though this may lighten or end nature's retaliation, we will be immediately conquered and subjugated by the other races (*hoka no minzoku*) and take a precipitous fall in world standing. . . ."[19] Thus, though there was no Judeo-Christian tradition to contradict it, and though it met with virtually none of the scandal or resistance attendant upon its introduction in the West, Darwin's theory of evolution did in fact present a major challenge to assumptions underlying the newly established political and commercial institutions of modern Japan—assumptions founded upon the industrial and colonial logic of centralization, objectification, and subjugation.

The brilliance of Darwin's idea, as with Einstein's theory in the next century, lay not in its complexity, but rather in its Neo-Copernican audacity. After reading *The Origin of Species*, Thomas Huxley is said to have exclaimed, "How stupid of me not to have thought of that!" As environmental historian Donald Worster observes, however, the major obstacle to the idea of evolution "was not stupidity; rather it was the traditional assumption of man's uniqueness. . . ."[20] By daring to remove humanity from its center, Darwin was able to recognize the natural world as a field of relations in which no single organism could reign supreme or exist autonomously: a world where an individual organism's identity and development were literally "socially determined."[21] While famously emphasizing the importance of deep linear time in the study of natural history, Darwin also, less famously, removed the usual teleological inflections from this diachronic framework. It was the reconceptualization of the *synchronic* structure of the natural scheme, far more than any specious contribution to Victorian ideas of "progress" commonly attributed to it, that made natural selection revolutionary, its emphasis on *location* in a network of relations: the enormous structure of the food web. For Darwin, Worster explains, "the economy of nature is more than a working composite of organisms; . . . considered abstractly, it is a system of 'places,' or what later ecologists would call 'niches.'"[22]

Against the tooth-and-claw image surrounding *The Origin of Species*—an image not exactly discouraged by the darkly suggestive subtitle "The Preservation of Favored Races in the Struggle for Life"—Darwin's ideas operated fundamentally by the logic of *interdependence*. The conceptualization of his infamous "struggle for existence" grew out of an apparently non-Darwinian insight, remindful of Buddhist cosmology: that "plants and animals remote in the scale of nature, are bound together by a web of complex relations."[23] The enormity of Darwin's vision astonishes readers even today. The language of evolution asked naturalists to consider what the *Lotus Sūtra* calls the "sum" of all living creatures "whether they are formed or formless, whether conscious or unconscious. . . ."[24] But it was not just this almost mystical inclusiveness that set Darwin's model apart. The crucial conclusions of the theory of evolution—that all life is interconnected, that humans are not privileged in this scheme, and that even seemingly insignificant organisms are important to the structure of the whole—articulate, in a sense, a biological version of Einstein's theory of relativity. Darwin's universe is a world with no center, a space where hierarchies must be recognized as observer dependent. While composing his work on human origins, Darwin scribbled a telling memo to himself to guide his thinking: "Never use the words *higher* and *lower*."[25]

Few would describe the children's stories of Miyazawa Kenji as "Darwinian." And yet the thematic content running through these tales—the relationship between human culture and the natural world that supports it—reflects the most basic insights of Darwin's understanding of wild systems. For Darwin, suffering, pain, and death were the conditions of nature, not so much as a *battlefield* defined by conquest and defeat (though his work tends to invite this interpretation by repeatedly invoking the language of warfare), but more accurately as an *arena of subsistence* involving both competition and mutual dependence. Despite its faintly Buddhist undertones, then, Darwinian holism bases itself not on universal "oneness" but on universal difference, embodied in conflict and cooperation. From this perspective, natural conflict becomes merely another form of cooperation, and the "conquest of nature" endemic to Victorian and Meiji ideology is shown to be not only inadvisable as a strategy, but patently absurd.

The short story I will treat in this chapter, "Oinomori to zarumori nusutomori" (The hills of Oino, Zaru, and Nusuto), is animated by the ethical consequences of this realization. This children's tale describes the establishment of a human settlement in a virgin clearing girded by wooded hills (*mori*) not far from present-day Morioka (the word *mori*, meaning "forest" in standard Japanese, signifies a "forested hill" in the dialect of the Tōhoku region).[26] Narrated by a rock in one of the forests, this piece depicts the fragile negotiations between the human settlers and the surrounding woods at a time when humanity still understood its dependence upon *and its membership in* the larger natural world. In important ways, the work narrates the mythical moment when that understanding begins to deteriorate, although it concludes with a final utopian gesture toward what we would call today "sustainability."

What makes this story "Darwinian," then, is its acknowledgement of the legitimacy of the nonhuman world, a world of organisms and processes that create with each other a constantly evolving web of relations too enormous ever to be perceived from any single perspective. It is Kenji's *realism* that links his work to Darwin's theory of natural selection. For it was nothing other than the workings of a realist imagination that allowed Charles Darwin himself to construct one of the most important materialist theories of the modern age, beginning from the unexpectedly saintly (and empirically unverifiable) insight that the animals of the wilderness and of the barnyard form with humans a brotherhood of agony and joy: "If we choose to let conjecture run wild, then animals, our fellow brethren in pain, diseases, death, suffering and famine—our slaves in the most laborious works, our companions in our amusements—they may partake [of] our origin in one common ancestor—we may be all netted together."[27]

This is exactly where Darwin reflected the anti-positivist spirit of his British contemporaries participating in the "energy revolution" in physics.[28] He worked from *empirical observation* to envision a system of relations *beyond* human perception. "The Grand Question, which every naturalist ought to have before him, when dissecting a whale, or classifying a mite, a fungus, or an infusorian," he wrote in one of his early notebooks, "is 'What are the laws of life.'"[29] To have imagined these underlying laws and *recognized them as real* is one of the great ethical achievements of Darwin's theory. Seven years after Faraday confirmed the reality of electromagnetic fields—the magic of "action at a distance"—Darwin provided a biological version of field theory with his notion of interconnectedness. His earliest suggestion that animals and humans might be "all netted together" emerged, by Darwin's own private admission, from a process of "conjecture run wild." For only by such rash imaginings could a naturalist, steeped in the discipline of rigid observation and classification, posit a world in which *inferred continuity* mattered as much as *observed difference.* It was precisely this continuity, however, that became the basis of his theory. "Let it also be borne in mind," he finally and famously wrote in *The Origin of Species*, "how infinitely complex and close-fitting are the mutual relations of all organic beings to each other and to their physical conditions of life."[30]

If it is the "privilege of poetry to conjoin the rational and the magical," as Norma Field has said, then Darwin's theory of evolution must be appreciated in part as a poetic achievement.[31] Although Darwin conceded that the effects of natural selection might prove "insuperable by our imagination"[32] when considered over the expanse of geological time, it was nothing other than an epoch-making feat of imagination that allowed him to subsume the infinite complexity of the organic and inorganic world under a single law. Unlike Faraday's proposal of a field of forces unobservable in *space*, however, Darwin's law of evolution proposed a system of relations immediately unobservable in everyday *time*: "We see nothing of these slow changes in progress, until the hand of time has marked the lapse of ages," he wrote, "and then so imperfect is our view into long-past geological ages, that we see only that the forms of life are now different from what they formerly were."[33]

With the rationalist confidence of a physicist or astronomer, Darwin constructed a worldview that transcended the bounds of everyday observation. "The undulatory theory of light has thus been arrived at," he wrote in response to charges of metaphysics, "and the belief in the revolution of the earth on its own axis was until lately supported by hardly any direct evidence."[34] Darwin's talent at observation and unmatched devotion to empiricism has led many to conclude, with biologists Richard Levins and Richard Lewontin in their classic work *The Dialectical Biologist*, that his theory was "devoid of any inferred but unobservable entities such as forces, fields, or atoms" and that the "Newtonian revolution of the seventeenth century, in which idealization played a central and essential role, was totally removed in spirit and method from the Darwinian revolution."[35] But Darwin himself understood and defended the centrality of the unobservable in his theory. It is indeed no accident that he repeatedly compared the essence of his own evolutionary model precisely to the spectral mystery at the heart of Newton's law of gravitation from which Levins and Lewontin saw him departing so fundamentally. In defending natural selection, Darwin explicitly invoked Newton's theory as an epistemological precedent, noting that the attraction of gravity remained a broadly accepted and reliable model, "notwithstanding that Leibnitz formerly accused Newton of introducing 'occult qualities and miracles into philosophy.'"[36]

There really *was* something miraculous, though, at the heart of evolutionary theory. After reading Darwin in 1867, the American naturalist John Muir wrote, "this star, our own good earth, made many a successful journey around the heavens ere man was made, and whole kingdoms of creatures enjoyed existence and returned to dust ere man appeared to claim them."[37] Muir's mystical vision of an "objective reality" undisturbed by humanity's absence—what Bhaskar called the world of "intransitive objects" existing "without any science to produce knowledge of them"[38]—forms the very foundation of ecological epistemology. Environmental historian Roderick Frazier Nash captures the power of this realist disposition in recounting the story of Muir's conversion to the notion that nature itself had "rights." Leaving his Wisconsin home in 1864 to avoid being called into the Union Army, Muir "followed a lonely trail into a wet and darkening swamp, where he suddenly came upon a cluster of rare white orchids, miles from anywhere." Confronted by their unexpected beauty, Muir sat down next to the flowers and wept. "Reflecting later on the experience," Nash tells us, "Muir realized his emotion sprang from the fact that the wilderness orchids did not have the slightest relevance to human beings. Were it not for Muir's chance encounter, they would have lived, bloomed, and died unseen."[39]

To imagine and to cherish *as real* a world that may live and die "unseen" by humans becomes one of the single most powerful ethical dispositions of the modern age: the essence of the scientific and artistic revolt from positivism. John Muir, like his contemporary Charles Darwin—and like Miyazawa Kenji a few generations later—lived his life in the subversive belief that *nature exists for itself.*

But what can it mean to speak of "nature" in the context of Kenji's literary world? In stories such as "Ginga tetsudō no yoru" and in much of his poetry, Kenji's portraits of nature often invoke the realm of energy fields and molecular activity. In a remarkable parallel to the work of Soviet geochemist and mineralogist V. I. Vernadsky (1863–1945)—whose 1926 "biosphere" concept "dismantled the rigid boundary between living organisms and a nonliving environment"—Kenji's poetic imagination brought rocks and gases as well as biota into a common order of interdependence and co-adaptation.[40] The author's own experience in soil research, where physics, chemistry, and biology coalesce, may have spurred this ambitiously "objective" position. Human beings, too, will have their "Carboniferous period" (*sekitanki*), he wrote in the poem "Seijika" (The politicians, 1927; cited in the epigraph above), when they will be reduced to fossilized deposits of coal and studied "by some invisible geologist." Indeed, the entire universe could be understood this way, as a field of evolving chemical states.

When imagining humanity's "Carboniferous period," Kenji's poetry seems to anticipate the concept of the "ecosystem," one of the central organizing principles of ecology today. The term itself, coined in 1935 by botanist Arthur Tansley (1871–1955), signified not only the "organism complex," in Tansley's words, but also the "multitudinous physical systems of the universe, which range from the universe as a whole down to the atom."[41] Steeped in the physics of energy systems, Tansley's work becomes a kind of practical rendition of the ethical system depicted a decade earlier in Kenji's poems and children's tales. For although they spoke the language of regional folk tales and invoked the cosmic opulence of continental Buddhism, Kenji's portrayals of forests and deer cannot be separated from the galactic or subatomic imagery of his more openly experimental work. Here is a cosmos bound together finally by matter and energy. Wild bears, telegraph lines, oak forests, and railroad engines: for Miyazawa Kenji, there was nothing in existence that could not be called "natural."

To argue that Kenji's work understands everything as *natural*, however, is not to suggest that everything for Kenji is the same. This is where the author's epistemology departs most significantly from the unifying impulse of Nichiren Buddhism. This poet of railroad ties and signal lamps managed to generate a "reading" of the universe that was as plausible as it was ambitious, succeeding where many in deep ecology still fail today. In this sense, the ethical thrust of Kenji's work can be usefully distilled to Christopher Belshaw's formula: "'everthing is connected' is true, while 'everything is one' is false."[42] For it is the *discontinuities* within the natural world—its conflicts and tensions—that animate Miyazawa Kenji's fiction and poetry:

> rain and clouds hang close to the ground
> washing the red ears of the pampas grass
> the plains are fresh and alive
> sparrows gather on the hundred insulators
> of the giant power line pole of Hanamaki
>
> they swoop down to pillage a rice-field
> into the light of clouds and rain
> then nimbly return to the hundred insulators
> at the fork in the road in Hanamaki[43]

This poem, "Gurando denchū" (The giant power line pole, 1922) provides a flashing glimpse of the border country of Kenji's literary world. The verse begins with the very essence of wild nature, which even the most urbanized reader confronts everyday: the wilderness of the sky above. In the opening image, rain and clouds reach down to the uncultivated plains (*nohara*) of Iwate, washing the ears of that region's ubiquitous "pampas grass" (*susuki*). By the end of this opening stanza, however, the jarring image of electrical insulators (*gaishi*) on a power line pole (*denchū*) opens onto a new reality, a different stratum of nature altogether. The word "insulator," which contains the character for the verb *samatageru* ("to interrupt," "to obstruct," "to hinder"), functions as a boundary of diction within the poem at the same time that it signifies the thematic borderline separating what is *wild* from what is *cultivated*. From an engineering standpoint, an insulator functions to corral electrical current within a designated circuit, to contain the dangers of its wild energy. In this deceptively modest poem, the "hundred insulators" also serve to suggest one of the central activities of human civilization:

the maintenance of boundaries between itself and the wild, the act of "obstruction," of *keeping at bay*. It is this frontier territory that serves as the site of crisis and revelation in much of Kenji's work.

As the poem goes on to suggest, however, even the most sophisticated civilized endeavor fails to provide a perfect seal. There is always leakage; there is interaction. Sparrows perch atop our power lines and pillage our cultivated fields. The wilderness encroaches, as evidenced by the ant poison in our cabinets, the snow shovels in our basements, the antibiotics dispensed by our physicians. It is the capacity to recognize beauty and value in this encroachment that becomes one of Kenji's lasting contributions. Historian of environmental literature Karen Colligan-Taylor underscores Kenji's stated preference for "dandelions in seed" over the cultivated refinement of cherry blossoms, noting a similar proclivity on the part of American conservationist, Aldo Leopold (1887–1948), who observed: "The weeds in a city lot convey the same lesson as the redwoods."[44] For Kenji, as for Leopold, the spheres of wild and domestic nature cannot and should not be perfectly separated from each other. What interested this author, rather, was the dialectical relation between the two, the state of ongoing negotiations.

The crucial distinction in many of Kenji's most interesting tales was not between "artificial" human society and nature, nor, to be sure, between "natural" Japanese culture and "unnatural" foreign culture, but rather, as in the poem cited above, between *wild* nature and *domestic* nature. Much of Kenji's fiction comes into focus when viewed in the context of this framework of wild and non-wild, an ecological disposition traceable to the writings of Charles Darwin, but articulated best by deep ecology activist and poet Gary Snyder in his collection of essays, *The Practice of the Wild*. Snyder—not coincidentally an early translator of Kenji's poetry—resists the temptation to replace the old connotations of wild as "desolate," "barren," and "savage," with an equally dualistic image of wilderness as a spectacular natural setting (usually set aside as a park) of pristine, Eden-like beauty. There is an arrogant and dangerous irony to today's popular notion of the wild as a place apart: untouched, though somehow also visited and "protected" by humans. For Snyder, as for Kenji, the wild is more than simply an uninhabited "place out in nature" (though it can be this, too). Where it counts most, the wild—a "self-propagating" and "self-maintaining" force of "exuberance"—*interpenetrates* the zone of human cultivation, interacts with it, and often conflicts with it.[45] The urgency of civilization's relations with this wild world—its ethical obligations toward it and its spiritual reliance upon it—makes up the thematic content of "Oinomori to zarumori, nusutomori."

The Wild and the Cultivated

The story begins with an enumeration of place-names, marking the boundaries of a geography, a setting: "North of Koiwai Farm, there are four mountains (*mori*) covered with black pine. The southernmost of these is Oinomori, next is Zarumori then Kurosakamori and, on the northern edge, Nusutomori." But it soon becomes clear that the "setting" of the story—the land and its features—is also its protagonist, one of its leading characters and, in fact, the primary agent of narration:

> One day a great rock deep in Kurosakamori boasted to me: "I am the only one who knows how these mountains came into being in the very beginning and how they got their strange names." It was this rock who told me the following story:
>
> A very long time ago, Iwate-san erupted over and over again. The whole area was buried in ash. (Of course, even the black rock telling me the story had been thrown up from that volcano, landing where it stands today.)
>
> When the eruption finally calmed, the hills and plains, beginning toward the south, gradually began to grow grasses—some with ears of grain-seed and some without—which eventually covered the area. Then oaks and pines sprang up until at last the four wooded mountains that stand there today were formed. But the mountains as yet had no names. Each one thought of itself simply as "I." It happened one year in autumn on a day when the wind, as cold and clear as water, rustled the dry oak leaves and a cloud cast a sharp black shadow upon the silver peak of Iwate-san.
>
> Four men—peasants wearing straw rain-gear—crossed over the rugged obsidian peaks to the east and arrived at a little field girdled by these mountains. They had hatchets and hoes and all the required "weaponry" for mountain and meadow strapped to their backs. If you looked carefully, you could see that they all were also brandishing large swords.[46]

With these opening lines, "Oinomori" identifies itself as a geographical autobiography, the story of a place *as told by the land itself.* The matter-of-fact idiom of the folk tale allows its narrator—with the help of his native informant (the rock)—to move across sweeping vistas of geological time, from the region's volcanic genesis to the appearance of ancient flora and finally the arrival of the first cultivators: the first encounter between the wilderness and agriculture.

In fact, the story is told for the benefit of human ears: those of the narrator, the formal "I" or *watakushi*, who first receives then "reports" each of the tales in this collection. So "Oinomori" must be understood finally as a human narrative, even if told from the curiously panoramic point of view of a geological formation. Time itself is made "visible" by the language of this passage, forming an elastic boundary expanding and contracting around its edges. At the center of this opening scene operates the mythic conceit that the beginning of an entire age can be traced unambiguously to a single day. Against this epic backdrop, a heartbreaking radiance seems to infuse the image of the last autumn afternoon when the leaves of the trees could rustle in the wind with no human ears to hear them. This taciturn description holds the understated power of a single idea: of a reality unencumbered by human witnesses. Imbued with the quiet ambition common to geology and children's tales, the language of the story asks its readers to picture the land before the burden of names, when each mountain "thought of itself simply as 'I'" (*ore wa ore da to omotteiru dake deshita*).

And so we are given the voice of a mountain, directly quoted and translated into human speech. With its ethnic, regional, and gendered (male) inflections, this technique underscores the limits of human language precisely by applying it to nonhuman experience. Assigning human language to a cliff or a mountain—complete with masculine pronoun (*ore*)—suggests a profound connection at the same time that it discloses an unbridgeable gulf between the human and nonhuman universe. It is this paradox that colors so much of Kenji's fiction thematically, but which also informs its deep structure. The reason we "recognize" (*ninshiki*) the world at all, wrote ecologist Imanishi Kinji (1902–92) in 1940, is that we are *part of it*. "It is not at all surprising then," Imanishi goes on to say, "that poets and priests can speak with and hear the voices of rocks and trees, and all sorts of other nonhuman things. *But the voices of these things are not like our own voices, and the ears they listen with are not like our own.*"[47] This shamanistic negotiation of identity and difference constitutes, in the very broadest sense, the posture of science itself. "Things are similar," write Levins and Lewontin, "this makes science possible.

Things are different: this makes science necessary."[48] The language of the natural universe, in other words, must be "translated."

Here I invoke a well-worn imperative of poststructuralist theory: that nature must be understood as a "discursive construct." This far-reaching assertion cannot be denied. Nature *is* a human construct—an "object of knowledge" produced by social, ideological, and linguistic convention. The problem for ecology emerges when this assertion implies the belief that this is *all* that nature is. To dismiss as metaphysical anything that exceeds the bounds of human language or perception constitutes the myopic failure of both positivism and poststructuralism in their most extreme versions. If nineteenth-century positivist physics refused to acknowledge a world outside of human sensation (Ernst Mach's "colors, space, tones"), many in humanistic disciplines in the last thirty years have assigned a similarly "final" status to the realm of human discourse. [49] By collapsing the *reality of the object depicted* with the *reality of the depiction*, this position tends to dismiss all scientific or descriptive labor as naïve objectivism, ignoring the dialectical relationship that has long been acknowledged by storytellers and scientists in the twentieth century. For environmental historian William Cronon, who has written on the historical interactions of the human and nonhuman worlds, to describe nature as a human construction "is not to say that the nonhuman world is somehow unreal or a figment of our imagination—far from it." For Cronon, this fundamental insight serves rather to remind ecologists, biologists, and cultural critics that "the way we describe and understand that world is so entangled with our own values and assumptions that the two can never be fully separated."[50] This supposedly postmodern observation is, in other words, the foundational insight of realism itself in its *modernist* form.

As such, it is also a common problem of early twentieth-century science and literature. If the storyteller "lends his voice to the experience of others," as Lloyd Spencer tells us, this is precisely where stories function most scientifically.[51] "Natural science does not simply describe or explain nature," wrote physicist Werner Heisenberg, "it is part of the interplay between nature and ourselves."[52] But much of contemporary (especially literary) theory denies the possibility of this sort of interplay, reverting instead to a classically homocentric belief system (a radically literal humanism) willing to acknowledge only what is human about nature: the language of its "translation."[53] This insistence upon the priority of human culture in a world increasingly hostile to nonhuman life betrays a posture that is not only disturbingly narcissistic but contrary to postmodernism's own stated aims. "If the world depends for its reality on our discourse about it," Terry Eagleton observes, "then this seems to lend the human animal, however 'decentred,' an imposing centrality."[54]

It is precisely his willingness to follow through on this fundamentally *realist* endeavor to "decenter" humankind that makes Miyazawa Kenji's work compelling to readers today. By subverting humanity's position as the universal reference point, much of Kenji's fiction and poetry preserves the ethical possibilities of Heisenberg's dialectic, working from the ecologically realist premise that nature is both *everything we are* as humans and *everything we are not*—a field of relations that defines but also exceeds human experience. This is why the term "nature" alone clarifies so little about the creative disposition of his work. In "Oinomori," it is not nature as an external "entity" that becomes the object of description, but rather the tensions, clashes, and interactions that occur within nature, that make up the *space between* (in the Cubist sense) the human and the nonhuman, the wild and the cultivated, the present-day landscape and its primal antecedents.

The grammar of this realist ambition demands the powerful juxtaposition in this story's opening passage between the familiar everyday world and its ancestral "other": between the sun-warmed surface of an obsidian peak and the molten violence of its ancient past; between "hills covered in black pine" and a wasteland "buried in ash"; between the dappled light of a single autumn afternoon and the inconceivable expanse of planetary time. Kenji gives us a portrait here of Darwin's self-confessed mystery of faith: the "hand of time" marking the "lapse of ages."[55]

These opening images suggest the simple evolutionary thesis that the nonhuman world has its own history, a history *connected to* but *not identical with* our own. "Oinomori" sets out to honor this history, and to describe the contours of a primal ecological crisis: when the evolutionary trajectory of a single wild system first becomes entangled with the forces of human domestication. The reader soon realizes that the darkness moving across the snowy peak of Iwate-san is meant to serve as a shadow-line marking the epochal instant of this transition—from the hour of the wilderness to the hour of the cultivator, the moment of human settlement.

> The lead farmer pointed here and there with his finger, showing everyone the magic-lantern landscape.
>
> "What do you think? It seems like a good place. We could easily make fields, and the forest is close. There's clean water. . . . And the light's good too. What do you think? I myself have already settled on this place."
>
> "But I wonder how the soil is," another farmer replied, stooping down to pull up a stalk of pampas grass. He let the earth fall from its root into his palm, kneading the soil with his fingers then tasting a little. "Well, the soil isn't great, but it's not bad either," he said.
>
> "So, shall we make it here then?" said another, looking around with the air of having returned home after a long time away.
>
> "Ok. It's decided," said the fourth peasant, who had been silent up to then.
>
> Happily, the four farmers dropped their loads with a thud, turned in the direction from which they had come, shouting "Oy! Oy! This is the place! Hurry on up! Hurry up!"
>
> At that, three women emerged red-faced from amid the pampas grass, carrying huge loads on their backs. And soon you could see nine children, none older than five or six, shouting cheerfully as they followed running up from behind.[56]

Human settlement. The phrase hardly captures the trauma of this biotic encounter, or the deadly promise of displacement, occupation, and control implied by a farmer's simple act of selection, of choosing a place to live. The lead farmer's finger *indicates* the land in much the same way human voices will later name it: in the interest of cultivation. That is why it is so significant, Komori Yōichi remarks in his analysis of this piece, that the events in the story—departing from the usual tradition of "tales about the origins of place names" (*chimei kigen setsuwa*)—are related by a nameless rock, by a voice that comes from a "side of nature" as yet "undominated by humans."[57] Only from such a position would the tools of farming and forestry be recognized as "weaponry" (*buki*). What is remembered as a settlement from one perspective is experienced as an invasion from another.

Indeed, the iron hoes and hatchets carried by the settlers foretell dire consequences for the surrounding forest, symbolizing not only the direct pressures of agriculture but also the depredation of hardwood stands that the manufacture of charcoal—required in the forging of metal tools—eventually brings to the Tōhoku region. "Humans, for their part," Komori asserts, "by calling these iron implements 'tools,' conceal the fact that they are used to wound, to murder nature (*shizen o kizutsuke, satsugai shiteiru to iu jijitsu*)."[58] Pursuing this theme of "nature's murder," Komori finally concludes that, from the point of view of the local vegetation and microorganisms, agriculture's inevitable "over-cultivation of the soil" amounts to "nothing other than a strategy of annihilation, a genocide."[59]

Komori's series of lectures on Miyazawa Kenji, which appeared as a book in 1996, include some of the most penetrating analyses of Kenji's work ever published. By identifying the "carnage" (*satsuriku*) of agriculture as the invisible theme haunting this and other of the author's children's tales, Komori removes a veil of quaintness obscuring the ideas of one of Japan's earliest ecological visionaries. In important ways, however, the theme of "nature's murder" and the language of "invasion," "colonization," and "genocide" so central to Komori's analysis distorts as much as it illuminates. For it is the opposition between nature and human civilization itself—or more exactly the assumption of civilization's power *over* nature—implied by the phrase "nature's murder" that Kenji's fiction worked so creatively to overcome. Komori's uncritical reliance upon the notion that civilization began as an "escape from the food chain," as a historical "separation from nature," strays subtly but crucially from the central insight of Kenji's masterful tale: that cultivated and wild systems are inalienably interdependent.[60] "Oinomori" tells the story not of humanity's tragic *dominance* over nature, but of its tragically misrecognized *embeddedness* in nature, a theme that betrays a heavy debt to evolutionary theory.

Miyazawa Kenji was sixteen years old when he read Oka Asajirō's *Shinkaron kōwa* (Lectures on evolution). Since its publication in 1904, Oka's Darwinian masterpiece had exerted an enormous influence on young lay readers at every level of society. For activist and anarchist intellectual Ōsugi Sakae, who was old enough to remember the excitement of the book's original publication, *Shinkaron kōwa* catalyzed a broad interest in the general applicability of the scientific method, signaling a move away from the "a priori reasoning" that had dominated the early education of Ōsugi's generation.[61] Though he ultimately recognized Oka's reductive conclusions as a paradoxical version of anthropocentrism,[62] Ōsugi acknowledged the unique importance of Oka's relativizing logic, his insistence that we view humanity as "merely another organism" rather than as "a special species completely separate from other organisms."[63] "We must imagine a single place in which all beings are gathered," Oka wrote, "from microscopic bacteria to higher organisms like primates. And while surveying this whole, we must learn to see humanity as one of its parts."[64]

It is easy to imagine the impact that statements like this would have had on a young Miyazawa Kenji. Even today, the chapter titles and subheadings in *Shinkaron kōwa* carry the allure of conceptual grandeur: "Seizon kyōsō" (The struggle for existence), "Seibutsu sōgo no fukuzatsu na kankei" (The complex mutual relations of life), "Seibutsu no kigen wa hitotsu de aru koto" (Life has one origin). One of the most practically significant subheadings comes toward the end of the book, in the chapter entitled "Shizen ni okeru jinrui no ichi" (The position of humanity in nature). It states simply, "Hito wa jūrui no isshu naru koto" (Humans are a species of animal).[65] In a certain sense, all of environmental ethics begins at the moment when this observation becomes a true conviction.

"Do you really believe you are an animal?" Gary Snyder asks his readers in *The Practice of the Wild* (1990). "We are now taught this in school. It is a wonderful piece of information. . . . But many people who have been hearing this since childhood have not absorbed the implications of it, perhaps feel remote from the nonhuman world, are not *sure* they are animals."[66] This uncertainty forms the most persistent intellectual barrier to meaningful environmental ethics in industrialized nations today. Scholars and intellectuals who will openly concede that human beings are biological organisms still struggle illogically to reconcile what Komori Yōichi describes as humanity's "privileged status"[67] in the food chain, to account for what they perceive as our unique position in nature.

Of course, human beings really *do* occupy a unique position in nature. But in this, they are like *any other organism on earth.* The premise of each organism's uniqueness or "specialization" underlies even the most primitive ecological models, going back to Darwin's concept of "place in the economy of nature" (what we call today "niches") and his later, more sophisticated, and lesser-known notion of "divergence."[68] In this limited and paradoxical sense, then, differentiation becomes the common unifying feature of all terrestrial life, including humans. Humanity's uniqueness emerges as a function of its competence to fill a particular "place" in a system of nutrient exchange. We are unique, in other words, but not *singular.* In matters of survival, nothing sets humans apart from what many still imagine to be some homogeneous "other" world of animality. Like any other organism, humans survive by perceiving and interpreting opportunities and dangers in the world around them, by *finding their place* in it.

What makes human survival singularly complex, however, is the cultural and technical relationship that has evolved between humans and their conditions of subsistence. According to Marx and Engels, humans "distinguish themselves from animals as soon as they begin to *produce* their means of subsistence. . . ." The authors go on to make clear, though, that the "way in which men produce their means of subsistence depends first of all on the nature of the means of subsistence they actually find in existence and have to reproduce."[69] What emerges as humanity's historical alienation from nature, in other words, should never be understood as *real autonomy* from nature, but rather as a uniquely human (ideological) experience of the biologically universal "struggle for existence."[70] From this perspective, humans do indeed enjoy a singular existence on the planet, but only in their historical practice of living *as if* they enjoyed a singular existence, free from the natural constraints of subsistence. "It is not the *unity* of living and active humanity with the natural, inorganic conditions of their metabolic exchange with nature, and hence their appropriation of nature, which requires explanation, or is the result of a historic process," Marx would write in the 1857–58 notebooks published as the *Grundrisse*, "but rather the separation between these inorganic conditions of human existence and this active existence, a separation which is completely posited only in the relation of wage labour and capital."[71]

The abstracting impulse driving this historic process of alienation, exemplified for Marx in "wage labour and capital," underlies what contemporary Marxist critic Terry Eagleton has identified as the centerpiece of his own thesis on human singularity: language. Humanity's linguistic capacity to *step back from* or *transcend* the data of biological perception—to interpret our bodies' more immediate "interpretations" of the world—prompts Eagleton to assert that, unlike the non-reflexive "sensuous response to reality" characteristic of beetles and monkeys, human engagement with the world involves a "second-order reflection on the 'language' of our bodies—of our sensory apparatus." It is in this sense, he tells us, that "all human language is meta-language."[72]

This argument inadvertently suggests to ecology-minded readers that the very abstracting impulse that Marx saw as responsible for humanity's alienation from nature might be the paradoxical key to its solution. Following Eagleton's logic, human discourse emerges as a central issue in ecology not because language makes the nonhuman world possible by "constructing" it, but because it makes nonhuman reality an *ethical problem* by ceaselessly interpreting humanity's real relationship to it. The notion that humanity enjoys a special position in nature may be nothing more than a discursive construct, in other words, but the extra-discursive effects of holding this belief upon the nonhuman world are very real indeed. The fact of nutrient exchange itself—Marx's "metabolic exchange with nature"—might easily be understood as the ultimate horizon of this ethical relationship, and this is where Marxism contributes most crucially to our understanding of Kenji's ecology. If Eagleton's radicalism leads him to conclude that "only a linguistic animal can be a moral one," it also compels him to insist later that all questions of ethics revolve fundamentally around the materiality of the body.[73] Humans may not share language with nonhuman animals, but they do share the fact of biological need.

Like any other organism, humans *select* and *modify* their environment; they *respond* to it and *transform* its statistical structure.[74] The farmers of ancient times who settled the valley north of the Koiwai pastures in Kenji's narrative were not the first to choose and to transform the land. The oaks and pines that sprang up in the region had also "chosen" this habitat through mechanisms of seed dispersal, and their occupation of the land had its own ripple effect. It is well known by now that a forest, if it is big enough, affects rainfall and atmospheric conditions. Even in small numbers, trees modify soil conditions around their roots and alter wind and temperature conditions to a distance of about ten times their height.[75]

So the act of selection (and the implied promise of modification) embodied in the lead peasant's index finger amounts to an act of recognition common to all life forms. Levins and Lewontin tell us not only that "organisms select their environments" but also that they "determine what aspects of their environment are relevant and which environmental variations can be lumped or ignored."[76] ("What we see as a steppe," writes Imanishi Kinji, "a grasshopper may see as a forest.")[77] Kenji's farmers taste the soil to assess its fertility; they check for availability of wood and clean water and the quality of sunlight for growing crops. In the Darwinian model, of course, this "local" act of selection (with specific organisms as agents) takes place in the context of the larger, anonymous law of *natural* selection. Organisms select their environment, but over time are themselves *selected by* a process that expresses itself in the statistical pronouncements of survival and extinction.

Darwin coined the term "natural selection" (Oka's *shizen tōta*) in part to distinguish it from what he called "selection by man" (Oka's "artificial selection" or *jin'i tōta*): the practice of crop improvement, crossbreeding, and husbandry that provided so much material for his research into variation and heredity.[78] From its beginnings, it seems, modern biology generated its central insights by studying the relationship between the wild and the cultivated. When he compared the shortsighted motives revealed by "improvements" that humans had made upon breeds of pigeon or sheep, Darwin openly marveled at the majestic "workmanship" evinced by the material laws of natural selection. "How fleeting are the wishes and efforts of man!" he wrote, "how short his time! and consequently how poor will be his results, compared with those accumulated by Nature during whole geological periods!"[79] It was not only the cosmic scale of its time frame, but the selfless comprehension of its "vision" that allowed natural selection to work so well: "It may metaphorically be said that natural selection is daily and hourly scrutinising, throughout the world, the slightest variations; rejecting those that are bad, preserving and adding up all that are good; silently and insensibly working, *whenever and wherever opportunity offers*, at the improvement of each organic being in relation to its organic and inorganic conditions of life."[80]

In a sense, though, by opposing human selection to "natural" selection, Darwin's language presented as somehow *unnatural* a range of civilizing activities—a multitude of transformative human pressures on the environment—that nevertheless necessarily unfold under the umbrella of "nature" and its laws. It would be more accurate to say that agriculture and industry have served to make the world less *wild* (and certainly more human), but no less *natural*. "So we can say that New York City and Tokyo are 'natural,'" writes Gary Snyder, clarifying this point, "but not 'wild.' They do not deviate from the laws of nature, but they are habitat so exclusive in the matter of who and what they give shelter to, and so intolerant of other creatures, as to be truly odd."[81]

Natural but not wild—this seemingly minor semantic distinction has led to enormous shifts in thinking about environmental crisis today and in the ethical responses it has generated. On the surface, the earth's accelerating extinction rate might suggest the fulfillment of an almost biblical prophecy: *the death of natural selection itself*—or Komori's "murder of nature" in its literal and apocalyptic version. "The extinction crisis is over," declares political scientist Stephen M. Meyer in a recent article. "We lost." Despite the rhetorical severity of this opening pronouncement, however, Meyer's article actually provides a bleakly nuanced analysis of the ways in which an anthropogenic incarnation of *nature* has won out over an ecocentric version of *wilderness*, characterized by biodiversity. "Today," he writes, "the guiding hand of evolution is unmistakably human, with earth shattering consequences."[82]

Predicting convincingly and with the support of overwhelming empirical data a 25 percent reduction in the earth's genetic stock in the next century, Meyer grimly envisions a world divided into "a three-tiered hierarchy of life built around human selection."[83] Meyer's "human selection" thesis clearly accounts for what he calls "relic species"—animals like elephants and pandas that linger in carefully managed "boutique populations" as nostalgic reminders of a richer biotic past. It also explains with relative transparency the ever-increasing number of "ghost species"—the vast majority of the earth's extinct or soon-to-be extinct life forms, driven out of existence through habitat loss or outright extermination campaigns.

But the final category in this three-tiered hierarchy, the newly thriving class of organisms Meyer refers to as "weedy species," reminds us that it is the inadvertent consequences of human *occupation* as much as deliberate acts of human *selection* that drives the devastation the author summarizes. "The land and the oceans will continue to teem with life," Meyer explains, "but it will be a peculiarly homogenized assemblage of organisms *naturally and unnaturally selected* for their compatibility with one fundamental force: us" (italics mine). Dandelions, cheatgrass,

English sparrows, the white-tailed deer, and the Norway rat all fall under this "weedy" category: plants and animals *naturally selected* for their capacity to thrive in "continually disturbed, human-dominated environments."[84] These species have continued to expand in population and distribution, and many are already labeled as pests. As Meyer's piece makes clear, in other words, it is not the process of natural selection that has failed and continues to fail—natural selection is alive and well (how could it be otherwise?)—but human civilization's material and cultural relationship to *the wild*.

On the other hand, Meyer's invocation of the concept of "weedy species" also serves inadvertently to remind us that contrary to Meyer's provocative title, "End of the Wild," the wilderness itself, broadly defined, is far from dead. If "human selection" has come to dominate the biosphere, as Meyer's piece suggests, this condition signals not exactly the *end* of the wild, but the emergence of a new manifestation of nature in which the wild is represented increasingly by "weeds" and "pests." In fact, the continuing threat of wild nature lurks behind Meyer's own assertion that "this human-selected biosphere will not necessarily be a human-friendly one."[85] From this perspective, the wilderness will continue to thrive as vigorously as it did in the past; the difference will be that now, instead of a grey wolf eating our children in the forests of Germany, the wild will be represented by a crow eating our garbage in the streets of Tokyo or a virus shutting down our immune systems in the slums of Johannesburg.

Wildness itself is a permeating phenomenon, extending far beyond the formal wilderness areas and national parks that stand for "the wild" in common imagination. "Shifting scales," writes Gary Snyder, wildness is literally everywhere: "ineradicable populations of fungi, moss, mold, yeasts, and such that surround and inhabit us. Deer mice on the back porch, deer bounding across the freeway, pigeons in the park, spiders in the corners."[86] What has ended, then, is neither natural selection nor the wild as such, but the broad diversity of wild systems that human populations managed to live creatively alongside throughout their Paleolithic past but have come increasingly to out-compete in the more recent history of civilization. In a fundamental sense, this too is "natural." The damage to biodiversity is the *result* of natural selection, as it has interacted dialectically with human culture, not the sign of its demise. It is the urgency of this dialectic—the unbalanced and troubled interactions among biotic systems (human and nonhuman alike)—that Kenji's "Oinomori" portrays so well.

The Sacramental Economy

The farmers who arrive in the valley north of Koiwai Farm to domesticate its wild fields carried with them (the story suggests) not only iron tools for breaking ground and clearing woods, but also the memory of an ancient code, the vital remnants of a fading system of etiquette expressed with the pedagogical transparency of the children's tale:

> At that moment each of the four men turned to face a different direction, and together they raised their voices in unison, "May we start our fields here?"
>
> "Go ahead!" the forest answered all at once.
>
> Then they shouted together, "May we build our houses here?"
>
> "All right," the forest simply replied.
>
> Again, the four farmers raised their voices and asked in unison, "May we make a fire here?"
>
> "Go ahead," the forest replied.
>
> And everyone shouted again, "May we help ourselves to a little wood?"
>
> "OK" answered the forest all at once.
>
> The men cheerfully clapped their hands and their faces flushed. The women and children who had been silent up to then suddenly began to create a great ruckus. The children started to tussle with each other in a fit of excitement and the women warmly boxed their ears.[87]

At the simplest level, Kenji's tale reminds his readers to say please and thank you. But the peculiar genius of "Oinomori" is to show its readers the ethical enormity of this imperative when it is extended to the mountains and to the woods. When the farmers ask the woods: "May we start our fields here?" their question acknowledges the human settlers' *difference* from the forest at the same time that it implies their inextricable *connection* to it. The coming of agriculture is felt as an ominous event by the land not because humans are specially endowed creatures who have somehow freed themselves from the food chain, as Komori Yōichi suggests, but precisely because they remain inalienably a part of it. (What better reminder of this than Kenji's own death by a bacterial lung infection at the age of 37?)

When Charles Elton introduced the concept of the "food chain" (translated *shokumotsu rensa*) in 1927, he made it clear that the *bottom* of the chain—plant life that produces food through photosynthesis—formed its most essential link. Even more significantly, Elton described the sum total of food chains in any biotic community as a "web" with neither top nor bottom: the very image of limitless relationality that was coming to dominate both biology and physics in the early twentieth century.[88] Producers, consumers, reducers, and decomposers: according to Elton's idea, the organisms that fulfill these roles form a vast and complex network of interdependence in the economy of nature. Fundamentally—and despite the vertical implications of most casual "food chain" references in English or in Japanese—Elton's Darwinian food web model departs from the logic of hierarchies. Evolutionary theory had finally if quietly rendered absurd the very notion of absolute relationships in nature, and Miyazawa Kenji seems to have absorbed this insight as an ethical conviction. Darwinian science seems to have instilled in Kenji, as it had in many of the leading figures in twentieth-century biology, the impulse to observe advantage in nature as relative, a disposition that retains today its subversive edge.

All rules of courtesy honor the ideal of shared dignity. In Kenji's tale, the farmers' observance of a sort of eco-etiquette—the securing of permission to make use of the land—suggests the preservation of a primal "equality" utterly at odds with liberal political ideology. Implied by their ritual language is the social contract of subsistence: the right to kill *but not to destroy*. But if Kenji's peasants really retain this primal ethic, what is the basis of the crisis that follows? When the settlers first begin the work of clearing the land and building shelter, humility and cooperation continue to characterize their relationship to the forest. From the forest's perspective, though, there is also something unprecedented and portentous in the industry exhibited by the cultivators:

> Starting the next day, the forest looked on as the people, seemingly possessed by madness, began their work. The men, with their hoes flashing in the sun, cleared pastures. The women gathered the chestnuts that had not yet been taken by squirrels or field mice, and cut up pine for firewood. Soon the ground was covered in snow.
>
> Throughout the winter, the forest did its best to protect the people from the northern winds.[89]

By the autumn of the following year, however, the settlers appear to have little need of such protection. Having built three structures and harvested their first crop of buckwheat and barnyard millet, they are no longer competing directly with woodland creatures for what the forest floor happens to provide. At exactly this moment, when the tiny community begins to move away from a subsistence economy (exemplified by gathering) and toward an economy of accumulation (exemplified by cultivation), the first in a series of crises occurs.

One morning that winter, "when the earth had frozen hard," four of the peasants' nine children are discovered missing. Again, the peasants react with a desperation that appears to the forest as the onset of "madness" (*kichigai no yō ni natte*). Of course, the "madness" of the farmers' panic over the missing children and the "mad" intensity of their labors in the previous autumn underscores the historical emergence of a perceived inseparability of development and survival. It is not merely the lives of the individual children or the success of the next crop that is at stake, but the survival of the settlement itself. The peasants find themselves, once again, appealing to the forest for assistance, turning in the four directions and asking the woods for some indication of their children's whereabouts. Claiming ignorance, the forest invites the farmers to come in and look. The scene that follows, which repeats itself twice with variations, following a formula reminiscent of folk tales, uses the spare idiom of dreams to suggest the community's knife-edge relationship to the wild:

> So they all took up their various farming tools and headed first toward Oinomori, the closest mountain. The moment they entered the forest, they were suddenly assaulted by a damp, cold wind and the smell of rotting leaves.
>
> They quickly marched on.
>
> As the farmers pushed forward, they noticed that deep in the forest, something was making a crackling sound.
>
> When they hurried over to look, they saw a transparent rose-colored fire blazing, and around the fire, nine wolves dancing and skipping.
>
> Slowly approaching, they spotted their four missing children facing the fire and eating roasted chestnuts and *hatsutake* mushrooms.
>
> The wolves were all singing and running around the fire as if it were a stone garden lantern in summer.
>
> "In the middle of Oino Forest
> The fire crackles and burns

The fire crackles and burns
The chestnuts crackle and cook
The chestnuts crackle and cook"

The wolves sang in unison at the top of their lungs.

"Mr. Wolf! Mr. Wolf!" the peasants cried out. "Please return our children to us!"

Taken by surprise, the wolves stopped singing all at once and frowned, turning in the direction of the peasants.

As they did this, the fire instantly extinguished itself. Since everything had suddenly fallen dark and silent, the children who had been by the fire began to cry.

The wolves looked around for a moment as if wondering what to do, but finally they all ran away into the depths of the forest.

At that, the peasants took their children by their hands to lead them out of the woods. As they began to walk, they could hear the voice of the wolves coming from deep in the forest: "Please don't think ill of us. We fed them lots of chestnuts and mushrooms!" When they got home, the peasants all prepared *awamochi* and left it at the edge of the Oinomori forest as a sign of their thanks.[90]

The last known wild wolf in Japan was killed on the Kii Peninsula by a lumber raftsman on January 23, 1905, about two decades before Kenji published this story.[91] But wolves—called *oino* in the dialect of Iwate—have remained emblematic of the mystery and danger of the wild, frequently appearing in folk tales and children's stories as they have in Europe and the United States. A subspecies of the grey wolf, the Hondo or Japanese wolf (*Canis lupus hodophylax*) disappeared from Japan's main islands of Honshu, Shikoku, and Kyushu under the shadow of rabies and distemper epidemics. Its northern cousin, Hokkaido's indigenous Ezo wolf (*Canis lupus hattai*), was eradicated more systematically by large-scale wolf-poisoning campaigns after the establishment of livestock ranches there in the late nineteenth century.[92] This familiar narrative of displacement and extermination belies the complex material and ritual relationship that held sway for generations in the Japanese hinterland between wolves and humans. In his sensitive study of people-wildlife relations, *Waiting for Wolves in Japan*, anthropologist John Knight reminds us that unlike its counterpart in Europe and the United States, where it often stood for pure evil, the wolf in Japan has long retained an ambiguous image: a terrifying and dangerous predator that was at the same time a powerful protector and a "messenger of the gods" (*kami no otsukai*).[93]

With no major tradition of raising livestock for food, pre-Meiji Japanese farming communities were predisposed to appreciate wolves as crucial agents in *controlling* rather than *contributing to* wildlife pestilence. For a peasant whose diet was grain-based and supplemented by fish and vegetables, the most direct wild threat to livelihood was posed by deer, boar, monkeys, and other crop-destroying herbivores.[94] Folklorist Chiba Tokuji reports that until the second half of the seventeenth century, the wolf's status as a "benign animal" (*ekijū*) rested precisely upon its skill as a predator. The protective function of the wolf in the symbolic economy of Japanese folklore and religion—its status as a "savior god" (*sukui no kami*) and its association with the "spirit of the mountain" (*yama no kami*)—cannot be separated from the animal's material position in the food chain.[95] Even today, long after the animal's extinction, wolf shrines in the Japanese countryside continue to offer, among other things, ritual—if not material—protection from farm pests.[96]

From the beginning, however, wolves represented the indeterminacy of a "double-edged sword," to borrow the words of Nomoto Kan'ichi.[97] A leading figure in the school of "environmental folklore" (*kankyō no minzoku*), Nomoto sees a nuanced understanding of predator-prey relations at work in the symbolic and material traditions of Japan's forest-edge cultivators. Livestock, though not raised for food, had long been kept for transport and draught purposes, and by the late seventeenth century with the transmission of rabies to the wolf population, lupine ferocity had begun to gain broad notice as a major threat to village horses and even to people throughout the countryside.[98] With attacks on the rise, John Knight tells us, "the image of the wolf as a benign spirit started to change to that of a mortal threat."[99] Today, an impressive lexicon attributing greed and savagery to wolves—a "wolfish look" (*rōko*), for example, might be translated as a "menacing glare"—has been superimposed over older connotations of benevolence and protection.[100]

Kenji's story mines the image of the wolf for all the creative potential of its ambiguity. Here is a predator that *polices* but also sometimes *violates* the border between forest and field. Whether benign or malignant, the symbolic valence of the wolf remains inseparable from its association with the primal compact between the hunter and the hunted. "'Your ass is somebody else's meal'—a blunt way of saying interdependence, interconnection, 'ecology,' on the level where it counts, also a teaching of mindfulness and preparedness."[101] Unlike the "firsthand true stories" that Gary Snyder invokes here—told presumably by modern day hikers, hunters, forest rangers, and backwoods residents—the visceral dimension of the peasants' ancient encounter with wolves in Kenji's story is relatively muted by the strangeness of its fairy-tale logic. The wolves do not threaten to attack or eat anyone directly, though their proximity to the peasants' children surely elicits thoughts of the kill. The danger they pose, the precise meaning of their bizarre prank, suggests heavier, more enigmatic demands.

The peasants' entry into the deep forest—the sacred "no rescue zone" of the pre-modern world, before wilderness had been appropriated as an arena of leisure and sport—retains the magical quality of an encounter with otherness, with a world that only children and mystics can penetrate. The reader imagines the peasants' chilled muscles shivering against the damp and cold, their hearts quickening at the smell of decomposing rot on the forest floor. Each careful image faintly suggests the truth of the sacramental economy: the exchange of life for food. Everything is eaten by something else eventually. The peasants have taken much from the forest in order precisely to escape its dangers, and they are worried now about what the forest might take from them. The emotional urgency of this scene, in other words, is generated by the paradox of civilization itself: that human beings no longer belong in the wild, though they continue to belong *to* it—dependent upon its gifts, living by its grace.

When Nomoto Kan'ichi describes wolves as the "watchdogs [*banken*] of the forest," he refers to legends that describe wolves protecting humans by warning them of "abnormalities in the natural world."[102] But for environmental groups today like the Nihon Ōkami Kyōkai (Japan Wolf Association), the wolf has taken on the expanded role of protector of the wilderness itself: the "wolf that will save the forest" (*mori o sukuu ōkami*).[103] Indeed, the creature's very indeterminacy has come to signify the workings of a higher order, only imperfectly represented by the mechanical model of the ecosystem. In important ways, Kenji's tale anticipates this broader view. The wolves care for the children, feed them mushrooms and chestnuts, but *only after displaying the power to kidnap them.* When the farmers glimpse the fantastic wolf-dance by firelight, amid the "rose-colored" glow that weirdly penetrates the shadows of the woods, the song of the wolves and their cryptic plea for kind thoughts could be understood as a request for fair play uttered on behalf of the mountain itself, of Oinomori. The wolves become emblems of Arne Næss's "total view"; they speak the language of a higher objectivity.

This motif of "catching the wilderness off guard," of civilized humans furtively witnessing what they are not supposed to see, recurs throughout this collection of stories and in much of Kenji's later fiction as well. These narrated experiences are always brief and they are always morally transformative. Compared to the ubiquitous fox of Japanese legend that "commutes" between mountain and village, the wolf is much more strongly associated with the deep mountains, the region beyond human activity.[104] A wolf sighting means a boundary has been breached. So when the peasants of Kenji's story make their presence known, the wolves do what is expected: they run away, they *keep their distance.* Characteristically, then, this scary encounter leads to the reestablishment of a frontier and the implied promise to recognize spatial order and territorial integrity. It represents, in other words, a renewed commitment to smooth relations, the foundation of all "courteous" behavior.

The offering of *awamochi* (cakes of pounded millet) carries the significance of its historic manufacture: grain that has been selected, sown, gathered, and prepared. If mushrooms and chestnuts suggest the Paleolithic candor of the forest's largesse, *awamochi* embodies the domestic organization of an agricultural community, its requirements of space, fuel, building materials, and the many other essentials the wild has surrendered to it. Presented first as a gift to the wolves of "Oinomori" this offering constitutes the concrete and pragmatic initiation of a sacred ritual. Something has now passed from the peasants to the wilderness. Not only a "thank you note" to the mountain, but a symbol of interdependence which it is practically essential for the peasants to remember.

So the crisis depicted here is far larger than "merely" the narrowly averted death of four children. With its sweeping mythical gestures, this story narrates the outlines of a sacred compact and hints darkly at its impending collapse. In 1993, the notion of the wolf as a sort of sentinel charged with maintaining the boundary between the wild and the cultivated—as protector of cultivated fields but also as savior of the forest itself—was given ecological expression through the Nihon Ōkami Kyōkai's campaign to reintroduce wolves to the "ecosystem" of Japan's forests. Wolf reintroduction is seen today by some as a practical and charismatic solution to the increasing problem of wildlife pestilence, a means of restoring the forest's ecological balance.[105] But behind the language of ecology, there persists a supernatural dimension to contemporary concerns about the consequences of wolf-extinction in Japan. A memorial rite for Japan's last wolf—initiated in 1905 by the hunter who killed him—continues to this day as an annual event.[106] John Knight reports that some farmers in Japan see increasing wildlife pestilence as "a manifestation of the curse of the wolf on the society that brought about its extinction."[107]

In fact, the final breakdown of the balance that Kenji's fictional peasants struggle to maintain would lead historically to the erosion of wild habitat throughout premodern and early modern Honshu, a trend that would intensify dramatically after the establishment of the modern Meiji state.

The Border Country

On the one hand, it would be foolish to attribute a twenty-first century eco-awareness to a late Taishō collection of children's tales or to the consciousness of its author. Kenji's optimism toward industrial technology, his faith in science, and his direct involvement in disseminating modern fertilizing techniques to Iwate farmers all suggest an enthusiasm about modern civilization in many ways typical of an educated progressive of the time. On the other hand, Kenji's assumption that a healthy civilization and fully functioning wilderness could and should coexist makes his work particularly relevant to readers today. Kenji witnessed in his lifetime, as I have suggested, the dramatic modernization of the Tōhoku region, exemplified by its rapid electrification. But even before this technical transformation, the rich woodlands straddling Japan's 40th parallel had undergone centuries of strain under the immediate pressures of local agriculture as well as under the more distant architectural demands of Japan's western urban centers.

By 1700, as Conrad Totman shows us in his detailed history of Japan's forests, nowhere in the entire northeastern half of Honshu remained untouched by logging activities.[108] Although the distant Tōhoku region had escaped the effects of what Totman calls the "ancient predation" of the Kinai basin—the logging of Honshu's watershed region near the ancient capital cities of Nara and Heian (later called Kyoto) in the seventh century—Japan's northeastern woodlands would strain under the far-reaching effects of the "early modern predation" beginning in the middle of the sixteenth century. "Logging was so intensive" during these centuries, Totman reports, "that when Japan entered the twentieth century only the northern island of Hokkaido still held major areas of virgin timber."[109] So when Kenji evoked in his stories and poems the untamed forests of Iwate, with its tangles of old-growth hardwoods populated by wolves, bears, and wild deer, he was reaching into the already distant and mythic past. By the end of the Tokugawa period, most of Japan's wild forests had been wholly domesticated: transformed under management policies of regenerative forestry, existing only "in plantations or as naturally seeded and supervised replacement growth."[110]

The early modern predation was driven by the monumental building projects of distant rulers, but a majority of the stress placed upon Japan's forests came from direct use by the 98 percent of the population who worked the fields.[111] As Kenji's tale synoptically suggests, local forests provided farmers with construction materials, brush and grass for fodder and green fertilizer, as well as food—chestnuts, mushrooms, game, and fish. But it was the harvesting of fuel wood that depleted local forests most substantially. In addition to the wood burned to heat and cook domestically, the rise of iron smelting, which in turn had made possible the spread of agriculture, required "substantial volumes of high-quality charcoal, which was made from oak, chestnut, or other dense hardwoods."[112]

The role of the forest in the manufacture of charcoal has special significance in Kenji's native Iwate Prefecture, where the woodlands of the northern mountains had long been noted for their deciduous trees. Before Japan's fossil-fuel revolution of the postwar period, Iwate had provided the bulk of the nation's charcoal for home cooking and heating. By the year 1912 (when Kenji was sixteen years old), even as the area was undergoing broad electrification, Iwate had become the nation's center of charcoal production, thanks to its still relatively plentiful supplies of oak (*kunugi*), white oak (*nara*, *konara*, and *kashiwa*) and chestnut (*kuri*).[113] In his research on Tōhoku's indigenous monkeys, primatologist Mito Yukihisa observes a direct link between charcoal production in Iwate and the dramatic diminishment of monkey habitat between the mid-nineteenth century and 1925.[114] Indeed, the erosion of wilderness habitat in general in Japan was profound enough to be legally (if weakly) acknowledged at the national level with the Shiseki meishō tennen kinenbutsu hozonhō (Historic and scenic natural monuments preservation law) of 1919, which, among other aims, was designed to protect threatened species and natural phenomena of particular scientific or cultural value—including, by 1934, Tōhoku's mountain-dwelling antelope or serow (*kamoshika*).[115]

But habitat destruction also sharply affected the plants and animals of the perimeter: that zone of confluence so central to Kenji's work, where the wild and the cultivated interact daily. Environmental historian Kawai Masao observes, for example, a precipitous drop in Iwate's population of wild deer between late Meiji and the Taishō periods, a decline alarming enough to have spurred a prefectural ban on deer hunting in 1919.[116] Kawai's quirky zoological analysis of Kenji's fiction notes that the author's work rarely features animals from the deep mountains—Iwate's famous serow never appears, for example—but focuses instead on what Stephen Meyer might identify as "weedy species" typical of an early twentieth century Japanese village: foxes, mice, *tanuki*, deer, rabbits, weasels, etc.[117] Kenji's stories and plays, Kawai concludes, are most concerned with those regions that would come to be called, in a postwar coinage, "*satoyama*" or "village mountains": the wooded hills on the edge of a village or hamlet that serve the needs of local farming communities.

When the geography of Iwate is divided into villages (*sato*), village mountains (*satoyama*), and deep mountains (*okuyama*), it is easy to recognize the strategic importance of the *satoyama*—where human civilization has historically exploited, defended, and *defended against* an alien wild. The "*mori*" of Tōhoku dialect that appears in the title of Kenji's "Oinomori" typically refers to a mountain of less than 1000 meters, exactly the sort of formation, Kawai tells us, that might be classified *satoyama*. It was these peripheral and low-lying hills that generations of Japanese peasants had harvested for fuel wood and fodder as well as other essentials such as *kuri* (chestnuts), *warabi* (a kind of bracken), *zenmai* (royal fern), *fuki* (butterbur), and *matsutake* (a variety of mushroom).[118] And it was also here, in these now-beleaguered border zones, that farmers would most visibly compromise their sacred compact with a diminishing wilderness during Kenji's lifetime.

If prewar and wartime charcoal production helped to erode the hardwood stands of Iwate's peripheral village forests, the rising use of oil, gas, and chemical fertilizers in the postwar period served to discourage their replacement. It is not that Japan is no longer covered in green woods. In fact, postwar reforestation policies ensured that the nation's forests actually increased in area over the twentieth century from the 22.5 million hectares that covered the islands in 1900 to today's 25 million hectares.[119] But government efforts to correct the large-scale denuding of hillsides and mountains that occurred during the war have fostered the replacement of hardwood trees with cedar (*sugi*) and Japanese cypress (*hinoki*)—fast-growing softwood timber species used in housing and construction. What has disappeared, in other words, is much of the wild vegetation of the deep forest (*okuyama*) as well as the transitional, semi-wild hardwood stands of the village forest (*satoyama*). Over 25 percent of Japan's total area of land today is taken up with monocultural, largely coniferous domesticated timber plantations, resulting in the seemingly paradoxical situation in which forest-area has *increased* while much of Japan's original or traditional wildlife habitat has *diminished*. As a result, the graduated separation of village and forest associated with the *satoyama* has given way, in John Knight's words, "to a sharp interface, with villages now surrounded by tall dark conifer forest."[120]

Today, the virtual disappearance of the *satoyama* combined with rural depopulation trends has made wildlife depredation in Japan's countryside especially acute. There is no more *space between*: no room for negotiation, no "demilitarized zone." Deer, boar, monkeys, and the nationally protected serow have become increasingly visible in forest-edge cultivating communities, raiding crops and damaging timber plantations. Even the most elusive deep forest creatures like the Japanese black bear (*tsukinowaguma*), when deprived of fruit- and acorn-bearing trees must resort to pillaging orchards and fields for their survival. Farmers resort to all the new and old techniques of fencing, field-guarding, trapping, and poisoning to keep the wild at bay—using everything from sensory repellents to charms and prayers.[121] With pestilence on the rise, the urgency depicted in Kenji's story begins to take on new meaning.

If "Oinomori" portrays the direct and undisguised competition between the human and the nonhuman world that must have held sway "when the mountains had yet to become *satoyama*," as Kawai Masao suggests, then the wildlife pestilence studied by anthropologists such as John Knight and Nomoto Kan'ichi today represents the reversal of this process.[122] The conflict between wilderness and cultivation dramatized in Kenji's tale continues to play itself out in contemporary forest-edge communities all over Japan, not because farmers are struggling to establish the culture of *satoyama*, but because they are grappling with the effect of its disappearance. It is no coincidence that anthropological descriptions of these conditions echo the conceptual framework of Kenji's children's story, with its emphasis on spatial order. In describing the anxieties expressed by human inhabitants of forest-edge communities, Iguchi Matoi reports: "When the wild beasts that are supposed to live in the forest start to appear in the village to such an extent, it suggests that 'something bad' [*warui koto*] is happening. . . ."[123] In Kenji's tale, that "something bad" is to be understood neither as the domination of wilderness over humans nor even its reverse, but rather as a *breakdown of negotiations* between the wild and the cultivated: the failure to thrive together. Whether the result is extinction or pestilence, the problem is evolutionary.

According to Conrad Totman, the history of Japan's human-forest relationship consists of two phases—"a thirty-thousand-year preagricultural phase, during which *Homo sapiens sapiens* used puny wood, bone, and stone tools to exploit a wooded landscape whose essential character he could not alter," and "a far shorter phase encompassing the past twenty-five hundred years, during which a swelling human population, equipped with an increasingly complex and demanding technology, has altered fundamentally the character of more and more woodland."[124] "Oinomori" outlines the ethical imperatives engendered at the moment of this epic transition. It must be noted, however, that if Kenji's stories take as one of their central themes the dream of a civilization capable of living creatively alongside the wild, the dreamscape he invented always speaks the language of dialectics.

Kenji's portrait of wild deer, for instance, in his famous tale, "Shishi odori no hajimari" (The first deer dance, 1924), operates precisely within this dialectical framework. Kajū, a traveler in Tōhoku's epic past, has crossed over the mountains from the cultivated lands east of the Kitakami river to heal his injured leg in a wilderness hot spring. Purposely leaving the remainder of his half-eaten lunch out for the deer, Kajū resumes his journey only to realize he has dropped his towel near the clearing where he had rested. Returning to retrieve it, the lone traveler finds a large group of deer circling around the woven cloth with awe and suspicion, confronting the enigma of an alien humanity. Kajū's ears begin to ring and, from his hiding place amid the pampas grass, he is gripped by a strangely heightened sensibility. After elaborate and cautious investigations, the deer determine that the cloth is harmless and begin to approach the chestnut dumpling itself. As Kajū looks on, he recognizes in the choreography of this original "deer dance" a primal kinship with these creatures at the same time that he perceives in their movements the mystery of an essential difference:

> The deer again formed a ring and began to walk round and round and round.
>
> Kajū was so engrossed in watching the deer that he began to feel as if he were one of them. Just as he was about to jump out from the bushes to join them, he caught a glimpse of his own bulky hand. "Of course, I couldn't!" he thought, and went back to holding his breath.[125]

An epiphany repeated throughout this collection of wilderness tales, Kajū's insight here echoes Christopher Belshaw's observation: to say that everything is *connected* is not to say that everything is *one*. At the very moment that Kajū recognizes a real connection with the deer, he is forced to see his "oneness" with them as an illusion. Morphologically and culturally, an evolutionary abyss stands between the hoof of a wild ungulate and his own prehensile hand. Although temporarily endowed with the ability to hear and understand the deer speaking to one another (another familiar refrain in these tales), Kajū's true connection to these animals exists not through language but through *food*. When the dumpling passes from the human world to the world of deer—from the space of cultivation to the order of the wild—the sense of awe is reciprocal, experienced by deer and human alike. The transmission of nutrients from human hands to the bodies of wild animals is depicted here as both spiritual and metabolic. More precisely, it is revealed as spiritual *because* it is metabolic. The sharing of food in this scene constitutes a "holy communion" because it acknowledges identical needs, continuous conditions of existence. In a sense, the deer's ingestion of the half-eaten dumpling made of horse chestnut becomes a sacrament honoring the interpenetration of the human and the nonhuman: an emblem of the dialectic between the wild and the cultivated.

The opening passage of "Oinomori" (collected in the same anthology) lays out the logical principle of this dialectic in a slightly different register. Just as there will always be "weeds" encroaching upon the garden of civilization, there must also have been "ears of grain seed" on some of the wild grasses of the land: the untamed cousins of wheat, rice, and millet. Environmentalists today often imagine a ghost wilderness hiding as tiny seeds of original vegetation in the soil of a modern-day farm or deep beneath the streets of Chicago and Tokyo. Kenji saw this too. But he also imagined a "ghost civilization," latent and unformed, beneath the volcanic plains of ancient Iwate, an incipient farm village waiting no less inevitably to rise up: natural but not wild. So the shock of an encounter between wilderness and cultivation depicted so pointedly in his children's stories is always tempered by the allure of recognition. This is the paradox at the heart of Kenji's dialectical imagination. If a profound and unbridgeable gap between the wild and the civilized makes Kenji's stories necessary (as Levins and Lewontin might observe), it is a deep and abiding connection between these two worlds that makes them possible.

In a sense, it was this vision of dialectical interpenetration that inspired Kenji's idealistic—and ultimately unsuccessful—attempt to become a farmer himself in 1926, and his simultaneous establishment of the Rasu Chijin Kyōkai. Convinced that practical engagement with agriculture would be the ultimate fulfillment of his cosmic and political vision, Kenji resigned his teaching position and moved (with all of his books, his cello, and his scientific instruments) to a family-owned house in Shimonekozakura to work the small parcel of land attached to it. The gesture was no doubt perceived by the struggling local farming community as highly suspect or, at best, merely eccentric. For Kenji himself, however, it was an opportunity to add depth to the artificiality of classrooms and textbooks. "I, too, have changed since our time in Morioka," he wrote to a friend in 1925, explaining his decision to resign. "Before, when I thought of the flow of water, it was a cold, transparent, quartz-like substance I thought of. But now, I want to repair irrigation gates, to sink my arms and feet in warm, muddy water, thick with rice-seedlings and grass, crowded with innumerable microbes drifting happily along."[126] This last sentence suggests the persistence of the author's ecological imagination. For Kenji the soil scientist, aquatic microbes represented another kind of wilderness, an invisible version of wolves in the forest.

From the beginning, the author's expertise in soil chemistry shaped his understanding of interactions between human and nonhuman life. Although the "Nōmin geijutsu" lecture notes, which he composed at this time, show the influence of Murobuse Kōshin's (1892–1970) enormously popular anti-scientific and anti-industrial works *Bunmei no botsuraku* (The decline of civilization, 1923) and *Tsuchi ni kaeru* (Return to the soil, 1924), Kenji's practical activities during this period suggest a more nuanced notion of sustainable metabolic relations between the land and its human occupants, in no way contradicted by science and its association with industry.[127] Indeed, although ostensibly engaged in farming, Kenji's greatest contribution to agriculture at the time was scientific. During the Rasu Chijin Kyōkai period, most of Kenji's time was taken up with a free fertilizer counseling service he had established and operated out of a relative's store in Hanamaki for the benefit of local farmers. Kenji distributed detailed questionnaires to address the conditions of individual plots and growing practices, took soil samples, analyzed them at home, then wrote up detailed agricultural plans for individual farmers, always favoring natural rather than chemically synthesized fertilizers, citing the exhaustion of the soil in the United States.[128] Indeed, it seems to have been part of Kenji's greater social vision to form an intimate partnership between the culture of science and the culture of farming. The scheduled activities at the Rasu Chijin Kyōkai in 1926 included lectures and discussions addressing such topics as "How can we make the science we need our own?" and "The principles of chemistry indispensable to us."[129] Kenji the chemist, the farmer, and the ecological visionary—tenderly aware of aquatic microbes "drifting happily along"—recognized the struggle for agricultural fertility as profoundly, if invisibly, rooted in the very processes of biological conflict and interpenetration that animate his children's tales.

It should not be surprising, then, that in "Oinomori," the zone of fertility is always also a zone of danger. By the spring following the resolution of the child abduction crisis, the human presence in the valley looms even larger. The number of children has increased to eleven—the first hints of a Malthusian shadow—and the village has acquired two horses. The presence of draft animals signals increased pressure upon the local woods through more efficient plowing and fertilization. "Because they mixed grass and rotten leaves with horse manure to put in the fields," the narrator tells us, "the millet and barnyard millet grew especially high."[130]

After a good harvest, however, the peasants wake up early one morning to clear new pastures and expand their fields only to find that their hatchets (*nata*), hoes, and all the other tools have been stolen. Again, their survival has come under threat. The forest appeal and search repeats itself, but this time the peasants venture as far as Zarumori (literally, "Basket Mountain") where they find their tools hidden in a mysterious woven basket resting at the foot of an old oak tree. Among the tools sits a new prankster, a "golden-eyed, red-faced mountain man" (*kin-iro no me o shita, kao no makka na yama-otoko*) who simply looks back at the peasants and, in a spirit of weird mischief, yells "Bah!"[131]

The "mountain man" (*yama-otoko*) figure, a deep-forest specter whose characteristically odd skin, eye, and hair color seems to suggest racial difference (among other things), makes frequent appearances not only in Kenji's fiction, but in many of the Tōhoku folk tales made famous by Yanagita Kunio's *Tōno monogatari* (Tales of Tōno, 1910), published fourteen years prior to Kenji's collection. Komori Yōichi recognizes a link between these mythical "wild" men and historical individuals known as *sanka* (or "mountain nomads") who lived in mountains, ravines, and other areas of the periphery, making their living by selling woven goods as they wandered from village to village.[132] For Komori, the basket-weaving mountain man in Kenji's tale represents the memory of a pre–Iron Age hunter-gatherer existence. More than simply another supernatural phenomenon, Kenji's *yama-otoko* becomes, from this perspective, a vestige of Totman's "thirty-thousand-year preagricultural phase" when humans are said to have lived in the woods without substantially altering them. But the mountain man also reminds the reader what the peasants are struggling to maintain: not merely a compact with "nature" or with the "animal world," but with *wildness itself*:

> "Mountain man, please don't play any more tricks on us. We're asking you as a favor, let this be the last of your pranks."
>
> The mountain man stood there very nervously, scratching his head. One by one, the farmers took up their tools and left the mountain.

As they did, the mountain man yelled from the middle of the woods, "How about bringing me some *awamochi*!" At that, he turned quickly and, hiding his head with his hands, retreated deep into the mountains at a run.

The peasants all laughed and went home. Again, they prepared some *awamochi* and took it as an offering to leave at Oinomori and Zarumori.[133]

At this point in the story, the mountains called Oino and Zaru have been irrevocably transformed. No longer thinking of themselves "simply as I," they have acquired names and reputations that bind them to the human world. They have entered into a new kind of history. These delicate mixtures of soil, rock, and gases that have co-evolved for millennia with an equally complex assembly of plants and animals now find themselves inextricably linked with a new type of organic complex: human cultivators who live in their shadow, gather firewood and mushrooms in their woods, leave offerings to their spirits. At the same time, the tiny farming village cannot imagine itself apart from of its wild counterpart. It, too, has been touched by an alien sort of "history," has come to feel the enormous weight of deep time. This is where Kenji's simple child's tale can be said to reflect a dialectical consciousness. In "Oinomori," the people and the land on which they live both evolve "as a consequence of their interpenetration."[134]

Progress and the Struggle for Existence

Inasmuch as "Oinomori" narrates environmental transformation, it speaks the language of Darwinian evolution—even if, in important ways, it moves beyond Darwin's original vision. The question arises: How can we reconcile the ideal of a negotiated balance with what is broadly understood as "evolutionary progress"? Change lies at the heart of the idea of evolution, and therefore entails a certain kind of instability or mutability. It has often proved tempting to assign a normative meaning to Darwin's notion of change, to attribute to Darwin himself a full-throated Victorian faith in progress according to which civilization's encroachment upon the wild might be justified as "advancement," the inevitable result of humanity's superior status over lower forms of life. The history of this misconception is long and no more deeply entrenched than in Japan.

The Japanese translation of the term "evolution" (*shinka*)—compounded of the characters for "advancement" and "change"—signifies "progress" even more explicitly than its English counterpart. Although the word "evolution" did not appear in the first edition of *The Origin of Species*, the term quickly descended, with all of its teleological weight, upon Darwin's theory of natural selection as its most widely recognized moniker.[135] In Japan, the word first appeared in scholarly treatments of Darwin's theory in the first and second decades of Meiji—including Izawa Shūji's *Seishu genshiron* (1879; a translation of Thomas Huxley's *Lectures on the Origin of Species*, 1862) and Ishikawa Chiyomatsu's *Dōbutsu shinkaron* (1883; a translation of Edward Morse's *Theory on the Evolution of Animals*). In his analysis of the importation of Western science into Japan, Scott L. Montgomery describes the newly minted term *shinka* as "an excellent choice" because it embodied both "Darwin's own Victorian view of evolution as a process of continual improvement and, more immediately, the ideology of the Japanese Enlightenment, with its call to a civilizing nationalism."[136] The appeal to Meiji-era ideology built into the term *shinka* prefigures the political and social inflection that would characterize early interpretations of Darwin's theory in Japan, a tendency embodied in the history of its translation and dissemination in the late nineteenth century.

Between 1877 and 1888, only four works on the subject of biological evolution were published in Japan. During these same eleven years, by contrast, at least twenty Japanese translations of Herbert Spencer's loosely "Darwinian" social theories made their appearance. The bulk of all scholarly articles published in Japanese on the subject of "evolution" in the 1880s, in fact, were in the social sciences.[137] It was not until 1896 that Darwin's original *The Origin of Species* appeared in translation as *Seibutsu shigen*, and even then it was published not by a scientific press but by the publisher of an economics journal.[138] It is not surprising then that by the early twentieth century, when Darwin's work began to make an impact as a biological rather than a "social" theory—through the technical and popular writings of scientists like Oka Asajirō—the terms "evolution" (*shinka*), "the struggle for existence" (*seizon kyōsō*), and "survival of the fittest" (*tekisha seizon*) had been indelibly marked as social and political principles. It was as if Darwin's famous oceanic journey and the meticulous research into the animal and plant kingdoms that he spent his life undertaking had all been staged as an elaborate excuse for composing a theory whose *true* object was Victorian society and the fate of the world's modern nations.

Of course, any scientific theory—no matter what it is "about"—is constructed from patterns of meaning and conventions of language inseparable from the historical and ideological conditions of its invention. The phrase "survival of the fittest," for example, which Darwin borrowed from Herbert Spencer and used interchangeably with his own "natural selection," could never be fully extricated from popular ideas about social domination, racial hierarchy, and national belligerence. With this expression, Darwin referred to the survival in nature—over great expanses of time—of features "most suitable" for a particular environment, the principle, he explained, "by which each slight variation, if useful, is preserved."[139] For many non-specialists, however, the term "fittest" came to be understood as a crude signifier for "strongest" (as if physical strength could ward against extinction) and was often misapplied to explain or to justify conflict within or between human societies.

Among Japanese scholars, evolutionary theory had its most reactionary "champion" in Katō Hiroyuki (1836–1916), who was president of Tokyo Imperial University when Edward Morse first introduced Darwin there.[140] In the name of evolution, Katō's *Jinken shinsetsu* (New theory of human rights, 1882) dismissed the very notion of freedom, self-government, or equality as natural rights, claiming to replace these "illusory" and "metaphysical" beliefs with the scientific and philosophical principles developed by Darwin and Spencer. Not satisfied with the term *tekisha seizon*, the literal translation of Spencer's "survival of the fittest," Katō coined his own blunt formula: "the victory of the superior and the defeat of the inferior" (*yūshō reppai*). This heavy-footed phrase, with its implications of improvement through predestined domination, gained enough currency in Meiji Japan to compel Oka Asajirō to address the term's inadequacy as a biological formula in his *Shinkaron kōwa* in 1904.[141]

Of course, even after accounting for these popular misapprehensions and scholarly distortions, Darwinian evolution remains rooted in the social and political conditions of its time. In a sense, what made evolutionary theory so endlessly fertile for later ecological thinking was precisely the ways in which it reflected the contradictions and ideological reversals of European bourgeois society in the mid-nineteenth century. If Darwin's theory of natural selection follows the logic of successive improvement found in Spencer's *Progress: Its Law and Cause*, it also continually counters this progressivism with a conceptual substratum emphasizing structural relationships and balanced interdependence. Even in its classic form, evolutionary theory always held the notion of diachronic progress in tension with the idea of synchronic equilibrium (Darwin's "web of complex relations").[142] Some scholars recognize the ideal of "dynamic stability" as the expression of an emergent bourgeois need to promote a more stable concept of change against the threat of a new and anti-bourgeois revolutionary fervor—the "specter" that was haunting Europe during the years that Darwin wrote his masterpiece.[143] Although the notion of "dynamic equilibrium" is commonly associated not with Darwin's work but with later versions of adaptationism, the image it implies of the natural world as a constantly shifting field of relations had its beginnings as a powerful undertow running through Darwin's original ideas.

So when Darwin speaks of the tendency of "all corporeal and mental endowments" to "progress toward perfection" in the final pages of *The Origin of Species*, his words must be taken as indicative of a relatively weak notion of progress, unmoored from any *absolute* vertical or linear framework.[144] The "onward and upward" thrust of Victorian progress that so many have attributed to Darwin's work was not finally an essential element of his theory. In one of the earlier chapters of *The Origin of Species*, Darwin makes this point clear, explaining that no difficulty presented itself by the "continual existence of lowly organisms" that might otherwise be expected to evolve out of existence, "for natural selection, or the survival of the fittest, does not necessarily include progressive development—it only takes advantage of such variations as arise and are beneficial to each creature under its complex relations of life." It may be for this reason that Darwin uses such terms as "lowly forms" so guardedly throughout this work. In this same passage, he reminds his readers that "every naturalist who has dissected some of the beings now ranked as very low in the scale, must have been struck with their really wondrous and beautiful organisation."[145]

Early on, Darwin evinced a profound awareness of the importance of his own relativizing perspective, his departure from the logic of absolute hierarchies. At times he seems to be moving toward a new relational understanding of objectivity itself, hinting at a biological version of what physicists today call "observer dependence."[146] "It is absurd to talk of one animal being higher than another," he wrote in 1837 in one of his earliest notebooks on the transmutation of species. "*We* consider those, where the cerebral structure/intellectual faculties most developed, as highest. A bee doubtless would when the instincts were."[147] Darwin could not have envisioned the vast network of organic relations so central to his theory of evolution without first accepting bees and other nonhuman beings as fully vested members of the assembly, legitimate "observers."

It remains one of the abiding paradoxes of the history of science that the most scandalously materialist theory of its time—openly exploited to legitimize race-thinking and to denounce universal human equality—seems to have been guided from the start by an equalizing impulse and a deep revulsion toward human arrogance, what Darwin denounced as "our admiration of ourselves."[148] Even as it was being deployed to justify imperialist ambitions in the human realm, Darwin's theory of evolution worked more quietly to dissolve the sacred seal that traditionally surrounded and separated the "human realm" itself. Ideologues like Katō Hiroyuki, willing to believe that humans were "no better than animals" when it came to their relations with each other, were utterly unprepared to accept the much more radical proposal that humans were "no better than animals" when it came to their relations with other animals. But this was at some level what natural selection asked us to believe. Behind Darwin's insistence that we accept species as an "artificial" category "made for convenience,"[149] lurked the specter of a radical kinship: the hypothesis that "all the organic beings which have ever lived on this earth may be descended from some one primordial form."[150] Darwin saw the tendency to privilege humans—our minds, our bodies, our societies—as a profound barrier to understanding speciation. More importantly, for Darwin this intellectual obstacle was itself rooted in a willful act of *ethical* blindness, as he suggests in an unguarded notebook entry, written in his characteristically elliptical and ungrammatical shorthand: "Animals—whom we have made our slaves we do not like to consider our equals. *Do not slave holders wish to make the black man other kind?*"[151]

In the context of this ethical commitment to relationality, Darwin's "progress toward perfection" in the organic world sheds its linear and vertical inflection and begins to acquire what might be called a spherical or radial structure, allowing for an entirely new, ecological grammar. "When we talk of higher orders," he wrote in the final pages of an early notebook, "we should always say, intellectually higher. But who with the face of the earth covered with the most beautiful savannahs & forests dare to say that intellectuality is [the] only aim in this world [?]"[152] At moments like this, Darwin seems on the verge of denying progress altogether, presenting a natural world that does not move through stages of improvement so much as it suffers metamorphoses: the earth as a sort of dream sequence.

And as with dreams, nature sometimes produces fantastic and wondrous results, such as those appurtenances Darwin called "organs of extreme perfection and complication."[153] The idea that the eye "with all of its inimitable contrivances for adjusting the focus to different distances, for admitting different amounts of light, and for the correction of spherical and chromatic aberration" could have been produced by random variations famously disturbed Darwin's faith in natural selection. This was not, however, because "organs of extreme perfection" represented a stage of final optimality that defied the eternal process of becoming at the heart of Darwin's supposedly progressive ideology, as Levins and Lewontin argue, but simply because the expansive time frame and statistical patience required for such complicated and refined results struck Darwin as "insuperable by our imagination."[154] It is not *perfection itself*, in other words, that Darwin describes here as "absurd in the highest degree," but the apparent unlikelihood of such complicated and refined *versions* of perfection ever appearing.

How can the concept of "improvement" be reconciled, then, with what I have called Darwin's departure from linear and vertical notions of progress? In Darwin's evolutionary model, the ceaseless "improvement of each organic being" by natural selection is always described explicitly as occurring "in relation to its organic and inorganic conditions of life."[155] From this point of view, even "perfection" itself must be understood as a *relative* and *unstable* phenomenon. For Darwin, refined sensitivity to light, like intellectuality, could only have been *one* of the world's many "aims," valuable in specific conditions at specific moments in evolutionary history. So life evolves, and thus "progresses" in this limited sense: not forward in a single straight line through absolute stages of improvement, but outward through innumerable, eternally shifting and relative incarnations of perfection.

"The eternally unfinished is the finished," as Kenji himself stated in the final sentences of his 1926 "Nōmin geijutsu" essay.[156] This aphoristic pronouncement highlights what is perhaps the most important parallel between Kenji's Buddhism and Darwinian biology—where the anti-teleological notion of "dynamic stability" meets the Buddhist doctrine of "immanence" captured in the "Nyorai-juryō-bon" chapter of the *Lotus Sūtra* on the "Revelation of the [Eternal] Life of the Tathagata." While the enlightenment of the Buddha is acknowledged in this chapter as a historical occurrence, it is also depicted as an event that transcends the limits of linear narrative: "But since I verily became Buddha, thus have I ever been. . . ."[157] Here, too, progress slips into paradox, emerging as a function of an *eternal* perfection. This is the truly mystical version of evolutionary models of "perfection" and "dynamic equilibrium." But for Kenji, the structural relations defining the contours of this dynamic stability served as the essential core of his literary cosmos.

The language of interdependence that runs throughout *The Origin of Species* is founded precisely on this structural epistemology, a prophetic anticipation of the modernist aesthetic enterprise. Darwin's notoriously Victorian-sounding "struggle for existence," as Oka Asajirō carefully noted in his *Shinkaron kōwa*, implied not only competition between and within species, but also interdependence and cooperation, what Ōsugi Sakae would later describe (after Pyotr Kropotkin) as "mutual aid" (*sōgo fujo*).[158] When understood in this broad sense—"including," as Darwin himself wrote, "dependence of one being on another"—the struggle for existence becomes the embodiment of relational truth extending even to the inorganic realm. The "plant on the edge of a desert is said to struggle for life against the drought," wrote Darwin, "though more properly it should be said to be dependent on the moisture."[159]

The final pages of Oka Asajirō's chapter on the "struggle for existence" (*seizon kyōsō*), a subsection entitled "Seibutsu sōgo no fukuzatsu na kankei" (The complex mutual relations of life), contains an anecdote lifted from Darwin's own experience on a family member's Staffordshire estate. On a broad area of barren land, untouched by cultivation, a single small section had been fenced off and planted with Scotch fir (*momi no ki*). After 25 years, the area inside the fence and the area outside the fence had evolved two entirely different ecosystems. Within the barrier, twelve species of plant that could not be found on the wild heath were thriving; vastly different types of insects lived there, inviting six new species of insectivorous birds unheard of outside the barrier. A single fence and a single species of plant had generated an entirely distinct bio-region.[160]

The teenage Miyazawa Kenji must have thrilled at what Darwin called the "ever-increasing circles of complexity"[161] revealed by this story and many others summarized in Oka's book. Oka outlined the ecological links from cats to mice to bees to flowers in a certain district of England, the interdependent relationship between cattle and a certain kind of fly in a region of Paraguay.[162] Perhaps the most persistent theme running through these ecological portraits was the far-reaching effects of human cultivation upon wild systems. A single fence, a single crop, a new universe.

In a sense, Kenji depicts in "Oinomori" exactly that: the evolution of a new universe. By the end of the tale, the peasants had firmly established their presence in the area: "The next summer arrived. Every flat space had been made into a field. The peasants' houses had wooden storage buildings attached to them and great barns had been built. . . . There were now three horses. Much to everyone's delight, the harvest that fall had been huge."[163]

When the third and final crisis occurs, this time it is the millet itself—every last grain—that disappears from the storage house. The culprit of course is the spirit of Nusutomori ("Thief Mountain"), appearing as a dark human figure who aggressively denies the charge until the gentle and judicious voice of Iwate-san—the volcanic progenitor of the entire region—intervenes.

As its name suggests, Nusutomori—the mountain that steals—might easily be understood as the embodiment of pestilence itself. By absconding with an entire harvest, Nusutomori stands in for every sort of crop invader that forest-edge cultivators might have had to endure then as now: deer that break through the fence, wolves that threaten the horses, sparrows that raid the fields. Although assigning the term "pest" to an animal or an insect might seem to remove it from all moral considerations—invoking the logic of eradication—John Knight has pointed out that "the starting-point of pestilence discourse, when applied to wildlife crop-raiders, is that of a problematic human-animal equivalence or parity." Wildlife pests must be killed or otherwise kept at bay not because they are strange outsiders, but precisely because "they occupy the same trophic level as Man himself." An animal is a pest, in other words, only when it inhabits a similar space and covets similar food. "It is because these animals are, in their material and ecological conditions of existence, continuous with human beings," Knight writes, "that they threaten human livelihoods."[164] If subsistence farmers tend to see crop-destroying wild animals as "essentially equals but in competition," as anthropologist Brian Morris argues, Kenji's tale depicts wildlife pests as equals *because* they are in competition.[165] It is the "because" in this sentence that hints most vividly at the underlying moral insight of Darwin's theory of natural selection.

The story ends here, with the glow of a mythical resolution gently contradicting the darkening horizon of twentieth-century reality. Iwate-san assures the peasants that the grain will be returned, explaining that "Nusutomori only wanted to try his hand at making *awamochi* himself. That's why he stole your millet."[166] Although told presumably to modern readers against the backdrop of expanding industry and the promise of unprecedented destruction of wilderness habitat, the narrative concludes with a portrait of the optimal stability of a legendary past: "From that time on, the mountains and the people were all good friends. And every year, at the beginning of winter, the mountains received their *awamochi*. . . . Depending on the harvest, the amount might be small, but there's nothing that can be done about that. And that is how the great black rock in the middle of Kurosakamori finished his story."[167]

Though characteristically utopian, this tale is clearly neither about "getting back to nature" nor "escaping into the wild," but rather about sustainability in all of its material and spiritual complexity. By the narrative's conclusion, Kenji's primal farming community is solidly established, the valley irreversibly altered by human occupation: this, indeed, is an essential (if not sufficient) element of the story's "happy ending." Though resonant in limited ways with contemporary depth ecology, Kenji's vision of wildlife-cultivator relations finally stands apart from today's high-profile eco-ideologies. Earth First! founder Dave Foreman, for example, also traces the root of environmental problems to the introduction of agriculture. In contrast to Kenji's relatively pragmatic logic, however, Foreman emphasizes the importance of preserving "the wilderness experience," of maintaining the possibility of an atavistic escape into the "Big Outside"—where those with sufficient leisure and physical health might enjoy the Paleolithic way of life.[168] If we view cultivation as essentially and inherently unnatural, William Cronon writes in his critical assessment of Foreman's ideas, "it is hard not to reach the conclusion that the only way human beings can hope to live naturally on earth is to follow the hunter-gatherers back into a wilderness Eden and abandon virtually everything that civilization has given us."[169]

Cronon himself promotes a far less spectacular environmentalism, one that begins at home, with "the wilderness in our own backyards." As with Kenji's fictional depictions of the intermediary *satoyama*, Cronon's ideas emphasize what he calls the "middle ground," the common territory of human and nonhuman occupation, important precisely because of its everyday proximity. "The middle ground is where we actually live. It is where we—all of us, in our different places and ways—make our homes."[170] Idiosyncratically, "Oinomori" seems to anticipate Cronon's position, offering a vision of a cultivating community that manages to live creatively and productively alongside the wild precisely by recognizing the conflicts and debts that join them. This story gives its readers a vision of human civilization that "knows its place" in every sense of that phrase: that knows where it belongs in the geography and knows also to say "please" and "thank you."

To acknowledge a debt is to recognize both difference and connection—Kenji's story allows us to see this paradox. The greatest contribution of this and other important tales in this collection, then, must be understood from the standpoint of epistemology. Narrated from within but also "above" the Darwinian web of relations, both inside and outside the continuum of geologic time, Kenji's simple children's tale exemplifies the paradoxical species of objectivity at the heart of aesthetic modernism and its counterpart in the physical sciences. I have suggested that it was one of Miyazawa Kenji's lasting marks of genius to recognize parallels between the cognitive habits of childhood and the science of relativity. This Einsteinian impulse finds its most powerful incarnation in the realist ambition that lay at the heart of the new science of ecology: to imagine a story *told by the land itself.*

FIVE

Brethren in Pain: Beauty, Objectivity, and the Lives of Bears

If we choose to let conjecture run wild, then animals, our fellow brethren in pain, diseases, death, suffering, and famine—our slaves in the most laborious works, our companions in our amusements—they may partake [of] our origin in one common ancestor—we may be all netted together.

—Charles Darwin, "Notebooks on Transmutation," 1837

Seen for what it is, nature has neither beauty nor ugliness.

—Oka Asajirō, "Iwayuru shizen no bi to shizen no ai," 1905

Oddly, love is the best guarantee against idealization.

—John Berger, *The Shape of a Pocket*, 2001

"Only the mountain has lived long enough to listen objectively to the howl of a wolf."[1] So concluded American conservationist and writer Aldo Leopold when, sometime in the early 1920s as a member of the U.S. Forest Service, he reversed his stance on predator eradication. His opinion was not widely held. In fact, it would not be shared by most game managers for another forty years, according to his biographers.[2] During the very years that Miyazawa Kenji was creating his literary dreamscape of Ihatov, where the organic and the inorganic formed a transparent social unity, Leopold was working in the still-wild Arizona territories evolving his own concept of the "social," promoting a moral vision that "enlarges the boundaries of the community to include soils, waters, plants, and animals. . . ."[3] Like Kenji, who mapped Iwate's frigid peaks, gave voice to its mountains, celebrated the molecular structure of its rivers, Aldo Leopold would famously extend the category of ethics not only to animals and plants, but also *to the land itself.*

In the section of his classic *A Sand County Almanac* (1949) subtitled "Thinking Like a Mountain," Leopold describes the moment of revelation that gave rise to this new ethical model. Although we cannot know the literal truth of this sudden conversion narrative, it is significant that its author traces the origins of his entire "land ethic" to a single instance of eye contact made with a dying wolf—a characteristically modernist conjunction of the visual with the visionary. With the neatness of a myth crafted retrospectively to account for what was almost certainly a more gradual process, Leopold's story attributes to this "ocular" experience the instantaneous force of a moral epiphany.

At the peak of the North American wolf extermination campaign, in which Leopold himself was an enthusiastic participant, the author and several companions had the occasion to shoot and kill from the height of a rimrock an adult wolf and her pups, "a melee of wagging tails and playful maulings," just as they were tumbling into the center of an open flat on the bank of a river. Leopold's description of the incident has the deadpan precision of a massacre remembered: "In those days we had never heard of passing up a chance to kill a wolf. In a second we were pumping lead into the pack, but with more excitement than accuracy: how to aim a steep downhill shot is always confusing. When our rifles were empty, the old wolf was down, and a pup was dragging a leg into impassable slide-rocks."[4]

A common enough occurrence, to be sure, in the early days of the U.S. Forest Service. For Leopold, though, this particular storm of smoke and blood was different from the many that had preceded it. This time, he tells us, something passed from the eyes of the wolf to his own, the shadow of some wordless knowledge. "We reached the old wolf in time to watch a fierce green fire dying in her eyes. I realized then, and have known ever since that there was something new to me in those eyes—something known only to her and to the mountain."[5] We are left to conclude that this "something new" Leopold describes is not merely the chilling recognition of a dark kinship, but the sudden and shocking awareness of the *limits of his own perception.* The remainder of the author's career can be described as the concrete exploration of this single epistemological insight: that the wolf and the land she lives on "know" the world with a mute clarity that rangers, scientists, and poets can only hope to imagine. The predatory single-mindedness reflected that day in the eyes of the wolf, measured against the enormous backdrop of terrestrial time *inscribed in the landscape itself,* left the author with a burning image of this geo-lupine objectivity.

Of course, Leopold was acting as a predator, too, and the reader is left wondering what atavistic feature of the hunt contributed to the author's own latent capacity to "listen objectively to the howl of the wolf." Crucially, Leopold is not renouncing hunting in this passage. Instead, he is revolting against the way in which modern game management—in collaboration with modern science and commerce—has come to objectify the world of living things, to follow the logic of the slaughter. So what can the term "objectively" really mean for Leopold? This chapter will attempt to answer that question by drawing connections between Leopold's notion of objectivity and the realist framework of aesthetic modernism recognizable in Miyazawa Kenji's work. Not coincidentally, a disposition of radical objectivity inherently opposed to the logic of the market finds vivid expression in Kenji's own story of the hunt, "Nametokoyama no kuma" (The bears of Nametokoyama). Resonant with Leopold's account, Kenji's story features its own moral epiphanies unveiled through the paradoxical intimacy of predatory antagonism. For Kenji's fictional hunter—as for the poet and the natural scientist—questions of "beauty" overlap with questions of "accuracy," and, by an apparent contradiction, objectivity is revealed as a stance of profound *involvement.* Human morality emerges finally in this piece as a function of observational clarity. Far from some caricature of holistic identity, however, the objective view of the nonhuman world presented here suggests an acknowledgment of continuity that doubles as a tender acceptance of difference: a simultaneous perception of proximity and distance that approaches what might otherwise be taken for everyday affection.

The Accurate and the Beautiful

Although rooted by his own account in a mystical encounter, Leopold's vision of ecological interdependence was nourished by an accumulation of empirical data cited in the many sketches and essays he would write over the following decades. By the mid-1920s, as the Division of Predatory Animal and Rodent Control in the Bureau of Biological Survey approached its goal of eradicating the wolf, Leopold observed and recorded the devastating effects of "newly wolfless" mountains, overrun by defoliating ungulates. "I now suspect," he wrote later, "that just as a deer herd lives in mortal fear of its wolves, so does the mountain live in mortal fear of its deer."[6]

So what possible connection can be drawn between Aldo Leopold's story about taming the rugged Gila Wilderness of 1920s Arizona, with its titular exhortation to "think like a mountain," and Miyazawa Kenji's children's tale about the primal forests of Tōhoku, told from the perspective of a geological formation? In her own discussion of this very connection between Kenji and Leopold, Karen Colligan-Taylor writes: "What is most remarkable about Kenji's ideas, from an environmental standpoint, is the degree to which they paralleled similar ideologies developed concurrently in the United States which were to form the philosophical basis of the American conservation movement."[7] Mutually innocent of one another's "influence," these historical contemporaries may nonetheless be described as united by the basic impulses of aesthetic modernism itself: not only the logic of material relationality, but also, and *especially*, the gesture toward a diagrammatic objectivity that both accommodates and reaches beyond the boundaries of immediate (or "local") perception.

Though ethical dispositions are notoriously difficult to relate to historical conditions, it may be enough to observe that, like the poets and artists of Japan's and Europe's literary avant-garde—from Hori Tatsuo to Ezra Pound—Kenji and Leopold shared a world of objects, texts, and events that referred, however obliquely, to a network of invisible forces and connections that scholars (myself included) have come to understand as inseparable from "modernity." A cosmos of power grids, train schedules, and telegraph networks, the industrial nation state itself might easily have been understood as both an abstract model for—and concrete evidence of—*natural* interconnectedness. As if echoing Darwin's metaphorically theistic portrait of natural selection "daily and hourly scrutinizing, throughout the world . . . silently and insensibly working, *whenever and wherever opportunity offers*,"[8] contemporary critic Paul Virilio describes "technological culture" as bringing into effect the "three traditional characteristics of the Divine: ubiquity, instantaneity, and immediacy."[9] As I have shown in earlier chapters, electromagnetic technology in the national and imperialist context, with its eerie capacities for "action at a distance," became one of the enabling "theological" conditions of modernity, exemplified and embodied in surrealism, Cubism, and New Sensationism. In important ways, it was also the cultural condition of early twentieth-century ecology.

If writers such as Yokomitsu Riichi experienced the industrial and colonial landscape of the 1920s as an enormous web of invisible forces, the unifying spirit of this geo-polity—its technological holy ghost—was energy. Electromagnetic energy coordinated the movements of armies, connected the fates of national economies, and helped to make possible what Lenin described in 1916 as the "socialization of production."[10] Through its practical effects, energy made "visible" a world of human and material relationships that had previously gone unseen. Paradoxically, though, energy also *embodied* the mysteries of this new observational power: an everyday practical object that itself existed somewhere beyond the reach of corporal perception and could only be depicted *in theory*. It was precisely this ontological flexibility that made energy the heuristic key for the emerging New Ecology and the ethics of environmentalism. In theorizing and promoting his 1949 "Land Ethic," for example, Aldo Leopold depicted the land itself as a sort of "energy circuit":

> Land, then, is not merely soil; it is a fountain of energy flowing through a circuit of soils, plants, and animals. Food chains are the living channels which conduct energy upward; death and decay return it to the soil. The circuit is not closed; some energy is dissipated in decay, some is added by absorption from the air, some is stored in soils, peats, and long-lived forests; but it is a sustained circuit, like a slowly augmented revolving fund of life.[11]

In this very real sense, then, twentieth-century ecology could never have been imagined without the mid-nineteenth-century transition from force physics to energy-field physics. Paradoxically, the practical efforts in nineteenth-century industry to improve efficiency in factory production spawned an energy revolution that ended up providing the most essential theoretical framework for early twentieth-century ecology: the language of interdependence distilled to the notion of energy exchange.[12] The moral insights of Aldo Leopold and Miyazawa Kenji must be understood in this context: not so much as reactions against industrial modernity—though both Leopold and Kenji were often actively critical of its deleterious effects—but rather as furtive expressions of its deep structure.

The New Physics and the New Ecology converged most conspicuously upon the concept of the ecosystem, conceived in 1935 by British botanist Arthur George Tansley. Thermodynamics and chemistry—the most "material" of the physical sciences—lay at the heart of Tansley's ecosystem model, which, according to J. Baird Callicott, "was expressly designed to be the 'field theory' of modern biology."[13] The notion of energy flow—clearly a crucial image for Aldo Leopold—came from several disciplinary sources in the early decades of the century. Geochemistry's focus on "chemical flows between biota, atmosphere, hydrosphere, and lithosphere" had begun to draw connections between the living and nonliving parts of the planet and introduced a literally global perspective to ecology.[14] Soviet geochemist V. I. Vernadsky pushed this holistic approach even further, beginning his now famous treatise *The Biosphere* (1926) with a discussion of the earth's "cosmic surroundings," where he traced the life of the planet to "an infinite diversity of radiations of which the luminous ones that we can see form only an insignificant part." It is not only the biosphere, Vernadsky wrote, "but all conceivable space" that is "penetrated by this immaterial substance, radiation." In this almost mystical opening passage, Vernadsky places at the center of his theory a permeating species of energy "ceaselessly diffused everywhere, round about us and through us."[15] Literally and metaphorically, for Vernadksy and his contemporaries all over the industrialized world, energy was in the air.

It is highly unlikely that Miyazawa Kenji ever read the works of Vernadsky, whose *Essays on Geochemistry* were not published in Japanese translation until 1933, the year of Kenji's death.[16] But the galactic imagery of Kenji's "Ginga tetsudō no yoru" and in his lecture outline, "Nōmin geijutsu gairon kōyō" (delivered in 1926, the year *The Biosphere* was published) share the cosmic ambition of Vernadsky's holism without losing sight of its *local* significance. If "to live justly and strongly means to be aware within ourselves of the Milky Way Galaxy," as Kenji proclaimed in his lecture on the rural arts, this awareness must make itself felt *on the ground*, so to speak.[17] For Kenji, what connects the dirt beneath the farmers' feet with the stars above their heads—the flesh of a living bird with the movement of distant galactic gases—was the cycle of energy and nutrient exchange. "A heron is made of congealed sand from the River of Heaven," the bird catcher explains to Giovanni in "Ginga tetsudō no yoru," "so they always come back to the river."[18] It is probably significant that both Kenji and Vernadsky first conceived of their respective visions of the world as soil scientists, for soil is where the barrier between the living and the nonliving is most ambiguous, where life seems most clearly embedded in the molecular dynamics of energy. The earth's crust, Vernadsky argued, "must not be considered as a domain of matter alone, but as a region of energy also, a place of transformation of the planet by external cosmic forces."[19]

Physiology, the second contributing discipline to the ecosystem concept, added the study of animal nutrition and plant growth to this geochemical perspective, culminating in the American zoologist Raymond Lindeman's classic 1942 study of Cedar Bog Lake near the University of Minnesota.[20] Focusing on the lake's dynamic processes, Lindeman concluded that the tiny body of water was indeed an ecosystem. Not surprisingly, as ecological historian Frank Benjamin Golley observes, the "idiom in which [Lindeman] expressed this process was energy."[21] For Kenji, understanding our own animal bodies as embedded in a network of "energy circuits" carried fundamentally ethical—even religious—implications. In the original draft of the poem "Gorin tōge" (Gorin pass, 1924), collected in revised form in the second volume of *Haru to shura: shinshō suketchi* (Spring and Asura: mental sketch, 1925), the author candidly (and somewhat hesitantly) struggles to reconcile Buddhist terminology with modern chemistry and physics.

The poem describes a journey along a path that crosses the mountainous border between the cities of Tōno and Esashi, southeast of Kenji's native Hanamaki.[22] A "five-ring" (*gorin*) pagoda looms at the crest of the trail, giving the pass its name. As the narrator begins to contemplate the meaning of this relatively common sight, he finds himself confronting the power of an ancient cosmic picture. The five rings of a "five-ring pagoda" are meant to represent what Buddhist cosmology identifies as the world's most basic material elements, the "Five Great Things" (*godai*): earth, water, fire, wind, and emptiness. Pagoda-shaped monuments and grave markers constructed from stacks of variously shaped stone blocks or "rings" had dotted the Japanese landscape since the Kamakura period (1185–1333), but the poet now looked upon the monument at Gorin Pass with the eyes of a modern artist, transformed by twentieth-century science.[23] Accepting each block as a stand-in for an essential material element, the narrator struggles to meet the five-ring pagoda on its own terms—as a compressive model of the universe itself:

> The Five Rings: earth, water, fire, wind, and emptiness
> The one called "emptiness" unites them all
> I guess we might call it "vacuum"
> And fire, "energy"
> Earth, perhaps, "the basis of all solids"
> Water, "the basis of liquids"
> And wind might be thought of as "the foundation of all gases"
> And all the world and all of us
> And mind itself is this
> Nothing has changed since long ago
>
> To say this even of a cloud
> Is to call it simply a vacuum
> But to our senses
> Its vapors are wind
> Its liquids, water
> Its solids, atomic particles
> And the energy of its motion
> Its heat and its electricity are its "fire"
> And I too am that
> And the village children too
> (Who boast that they can split this oak tree)
> I and he
> The cloud, the rock
> Are all just *karma*
> The world, in short
> Is simply *karma*
>
> When I consider each flake of snow
> Its substance, its shape, its course, position, and time
> As nothing other than *karma* itself
> My heart falls silent[24]

In the final version of this poem—included in published collections today—the substance of this baroque (and relatively clumsy) meditation is distilled to four elegant lines:

A wonderful taxonomy
All matter reduced to electrons
Electrons to another form of vacuum
Nothing at all has changed today[25]

What could be at stake in this transparent effort to reconcile chemistry with *karma*? From the final quoted lines of the earlier draft, it becomes clear that this much-cited poem emerges from a struggle that is "environmental" in the most basic sense. This poem's portrait of the natural world depends on the inseparability of the material and the ethical, a disposition echoed by the unsentimental and counter-teleological laws of *karma* itself. What sends the poet into awe-struck silence (*kokoro ga bō to naru*) when he considers the shape and position of a single snowflake—and the path it follows as it floats to earth—is its connection *through unseen physical laws* to an enormous, equally invisible network of *moral* relations. If much of green theory has reduced modernity's environmental crisis to a question of values, as John Bellamy Foster has argued, the power of Kenji's work lay in its poetic capacity to recognize the roots of these values in material interrelations, an insight that Foster identifies with Marx himself: the capacity to "understand how spiritual conceptions, including our spiritual connections to the earth, are related to our material, earthly conditions."[26] The cloud, the rock, and "all the world and all of us" live ethically significant lives by virtue of material interconnectedness, what Marx called "metabolic relations."[27] It is in *this* sense that the modern notion of "vacuum" and the Buddhist concept of "emptiness" (*kū*) become particularly productive. Modern physics understands objects and events as rooted in an evolving network of relations, and Buddhism's "emptiness" applies a similar logic to the realm of ethics. "According to Buddhist philosophy," writes Sarah Strong in her analysis of this poem, "emptiness (*sūnyata*) is not 'nothingness' or 'empty space' but rather the absence of any *independently* existent things."[28]

Critic and physicist Saitō Bun'ichi recognizes in this early draft of "Gorin tōge" the enormous influence of Kenji's well-thumbed chemistry textbook *Kagaku honron* by Katayama Masao. By depicting the material composition of a cloud as ontologically continuous with the physical substance of the narrator himself, Saitō argues, this poem reflects the "principle of continuity" (*renzoku no hōsoku*) at the heart of chemical thermodynamics—in particular, the law of the conservation of energy, which reveals the formal "state" of any object to be ephemeral. As molecules gather energy ice becomes water, water becomes vapor, cooling again to crystallize into a snowflake: energy *moves* but never diminishes. "Matter can change shape, over and over," Saitō observes. "It has that Protean character. Kenji saw this. And living things too, are they not also made of matter?"[29] Just below the surface of the poem's openly Buddhistic theme, then, is the outline of a far-reaching ecological vision. If Arthur Tansley's ecosystem model was born not of biology but of "thermodynamic physics," as Donald Worster has suggested, Kenji's own ethical vision seems, in important ways, to have shared this theoretical parentage.[30]

As with the writings of his American contemporary Aldo Leopold, Miyazawa Kenji's portrait of the material world departs from what J. Baird Callicott calls "object-ontology": the habit of viewing the world as made up of distinct, independently existing objects. Such a habit, Callicott observes in his discussion of Leopold, "is inappropriate to an ecological description of the natural environment," which more properly regards objects as "ontologically subordinate to 'events' and/or 'flow patterns' and/or 'field patterns.'"[31] This observation is given a broader cultural reading in as comparative analysis by philosopher Steve Odin, who identifies deep parallels between Leopold's "Land Ethic" and Japanese Buddhism. For Odin, though, it is not merely the inclusiveness of Leopold's ethic or his reliance on a "field paradigm of reality" that underscores his affinities with Japanese Buddhism, but that the world he describes acquires a fundamentally *aesthetic* meaning. According to Odin, Leopold's ecological masterpiece *A Sand County Almanac* is first and foremost an aesthetic treatise, reducible to the proposition that, in Odin's words, "our moral love and respect for nature is based on an aesthetic appreciation of the beauty and value of land."[32]

But this formulation that links "aesthetic appreciation" directly and unproblematically to "beauty" misses what is truly revolutionary—and truly modernist—about early twentieth-century ecology. In a certain sense, Odin's assessment of Aldo Leopold remains rooted in the very opposition that Leopold's ecology was striving to overcome: between factual accuracy as the domain of science and beauty as the domain of art. While Leopold does indeed refer in the "Foreword" to the 1949 edition of this work to a potential "esthetic harvest" of the land (and "esthetic" concerns remain central throughout), it soon becomes clear that one of the basic accomplishments of this rhetorical masterpiece is a redefinition of "beauty" itself as inseparable from "accuracy," a position consistent with the realist impulse I have identified with high modernism.[33] For Leopold, the central achievement of ecology's radical logic was the cultivation of an *ocular reorganization*—a new way of seeing the land as a coalescence of previously hidden material connections that are at once ethical, aesthetic, and scientific.[34]

Leopold's reassessment of the romantic figure of Daniel Boone, for example, presents the American frontiersman as laboring under the severe limitations of his own historically conditioned senses. For Leopold, Boone's reaction to the outdoors of eighteenth-century America was necessarily rooted in the literalist empirical data of an uninformed "mental eye":

> Daniel Boone's reaction depended not only on the quality of what he saw, but on the quality of the mental eye with which he saw it. Ecological science has wrought a change in the mental eye. It has disclosed origins and functions for what to Boone were only facts. It has disclosed mechanisms for what to Boone were only attributes. We have no yardstick to measure this change, but we may safely say that, as compared with the competent ecologist of the present day, Boone saw only the surface of things. The incredible intricacies of the plant and animal community—the intrinsic beauty of the organism called America, then in the full bloom of her maidenhood—were as invisible and incomprehensible to Daniel Boone as they are today to Mr. Babbitt.[35]

For Leopold, it is precisely the "development of the perceptive faculty"[36] that constitutes the primary ethical labor of ecology. As with Miyazawa Kenji's chemical excursus in "Gorin tōge," Leopold's *A Sand County Almanac* depended upon the observational expansion of twentieth-century science to promote its ethical program, a new willingness to theorize underlying laws and forces, to support (without the benefit of direct observation) the reality of invisible entities, processes, and fields. Inseparably "scientific" and "aesthetic," the essential contribution of this work revolves around the ethical implications enabled (but not necessitated) by this modernist epistemology. "When we see the land as a community to which we belong," Leopold explains, "we may begin to use it with love and respect. There is no other way for land to survive the impact of mechanized man, nor for us to reap from it the esthetic harvest it is capable, under science, of contributing to culture."[37]

It is the phrase "under science" that highlights the modernist inflection of Leopold's "esthetic harvest." It is no longer enough to be beautiful, in other words; an "esthetic harvest" has also to be "true," and in this sense facticity occupies the center of a new species of aesthetic pleasure. Leopold's work calls for a *scientifically informed* aesthetic imagination as the starting point of an expanded ethics: a fusion of the visual with the visionary. Leopold and Kenji share striking similarities, then, precisely through their common promotion of an aesthetics of accuracy. Behind Kenji's struggle with proper terminology in "Gorin tōge" operates not only a clear belief in a reality beyond direct observation—real connections articulated by the convenience of a spectral, overarching "law"—but also an utterly sincere commitment to referential accuracy:

> To say this even of a cloud
> Is to call it simply a vacuum
> But to our senses
> Its vapors are wind
> Its liquids, water
> Its solids, atomic particles
> And the energy of its motion
> Its heat and its electricity are its "fire"[38]

It is no mere metaphor that the poet is wrestling with here, but the *literal* composition of reality: solid, liquid, gas, energy—and connecting them all, the vacuum of space. Reflecting Ezra Pound's quintessentially modernist identification of "bad art" with "inaccurate art," Kenji's descriptive struggle makes clear the connection between this aesthetic disposition and arguably the most important ethical development of the twentieth century.

The modernist fusion of art and accuracy and the deep relationship between science and aesthetics that it suggests is foreshadowed by some of Japan's earliest figures in evolutionary theory. Darwinian biologist Oka Asajirō—whose work formed the foundation of Kenji's understanding of natural selection—engaged directly with this question in a 1905 essay, "Iwayuru shizen no bi to shizen no ai" (Nature's so-called beauty and the so-called love of nature, 1905).[39] Oka rejected as a scientific fallacy the pedagogical consensus of his Meiji contemporaries that one of the goals of teaching natural history (*hakubutsugaku*) should be to "get the students to admire the beauty of nature and, accordingly, to awaken in them a feeling of love for natural things."[40] However widely held even among Japanese natural scientists themselves, he argued, such a view perpetuates the erroneous idea that nature is, in fact, "beautiful" and should be loved as such. "If one observes nature without prejudice (*kyoshin heiki de*)," Oka wrote, "there are of course aspects that seem beautiful; but at the same time there are also many parts of nature by which we cannot help being repelled."[41] It is precisely because the term "nature" (*shizen*) in Oka's argument is all-inclusive that the notion of its beauty is rendered absurd. Demonstrating this inclusiveness with a brief portrait of nature as it might be encountered in any suburb of late Meiji Tokyo, Oka's "objective" depiction produces a jarring and compressive effect that can only be described (significantly) as *surreal*:

> If one ventures to the outskirts of the city in order to observe nature, one might find scattered in a wild meadow next to the bones of a cow or a horse, the corpse of a cat in the first stages of decay—with its hide torn open and its bowels spilling out, all of it releasing an incredible stench. And next to that, a beautiful violet might be blooming. And alongside of that, some fresh dog feces might be piled high. In other words, a small-scale model (*mihon*) of nature.[42]

On the one hand, Oka is engaging here in a familiar struggle to introduce into Meiji educational debate the relatively new—and still counterintuitive—notion of the disciplinary limits of scientific endeavor, to remind his fellow scientists and educators that questions of beauty are simply beyond the scope of natural science, the "goal" of which, he observed, "is simply to understand nature just as it is" (*ari no mama*).[43] On the other hand, and more furtively, this essay seems to offer what amounts to a redefinition of beauty itself, informed precisely by the values of objectivity and accuracy at the heart of scientific inquiry.

Even while Oka characterizes aesthetic concerns as wholly determined by history and culture ("time" and "place")—and thus distinct from the presumably universal and permanent "truths" of science—his essay is most interesting when it is describing the aesthetic effects of scientific endeavor itself.[44] Natural science, with its habits of penetrating "more deeply" and with greater "precision" into nature than nonscientific activity, he wrote, is apt to discover beauty hidden in phenomena commonly viewed as ugly, as well as ugliness in phenomena that—"when viewed on the surface only"—are commonly seen as beautiful.[45] This passage serves to remind readers that evolutionary science is concerned not merely with empirically literal renderings of sensory details, but with underlying laws and mechanisms. The natural scientist *magnifies* details in order to extrapolate hidden structures; invisible truths are mined from visible deceptions. It is possible to see here the faint shadow of a modernist disposition, of an aesthetics that has lost its traditional connection with beauty and taken on another value altogether: a profound faith in a *higher* form of referential fidelity. Accuracy means precision (*seisai*)—an ever finer rendering of the world around us—but it also means "truth" (*shin*) in this realist sense. Oka's celebration of the supremacy of science hints subtly at the possibility of an "aesthetic" that operates beyond beauty and ugliness. "In the end," Oka concludes, "nature contains merely what it contains. Seen for what it is, nature has neither beauty nor ugliness."[46]

For Oka, this move from beauty to "truth" represents the transcendent hope of a thoroughgoing objectivity, squarely in the Enlightenment tradition. Not surprisingly, he sees the rise of science as suffused with ethical consequences as well. Referring to the classic triumvirate of truth, goodness, and beauty, Oka depicts truth (in the sense of scientific factuality) as the only human value independent of history and culture: "It is by standards we carry ourselves that we measure a thing and describe its beauty or its moral quality. By contrast, it is with truth alone that the standard exists in nature and not in ourselves."[47] Accordingly, Oka argues, science ought to be understood not merely as one discipline among others, but as the foundation of aesthetics and ethics.

It is even more important, however, that for Oka it is not only science's commitment to factuality, but its capacity for *reflexivity* that constitutes this supremacy. "Knowing humanity's position in nature (*shizen ni okeru jinrui no ichi o shiru no wa*) is the foundation of all ethical thought," Oka asserts toward the end of the essay, invoking a refrain that runs through much of his work on evolution. "But in order to know this, we must first know nature just as it is, and humans just as they are."[48] Thus, however problematic Oka's reliance upon a Platonic ideology of "objectivity" appears to us today—an ideology embodied in the much-repeated mimetic phrase "just as it is" (*ari no mama*)—it is important to note a powerful anti-idealism at work in this essay, an uncanny (if inadvertent) anticipation of modernist epistemology. For Oka, seeing an object in nature "for what it is" means first seeing ourselves for what *we* are *in relation to* that object. Just below the surface of Oka's naïve metaphysics of "universal and eternal truth," then, runs a Darwinian undertow that acts to relativize this objective world, presenting all human experience as a "local" rendering of the larger scheme. By acknowledging the limits of human perception—and by understanding these limits as governed by an accurately knowable "position in nature"—Oka's work begins to resemble modernism's idiosyncratically *realist* disposition: the ambition both to accommodate and to transcend the boundaries of human experience.

Compare Darwin's own discussion of nature's beauty in *The Origin of Species* more than four decades earlier. In a passage that defends his theory against the belief of his detractors that certain structures in nature "have been created for the sake of beauty, to delight man or the Creator," Darwin reveals the most subversive dimension of his theory. Admitting that such a doctrine "if true, would be absolutely fatal to my theory," he responds not by denying beauty in nature, but by removing beauty from its anthropocentric (and theistic) moorings, placing it squarely at the center of his own ecocentrically utilitarian doctrine.[49] "Flowers rank amongst the most beautiful productions of nature," he observes, "but they have been rendered conspicuous in contrast with the green leaves, and in consequence at the same time beautiful, so that they may be easily observed by insects." He makes a similar argument for fruit, such as ripe strawberry or cherry, whose beauty he considers beyond question. "But this beauty serves merely as a guide to birds and beasts, in order that the fruit may be devoured and matured seeds disseminated." Paradoxically, then, Darwin's emphasis on the instrumental dimension of beauty ends up underscoring the *aesthetic* inflection of his own utilitarianism. By understanding "the sense of beauty in its simplest form"—that is, as a response common to humans, insects, birds, and other animals—Darwin introduces a radical expansion of Kant's *sensus communis*, indicating a primal sensibility that unites humans not only with each other, but also with the greater nonhuman community.[50]

Few passages in *The Origin of Species* reflect more clearly the differences between Darwin's utilitarianism and the instrumental principle associated with industrial capitalism. It is not simply that "form follows function" in the sense of Louis H. Sullivan's famous 1896 modernist design dictum, but that form and function stand in a dialectical relation to one another, that they evolve together.[51] In fact, as Darwin's notion of "divergence" suggests, it would be more accurate to say that, in nature, form and function *find* each other. The narrow instrumentalism implied by the idea of "design" itself is wholly inadequate to the logic of evolution. Thus, even while arguing that beauty exists neither for its own sake nor for the sake of human enjoyment but rather as a function of the struggle for survival, Darwin leaves conspicuously open the final question: what is the function of survival? For what could be less instrumentally explicable than the image of life itself? By accepting the flourishing of life as its unquestioned foundation—*survival for its own sake*—Darwin's vision of the natural world stands profoundly opposed to the goal-oriented ethos of industrial capitalism. From Darwin's "utilitarian" perspective, wild nature in all its fecundity and diversity replaces artistic beauty as a powerful, if latent, critique of the modern world. Terry Eagleton hints at this critical connection between aesthetics and the "idea of nature" in a passage from his book, *After Theory*:

> In its ruthlessly instrumental logic, [capitalism] has no time for the idea of nature—for that whose whole existence consists simply in fulfilling and unfolding itself, purely for its own sake and without any thought of a goal. This is one reason why this social order has a boorish horror of art, which can be seen as the very image of such gloriously pointless fulfillment. It is also one reason why aesthetics has played such a surprisingly important moral and political role in the modern age.[52]

Thus speaks modern art to evolutionary science, and each gives to each a defensive stance against modernity. Art provides the boldness of a "gloriously pointless fulfillment," while science offers the humble awareness of the provincialism of human experience. It is important to remember in this context that Darwin did not merely absorb the logic of aesthetics into his theory, but offered a reflexively "objective" view of beauty itself—one of his boldest statements against homocentrism:

> Were the beautiful volute and cone shells of the Eocene epoch, and the gracefully sculptured ammonites of the Secondary period, created that man might

ages afterwards admire them in his cabinet? Few objects are more beautiful than the minute siliceous cases of the diatomacae: were these created that they might be examined and admired under the higher powers of the microscope?[53]

Yet this radical decentering of the human perspective only seems to intensify the poignancy of the human experience depicted here. Millennia of evolution gather toward the moment when the scientist admires a shell in her cabinet or wonders at the symmetry of an alga's secretions. Far from denying these uniquely human responses, Darwin seems rather to attribute new meaning to their singularity. Beauty serves a function in the larger "struggle for existence," but it is also always *experienced* locally, where it is not apparently *for* anything. In the field or in the laboratory an object is encountered "up close," disjoined from the big picture. And although it is part of the natural scientist's observational discipline to reconcile local experience to global function, Darwin's illustration serves to remind us that neither view is wholly reducible to the other. If all objects and creatures play a role in the system, this can never fully explain the unique presence of each. In fact, it is only by accommodating *both* of these aspects that the ecologist arrives at the sort of "objectivity" theorized by Leopold and practiced by Kenji. Through the poetry of "gracefully sculptured ammonites" and the classic harmonies of "siliceous cases of the diatomacae," Darwin's reader confronts the seemingly unscientific yet irrepressible phenomenon named in the second half of Oka Asajirō's title: the "so-called love of nature."

Love and Objectivity

If Oka expected his fellow scientists to view human beings as merely a tiny part of a larger web of organic and inorganic relations, the emotional and cognitive disposition required by such a self-effacing objectivity comes close to the very "love of nature" he denied. Here, too, the poet and the biologist share the profound discipline of daily practice: the modernist vigilance against idealization. "Contrary to the adage that love is blind," writes Terry Eagleton in his own discussion of ethics and objectivity, "it is because love involves a radical acceptance that it allows us to see others for what they are."[54] To see an object or a being as a fragment in a larger network of relations, without losing sight of the thing itself in all of its everyday particularity, requires an observational honesty familiar to both scientist and poet—and certainly shared by Aldo Leopold and Miyazawa Kenji. It is exactly this attitude that art critic John Berger refers to as "the toughness of an everyday tenderness" when describing the drawings of Vincent Van Gogh. "I can think of no other European painter," Berger observes, "whose work expresses such a stripped respect for everyday things without elevating them, in some way, without referring to salvation by way of an ideal which the things embody to serve."[55] When applied to Berger's analysis, the term "realism" takes on the deep significance of its colloquial usage: the realism associated with farmers, carpenters, and groundskeepers. "The chair is a chair, not a throne. The boots have been worn by walking. The sunflowers are plants, not constellations. The postman delivers letters. The irises will die." It was this observational nakedness, Berger tells us, from which emerged Van Gogh's "capacity to love, suddenly and at any moment, what he saw in front of him," this nakedness that explains why the painter himself is loved by so many.[56]

Berger's discussion of Van Gogh captures the baffled tenderness of Darwin's own observational posture evident in the passage quoted above. Across the dark expanse of deep time, the evolutionary biologist admires a shell's beauty even while recognizing it "for what it is" (to borrow Oka's phrase): neither beautiful nor ugly in the conventional sense. Beauty here amounts to a flash of insight not only into an object's structural elegance but also into its self-sufficiency, its relative indifference to human appreciation. It is the peculiar yield of Darwin's discussion of beauty that a specimen's appeal to human sensibility is revealed as *both* accidental and profoundly meaningful. The scientist's eye, no less than the painter's, must struggle to make sense of a world that *exists for itself*, yet is at the same time deeply connected to human history. Aldo Leopold and Miyazawa Kenji seem both to have absorbed this insight as a far-reaching ethical conviction: an "ocular" disposition that focuses not upon idealized objects and beings, but upon the *relations* of those objects and beings to ourselves and to each other.

No story better illustrates the politics of this form of "objectivity" than Miyazawa Kenji's darkly beautiful "Nametokoyama no kuma" (The bears of Nametokoyama). Unpublished during his lifetime, this children's tale represents both a culmination of Kenji's literary meditation on human-wildlife relations and a significant departure from many of the author's other fictional pieces. Set in the modern (though faintly legendary) past, "Nametokoyama" tells the story of a hunter named Fuchizawa Kojūrō who works the inaccessible mountainous region above Ōzora Falls northwest of Hanamaki, making his living selling bearskins and bear's gallbladder (*kuma no i*) to a merchant in town. Plagued by doubts about his trade but also trapped by a poverty specific to the new institutional and economic organization of the Meiji state, Kojūrō's great love for the animals he kills and his uncanny ability to understand their thoughts generates both the drama and the political content of this story.

Critical less of hunting per se than of the trading of body parts for cash, "Nametokoyama" can be read finally as a keenly insightful attack on capitalism and the modern state. The essence of Kenji's radicalism is contained in the story's central and charismatic figure of Kojūrō himself, a human predator endowed with the tragic capacity to understand the needless suffering and destruction generated when living things are made into commodities. Persuaded to spare the life of one bear on the condition that the animal give itself up for slaughter in two years' time, Kojūrō evinces a profoundly "un-modern" commitment to interspecific fair play, accepting his own death by mauling with equanimity at the story's end. Elegant and spare, the narrative itself reflects this tenderly objective "total view." The story of the hunter is also necessarily a story of the *hunted* and of the *place* they both inhabit in the land:

> It's really something, all this business about the bears of Nametokoyama. Nametokoyama is a large mountain, and it is up there where the Fuchizawa River begins. For most of the year on a typical day, this mountain breathes in and out cold mists and clouds. All around it too, the peaks are like blue-black sea slugs or green sea turtles. Somewhere in the middle of this mountain, a great cavern opens up. At the mouth of that cavern, the Fuchizawa River becomes a waterfall, suddenly dropping with a roar about 300 feet into a thicket of cypress and maple.
>
> These days no one ever walks along the Nakayama Highway, so it is full of nettles and butterburs, and there are fences in the road to keep cows from climbing up its slope. But if you were to trudge through the brush for just six miles or so, you would hear something like the sound of wind crossing the peak of the mountain. Looking carefully, you would see something strange and slender and white tumbling down the mountain, raising a cloud of mist. That would be Nametokoyama's Ōzora Falls. And people say that a long time ago, there were all kinds of bears tramping around up there. The truth is, I have never seen Nametokoyama myself, nor any bear's gallbladder. I have

only imagined these things from what people tell me. All of this could be untrue, for all I know, but I myself believe it. Anyway, bear's gallbladder from Nametokoyama is quite well-known.

The gallbladder of a bear is good for curing stomach aches and healing injuries. For ages, there has been a sign hanging at the entrance to the Namari hot springs: "We sell bear's gallbladder from Nametokoyama." So it must be true that there are bears up there roaming the valleys of Nametokoyama with their red tongues hanging out and their cubs wrestling with each other until one of them gets annoyed and boxes the other's ears. It was these animals that the famous bear hunter Fuchizawa Kojūrō used to kill, one after the other.[57]

These opening paragraphs display both typicality and singularity in Kenji's body of work. Characteristic of the author's tales of Ihatov, the setting for "Nametokoyama" is a conglomeration of real and imagined geography. Although there does exist a mountain known by locals as Nametoko northwest of the Toyosawa dam, near the headwaters of the Toyosawa River (called the Fuchizawa River in this story), the name "Nametokoyama" does not appear officially on any map of the region. Kenji scholar Hara Shirō tells us that in Kenji's fictional world it is more accurate to think of Nametokoyama as the whole area encompassing Nakayama Pass, Ōzora Falls, and Katsurazawa.[58] Whatever the geographical referents, this passage is clearly meant to evoke the most remote forests of the region. We are given a rugged and lonely landscape shrouded in cold fogs, fenced off from wandering livestock, protected by thorny undergrowth, and inhabited by bears. Known in Japanese as *tsukinowaguma* ("crescent moon bear" for the characteristic white mark decorating its chest)—and not to be confused with the larger brown bear, or *higuma*, of Hokkaido (*Ursus arctos yezoensis*)—the Japanese black bear (*Ursus thibetanus japonicus*) originally ranged across the islands of Honshu, Kyushu, and Shikoku. Throughout the twentieth century, as suitable habitats have atrophied, black bear distribution has grown uneven, confining itself largely to the elevated forests of central and eastern Japan, including those of Kenji's native Iwate Prefecture. This animal's need for space (with annual home ranges reported between 30 and 70 square kilometers) makes it particularly vulnerable to the effects of modernization. Today the black bear has disappeared completely from Kyushu and Shikoku.[59] This history of decline—of ursine incompatibility with human settlement—infuses Kenji's story from the beginning. Through their association with solitude and remoteness, the image of bears "tramping around up there" serves as an organic embodiment of what Roy Bhaskar calls "intransitive objects of knowledge."[60] From its opening sentences, the tale draws our attention to the connection between objective knowledge and imagination.

It has long been understood among the farmers and foresters of Tōhoku that the black bear's invisibility is an essential part of its existence and a key to its survival. The Japanese black bear lives—or attempts to live—its life beyond the reach of direct human detection, a living symbol of the deep wild or *okuyama.* Increased bear sightings in Iwate today are indicative of a *decline* in numbers, not an increase: a sign of displacement from traditionally remote habitats that are disappearing with monocultural forestry methods, the construction of ski slopes, and other effects of capitalist development.[61] The casually healthy bear population implied by the opening lines of Kenji's story (*kuma ga gocha-gocha ita sō da*) carries the mystery of this intransitive existence, suggesting a phenomenon that is "truest" when *unseen* by human eyes. Anthropologist John Knight has remarked that, in his many years researching human-wildlife relations on the Kii Peninsula—much of that time spent "in and around the forest"—neither he nor the majority of local residents has ever seen a wild bear. "Despite this," he continues, "the bear remains the most impressive animal in the forest, one that is much talked about by villagers."[62]

It is critical to Kenji's story that the world of these secretive creatures can only be comprehended through an act of *imagined* infiltration. The narrator asks the reader to imagine crossing fences, trudging miles through the bush to listen for the sound of Ōzora Falls. Highlighting the speculative nature of the story to follow, the work structures its contents around an act of *belief.* "All of this could be untrue, for all I know," the narrator announces, "but I myself believe it." In contrast with many of Kenji's other wilderness tales, there is no nonhuman informant to "record" and "translate" here. The story of Kojūrō has been imparted to the narrator neither by a rock (as in "Oinomori") nor by the wind (as in "Shishi odori no hajimari"). In fact, as Amazawa Taijirō has observed, although the content of the story reaches the narrator indirectly—"I have never seen Nametokoyama myself, nor any bear's gallbladder"—its original source, the "true master narrator" (*shin no katari nushi*), is never disclosed.[63]

This transformation of hearsay into imagined reality also generates the mythically ambiguous time frame of the tale, what Amazawa calls a "trans-temporal present" (*chōjiteki genzai*).[64] The statement "people say that a long time ago, there were all kinds of bears tramping around up there" is followed by a description of the signboard advertising bear's gallbladder, taken to indicate the bears' *continuing presence.* The narrative makes clear here the connection not only between a conceivable past and a living present, but also—and more powerfully—between bear cubs horsing around in the back country far beyond the purview of village life, and the observable "evidence" of dusky medicinal cures stored in shadowy cabinets at hot spring inns in the author's time (or sold by traditional apothecaries in our own). Built into the very structure of the tale, in other words, are all the uncertainties and ambiguities associated with the paradoxically human struggle to grasp the intransitive: the effort to depict "objectively" the experience of nonhuman beings, to conceptualize the historical relevance of unobservable entities and events.

The essential humanness of this impulse emerges too in the roughness of the story's language and tone. The use of informal grammatical endings in "Nametokoyama," distinct from the more distant *desu/masu* endings of his *Chūmon no ōi ryōriten* collection (a common style for children's fiction), accompanies the narrator's occasional indulgences in emotional interjection marked by the boyish first-person masculine pronoun "*boku.*" The narrator is intimately involved with the characters and events of this tale. Amazawa sees the "roughness" (*araarashisa*) of this approach as a response to the story's protagonist, Fuchizawa Kojūrō himself. Indeed, the image of Kojūrō constitutes another divergence from common patterns in Kenji's fiction. Neither a farmer who has ventured into a wild frontier in order to "settle" it (as in "Oinomori"), nor a civilized pilgrim glimpsing the wild during a limited sojourn (as in "Shishi odori no hajimari"), Kojūrō is a hunter who makes his living in the deep forest, is at ease with wildness, and is a recognized member of the wild community:

> Fuchizawa Kojūrō was a sturdy old man with squinted eyes and a swarthy complexion. His chest was like a barrel and his palms were as big and thick as the handprints of Bishamon used to cure the sick at shrines in Kitajima. In the summer, Kojūrō would put on leggings and raingear made from the bark of a linden tree. Taking up a forester's hatchet of the sort used by the wild moun-

tain natives of Taiwan and an enormous blunderbuss resembling those introduced to Japan by the Portuguese, he would walk with his powerful golden-haired hound by his side, covering the whole area from Nametokoyama to Shidoke Valley, from Mitsumata to Mount Sakai, from Mamiana Woods to Shirazawa. The area was thick with trees, so climbing into the valley was like passing through the center of a dark tunnel. At times, there would be a sudden burst of green and yellow light, and sometimes the sun would shine down like a flower in bloom. Through this place Kojūrō moved along deliberately just as if he were walking through his own house. His dog would run ahead, scrambling along cliffs, plunging into the eerie, sluggish waters of a deep pool and swimming with all his might until he climbed out onto the rock of the opposite shore. There, with his body shivering and his hair on end, he would shake off the water, twitch his nose, and wait for his master. Kojūrō followed, moving through the water with a white wave curling above his knees like the ones depicted on folding screens. He moved with his legs straight out like the points of a drafting compass, wincing a little as he went. It is probably not right for me to say it so abruptly, but the bears around Nametokoyama were fond of Kojūrō. One proof of this is that they would gaze silently down on him from some high place as he sloshed his way through valleys or moved along narrow banks tangled with thistles. They watched Kojūrō with great interest from the tops of trees with both paws around a branch or hugging their knees at the top of a cliff. Indeed, these bears even seemed to like Kojūrō's dog.[65]

Through the center of the story moves this remarkable human figure, a hunter who routinely infiltrates the deepest reaches of Tōhoku's wild forests. Robust, enormously mobile, and eminently confident, Kojūrō strolls through the gloom of tangled thickets "as if he were walking through his own house." This hunter's mastery of the geography implies a heroic sort of physical stamina ("he would walk . . . covering the whole area from Nametokoyama to Shidoke Valley," etc.), but it also suggests a species of toughness, the vaguely supernatural dimensions of which have long been displaced by the athletic ethos of contemporary outdoor culture. Reflecting a more primal relationship, Kojūrō can hunt bears, it seems, not merely because he is apparently in excellent physical condition, but also in part because he is willing to pass through the "dark tunnel" of the forest and enter into a *different order of survival*: to follow his dog through the depths of faintly sinister mountain pools, described here as "eerie" in their stillness (*fuchi no noronoroshita kimi no warui toko*). It is important to remember that the Gothic strangeness suffusing the wilderness in this passage refers to dangers that are, for all their mystery, undeniably real. By the end of the story, Kojūrō will be dead. Even today, as John Knight observes, although only a very small number of people has ever seen a wild bear in Japan's rural uplands, "[e]veryone knows that there are bears out there in the *yama*, that there are occasional encounters with them, and that bear attacks on people can have serious, even lethal consequences."[66] In important ways, the "eeriness" of this scene, while tinged with the magical aura of a Tōhoku folk tale, is closer to what astronauts might experience on routine missions into space: the weird thrill of entering an alien environment.

Indeed, it may be one of Miyazawa Kenji's greatest environmental achievements to have preserved through his fiction and poetry the sheer *strangeness* of the wilderness. In Kenji's literary universe the wild remains, and is meant to remain, a foreign country. For most of his potential readers, too—farmers, townspeople, and urban poets—the foreignness of the deep wild was its central feature. To the extent that he makes his living in the deep woods, Kojūrō himself appears to the reader as a kind of foreigner. Equipped with his primitive mountain hatchet or *yamagatana* (literally "mountain sword"), which the narrator frankly compares to gear used by "wild mountain natives"—*seiban*, a racist term for the mountain-dwelling peoples of Taiwan who resisted assimilation into Chinese culture and civilization[67]—Kojūrō's competence to navigate the wilderness becomes itself a sign of wildness, marking him as a local shadow of colonial "otherness." But his wildness is duplicitous. No matter how comfortably he moves through the forest, Kojūrō's "business" there is to procure bearskins and gallbladders to sell in town.[68] His extravagantly antiquated musket, suggestive of early European conquest and colonization, reminds readers that Kojūrō is himself an invading predator, a human hunter who has penetrated the forest in order to exploit another kind of "colonized other": the feared and unpredictable wild bear.[69]

Kojūrō's simultaneous *identity with* and *exploitation of* the animals he hunts touches upon the central problem dramatized by this tale. As the story unfolds, its protagonist evinces a troubled awareness of the paradoxical intimacy that unites him with his prey. A combination of tenderness and ruthlessness colors his outlook, a desire to atone for his own violence expressed alongside a cool acceptance of its necessity. Among hunting peoples, confronting the *moral* dangers of sustenance is often understood as the fundamental requirement of "courage." As an Iglulik hunter once observed: "The greatest peril in life lies in the fact that human food consists entirely of souls."[70] But it is not, strictly speaking, "food" that Kojūrō is after. So what does predatory courage mean in *this* context, and why—apart from its atavistic appeal—should such an archaic ethos matter to Kenji's contemporaries, or to readers today?

On the one hand, there is the sheer magnificence of Kojūrō's ease with the prospect of encountering a bear—clearly linked to the masculinist bear-hunting tradition of Japan's northeast, which defined a man's ability to face a bear as the ultimate test of pluck (*dokyō*) or of his "hunter's spirit" (*matagi no konjō*).[71] The deadly potential of a bear attack coupled with the animal's charismatic reputation, its special significance as a "mountain deity" (*yama no kami*) in many parts of Japan, works here to form an attractive image of epic bravery.[72] The reader learns less about the nature of Kojūrō's fearlessness from observing him directly, however, than from considering the assessment of the animals themselves. The bears of Nametokoyama "were fond of Kojūrō" (*Kojūrō o suki nano da*) and "proof" of this enigmatic affection is contained in their silent gaze, directed tenderly "from some high place" as they consider from afar the one who has come to hunt them down. If Kojūrō's character is defined practically and ideally in relation to the creatures he kills, this passage injects new meaning into the idea of courage in the modern world, derived from the premodern logic of the hunt itself. As critic Nakachi Aya has observed, the narrator's simple statement, "the bears around Nametokoyama were fond of Kojūrō," is more than merely an interesting detail; it is the story's central insight, inextricably linked to the narrative's "essential foundation" (*konkan*).[73] Explaining the nature of this "fondness"—its ethical and political significance—emerges as the critic's central task.

It cannot be overlooked, for example, that this ursine affection plays itself out in the very next scene through a pitiless and bloody confrontation, expressed in the spare lines of action under pressure. Having observed that the bears "even seemed to like Kojūrō's dog," the narrative continues with one of the most violent passages of Kenji's body of work:

> But no bear liked it much when it came face to face with Kojūrō, or when his dog came flying at it like a ball of fire and Kojūrō raised his gun with a

strange glint in his eye. When this happened, most bears would wave their paws with annoyance and in protest against such treatment. But there are many different sorts of bears, and the fiercer ones might stand up on their hind legs, let out a roar and—as if meaning to trample right over the dog—come straight toward Kojūrō with both paws out. At times like this, Kojūrō would calmly brace himself against a tree, take aim at the crescent moon pattern on the bear's chest, and—*tharong!*—fire a shot that would echo throughout the forest. The bear would then fall heavily to the ground, dark-red blood gurgling from its mouth, and with its nose making sniffling noises, would die. Resting his rifle against a tree, Kojūrō would very cautiously approach the bear, saying: "Bear, I didn't kill you because I hated you. I killed you because it's my trade and I had to. I would do less sinful work, but I have no fields and they say the trees belong to the authorities, and I am shunned whenever I go into town. I am a hunter and there's nothing I can do about it. It was your fate to be born a bear, and this trade is my own. Listen! Next time, don't be born a bear!"

When Kojūrō spoke like this, even his dog seemed remorseful, making himself small and narrowing his eyes as he sat there.

Out of everyone who had gotten sick with dysentery in the summer of Kojūrō's fortieth year, with his son and his son's wife eventually dying of it, it was this dog alone who remained healthy throughout.

Next, Kojūrō would take a well-sharpened knife from his pocket and, slicing from the bear's jaw to its chest and down to its belly, would remove its hide. The scene that follows really disgusts me. But in any event, Kojūrō would finally place the bear's crimson gallbladder into a wooden box, and after washing the bearskin—with its dripping bloody tassels—in the river, would roll it up and pack it out of the valley, looking exhausted and depressed.[74]

In his remarkable study *In the Company of Animals*, James Serpell notes that "the undercurrent of guilt and the need for some form of atonement for animal slaughter is widespread, if not universal, among hunting peoples."[75] The danger posed to humans by the prospect of ontological continuity with the animals they eat—the notion, as the Iglulik hunter put it, that "the creatures that we have to kill . . . have souls, like we have, souls that do not perish with the body"—has spurred the evolution of a broad range of propitiatory rites and "sending ceremonies," of which Kojūrō's Buddhist-inflected apology must count as one.[76] There is, moreover, a causal connection commonly perceived between these acts of restitution and the success of the hunt. Far from adversarial, the hunt becomes a ritualized expression of mutual respect and affection.

Serpell explains that "the animal that is killed for food is almost never regarded as a mere object; a passive victim of human predation." On the contrary, he tells us, the prey itself is typically seen as "an active and, hopefully, willing agent of its own slaughter."[77] Anthropologists have often noted that the quarry's willingness to be killed amounts to a form of approbation: proof of the hunter's worthiness as a reverent, grateful, and courteous predator. In his study of early modern Ainu-Japanese relations, historian Brett Walker identifies a similar belief expressed in Ainu folklore, especially relevant to bear hunting. Oral narratives "stressed that only virtuous hunters, those who had high moral character and conducted rituals aimed at the myriad deities, were able to kill game such as brown bear." The bear is not simply killed, Walker explains, but rather it was "the bear god that willingly made itself available to hunters of such worthy character."[78]

Understood in this context, the bears' "fondness" for Kojūrō acquires both practical and ethical significance. Why is Kojūrō worthy? According to Nakachi Aya, the bears' affectionate gaze suggests approval of Kojūrō's competence to leave the protection of town and to cross over into the "simple and honest natural environment" (*junbokuna shizenkai*) to which the bears themselves belong.[79] For Nakachi, Kojūrō's everyday willingness to expose himself to attack—to accept the raw equality of a food chain as yet not dominated by human occupation—counts as a kind of primal righteousness. Most importantly, though, Nakachi reads the affinity between the bears of Nametokoyama and Kojūrō the hunter as evidence of the karmic connection alluded to in Kojūrō's rite of appeasement. The hunter and the hunted, according to this view, recognize each other as connected by the suffering of life itself: joined by the conditions of a sacramental economy. Given the language of cosmic destiny (*inga*) invoked by the protagonist here, it is indeed tempting to read this story metaphysically, as an exploration of the "problem of the sin of existence," to borrow Nakachi's words.[80] In part, of course, it *is* that—as nearly all of Kenji's fiction and poetry is. But the ecological insights of Nakachi's own observations inadvertently reveal the ultimate inadequacy of this Buddhist reading. The circumstances to which Kojūrō himself attributes the "sin" (*tsumi*) of his labor remind the reader that the moral crime staining the surface of this story must be understood finally not as a *condition of existence* to be recognized and accepted, but rather as a *historical problem* to be identified, criticized and somehow overcome.

To begin with, Kojūrō kills his bears not for food but for body parts, taking only the hide and the gallbladder because of their exchange value in town. Leaving the rest of the carcass behind unused—a moral felony from a subsistence hunter's point of view—vividly identifies Kojūrō's labor as a "market" activity, what he himself refers to as *shōbai* ("business" or "trade"). His guilt reflects the sin of an economic exchange, not a sacramental one. Unexpectedly, the most ritualistic moment in the story—Kojūrō's improvised sending ceremony—is also the most explicit indicator of the story's economic and historical setting, hinting at circumstances identifiable with the early Meiji state. New institutional and economic arrangements seem to have intensified Kojūrō's dependence upon a relatively distant town-centered economy, and the hunter's apology to the soul of the bear—"I would do less sinful work, but I have no fields and they say the trees belong to the authorities"—encapsulates what modernization might have meant for the most impoverished people of Japan's hinterlands. In a variation on the "tragedy of the commons" that has attracted so much attention among Western environmental historians, the Meiji government's early efforts to place the nation's geography under unambiguously private or national ownership—an effort initiated most notably with the 1873 "land tax amendment" (*chiso kaisei*)—effectively suppressed use-rights to what had previously functioned as communal land (*iriaichi*).[81] The reader is left to assume that the landless Kojūrō, having lost the right to harvest timber, for instance, or to produce charcoal in the local woods, has been left with little choice but to apply for a rifle permit and to harvest what he can of the forest's most lucrative species. It is the mark of his modernity that Kojūrō's relation to the bears is mediated in this way by the institution of private property.[82]

Of course, Japan had a commercial market long before the establishment of the Meiji state. For centuries, the sale of bearskins, organs, and other body parts played an important role in the economics of remote regions of Japan's northeast. Sometimes compared to gold, the gallbladder of a bear—regarded throughout East Asia as a sort of panacea—was the most coveted of any bear part, and hunters have been known to starve or club a bear to death in order to inflate this organ and increase its market value.[83] Conservationist Hazumi Toshihiro reports that bear gallbladders continue today to "have the highest commercial value of all Japanese wildlife products," further emphasizing the contemporary relevance of Kenji's story.[84] What is at issue here is the very logic of the terms "commercial value" and "wildlife product," and the consequences these terms carry for human culture when applied to the living world that supports it.

Recalling Richard White's analysis of the transformation from subsistence to "dependency" among North American Indian nations when they began to trade with Europeans, Brett Walker's discussion of the seventeenth- and eighteenth-century development of trade between the Ainu and the Japanese makes clear the cultural and ecological degradation that results when local fauna, previously depended upon for subsistence, become commodified—identified, in White's terms, as "animals of enterprise."[85] Not only does social autonomy erode as productive systems change, but the very purpose and conceptual framework of the hunt undergo transformation as animals that had once themselves provided food and clothing are killed for export, "to satisfy new Ainu wants as well as commercial demand in Japan." Inevitably, what Walker describes as "shifts in deeper sentiments about killing animals" brings about changes in environmental conditions. "In time," he tells us, "deer and salmon, critical to Ainu survival, become overhunted and overfished."[86]

It is important to recognize in the context of Kenji's story, though, that bear hunting in Japan was never undertaken for subsistence. Bear gallbladder, considered medicinally beneficial for many centuries in China, has been traded in Japan since the late seventeenth century, and demand for this pharmaceutical increased steadily throughout the Tokugawa period.[87] Whether killed as pests—today, mostly to protect timber plantations from "bark-stripping"—or as game animals with valuable body parts, the Japanese black bear has long been an "animal of enterprise" whose slaughter was motivated by a fundamentally commercial logic. Until the twentieth century, however, when remote bear habitats came under unprecedented development, the culling of bears as pests—a major factor in the decline of the Japanese black bear population today as well as a source of bear gallbladder—was bound to be limited. In addition, the legally sanctioned status system of the

Tokugawa government tended, in important ways, to counter the runaway effect of market dynamics. As long as hunting was restricted to the tradition-bound practices of a mountain-dwelling caste of hunters known as *matagi*, associated especially with the Tōhoku region, hunting pressure on bear populations would remain low. According to Hazumi, the Japanese black bear was widely distributed throughout the three main islands of Japan until the early 1900s, owing not only to the abundance of "underdeveloped bear habitats," but also, in part, to "simple and traditional hunting methods such as the use of spears, snares with fiber ropes, and traps that crushed animals with the weight of stones."[88] In their report on Japan's contemporary market in bear parts, Togawa Kumi and Sakamoto Masayuki observe that Japanese bears live today under the shadow of the Meiji government's dissolution of the *matagi* class. Since the establishment of the modern Japanese state, they tell us, virtually anyone may engage in hunting activities, "if carried out within the legal framework."[89] So the gun-wielding Kojūrō of Kenji's story, who kills bears "one after the other," is finally a *modern* figure, however redolent he remains of an archaic ethos.

Modernization during Meiji carried profound consequences for the livelihood of individuals like Kojūrō as well as for the health of nonhuman populations. The reader learns, for example, that Kojūrō's struggle to support single-handedly a brood of five grandchildren and his own 90-year-old mother is made nearly impossible by the unfairly low price of bear parts (signaling an oversupply of dead bears). When Kojūrō goes into town to trade, we are confronted with a new and shocking picture of the fearless hunter, bargaining pitifully among the commodities of a small-town general store. The narrator's voice underscores the contrast:

> But when this magnificent Kojūrō went into town to sell his bearskins and gallbladders, the wretchedness of it all was really too sad to contemplate.
>
> Right in the middle of town was a large general store with baskets and sugar, whetstones, metal *tengu* masks, Chameleon brand cigarettes, and even glass flytraps lining its shelves. As soon as Kojūrō took a single step inside the shop with his mountain of bearskins on his back, the people there smiled sardonically as if to say "You again?" The owner of the shop was sitting in the next room, stationed in front of a big iron *hibachi*.
>
> Kojūrō, the great master of the forest, set his load of bearskins beside him, kneeled down and bowed deeply, saying, "Sir, thank you for your business last time."[90]

The "wretchedness" (*mijimesa*) of this scene taints not only the image of Kojūrō's "magnificence" (*gōgi*), brought low by the craven arrogance of the marketplace, but also the figure of the wild bears themselves, whose skin and organs are transformed here into objects of trade, equivalent to factory-made cigarettes, a sack of sugar, or a glass flytrap. After a pitiful bargaining session during which the shop owner's calm refusals ("However cheap they are, I don't need any") contrast sharply with Kojūrō's increasing desperation ("Sir, I ask you as a favor, please buy them at any price you like"), the hunter finally receives outrageously unfair payment for his bearskins. "However low prices are running," the narrator remarks, "anyone knows that two yen for two bearskins is far too low."[91]

Naked disgust permeates the narrator's portrayal of this transaction, an open revolt against the indignity of an unfair bargain. Bargaining itself is not the issue; even the most basic transaction of existence—the taking of life for food—is a sort of bargain. Rather, it is the lopsided structure of bargaining conditions *in town* that become the object of the narrator's derision. If Kojūrō himself knows the deal is unfair, then why should he accept it? Here is the narrator's enigmatic answer: "Well, in Japan there is a system in place much like the game of *kitsuneken* in which the fox loses to the hunter, and the hunter loses to the lord. Here, the bears lose to Kojūrō and Kojūrō loses to the shopkeeper. But since the shopkeeper is right in the middle of a crowded town, he cannot be eaten by the bears. . . ."[92]

A version of the internationally recognized "rock-paper-scissors" (*janken*) game, the Edo-period *kitsuneken* traces through its hand gestures a more literal food chain, according to which the "village headman" (*shōya*) wins out over the "hunter," the hunter over the "fox," and (most relevantly here) the *fox over the village headman.*[93] In Kenji's story, the significance of the broken circle—the shopkeeper's immunity from bear attack—cannot be overstated. The marketplace is shown as a place of cowardly delusion, where the shopkeeper's own dependence upon nutrient exchange is obscured by an ideology of transcendence and domination. Directing the reader's attention explicitly to this mercantile interruption of the *kitsuneken* wheel of sacrifice—what Marx identified as the "rift" in the "metabolic interaction between man and the earth"[94]—Kenji's tale offers an abstract picture of the historical emergence of the market economy's self-perception: a move from the finite (though limitless) shape of a *circle* to the illusion of infinite domination suggested by the open-ended *pyramid*. The shopkeeper always "wins." Carolyn Merchant's classic analysis of the shift in European culture from the normative restraints of Renaissance-era vitalism to the modern emphasis on exploiting the earth as a "material resource" presents a history similarly haunted by images of infinity. Renaissance critics of mining activities, for example, pointed to *locally* deleterious effects upon a "nurturing earth"—the pollution of local fields or the destruction of a local forest with all the valuable animal and plant life it held—to argue against the efficacy of a mine. But for Georgius Agricola (1454–1555), Europe's first promoter of "modern" mining techniques, this emphasis on local limits was shortsighted and backward. "Where the birds and animals had been destroyed by mining operations," Merchant writes, summarizing Agricola's argument, "the profits could be used to purchase 'birds without number' and 'edible beasts and fish elsewhere' and refurbish the area."[95]

We know today that one of the most robust illusions of capitalism is the idea that there exist "birds without number" that can always be purchased *from someplace else*. It is an illusion that announces itself as such in any Japanese supermarket, where shoppers buy fish for "local" seasonal dishes that today must be flown in from the coasts of Portugal, Chile, or Alaska. The induction of any wild species into capitalism's "infinite" universe of exchange casts a shadow on its future. "This was the situation," the narrator writes, concluding the scene in the general store, "and so, Kojūrō went on killing his bears, feeling absolutely no malice toward them."[96] The sentence radiates a haunting relevance today, for although the Japanese black bear is not officially endangered, many experts believe that it faces an impending crisis. According to the Japan Wildlife Conservation Society, there are about 7,000 black bears left in Japan, but over a thousand are killed every year through sport hunting and pest control.[97] Some critics argue that it is the high market value of bear parts more than the cost of bear-related damage to timber plantations and orchards that motivates most bear culling operations.[98] Japan remains one of the world's largest consumers of bear gall and bile and "there is virtually no regulation in the current Japanese legislation to restrict domestic trade in bear gallbladders."[99] Moreover, as Japanese black bears disappear, the national consumption of bear gall for "traditional medicine" (200 kg a year, equal to about 10,000 bears), puts increasing pressure on bear populations around the world, including those found in China, the Himalayas, Canada, and Russia.[100]

The illusion of "bears without number" animates the market scene in "Nametokoyama," with its calculating shopkeeper—hungry for the best possible deal—and the desperate hunter left with no choice but to increase his yield. The burden of injustice generated by this transaction falls most heavily on the bears themselves, whose only means of protest is extinction. In a certain abstract sense, then, the many modern instances of extinction could be interpreted as innumerable acts of protest: desperately objective reminders of an ecological interdependence that the ideology of infinite economic growth has worked so hard to deny.

But what might Miyazawa Kenji's cryptic tale be suggesting as an ethical solution to historical conditions under which wild animals will never have a chance to "eat the shopkeeper[s]" of the world? In one of the strangest sentences of the story (as evidenced by John Bester's decision to ignore it in his 1993 translation), the narrator hints at an answer to this question when he speculates that "disgusting and slimy characters" like the shopkeeper "will naturally disappear as the world gradually progresses."[101] Serious readers of this posthumously published—and therefore possibly unpolished—manuscript must address the meaning of this intrusive remark and the idea of "progress" (*shinpo*) to which it alludes. Any theory of progress radical enough to encompass the ecological crisis haunting this story is surely not to be found in standard leftist political discourse of 1920s Japan. As I have suggested, however, the shadow of a solution did exist in embryonic form in newly emergent notions of observation and objectivity characteristic of the most daring movements in science of Kenji's day. In this deceptively simple tale, however, the epistemological revolution of early twentieth-century science, to which the author was clearly indebted throughout his career, is distilled to a single ethical relationship embodied in the hunt.

Far from the sort of self-consciously ecological message that a piece of creative fiction might deliver today, the real political content of Kenji's story—and the only reasonable interpretation of what "progress" might mean to its author—emerges from its remarkable portrait of the hunter's *way of seeing*. Resonant with Aldo Leopold's self-confessed predatory epiphany, Kenji's portrayal of Kojūrō's ocular stance generates the story's most powerful ethical assertion by showing the deep connection between *objectivity* and *involvement.* Inseparably pragmatic and imaginative, Kojūrō's empathy with the animals he hunts suggests an observational clarity common to the scientist, the poet, and John Berger's painter: the "capacity to love, suddenly and at any moment, what he saw in front of him."[102] That the bears "liked" Kojūrō cannot be understood apart from the equally scandalous notion that *he liked them*:

> Kojūrō even seemed to understand the bears' language. One spring, before any of the trees had turned green, Kojūrō took his dog and climbed all the way to Shirazawa. When evening came, he decided to spend the night in a bamboo grass hut he had built the previous summer, so he headed up toward the peak that crosses over into Bakkaizawa. For some reason, and unusually for him, Kojūrō took the wrong trailhead.
>
> Several times over, they descended into the valley and climbed back up the mountain. When they finally found the hut from the previous year the dog was exhausted and even Kojūrō was halfway done in, breathing out of the side of his mouth. Kojūrō remembered that there was a spring just below the hut, but he had only gone a little way down the mountainside when, to his surprise, he came upon a mother bear and a cub not yet one year old. The two animals seemed to be gazing into the distance with their paws shading their eyes exactly the way people do, staring intently toward the valley beyond in the pale light of a six-day-old moon. It seemed to Kojūrō as if there was a halo of light shining from the bodies of the two bears, and he stopped in his tracks and stood transfixed. Just then, the bear cub said to its mother in a wheedling sort of voice: "It's snow, Mother. 'Cuz only the near side of the valley's white. I'm sure it's snow." Then the mother bear, still staring intently, finally said, "It's not snow. It wouldn't fall just over there."
>
> "Maybe it just hasn't melted yet."
>
> "No, I passed through there just yesterday looking for thistle buds."
>
> Kojūrō looked hard in the same direction.
>
> The moonlight was streaming pale down the mountainside, which gleamed like a suit of silver armor. After a while, the cub said: "If it's not snow, it must be frost. I'm sure of it." It really will frost tonight, Kojūrō thought to himself, since the star of Aries is shimmering so blue right next to the moon, and the moon itself is the color of ice.[103]

After the two bears conclude that the whiteness on the distant slope must be cherry blossoms, Kojūrō finds himself deeply and inexplicably moved:

> For some reason, Kojūrō's heart felt full. Stealing one last glance at the snowy white flowers on the distant slope and at the mother bear and cub standing bathed in moonlight, he began to sneak away, careful not to make a sound. He retreated slowly, thinking "Please wind, don't blow this way. Don't blow this way." Moonlight and the smell of spice bush penetrated the air.[104]

This memorable scene follows a familiar pattern in Kenji's work: unapologetic anthropomorphism. The narrator gives us talking bears, bears that puzzle over a visual mystery, bears joined by filial affection. An object of wide-ranging anthropomorphism in Japan, the bear functions easily in fiction and folklore as a crossover species, metaphorically well-adapted to communicating with the human realm. Here is a creature that uses "both hands" (*ryōte*) to grasp a tree branch or to wave at its attacker (although throughout my translation, I render the term *te*, "hands," as "paws" for clarity), an animal that hugs its "knees," that "stands up" to confront an intruder: an animal that, when skinned, resembles very closely the naked corpse of a human being.[105] Kojūrō's own resemblance—physical and otherwise—to the bears he hunts further underscores this parity. Unusually comfortable in the wilderness and poised to understand "the bear's language," Kojūrō serves as the reader's instrument of encounter, singularly sensitive to a normally unobservable ursine existence. There is something poignant about the hunter's heightened senses being deployed not to track and to kill, but merely to witness. Kojūrō's predatory silence enables a radical openness: a readiness to perceive the miraculous in the simple fact of two bears looking across a moonlit valley. The bear's conversation seems beside the point here, for the true content of this scene is the relationship it reveals between the hunter and his prey, between the observer and the observed.

Why then do Kenji's animals talk? What could be less scientific or more ecologically misguided than the saccharine sentiment of a talking bear? The garrulous flora and fauna that populate Kenji's literary world may indeed account for the relative lack of attention his work has received from North American and European scholars, whose every instinct resists what might be construed as an endorsement of some "Walt Disney" ideology of animal cuteness. Kenji scholarship suffers, in other words, from a prejudice against anthropomorphism as a serious epistemological stance. "Since the early nineteenth century," Lorraine Daston and Gregg Mitman tell us, "historians, philosophers, and anthropologists have repeatedly linked the rise of modern science with the waning of anthropomorphic attitudes toward the natural world."[106] In their introductory essay to *Thinking with Animals*, however, Daston and Mitman argue for a reconsideration of the usefulness of this phenomenon to science and philosophy, observing crucially that *anthropomorphism* must not be equated with *anthropocentrism.* In fact, they write, the effort to "think with animals"—implying all the semantic richness that this phrase contains—often serves as a useful *guard against* the dangers of a homocentric worldview. By definition, the anthropomorphic impulse involves a projection of human meaning onto a nonhuman world. On the other hand, any attempt at all to "capture the agency of another being that cannot speak" inevitably falls into this category.[107] Even the most abstract theories of organic continuity, including Darwin's theory of natural selection, derive from anthropomorphic insights.

For James Serpell, anthropomorphism is not only the "normal and immediate response of the vast majority of people to animals"—explaining the need for warnings against it—but it also constitutes an effective and useful observational strategy among natural scientists.[108] John Garcia, a behavioral scientist specializing in rats, admits to using anthropomorphism not out of some human weakness, but precisely because it "works better" than most learning theories. "I could rationalize this heresy by pointing to our common neurosensory systems or to convergent evolutionary forces," Garcia remarks. "But, in truth, I merely put myself in the animal's place."[109] Garcia's candid admission points toward a paradigm of objective observation based not upon an ideology of distance, but rather upon a perception of proximity made possible by temporary creative dislocation. If "reason respects the differences and imagination the similitude of things," as Shelley once wrote, then any effective observational stance—for the poet, for the natural scientist, or for the hunter—must be both rational and imaginative.[110] "To be really successful at hunting," Serpell writes, "one needs to know a great deal about the habits of the quarry; the kinds of places where it is likely to make its den, the territory it occupies, its seasonal movements, what it likes to eat, where it drinks, when it breeds, how it behaves when threatened, and how best to approach it without causing alarm." Knowledge for the hunter, in other words, as for the natural scientist, consists of more than raw data. True knowledge implies an act of imagination of the kind only a story can contain. "One needs in a sense to get inside the animal and see the world from its point of view; to empathize with it."[111]

Remarkably, what Kenji's story finally reveals to attentive readers is the unlikely connection between a modernist style of objectivity, associated with new scientific theory, and the practical and ethical clarity of the hunt. It is no accident that both Aldo Leopold and Miyazawa Kenji found in hunting occasion for their most powerful ethical and epistemological assertions. Kojūrō the hunter sees his bears with an openness remindful of Darwin's early notebooks on transmutation. In the most abstract sense, what Kojūrō sees and hears in the bears' "conversation" is evidence of kinship: not sameness, but relatedness. The bears are recognized by their predator as "fellow brethren in pain, diseases, death, suffering, and famine," to borrow Darwin's language, but also as companions in wonder and mentors of perception. "Bears are made of the same dust as we," wrote John Muir, who frequently encountered them on his mountain hikes, "and breathe the same winds and drink the same waters. A bear's days are warmed by the same sun, his dwellings are overdomed by the same blue sky. . . ."[112] And yet, despite these commonalities, it is equally true that bears know the land in a way only bears can know it: "I passed through there just yesterday looking for thistle buds." They gaze toward the distant slope in a way that only bears can gaze, and when Kojūrō follows suit, his sensible world is momentarily enlarged. "The moonlight was streaming pale down the mountainside, which gleamed like a suit of silver armor." Anyone who has walked a dog through a foggy city park or shared a sunny room with a cat will understand the trans-specific *sensus communis* that Kojūrō seems to experience in this scene. Animals can open our eyes to the poetry of the world. But what that tells us about animals is less important than what it tells us about humanity's *relationship* to animals and to the entire nonhuman universe. In a sense, it is the story of this relationship that Miyazawa Kenji spent so much of his life trying to tell.

For Kojūrō, the bears' appreciation of the moonlit world enhances his own: "Moonlight and the smell of spice bush penetrated the air."[113] But here, as with much of Kenji's fiction and poetry, the relationship between animals and people—and, more generally, between the wild and the cultivated—is imbued with conflict. It is not simply because Kojūrō witnesses unexpectedly a moment in the everyday life of wild bears that he feels a sudden tenderness, but because he experiences this encounter self-consciously as the agent of a marketplace that demands their slaughter. "For some reason, Kojūrō's heart felt full." This sentence communicates far more than mere sentimentalism; the hunter's affection suggests a clarity, not a cloudiness, of vision. Although rooted in archaic skills and sensitivities, Kojūrō's objectivity in this scene emerges as a wholly modern virtue: the courage to *open his eyes* to the historical relationship of exploitation that he has come to uphold between the market and the wild.

In important ways, then, what Hagiwara Takao has described as the "innocence" at the center of Miyazawa Kenji's children's fiction may be more usefully categorized under this expanded rubric of objectivity.[114] If innocence implies the opposite of knowledge—the Blakean counter to experience—then Kenji's characters seem to operate based on an inversion of this concept. Think of Giovanni touching the closed eye of a dead heron, tenderly appreciating the bird's transformation by death into food. Similarly, the "innocence" embodied in Kojūrō's gaze functions in this scene not as a barrier to knowledge, but as the *condition of knowledge*. That is, Kojūrō's empathy with the bears he hunts guarantees *against* their idealization. The reader is faced here with the far-reaching ethics of objectivity in the Leopoldian sense, which accounts for the emotional weight of its depiction. "Objectivity can mean a selfless openness to the needs of others," writes Eagleton, one that "lies very close to love."[115]

When, near the end of the story, Kojūrō faces another bear at the end of his gun barrel, it is no surprise that the historical "sin" of his trade erupts again, this time preventing him from following through in the kill. Just as he is about to fire, his quarry speaks—this time, directly to Kojūrō. "What is it you want from me? Why do you kill me?" Kojūrō is hard-pressed to answer. "For nothing but your hide and your gallbladder. Not that I'll get much for them in town. It's a shame, but there you have it." This halting justification causes a crucial moment of self-doubt: "When you ask me that question, I feel as if I'd be better off eating chestnuts or ferns, even if it means the end of me."[116] When the bear offers to give himself up in two years' time, Kojūrō does not answer, but finds himself simply watching the animal retreat into the forest: a heavy sacrifice for the hungry breadwinner. So two years later, when the bear returns as promised, appearing before him as an offering, the hunter responds with reverence. "Without thinking, Kojūrō put his hands together in supplication" (*ogamu yō ni shita*).[117]

Throughout this story, the etiquette of the sacramental economy struggles against the demands of its capitalist counterpart. The bear's interrogation of the hunter places the puny imagination of capitalist exchange explicitly against the enormity of life itself. If Kojūrō must kill a bear, the episode seems to suggest, he should know—beyond the exchange value of its carcass, beyond even its practical use—what the life of a bear is *worth*. The story finally culminates around this question of value. Behind the bear's demand to know what will be gained by his death, readers today will hear echoes of a still larger question: What will be lost when the whole species disappears? The problem is basic enough to set off a barrage of further interrogations: Lost to whom? To human civilization? To the forest? To the bears themselves? The goal-oriented ethos of capitalism is so deeply entrenched that environmentalists today typically rely on utilitarian logic to make the case for conservation and protection, emphasizing the smooth functioning of ecosystems, for example, or the thriving of healthy human food supplies. These arguments are by no means insignificant, but Kenji's story reminds readers that there remains yet another dimension to human-wildlife relations, connected with the logic of function but not reducible to it: the experience of beauty and affection. The bears are fond of Kojūrō, and Kojūrō likes them too. In the end, Kenji's poetic effort to depict this mutual affection emerges as his most subversive maneuver.

When Kojūrō faces his last bear in the story's final episode, standing bravely against the animal's seeming immunity to gunfire, the last thing he hears as he is being attacked and killed is the voice of the bear itself:

> "Oh Kojūrō, I didn't mean to kill you."
>
> I am dead, thought Kojūrō. And then he could see lights all around him like shimmering blue stars.
>
> "These lights must be the sign I'm dead, the fires you see when you die. Bears, forgive me." What Kojūrō felt after that, I have no idea.[118]

Immediately following this, the story's concluding image—a final portrait of honor between species—stands as one of the strangest passages in all of Kenji's work:

It was the night of the third day after that. The moon hung in the sky like a ball of ice. The snow shined cold and white, and the water threw off a phosphorescent glow. The stars of the Pleiades and Orion's belt seemed to flicker from green to orange as if they were breathing.

On a mountain plateau, surrounded by chestnut trees and white snowy peaks, a number of large black shapes were gathered in a circle, each casting a dark shadow. They were motionless, bowing low in the snow like worshipers in prayer, absolutely still. If you looked by the light of the moon and snow, you could see on the highest part of the plateau Kojūrō's corpse placed in a kneeling position.

The frozen face on Kojūrō's dead body appeared as healthy as it had in life. He even seemed to be smiling about something. The stars of Orion's belt moved to the center of the sky, then still further west, but the large black shapes remained still, as if they had turned to stone.[119]

This scene of mourning—of paying respects—bleeds easily into an image of worship. As with any political belief that is truly felt, the author's plea for the recognition of nature's rights must guard against the metaphysics of its own religiosity. At the same time, it is this "religious" impulse that allows the author to conceptualize an ecological vision that reaches beyond the purely mechanistic boundaries of goal-oriented, material politics. If Kenji's work helps us to see a relationship of interdependence between the material and the spiritual—a dialectical link between function and affection—it is precisely through this conjunction that his work expresses the possibility of social change. "What counts," Italo Calvino once remarked, "is what we are, and the way we deepen our relationship with the world and with others, a relationship that can be one of *both love for all that exists and of desire for its transformation*."[120] For Calvino, in other words, "love for all that exists" never amounts merely to a legitimation or approbation of the way things are, but constitutes instead a basic condition for meaningful change. From this perspective, "Nametokoyama no kuma" accomplishes something essential with its portrait of affection between bear and human: the creative beginnings of a profound opposition to the market forces that otherwise define human relations with the wild. In a broad sense, the hunter's empathy for his prey and the respect that is returned to him, amounts to the essential "political content" of this tale. The story's final shadowy portrait of an ursine ritual unwitnessed by human eyes, with its galactic backdrop and lunar luminescence, is the narrator's imagined picture of what human-wildlife relations might "look like" to the bear and to the mountain if antagonism with human life culminated not in destruction but in an awareness of mutual dependence and respect. It is a picture of continuity recognized in the face of difference. In some essential way, it portrays what Aldo Leopold would call "objectivity." Others would call it love.

Epilogue

In their textbook *What Is Mathematics?* (1941), Richard Courant and Herbert Robbins describe the emergence of a "modern point of view" underlying the great achievements in nineteenth- and twentieth-century mathematics. They characterize this approach as identifiable with "a universal scientific attitude" that revolves around a disciplined restriction of its own truth claims to those phenomena that are directly and physically *observable*.[1] To move beyond this, the authors explain, to make reference "to some underlying entity, a 'thing in itself,'" is to defy the limits of what constitutes scientific knowledge and insight.

The greatest achievements in physics, Courant and Robbins go on to assert, have come precisely as a reward for this "courageous adherence to the principle of eliminating metaphysics." Citing Einstein's theory of relativity, the discovery in quantum mechanics of mutual interaction between the "observing instrument" and the "observed object," as well as those nineteenth-century discoveries concerning light and electricity that eventually led to the discarding of the concept of the ether, Courant and Robbins present the realist revolution in science, which has played such an important part of this study, as the culminating achievement of modernity, centered on an abiding faith in the power of direct observation. For mathematics too, they argue, no less than for scientific procedure in general, "it is important to discard elements of metaphysical character and to consider observable facts always as the ultimate source of notions and constructions."[2]

On the one hand, there is nothing surprising about this anti-metaphysical stance or about the rhetorical invocation of "direct observation" in what is clearly an effort to claim for mathematics a place in the sciences. But what can it mean to hold up the cosmic paradoxes of relativity theory and the subvisible uncertainties of quantum mechanics as strongholds of "direct observation"? Even more crucially, what do the authors mean to suggest by applying this empirical disposition to that most *abstract* realm of all: the realm of mathematics? In fact, what Courant and Robbins inadvertently present to their readers in this opening essay is not simply the modern triumph of empiricism over metaphysics, but the historical transfiguration of the concept of "direct observation" itself. For centuries, they tell us, mathematicians considered their objects of study—numbers, points, lines, etc.—as "substantial things in themselves." The nineteenth-century departure from this notion stands as one of the great discoveries of modern mathematics:

> Since these entities had always defied attempts at an adequate description, it slowly dawned on mathematicians of the nineteenth century that the question of the meaning of these objects as substantial things does not make sense within mathematics, if at all. The only relevant assertions concerning them do not refer to substantial reality; they state only the interrelations between mathematically "undefined objects" and the rules governing operations with them. What points, lines, numbers "actually" *are* cannot and need not be discussed in mathematical science. What matters and what corresponds to "verifiable" fact is structure and relationship, that two points determine a line, that numbers combine according to certain rules to form other numbers, etc.[3]

It is important to recognize here that for the authors to take as an equivalent to "verifiable fact" the interrelations between undefined objects amounts to far more than another manifestation of empiricism. "Whatever our philosophical standpoint may be," they write, "for all purposes of scientific observation an object exhausts itself in the totality of possible relations to the perceiving subject or instrument." In this modest statement alone is embodied an epochal shift in the very meaning of observation. A distinction has been discarded, it seems, between the positivist image of the empirically verifiable and what philosopher of psychology Jean Piaget called the realm of "logico-mathematical knowledge." For Piaget, who found it necessary to preserve this distinction, mathematical relationships can be known, but not "observed." Although a child may know objects numerically, he argued, knowledge of numbers remains outside the realm of observation. When two chips are shown to a child, explains Constance Kamii in a summary of Piaget's position, "[t]he two chips are observable, but the 'two-ness' is not."[4] Despite this distinction in terminology, however, Piaget, Courant, and Robbins all agree on one thing: what is knowable and verifiable—even if not *organically perceivable*—in no way confines itself to the "substantial things" of the world, but extends necessarily to the *relations between them.*

It is precisely this modern insight that runs through the fiction and poetry of Japan's modernist moment in literature. From Tanizaki's diagrammatic portrait of Naomi—who becomes the "effect" of an observational relationship, which is itself defined by a larger social universe—to Yokomitsu's relational vision of the imperial cosmos, a spirit of relational realism drives the most creative works of the late Taishō and early Shōwa years. I have tried to show that the "mathematical" dimension of this aesthetic finds its greatest expression in the poetry and fiction of Miyazawa Kenji, where it absorbs as its ethical underpinning the Darwinian concept of interdependence.

Over and over, Miyazawa Kenji's work seems to clarify this most essential, if sometimes hidden, lesson of aesthetic modernism: that the scientific and materialist rejection of metaphysics does not mean the end of imagination, but rather its rejuvenation. For Japanese literary modernism, as for the mathematicians Courant and Robbins, interconnection must be understood neither as a metaphysical figment, nor as a sentimental dream, but as a *fact of existence.* In our century, as weather patterns change, as organisms disappear or thrive, problematically, with new vigor, this realist vision at the heart of Japan's modernist moment seems to speak with renewed authority. The fact of interconnection—what we "see" with our minds as well as our bodies—presents itself today as the first and last evidence that the world is real: the one thing, finally, that matters.

Reference Matter

Notes

Prologue

EPIGRAPH. Marx, *The Marx-Engels Reader*, 116. Italics in original.

1. In his introductory overview of Japanese modernism, for example, Seiji Lippit underscores the "unsettling experience of the 'unreal'" and "spaces characterized by fragmentation and abjection" as central to this aesthetic movement. See Lippit, 3, 32.

2. Similarly, the Japanese word "to understand" (*wakaru*; 分かる) is written with a Chinese ideograph which also carries the meaning "to divide," "to segment," "to isolate," or "to separate."

3. Engels, 26.

4. Berman, 15. Citations are to the Penguin edition.

5. Ibid., 23.

6. My debt to Berman is reflected openly, if at first unconsciously, in the syntax of my own opening two sentences.

7. Berman, 21.

8. Nietzsche, 45. Citations are to the Vintage edition.

9. Ibid.

10. Ibid.

11. Marx, *The Marx-Engels Reader*, 116. Italics in original.

12. See ibid., note 8.

13. Sakata, "Watakushi no koten," 137.

14. Marx, *The Marx-Engels Reader*, 89.

15. Murphy, 14.

16. See "Introduction: Fissures of Japanese Modernity" in Lippit, 3–36.

17. Ibid., 3.

18. Ibid., 7.

19. Marx, *The Marx-Engels Reader*, 91. Italics in original.

20. Foster, 6. Italics in original.

Introduction

EPIGRAPH 1. "Butsurigaku to kankaku" (Physics and perception) in Terada, 5: 69. This essay first appeared in *Tōyō gakugei zasshi* (November 1917). Unless otherwise indicated, all translations are mine.

EPIGRAPH 2. Einstein, *Autobiographical Notes*, 8. This is a corrected edition of a version published in 1947. Cited by John Stachel in his introduction to Einstein, *Einstein's Miraculous Year*, xliii. This is the centenary edition of a book originally published in 1998.

1. "Gendai Nihon no kaika" (The civilization of modern Japan) in Natsume, 11: 319–43. Subsequent references to this work will hereafter be cited as *SZ* with volume and page numbers.

2. *SZ* 11: 321.

3. Ibid., 322.

4. Ibid., 322–23.

5. See Hynes, xiv.

6. Sōseki's understanding of consciousness is essential to his understanding of the function of literary language, as he makes clear in his famous essay "Bungakuron" (A theory of literature), *SZ* 9 (entire volume). Also see his summary of this position in "Bungei no tetsugakuteki kiso" (The philosophical foundation of literature) in *SZ* 11: 39. For a recent study of the problem of "the real" in Sōseki's work, see Wakabayashi, *Sōseki no riaru.*

7. *SZ* 11: 337. It is significant that the author places these "waves" beyond the grasp of quantification. Like his contemporary, Henri Bergson, Sōseki evinced a persistent suspicion toward mathematical renderings of reality. In the novel *Sanshiro*, for example, the scientist Nonomiya's disconnection from the "real world" (*genjitsu sekai*) is epitomized by his comic (but also dangerously insensitive) preoccupation with measuring the numerical values of "light pressure" in his darkened laboratory. "However much the scale moved inside his telescope," the narrator tells us, "it was clear it had nothing to do with the real world." See *SZ* 4: 28.

8. Jay Rubin, "Sōseki as Lecturer," 239.

9. For more on the Katsura government, see Jay Rubin, *Injurious to Public Morals.*

10. Jay Rubin, "Sōseki as Lecturer," 237.

11. *SZ* 11: 335.

12. Ibid., 324.

13. Ibid., 341.

14. Ueda, 62.

15. Nishi Amane's essay "Bimyōgaku setsu" (The theory of aesthetics; 1877) and Tsubouchi Shōyō's "Bi towa nanzo ya?" (What is beauty?; 1886) further demonstrate the purposefulness with which early Meiji intellectuals strove to establish modern institutions of art and literature as "autonomous" fields. Both of these essays appear in translation in Marra, 26–37; 48–64.

16. I am borrowing this turn of phrase from Seed, xiii.

17. Hughes, 37. Cited in Ross, 4.

18. Raymond Williams, 33.

19. Ross, 6.

20. Both Shinoda Kōichirō and Komori Yōichi, for example, argue that Yokomitsu Riichi's essays on poetics from the late 1920s anticipate French semiotic theory. See Shinoda, 100. See also Komori, *Kōzō to shite no katari*, 470.

21. Crary, 14.

22. Ibid., 70.

23. Dale, 9.

24. Positivism, Dale tells us, "maintains with Locke, Hume, Turgot, Condillac, and others, that the experience of the senses must be the basis of all knowledge." Ibid., 12. For a very clear explanation of positivism's anti-realist role in the sciences, see Hacking, 41–57.

25. Mach's insistence that the physical sciences must focus upon describing immediate experience was echoed in a different register—and with different results—in Edmund Husserl's (1859–1938) philosophy of phenomenology. See Husserl, *The Crisis of European Sciences and Transcendental Phenomenology.*

26. Crary, 14.

27. Crary, 39.

28. Quoting from *Consciousness and Society*, Dorothy Ross shows us that H. Stuart Hughes used the word "positivism" to suggest a broadly defined "scientism": "the whole tendency to discuss human behavior in terms of analogies drawn from natural science." See Ross, 4.

29. Karatani, "One Spirit, Two Nineteenth Centuries," 618. Also see his discussion of the I-novel in Karatani, *Origins of Modern Japanese Literature*, 158.

30. Karatani, "One Spirit, Two Nineteenth Centuries," 627.

31. I refer here to Karatani's famous opening chapter in *Origins of Modern Japanese Literature*, which I will discuss later in this Introduction.

32. Morris-Suzuki, 72.

33. Ibid., 111.

34. Wolfgang Schivelbusch explains the crucial role that telegraphic signaling systems played in allowing the railroad as a "machine ensemble" to function.

"The most important technological addition to the railways," he writes, "was the electrically operated telegraph system." Telegraph, which "played a vital part from the beginning," allowed the separate parts of the ensemble to be "minutely adjusted to each other" in order to avoid catastrophes. See Schivelbusch, 29–30.

35. Yoshimi, 147.

36. Cited in Minami, 119.

37. For a discussion of the role of models in modern physics, see Porter, 130–36.

38. Yoshimi, 140–45.

39. Smith, 326.

40. Wise, 342.

41. Porter, 128.

42. Boltzmann's discussion of Maxwell was part of an article entitled "Model," which appeared as a new entry in the tenth edition of the *Encyclopedia Britannica* in 1902. See Boltzmann, 214. Cited in Porter, 130.

43. Porter, 132.

44. Ibid., 131.

45. Roger Penrose tells us that nineteenth century electrodynamics represented the first of three "revolutions in our physical picture of the world . . . when Faraday and Maxwell showed us that particles were not enough, and we must consider, also, that there are continuous fields pervading space, with a reality as great as that of the particles themselves." See "Foreword" in Einstein, *Einstein's Miraculous Year*, vii–viii.

46. Morris-Suzuki, 105.

47. For an analysis of Faraday's role in creating "field theory," see Wise, 349: "Objects in the field . . . are not so much acted on by the field as they participate in it, and the action they experience expresses the effect they have on the distribution of force in the field, which obeys an overall principle of economy."

48. Cited in Hacking, 34.

49. Ibid., 37.

50. Nagaoka's account originally appeared in *Tōyō gakugei zasshi* 28 (1911). Cited in Kaneko, *Ainshutain shokku 2*, 22. Nagaoka also published an essay on quantum mechanics this same year, entitled "Kuwanten kasetsu ni tsuite" (On the quantum hypothesis) in *Tetsugaku zasshi*, no. 294.

51. James R. Bartholomew reports that Nagaoka's "Saturn model" of 1903 "reflected some cogent analysis and was taken rather seriously in Europe. Henri Poincaré called it a 'very interesting attempt.' Ernest Rutherford, who received greater credit for modeling work, conceded that Nagaoka had partly anticipated

the atomic structure assumed in his model." Bartholomew, 193. See also Kaneko, *Ainshutain shokku* 2, 22.

52. See Bohr, 203.

53. Relativity and quantum theory are what Roger Penrose identifies as the second and third "revolutions" in modern physics, after electromagnetism. See "Foreword" in Einstein, *Einstein's Miraculous Year*, vii–xiv.

54. Kaneko, *Ainshutain shokku* 2, 22.

55. Kuwaki's "Rikigakuteki shizenkan ni tai suru shinbutsurigaku no ichi," a translation of Planck's essay "The Position of the New Physics Regarding the Mechanical View of Nature," appeared in *Tōyō gakugei zasshi*, no. 352–53 (1911). His essay on Relativity, "Sōtaigensoku ni okeru jikan oyobi kūkan no kannen" ("The concept of time and space within the principle of relativity") appeared in *Tōkyō butsurigakkō zasshi*, no. 232 (1911).

56. Kaneko, 48.

57. The most exhaustive examination of the impact of Einstein's theory upon the culture of interwar Japan is Kaneko Tsutomu's two-volume history, *Ainshutain shokku*.

58. "Sōtaisei no mondai" (The problem of relativity) in Tanabe, *Tanabe Hajime zenshū*, 14: 33–48. In this 1912 essay, Tanabe discusses at length the importance of both Kuwaki's and Nagaoka's work to his own ideas.

59. See Galison, *Image & Logic*, 112.

60. Kuhn described "the recourse to philosophy" as one of the "symptoms of a transition from normal to extraordinary research." Normal science, by contrast, "is predicated on the assumption that the scientific community knows what the world is like." See Kuhn, 5, 91.

61. Sakata, "Butsurigaku to shizen benshōhō," 2.

62. Ibid.

63. Ibid.

64. Kikuchi Seishi, *Busshitsu no kōzō*. Cited in Sakata, "Butsurigaku to shizen benshōhō," 3.

65. Ibid., 4.

66. Ibid.

67. Einstein, *Autobiographical Notes*, 8.

68. Sakata, "Butsurigaku to shizen benshōhō," 5.

69. Ibid., 10.

70. Sakata, "Watakushi no koten," 134–35. It was a friend of Sakata's, Katō Tadashi, together with Kako Yūjirō, who translated Engels' *Dialectics of Nature* into Japanese. Kato's co-translator Kako, who would go on to teach at Kyoto Imperial University, would later be fired during the notorious faculty purge of 1933, the "Kyoto University Incident" (*Kyōdai jiken*). See ibid., 135.

71. Ibid., 136–37.

72. Sakata, "Taketani's 'Three-Stage Theory,'" 9. English versions of Taketani's two *Sekai bunka* articles are also included in this volume.

73. Tani, "Shizen no benshōhō," 10.

74. The two essays were "Shizen no benshōhō" (Nature's dialectics) in *Sekai bunka* 15 (March 1936) and "Nōberushō jushōsha Jorio-Kyūrii fusai no gakuteki gyōseki ni tsuite" (On Nobel Prize winners Mr. and Mrs. Joliot-Curie's scholarly achievements) in *Sekai bunka* 16 (April 1936). For a discussion of the politics surrounding the publication of these two essays, see Taketani, 22.

75. Ibid., 19.

76. Tani, "Shizen no benshōhō," 3.

77. Sakata, "Watakushi no koten," 137.

78. Sakata, "Butsurigaku to shizen benshōhō," 9.

79. Ibid., 4–5.

80. Kaku, 71.

81. Holton, 237.

82. "Bungaku igai" (Besides literature) in Tsuji, *Tsuji Jun zenshū*, 1: 327.

83. Kaneko, "Ainshutain," 12.

84. Kaneko, *Ainshutain shokku 2*, 287–88. Ishiwara Jun's key role in explaining Einstein's theory to the general public will be discussed in Chapter 2.

85. For an explanation of the relationship between Mach's positivism and Einstein, see "Mach, Einstein, and the Search for Reality" in Holton, 237–77.

86. Ibid., 239.

87. Smolin, 25.

88. Ibid., 72.

89. For an historical and theoretical discussion of the links between Einstein and Cubism, see Miller, *Einstein, Picasso.*

90. Feuer, 59–60.

91. Einstein, "Physics and Reality," 73–77; reprinted in Einstein, *Out of My Later Years*, 59. Cited in Miller, 187.

92. Tani, "Shizen no benshōhō," 8.

93. Holton, 260.

94. Kuwaki Ayao's "Setsumei to kisai" (Explanation and description) appeared in *Rigakkai* (January 1912). The essay "Butsurigakujō no ninshiki no mondai" (The problem of knowledge in physics) appeared in *Rigakkai* in March of the same year. The latter essay as well as a 1915 article called "Bungeijō no byōsharon to kagaku" (Science and the theory of description in literature) were anthologized in the 1922 collection of Kuwaki essays, *Butsurigaku to ninshiki* (Physics and knowledge). See Kuwaki, 33–61.

95. Kuwaki, 34.

96. Ibid., 33–34.

97. Ibid., 20.

98. Ibid.

99. Ibid., 26.

100. Ibid., 29. In 1924, Einstein's champion in Japan, Ishiwara Jun, would write in a similar vein: "to the extent that it is a perception of the eye, we cannot know whether the red we perceive and the red others perceive is the same or different. Our perceptions are individual and different for everyone. That is why matters of the senses can never be universal. Accordingly, [sensation itself] does not amount to a scientific concept." See Ishiwara, 7.

101. According to Crary, nineteenth-century Europe saw the end of eighteenth-century notions of transcendental, objective vision and the rise of a more "subjective" or "physiological" model of vision. "Vision, rather than a privileged form of knowing, becomes itself an object of knowledge, of observation." See Crary, 70.

102. Holton, 247.

103. This link to complexity theory is discussed in Joseph Murphy's useful introduction to Terada Torahiko's career (Murphy, 57).

104. Ibid., 66, 68.

105. Cited in "Tetsugaku kei no kenkyū" (Philosophical research) in Nakaya, *Nakaya Ukichirō zuihitsu senshū*, 3: 329.

106. Ibid.

107. "The Metaphysical Poets" in Eliot, 247.

108. "Butsurigaku to kankaku" (Physics and perception) first appeared in *Tōyō gakugei zasshi* (November 1917). The essay I cite here appears in Terada, 5: 68–80.

109. Ibid., 72.

110. Ibid.

111. Ibid., 74.

112. Cited in Kaneko, *Ainshutain shokku 2*, 124.

113. *Concise Dictionary of Modern Japanese History*, comp. Janet E. Hunter (Berkeley: University of California Press, 1984), s.v. "Kantō Earthquake."

114. Compiled in Kikuchi Yasuo, 152–54. The words "dynamo electric" appear as transliterated English words rendered in *katakana*. See ibid., 152.

115. Ibid., 152–53.

116. Virilio, 36. I thank Mike Yong for pointing out the relevance of this essay.

117. Kikuchi Yasuo, 153.

118. See Yoshimura, *Kantō daishinsai.*

119. "Shizenryoku to ningenryoku to no kōshō" (The negotiation between natural and human power) in Hirabayashi, 3: 739.

120. For an analysis of the role of the earthquake on modern Japanese technical and consumer culture, see Minami, 350–69. See also Seidensticker, 3–87.

121. See Gardner, 3–4. Gardner's useful study focuses on the commercial and political changes implied by this image. It is my intention to address the full importance of their "electric-radio" character.

122. Perry Anderson, 325.

123. Kataoka, "Tsūshin kōshu," 187. I am indebted to Heather Bowen-Struyk for alerting me to the significance of this work. The story is also collected in Kataoka, *Kataoka Teppei zenshū*, 1: 213–18. In the discussion that follows, however, I will cite the less censored original text from *Senki*.

124. Ibid., 188.

125. Ibid., 190.

126. Ibid., 191.

127. Ibid., 193.

128. Yoshimi, 147.

129. Ibid., 149.

130. See Yamaguchi, 120.

131. "Saikin no bungaku shichō" (Recent trends in literature) in Hirabayashi, 3: 639.

132. Eagleton, *After Theory*, 135.

133. Ibid., 135–36.

134. This story is collected in Yokomitsu, *Teihon: Yokomitsu Riichi zenshū*, 1: 396–403.

135. Kataoka, "Wakaki dokusha ni kou," 223. The essay originally appeared in *Bungei jidai* (December 1924).

136. Ibid.

137. Quoted in Reynolds, 30.

138. Lippit, 69.

139. For a discussion of the effect of Akutagawa's death on writers of this generation, including Kataoka and Yokomitsu, see Miyoshi, 204–24.

140. Galison, *Einstein's Clocks, Poincaré's Maps*, 14.

141. Ibid., 31.

142. Ibid., 34.

143. Ibid., 37.

144. Ibid., 41.

145. Ibid., 78, 82. See also Miller, 100–6.

146. In his classic survey, *Dawn to the West*, Donald Keene refers to Tanizaki's sudden wealth and popularity during the mid-1920s, noting that, thanks to contracts with Kaizōsha, "popular authors like Tanizaki made a fortune." See Keene, 757.

147. Sontag, 88.

148. Jeremy Hawthorn, *A Glossary of Contemporary Literary Theory*, 4th ed., (London: Oxford University Press, 2000), s.v. "Diegesis and mimesis."

149. The title of Tanizaki's famous novel, *Chijin no ai*, means "Love of a Fool," but it has come to be known in English by the title *Naomi* based on the excellent translation by Anthony H. Chambers. The version I cite throughout this book is collected in Tanizaki, *TJZ* 10.

150. Stein, 19.

151. Cited in Berger, *The Sense of Sight*, 176.

152. Crary, 14.

153. Ibid., 13.

154. Karatani Kōjin's book was originally published as *Nihon kindai bungaku no kigen* (Tokyo: Kōdansha, 1980). I quote here from the extraordinarily influential English translation *Origins of Modern Japanese Literature.*

155. Karatani, *Origins of Modern Japanese Literature*, 27.

156. *Bungakuron* (A theory of literature) in Natsume, 9: 27.

157. Karatani, *Origins of Modern Japanese Literature*, 11.

158. Nakamura Murao's essay "Honkaku shōsetsu to shinkyō shōsetsu to" (The authentic novel and the state-of-mind novel) was published in *Shin shōsetsu* (January 1924). For a discussion of this essay and its complex relations to a retrospective understanding of the Japanese I-novel, see Suzuki, 49–52.

159. This argument is especially vivid in Karatani's discussion of the development of Masaoka Shiki's poetic "sketching" (*shasei*) techniques. See Karatani, *Origins of Modern Japanese Literature*, 26–27.

160. Ibid., 27.

161. Takahashi, *Kankaku no modan*—a study of Hagiwara Sakutarō, Tanizaki Jun'ichirō, Miyazawa Kenji, and Edogawa Rampo—represents a growing effort among Japanese scholars today to reassess the relationship of sensation to language in the literature of this period and the importance of new technologies to the transformation of this relationship.

162. "Kaisetsu ni kaete" (In lieu of commentary) in Yokomitsu, *Teihon: Yokomitsu Riichi zenshū*, 13: 584.

163. "Shin shinsakka no shinkeikō kaisetsu" (An explanation of new trends among avant-garde authors) in Kawabata, *Kawabata Yasunari zenshū*, 16: 276.

164. Ibid., 278.

165. Ibid., 276.

166. Ibid., 280.

167. Ibid., 279.

168. Ibid.

169. "Bungei jihyō" (Literary commentary) in Miyamoto, 10: 71–75.

170. "Yuibutsuronteki bungakuron ni tsuite" (On a materialist theory of literature) in Yokomitsu, *Teihon*, 13: 99. The following quotations on language and literature are taken from a series of essays written in the context of what later became known as the "formalist literature debate" (*keishiki shugi bungaku ronsō*, 1928–29).

171. "Moji ni tsuite" (On script) in ibid., 115.

172. "Bungei jihyō, 1" (Literary commentary, 1) in ibid., 152.

173. "Bungei jihyō, 2" (Literary commentary, 2) in ibid., 161.

174. *Economic and Philosophic Manuscripts of 1844*, in Marx, *The Marx-Engels Reader, Second Edition*, 116.

175. Ibid., 75.

176. Jameson, *Postmodernism*, 95–96.

177. Bell, 9.

178. Komori, "Shimpojiumu," 6.

179. Maeda, "Tōkyō sen kyūhyaku nijūgo nen," 72.

180. Karatani, *Origins of Modern Japanese Literature*, 169.

181. "Bungei jihyō 1" in Yokomitsu, *Teihon*, 144.

182. Originally serialized in the journal *Kaizō* between 1928 and 1932, *Shanhai* is reprinted in *Teihon: Yokomitsu Riichi zenshū*, vol. 3. Dennis Washburn's English translation, *Shanghai*, appeared in 2001.

183. Guillory, 475.

184. Ibid., 485.

185. Ibid., 496.

186. Ibid., 486.

187. "Kokyō o ushinatta bungaku" (Literature of the lost home) in Kobayashi, *Kobayashi Hideo zenshū*, 2: 370. Although the title of this essay literally means "literature that has lost its home," it has come to be known in the English-speaking world by the more poetic title assigned to it by its translator, Paul Anderer. See Kobayashi, *Literature of the Lost Home*. To retain linguistic consistency in the following analysis, however, I provide my own translations of the text.

188. Kobayashi, *Kobayashi Hideo zenshū*, 2: 375.

189. Ibid., 370.

190. Ibid., 369.

191. Ibid.

192. Ibid., 370.

193. Ibid., 368.

194. Ibid., 375.

195. "Gendai bungaku no fuan" (The anxiety of modern literature) in Kobayashi, *Kobayashi Hideo zenshū*, 2: 212–13.

196. Ibid., 214.

197. Berman, 21.

198. Kobayashi, *Kobayashi Hideo zenshū*, 2: 214.

199. For a discussion of the importance of thermodynamics and chemistry in the ecosystem model, see Frank Benjamin Golley, *A History of the Ecosystem Concept in Ecology*.

200. Callicott, "The Metaphysical Implications of Ecology," 56.

201. Kobayashi, *Kobayashi Hideo zenshū*, 2: 215.

202. Lippitt, 3.

203. See Iwamoto, 180.

204. See Doak, 107–30.

205. Harootunian, *Overcome by Modernity*, 37.

206. Although Japanese scholars usually refer to modern authors either by the writer's family name (as with Tanizaki) or by penname (as with Sōseki), it is normal for scholars to refer to Miyazawa Kenji by his given name, Kenji—a practice I have adopted here. The almost universal application of this usage among literary scholars diminishes somewhat the intimacy it implies.

207. See Katz, Light, and Rothenberg, eds., xi.

208. On Marx's concept of "metabolic relations," see Foster, 141–77.

209. Ibid., 1.

210. Ibid., 11.

211. Smolin, 19–20.

212. Spender, 107.

Chapter 1

EPIGRAPH. "Jōzetsuroku" (Annals of verbosity) in Tanizaki, *Tanizaki Jun'ichirō zenshū*, vol. 20, 72. Hereafter, this work will be cited as *TJZ* followed by volume and page numbers. All translations, unless otherwise indicated, are mine.

1. John Updike's reviews of the translated fiction of Natsume Sōseki, Tanizaki Jun'ichirō, Endō Shūsaku, and Abe Kōbō are collected in Updike, 723–42. For Jorge Luis Borges's essay on Akutagawa Ryūnosuke, see Borges, 437–38.

2. Borges's "Prologue" for *Kappa* originally appeared in *Kappa/Los Engranajes* (Buenos Aires: Mundonuevo, 1959). See Borges, 437.

3. For both the presentation speech and Japanese and English versions of Kawabata's Nobel lecture delivered on December 12, 1968, see the website of the Nobel Foundation at http://nobelprize.org/nobel_prizes/literature/laureates/1968/index.html [accessed April 27, 2007].

4. For a useful discussion of the ideological function of postwar translation practices of Japanese fiction, see Fowler, "Rendering Words, Traversing Cultures." See also Venuti, 71–75.

5. For Ōe's English-language Nobel lecture delivered December 7, 1994, see the Nobel Foundation website at http://nobelprize.org/nobel_prizes/literature/laureates/1994/oe-lecture.html [accessed April 27, 2007]. For a Japanese version of this speech, see Ōe, *Aimai na Nihon no watakushi.*

6. For a discussion of Tanizaki's complex role in the "return to Japan" phenomenon, see Gregory Golley, "Tanizaki Junichirō: The Art of Subversion and the Subversion of Art."

7. "In'ei raisan" (In praise of shadows) in *TJZ* 20: 523. For an English translation of this entire essay, see Tanizaki, *In Praise of Shadows.*

8. *TJZ* 20: 530.

9. Heisenberg, 75.

10. *Chijin no ai*, in *TJZ* 10: 3. I provide my own translations of Tanizaki's novel, as I do for primary and secondary sources throughout this book. This is to maintain linguistic consistency for the purpose of analysis and is in no way meant to cast doubt upon Anthony H. Chambers' inspired translation, to which I am clearly indebted. It is because of Chambers' translation, in fact, that *Chijin no ai* (literally, "Love of a Fool") has come to be known among English readers by the title *Naomi*, which I use throughout this essay.

11. "*Chijin no ai* hashigaki" (A foreword to *Naomi*), *TJZ* 23: 83.

12. Tomi Suzuki's work has alerted scholars to the historical genesis of the I-novel as a central category of literary legitimacy in Japan, underscoring its dependence upon a "discursive field in which the corpus of the I-novel was retroactively created and defined and from which the standard literary histories emerged." See Suzuki, 10. Suzuki's reading of *Naomi* (which she translates as *Fool's Love*) emphasizes its parodic elements. See ibid., 151–74.

13. For a discussion of the historical relationship between literary fiction and "lies" in Japan, see Fowler, *The Rhetoric of Confession*, 23–27.

14. Ibid., 128–29.

15. Bourdieu, 40.

16. The convoluted power dynamics of masochism in Tanizaki's fiction have been addressed by an array of scholars. See, for example, Chiba Shunji, *Tanizaki Jun'ichirō* and Noguchi, 43–90. Ken K. Ito cites pornographer Pauline Réage to remind us that, in a masochistic relationship, it is the "degraded partner who exercises control." See Ken K. Ito, 94.

17. *TJZ* 10: 62.

18. "Jōzetsuroku" in *TJZ* 20: 72.

19. The content of this debate is collected in Hirano, Odagiri, and Yamamoto, eds., 1: 139–60.

20. *TJZ* 20: 72.

21. Ibid., 73.

22. Ibid., 76.

23. See Karatani, *Origins of Modern Japanese Literature*, 169.

24. *TJZ* 20: 78.

25. Akutagawa Ryūnosuke, "Bungeiteki na, amari ni bungeiteki na" (Artistic, all too artistic) in Hirano, Odagiri, and Yamamoto, eds., 1: 150. The entirety of this essay is included in Akutagawa, *Akutagawa Ryūnosuke zenshū*, vol. 9.

26. Ibid.

27. *TJZ* 20: 107.

28. Satō Haruo, "Jun'ichirō: hito oyobi geijutsu" (Jun'ichirō: the man and his art) in Satō, *Satō Haruo zenshū*, 11: 361. This essay was originally published in *Kaizō* (March 1927), a month after Tanizaki's initial comments, which sparked the "plot debate," appeared in the same journal.

29. Ibid., 364.

30. Ibid., 372.

31. Ibid.

32. Nakamura Mitsuo, 162.

33. Itō Sei, "Tanizaki Jun'ichirō no geijutsu to shisō," 57–60. This essay originally appeared in *Gendai bungō meisaku zenshū* (Tokyo: Kawade shobō, 1953).

34. Maeda, "Tōkyō sen kyūhyaku nijūgo nen," 72.

35. Minami, 118.

36. See Silverberg, *Changing Song*, 122–40.

37. Ōya, 2: 7.

38. Ibid., 18.

39. Nakai, 2: 43–45.

40. Ibid., 57.

41. Ibid., 45.

42. Huyssen, vii.

43. Moretti, 340. Moretti refers here to Lautréamont's much-cited phrase: "beau comme la rencontre fortuite sur une table de dissection d'une machine à coudre et d'un parapluie," from *Les Chants de Maldoror*. Although Moretti translates "table de dissection" as "anatomical table," the words are more often rendered as "dissection table" or "operating table."

44. I refer here to Hansen's seminal article "The Mass Production of the Senses: Classical Cinema as Vernacular Modernism."

45. Berman, 16.

46. Hansen, 59.

47. For Naomi's publication history, see Nomura, 295–98.

48. See Yamada Yūsaku's remarks in Komori, "Shinpojiumu," 18.

49. Minami, 353–54.

50. Ibid., 351–64.

51. Ibid., 354.

52. Ibid., 351.

53. Gregory J. Kasza reports, for example, that the circulation of the *Ōsaka mainichi shinbun* grew from 260,000 in 1912 to 670,000 in 1921, and 1,500,000 in 1930. See Kasza, 28. See also Minami, 362.

54. Minami, 355.

55. See Yamada Yūsaku's comments in Komori, "Shinpojiumu," 17–19.

56. *TJZ* 10: 4.

57. Ibid.

58. See Komori's comments in "Shimpojiumu," 6.

59. *TJZ* 22: 38–40.

60. Ibid., 38.

61. Ibid.

62. Ibid., 39.

63. Ibid.

64. See the present book's Introduction.

65. LaMarre, 29. This landmark contribution to the scholarship on Tanizaki contains a series of translations and commentaries, including this and other film-related essays and fictional works by Tanizaki.

66. Ibid., 29–30.

67. See the present book's Introduction. Yokomitsu's "materialist" theory of language is discussed further in the next chapter.

68. Abel Gance, "Le Temps de l'image est venu!" in *L'Art cinématographique*, vol. 2, 1. Cited in Benjamin, *Walter Benjamin*, 110.

69. See "The Cinematographic Principle and the Ideogram" in Eisenstein, 28–30. Thomas LaMarre invokes this connection as well, though he distinguishes Tanizaki's focus upon "phantasm" as distinct from Eisenstein's emphasis on "[c]ombining images into a concept." See LaMarre, 30.

70. Keller, 156.

71. Nagai Kafū's essay "Tanizaki Jun'ichirō shi no sakuhin" [The Works of Mr. Tanizaki Jun'ichirō] originally appeared in *Mita bungaku* (October 1912). The version I cite here appears in Nagai, 92–98. Praise from this established writer provided an invaluable public endorsement of the unorthodox style and themes of Tanizaki's early stories. For Tanizaki's own account of this turning point in his early career, see "Seishun monogatari" (Tale of youth), *TJZ* 13: 365–67.

72. Nagai, 95–97.

73. See "Shisei" (Tattoo), *TJZ* 1: 63–72.

74. Tanizaki's story was published in the journal *Shin shichō*, which dedicated itself to resisting the stylistic homogeny of literary Naturalism. For Kafū, Tanizaki's piece was a breath of fresh air that answered to the general neglect of

style he recognized in the work of "contemporary members of Japan's *bundan*," obsessed with the prosaic documentation of "life." See Nagai, 97.

75. See Yomota, 45.

76. Speculation often points to Seiko, moreover, as the reason for the breakup of the author's marriage. For a thorough account of Tanizaki's personal and professional relationship to the movie industry in English, see Bernardi, 141–65.

77. In the following discussion of the "ontology of the obscene," I am especially indebted to the chapter "Power, Pleasure, and Perversion: Sadomasochistic Film Pornography" in Linda Williams, 184–228.

78. *TJZ* 10: 34.

79. The words that Naomi uses to ask that Jōji fasten the buttons on her swimming suit, for example—"*hamete chōdai*"—are loaded with sexual overtones. *TJZ* 10: 35.

80. Ibid.

81. Cavell, 45. Cited in Linda Williams, 185.

82. Cited in Linda Williams, 184.

83. As Williams' analysis suggests, it is film's capacity to "abstract" the thing from the world that allows for the other side of Bazin's "naïve realism": the concession that cinema is also a *language*. See Linda Williams, 185.

84. Crary, 13.

85. Sontag, 5.

86. Crary, 13.

87. Julia Adeney Thomas made this remark in the course of a presentation she gave at the Association for Asian Studies Annual Conference in San Diego in the spring of 2003.

88. *TJZ* 10: 34.

89. Ibid. Photographs of Annette Kellerman's famous publicity pose, together with Hayama Michiko's imitation of it in the film *Amachua kurabu*, based on Tanizaki's scenario, are reproduced in both LaMarre, 54–55 and Bernardi, 212–13.

90. Joanne Bernardi's *Writing in Light* contains a thorough history of Tanizaki's scenario-writing career, including a translation of *Amachua kurabu* and an excerpt from *Jasei no in* (The lust of the white serpent, 1921), a film adaptation of a story by Ueda Akinari. See also Chiba Nobuo, 7–22.

91. The first form of animated photography was introduced to Japan in 1896, two years after its invention, when Tanizaki was ten years old. Known as Kinetoscope, this early apparatus was one of many technical novelties popular among urban populations of modernizing Japan, especially in Tanizaki's native Tokyo. Equipped with a single eyepiece for an individual viewer, the Kinetoscope was soon displaced by a second generation of devices that projected

images on a screen for viewers to watch in groups. Lumière's Cinematographe, followed by Edison's Vitascope, enjoyed huge popularity among late nineteenth-century Japanese audiences, and demonstrations of these devices were frequented by members of all classes. Tanizaki himself was taken in 1899 to see one of the first Vitascope performances at the Kinkikan, a theater in the Nishikichō district of Kanda that had been made into a permanent Vitascope venue. For a history of the development of cinema in Japan, see Ishikawa, ed., 40–45. See also Anderson and Richie, 21–34. Tanizaki's first exposure to cinema is described in his *Yōshō jidai* (Childhood days), *TJZ* 29: 111–12. For an English translation, see Tanizaki, *Childhood Years*, 97–98.

92. "Katsudō shashin no genzai to shōrai," *TJZ* 20: 13–15.

93. Ibid., 16–17.

94. Ibid., 16.

95. Kano, 31.

96. *TJZ* 20: 18.

97. *TJZ* 5: 283–84. A complete translation of this story is included—under the title "The Tumor with a Human Face"—in LaMarre, 86–101.

98. Ibid., 314.

99. Ibid., 315.

100. Luigi Pirandello, *Il turno* (The Turn). Cited in Benjamin, *Walter Benjamin: Selected Writings, Volume 3, 1935–1938*, 112.

101. Ibid., 113.

102. Ibid.

103. Gunning, 19.

104. Terry Eagleton, "Discourse and Discos." Cited in Wolin, 1.

105. *TJZ* 5: 302.

106. *Kenkyusha's New Japanese-English Dictionary*, 5th ed., s.v. "*haikara*."

107. *TJZ* 10: 21.

108. Ibid., 20–21.

109. Satō, *Satō Haruo zenshū*, 11: 364.

110. *TJZ* 10: 7–8.

111. Ken K. Ito, 67–68.

112. Harootunian, "Introduction," 14.

113. Ken K. Ito, 68.

114. Ibid., 67–68.

115. Silverberg, "The Modern Girl as Militant," 239.

116. Nomura, 295–97.

117. Ibid., 295–98. For Tanizaki's remarks on finding another publisher, see "*Chijin no ai* no sakusha yori dokusha e" (From the author of *Naomi* to its readers), *TJZ* 23: 80. According to Komori Yōichi, it was the unexpected

artistic maturity of Tanizaki's stance that surprised his fellow writers. Hasumi and Komori, 11.

118. Nomura, 298. For a history of the journal *Josei* (1922–28), see Nihon Kindai Bungakukan, ed., 5: 176.

119. Huyssen, 47. For a discussion of gender in *Naomi*, see Ueno, Ogura, and Tomioka, 162–66.

120. Kitazawa Shūichi first introduced the term "modern girl" (*modan gāru*) in the journal *Josei* in 1924 (the same journal and year in which *Naomi* began its second phase of publication), characterizing her, in Miriam Silverberg's summary, as "apolitical but militantly autonomous, neither an advocate of expanded rights for women nor a suffragette." At the same time, though, for Kitazawa, the modern girl "had no intention of being a slave to men." See Silverberg, "The Modern Girl as Militant," 240–41.

121. Silverberg, "The Modern Girl as Militant," 260–61.

122. The "competence" of the modern Japanese woman was acknowledged by the state in 1925 in proposed changes to the Meiji Civil Code that would "seemingly eliminate the requirement of parental consent before marriage, make divorce easier for women, expand the parental rights of women, and grant women the right to manage their own property." See Silverberg, "The Modern Girl as Militant," 259.

123. "Hyaku pāsento moga" (One hundred percent *moga*) in Ōya, 2: 13–14.

124. "Modansō to modansō," in ibid., 8.

125. "Hyaku pāsento moga," in ibid., 14.

126. "Kindaibi to yabanbi" (Modern beauty and barbarian beauty), in ibid., 29.

127. "Modansō to modansō," in ibid., 8.

128. For a thorough discussion of the modern girl's relationship to consumer culture, see Sato, *The New Japanese Woman.*

129. *TJZ* 10: 47.

130. Ibid.

131. Ibid., 29.

132. Ibid., 48.

133. Ibid.

134. Berger, *Ways of Seeing*, 131.

135. *TJZ* 10: 47.

136. Ibid., 18.

137. Ibid., 39.

138. Maeda, "Tōkyō sen kyūhyaku nijūgo nen," 72.

139. *TJZ* 10: 38–39.

140. Ibid., 224–25.

141. For a summary of the history of advertising in Japan, see Minami, 130–33.

142. Kinreisha was not launched until 1926, but the two founding members were active commercial photographers in the early 1920s as well. Suzuki started his journal *Shashin hyōgen* (Photographic expression), dedicated to the future of commercial photography, in 1924, the year of *Naomi*'s publication. See Iizawa, 206–8, 210.

143. Both of these photographs are reproduced in Iizawa, 207.

144. Berger, *Ways of Seeing*, 132.

145. Minami, 137–38.

146. *TJZ* 10: 58.

147. Ibid., 19.

148. Isoda, 195–96.

149. For Isoda Kōichi, who describes Naomi as the character Midori (the child protagonist of *Takekurabe*) "grown up," it is the "shame" of Naomi's birth that drives her to "pursue the limit of modernity's spell." See ibid., 196. For a classic analysis of the role of Senzoku in *Takekurabe*, see "Kodomotachi no jikan" (The time of children) in Maeda, *Toshi kūkan no naka no bungaku*, 339–78. For the area's association with ritual pollution, see Tamura, 107–8.

150. Ken K. Ito, 89.

151. *TJZ* 10: 155.

152. Foucault, 63.

153. Linda Williams, 4.

154. *TJZ* 10: 224–25.

155. See the Introduction in the present study.

156. Crary, 127.

157. *TJZ* 10: 281–82.

158. Sontag, 51.

159. Galison, "Judgement Against Objectivity," 332.

160. Ibid., 329.

161. Ibid., 347.

162. Cited in "Tanizaki Jun'ichirō ron (2): Tanizaki shi wa riaristo dearu ka—Hashizume Ken shi no hihyō ni tsuite" (Tanizaki Jun'ichirō (2): Is Tanizaki a realist? On the criticism of Hashizume Ken), Hirabayashi, 3: 272–73. This essay was originally published in the journal *Bunshō ōrai* (April 1926).

163. Ibid., 273.

164. Ibid.

165. Ibid.

166. *TJZ* 20: 16–17

167. Joel Snyder, "Benjamin on Reproducibility and Aura," 161. Snyder further discusses the relationship between machine technology and accuracy in Joel Snyder, "Visualization and Visibility," 379–97.

168. Dziga Vertov, cited in Berger, *Ways of Seeing*, 17.
169. Miller, 221–22.
170. Berger, *Ways of Seeing*, 18.
171. Slayter, *Optical Methods in Biology*. Cited in Hacking, 190.
172. Ibid. Italics in original.
173. Sontag, 4.
174. *TJZ* 10: 206–7.
175. Eagleton, *The Ideology of the Aesthetic*, 208.
176. *TJZ* 10: 266.

Chapter 2

EPIGRAPH. "Yuibutsuronteki bungakuron ni tsuite" (On a materialist theory of literature) in Yokomitsu, *Teihon* 13: 99. Subsequent references to this work will hereafter be cited as *YRZ* with volume and page numbers. Translations, unless otherwise indicated, are mine.

1. *Shanhai* (Shanghai) in *YRZ* 3: 4. Although I provide my own translations of this novel throughout this chapter, I am greatly indebted to Dennis Washburn's important translation, *Shanghai: A Novel by Yokomitsu Riichi.*

2. See Engels, 26.

3. Raymond Williams describes the importance of metropolitan linguistic multiplicity to the aesthetics of modernism in his essay "The Emergence of Modernism" in Williams, 45–46.

4. *YRZ* 3: 3.

5. Shklovsky, 19.

6. For a discussion of this concept, see Boym, 511–24.

7. Shklovsky, 219.

8. Ibid. Emphasis in original.

9. I am borrowing this term from Shklovsky himself, who compares the relationship that develops between word and object to the abstractions associated with the "method of algebra." He writes: "By this 'algebraic' method of thought . . . we apprehend objects only as shapes with imprecise extensions. . . ." Ibid., 218.

10. Tansley, 299.

11. Worster, 257,473.

12. Callicott, "The Metaphysical Implications of Ecology," 56.

13. My understanding of the role of "the body" in this novel originates in many hours of discussion with Komori Yōichi at the University of Tokyo in the winter of 1996. The fruits of those discussions were first published in Japanese as Gregory Golley, "Shokumin toshi Shanhai ni okeru shintai."

14. See Lippit, 69.

15. See Horio, 285.

16. See "Jo" (Introduction) to *Kakikata sōshi*, in *YRZ* 16: 369.

17. For the dates and titles of *Shanghai*'s serial installments, see *YRZ* 3: 591–92.

18. See "Yokomitsu Riichi: Shōwa bungaku saikentō no shiten" (Yokomitsu Riichi: some viewpoints for a reexamination of Shōwa literature) in Odagiri, 637.

19. See "Jo" (Introduction) to *Shanhai* in *YRZ* 16: 370.

20. See Goto-Shibata, xiii–5.

21. This term can be traced to Jürgen Osterhammel who describes the "informal" empire as characterized by the exploitation of a power differential without direct rule. According to Osterhammel, the informal imperial relation typically manifests itself in the occupying nation's ability to impose upon the occupied nation basic guidelines for foreign policy orientation, in its freedom to maintain a military presence there, and in its reliance upon a degree of collaboration by indigenous rulers. See "Semi-Colonialism and Informal Empire in Twentieth Century China: Toward a Framework of Analysis," in Mommsen and Osterhammel, eds., 290–314. See also "Overview" in Duus, Myers, and Peattie, eds., xv, note 4.

22. Duus, Myers, and Peattie, eds., xii.

23. Ibid., xii–xiii.

24. Kamikawa, ed., 345. Cited in Duus, Myers, and Peattie, eds., xxvi–xxvii.

25. Goto-Shibata, 5.

26. Duus, Myers, and Peattie, eds., 204.

27. See Shimamura, 128–31.

28. The list of Japanese authors who visited Lu Xun in Shanghai during these years includes Hayashi Fumiko, Mushanokōji Saneatsu, and Yokomitsu himself. For a discussion of Lu Xun's influence in interwar Japan, see Maruyama, 216–41.

29. Goto-Shibata, 5.

30. Ibid.

31. For a comprehensive history of Japan's relationship to imperialism, see Myers and Peattie, eds., *The Japanese Colonial Empire, 1895–1945*.

32. The following is based on Elizabeth J. Perry's summary and analysis of the May 30 Incident in Perry, 80–82.

33. "Japanese Treaty Port Settlements in China, 1895–1937," in Duus, Myers, and Peattie, eds., 192. For a map of the Hongkou district, see 185. The great Japanese cotton mills that dominated the southern side of Suzhou Creek on the western edge of the International Settlement featured mess halls and dormitories, company nurseries, and infirmaries. The largest cotton manufacturer in Shanghai, Nagai-men, also offered its employees spacious residential quar-

ters and a company park. At the nine textile mills operated by Nagai-men, "tidiness and order prevailed," writes Peter Duus, "and looking down benignly on it all was a bronze statue of Kawamura Rihei, third president of the company." See "Zaikabo: Japanese Cotton Mills in China, 1895–1937," in ibid., 65.

34. For a description of life and entertainment in Shanghai during the 1920s and 30s, see Sergeant, *Shanghai*. Many of the details I cite here come from its introduction, 1–9. See also Lee, *Shanghai Modern*.

35. Sergeant, 3.

36. Ibid., 3–4.

37. Huxley, 241.

38. Kaneko Mitsuharu, "Shanhai tan"(Shanghai: an open sea). Cited in Maeda, *Toshi kūkan no naka no bungaku*, 458.

39. Ibid., 495.

40. See Maeda, *Toshi kūkan no naka no bungaku*, 467–69. See also Shimamura, 128–31.

41. *YRZ* 16: 98.

42. Yokomitsu used this expression retrospectively in his 1939 essay "Shinakai" (China sea) to describe his relation to the Concessions area. *YRZ* 13: 439.

43. Kuritsubo, 20–21.

44. *YRZ* 3: 7.

45. Ibid., 33.

46. Gayle Rubin, "The Traffic in Women." To explain the historical subordination of women, Rubin replaces Marxist concepts with the notion of a "sex/gender system," rooted in very old kinship conventions that have outlived their organizational usefulness and have come to function solely to reproduce ontological categories based on sexual anatomy.

47. "Japanese Treaty Port Settlements in China" in Duus, Myers, and Peattie, eds., 195–96.

48. Hershatter, 52–53.

49. *YRZ* 3: 35–26.

50. Ibid., 69.

51. "Shinkankakuha to conminizumu bungaku" in *YRZ* 13: 97.

52. Ibid., 93.

53. Ibid., 94–95.

54. Ibid., 97.

55. Adorno, 144. Cited in Larsen, 7.

56. Itō Sei, "Kaisetsu," 430–31.

57. *YRZ* 3: 19.

58. Komori, *Kōzō to shite no katari*, 507.

59. See Kamei, *Shintai*, 125–46. See also Shinoda, 100–48.

60. Linguistic scholar Kobayashi Hideo's Japanese translation of Saussure's now famous collection of lectures was the first translation from the French original to appear in any language. See translator's note in Kamei, *Transformations of Sensibility*, xxx.

61. Komori, *Kōzō to shite no katari*, 523.

62. *YRZ* 3: 49.

63. Ibid.

64. *YRZ* 13: 100.

65. Ibid.

66. *YRZ* 3: 37.

67. *YRZ* 3: 39.

68. Lenin, 730. Cited in Kern, 231.

69. Leftist political and artistic organizations during these years often went by the initials of their Esperanto names. My understanding of NAPF, its role in the "artistic massification debate" and in the "formalist literature debate," is based on Hirano, 65–75; and Moriyama, 102–63.

70. See "Bungei jihyō (2)" in *YRZ* 13: 152.

71. See "Bungei jihyō (1)" in *YRZ* 13: 144.

72. Advocating what Moriyama Shigeo calls a "revolution in sensibility" (*kansei no henkaku*), Yokomitsu departed from "consciousness" in its traditional form, focusing instead upon consciousness as a physical relationship to material reality. See Moriyama, 124.

73. *YRZ* 13: 144.

74. Ibid.

75. *YRZ* 13: 152.

76. Ibid., 151.

77. Ibid.

78. Nakagawa, 42.

79. Ishiwara Jun, "Busshitsu to kūkanjikan to no hitsuzenteki kankei" (The necessary relation of matter to space-time), cited in Nakagawa, 97–98.

80. For an account of Ishiwara's life, see Kaneko, *Ainshutain shokku 2*, 54–66.

81. For an account of Ishiwara's scientific research, see Kenji Ito, 51–54.

82. Other newly established science journals included: *Kagaku to bungei* (Science and literature, 1914), *Rika kyōiku* (Science education, 1917), *Kodomo to kagaku* (Youth and science, 1917), *Shonen kagaku* (Science for boys, 1917), *Kagaku gahō* (Science illustrated, 1923), *Kodomo no kagaku* (Science for kids, 1924) *Shizen kagaku* (Natural science, 1926), and *Butsuri kagaku no shinpo* (Progress in the physical sciences, 1926). See Kenji Ito, 389. For a discussion of how quantum ideas about causation were reported in science journals, see ibid., 383–95.

83. "Yuibutsuronteki bungakuron ni tsuite" (On a materialist theory of literature, 1928) in *YRZ* 13: 99.

84. Ibid., 114.

85. Ibid., 115.

86. "Keishikiron no hihan" (A critique of formalist theory, 1929) in *YRZ* 13: 135.

87. Komori, *Kōzō to shite no katari*, 473.

88. Ibid., 479.

89. "Bungei jihyō (3)" in *YRZ* 13: 161.

90. *YRZ* 3: 84.

91. Ibid., 161.

92. Ibid., 162.

93. Ibid.

94. Ibid.

95. Lukács, 36.

96. Ibid., 36–37.

97. I take this phrase from R. S. Livingstone's excellent summary of Bloch's position in this debate. Livingstone, 9.

98. Bloch, 22.

99. Jameson, "Cognitive Mapping," 349.

100. Ibid., 353.

101. Lukács, 33.

102. Ibid., 37.

103. Ibid., 31.

104. *YRZ* 3: 119.

105. See "Junsui shōsetsuron" in *YRZ* 13: 240–42.

106. *YRZ* 3: 174.

107. For a discussion of the importance of this essay to the "cultural renaissance," see Doak, 111–14.

108. *YRZ* 13: 244.

109. *YRZ* 3: 232.

110. Ibid.

111. Perry, 84.

112. For a discussion of this crisis, see Henriot, 65–102.

113. Ibid., 67.

114. Ibid., 86.

115. The Shanghai Incident ended when, faced with international disapproval, the Japanese government agreed to a cease-fire on May 5 1932. The incident did intensify Japan's isolation in the world, however, and irrevocably

damaged its relations with China. See *Concise Dictionary of Modern Japanese History* (1984), s.v. "Shanghai Incident."

116. Albert Feuerwerker, "Japanese Imperialism in China: A Commentary," in Duus, Myers, and Peattie, eds., 433.

117. Marx, *Capital*, 1: 637–38. Cited in Foster, 155.

118. Marx, *Capital*, 1: 92. Cited in Foster, 7.

Chapter 3

EPIGRAPH 1. "Indora no ami" (Indra's net) in Miyazawa Kenji, *Kohon: Miyazawa Kenji zenshū*, 8: 276. Subsequent references to this work will be cited as *KMKZ* with volume and page numbers. All translations are mine.

EPIGRAPH 2. Marx, *The Marx-Engels Reader*, 85.

1. The "Kenji boom" of 1996, occasioned by the centennial of his birth, spurred newly invigorated promotions of Kenji-related museums, gifts shops, and parks in and around the city of Hanamaki. The mid-1990s also witnessed renewed popular interest in animated features, paperback collections, and illustrated editions of Kenji's work.

2. In addition to Chikuma shobō's *Shin kōhon Miyazawa Kenji zenshū* (1995), a revised edition of that publisher's extraordinary 1974 *zenshū*, Chikuma also released a paperback (*bunko*) collection, *Miyazawa Kenji zenshū*, in 1986. Six additional volumes of collected stories, poetry, and plays by Kenji have also been published as part of a popular paperback series by Shinchōsha, and ten others by Kadokawa shoten.

3. Fromm, 6. Fromm later writes: "Kenji was not a devotee of the Lotus sutra out of blind faith. His poetic eye and scientifically trained mind perceived that the universe physically confirms its own unity." Ibid., 165.

4. For a discussion of the content of Katayama's chemistry text and its influence on Kenji, see Saitō, *Miyazawa Kenji to sono tenkai*, 77–115.

5. During Kenji's life, Hienuki County covered territory just southwest of the center of Iwate Prefecture and included the township (*chō*) of Hanamaki, which served as its administrative center. In 1929, Hanamaki-chō absorbed its neighboring township of Kawaguchi, and finally, in 1954, became Hanamaki City, reducing the size of Hienuki County territory substantially. See "Hienuki," in Hara, ed., 581–82. Also, see map in ibid., 875. Suffering from a lung condition, Kenji was initially unenthusiastic about undertaking this survey, though he recognized in it a chance to delay returning to a family business he deplored. The project did indeed prove to be a physically grueling experience, but he managed to complete the survey under the supervision of Professor Seki Toyotarō. The published results were included as supplements in the

county geological and topographical report. See Miyazawa Seiroku, "Kaisetsu," 180. See also Hara, ed., 456.

6. For a discussion of Kenji's relationship to the bio-region of Japan's fortieth parallel, see Saitō, *Gingakei to Miyazawa Kenji*, 34–38.

7. Later, this school would become the Iwate Kenritsu Hanamaki Nōgakkō (Iwate Prefectural School of Agriculture at Hanamaki). Today, it survives as the Hanamaki Nōgyō Kōtō Gakkō (Hanamaki Agricultural High School). See Miyazawa Seiroku, "Kaisetsu," 226–27. Kenji also taught, among other things, algebra, English, and meteorology. See Horio, 281–82.

8. Tsuji called him "the possessor of an idiosyncratic individuality" (*tokui na kosei no mochinushi*). His comments originally appeared in the *Yomiuri Shinbun* on July 23, 1924. See Tsuzukihashi, 1: 4.

9. Ibid., 6.

10. Amazawa, "Kaisetsu," 406.

11. *KMKZ* 11: 7.

12. Ibid.

13. Bhaskar, *A Realist Theory of Science*, 21.

14. Ibid., 22.

15. Both of these stories are collected in *Chumon no ōi ryōriten*. See *KMKZ* 11: 19–27, 87–98.

16. In navigation or in land-surveying, triangulation means to locate an unknown point by forming a triangle that has the unknown point and two known points as the vertices.

17. Inoue, 2.

18. This experimental educational association offered a place for adult citizens of Iwate to discuss agricultural issues in a broader cultural and aesthetic context. Kenji gave phonograph record "concerts" there, for example, and presided over music recitals. See Miyagi, 178–219.

19. *KMKZ* 12.1: 9, 11.

20. Kenji's family privileges, as he was painfully and guiltily aware throughout his life, were built on the economic misfortunes of the poorest members of the farming community in Hanamaki. The author's disapproval and eventual renunciation of the family business was the source of lifelong tension between himself and his father. For a good summary in English of this family conflict, see Strong, "The Poetry of Miyazawa Kenji," 14–67.

21. *KMKZ* 12.1:. 11.

22. For a discussion of the differences between Kenji's notion of "rural art" and the various agro-nationalist movements flourishing in the 1920s and 30s, see Oshino, 149–50.

23. *KMKZ* 12.1: 9.

24. Saitō, *Gingakei to Miyazawa Kenji*, 18.

25. *KMKZ* 12.1: 15. Hermann Minkowski used the mathematical formalism of Henri Poincaré as the basis for his geometrical formulations to represent Einstein's theory in four-dimensional space. "He realized," writes Arthur I. Miller, "that the velocity of light is what connects the three spatial dimensions with time." See Miller, 221–22.

26. For a discussion of the importance of Steinmetz's book to Kenji, see Saitō, *Miyazawa Kenji to sono tenkai,* 99–115. See also, Ogura, 202.

27. Smolin, 19–20.

28. *KMKZ* 12.1: 9.

29. Ibid., 15. What I have translated here as "atoms" is not the scientific word *genshi* but the Buddhist word *mijin*, used to refer to the smallest unit of matter in religious cosmology. The word Rikuchū is a Meiji-era regional designation that included today's Iwate Prefecture.

30. Katō, Tamura, and Miyasaka, trans., 270.

31. I understand "environmental ethics" as it is broadly defined by Roderick Frazier Nash: "the idea that morality ought to include the relationship of humans to nature." See Nash, 4.

32. Dreyfus, 26.

33. Stein, 19. Cited by Miller, 8.

34. Miller, 111. "While art was moving toward a highly abstractive phase," Miller writes, "physics underwent a parallel movement after the geometrization of space and time in Einstein's general relativity theory of 1915, and then even more dramatically in the 1920s with the development of quantum theory. Yet pure abstraction was a Rubicon that Picasso never crossed, and Einstein never agreed with the high abstractions of quantum theory. Each man ultimately lost contact with the implications of his own revolution." Miller, 6.

35. *KMKZ* 10: 123. All translations of this and other texts in this chapter are my own. But several English translations, of varying success, do exist of "Night of the Milky Way Railroad." They are: *Night on the Milky Way Train*, translated by Roger Pulvers; *Milky Way Railroad*, translated and adapted from the Japanese by Joseph Sigrist and D. M. Stroud; *Night of the Milky Way Railway: A Translation and Guide*, translated by Sarah M. Strong; and *Night Train to the Stars and Other Stories,* translated by John Bester.

36. Kenji continued to revise this story even on his deathbed. See Miyazawa Seiroku, "Kaisetsu," 186. The biggest change in the manuscript occurred between the first draft and the third, when Kenji added the first three chapters, including this classroom scene. For a thorough discussion of the transformations of this manuscript, see Irisawa and Amazawa, *Tōgi: "Ginga tetsudō no yoru" to wa nanika.*

37. *KMKZ* 10: 123.

38. Ibid., 124.

39. Jameson, "Cognitive Mapping," 347.

40. "The Production of the World," in Berger, *John Berger, Selected Essays*, 461. Italics in original.

41. Jameson, "Cognitive Mapping," 348.

42. I borrow these terms from Jameson, "Cognitive Mapping," 347.

43. In the late Taishō period (1912–26), magazines like *Kagaku chishiki* (Scientific knowledge") and *Kagaku gahō* (Science illustrated) often carried pictorial articles on the latest developments in astronomy. See Ikeno, 38–39.

44. *KMKZ* 10: 124.

45. "The Storyteller," in Benjamin, *Illuminations*, 84–88.

46. *KMKZ* 10: 124.

47. Ōsawa, 104. According to literary scholar Ono Ryūshō, Kenji probably read about Campanella and his utopian work *City of the Sun* in Ōnishi Hajime's *Seiyō tetsugakushi* (History of western philosophy, 1903–04). See Hara, ed., 161.

48. *KMKZ* 10: 123–124.

49. *Novum Organum*. Cited in Hacking, 169.

50. The "prime requirement" of information, Benjamin writes, "is that it appear 'understandable in itself.'" See Benjamin, *Illuminations*, 89.

51. Galison, "Judgment against Objectivity," 332.

52. One popular stellar atlas of the time, a book of fold-out maps called *Hoshi* (The stars, 1910) was compiled by Ichinohe Naozō, whose *Saikin no uchūkan* (a translation of S. A. Arrhenius's *The Life of the Universe: As Conceived by Man from the Earliest Ages to the Present Time, 1909*) was published in 1920. A hanging astronomical map, *Shinsen kōseizu* (New map of the fixed stars) had also been available since 1910. Two of Kenji's known sources for astronomical information were Yoshida Genjirō's 1922 *Nikugan ni mieru hoshi no kenkyū* (Studies of the stars visible to the naked eye, 1922), and *Kagaku taikei* (1922; the translation of A. Thompson's *Scientific Compendium*). See Ikeno, 38.

53. Galison, "Judgment against Objectivity," 329.

54. *KMKZ* 10: 124–25.

55. Hara, ed., 230.

56. *KMKZ* 10: 125.

57. See footnote by Ōtsuka Tsuneki in Miyazawa, *Ginga tetsudō no yoru*, 235.

58. Ōtsuka, 120.

59. Saitō, *Gingakei to Miyazawa Kenji*, 19.

60. Thompson's book, for example, also compared the shape of our galaxy to a "lens" (the word *rensu* was used in the Japanese translation) and located our sun "approximately in the middle of this lens." Cited in Ōtsuka, 123–24.

61. Mita, 5, 11–12.

62. Jean Metzinger wrote in his "Note sur la peinture" (1910): "[Picasso] lays out a free, mobile perspective, from which that ingenious mathematician Maurice Princet has deduced a whole new geometry." Cited in Miller, 167.

63. Miller, 208.

64. Kaneko Tsutomu, *Ainshutain shokku 2*, 158.

65. Kaneko Tsutomu, "Ainshutain," 12.

66. Dingle, 537.

67. Guillory, 486.

68. The results of this 1887 experiment suggested that the velocity of light does not change the way it would be expected to in a Newtonian universe. Light does not speed up or slow down in relation to the initial velocity of the light-emitting source relative to its observer, but rather remains constant. For a summary of the Michelson-Morley experiment and Einstein's solution to the problem it posed, see Feynman, *Six Not-So-Easy Pieces*, 54–58.

69. Latour, "A Relativistic Account of Einstein's Relativity," 24.

70. Ibid., 3–4.

71. Ibid., 5. Italics in original.

72. Ibid.

73. Ibid., 9.

74. Ibid., 23–24.

75. Ibid., 23.

76. Ibid., 35.

77. Latour describes the postmodern position as a "clever sleight of hand" that turns anxiety over the loss of absolute certainty into a reason to rejoice. "Yes, we have lost the world. Yes, we are forever prisoners of language. No, we will never regain certainty. No, we will never get beyond our biases. Yes, we will forever be stuck within our own selfish standpoint. Bravo! Encore!" See Latour, *Pandora's Hope*, 8.

78. Ibid., 4.

79. Kaneko Tsutomu, *Ainshutain shokku 2*, 158.

80. Apollinaire, 62. Cited in Miller, 164. Italics in original.

81. Bhaskar, *A Realist Theory of Science*, 34.

82. Foster, 6–7.

83. Ibid., 77.

84. Kaneko Tsutomu, "Ainshutain," 12–13. See also discussion of Kenji and the fourth dimension in Kaneko Tsutomu, *Ainshutain shokku 2*, 154–70.

85. Mita, 22–23.

86. Kaneko Tsutomu, *Ainshutain shokku 2*, 155.

87. *KMKZ* 2: 8.

88. *KMKZ* 12.1: 15.

89. Mita Munesuke, for example, has drawn essential connections between Kenji's notion of "four-dimensional perception" and the death of his sister, the author's most agonizing encounter with "eternity." The trauma of loss, the mystery of an existence that comes to an end, Mita suggests, finds potential resolution in Einstein's counterintuitive "invisible" dimension that overturns the progressive concept of time as an irreversible and all-encompassing flow. "In Minkowski space," Mita writes, outlining what may have been a popular (if misguided) understanding of non-Euclidean geometry, "since time and space are joined in a single dimension, what existed in the *past* and what will exist in the *future* both *continue to exist* latently in this fourth dimensional world" (emphasis in original). See Mita, 24–25. The transient things of this world never really die, according to this reading, but merely join what Kenji called elsewhere "the great invisible past." See "Kaze no henki" in *KMKZ* 2: 197. Saitō Bun'ichi makes a similar argument, citing poems like "Aomori banka" (Aomori elegy, 1923) and "Funka wan (nokutaan)" (Bay of eruption [A nocturn], 1923), in which death itself is rendered not in temporal language, but in terms of a "different space" (*chigatta kūkan*). See Saitō, *Gingakei to Miyazawa Kenji*, 42.

90. Saitō, *Gingakei to Miyazawa Kenji*, 55–62.

91. Katō, Tamura, and Miyasaka, trans., 249–56.

92. Ōtsuka, 134.

93. Saitō, *Gingakei to Miyazawa Kenji*, 132.

94. To get a sense of this line of Kenji criticism and its characteristic dismissal of textual analysis, see the roundtable discussion in Karatani, Kani, Murai, and Yoshida, 6–41.

95. Komori, *Kōzō to shite no katari*, 4.

96. "The Work of Art in the Age of Its Technological Reproducibility" in Benjamin, *Walter Benjamin: Selected Writings*, 105. Italics in original.

97. Walter Benjamin used the word "aura" (adj. auratic) to describe the mystical sense that surrounds ritual and artistic objects. The aura is, for Benjamin, that which is destroyed by techniques of mechanical reproduction such as photography. For a full explanation and discussion of this concept, see Jeremy Hawthorn, *A Glossary of Contemporary Literary Theory*, 4th ed. (London: Oxford University Press, 2000), s.v. "aura."

98. Komori, *Kōzō to shite no katari*, 4.

99. *KMKZ* 10: 130–31.

100. For details on Kenji's studies in astronomy and physics, see Ōtsuka, 120–35.

101. For a photograph of the revolving star chart that Kenji himself used, see Ikeno, 36.

102. For a photograph of this map, see ibid., 39.

103. *KMKZ* 10: 131–32.

104. Saitō, *Gingakei to Miyazawa Kenji*, 52.

105. See Chapter 1 of the present study.

106. Steinmetz, 69–70.

107. Ibid., 70.

108. Ibid., 76.

109. Ibid., 79.

110. Haraway, 184–85.

111. Ibid., 200.

112. Also called *jizō guruma*, *nenbutsu guruma*, *bodai guruma*, and *ketsuen guruma*, depending on the area, these columns were fitted with round iron rings to be turned while performing one's devotions. See Hara, ed., 483.

113. Grapard, 197–98. Regarding this notion of a cosmic center, Mircea Eliade has written: "Every microcosm, every inhabited region, has what may be called a 'Centre'; that is to say, a place that is sacred above all." Moreover, Eliade goes on to explain, Asian civilizations all recognized an "unlimited number of 'Centres'" and "each one of these 'Centres' was considered and even literally called the 'Centre of the World.'" Curiously, this "plurality of 'Centres of the Earth' . . . presented no difficulty." The links here with an Einsteinian cosmos would be easy to make, but misleading. Whereas ancient religious practice replaces what Eliade calls "a profane, homogeneous, geometrical space," with "sacred space," Einstein's theory has replaced the Euclidean worldview not with an ontologically disparate *sacred* space, but simply with a more *accurate* four-dimensional geometrical system. See Eliade, 39.

114. *KMKZ* 10: 134.

115. Ibid., 135.

116. Ibid., 124–25.

117. Ether amounted to a nondescript substance which physicists proposed as the medium that filled all space in order to explain the otherwise inconceivable transmission of electromagnetic energy through "empty" vacuums.

118. *KMKZ* 3: 15.

119. For example, the *Heart Sūtra* (*Hannya shingyō*) claims famously that "all the phenomena of the world is emptiness, and emptiness is the phenomena of the world" (*shiki soku ze kū kū soku ze shiki*). Kenji's poem "Gorin tōge," like most in this collection, refers directly to Buddhist philosophy. *Gorin* itself, here, refers to the "five rings" representing the five component elements of all matter—earth, water, fire, wind, and air—in Buddhist tradition.

120. *KMKZ* 10: 136.

121. Ibid., 136–37.

122. Ibid., 140–41.

123. Cited in Miller, 130.

124. While noting the difficulties of determining the exact nature of the relationship between Braque's Cubism and contemporary theories in science, Arthur I. Miller writes: "Braque's usage of 'tactile space,' however, is so close to Poincaré's that I would wager he was influenced mainly by Princet's discourses about *La Science et l'hypothese*." Ibid., 131.

125. I take this phrase from John Berger's the essay on Renaissance art, "The Clarity of the Renaissance," in Berger, *John Berger, Selected Essays*, 43.

126. "The Moment of Cubism," in Berger, *The Sense of Sight*, 176. Italics in original.

127. Ibid., 178.

128. Smolin, 18.

129. *KMKZ* 10: 138.

130. Ōtsuka, 20. For a discussion in English on Kenji's early poetic influences, see Sarah Strong, "The Poetry of Miyazawa Kenji," 125–82.

131. Ōtsuka, 25.

132. Ibid., 29.

133. Ibid., 240.

134. Cited in ibid., 29–30.

135. These are chapter headings taken from one of Kenji's favorite books, Katayama Masao's chemistry text *Kagaku honron*.

136. The electron theory was a matter of debate throughout the latter half of the nineteenth century. See Wise, 342–56.

137. *Tōhoku no denshin denwa shi* (History of telephone and telegraph in Tōhoku), cited in Yoshimi, 142.

138. This information is based on tables published in 1936 in *Tōkyō dentō kabushikigaisha kaigyō gojūnen shi* (Tokyo electric light company: fifty years of business), reprinted in Ōtsuka, 194.

139. Ōtsuka, 193–94.

140. Ibid., 195.

141. Ibid., 188. Kenji wrote poems with titles like "Hatsudensho" (Power generating station, 1925) and "Densen kōfu" (Power line worker, 1922).

142. Steinmetz, 23.

143. Ibid., 23–24.

144. *KMKZ* 2: 62.

145. Morgan, 500. For Kenji's link with colloid science, see Ōtsuka, 28–42.

146. The title of the paper was "On the Movement of Small Particles Suspended in Stationary Liquids Required by the Molecular-Kinetic Theory of Heat." See Kaku, 70–71.

147. On Einstein and Brownian movement, see Holton, 192–94. For an analysis of the importance of Katayama Masao's chemistry text to Kenji, see Saitō, *Miyazawa Kenji to sono tenkai*, 77–115.

148. Feynman, *Six Easy Pieces*, 20. Italics in original.

149. Ibid. Italics in original.

150. Ōtsuka, 135.

151. Bhaskar, *The Possibility of Naturalism*, 3; Bhaskar, "General Introduction," xiii. Cited in Foster, 7.

152. Miyazawa Seiroku, "Kaisetsu," 180.

153. Foster, 72.

154. Ibid., viii.

155. Marx, *Karl Marx: Early Writings*, 328. Cited in Foster, 72.

156. *KMKZ* 10: 142.

157. "Butsurigaku to kankaku" (Physics and perception) in Terada, 5: 72.

158. Bhaskar, *A Realist Theory of Science*, 26.

159. Ibid., 28.

160. Gary Snyder, *The Practice of the Wild*, 184.

161. On the centrality of Marx's notion of "metabolic relations," see Foster, 141–77.

162. *KMKZ* 10: 142.

163. Ibid., 144–45.

164. The meat that Giovanni and Campanella actually taste is not from the heron they examine in this scene, but from cranes. See ibid., 145.

165. Gary Snyder, *The Practice of the Wild*, 184.

166. *KMKZ* 10: 147.

167. Ibid., 155.

168. Ibid., 156.

169. See Strong, "Reader's Guide," 110.

170. Ibid., 109.

171. *KMKZ* 10: 160–61.

172. Strong, "Reader's Guide," 112.

173. *KMKZ* 10: 162.

174. Ibid., 163.

175. Hara, ed., 395.

176. *KMKZ* 10: 168.

177. Ibid., 170.

178. Nash, 7.

179. Nash attributes this term to Richard Ryder, who coined it in his essay, "Experiments on Animals" (1972). See Nash, 5.

Chapter 4

EPIGRAPH 1. "Seijika" (The politicians) in Miyazawa Kenji, *Shinpen Miyazawa Kenji shishū*, 259. All translations, unless otherwise indicated, are mine.

EPIGRAPH 2. Darwin, *Charles Darwin's Notebooks*, 189.

1. Introduced in 1935 by British ecologist Arthur George Tansley, the "ecosystem" model treated biological and non-biological aspects of the environment as inseparable, with special emphasis on the cycling of nutrients and the flow of energy in the system. This idea remains today a central organizing principle of ecology. For a history of its genesis in the interwar and early postwar years in England and the United States, see Frank Benjamin Golley, *A History of the Ecosystem Concept in Ecology*, 8–34.

2. Katz, Light, and Rothenberg, eds., xi.

3. This English translation of Haeckel's definition of "ecology," taken from *Generelle Morpholgie der Organismen* (1866), appeared as the frontispiece in Allee, Emerson, Park, Park, and Schmidt, eds., *Principles of Animal Ecology*.

4. Bramwell, 41. For a full discussion of Haeckel's role in the development of ecology in the West, see Bramwell, 39–53.

5. For a discussion of Ernst Haeckel's influence on Kenji, see Ono, 266–76. See also "Hekkeru" (Haeckel) in Hara, ed., 624–25.

6. Collected in Miyazawa Kenji, *Kohon: Miyazawa Kenji zenshū*, 11: 5–98. Hereafter, this work will be cited as *KMKZ* with volume and page number.

7. The problem of ecology's origins is, predictably, a subject of dispute among environmental historians. Donald Worster, for example, traces ecology's roots to such varied figures as the eighteenth-century English naturalist, Gilbert White, Swedish botanist Carl Linnaeus, and nineteenth-century American essayist, Henry David Thoreau. See Worster, 1–111. Anna Bramwell, on the other hand, argues that the "true ecologist could not have arisen until the middle of the last (nineteenth) century." See Bramwell, 22.

8. In *The Wonders of Life*, for example, Haeckel critiques the "mystic" and "dualistic" doctrine of vitalism, which characterized several influential works in theoretical biology at the time. Vitalism proposed an independently existing life-force that animated physical bodies to give them life. See Haeckel, 47–53.

9. For a discussion of the connection between Haeckel's ideas and Nazism, see Gould, 77–78.

10. Worster, 192.

11. For a discussion of the importance of Darwin's theory to the development of a "biocentric" approach to natural science, see Worster, 179–87.

12. According to Richard Levins and Richard Lewontin, Darwin's recognition of the link between individual differences and speciation was one of his most "revolutionary" contributions to science. See Levins and Lewontin, 31.

13. Thomas observes that, between 1877 and 1890, "there were at least thirty-two translations of Spencer's work published in Japanese." See Thomas, 117.

14. Shibatani, 336–37.

15. Ishikawa Chiyomatsu, a student of Edward Morse, published *Dōbutsu shinkaron* (The evolution of animals) in 1883, based on Morse's lectures. He also published a translation of the writings of German zoologist August Weissmann under the title *Banbutsu taika shinsetsu* (New theories of natural retrogression) in 1889, and his own *Shinka shinron* (New theories in evolution) in 1891. Oka Asajirō, an internationally recognized biologist, published several books and over a hundred articles in Japanese and European languages. A dedicated defender of evolutionary theory, he played a major role in explaining Darwin's model as a scientific theory to a popular Japanese audience in the early twentieth century. See Watanabe, 66–98. Also see Montgomery, 232–35.

16. See "Daauin" (Darwin) in Hara, ed., 432–33.

17. Oka, "Jinrui no seifuku ni tai suru shizen no fukushū," 13–14.

18. Oddly, the main consequence of progress that Oka emphasizes in this essay is the weakening of the human body itself due to the overprotection enabled by material advancement.

19. Ibid., 20.

20. Worster, 182.

21. Ibid., 156.

22. Ibid., 156–57.

23. Darwin, *The Origin of Species*, 101. The link between ecology and Buddhism has been observed by many scholars. See, for example, William R. LaFleur's "Saigyō and the Buddhist Value of Nature" or Francis Cook's "The Jewel Net of Indra" in Callicott and Ames, eds., 183–229.

24. Katō, Tamura, and Miyasaka, trans., 270.

25. Cited in Nash, 42.

26. Amazawa Taijirō, footnote to "Oinomori to zarumori, nusutomori," in Miyazawa Kenji, *Chūmon no ōi ryōriten*, 305.

27. Darwin, *Charles Darwin's Notebooks*, 228–29.

28. To the extent that Darwin's theory enabled the idea of ecology, his work shares a deep structure with the "energy revolution" in physics. The complementary relationship between ecology and the physics of energy has been observed by several scholars. J. Baird Callicott, for example, writes: "Ecology and contemporary physics, interestingly, complement one another conceptually and converge toward the same metaphysical notions. Hence . . . the 'New Ecol-

ogy' and the 'New Physics,' respectively, draw mutually consistent and mutually supporting abstract pictures of nature in its most elementary and universal and in its most complex and local manifestations." See Callicott, "The Metaphysical Implications of Ecology," 51–52. For further discussion of the links between the New Physics and New Ecology, see Callicott, "Intrinsic Value, Quantum Theory, and Environmental Ethics."

29. Darwin, *Charles Darwin's Notebooks*, 228.

30. Darwin, *The Origin of Species*, 108.

31. Field, 173.

32. Darwin, *The Origin of Species*, 228.

33. Ibid., 112–13.

34. Ibid., 637.

35. Levins and Lewontin, 33.

36. Darwin wrote: "Who can explain what is the essence of the attraction of gravity? No one now objects to following out the results consequent on this unknown element of attraction. . . ." See Darwin, *The Origin of Species*, 637–38. See also ibid., 109 and Darwin, *Charles Darwin's Notebooks*, 195, 219, for similar invocations of the law of gravity.

37. Muir, 357–58. Cited in Nash, 42–43.

38. Bhaskar, *A Realist Theory of Science*, 22.

39. Nash, 39.

40. Lapo, 47. It is highly unlikely, however, that Miyazawa Kenji was aware of Vernadsky's work. Vernadsky's book *Essays on Geochemistry* was not published in Japanese translation until 1933, the year of Kenji's death.

41. Tansley, 299. Cited by Frank Benjamin Golley, *A History of the Ecosystem Concept in Ecology*, 8. Three decades later, Francis Crick, co-discoverer of the DNA code, would push this synthesis even further. "The ultimate aim of the modern movement in biology," he wrote in a 1966 lecture, "is in fact to explain *all* biology in terms of physics and chemistry." See Crick, 10.

42. Belshaw, 187.

43. "Gurando denchū" in *KMKZ* 2: 108.

44. See "Aru nōgakusei no nikki" (The diary of an agronomy student), in Miyazawa Kenji, *Shinshū: Miyazawa Kenji zenshū*, 14: 124–25. See also Leopold, *A Sand County Almanac and Sketches Here and There*, 292. Both are cited in Colligan-Taylor, 38–39.

45. Gary Snyder, *The Practice of the Wild*, 9–10. For a discussion of Gary Snyder's translations of Kenji's poetry, see Tomiyama, 1–37.

46. "Oinomori to zarumori, nusutomori" in *KMKZ* 11: 19. A full translation of this story appears as "Appendix A" in Colligan-Taylor, 242–49. All translations provided here, however, are my own.

47. *Seibutsu no sekai* (The world of living things) in Imanishi, 1: 18. Italics mine.

48. Levins and Lewontin, 141.

49. In an essay called "Is Nature Real?" Gary Snyder angrily denounces this extreme position "put forth by high-paid intellectuals trying to knock nature and knock the people who value nature and still come out smelling smart and progressive." Taking an approach he traces back to Mahayana Buddhism, Snyder reminds his readers that to understand nature as a "social construction" is not to deny its independent reality, but only to acknowledge a need to "examine one's own seeing, so as to see the one who sees and thus make seeing more true." See Gary Snyder, "Is Nature Real?" 387.

50. Cronon, "Introduction," 25.

51. Spencer, xvii.

52. Heisenberg, *Physics and Philosophy*. Cited in Berger, *The Success and Failure of Picasso*, 68.

53. Cary Wolfe describes this posture as "speciesism": a fundamental blindness at the heart of cultural studies that consistently represses "the question of nonhuman subjectivity, taking it for granted that the subject is always already human." Wolfe goes on to say: "Most of us remain humanists to the core, even as we claim for our work an epistemological break with humanism itself." See Wolfe, 1.

54. Eagleton, *After Theory*, 162.

55. Darwin, *The Origin of Species*, 112–113.

56. *KMKZ* 11: 20.

57. Komori, *Saishin*, 38.

58. Ibid., 42.

59. Ibid., 43.

60. Ibid., 50.

61. Ōsugi, 413.

62. Ibid., 428.

63. Ibid., 413.

64. Ibid., 414.

65. *Shinkaron kōwa*, in Oka, *Kindai Nihon shisō taikei* 9, 56, 67, 232, 236, 248.

66. Gary Snyder, *The Practice of the Wild*, 15–16.

67. Komori, *Saishin*, 50.

68. Worster, 157–61.

69. Marx and Engels, 5: 31–32. Cited in Foster, 115.

70. For a discussion of the importance to Marx and Engels of the Darwinian "struggle for existence" and their understanding of "man's struggle with nature," see Foster, 123–26.

71. Marx, *Grundrisse*, 489. Cited in Foster, 159.

72. Eagleton, *After Theory*, 60.

73. Ibid., 61, 155. "The material body is what we share most significantly with the whole of the rest of our species," Eagleton writes, "extended both in time and space." It is only a short distance from this statement to the observation that this "material body" is precisely what we share with *all* species.

74. Levins and Lewontin, 51–58.

75. Ibid., 55.

76. Ibid.

77. Imanishi, 1: 87.

78. *Shinkaron kōwa* in Oka, *Kindai Nihon shisō taikei 9*, 30. Darwin, *The Origin of Species*, 49.

79. Darwin, *The Origin of Species*, 112.

80. Ibid. Italics in original.

81. Gary Snyder, *The Practice of the Wild*, 11–12.

82. Meyer, 20.

83. Ibid.

84. Ibid.

85. Ibid., 24.

86. Gary Snyder, *The Practice of the Wild*, 14.

87. *KMKZ* 11: 20–21.

88. Worster, 294–99.

89. *KMKZ* 11: 21.

90. *KMKZ* 11: 22–23.

91. Knight, 195.

92. Knight, 3. For an examination of the extermination of the Hokkaido wolf, see Walker, "Meiji Modernization, Scientific Agriculture, and the Destruction of Japan's Hokkaido Wolf" and Walker, *The Lost Wolves of Japan*.

93. Knight, 194.

94. Ibid., 12.

95. Chiba Tokuji, 183. Cited in Knight, 203.

96. Knight, 197.

97. Nomoto, "Shin'i no naka no dōbutsu," 225.

98. Hiraiwa, 128.

99. "Between 1644 and 1672," Knight reports, "over 270 horses were attacked and killed by wolves in one area of Tōhoku." See Knight, 199.

100. Ibid., 200.

101. Gary Snyder, *The Practice of the Wild*, 18.

102. Nomoto, *Kumano sankai minzokukō*, 66. Cited in Knight, 206.

103. Knight, 219.

104. Nomoto, "Shin'i no naka no dōbutsu," 224.

105. Knight, 3.
106. Ibid., 195.
107. Ibid., 209.
108. Map 2 in Totman, xxii.
109. Ibid., 4.
110. Ibid.
111. Ibid., 23.
112. Ibid., 9.
113. Kawai, 18. See also Mito, 93–94.
114. Mito, 90.
115. Kawai, 19.
116. Ibid.
117. Ibid., 17.
118. Ibid., 16.
119. Knight, 32.
120. Ibid., 30.
121. Ibid., 1.
122. Kawai, 19.
123. Ibid.
124. Totman, 2–3.
125. *KMKZ* 11: 95.
126. *KMKZ* 13: 226.
127. "Science is slavery of the intellect," as Murobuse wrote in Murobuse, 55. Cited and translated in Fromm, 101. For a full discussion of Murobuse's influence on Kenji, see Fromm, 99–101.
128. Ibid., 186.
129. *KMKZ* 12.2: 168.
130. *KMKZ* 11: 23.
131. Ibid., 24.
132. Komori, *Saishin,* 61.
133. *KMKZ* 11: 24–25.
134. I borrow this phrase from Levins and Lewontin, 3.
135. Foster, 188.
136. Montgomery, 233–34.
137. Watanabe, 68–69.
138. Darwin's masterpiece was first translated by Tachibana Senzaburō (identified as a "Doctor of Japanese Letters") and published by Keizai Zasshisha. For a photograph of its cover page, see Montgomery, 233.
139. Darwin, *The Origin of Species*, 88.
140. Watanabe, 71–75.

141. Oka, *Kindai Nihon shisō taikei 9*, 70. For a detailed discussion of the paradoxes of Katō Hiroyuki's philosophy, see Thomas, 84–110.

142. Darwin, *The Origin of Species*, 101.

143. Levins and Lewontin, 83–84.

144. Darwin, *The Origin of Species*, 648.

145. Ibid., 162.

146. Smolin, 72.

147. Darwin, *Charles Darwin's Notebooks*, 189.

148. Ibid., 291.

149. Darwin, *The Origin of Species*, 644.

150. Ibid., 642.

151. Darwin, *Charles Darwin's Notebooks*, 228.

152. Ibid., 233.

153. Darwin, *The Origin of Species*, 227. Levins and Lewontin point out that the existence of "organs of extreme perfection and complication" was "a difficulty for (Darwin's) theory, not a proof of it." See Levins and Lewontin, 83.

154. Darwin, *The Origin of Species*, 228.

155. Ibid., 112.

156. *KMKZ* 12.1: 16.

157. Katō, Tamura, and Miyasaka, trans., 251.

158. See Ōsugi, 426. Ōsugi was the Japanese translator of Pyotr Kropotkin's *Mutual Aid: A Factor of Evolution* (1902), translated as *Sōgo fujoron: shinka no ichi yōso* (Shun'yōdō, 1917).

159. Darwin, *The Origin of Species*, 90.

160. Oka, *Kindai Nihon shisō taikei 9*, 67.

161. Darwin, *The Origin of Species*, 100.

162. Oka, *Kindai Nihon shisō taikei 9*, 68.

163. *KMKZ* 11: 25.

164. Knight, 244.

165. Morris, 120.

166. *KMKZ* 11: 27.

167. Ibid.

168. Foreman, *Confessions of an Eco-Warrior*, 65. See also Foreman and Wolke, *The Big Outside*. Both are cited in Cronon, "The Trouble with Wilderness," 84.

169. Cronon, "The Trouble with Wilderness," 83–84.

170. Ibid., 85–86.

Chapter 5

EPIGRAPH 1. Darwin, *Charles Darwin's Notebooks*, 228–29.

EPIGRAPH 2. "Iwayuru shizen no bi to shizen no ai" in Oka, *Kindai Nihon shisō taikei 9*, 318.

EPIGRAPH 3. Berger, *The Shape of a Pocket*, 151.

1. Leopold, *A Sand County Almanac*, 129.

2. See editors' notes on "Ten New Developments in Game Management" in Leopold, *Aldo Leopold's Southwest*, 124. According to his own account, Leopold developed the rudiments of his idea of the land ethic during his tenure in the Forest Service in the Southwest. He left that position on June 3, 1924.

3. Leopold, *A Sand County Almanac*, 204

4. Ibid., 130.

5. Ibid.

6. Ibid., 132.

7. Colligan-Taylor, 35.

8. Darwin, *The Origin of Species*, 112. Italics in original.

9. Virilio, 36.

10. Lenin, 231

11. Leopold, *A Sand County Almanac*, 216.

12. See Smith, 326–41.

13. Callicott, "The Metaphysical Implications of Ecology," 56. See also Worster, 303.

14. Frank Benjamin Golley, *A History of the Ecosystem Concept in Ecology*, 56–59. Golley outlines the significance of work by soil scientists and geochemists such as A. E. Fersman (1883–1945), V. M. Goldschmidt (1888–1947), V. V. Dokuchaev (1846–1903), and Alfred Lotka (1880–1949).

15. Vernadsky, 6.

16. Lapo, 47.

17. *KMKZ* 12.1: 9. All translations are mine.

18. *KMKZ* 10: 144.

19. Vernadsky, 7.

20. Frank Benjamin Golley, 48–56.

21. Ibid., 59.

22. See note 93 in Miyazawa Kenji, *Shinpen*, 391.

23. Nakamura Hajime, 371, 377.

24. *KMKZ* 3: 276–77.

25. Ibid., 15.

26. Foster, 10–11.

27. Ibid., 11.

28. Strong, "The Poetry of Miyazawa Kenji," 261–62.

29. Saitō, *Miyazawa Kenji to sono tenkai*, 109.

30. Worster, 303.

31. Callicott, "The Metaphysical Implications of Ecology," 58.

32. Odin, 348.

33. Leopold, *A Sand County Almanac*, viii.

34. Karen Colligan-Taylor notes that for Kenji, too, the natural world acquired a broad array of meanings, serving as "the fountainhead of both religious insight and scientific knowledge." See Colligan-Taylor, 34.

35. Leopold, *A Sand County Almanac*, 173–74.

36. Ibid., 174.

37. Ibid., viii.

38. *KMKZ* 3: 276.

39. This essay was originally published in *Jidai shichō* (1905). Oka, *Kindai Nihon shisō taikei 9*, 458.

40. Ibid., 316.

41. Ibid.

42. Ibid.

43. Ibid., 317.

44. Ibid., 318, 322.

45. Ibid., 317.

46. Ibid., 318.

47. Ibid., 322.

48. Ibid., 321.

49. Darwin, *The Origin of Species*, 251–52.

50. Darwin described "beauty in its simplest form" as "the reception of a peculiar kind of pleasure from certain colours, forms, and sounds." See ibid., 253–55.

51. In spite of this fundamental difference, however, Sullivan shows the influence of evolutionary theory in the very essay in which he introduces what would become a commonplace modernist adage. "Whether it be the sweeping eagle in his flight," he wrote, "or the open apple-blossom, the toiling workhorse, the blithe swan, the branching oak, the winding stream at its base, the drifting clouds, over all the coursing sun, *form ever follows function*, and this is the law." See Sullivan, "The Tall Office Building Artistically Considered," available online at www.njit.edu/v2/Library/archlib/pub-domain/Sullivan–1896-tall-bldg.html [accessed 5/18/07].

52. Eagleton, *After Theory*, 119.

53. Darwin, *The Origin of Species*, 253.

54. Eagleton, *After Theory*, 131.

55. Berger, *The Shape of a Pocket*, 88.

56. Ibid.

57. *KMKZ* 9: 232.

58. Hara, ed., 520.

59. For an introduction to the Japanese black bear and a survey of its status, see Hazumi, "Status and management of the Asiatic black bear in Japan." See also Knight, 159–93.

60. Bhaskar, *A Realist Theory of Science*, 21–22.

61. Knight, 192–93.

62. Ibid., 159.

63. Amazawa, "Shijin Miyazawa Kenji no seiritsu," 17.

64. Ibid., 18.

65. *KMKZ* 9: 232–33.

66. Knight, 159.

67. *Kōjien*, 5th ed., s.v. "seiban" (Tokyo: Iwanami Shoten, 1998), 1477.

68. In fact, the word "business," or *shōbai*, will later by used by Kojūrō himself to describe his activities.

69. I am indebted here to Komori Yōichi's analysis of the different levels of meaning of Kojūrō's "foreignness" (*ijinsei*) as it might have been understood by a 1920s Japanese readership. See Komori, *Saishin*, 138.

70. Tuan, 91. Cited in Serpell, 178.

71. Knight, 180–81.

72. Ibid., 162–63. Knight tells the story of a roadside billboard warning of wild animals crossing the road in Iwate Prefecture that "had to be replaced by an image of a raccoon-dog because the bear image was deemed to be too shocking to passing drivers and a possible cause of road accidents."

73. Nakachi, 170.

74. *KMKZ* 9: 233–34.

75. Serpell, 180.

76. Ibid., 178.

77. Ibid., 181.

78. Walker, *The Conquest of Ainu Lands*, 78.

79. Nakachi, 170.

80. Ibid., 171.

81. For an exhaustive explanation of this transition, see Hōjō, "Kanrin no seiritsu to shoki kanrin seisaku."

82. As Komori Yōichi explains with characteristic succinctness: "The reason that Kojūrō must kill bears is itself profoundly connected with the establishment of the modern nation-state of 'Japan,' a fact made clear by Kojūrō's owns words." See Komori, *Saishin*, 141.

83. Knight, 179–80.

84. Hazumi, "Status of the black bear," 147. Cited in Knight, 180.

85. White, 238. Cited in Walker, *The Conquest of Ainu Lands*, 75.

86. Walker, *The Conquest of Ainu Lands*, 75.

87. Togawa and Sakamoto, 129. Also available online at http://www.wspa-international.org/publicfiles/191102_110942_BearBileJapan.pdf [accessed 5/18/07].

88. Hazumi, "Status and management of the Asiatic black bear in Japan," 208.

89. Togawa and Sakamoto, 124.

90. *KMKZ* 9: 235.

91. Ibid., 236–37.

92. Ibid., 237

93. *Kōjien*, 5th ed., s.v. "*kitsuneken*" (Tokyo: Iwanami Shoten, 1998), 657. See also Hara, ed., 174.

94. For an explanation of this concept as it was developed in Marx's *Capital*, see Foster, 155–56.

95. Merchant, 38

96. *KMKZ* 9: 237.

97. Togawa and Sakamoto, 121.

98. Mizoguchi, 33. Cited by Knight, 186.

99. Togawa and Sakamoto, 121.

100. Ibid., 122.

101. *KMKZ* 9: 237.

102. Berger, *The Shape of a Pocket*, 88.

103. *KMKZ* 9: 234–35.

104. Ibid., 235.

105. If it is true that "mountain men" (*yamaotoko*) like Kojūrō often carry ethnically foreign associations (see Komori, *Saishin: Miyazawa Kenji kōgi*, 61), it is equally useful to note in this context the colloquial reference in many parts of Japan to bears themselves as *yamaotoko* ("mountain men") or *yama no oyaji* ("old men of the mountain"). See Knight, 163–64.

106. Daston and Mitman, eds., 3.

107. Ibid., 4–5.

108. Serpell, 172.

109. Ibid., 174.

110. Cited in Berger, *Another Way of Telling*, 83.

111. Serpell, 175–76.

112. See Fox, 374. This beautiful passage is cited by Karen Colligan-Taylor in her discussion of "Nametokoyama." See Colligan-Taylor, 55.

113. The Japanese black bear's traditional association with the moon resonates with the lunar imagery that runs throughout this story.

114. See, for example, Hagiwara, "Innocence and the Other World: The Tales of Miyazawa Kenji."

115. Eagleton, *After Theory*, 131.

116. *KMKZ* 9: 237.

117. Ibid., 238.

118. Ibid., 239–40.

119. Ibid., 240.

120. "The Cloven Communist," in Calvino, 124. Italics mine.

Epilogue

1. Courant and Robbins, *What Is Mathematics?* The quotations that follow come from the unpaginated five-page introductory essay, "What Is Mathematics?"

2. Ibid.

3. Ibid.

4. "The Nature of Number" in Kamii, 8.

Works Cited

Unless otherwise noted, place of publication for Japanese-language works is Tokyo.

Adorno, Theodor. *Minima Moralia: Reflections from a Damaged Life.* Translated by E. F. N. Jephcott. London: New Left Books, 1974.

Akutagawa Ryūnosuke 芥川龍之介. *Akutagawa Ryūnosuke zenshū* 芥川龍之介全集 (Collected works of Akutagawa Ryūnosuke). 12 vols. Iwanami shoten, 1977–78.

Allee, W. C., Alfred E. Emerson, Orlando Park, Thomas Park, and Karl P. Schmidt, eds. *Principles of Animal Ecology.* Philadelphia, PA: W. B. Saunders, 1949.

Amazawa Taijirō 天沢退二郎. "Kaisetsu" 解説 (Commentary). In *Shinpen: Miyazawa Kenji shishū* 新編・宮沢賢治詩集 (Collected poems of Miyazawa Kenji: new edition). Edited by Amazawa Taijirō, 406–20. Shinchōsha, 1991.

———. "Shijin 'Miyazawa Kenji' no seiritsu" 詩人〈宮沢賢治〉の成立 (The making of Miyazawa Kenji, poet). In *Bungei tokuhon: Miyazawa Kenji* 文芸読本・宮沢賢治 (Miyazawa Kenji: a literary reader), 10–25. Kawade shobō shinsha, 1977.

Anderson, Joseph L. and Donald Richie. *The Japanese Film: Art and Industry.* Princeton, NJ: Princeton University Press, 1982.

Anderson, Perry. "Modernity and Revolution." In *Marxism and the Interpretation of Culture.* Edited by Cary Nelson and Lawrence Grossberg, 317–33. Urbana and Chicago, IL: University of Illinois Press, 1988.

Apollinaire, Guillaume. *Les Peintres cubists: meditations esthetiques.* Paris: Hermann, 1980.

Bartholomew, James R. *The Formation of Science in Japan.* New Haven, CT: Yale University Press, 1989.

Bell, Michael. "The Metaphysics of Modernism." In *The Cambridge Companion to Modernism.* Edited by Michael Levenson, 9–32. Cambridge, UK: Cambridge University Press, 1999.

Belshaw, Christopher. *Environmental Philosophy: Reason, Nature and Human Concern.* Montreal & Kingston: McGill-Queen's University Press, 2001.

Benjamin, Walter. *Illuminations.* Edited by Hannah Arendt. Translated by Harry Zohn. New York: Schocken Books, 1968.

———. *Walter Benjamin: Selected Writings, Volume 3 1935–1938.* Edited by Howard Eiland and Michael W. Jennings. Translated by Edmund Jephcott, Howard Eiland, and others. Cambridge, MA: The Belknap Press of Harvard University Press, 2002.

Berger, John. *Another Way of Telling.* New York: Vintage, 1982.

———. *John Berger, Selected Essays.* New York: Pantheon, 2001.

———. *The Sense of Sight.* New York: Vintage, 1985.

———. *The Shape of a Pocket.* New York: Vintage, 2001.

———. *The Success and Failure of Picasso.* New York: Vintage, 1965.

———. *Ways of Seeing.* London: British Broadcasting Corporation and Penguin, 1972.

Berman, Marshall. *All That Is Solid Melts Into Air: The Experience of Modernity.* New York: Penguin Books, 1988. First published by Simon & Schuster, 1982.

Bernardi, Joanne. *Writing in Light: The Silent Scenario and the Japanese Pure Film Movement.* Detroit, MI: Wayne State University Press, 2001.

Bhaskar, Roy. "General Introduction." In *Critical Realism: Essential Readings.* Edited by Margaret Archer, Roy Bhaskar, Andrew Collier, Tony Lawson, and Alan Norrie, ix–xxiv. New York: Routledge, 1998.

———. *The Possibility of Naturalism.* Atlantic Highlands, NJ: Humanities Press, 1979.

———. *A Realist Theory of Science.* New York: Verso, 1975.

Bloch, Ernest. "Discussing Expressionism." In *Aesthetics and Politics.* Edited by Ronald Taylor, 16–27. London: Verso, 1980.

Bohr, Niels. "Discussion with Einstein on Epistemological Problems in Atomic Physics." In *Albert Einstein: Philosopher-Scientist.* Edited by P. A. Schlipp, 200–41. LaSalle, IL: Open Court Publishing, 1970.

Boltzmann, Ludwig. *Theoretical Physics and Philosophical Problems: Selected Writings.* Edited by Brian McGuinness. Translated by Paul Foulkes. Boston, MA: R. Reidel, 1974.

Borges, Jorge Luis. *Jorge Luis Borges: Selected Non-Fictions.* Edited by Eliot Weinberger. Translated by Esther Allen, Suzanne Jill Levine, and Eliot Weinberger. New York: Penguin, 1999.

Bourdieu, Pierre. *The Field of Cultural Production.* Translated by Richard Nice. New York: Columbia University Press, 1993.

Boym, Svetlana. "Estrangement as a Life Style: Shklovsky and Brodsky." In *Poetics Today: International Journal of Theory and Analysis of Literature and Communication* 17, no. 4 (Winter 1996): 511–24.

Bramwell, Anna. *Ecology in the 20th Century: A History.* New Haven, CT: Yale University Press, 1989.

Callicott, J. Baird. "Intrinsic Value, Quantum Theory, and Environmental Ethics." *Environmental Ethics* 7 (1985): 257–75.

———. "The Metaphysical Implications of Ecology." In *Nature in Asian Traditions of Thought: Essays in Environmental Philosophy.* Edited by J. Baird Callicott and Roger T. Ames, 51–64. Albany, NY: State University of New York Press, 1989.

Callicott, J. Baird and Roger T. Ames, eds. *Nature in Asian Traditions of Thought: Essays in Environmental Philosophy.* Albany, NY: State University of New York Press, 1989.

Calvino, Italo. *Hermit in Paris: Autobiographical Writings.* Translated by Martin McLaughlin. New York: Vintage International, 2004. First published London: Jonathan Cape, 2003.

Cavell, Stanley. *The World Viewed: Reflections on the Ontology of Film.* Cambridge, MA: Harvard University Press, 1979.

Chiba Nobuo 千葉伸夫. *Eiga to Tanizaki* 映画と谷崎 (Film and Tanizaki). Seiabō, 1989.

Chiba Shunji 千葉俊二. *Tanizaki Jun'ichirō: kitsune to mazohizumu* 谷崎潤一郎—狐とマゾヒズム (Tanizaki Jun'ichirō—the fox and masochism). Ozawa shoten, 1994.

Chiba Tokuji 千葉徳爾. *Ōkami wa naze kieta ka* オオカミはなぜ消えたか (Why did the wolf disappear?). Shinjinbutsu ōraisha, 1995.

Colligan-Taylor, Karen. *The Emergence of Environmental Literature in Japan.* New York: Garland Publishing, 1990.

Courant, Richard and Herbert Robbins. *What Is Mathematics? An Elementary Approach to Ideas and Methods.* Oxford, UK: Oxford University Press, 1941.

Crary, Jonathan. *Techniques of the Observer: On Vision and Modernity in the Nineteenth Century.* Cambridge, MA: The MIT Press, 1990.

Crick, Francis. *Of Molecules and Men.* Seattle, WA: University of Washington Press, 1966.

Cronon, William. "Introduction: In Search of Nature" and "The Trouble with Wilderness; or, Getting Back to the Wrong Nature." In *Uncommon Ground: Rethinking the Human Place in Nature.* Edited by William Cronon, 23–90. New York: W.W. Norton, 1996.

Dale, Peter Allan. *In Pursuit of a Scientific Culture: Science, Art, and Society in the Victorian Age.* Madison, WI: University of Wisconsin Press, 1989.

Darwin, Charles. *The Origin of Species By Means of Natural Selection, or, the Preservation of Favored Races in the Struggle for Life.* New York: Modern Library, 1998.

———. *Charles Darwin's Notebooks, 1836–1844: Geology, Transmutation of Species, Metaphysical Inquiries.* Edited by Paul H. Barrett, Peter J. Gautrey, Sandra Herbert, David Kohn, and Sydney Smith. Ithaca, NY: Cornell University Press, 1987.

Daston, Lorraine and Gregg Mitman, eds. *Thinking With Animals: New Perspectives on Anthropomorphism.* New York: Columbia University Press, 2005.

Dingle, Herbert. "Scientific and Philosophical Implications of the Special Theory of Relativity." In *Albert Einstein: Philosopher-Scientist.* Edited by Paul Arthur Schilpp, 535–54. La Salle, IL: Open Court Publishing, 1949.

Doak, Kevin Michael. *Dreams of Difference: The Japan Romantic School and the Crisis of Modernity.* Berkeley, CA: University of California Press, 1994.

Dreyfus, Hubert L. "Heidegger's Hermeutic Realism." In *The Interpretive Turn: Philosophy, Science, Culture.* Edited by David R. Hiley, James F. Bohman, and Richard Shusterman, 25–41. Ithaca, NY: Cornell University Press, 1991.

Duus, Peter, Ramon H. Myers, and Mark R. Peattie, eds. *The Japanese Informal Empire in China, 1895–1937.* Princeton, NJ: Princeton University Press, 1989.

Eagleton, Terry. *After Theory.* New York: Basic Books, 2003.

———. *The Ideology of the Aesthetic.* Oxford, UK: Basil Blackwell, 1990.

Einstein, Albert. *Autobiographical Notes.* Edited and translated by P. A. Schlipp. LaSalle, IL: Open Court Publishing, 1979.

———. *Einstein's Miraculous Year: Five Papers That Changed the Face of Physics.* Edited by John Stachel. Princeton, NJ: Princeton University Press, 2005.

———. *Out of My Later Years.* Totown, NJ: Littlefield, Adams & Co., 1967.

———. "Physics and Reality." *Franklin Institute Journal* 221 (1936): 73–77.

Eisenstein, Sergei. *Film Form: Essays in Film Theory.* Edited and translated by Jay Leyda. New York: Harcourt and Brace, 1949.

Eliade, Mircea. *Images and Symbols: Studies in Religious Symbolism.* Translated by Philip Mairet. Princeton, NJ: Princeton University Press, 1991. First published 1952.

Eliot, T. S. *Selected Essays, 1917–1932.* New York: Harcourt Brace, 1932.

Engels, Friedrich. *Dialectics of Nature.* Translated by Clemens Dutt. New York: International Publishers, 1940.

Feuer, Lewis S. *Einstein and the Generations of Science.* New Brunswick, NJ: Transaction Books, 1982.

Feynman, Richard P. *Six Easy Pieces: Essentials of Physics Explained by Its Most Brilliant Teacher.* Cambridge, MA: Perseus Books, 1995.

———. *Six Not-So-Easy-Pieces: Einstein's Relativity, Symmetry and Space-Time.* Reading, MA: Perseus Books, 1997.

Field, Norma. *In the Realm of a Dying Emperor: Japan at Century's End.* New York: Vintage Books, 1991.

Foreman, Dave. *Confessions of an Eco-Warrior.* New York: Harmony Books, 1991.

Foreman, Dave and Howie Wolke. *The Big Outside: A Descriptive Inventory of the Big Wilderness Areas of the U.S.* Tucson, AZ: Ned Ludd Books, 1989.

Foster, John Bellamy. *Marx's Ecology: Materialism and Nature.* New York: Monthly Review Press, 2000.

Foucault, Michel. *The History of Sexuality, Volume I: An Introduction.* Translated by Robert Hurley. New York: Vintage Books, 1978.

Fowler, Edward. "Rendering Words, Traversing Culture: On the Art and Politics of Translating Modern Japanese Fiction." *Journal of Japanese Studies* 18, no. 1 (Winter 1992): 1–44.

———. *The Rhetoric of Confession: Shisōsetsu in Early Twentieth-Century Japanese Fiction.* Berkeley, CA: University of California Press, 1988.

Fox, Stephen. *John Muir and His Legacy: the American Conservation Movement.* Boston, MA: Little, Brown and Company, 1981.

Fromm, Mallory Blake. "The Ideals of Miyazawa Kenji—A Critical Account of Their Genesis, Development, and Literary Expression." Ph.D. diss., University of London, 1980.

Galison, Peter. *Einstein's Clocks, Poincaré's Maps: Empires of Time.* New York: W.W. Norton & Company, 2003.

———. *Image & Logic: A Material Culture of Microphysics.* Chicago, IL: University of Chicago Press, 1997.

———. "Judgment against Objectivity." In *Picturing Science, Producing Art.* Edited by Caroline A. Jones and Peter Galison, 327–59. New York: Routledge, 1998.

Gardner, William O. *Advertising Tower: Japanese Modernism and Modernity in the 1920s.* Cambridge, MA: Harvard University Asia Center, 2006.

Golley, Frank Benjamin. *A History of the Ecosystem Concept in Ecology.* New Haven, CT: Yale University Press, 1993.

Golley, Gregory. "Shokumin toshi Shanhai ni okeru shintai," 植民都市上海における身体 (The body in colonial Shanghai). *Shiso* 12, no. 882 (December 1997): 242–61.

———. "Tanizaki Junichirō: The Art of Subversion and the Subversion of Art." *Journal of Japanese Studies* 21, no. 2 (Summer 1995): 365–404.

Goto-Shibata, Harumi. *Japan and Britain in Shanghai, 1925–31.* London: Macmillan Press Ltd., 1995.

Gould, Stephen Jay. *Ontogeny and Phylogeny.* Cambridge, MA: Harvard University Press, 1977.

Grapard, Allan G. "Flying Mountains and Walkers of Emptiness: Toward a Definition of Sacred Space in Japanese Religions." *History of Religions* 21, no. 3 (February 1982): 195–221.

Guillory, John. "The Sokal Affair and the History of Criticism." *Critical Inquiry* 28 (Winter 2002): 470–508.

Gunning, Tom. "Tracing the Individual Body: Photography, Detectives and Early Cinema." In *Cinema and the Invention of Modern Life*. Edited by Leo Charney and Vanessa R. Schwartz, 15–45. Berkeley, CA: University of California Press, 1995.

Hacking, Ian. *Representing and Intervening: Introductory Topics in the Philosophy of Natural Science*. Cambridge, UK: Cambridge University Press, 1983.

Haeckel, Ernst. *The Wonders of Life: A Popular Study of Biological Philosophy*. Translated by Joseph McCabe. New York: Harper & Brothers, 1905.

Hagiwara, Takao. "Innocence and the Other World: The Tales of Miyazawa Kenji." *Monumenta Nipponica* 47, no. 2 (Summer 1992): 241–63.

Hansen, Miriam Bratu. "The Mass Production of the Senses: Classical Cinema as Vernacular Modernism." *Modernism/Modernity* 6, no. 2 (1999): 59–77.

Hara Shirō 原子朗, ed. *Miyazawa Kenji goi jiten* 宮沢賢治語彙辞典 (A Miyazawa Kenji lexicon). Tōkyō shoseki, 1989.

Harootunian, Harry. "Introduction: A Sense of an Ending and the Problem of Taishō." In *Japan in Crisis: Essays on Taishō Democracy*. Edited by Bernard Silberman and H. D. Harootunian, 3–28. Princeton, NJ: Princeton University Press, 1974.

———. *Overcome by Modernity: History, Culture, and Community in Interwar Japan*. Princeton, NJ: Princeton University Press, 2000.

Haraway, Donna. "Deanimations: Maps and Portraits of Life Itself." In *Picturing Science, Producing Art*. Edited by Caroline A. Jones and Peter Galison, 181–207. New York: Routledge, 1998.

Hasumi Shigehiko 蓮實重彦 and Komori Yōichi 小森陽一. "Tanizaki raisan: tōsō suru deisukuuru" 谷崎礼讃・闘争するディスクール (In praise of Tanizaki: competing discourses). *Kokubungaku: kaishaku to kyōzai no kenkyū* 国文学・解釈と教材の研究 38, no. 14 (1993): 6–29.

Hazumi, Toshihiro. "Status and Management of the Asiatic Black Bear in Japan." In *Bears: Status Survey and Conservation Action Plan*. Compiled by Christopher Servheen, Stephen Herrero and Bernard Peyton, 207–11. Oxford, UK: Information Press, 1999.

———. "Status of the Black Bear." *International Conference on Bear Research and Management* 9, no. 1 (1994): 145–48.

Heisenberg, Werner. *Physics and Philosophy: The Revolution in Modern Science*. London: Allen & Unwin, 1959.

Henriot, Christian. *Shanghai, 1927–1937: Municipal Power, Locality and Modernization*. Translated by Noel Castelino. Berkeley, CA: University of California Press, 1993.

Hershatter, Gail. *Dangerous Pleasures: Prostitution and Modernity in Twentieth-Century Shanghai*. Berkeley, CA: University of California Press, 1997.

Hirabayashi Hatsunosuke 平林初之輔. *Hirabayashi Hatsunosuke bungei hyōron zenshū* 平林初之輔文芸評論全集 (Collected literary criticism of Hirabayashi Hatsunosuke). 3 vols. Bunsendō, 1975.

Hiraiwa Yonekichi 平岩米吉. *Ōkami—sono seitai to rekishi* 狼—その生態と歴史 (The wolf—its ecology and history). Tsukiji shokan, 1992.

Hirano Ken 平野謙. *Shōwa bungakushi* 昭和文学史 (A history of Shōwa literature). Chikuma shobō, 1963.

Hirano Ken, Odagiri Hideo 小田切秀雄, and Yamamoto Kenkichi 山本健吉, eds. *Gendai Nihon bungaku ronsōshi* 現代日本文学論争史 (A history of modern literary debates). 3 vols. Miraisha, 1957.

Hirato Renkichi 平戸廉吉. "Nihon miraiha sengen undō" 日本未来派宣言運動 (The Japanese futurist manifesto movement). In *Gendaishi no taidōki* 現代詩の胎動期 (An age of change in modern poetry). Edited by Kikuchi Yasuo, 152–54. Genbunsha, 1967.

Hōjō Hiroshi 北條浩. "Kanrin no seiritsu to shoki kanrin seisaku" 官林の成立と初期官林政策 (The establishment of Meiji government forests and the initial Meiji forest policy). In *Tokugawa rinseishi kenkyūjo kenkyū kiyō* 徳川林政史研究所研究紀要 (Bulletin of the Tokugawa institute for the history of forest administration), (March, 1977): 144–73.

Holton, Gerald. *Thematic Origins of Scientific Thought: Kepler to Einstein*. Cambridge, MA: Harvard University Press, 1973.

Horio Seishi 堀尾青史. "Miyazawa Kenji nenpu" (A biographical timeline of Miyazawa Kenji). In *Bungei tokuhon: Miyazawa Kenji* 文芸読本・宮沢賢治 (Miyazawa Kenji: a literary reader), 281–85. Kawade shobō shinsha, 1977.

Hughes, Stuart H. *Consciousness and Society: The Reorientation of European Social Thought, 1890–1930*. New York: Vintage Books, 1961. First published Alfred A. Knopf, 1958.

Husserl, Edmund. *The Crisis of European Sciences and Transcendental Phenomenology*. Translated by David Carr. Evanston, IL: Northwestern University Press, 1970.

Huxley, Aldous. *Jesting Pilate: The Diary of a Journey*. London: Chatto & Windus, 1927.

Huyssen, Andreas. *After the Great Divide: Modernism, Mass Culture, Postmodernism*. Bloomington, IN: Indiana University Press, 1986.

Hynes, Samuel. "The Art of Unrest: An Introduction to Conrad's Stories." In *The Collected Stories of Joseph Conrad*. Edited by Samuel Hynes, xi–xx. Hopewell, NJ: The Ecco Press, 1991.

Iizawa Kotarō 飯沢耕太郎. *Nihon shashinshi o aruku* 日本写真史を歩く (A journey through Japan's photographic history). Shinchōsha, 1992.

Ikeno Masaki 池野正樹. "Kenji no mita hoshi" 賢治の見た星 (The stars Kenji saw). In *Zusetsu: Miyazawa Kenji* 図説：宮沢賢治 (The illustrated Miyazawa Kenji), by Ueda Akira 上田哲, Sekiyama Fusahei 関山房兵, Ōya Kuninori 大矢邦宣, and Ikeno Masaki, 36–41. Kawade shobō shinsha, 1996.

Imanishi Kinji 今西錦司. *Imanishi Kinji zenshū* 今西錦司全集 (Collected works of Imanishi Kinji). 10 vols. Kōdansha, 1974–75.

Inoue Hisashi 井上ひさし. *Miyazawa Kenji ni kiku* 宮沢賢治に聞く (Asking Miyazawa Kenji). Bungei shunjū, 1995.

Irisawa Yasuo 入沢康夫 and Amazawa Taijirō 天沢退二郎. *Tōgi: "Ginga tetsudō no yoru" to wa nanika* 討議：『銀河鉄道の夜』とは何か (Discussion: what is "Night of the milky way railroad"?). Seidosha, 1979.

Ishikawa Hiroyoshi 石川弘義, ed. *Goraku no senzenshi* 娯楽の戦前史 (A prewar history of entertainment). Tōkyō shoseki, 1981.

Ishiwara Jun 石原純. *Gendai no shizen kagaku* 現代の自然科学 (Contemporary natural science). Iwanami shoten, 1924.

Isoda Kōichi 磯田光一. "*Chijin no ai* no bunmei hihyō" 『痴人の愛』の文明批評 (The critique of civilization in *Chijin no ai*). In *Tanizaki Jun'ichirō* 谷崎潤一郎, 194–98. Vol 8 of *Gunzō: Nihon no sakka* 群像・日本の作家 (Writers of Japan). Shōgakukan, 1991.

Ito, Kenji. "Making Sense of *Ryōshiron* (Quantum theory): Introduction of Quantum Mechanics into Japan, 1920–1940." Ph.D. diss., Harvard University, 2002.

Ito, Ken K. *Visions of Desire: Tanizaki's Fictional Worlds*. Stanford, CA: Stanford University Press, 1991.

Itō Sei 伊藤整. "Kaisetsu" 解説 (Commentary). In *Gendai Nihon bungaku zenshū 36: Yokomitsu Riichi shū* 現代日本文学全集 36: 横光利一集 (Collected works of modern Japanese literature, volume 36: works by Yokomitsu Riichi), 425–32. Chikuma shobō, 1954.

———. "Tanizaki Jun'ichirō no geijutsu to shisō" 谷崎潤一郎の芸術と思想 (The art and thought of Tanizaki Jun'ichirō). In *Tanizaki Jun'ichirō* 谷崎潤一郎, 53–61. Vol 8 of *Gunzō: Nihon no sakka* 群像・日本の作家 (Writers of Japan). Shōgakukan, 1991.

Iwamoto, Yoshio. "Aspects of the Proletarian Literary Movement in Japan." In *Japan in Crisis: Essays on Taishō Democracy*. Edited by Bernard S. Silberman and H. D. Harootunian, 156–82. Ann Arbor, MI: Center for Japanese Studies, University of Michigan, 1974.

Jameson, Frederic. "Cognitive Mapping." In *Marxism and the Interpretation of Culture*. Edited by Cary Nelson and Lawrence Grossberg, 347–57. Urbana and Chicago, IL: University of Illinois Press, 1988.

———. *Postmodernism, or, The Cultural Logic of Late Capitalism*. Durham, NC: Duke University Press, 1994.

Kaku, Michio. *Einstein's Cosmos: How Albert Einstein's Vision Transformed Our Understanding of Space and Time*. New York: W. W. Norton, 2004.

Kamei Hideo 亀井秀雄. *Shintai: kono fushigi naru mono no bungaku* 身体・この不思議なるものの文学 (The body: the literature of this astonishing thing). Renga shobō shinsha, 1984.

———. *Transformations of Sensibility: The Phenomenology of Meiji Literature*. Translated by Michael Bourdaghs. Ann Arbor, MI: Center for Japanese Studies, University of Michigan, 2002.

Kamii, Constance. *Number in Preschool and Kindergarten: Educational Implications of Piaget's Theory*. Washington, D.C.: National Association for the Education of Young Children, 1982.

Kamikawa, Hikomatsu, ed. *Japanese-American Diplomatic Relations in the Meiji-Taishō Era*. Pan-Pacific Press, 1958.

Kaneko Tsutomu 金子務. "Ainshutain" アインシュタイン (Einstein). In *Miyazawa Kenji handobukku* 宮沢賢治ハンドブック (Miyazawa Kenji handbook). Edited by Amazawa Taijirō 天沢退二郎, 12–13. Shinshokan, 1996.

———. *Ainshutain shokku 1: Taishō Nihon o yuragaseta yonjūsannichikan* アインシュタイン・ショック 1: 大正日本を揺がせた四十三日間 (Einstein shock 1: forty-three days that shook Taishō Japan). Kawade shobō shinsha, 1991.

———. *Ainshutain shokku 2: Nihon no bunka to shisō e no shōgeki* アインシュタイン・ショック 2: 日本の文化と思想への衝撃 (Einstein shock 2: the impact upon Japanese culture and thought). Kawade shobō shinsha, 1991.

Kano, Ayako. *Acting Like a Woman in Modern Japan: Theater, Gender, and Nationalism*. New York: Palgrave, 2001.

Karatani, Kōjin. *Origins of Modern Japanese Literature*. Translated by Brett De Bary. Durham, NC: Duke University Press, 1993.

———. "One Spirit, Two Nineteenth Centuries." *The South Atlantic Quarterly*, 87, no. 3 (Summer 1988): 615–28.

Karatani Kōjin 柄谷行人, Sekii Mitsuo 関井光男, Murai Osamu 村井紀, and Yoshida Tsukasa 吉田司. "Miyazawa Kenji o megutte" 宮沢賢治をめぐって (Revisiting Miyazawa Kenji). *Hihyō kūkan* 批評空間 II, no. 14 (1997): 6–41.

Kasza, Gregory J. *The State and the Mass Media in Japan, 1918–1945*. Berkeley, CA: University of California Press, 1988.

Kataoka Teppei 片岡鉄平. *Kataoka Teppei zenshū* 片岡鉄平全集 (Collected works of Kataoka Teppei). 9 vols. Nihon tosho sentā, 1995.

———. "Tsūshin kōshu" 通信工手 (The linesmen), *Senki* 戦旗 (May 1930): 187–99.

———. "Wakaki dokusha ni uttau" 若き読者に訴ふ (An appeal to young readers). In *Yokomitsu Riichi to Shin kankakuha* 横光利一と新感覚派 (Yokomitsu Riichi and New Sensationism). Edited by Nihon Bungaku Kenkyū Shiryō Kankōkai 日本文学研究資料刊行会, 222–26. Yūseidō, 1991.

Katayama Masao 片山正夫. *Kagaku honron* 化学本論 (Fundamental issues in chemistry). Uchida rōkakuho, 1915.

Katō, Bunnō, Yoshirō Tamura, and Kōjirō Miyasaka, trans. *The Three Fold Lotus Sutra*. Kosei Publishing, 1975.

Katz, Eric, Andrew Light, and David Rothenberg, eds. *Beneath the Surface: Critical Essays in the Philosophy of Deep Ecology*. Cambridge, MA: The MIT Press, 2000.

Kawabata Yasunari 川端康成. *Kawabata Yasunari zenshū* 川端康成全集 (Collected works of Kawabata Yasunari). 19 vols. Shinchōsha, 1969–74.

———. "Utsukushii Nihon no watakushi" 美しい日本の私 (Japan, the Beautiful and Myself). Stockholm, Sweden: The Nobel Foundation, 1968. http://nobelprize.org/nobel_prizes/literature/laureates/1968/index.html.

Kawai Masao 河合雅雄. "Miyazawa Kenji no dōbutsu no sekai—joshō" 宮沢賢治の動物の世界—序章 (Miyazawa Kenji's animal world—an introduction). In *Kōza: bunmei to kankyō 8—Dōbutsu to bunmei* 講座・文明と環境 8—動物と文明 (Lectures: civilization and environment, volume 8—Animals and civilization). Edited by Kawai Masao 河合雅雄 and Haniwara Kazuo 埴原和郎, 8–25. Asakura shoten, 1995.

Keene, Donald. *Dawn to the West: Japanese Literature of the Modern Era*. New York: Henry Holt and Company, 1984.

Keller, Alexandra. "Disseminations of Modernity: Representation and Consumer Desire in Early Modern Mail-Order Catalogs." In *Cinema and the Invention of Modern Life*. Edited by Leo Charney and Vanessa R. Schwartz, 156–82. Berkeley, CA: University of California Press, 1995.

Kern, Stephen. *The Culture of Time and Space: 1880–1918*. Cambridge, MA: Harvard University Press, 1983.

Kikuchi Seishi 菊池正士. *Busshitsu no kōzō* 物質の構造 (The structure of matter). Sōgansha, 1948.

Kikuchi Yasuo 菊地康雄. *Gendaishi no taidōki* 現代詩の胎動期 (An age of change in modern poetry). Genbunsha, 1967.

Knight, John. *Waiting for Wolves in Japan: An Anthropological Study of People-Wildlife Relations*. Oxford, UK: Oxford University Press, 2003.

Kobayashi Hideo 小林秀雄. *Kobayashi Hideo zenshū* 小林秀雄全集 (Collected works of Kobayashi Hideo). 16 vols. Shinchōsha, 2001–2.

———. *Literature of the Lost Home: Kobayashi Hideo—Literary Criticism, 1924–1939*. Translated by Paul Anderer. Stanford, CA: Stanford University Press, 1995.

Komori Yōichi 小森陽一. *Kōzō to shite no katari* 構造としての語り (Narrative as structure). Shin'yōsha, 1988.

———. *Saishin: Miyazawa Kenji kōgi* 最新・宮沢賢治講義 (Lectures on Miyazawa Kenji). Asahi sensho, 1996.

———. "Shinpojiumu: hōhō no kanosei o motomete" シンポジウム・方法の可能性を求めて (Symposium: toward the possibility of method). *Nihon kindai bungaku* 日本近代文学 35 (October 1986): 1–49.

Kuhn, Thomas S. *The Structure of Scientific Revolutions*. Chicago, IL: University of Chicago Press, 1996. First published 1962.

Kuritsubo Yoshiki 栗坪良樹. "Yokomitsu Riichi no hito to sakuhin" 横光利一の人と作品 (Yokomitsu Riichi: the man and his works). In *Kanshō Nihon gendai bungaku 14: Yokomitsu Riichi* 鑑賞現代日本文学 14: 横光利一 (Appreciating modern Japanese literature, volume 14: Yokomitsu Riichi). Edited by Kuritsubo Yoshiki, 5–38. Kadokawa shoten, 1981.

Kuwaki Ayao 桑木彧雄. *Butsurigaku to ninshiki* 物理学と認識 (Physics and knowledge). Kaizōsha, 1922.

LaMarre, Thomas. *Shadows on the Screen: Tanizaki Jun'ichirō on Cinema and "Oriental" Aesthetics*. Ann Arbor, MI: Center for Japanese Studies, University of Michigan, 2005.

Lapo, Andrei V. "Vladimir I. Vernadsky (1863–1945), founder of the biosphere concept." *International Microbiology* 4 (2001): 47–49.

Larsen, Neil. *Modernism and Hegemony: A Materialist Critique of Aesthetic Agencies*. Minneapolis, MN: University of Minnesota Press, 1990.

Latour, Bruno. *Pandora's Hope: Essays on the Reality of Science Studies*. Cambridge, MA: Harvard University Press, 1999.

———. "A Relativistic Account of Einstein's Relativity." *Social Studies of Science* 18, no. 1 (February 1988): 3–44.

Lee, Leo Ou-fan. *Shanghai Modern: The Flowering of a New Urban Culture in China, 1930–1945*. Cambridge, MA: Harvard University Press, 1999.

Lenin, V. I. "Imperialism, the Highest Stage of Capitalism." In *Selected Works*, vol. 1, 667–766. Moscow: Progress Publishers, 1977.

Leopold, Aldo. *Aldo Leopold's Southwest*. Edited by David E. Brown and Neil B. Carmony. Albuquerque, NM: University of New Mexico Press, 1999. First published Stackpole Books, 1990.

———. *A Sand County Almanac and Sketches Here and There.* New York: Oxford University Press, 1989. First published 1949.

Levins, Richard and Richard Lewontin. *The Dialectical Biologist.* Cambridge, MA: Harvard University Press, 1985.

Lippit, Seiji M. *Topographies of Japanese Modernism.* New York: Columbia University Press, 2002.

Livingstone, R. S. "Ernst Bloch." In *Proceedings of the Essex Conference on the Sociology of Literature.* Edited by Francis Barker, Jay Bernstein, John Coombes, Peter Hulme, David Musselwhite, and Jennifer Stone, 3–11. Colchester, UK: University of Essex, 1979.

Lukács, Georg. "Realism in the Balance." In *Aesthetics and Politics.* Edited by Ronald Taylor, 28–59. London: Verso, 1980.

Maeda Ai 前田愛. "Tōkyō sen kyūhyaku nijūgo nen" 東京 1925 年 (Tokyo 1925). *Gendai shisō* 現代思想 7 (June 1979), no. 8: 72–80.

———. *Toshi kūkan no naka no bungaku* 都市空間のなかの文学 (Literature in city space). Chikuma gakugei bunko, 1992.

Marra, Michele, ed. *Modern Japanese Aesthetics: A Reader.* Honolulu, HI: University of Hawai'i Press, 1999.

Maruyama, Noboru. "Lu Xun in Japan." In *Lu Xun and His Legacy.* Edited by Leo Ou-fan Lee, 216–41. Berkeley, CA: University of California Press, 1985.

Marx, Karl. *Capital*, vol. 1. Translated by Ben Fowkes. New York: Vintage (Random House), 1976.

———. *Grundrisse.* Translated by Martin Nicolaus. New York: Vintage, 1973.

———. *Karl Marx: Early Writings.* Translated and edited by T. B. Bottomore. New York: McGraw-Hill, 1964.

———. *The Marx-Engels Reader: Second Edition.* Edited by Robert C. Tucker. New York: W. W. Norton, 1978.

Marx, Karl and Friedrich Engels. *Collected Works.* Translated by Richard Dixon and others. 50 vols. New York: International Publishers, 1975–2004.

Merchant, Carolyn. *The Death of Nature: Women, Ecology and the Scientific Revolution.* San Francisco, CA: HarperCollins, 1980.

Meyer, Stephen M. "End of the Wild." *Boston Review* 29, no. 2 (April/May 2004): 20–26.

Miller, Arthur I. *Einstein, Picasso: Space, Time and the Beauty that Causes Havoc.* New York: Basic Books, 2001.

Minami Hiroshi 南博. *Taishō bunka* 大正文化 (Taisho culture). Keisō shobō, 1965.

Mita Munesuke 見田宗介. *Miyazawa Kenji: sonzai no matsuri no nake e* 宮沢賢治・存在の祭りの中へ (Miyazawa Kenji: toward the center of a festival of existence). Iwanami shoten, 1984.

Mito Yukihisa 三戸幸久. "Nihonzaru no bunpu hensen ni miru Nihonjin no dōbutsukan henten—Tōhoku chihō no baai o rei ni" ニホンザルの分布変遷にみる日本人の動物観の変転—東北地方の場合を例に (Transformation of the Japanese view of animals as reflected in the shifting distribution of Japanese monkeys—taking Tōhoku as an example). In *Kōza: bunmei to kankyō 8—dōbutsu to bunmei* 講座・文明と環境 8—動物と文明 (Lectures: civilization and environment, volume 8—animals and civilization). Edited by Kawai Masao 河合雅雄 and Haniwara Kazuo 埴原和郎, 89–105. Asakura shoten, 1995.

Miyagi Kazuo 宮城一男. *Miyazawa Kenji no shōgai: ishi to tsuchi e no yume* 宮沢賢治の生涯・石と土への夢 (The life of Miyazawa Kenji: dreams of rock and earth). Chikuma shobō, 1980.

Miyamoto Yuriko 宮本百合子. *Miyamoto Yuriko zenshū* 宮本百合子全集 (Collected works of Miyamoto Yuriko). 30 vols. Shin Nihon shuppansha, 1979–86.

Miyazawa Kenji 宮沢賢治. *Chūmon no ōi ryōriten* 注文の多い料理店. Shinchō bunko, 1990.

———. *Ginga tetsudō no yoru* 銀河鉄道の夜. Kadokawa bunko, 1996.

———. *Kōhon: Miyazawa Kenji zenshū* 校本・宮沢賢治全集 (Collected works of Miyazawa Kenji). 14 vols. Chikuma shobō, 1973–77.

———. *Milky Way Railroad.* Translated and adapted by Joseph Sigrist and D. M. Stroud. Berkeley, CA: Stone Bridge Press, 1996.

———. *Night of the Milky Way Railway: A Translation and Guide.* Translated by Sarah M. Strong. New York: M.E. Sharpe, 1991.

———. *Night on the Milky Way Train.* Translated by Roger Pulvers. Chikuma shobō, 1996.

———. *Night Train to the Stars and Other Stories.* Translated by John Bester. Kodansha International, 1987.

———. *Shinpen: Miyazawa Kenji shishū* 新編・宮沢賢治詩集 (Collected poems of Miyazawa Kenji: new edition). Edited by Amazawa Taijirō 天沢退二郎, 406–20. Shinchōsha, 1991.

———. *Shinshū: Miyazawa Kenji zenshū* 新修：宮沢賢治全集. 16 vols. Chikuma shobō, 1974.

Miyazawa Seiroku 宮沢清六. "Kaisetsu" 解説 (Commentary). In *Chūmon no ōi ryōiten* 注文の多い料理店 (The restaurant of many orders), 176–87. Kadokawa shoten, 1996.

Miyoshi Yukio 三好行雄. *Nihon bungaku no kindai to hankindai* 日本文学の近代と反近代 (The modern and the anti-modern in Japanese literature). Tōkyō daigaku shuppankai, 1972.

Mizoguchi Masahito 溝口雅仁. *Mori no dōbutsu to ikiru gojū no hōhō* 森の動物と生きる50の方法 (Fifty ways of coexisting with forest animals). Buronzu shinsha, 1992.

Mommsen, Wolfgang J. and Jürgen Osterhammel, eds. *Imperialism and After: Continuities and Discontinuities*. London: Allen and Unwin, 1986.

Montgomery, Scott L. *Science in Translation: Movements of Knowledge Through Culture and Time*. Chicago, IL: University of Chicago Press, 2000.

Moretti, Franco. "The Spell of Indecision." In *Marxism and the Interpretation of Culture*. Edited by Cary Nelson and Lawrence Grossberg, 339–44. Urbana and Chicago, IL: University of Illinois Press, 1988.

Morgan, Neil. "From Physiology to Biochemistry." In *Companion to the History of Modern Science*. Edited by R. C. Olby, G. N. Cantor, J. R. R. Christie, and M. J. S. Hodge, 494–502. New York: Routledge, 1990.

Moriyama Shigeo 森山重雄. *Josetsu: tenkanki no bungaku* 序説転換期の文学 (Introduction: literature in an age of transition). San'ichi shobō, 1974.

Morris, Brian. *The Power of Animals: An Ethnography*. Oxford, UK: Berg, 1998.

Morris-Suzuki, Tessa. *The Technological Transformation of Japan: From the Seventeenth to the Twenty-First Century*. Cambridge, UK: Cambridge University Press, 1994.

Muir, John. *A Thousand-Mile Walk to the Gulf*. Edited by William F. Bade. Boston and New York: Houghton Mifflin Company, 1916.

Murobuse Kōshin 室伏高信. *Tsuchi ni kaeru* 土に還る (Return to the soil). Hihyōsha, 1924.

Murphy, Joseph A. *Metaphorical Circuit: Negotiations between Literature and Science in 20th Century Japan*. Ithaca, NY: East Asia Program, Cornell University, 2004.

Myers, Ramon H. and Mark R. Peattie, eds. *The Japanese Colonial Empire, 1895–1945*. Princeton, NJ: Princeton University Press, 1984.

Nagai Kafū 永井荷風. "Tanizaki Jun'ichirō shi no sakuhin" 谷崎潤一郎氏の作品 (The works of Mr. Tanizaki Jun'ichirō). In *Tanizaki Jun'ichirō* 谷崎潤一郎, 92–98. Vol. 8 of *Gunzō: Nihon no sakka* 群像・日本の作家 (Writers of Japan). Shōgakukan, 1991.

Nakachi Aya 中地文. "Fuchizawa Kojūrō" 淵沢小十郎. In *Miyazawa Kenji handobukku* 宮沢賢治ハンドブック (Miyazawa Kenji handbook). Edited by Amazawa Taijirō 天沢退二郎, 170–71. Shinshokan, 1996.

Nakagawa Yoichi 中河与一. *Keishiki shugi geijutsuron* 形式主義芸術論 (A theory of formalist art). Shinchōsha, 1930.

Nakai Masakazu 中井正一. *Nakai Masakazu zenshū* 中井正一全集 (Collected works of Nakai Masakazu). 4 vols. Bijutsu shuppansha, 1965.

Nakamura Hajime 中村元. *Bukkyōgo daijiten* 仏教語大辞典 (Encyclopedia of Buddhist terminology). Tōkyō shoseki, 1981

Nakamura Mitsuo 中村光夫. *Tanizaki Jun'ichirō ron* 谷崎潤一郎 (On Tanizaki Jun'ichirō). Kawade shobō, 1952.

Nakamura Murao 中村武羅夫. "Honkaku shōsetsu to shinkyō shōsetsu to" 本格小説と心境小説と (The authentic novel and the state-of-mind novel). In *Gendai Nihon bungaku ronsō shi 1* 現代日本文学論争史 1 (A history of modern Japanese literary debates 1). Edited by Hirano Ken 平野謙, Odagiri Hideo 小田切秀雄, Yamamoto Kenkichi 山本健吉. Miraisha, 1957.

Nakaya Ukichirō 中谷宇吉郎. *Kagaku no hōhō* 科学の方法 (Methods of science). Iwanami shinsho, 2004. First published 1958.

———. *Nakaya Ukichirō zuihitsu senshū* 中谷宇吉郎随筆選集 (Selected writings of Nakaya Ukichirō). Edited by Oka Kiyoshi 岡潔, Kaya Seiji 茅誠司, and Fujioka Yoshio 藤岡由夫. 3 vols. Asahi shinbunsha, 1966.

Nash, Roderick Frazier. *The Rights of Nature: A History of Environmental Ethics*. Madison, WI: University of Wisconsin Press, 1989.

Natsume Sōseki 夏目漱石. *Sōseki zenshū* 漱石全集 (Collected works of Natsume Sōseki). 19 vols. Iwanami shoten, 1965–76.

Nietzsche, Friedrich. *On the Genealogy of Morals and Ecce Homo*. Translated by Walter Kaufmann and R. J. Hollingdale. New York: Vintage, 1989. First published Random House, 1967.

Nihon Kindai Bungakukan 日本近代文学館, ed. *Nihon kindai bungaku daijiten* 日本近代文学大事典. 6 vols. Kōdansha, 1977–78.

Noguchi Takehiko 野口武彦. *Tanizaki Jun'ichrō ron* 谷崎潤一郎論. Chūō kōronsha, 1973.

Nomoto Kan'ichi 野本寛一. *Kumano sankai minzokukō* 熊野山海民俗考 (A treatise on the mountain and coastal folk customs of Kumano). Kyoto: Jinbun shoin, 1990.

———. "Shin'i no naka no dōbutsu" 心意のなかの動物 (Animals in folk consciousness). In *Kōza: Nihon no minzokugaku 4—kankyō no minzoku* 講座：日本の民俗学—環境の民俗 (Lectures: Japanese folklore studies—environmental folklore). Edited by Akata Mitsuo 赤田光男, Katsuki Yōichirō 香月洋一郎, Komatsu Kazuhiko 小松和彦, Nomoto Kan'ichi 野本寛一, and Fukuda Ajio 福田アジオ, 221–34. Yūzankaku, 1996.

Nomura Shōgo 野村尚吾. *Denki: Tanizaki Jun'ichirō* 伝記・谷崎潤一郎. Rokkō shuppan, 1972.

Odagiri Hideo 小田切秀雄. In *Kindai Nihon no sakkatachi* 近代日本の作家たち (Modern writers of Japan). 2 vols. Hōsei daigaku shuppankyoku, 1973.

Odin, Steve. "The Japanese Concept of Nature in Relation to Environmental Ethics and Conservation Aesthetics of Aldo Leopold." *Environmental Ethics* 13, no. 4 (Winter 1991): 345–60.

Ōe Kenzaburō 大江健三郎. *Aimai na Nihon no watakushi* 曖昧な日本の私 (Iwanami shoten, 1995).

———. "Japan, the Ambiguous, and Myself." Stockholm, Sweden: The Nobel Foundation, 1994. http://nobelprize.org/nobel_prizes/literature/laureates/1994/oe-lecture.html.

Ogura Toyofumi 小倉豊文. "Kenji no yonda hon" 賢治の読んだ本 (Books Kenji read). In *Nihon bungaku kenkyū shiryō shinshū 26—Miyazawa Kenji: dōwa no uchū* 日本文学研究資料新集 26—宮沢賢治・童話の宇宙 (New collection of research material in Japanese literature 26—Miyazawa Kenji: the universe of children's stories). Edited by Kurihara Atsushi 栗原敦, 200–3. Yūseido, 1990.

Oka Asajirō 丘浅次郎. "Jinrui no seifuku ni tai suru shizen no fukushū" 人類の征服に対する自然の復讐 (Nature's retaliation against human conquest). *Chūō kōron* 中央公論 27, no. 1 (1912): 13–20.

———. *Kindai Nihon shisō taikei 9—Oka Asjirō shū* 近代日本思想大系 9—丘浅次郎集 (A compendium of modern Japanese thought, volume 9—an Oka Asajirō collection). Edited by Tsukuba Hisaharu 筑波常治. Chikuma shobō, 1979.

Ono Ryūshō 小野隆祥. "'Aomori banka' to Hekkeru hakushi" 「青森挽歌」とヘッケル博士 ('Aomori elegy' and Dr. Haeckel). In *Miyazawa Kenji*, 266–76. Vol 12 of *Gunzō: Nihon no sakka* 群像・日本の作家 (Writers of Japan). Shogakukan, 1990.

Ōsawa Masayoshi 大沢正善. "Jyobanni & Kamupanerura" ジョバンニ＆カムパネルラ (Giovanni and Campanella). In *Miyazawa Kenji handobukku* 宮沢賢治ハンドブック (Miyazawa Kenji handbook). Edited by Amazawa Taijirō 天沢退二郎, 104–5. Shishokan, 1996.

Oshino Takeshi 押野武志. "Nōmin geijutsu" 農民芸術 (Art of the farmer). In *Miyazawa Kenji handobukku* 宮沢賢治ハンドブック (Miyazawa Kenji handbook). Edited by Amazawa Taijirō 天沢退二郎, 149–50. Shinshokan, 1996.

Ōsugi Sakae 大杉栄. "Oka hakase no seibutsugakuteki jinsei shakaikan o ronzu" 丘博士の生物学的人生社会観を論ず (On Professor Oka's biological view of human society). In *Kindai Nihon shisō taikei 9—Oka Asajirō shū* 近代日本思想大系 9—丘浅次郎集 (A compendium of modern Japanese thought volume 9—an Oka Asajirō collection). Edited by Tsukuba Hisaharu 筑波常治, 411–29. Chikuma shobō, 1979.

Ōtsuka Tsuneki 大塚常樹. *Miyazawa Kenji shinshō no kosumorojī* 宮沢賢治・心象の宇宙論 (The cosmology of Miyazawa Kenji's "mental sketch"). Chōbunsha, 1993.

Ōya Sōichi 大宅壮一. *Ōya Sōichi zenshū* 大宅壮一全集 (Collected works of Ōya Sōichi). 31 vols. Sōyōsha, 1981–82.

Perry, Elizabeth J. *Shanghai on Strike: The Politics of Chinese Labor.* Stanford, CA: Stanford University Press, 1993.

Porter, Theodore M. "The Death of the Object: *Fin de siecle* Philosophy of Physics." In *Modernist Impulses in the Human Sciences.* Edited by Dorothy Ross, 128–51. Baltimore, MD: Johns Hopkins University Press, 1994.

Reynolds, Michael. *Hemingway: The Paris Years.* New York: W. W. Norton & Company, 1989.

Ross, Dorothy. "Modernism Reconsidered." In *Modernist Impulses in the Human Sciences: 1870–1930.* Edited by Dorothy Ross, 1–25. Baltimore, MD: Johns Hopkins University Press, 1994.

Rubin, Gayle. "The Traffic in Women: Notes on the 'Political Economy' of Sex." In *Feminist Frameworks: Alternative Theoretical Accounts of the Relations between Women and Men.* Edited by Alison M. Jaggar and Paula Rothenburg, 157–210. New York: McGraw-Hill, 1993.

Rubin, Jay. *Injurious to Public Morals: Writers and the Meiji State.* Seattle, WA: University of Washington Press, 1984.

———. "Sōseki as Lecturer: Autonomy and Coercion." In *Kokoro: A Novel and Selected Essays*, by Natsume Sōseki, 237–56. Translated by Edwin McClellan and Jay Rubin. New York: Madison Books, 1992.

Saitō Bun'ichi 斎藤文一. *Gingakei to Miyazawa Kenji* 銀河系と宮沢賢治 (The Milky Way galaxy and Miyazawa Kenji). Kokubunsha, 1996.

———. *Miyazawa Kenji to sono tenkai* 宮沢賢治とその展開 (Miyazawa Kenji and his development). Kokubunsha, 1976.

Sakata Shōichi 坂田昌一. "Butsurigaku to shizen benshōhō" 物理学と自然弁証法(Physics and natural dialectics). *Chōryū* 潮流 2, no. 8 (September-October 1947): 1–12.

———. "Taketani's 'Three-Stage Theory.'" *Supplement of the Progress of Theoretical Physics*, 50 (1971): 9–11.

———. "Watakushi no koten: Engerusu no *Shizen benshōhō*" 私の古典:エンゲルスの『自然弁証法』(My classics: Engels' *Dialectics of Nature*). *Kagaku* 科学 41, no. 3 (March 1971): 134–37.

Sato, Barbara. *The New Japanese Woman: Modernity, Media, and Women in Interwar Japan.* Durham, NC: Duke University Press, 2003.

Satō Haruo 佐藤春夫. *Satō Haruo zenshū* 佐藤春夫全集 (Collected works of Satō Haruo). 12 vols. Kōdansha, 1966–70.

Schivelbusch, Wolfgang. *The Railway Journey: The Industrialization of Time and Space in the 19th Century.* Berkeley, CA: University of California Press, 1977.

Seed, David. Introduction to *The Inheritors: An Extravagant Story*, by Joseph Conrad and Ford Madox Ford, ix–xxviii. Liverpool, UK: Liverpool University Press, 1999.

Seidensticker, Edward C. *Tokyo Rising: The City Since the Great Earthquake.* Cambridge, MA: Harvard University Press, 1991.

Sergeant, Harriet. *Shanghai.* London: Jonathan Cape, 1991.

Serpell, James. *In the Company of Animals: A Study of Human-Animal Relationships.* Cambridge, UK: Cambridge University Press, 1996.

Shibatani, Atsuhiro. "The Anti-Selectionism of Kinji Imanishi and Social Anti-Darwinism in Japan." *The Journal of Social and Biological Structures* 6 (1983): 335–43.

Shimamura Teru 島村輝. "Kondō Azuma ron" 近藤東論 (On Kondō Azuma). In *Toshi modanizumu no honryū: "Shi to shiron" no resupurinūbō* 都市モダニズムの奔流:「詩と詩論」のレスプリ・ヌーボー (A torrent of urban modernism: the *esprit nouveau* of the journal *Shi to shiron*). Edited by Sawa Masahiro 澤正宏 and Wada Hirofumi 和田博文, 124–31. Kanrin shobō, 1996.

Shinoda Kōichirō 篠田浩一郎. *Shōsetsu wa ika ni kakareta ka* 小説はいかに書かれたか (How have novels been written?). Iwanami shinsho, 1982.

Shklovsky, Victor. "Art as Technique." In *Modernism: An Anthology of Sources and Documents.* Edited by Vassiliki Kolocotroni, Jane Goldman, Olga Taxidou. Translated by Lee T. Lemon and Marion J. Reis, 217–21. Chicago, IL: University of Chicago Press, 1998.

Silverberg, Miriam. *Changing Song: The Marxist Manifestos of Nakano Shigeharu.* Princeton, NJ: Princeton University Press, 1990.

———. "The Modern Girl as Militant." In *Recreating Japanese Women, 1600–1945.* Edited by Gail Lee Bernstein, 239–66. Berkeley, CA: University of California Press, 1991.

Slayter, Elizabeth M. *Optical Methods in Biology.* New York: Wiley-Interscience, 1970.

Smith, Crosbie. "Energy." In *Companion to the History of Modern Science.* Edited by R. C. Olby, G. N. Cantor, J. R. R. Christie, and M. J. S. Hodge, 326–41. London: Routledge, 1990.

Smolin, Lee. *Three Roads to Quantum Gravity.* New York: Basic Books, 2001.

Snyder, Gary. "Is Nature Real?" In *The Gary Snyder Reader: Prose, Poetry, and Translations.* Washington, D.C.: Counterpoint, 1999.

———. *The Practice of the Wild.* New York: North Point Press, 1990.

Snyder, Joel. "Benjamin on Reproducibility and Aura: A Reading of 'The Work of Art in the Age of its Technical Reproducibility.'" In *Benjamin: Philosophy,*

Aesthetics, History. Edited by Gary Smith, 158–74. Chicago, IL: University of Chicago Press, 1989.

———. "Visualization and Visibility." In *Picturing Science, Producing Art*. Edited by Caroline A. Jones and Peter Galison, 379–96. New York: Routledge, 1998.

Sontag, Susan. *On Photography*. New York: Anchor Books, 1990. First published Farrar, Straus & Giroux, 1977.

Spencer, Lloyd. Introduction to *The Sense of Sight* by John Berger. Edited by Lloyd Spencer, xi–xix. New York: Vintage, 1985.

Spender, Stephen. *World Within World: The Autobiography of Stephen Spender*. New York: The Modern Library, 2001.

Stein, Gertrude. *Picasso*. New York: Dover, 1938.

Steinmetz, Charles. *Four Lectures on Relativity and Space*. New York: McGraw-Hill, 1923.

Strong, Sarah M. "The Poetry of Miyazawa Kenji." Ph.D. diss., University of Chicago, 1984.

———. "Reader's Guide." In *Night of the Milky Way Railway: A Translation and Guide*. Translated by Sarah M. Strong, 83–120. New York: M.E. Sharpe, 1991.

Sullivan, Louis H. "The Tall Office Building Artistically Considered." Available online at http://www.njit.edu/v2/Library/archlib/pub-domain/Sullivan-1896-tall-bldg.html. First published in *Lippincott's Magazine* (March 1896).

Suzuki, Tomi. *Narrating the Self: Fictions of Japanese Modernity*. Stanford, CA: Stanford University Press, 1996.

Takahashi Seori 高橋世織. *Kankaku no modan* 感覚のモダン (The modern of the senses). Serika shobō, 2003.

Taketani, Mitsuo. "Methodological Approaches in the Development of the Meson Theory of Yukawa in Japan." *Supplement of the Progress of Theoretical Physics* 50 (1970): 12–24.

Tamura Eitarō 田村栄太郎. *Asakusa, Yoshiwara, Sumidagawa* 浅草・吉原・隅田川. Yūzankaku, 1964.

Tanabe Hajime 田辺元. *Tanabe Hajime zenshū* 田辺元全集 (Collected works of Tanabe Hajime). 15 vols. Chikuma shobō, 1963–64.

Tani Kazuo (Taketani Mitsuo) 武谷三男. "Nōberushō jushōsha Jorio-Kyurī fusai no gakuteki gyōseki ni tsuite" ノーベル賞受賞者ジョリオキュリー夫妻の学的業績について (On Nobel Prize winners Mr. and Mrs. Joliot-Curie's scholarly achievements). *Sekai bunka* 世界文化 16 (April 1936): 10–20.

———. "Shizen no benshōhō" 自然の弁証法 (Nature's dialectics). *Sekai bunka* 世界文化 15 (March 1936): 2–11.

Tanizaki Jun'ichirō 谷崎潤一郎. *Childhood Years: A Memoir.* Translated by Paul McCarthy. Kodansha International, 1988.

———. *In Praise of Shadows.* Translated by Thomas J. Harper and Edward G. Seidensticker. Stony Creek, CT: Leete's Island Books, 1977.

———. *Naomi.* Translated by Anthony H. Chambers. San Francisco, CA: North Point Press, 1990.

———. *Tanizaki Jun'ichirō zenshū* 谷崎潤一郎全集 (Collected works of Tanizaki Jun'ichirō). 28 vols. Chūō kōronsha, 1966–70.

Tansley, Arthur G. "The Use and Abuse of Vegetational Concepts and Terms." In *Ecology* 16, no. 3 (1935): 284–307.

Terada Torahiko 寺田寅彦. *Terada Torahiko zenshū* 寺田寅彦全集 (Collected works of Terada Torahiko). 20 vols. Iwanami shoten, 1996–97.

Thomas, Julia Adeney. *Reconfiguring Modernity: Concepts of Nature in Japanese Political Ideology.* Berkeley, CA: University of California Press, 2001.

Togawa, Kumi and Masayuki Sakamoto. "Bear Markets: Japan." *Japan Wildlife Conservation Society* (February 2002): 121–52.

Tomiyama Hidetoshi 富山英俊. "Gērī Sunaidā no Miyazawa Kenji" ゲーリー・スナイダーの宮沢賢治 (Gary Snyder's Miyazawa Kenji). *Meiji gakuin ronsō* 明治学院論叢 537, no. 89 (March, 1994): 1–37.

Totman, Conrad. *The Green Archipelago: Forestry in Pre-Industrial Japan.* Athens, OH: Ohio University Press, 1989.

Tsuji Jun 辻潤. *Tsuji Jun zenshū* 辻潤全集 (Collected works of Tsuji Jun). 9 vols. Satsuki shobō, 1982.

Tsuzukihashi Tatsuo 続橋達雄, ed. *Miyazawa Kenji kenkyū shiryō shūsei* 宮沢賢治研究資料集成 (Collected research material on Miyazawa Kenji). 23 vols. Nihon tosho sentā, 1990.

Tuan, Yi-Fu. *Dominance and Affection: The Making of Pets.* New Haven, CT: Yale University Press, 1984.

Ueda, Atsuko. "The Production of Literature and the Effaced Realm of the Political." *Journal of Japanese Studies* 31, no. 1 (Winter 2005): 61–88.

Ueno Chizuko 上野千鶴子, Ogura Chikako 小倉千加子, and Tomioka Taeko 富岡多恵子. *Danryū bungaku ron* 男流文学論 (A theory of men's literature). Chikuma shobō, 1992.

Updike, John. *Hugging the Shore: Essays and Criticism.* New York: Alfred A. Knopf, 1983.

Venuti, Lawrence. *The Scandals of Translation: Towards an Ethics of Difference.* New York: Routledge, 1998.

Vernadsky, Vladimir I. *The Biosphere.* London: Synergetic Press, 1986.

Virilio, Paul. *Virilio Live: Selected Interviews.* Edited by John Armitage. London: Sage Publications, 2001.

Wakabayashi Mikio 若林幹夫. *Sōseki no "riaru"—sokuryō to shite no bungaku* 漱石のリアル—測量としての文学 (The "real" in Sōseki: literature as measurement). Kinokuniya shoten, 2002.

Walker, Brett. *The Conquest of Ainu Lands: Ecology and Culture in Japanese Expansion, 1590–1800.* Berkeley, CA: University of California Press, 2001.

———. *The Lost Wolves of Japan.* Seattle, WA: University of Washington Press, 2005.

———. "Meiji Modernization, Scientific Agriculture, and Destruction of Japan's Hokkaido Wolf." *Environmental History* 9, no. 2 (April 2004): 248–74.

Watanabe, Masao. *The Japanese and Western Science.* Translated by Otto Theodor Benfey. Philadelphia, PA: University of Pennsylvania Press, 1988.

White, Richard. "Animals and Enterprise." In *The Oxford History of the American West.* Edited by C. A. Milner II, C. A. O'Connor, and M. Sandweiss, 237–73. New York: Oxford University Press, 1994.

Williams, Linda. *Hard Core: Power, Pleasure, and the "Frenzy of the Visible."* Berkeley, CA: University of California Press, 1989.

Williams, Raymond. *The Politics of Modernism: Against the New Conformists.* New York: Verso, 1989.

Wise, Norton M. "Electromagnetic Theory in the Nineteenth Century." In *Companion to the History of Modern Science.* Edited by R. C. Olby, G. N. Cantor, J. R. R. Christie, and M. J. S. Hodge, 342–56. London: Routledge, 1990.

Wolfe, Cary. *Animal Rites: American Culture, the Discourse of Species, and Posthumanist Theory.* Chicago, IL: University of Chicago Press, 2003.

Wolin, Richard. *Labyrinths: Exploration in the Critical History of Ideas.* Amherst, MA: University of Massachusetts Press, 1995.

Worster, Donald. *Nature's Economy: A History of Ecological Ideas, Second Edition.* Cambridge, UK: Cambridge University Press, 1994. First published San Francisco: Sierra Club Books, 1977.

Yamaguchi Osamu 山口修. "Jōhōka jidai no tōrai" 情報化時代の到来 (The advent of the information age). In *Zusetsu Nihon bunka no rekishi 12: Taishō/Shōwa* 図説日本文化の歴史 12：大正・昭和. Edited by Kano Masanao 鹿野政直, et al. 26–34. Shōgakukan, 1981.

Yokomitsu Riichi. *Shanghai: A Novel by Yokomitsu Riichi.* Translated by Dennis Washburn. Ann Arbor, MI: Center for Japanese Studies, University of Michigan, 2001.

——— 横光利一. *Teihon: Yokomitsu Riichi zenshū* 定本：横光利一全集 (Collected works of Yokomitsu Riichi). 16 vols. Kawade shobō shinsha, 1981–87.

Yomota Inuhiko 四方田犬彦. "Tanizaki Junichirō no eiga taiken" 谷崎潤一郎の映画体験 (Tanizaki Junichirō's experience with cinema). *Kokubungaku:*

kaishaku to kyōzai no kenkyū 国文学・解釈と教材の研究 43, no. 6 (1998): 40–48.

Yoshimi Shun'ya 吉見俊哉. *"Koe" no shihonshugi: denwa, rajio, chikuonki no shakai shi* 「声」の資本主義—電話・ラジオ・蓄音機の社会史 (The capitalism of voice: a social history of telephones, radio, and the phonograph). Kōdansha, 1995.

Yoshimura Akira 吉村昭. *Kantō daishinsai* 関東大震災 (The great Kantō earthquake). Bungei shunjū, 1977.

List of Characters

"Aimai na Nihon no watakushi"
曖昧な日本の私
"Ainshutain no shin gakusetsu ni tsuite" アインシュタインの新学説に就いて
Akutagawa Ryūnosuke
芥川龍之介
Amachua kurabu
アマチュア倶楽部
"Aomori banka" 青森挽歌
"Aru nōgakusei no nikki"
或る農学生の日記
"Atama narabi ni hara"
頭ならびに腹

Banbutsu taika shinsetsu
万物退化新説
"Bijiterian taisai"
ビジタリアン大祭
"Bungakuron" 文学論
bungei fukkō 文芸復興
Bungei jidai 文芸時代
"Bungei jihyō" 文芸時評
"Bungeijō no byōsharon to kagaku"
文芸上の描写論と科学
bungo 文語
bunka 文化
bunmei 文明
Bunmei no botsuraku 文明の没落
"Butsurigakujō no ninshiki no mondai"
物理学上の認識の問題
"Butsurigaku to kankaku"
物理学と感覚

Chiba Kameo 千葉亀雄
Chijin no ai 痴人の愛
Chijin no yume 痴人の夢
chiso kaisei 地租改正
Chūmon no ōi ryōriten
注文の多い料理店
Chūō kōron 中央公論

Dai Nihon Seruroido
大日本セルロイド
Dentsū 電通
Dōbutsu shinkaron 動物進化論

ekijū 益獣
Esashi 江刺
Ezo 蝦夷

Fukushima 福島
"Futon" 布団
fūzoku shōsetsu 風俗小説

genbun itchi 言文一致
"Gendai bungaku no fuan" 現代文学の不安
"Gendai Nihon no kaika" 現代日本の開化
Gendai shisō 現代思想
"Genjitsu no sokudo to yuibutsuronteki bungakuron" 現実の速度と唯物論的文学論
gesaku 戯作
"Ginga tetsudō no yoru" 銀河鉄道の夜
godai 五大
"Gorin tōge" 五輪峠
Gunritsu Hienuki Nōgakkō 群立稗貫農学校
"Gurando denchū" グランド電柱

Hagiwara Kyōjirō 萩原恭次郎
Hagiwara Sakutarō 萩原朔太郎
haikara ハイカラ
hakubutsugaku 博物学
Hanamaki 花巻
Hara Asao 原阿佐緒
Haru to shura: shinshō suketchi 春と修羅：心象スケッチ
Hashizume Ken 橋爪健
Hayama Michiko 葉山三千子
Hienuki 稗貫
Higuchi Ichiyō 樋口一葉
higuma ヒグマ（羆、樋熊）
Hirabayashi Hatsunosuke 平林初之輔
Hirato Renkichi 平戸廉吉
Hongkou 虹口
Hori Tatsuo 堀辰雄
Huangpu 黄浦

Imanishi Kinji 今西錦司
Inawashiro 猪苗代
"In'ei raisan" 陰翳礼賛
inga 因果
iriaichi 入会地
Ishii Kikujirō 石井菊次郎
Ishikawa Chiyomatsu 石川千代松
Ishiwara Jun 石原純
Itō Noe 伊藤野枝
Itō Sei 伊藤整
Iwate 岩手
Iwate-san 岩手山
"Iwayuru shizen no bi to shizen no ai" 所謂自然の美と自然の愛
Izawa Shūji 伊沢修二

"Jashūmon" 邪宗門
jin'i tōta 人為淘汰
Jinken shinsetsu 人権新説
"Jinmenso" 人面疽
Jinrui no kako genzai oyobi mirai 人類の過去現在及び未来
"Jinrui no seifuku ni taisuru shizen no fukushū" 人類の征服に対する自然の復讐
Jōdoshinshū 浄土真宗
Josei 女性
jūjū mujin 重重無尽
junbungaku 純文学
"Junsui shōsetsuron" 純粋小説論

Kagaku 科学
Kagaku honron 化学本論
Kagaku taikei 科学大系
Kaizō 改造
Kamakura 鎌倉
Kamera カメラ
Kanamaru Shigene 金丸重嶺
kanbun 漢文
Kaneko Mitsuharu 金子光晴
kanji 漢字
Kappa 河童
katakana 片仮名
Kataoka Teppei 片岡鉄平
Katayama Masao 片山正夫
Katō Hiroyuki 加藤弘之
"Katsudō shashin no genzai to shōrai"
活動写真の現在と将来
Katsurazawa 桂沢
Kawabata Yasunari 川端康成
Keishiki shugi geijutsu ron
形式主義芸術論
Keizai Zasshisha 経済雑誌社
Kii 紀伊
Kikuchi Seishi 菊池正士
Kinai 畿内
Kingu キング
Kinreisha 金鈴社
Kitahara Hakushū 北原白秋
kitsuneken 狐拳
Kobayashi Hideo 小林秀雄
Kobayashi Takiji 小林多喜二
"Koiwai nōjō" 小岩井農場
"Kokyō o ushinatta bungaku"
故郷を失った文学
kokubungaku 国文学
Kokuchūkai 国柱会
kū 空
Kuki Shūzō 九鬼周造
Kurahara Korehito 蔵原惟人
Kurihara Kisaburō
栗原喜三郎
Kuwaki Ayao 桑木彧雄

Mannensha 万年社
matagi またぎ
Meiji 明治
Miyamoto Yuriko
宮本百合子
Miyazawa Kenji 宮沢賢治
Modansō to modansō
モダン層とモダン相
"Moji ni tsuite"
文字について
Morioka Kōtō Nōrin Gakkō
盛岡高等農林学校
mujō 無常
Murobuse Kōshin 室伏高信
Myōhō renge kyō 妙法蓮華経

Nagai Kafū 永井荷風
Nagaoka Hantarō
長岡半太郎
Nakagawa Yoichi 中河与一
Nakai Masakazu 中井正一
Nakamura Mitsuo 中村光夫
Nakamura Murao
中村武羅夫
Nakano Shigeharu 中野重治
Nakaya Ukichirō
中谷宇吉郎
Nakayama 中山
"Nametokoyama no kuma"
なめとこ山の熊
Natsume Sōseki 夏目漱石
Nichiren 日蓮
Nihonjin shijin 日本人詩人
Nihon Kōgaku Kōgyō
日本光学工業
Nihon Kōkoku 日本広告

"Nihon miraiha sengen undō"
日本未来派宣言運動
Nihon Ōkami Kyōkai
日本オオカミ協会
Nikugan ni mieru hoshi no kenkyū
肉眼に見える星の研究
Nishiwaki Junzaburō
西脇順三郎
"Nōmin geijutsu gairon kōyō"
農民芸術概論綱要
"Nyorai-juryō-bon"
如来寿量品

Ōe Kenzaburō 大江健三郎
"Oinomori to zarumori, nusutomori"
狼森と笊森、盗森
Oka Asajirō 丘浅次郎
okuyama 奥山
Ōsaka asahi shinbun
大阪朝日新聞
Ōsugi Sakae 大杉栄
Ōya Sōichi 大宅壮一
Ōzora 大空

Rasu Chijin Kyōkai
羅須地人協会
rōko 狼顧

Sakata Shōichi 坂田昌一
Satō Haruo 佐藤春夫
Satō Sōnosuke 佐藤惣之助
satoyama 里山
seiban 生蕃
Seibutsu shigen 生物始源
"Seijika" 政治家
Seimei no fukashigi
生命の不可思議
Seishu genshiron 生種原始論
seizon kyōsō 生存競争
Sekai bunka 世界文化
Senki 戦旗
seitaigaku 生態学
"Setsumei to kisai"
説明と記載
Shanhai 上海
Shiga Naoya 志賀直哉
Shimonekozakura 下根子桜
"Shina yūki" 支那遊記
Shin kankakuha 新感覚派
"Shin kankakuha to conminizumu bungaku" 新感覚派とコンミニズム文学
shinka 進化
Shinkaron kōwa 進化論講話
Shinka shinron 進化新論
"Shinkū yōbai" 真空溶媒
shinkyō shōsetsu 心境小説
shinpo 進歩
Shinsen kōseizu 新撰恒星図
Shin shōsetsu 新小説
Shirakaba 白樺
Shiseki meishō tennen kinenbutsu hozonhō
史跡名勝天然記念物保存法
"Shishi odori no hajimari"
鹿踊りのはじまり
Shisō 思想
"Shi to moji to" 詩と文字と
Shi to shiron 詩と詩論
Shizen benshōhō 自然弁証法
shizen tōta 自然淘汰
shōbai 商売
shokumotsu rensa 食物連鎖
Shomotsu Tenbōsha
書物展望社
Shōsetsu shinzui 小説神髄
Shōwa 昭和
shōya 庄屋
sōgo fujo 相互扶助

Sōgo fujoron: shinka no ichi yōso
相互扶助論:進化の一要素
"Sōtaisei no mondai"
相対性の問題
Suzhou 蘇州
Suzuki Hachirō 鈴木八郎

Tachibana Senzaburō
立花銑三郎
Tade kuu mushi 蓼食う虫
Taishō 大正
Taishō Katsudō Shashin
大正活動写真
taishū bungaku 大衆文学
Takekurabe たけくらべ
Taketani Mitsuo 武谷三男
Tanabe Hajime 田辺元
Tane maku hito 種蒔く人
Tanizaki Jun'ichirō
谷崎潤一郎
Tayama Katai 田山花袋
tekisha seizon 適者生存
Terada Torahiko 寺田寅彦
Tetsugaku zasshi 哲学雑誌
Tōhoku 東北
Tokugawa 徳川
Tōno 遠野
Tōno monogatari 遠野物語
Tosaka Jun 戸坂潤
Toyama Usaburō 外山卯三郎
Toyosawa 豊沢
Tsubouchi Shōyō 坪内逍遥
Tsuchi ni kaeru 土に還る
Tsuji Jun 辻潤
Tsukiji 築地
tsukinowaguma
ツキノワグマ(月輪熊)
"Tsūshin kōshu" 通信工手

"Utsukushii Nihon no watakushi"
美しい日本の私

Wakayama 和歌山
watakushi shōsetsu 私小説

yamagatana 山刀
yamaotoko 山男
Yanagita Kunio 柳田國男
Yokomitsu Riichi 横光利一
yorishiro 依代
"Yuibutsuronteki bungakuron ni tsuite"
唯物論的文学論について
Yuibutsuron to keiken hihanron
唯物論と経験批判論
Yukawa Hideki 湯川秀樹
yūshō reppai 優勝劣敗

Zen Nihon Musansha Geijutsu Renmei
全日本無産者芸術連盟
Zhabei 閘北

Index

Harvard East Asian Monographs
(*out-of-print)

*1. Liang Fang-chung, *The Single-Whip Method of Taxation in China*
*2. Harold C. Hinton, *The Grain Tribute System of China, 1845–1911*
3. Ellsworth C. Carlson, *The Kaiping Mines, 1877–1912*
*4. Chao Kuo-chün, *Agrarian Policies of Mainland China: A Documentary Study, 1949–1956*
*5. Edgar Snow, *Random Notes on Red China, 1936–1945*
*6. Edwin George Beal, Jr., *The Origin of Likin, 1835–1864*
7. Chao Kuo-chün, *Economic Planning and Organization in Mainland China: A Documentary Study, 1949–1957*
*8. John K. Fairbank, *Ching Documents: An Introductory Syllabus*
*9. Helen Yin and Yi-chang Yin, *Economic Statistics of Mainland China, 1949–1957*
10. Wolfgang Franke, *The Reform and Abolition of the Traditional Chinese Examination System*
11. Albert Feuerwerker and S. Cheng, *Chinese Communist Studies of Modern Chinese History*
12. C. John Stanley, *Late Ching Finance: Hu Kuang-yung as an Innovator*
13. S. M. Meng, *The Tsungli Yamen: Its Organization and Functions*
*14. Ssu-yü Teng, *Historiography of the Taiping Rebellion*
15. Chun-Jo Liu, *Controversies in Modern Chinese Intellectual History: An Analytic Bibliography of Periodical Articles, Mainly of the May Fourth and Post-May Fourth Era*
*16. Edward J. M. Rhoads, *The Chinese Red Army, 1927–1963: An Annotated Bibliography*
*17. Andrew J. Nathan, *A History of the China International Famine Relief Commission*
*18. Frank H. H. King (ed.) and Prescott Clarke, *A Research Guide to China-Coast Newspapers, 1822–1911*
*19. Ellis Joffe, *Party and Army: Professionalism and Political Control in the Chinese Officer Corps, 1949–1964*

*20. Toshio G. Tsukahira, *Feudal Control in Tokugawa Japan: The Sankin Kōtai System*
*21. Kwang-Ching Liu, ed., *American Missionaries in China: Papers from Harvard Seminars*
*22. George Moseley, *A Sino-Soviet Cultural Frontier: The Ili Kazakh Autonomous Chou*
23. Carl F. Nathan, *Plague Prevention and Politics in Manchuria, 1910–1931*
*24. Adrian Arthur Bennett, *John Fryer: The Introduction of Western Science and Technology into Nineteenth-Century China*
*25. Donald J. Friedman, *The Road from Isolation: The Campaign of the American Committee for Non-Participation in Japanese Aggression, 1938–1941*
*26. Edward LeFevour, *Western Enterprise in Late Ching China: A Selective Survey of Jardine, Matheson and Company's Operations, 1842–1895*
27. Charles Neuhauser, *Third World Politics: China and the Afro-Asian People's Solidarity Organization, 1957–1967*
*28. Kungtu C. Sun, assisted by Ralph W. Huenemann, *The Economic Development of Manchuria in the First Half of the Twentieth Century*
*29. Shahid Javed Burki, *A Study of Chinese Communes, 1965*
30. John Carter Vincent, *The Extraterritorial System in China: Final Phase*
31. Madeleine Chi, *China Diplomacy, 1914–1918*
*32. Clifton Jackson Phillips, *Protestant America and the Pagan World: The First Half Century of the American Board of Commissioners for Foreign Missions, 1810–1860*
*33. James Pusey, *Wu Han: Attacking the Present Through the Past*
*34. Ying-wan Cheng, *Postal Communication in China and Its Modernization, 1860–1896*
35. Tuvia Blumenthal, *Saving in Postwar Japan*
36. Peter Frost, *The Bakumatsu Currency Crisis*
37. Stephen C. Lockwood, *Augustine Heard and Company, 1858–1862*
38. Robert R. Campbell, *James Duncan Campbell: A Memoir by His Son*
39. Jerome Alan Cohen, ed., *The Dynamics of China's Foreign Relations*
40. V. V. Vishnyakova-Akimova, *Two Years in Revolutionary China, 1925–1927,* trans. Steven L. Levine
41. Meron Medzini, *French Policy in Japan During the Closing Years of the Tokugawa Regime*
42. Ezra Vogel, Margie Sargent, Vivienne B. Shue, Thomas Jay Mathews, and Deborah S. Davis, *The Cultural Revolution in the Provinces*
43. Sidney A. Forsythe, *An American Missionary Community in China, 1895–1905*
*44. Benjamin I. Schwartz, ed., *Reflections on the May Fourth Movement.: A Symposium*
*45. Ching Young Choe, *The Rule of the Taewŏngun, 1864–1873: Restoration in Yi Korea*
46. W. P. J. Hall, *A Bibliographical Guide to Japanese Research on the Chinese Economy, 1958–1970*
47. Jack J. Gerson, *Horatio Nelson Lay and Sino-British Relations, 1854–1864*

48. Paul Richard Bohr, *Famine and the Missionary: Timothy Richard as Relief Administrator and Advocate of National Reform*
49. Endymion Wilkinson, *The History of Imperial China: A Research Guide*
50. Britten Dean, *China and Great Britain: The Diplomacy of Commercial Relations, 1860–1864*
51. Ellsworth C. Carlson, *The Foochow Missionaries, 1847–1880*
52. Yeh-chien Wang, *An Estimate of the Land-Tax Collection in China, 1753 and 1908*
53. Richard M. Pfeffer, *Understanding Business Contracts in China, 1949–1963*

*54. Han-sheng Chuan and Richard Kraus, *Mid-Ching Rice Markets and Trade: An Essay in Price History*

55. Ranbir Vohra, *Lao She and the Chinese Revolution*
56. Liang-lin Hsiao, *China's Foreign Trade Statistics, 1864–1949*

*57. Lee-hsia Hsu Ting, *Government Control of the Press in Modern China, 1900–1949*

*58. Edward W. Wagner, *The Literati Purges: Political Conflict in Early Yi Korea*

*59. Joungwon A. Kim, *Divided Korea: The Politics of Development, 1945–1972*

60. Noriko Kamachi, John K. Fairbank, and Chūzō Ichiko, *Japanese Studies of Modern China Since 1953: A Bibliographical Guide to Historical and Social-Science Research on the Nineteenth and Twentieth Centuries, Supplementary Volume for 1953–1969*
61. Donald A. Gibbs and Yun-chen Li, *A Bibliography of Studies and Translations of Modern Chinese Literature, 1918–1942*
62. Robert H. Silin, *Leadership and Values: The Organization of Large-Scale Taiwanese Enterprises*
63. David Pong, *A Critical Guide to the Kwangtung Provincial Archives Deposited at the Public Record Office of London*

*64. Fred W. Drake, *China Charts the World: Hsu Chi-yü and His Geography of 1848*

*65. William A. Brown and Urgrunge Onon, translators and annotators, *History of the Mongolian People's Republic*

66. Edward L. Farmer, *Early Ming Government: The Evolution of Dual Capitals*

*67. Ralph C. Croizier, *Koxinga and Chinese Nationalism: History, Myth, and the Hero*

*68. William J. Tyler, tr., *The Psychological World of Natsume Sōseki*, by Doi Takeo

69. Eric Widmer, *The Russian Ecclesiastical Mission in Peking During the Eighteenth Century*

*70. Charlton M. Lewis, *Prologue to the Chinese Revolution: The Transformation of Ideas and Institutions in Hunan Province, 1891–1907*

71. Preston Torbert, *The Ching Imperial Household Department: A Study of Its Organization and Principal Functions, 1662–1796*
72. Paul A. Cohen and John E. Schrecker, eds., *Reform in Nineteenth-Century China*
73. Jon Sigurdson, *Rural Industrialism in China*
74. Kang Chao, *The Development of Cotton Textile Production in China*

75. Valentin Rabe, *The Home Base of American China Missions, 1880–1920*
*76. Sarasin Viraphol, *Tribute and Profit: Sino-Siamese Trade, 1652–1853*
77. Ch'i-ch'ing Hsiao, *The Military Establishment of the Yuan Dynasty*
78. Meishi Tsai, *Contemporary Chinese Novels and Short Stories, 1949–1974: An Annotated Bibliography*
*79. Wellington K. K. Chan, *Merchants, Mandarins and Modern Enterprise in Late Ching China*
80. Endymion Wilkinson, *Landlord and Labor in Late Imperial China: Case Studies from Shandong by Jing Su and Luo Lun*
*81. Barry Keenan, *The Dewey Experiment in China: Educational Reform and Political Power in the Early Republic*
*82. George A. Hayden, *Crime and Punishment in Medieval Chinese Drama: Three Judge Pao Plays*
*83. Sang-Chul Suh, *Growth and Structural Changes in the Korean Economy, 1910–1940*
84. J. W. Dower, *Empire and Aftermath: Yoshida Shigeru and the Japanese Experience, 1878–1954*
85. Martin Collcutt, *Five Mountains: The Rinzai Zen Monastic Institution in Medieval Japan*
86. Kwang Suk Kim and Michael Roemer, *Growth and Structural Transformation*
87. Anne O. Krueger, *The Developmental Role of the Foreign Sector and Aid*
*88. Edwin S. Mills and Byung-Nak Song, *Urbanization and Urban Problems*
89. Sung Hwan Ban, Pal Yong Moon, and Dwight H. Perkins, *Rural Development*
*90. Noel F. McGinn, Donald R. Snodgrass, Yung Bong Kim, Shin-Bok Kim, and Quee-Young Kim, *Education and Development in Korea*
*91. Leroy P. Jones and II SaKong, *Government, Business, and Entrepreneurship in Economic Development: The Korean Case*
92. Edward S. Mason, Dwight H. Perkins, Kwang Suk Kim, David C. Cole, Mahn Je Kim et al., *The Economic and Social Modernization of the Republic of Korea*
93. Robert Repetto, Tai Hwan Kwon, Son-Ung Kim, Dae Young Kim, John E. Sloboda, and Peter J. Donaldson, *Economic Development, Population Policy, and Demographic Transition in the Republic of Korea*
94. Parks M. Coble, Jr., *The Shanghai Capitalists and the Nationalist Government, 1927–1937*
95. Noriko Kamachi, *Reform in China: Huang Tsun-hsien and the Japanese Model*
96. Richard Wich, *Sino-Soviet Crisis Politics: A Study of Political Change and Communication*
97. Lillian M. Li, *China's Silk Trade: Traditional Industry in the Modern World, 1842–1937*
98. R. David Arkush, *Fei Xiaotong and Sociology in Revolutionary China*
*99. Kenneth Alan Grossberg, *Japan's Renaissance: The Politics of the Muromachi Bakufu*
100. James Reeve Pusey, *China and Charles Darwin*

101. Hoyt Cleveland Tillman, *Utilitarian Confucianism: Chen Liang's Challenge to Chu Hsi*
102. Thomas A. Stanley, *Ōsugi Sakae, Anarchist in Taishō Japan: The Creativity of the Ego*
103. Jonathan K. Ocko, *Bureaucratic Reform in Provincial China: Ting Jih-ch'ang in Restoration Kiangsu, 1867–1870*
104. James Reed, *The Missionary Mind and American East Asia Policy, 1911–1915*
105. Neil L. Waters, *Japan's Local Pragmatists: The Transition from Bakumatsu to Meiji in the Kawasaki Region*
106. David C. Cole and Yung Chul Park, *Financial Development in Korea, 1945–1978*
107. Roy Bahl, Chuk Kyo Kim, and Chong Kee Park, *Public Finances During the Korean Modernization Process*
108. William D. Wray, *Mitsubishi and the N.Y.K, 1870–1914: Business Strategy in the Japanese Shipping Industry*
109. Ralph William Huenemann, *The Dragon and the Iron Horse: The Economics of Railroads in China, 1876–1937*
*110. Benjamin A. Elman, *From Philosophy to Philology: Intellectual and Social Aspects of Change in Late Imperial China*
111. Jane Kate Leonard, *Wei Yüan and China's Rediscovery of the Maritime World*
112. Luke S. K. Kwong, *A Mosaic of the Hundred Days:. Personalities, Politics, and Ideas of 1898*
*113. John E. Wills, Jr., *Embassies and Illusions: Dutch and Portuguese Envoys to K'ang-hsi, 1666–1687*
114. Joshua A. Fogel, *Politics and Sinology: The Case of Naitō Konan (1866–1934)*
*115. Jeffrey C. Kinkley, ed., *After Mao: Chinese Literature and Society, 1978–1981*
116. C. Andrew Gerstle, *Circles of Fantasy: Convention in the Plays of Chikamatsu*
117. Andrew Gordon, *The Evolution of Labor Relations in Japan: Heavy Industry, 1853–1955*
*118. Daniel K. Gardner, *Chu Hsi and the "Ta Hsueh": Neo-Confucian Reflection on the Confucian Canon*
119. Christine Guth Kanda, *Shinzō: Hachiman Imagery and Its Development*
*120. Robert Borgen, *Sugawara no Michizane and the Early Heian Court*
121. Chang-tai Hung, *Going to the People: Chinese Intellectual and Folk Literature, 1918–1937*
*122. Michael A. Cusumano, *The Japanese Automobile Industry: Technology and Management at Nissan and Toyota*
123. Richard von Glahn, *The Country of Streams and Grottoes: Expansion, Settlement, and the Civilizing of the Sichuan Frontier in Song Times*
124. Steven D. Carter, *The Road to Komatsubara: A Classical Reading of the Renga Hyakuin*
125. Katherine F. Bruner, John K. Fairbank, and Richard T. Smith, *Entering China's Service: Robert Hart's Journals, 1854–1863*

126. Bob Tadashi Wakabayashi, *Anti-Foreignism and Western Learning in Early-Modern Japan: The "New Theses" of 1825*
127. Atsuko Hirai, *Individualism and Socialism: The Life and Thought of Kawai Eijirō (1891–1944)*
128. Ellen Widmer, *The Margins of Utopia: "Shui-hu hou-chuan" and the Literature of Ming Loyalism*
129. R. Kent Guy, *The Emperor's Four Treasuries: Scholars and the State in the Late Chien-lung Era*
130. Peter C. Perdue, *Exhausting the Earth: State and Peasant in Hunan, 1500–1850*
131. Susan Chan Egan, *A Latterday Confucian: Reminiscences of William Hung (1893–1980)*
132. James T. C. Liu, *China Turning Inward: Intellectual-Political Changes in the Early Twelfth Century*

*133. Paul A. Cohen, *Between Tradition and Modernity: Wang T'ao and Reform in Late Ching China*

134. Kate Wildman Nakai, *Shogunal Politics: Arai Hakuseki and the Premises of Tokugawa Rule*

*135. Parks M. Coble, *Facing Japan: Chinese Politics and Japanese Imperialism, 1931–1937*

136. Jon L. Saari, *Legacies of Childhood: Growing Up Chinese in a Time of Crisis, 1890–1920*
137. Susan Downing Videen, *Tales of Heichū*
138. Heinz Morioka and Miyoko Sasaki, *Rakugo: The Popular Narrative Art of Japan*
139. Joshua A. Fogel, *Nakae Ushikichi in China: The Mourning of Spirit*
140. Alexander Barton Woodside, *Vietnam and the Chinese Model: A Comparative Study of Vietnamese and Chinese Government in the First Half of the Nineteenth Century*

*141. George Elison, *Deus Destroyed: The Image of Christianity in Early Modern Japan*

142. William D. Wray, ed., *Managing Industrial Enterprise: Cases from Japan's Prewar Experience*

*143. T'ung-tsu Ch'ü, *Local Government in China Under the Ching*

144. Marie Anchordoguy, *Computers, Inc.: Japan's Challenge to IBM*
145. Barbara Molony, *Technology and Investment: The Prewar Japanese Chemical Industry*
146. Mary Elizabeth Berry, *Hideyoshi*
147. Laura E. Hein, *Fueling Growth: The Energy Revolution and Economic Policy in Postwar Japan*
148. Wen-hsin Yeh, *The Alienated Academy: Culture and Politics in Republican China, 1919–1937*
149. Dru C. Gladney, *Muslim Chinese: Ethnic Nationalism in the People's Republic*
150. Merle Goldman and Paul A. Cohen, eds., *Ideas Across Cultures: Essays on Chinese Thought in Honor of Benjamin L Schwartz*
151. James M. Polachek, *The Inner Opium War*
152. Gail Lee Bernstein, *Japanese Marxist: A Portrait of Kawakami Hajime, 1879–1946*

*153. Lloyd E. Eastman, *The Abortive Revolution: China Under Nationalist Rule, 1927–1937*
154. Mark Mason, *American Multinationals and Japan: The Political Economy of Japanese Capital Controls, 1899–1980*
155. Richard J. Smith, John K. Fairbank, and Katherine F. Bruner, *Robert Hart and China's Early Modernization: His Journals, 1863–1866*
156. George J. Tanabe, Jr., *Myōe the Dreamkeeper: Fantasy and Knowledge in Kamakura Buddhism*
157. William Wayne Farris, *Heavenly Warriors: The Evolution of Japan's Military, 500–1300*
158. Yu-ming Shaw, *An American Missionary in China: John Leighton Stuart and Chinese-American Relations*
159. James B. Palais, *Politics and Policy in Traditional Korea*
*160. Douglas Reynolds, *China, 1898–1912: The Xinzheng Revolution and Japan*
161. Roger R. Thompson, *China's Local Councils in the Age of Constitutional Reform, 1898–1911*
162. William Johnston, *The Modern Epidemic: History of Tuberculosis in Japan*
163. Constantine Nomikos Vaporis, *Breaking Barriers: Travel and the State in Early Modern Japan*
164. Irmela Hijiya-Kirschnereit, *Rituals of Self-Revelation: Shishōsetsu as Literary Genre and Socio-Cultural Phenomenon*
165. James C. Baxter, *The Meiji Unification Through the Lens of Ishikawa Prefecture*
166. Thomas R. H. Havens, *Architects of Affluence: The Tsutsumi Family and the Seibu-Saison Enterprises in Twentieth-Century Japan*
167. Anthony Hood Chambers, *The Secret Window: Ideal Worlds in Tanizaki's Fiction*
168. Steven J. Ericson, *The Sound of the Whistle: Railroads and the State in Meiji Japan*
169. Andrew Edmund Goble, *Kenmu: Go-Daigo's Revolution*
170. Denise Potrzeba Lett, *In Pursuit of Status: The Making of South Korea's "New" Urban Middle Class*
171. Mimi Hall Yiengpruksawan, *Hiraizumi: Buddhist Art and Regional Politics in Twelfth-Century Japan*
172. Charles Shirō Inouye, *The Similitude of Blossoms: A Critical Biography of Izumi Kyōka (1873–1939), Japanese Novelist and Playwright*
173. Aviad E. Raz, *Riding the Black Ship: Japan and Tokyo Disneyland*
174. Deborah J. Milly, *Poverty, Equality, and Growth: The Politics of Economic Need in Postwar Japan*
175. See Heng Teow, *Japan's Cultural Policy Toward China, 1918–1931: A Comparative Perspective*
176. Michael A. Fuller, *An Introduction to Literary Chinese*
177. Frederick R. Dickinson, *War and National Reinvention: Japan in the Great War, 1914–1919*

178. John Solt, *Shredding the Tapestry of Meaning: The Poetry and Poetics of Kitasono Katue (1902–1978)*
179. Edward Pratt, *Japan's Protoindustrial Elite: The Economic Foundations of the Gōnō*
180. Atsuko Sakaki, *Recontextualizing Texts: Narrative Performance in Modern Japanese Fiction*
181. Soon-Won Park, *Colonial Industrialization and Labor in Korea: The Onoda Cement Factory*
182. JaHyun Kim Haboush and Martina Deuchler, *Culture and the State in Late Chosŏn Korea*
183. John W. Chaffee, *Branches of Heaven: A History of the Imperial Clan of Sung China*
184. Gi-Wook Shin and Michael Robinson, eds., *Colonial Modernity in Korea*
185. Nam-lin Hur, *Prayer and Play in Late Tokugawa Japan: Asakusa Sensōji and Edo Society*
186. Kristin Stapleton, *Civilizing Chengdu: Chinese Urban Reform, 1895–1937*
187. Hyung Il Pai, *Constructing "Korean" Origins: A Critical Review of Archaeology, Historiography, and Racial Myth in Korean State-Formation Theories*
188. Brian D. Ruppert, *Jewel in the Ashes: Buddha Relics and Power in Early Medieval Japan*
189. Susan Daruvala, *Zhou Zuoren and an Alternative Chinese Response to Modernity*
*190. James Z. Lee, *The Political Economy of a Frontier: Southwest China, 1250–1850*
191. Kerry Smith, *A Time of Crisis: Japan, the Great Depression, and Rural Revitalization*
192. Michael Lewis, *Becoming Apart: National Power and Local Politics in Toyama, 1868–1945*
193. William C. Kirby, Man-houng Lin, James Chin Shih, and David A. Pietz, eds., *State and Economy in Republican China: A Handbook for Scholars*
194. Timothy S. George, *Minamata: Pollution and the Struggle for Democracy in Postwar Japan*
195. Billy K. L. So, *Prosperity, Region, and Institutions in Maritime China: The South Fukien Pattern, 946–1368*
196. Yoshihisa Tak Matsusaka, *The Making of Japanese Manchuria, 1904–1932*
197. Maram Epstein, *Competing Discourses: Orthodoxy, Authenticity, and Engendered Meanings in Late Imperial Chinese Fiction*
198. Curtis J. Milhaupt, J. Mark Ramseyer, and Michael K. Young, eds. and comps., *Japanese Law in Context: Readings in Society, the Economy, and Politics*
199. Haruo Iguchi, *Unfinished Business: Ayukawa Yoshisuke and U.S.-Japan Relations, 1937–1952*
200. Scott Pearce, Audrey Spiro, and Patricia Ebrey, *Culture and Power in the Reconstitution of the Chinese Realm, 200–600*
201. Terry Kawashima, *Writing Margins: The Textual Construction of Gender in Heian and Kamakura Japan*
202. Martin W. Huang, *Desire and Fictional Narrative in Late Imperial China*

203. Robert S. Ross and Jiang Changbin, eds., *Re-examining the Cold War: U.S.-China Diplomacy, 1954–1973*
204. Guanhua Wang, *In Search of Justice: The 1905–1906 Chinese Anti-American Boycott*
205. David Schaberg, *A Patterned Past: Form and Thought in Early Chinese Historiography*
206. Christine Yano, *Tears of Longing: Nostalgia and the Nation in Japanese Popular Song*
207. Milena Doleželová-Velingerová and Oldřich Král, with Graham Sanders, eds., *The Appropriation of Cultural Capital: China's May Fourth Project*
208. Robert N. Huey, *The Making of 'Shinkokinshū'*
209. Lee Butler, *Emperor and Aristocracy in Japan, 1467–1680: Resilience and Renewal*
210. Suzanne Ogden, *Inklings of Democracy in China*
211. Kenneth J. Ruoff, *The People's Emperor: Democracy and the Japanese Monarchy, 1945–1995*
212. Haun Saussy, *Great Walls of Discourse and Other Adventures in Cultural China*
213. Aviad E. Raz, *Emotions at Work: Normative Control, Organizations, and Culture in Japan and America*
214. Rebecca E. Karl and Peter Zarrow, eds., *Rethinking the 1898 Reform Period: Political and Cultural Change in Late Qing China*
215. Kevin O'Rourke, *The Book of Korean Shijo*
216. Ezra F. Vogel, ed., *The Golden Age of the U.S.-China-Japan Triangle, 1972–1989*
217. Thomas A. Wilson, ed., *On Sacred Grounds: Culture, Society, Politics, and the Formation of the Cult of Confucius*
218. Donald S. Sutton, *Steps of Perfection: Exorcistic Performers and Chinese Religion in Twentieth-Century Taiwan*
219. Daqing Yang, *Technology of Empire: Telecommunications and Japanese Expansionism, 1895–1945*
220. Qianshen Bai, *Fu Shan's World: The Transformation of Chinese Calligraphy in the Seventeenth Century*
221. Paul Jakov Smith and Richard von Glahn, eds., *The Song-Yuan-Ming Transition in Chinese History*
222. Rania Huntington, *Alien Kind: Foxes and Late Imperial Chinese Narrative*
223. Jordan Sand, *House and Home in Modern Japan: Architecture, Domestic Space, and Bourgeois Culture, 1880–1930*
224. Karl Gerth, *China Made: Consumer Culture and the Creation of the Nation*
225. Xiaoshan Yang, *Metamorphosis of the Private Sphere: Gardens and Objects in Tang-Song Poetry*
226. Barbara Mittler, *A Newspaper for China? Power, Identity, and Change in Shanghai's News Media, 1872–1912*
227. Joyce A. Madancy, *The Troublesome Legacy of Commissioner Lin: The Opium Trade and Opium Suppression in Fujian Province, 1820s to 1920s*

228. John Makeham, *Transmitters and Creators: Chinese Commentators and Commentaries on the Analects*
229. Elisabeth Köll, *From Cotton Mill to Business Empire: The Emergence of Regional Enterprises in Modern China*
230. Emma Teng, *Taiwan's Imagined Geography: Chinese Colonial Travel Writing and Pictures, 1683–1895*
231. Wilt Idema and Beata Grant, *The Red Brush: Writing Women of Imperial China*
232. Eric C. Rath, *The Ethos of Noh: Actors and Their Art*
233. Elizabeth Remick, *Building Local States: China During the Republican and Post-Mao Eras*
234. Lynn Struve, ed., *The Qing Formation in World-Historical Time*
235. D. Max Moerman, *Localizing Paradise: Kumano Pilgrimage and the Religious Landscape of Premodern Japan*
236. Antonia Finnane, *Speaking of Yangzhou: A Chinese City, 1550–1850*
237. Brian Platt, *Burning and Building: Schooling and State Formation in Japan, 1750–1890*
238. Gail Bernstein, Andrew Gordon, and Kate Wildman Nakai, eds., *Public Spheres, Private Lives in Modern Japan, 1600–1950: Essays in Honor of Albert Craig*
239. Wu Hung and Katherine R. Tsiang, *Body and Face in Chinese Visual Culture*
240. Stephen Dodd, *Writing Home: Representations of the Native Place in Modern Japanese Literature*
241. David Anthony Bello, *Opium and the Limits of Empire: Drug Prohibition in the Chinese Interior, 1729–1850*
242. Hosea Hirata, *Discourses of Seduction: History, Evil, Desire, and Modern Japanese Literature*
243. Kyung Moon Hwang, *Beyond Birth: Social Status in the Emergence of Modern Korea*
244. Brian R. Dott, *Identity Reflections: Pilgrimages to Mount Tai in Late Imperial China*
245. Mark McNally, *Proving the Way: Conflict and Practice in the History of Japanese Nativism*
246. Yongping Wu, *A Political Explanation of Economic Growth: State Survival, Bureaucratic Politics, and Private Enterprises in the Making of Taiwan's Economy, 1950–1985*
247. Kyu Hyun Kim, *The Age of Visions and Arguments: Parliamentarianism and the National Public Sphere in Early Meiji Japan*
248. Zvi Ben-Dor Benite, *The Dao of Muhammad: A Cultural History of Muslims in Late Imperial China*
249. David Der-wei Wang and Shang Wei, eds., *Dynastic Crisis and Cultural Innovation: From the Late Ming to the Late Qing and Beyond*
250. Wilt L. Idema, Wai-yee Li, and Ellen Widmer, eds., *Trauma and Transcendence in Early Qing Literature*
251. Barbara Molony and Kathleen Uno, eds., *Gendering Modern Japanese History*

252. Hiroshi Aoyagi, *Islands of Eight Million Smiles: Idol Performance and Symbolic Production in Contemporary Japan*
253. Wai-yee Li, *The Readability of the Past in Early Chinese Historiography*
254. William C. Kirby, Robert S. Ross, and Gong Li, eds., *Normalization of U.S.-China Relations: An International History*
255. Ellen Gardner Nakamura, *Practical Pursuits: Takano Chōei, Takahashi Keisaku, and Western Medicine in Nineteenth-Century Japan*
256. Jonathan W. Best, *A History of the Early Korean Kingdom of Paekche, together with an annotated translation of* The Paekche Annals *of the* Samguk sagi
257. Liang Pan, *The United Nations in Japan's Foreign and Security Policymaking, 1945–1992: National Security, Party Politics, and International Status*
258. Richard Belsky, *Localities at the Center: Native Place, Space, and Power in Late Imperial Beijing*
259. Zwia Lipkin, *"Useless to the State": "Social Problems" and Social Engineering in Nationalist Nanjing, 1927–1937*
260. William O. Gardner, *Advertising Tower: Japanese Modernism and Modernity in the 1920s*
261. Stephen Owen, *The Making of Early Chinese Classical Poetry*
262. Martin J. Powers, *Pattern and Person: Ornament, Society, and Self in Classical China*
263. Anna M. Shields, *Crafting a Collection: The Cultural Contexts and Poetic Practice of the* Huajian ji 花間集 *(Collection from Among the Flowers)*
264. Stephen Owen, *The Late Tang: Chinese Poetry of the Mid-Ninth Century (827–860)*
265. Sara L. Friedman, *Intimate Politics: Marriage, the Market, and State Power in Southeastern China*
266. Patricia Buckley Ebrey and Maggie Bickford, *Emperor Huizong and Late Northern Song China: The Politics of Culture and the Culture of Politics*
267. Sophie Volpp, *Worldly Stage: Theatricality in Seventeenth-Century China*
268. Ellen Widmer, *The Beauty and the Book: Women and Fiction in Nineteenth-Century China*
269. Steven B. Miles, *The Sea of Learning: Mobility and Identity in Nineteenth-Century Guangzhou*
270. Lin Man-houng, *China Upside Down: Currency, Society, and Ideologies, 1808–1856*
271. Ronald Egan, *The Problem of Beauty: Aesthetic Thought and Pursuits in Northern Song Dynasty China*
272. Mark Halperin, *Out of the Cloister: Literati Perspectives on Buddhism in Sung China, 960–1279*
273. Helen Dunstan, *State or Merchant? Political Economy and Political Process in 1740s China*
274. Sabina Knight, *The Heart of Time: Moral Agency in Twentieth-Century Chinese Fiction*

275. Timothy J. Van Compernolle, *The Uses of Memory: The Critique of Modernity in the Fiction of Higuchi Ichiyō*
276. Paul Rouzer, *A New Practical Primer of Literary Chinese*
277. Jonathan Zwicker, *Practices of the Sentimental Imagination: Melodrama, the Novel, and the Social Imaginary in Nineteenth-Century Japan*
278. Franziska Seraphim, *War Memory and Social Politics in Japan, 1945–2005*
279. Adam L. Kern, *Manga from the Floating World: Comicbook Culture and the* Kibyōshi *of Edo Japan*
280. Cynthia J. Brokaw, *Commerce in Culture: The Sibao Book Trade in the Qing and Republican Periods*
281. Eugene Y. Park, *Between Dreams and Reality: The Military Examination in Late Chosŏn Korea, 1600–1894*
282. Nam-lin Hur, *Death and Social Order in Tokugawa Japan: Buddhism, Anti-Christianity, and the* Danka *System*
283. Patricia M. Thornton, *Disciplining the State: Virtue, Violence, and State-Making in Modern China*
284. Vincent Goossaert, *The Taoists of Peking, 1800–1949: A Social History of Urban Clerics*
285. Peter Nickerson, *Taoism, Bureaucracy, and Popular Religion in Early Medieval China*
286. Charo B. D'Etcheverry, *Love After* The Tale of Genji*: Rewriting the World of the Shining Prince*
287. Michael G. Chang, *A Court on Horseback: Imperial Touring & the Construction of Qing Rule, 1680–1785*
288. Carol Richmond Tsang, *War and Faith:* Ikkō Ikki *in Late Muromachi Japan*
289. Hilde De Weerdt, *Competition over Content: Negotiating Standards for the Civil Service Examinations in Imperial China (1127–1279)*
290. Eve Zimmerman, *Out of the Alleyway: Nakagami Kenji and the Poetics of Outcaste Fiction*
291. Robert Culp, *Articulating Citizenship: Civic Education and Student Politics in Southeastern China, 1912–1940*
292. Richard J. Smethurst, *From Foot Soldier to Finance Minister: Takahashi Korekiyo, Japan's Keynes*
293. John E. Herman, *Amid the Clouds and Mist: China's Colonization of Guizhou, 1200–1700*
294. Tomoko Shiroyama, *China During the Great Depression: Market, State, and the World Economy, 1929–1937*
295. Kirk W. Larsen, *Tradition, Treaties and Trade: Qing Imperialism and Chosŏn Korea, 1850–1910*
296. Gregory Golley, *When Our Eyes No Longer See: Realism, Science, and Ecology in Japanese Literary Modernism*

FOR THE KING

Roger L'Estrange and the Siege of King's Lynn

EVELYN TIDMAN

Berforts Information Press

FOR THE KING

Roger L'Estrange and the Siege of King's Lynn

Fiction
First Edition

First Published 2014

ISBN 978-1-910693-01-8

Printed and bound in Great Britain by
Berforts Information Press
www.bookprinting.co.uk

FOR THE KING

Roger L'Estrange and the Siege of King's Lynn

My soul is free as ambient air,
Although my baser parts immew'd
Whilst loyal thoughts do still repair
T'accompany my solitude;
Although rebellion do my body binde,
My King alone can captivate my minde.

--Roger L'Estrange
Loyalty Confined

ONE

Newburn, near Newcastle-upon-Tyne, August 1640

As he watched the sea of blue hats of the ranked masses of Scottish Covenanters across the Tyne valley Roger's heart shuddered in his chest. They outnumbered the King's army and were better prepared, more experienced.

''Sblood, we'll be slaughtered!' someone along the line swore and Roger glanced towards him. No-one smiled. They sat on their restless horses grim-faced, staring at imminent death, mechanically struggling to keep in the rank.

Roger's gloved hand shook as it held the rein. No wonder his horse sidestepped.

'You know what Leslie intends to do, don't you?' His father's deep voice beside him caused him to turn his head sharply to look at him. As ever, Sir Hamon was cool, matter-of-fact. His grey eyes briefly held the ghost of a smile and he calmed Roger.

Roger took a steadying breath. 'He wants to take Newcastle.' The Scottish target, the town of Newcastle, with its fortifications was no more than five miles to the east but here at Newburn with its ford was the crossing point over the Tyne.

'Indeed.' Sir Hamon squinted in the bright August sun at the opposite bank. 'They've got artillery in the tower.'

Roger's eyes followed his gaze to the top of the square church tower where shadowy dots moved about behind the battlements. He could not see the guns, but he knew they were there ready to rain death on the King's men. 'I see them,' he said. 'How in the name of all that is sacred did they get them up there?'

'A lot of heave-ho-ing I shouldn't wonder!' Sir Hamon turned his attention to the King's army, the infantry, the pikemen, the gunners massed on the slopes below them. 'Damn shambles!' he grumbled. He referred to the troops Viscount Conway had mustered for the king, a ramshackle army of raw and largely untrained recruits, ordinary men who had marched from the south of the country to arrive exhausted and demoralised in the borderlands. Many of them had no heart for the fight. They were there because of loyalty to their 'lords of the manor' who had been summoned to the King's army. An undisciplined and unwilling rabble, Roger thought. They had no idea of the cause of the argument, no grasp of the politics, no pay and no reason to fight.

Sweat trickled down Roger's back and stood out on his clean-shaven lip. He wore a thick, padded gambeson beneath his coat so that the armour did not chafe through to his skin.

They lapsed into silence, father and son. Tension swaddled the waiting troops. Beyond their own artillery the grassy bank shimmered in the heat. On the opposite bank the Scots lined up their men behind the guns. On the King's side too, men were lined up in ranks. They moved around as though they were out for a Sunday stroll, shuffling in the heat, weighed down with glinting armour, those that had it, forming into ragged lines, while the officers rode up and down bellowing orders. The King should have had a retained army, trained, ready, but with Parliament withholding payment, he simply could not afford it. As it was, he could not pay the troops. The lords had seen to it instead, paying their own men.

'What's this?' Sir Hamon moved away a little and stood up in the stirrups to get a better look. Roger followed his example. A rider, no three riders, came out from the Scottish ranks, splashing across the river Tyne at the Newburn Ford and galloped into the English camp.

Sir Hamon immediately dismounted, handing the reins to his son and marched across flattened grass to Viscount Conway's tent. As a mere younger son, Roger was not privy to the conversations of his commanders, whereas Sir Hamon was. However, as Lord Conway emerged from his tent to meet the riders, Roger jumped down from his horse, handed the reins of both animals to a servant who had magically appeared from behind him and followed at a run behind his father. He found himself at the rear of Lord Conway's men but although he was considered a tall man, their hats obscured his vision, so that he moved to the side to see what was happening.

The messengers dressed in tartan skirts and sashes and blue coats did not dismount, but one of them, sporting an impressive red beard, walked his fine chestnut mare forward. Even then he stayed mounted, staring haughtily down on the English lord. The Scottish heathens lacked common manners!

'General Leslie sends his compliments to Lord Conway,' he bellowed in a thick lilting Scottish brogue so that Roger had to concentrate hard in order to understand him.

Viscount Conway, an elegant man with long flowing light brown hair, an immaculate moustache and small beard, graciously inclined his head in stark contrast to the uncouth Scottish messenger who continued:

'We, the Covenanters do not wish to fight the English but General Leslie requests free passage so that we may petition the King.' He leaned forward and held out a scroll of paper so that Lord Conway could reach it.

Breaking the seal, Lord Conway took a minute to read while the messengers waited and everyone else held their breath. He pursed his lips. 'Tell the General that I cannot accede to his wishes,' he said and turned his back on the messenger to return to his tent, contemptuously dismissing him.

The Scotsman's eyes flashed in anger and all of Conway's men reached for the swords on their hips, but although the man grumbled something incomprehensible he turned his horse's head and spurred the animal into a gallop down the slope towards the Tyne, his companions following behind.

Conway stopped at the tent entrance and turned to Colonel Lunsford in command of the artillery. 'Make ready the guns.'

Sir Hamon left Conway's men and Roger joined him as they returned to the cavalry. Sir Hamon shot him a censuring look, but chose not to mention Roger's impertinence. The drummers began to beat the advance and Roger felt a roll in his belly of fear and excitement.

'This is it,' Sir Hamon said to Roger. 'Remember what I taught you. No heroics. Do not risk your life. Make your sword thrusts true.'

He walked quickly, but Roger kept pace. 'I will watch your back, sir.'

He stopped and looked at his son, tenderness in his eyes. 'If I do not come home, take care of your lady mother,' he said.

Roger nodded and swallowed. Of course Nick, his brother, would do that, but it touched him that his father placed such confidence in him.

Shouts from behind warned them as the first cannon fired. Turning around, Roger's heart missed a beat as he saw the Scottish cavalry advancing towards the ford. A plume of spray in the Tyne showed where a cannonball from the Royalist's side hit the water, the aim too short, but the English adjusted their aim and continued to fire on the Cavalry with the boom of cannon, spewing smoke in the shuddering hot August air. The smell of burning gunpowder wafted towards them and all at once Roger and Sir Hamon ran for their horses.

Scottish horses collapsed beneath their riders, mown down by the barrage of fire from the Royalists. The Scots retreated. However the small victory was short lived. From their vantage points on the slightly higher ground, the Scots retaliated by pounding the English guns.

By now Roger and Sir Hamon had reached their positions and took possession of their mounts, Roger leaping into the saddle, Sir Hamon hopping up stiffly from the stirrup.

The bombardment was relentless and the gunners turned and fled. 'Look at them!' Roger cried in disgust. 'They run from the Scots!'

Frowning at the retreating figures of English artillery running from the enemy, Sir Hamon merely said: 'Raw recruits. Even Colonel Lunsford cannot keep them.' From this higher point they could see the Scots pouring across the dark river at the ford, could see the whole battle being played out beneath them.

Frustration made Roger grind his teeth. 'We need to give fire!' But there was no-one left to give fire, they had fled.

'Here they come!'

The cry from along the ranks made Roger draw breath. Beneath him Achilles fidgeted and nodded his head. With an effort Roger held him, patted and stroked the animal's neck with a black gloved hand and spoke to him in low tones, but his eyes were on the oncoming Scottish hordes.

'Hold you hard there, boy.' Sir Hamon's voice was low. Roger took a steadying breath. All along the cavalry line the king's men drew their swords with the ring of metal, holding them upright in their hands, ready for the order.

They waited as the Scottish cavalry charged down the hill.

'We should go,' Sir Hamon muttered. 'He's leaving it too late.'

Then as the Scots crossed the river, the order came from Henry Wilmot, in command of the cavalry. '*Charge*!'

Digging his heels into his horse's flanks, with his father at his side, Roger leaned forward in the saddle as his black stallion sprang into action like a suddenly released spring, hurtling headlong down the grassy slope, hooves thundering over the uneven turf. Roger kept pace with everyone else, his sword held out in front of him. No man wanted to be the one out in front when they met with the enemy, but neither did he want to be the last man.

The Scottish musketeers had already taken up their positions.

Suddenly confronted with two ranks of black muzzles, the first of the cavalry came to a sudden halt in front of Roger and his father. Quickly they pulled up on the reins as the upper rank of Scottish muskets belched smoke and popped. A whisper of hot air next to Roger's ear, felt rather than heard, was too close for comfort.

In the confusion, men and horses fell beneath the hail of gunfire.

It was too much for the inexperienced English. They too broke ranks and began to retreat to get out of the murderous, death-dealing fire. Sizing up the situation, Roger grabbed the reins on Sir Hamon's mount and pulled him round.

'Let's get out of here,' he bellowed above the din.

Once more digging his heels into his horse's flanks, Roger galloped away from the muskets with the rest of the cavalry, his father right behind him, not stopping until they were out of range.

It was a far cry from the victory Roger had envisioned and his disappointment was intense. 'Damn them! Damn them to hell.'

'At least you have your life and you still have your horse,' Sir Hamon retorted, but he spoke through his teeth as they dismounted and handed the reins to the servant. 'Others may not have been so privileged.'

Anger flushed through Roger as he too dismounted. 'Wilmot left it too late!'

'He did. Come with me.'

Together they strode towards a knot of men to seek out Henry Wilmot, but he had sought the sanctuary of his tent. Sir Hamon followed him there and found him packing up his things into a chest. They were not the only ones seeking him and the tent was crowded, Wilmot besieged by complaints all around him.

Determined to air his own views Sir Hamon cried above the din: 'You left it too late, sir! Now they have control of the Tyne. They'll take Newcastle next.'

'We had already lost,' Wilmot told him shortly, breaking off from bending to the chest and meeting Sir Hamon's eyes. 'We were defeated when the infantry fled.'

''Tis no wonder they took off,' Sir Hamon retorted scathingly. 'Raw recruits facing intense artillery bombardment. No-one, not even Colonel Lunsford could not stop them. These men need training.'

'Then you do it!' Wilmot fumed at him, and turned his back again.

Roger was as furious as his father. He hated defeat. He hated the ignominy of it. And he hated the Scots too. He was unimpressed also by the commanders of the King's army who seemed to have little idea of what they were about. And why? Simply put, they had no experience of war or battle of any kind. It had never before been necessary, whereas the Scots were always fighting each other—well so it seemed to Roger—so they had experience and training.

Effectively dismissed, Sir Hamon and Roger left the tent. Outside, men gathered the equipment and artillery and they were already pouring out of the camp.

'We need to get our things,' Roger said to Sir Hamon. The Scots were coming and they had to make good their escape.

TWO

York, September 1640

Sir Hamon closed the door with a snap, the latch dropping home with a clatter and took off his cloak, shaking off the rain onto the wooden floor.

Roger, stretched out on the bed with his ankles crossed, awoke from his nap with a start. This was his room, paid for out of his own allowance so that he did not have to suffer his father's snoring and Sir Hamon had not knocked. However, a glance at his father's face made him think better of mentioning it.

'Fools!'

Roger rubbed his face to clear away the sleep befuddlement as his father threw his cloak on the back of a chair and began to pace the room.

'Idiots!'

Roger sat up and swung his long legs over the edge of the bed, struggling to gather his wits. 'I collect the meeting did not go well, sir?'

Sir Hamon stopped pacing and pulled up a chair to sit in front of his son and look directly into his face. 'Never in all my life have I been so amazed at the incompetence of my fellow Englishmen.'

Seeing that his father wished to unburden himself, Roger said: 'Of whom are you speaking sir?'

'The King's advisors, who else?'

Since the King had seen fit to summon a Great Council of Peers—the first since Edward III—and all of them therefore the King's advisors, Roger remained unenlightened as to the culprits. Wisely he held his peace and waited. He knew his father would tell him all.

Sir Hamon ran his fingers through his faded upstanding auburn hair, which did nothing to flatten it into submission and said: 'The King was all for continuing the fight against the Scots. His advisors are giving him wrong advice. How can he win in a war against the Scots? They have far more troops than we have and the King cannot pay even what he does have.'

''Tis unsurprising when Parliament refuses to give him any funds.'

'And why do they do that, pray?'

Roger thought about it. 'They do not want the King to have an army.'

An arrested look came into Sir Hamon's dark eyes as he stared at his son. 'No. They don't. They are of Puritan bent themselves. They are on the side of the Scots.' Parliament was largely run by the Puritans. They favoured church rule by elders or presbyters, as did the Scottish Covenanters. The King, however, was head of the English Church, which favoured episcopacy, that is rule by bishops and priests who had much power and exerted much influence over the King. Parliament resented the power of the bishops. The bishops in turn loathed the direct attack on their supremacy by the Puritan ethics and designated it an attack on the King. Each side called the other traitors. It had been the King's insistence on imposing episcopacy on the Scots who were largely Presbyterian, that had caused the so-called Bishops' War which Roger and Sir Hamon found themselves mixed up in.

Roger frowned. 'You are thinking it could come to war between the King and Parliament?'

Taking an agitated breath Sir Hamon stood up and began to pace the floorboards again. 'I think it has already started. I think this skirmish with the Scots was the opening salvo. And I think Parliament intends to turn this into a fight.'

Roger frowned. 'Surely it must be treason to war against the anointed King?'

'So it ought to be.' Sir Hamon shook his head.

Roger's pulse quickened. A war meant action. And for a younger son with little to occupy him since leaving Cambridge, a career in the army beckoned. 'What happened at the Council?' he invited.

Sir Hamon continued his agitated pacing and Roger's eyes followed him. 'The King has been advised to negotiate a truce with the Scots. It has to be. You saw it at Newburn. The Scots heavily outnumber and outgun the English. But the King didn't like it.'

'You think it was the King's advisors who influenced him against it, then?'

'Who else?' It was unthinkable that his king could err in his judgement. After all, Charles was king by Divine right. He had right on his side. 'It has to be Strafford behind this.' The Earl of Strafford, Thomas Wentworth, was a close friend of the King, his principle advisor.

Roger said: 'The King cannot win a war with the Scots. Anyone can see that.' He thought for a moment. 'He needs funds.'

'He needs to summon Parliament again. He's got to get some money out of them. 'Tis outrageous that they withhold funds from him.

He's the King, for heaven's sake!'

'How long are we to be kicking our heels here in York?' Roger asked.

Sir Hamon resumed his seat and rubbed his face in a weary gesture. 'Damned if I know! The King isn't done with us yet.'

Roger got up from the bed. 'Well I am sure I can find plenty to amuse myself with,' he said grabbing his hat.

Sir Hamon also stood. 'Wenching and drinking and gaming, I shouldn't wonder.'

Putting his hat on his head so that the large white feather floated around the crown, he grinned at his father. 'Not gaming, sir. You know I don't gamble. 'Tis the occupation of fools. 'Tis supper I have in mind—first. Can't go wenching and drinking on an empty stomach now! Do you come with me?'

'Mind you don't get more than you bargained for,' Sir Hamon warned darkly and, picking up his cloak followed his son from the room.

The taproom was packed with people, all of the men being from the King's army, but there were a good many women as well. Wenches, his father called them. Buxom ladies intent on having a good time with men who might have money to throw in their direction.

Roger and Sir Hamon sat down at a table and a comely young woman with bold eyes and too much exposed bosom soon came over. 'What'll it be, gents?'

'What have you got?' Roger countered with a cheeky grin.

The woman smiled showing even white teeth. 'Stew,' she said. 'Rabbit stew, if your lordship pleases.'

'He's no lord,' Sir Hamon said depressingly. 'Two bowls of stew will do us fine. And some bread.'

'And beer,' Roger added again grinning at the woman.

Her cheeks dimpled appreciatively as she turned away and Roger watched her hips as they swayed from side to side, a slow smile on his lips. At the door she turned, caught his eye and smiled that slow provocative smile.

'Don't get tangled with serving wenches,' Sir Hamon warned and Roger turned his attention back to his father. 'They're out to trap a rich husband.'

'I'm not rich.'

'To them you are. They've been born in poverty. Anyone who has a decent suit of clothes is rich to them. And that one will trap you, if you are not careful.'

'I will be careful,' he replied in all seriousness. He knew his father had Puritanical ideas, if not allegiance, and it did not do to upset him.

''Twould be better if you were to return home ahead of me,' Sir Hamon said.

Roger met his eyes. 'And leave you here to fend for yourself? Now what kind of son would leave his aging father in the wilds of Yorkshire all alone?'

'You insolent pup!' But Sir Hamon's eyes danced. 'Damned if I won't whip you for that.'

Roger grinned at his father. 'You'd need to catch me first, and at your age . . .' He shook his head in exaggerated doubt. He knew he could get away with a little banter, whereas neither of his older brothers could. They were far too serious to tease their father, but Roger and Sir Hamon were alike in more than looks. Perhaps Sir Hamon saw himself in his youngest son, or perhaps he was won by Roger's youthful exuberance. Either way, Roger knew, as his brothers also reluctantly knew, that he, the youngest surviving child of Sir Hamon and his wife Alice, was their parents' favourite, but because the age gap was great, eleven and twelve years between them, sibling rivalry was short-lived. 'You have been to Scotland, sir?' Roger asked as they waited for their food.

'Indeed I have. I was younger than you are, just after I married your mother, when the old Queen died. My dear friend Sir John Carey and myself rode to Edinburgh to inform King James that he was now King of England as well as Scotland.'

The woman had brought the beer, but Roger had been intent on his father and hardly noticed her, but he did pick up the tankard and took a large swallow. 'I never heard of this!'

'You don't know everything, my son.'

'What was he like, the King?'

'Scottish!' Sir Hamon frowned, thoughtfully. 'A peaceful man, not like the old queen who was warlike.'

'But you did not continue at court, obviously.'

Sir Hamon shrugged. 'I had just married and my young wife, your mother, was at home in Hunstanton all alone and expecting her first child. That was your brother Nicholas of course. I did not wish to be apart from her at that time and she was not able to manage the estates on her own, so I came home to Norfolk and I settled down and found that the life of a country squire suited me very well indeed. Your dear mother never did like life in London. She was a Norfolk lass, country born and bred and so we rarely go there. If it had not been for the war, I doubt I would have set eyes on royalty again.'

The stew arrived now, two large steaming bowls full and two wooden spoons. They both bowed their heads as Sir Hamon said a brief prayer of thanks. It was common enough practice and common at home. As Roger took piece of ordinary brown bread and dipped it in the stew he said: 'I think I should like London above all things. Norfolk is all very well, but it is so quiet. Nothing ever happens there! One can make one's fortune in London. And as a younger son, you know I need to make my fortune.'

'You will receive a sizeable inheritance and you already get a decent allowance. It is more than a younger son could rightfully expect.'

'For which I am truly grateful. But it is not enough for my tastes. I need to make my own way in the world, find my own path. I am not ever going to be a country squire.'

Sir Hamon swallowed a mouthful of steaming stew, but his grey eyes danced. 'That I can readily believe! No, the life of a country squire is not your calling,' he acknowledged. 'At least, not until you marry.'

'I don't intend to marry until I have made my way in the world.'

'Then I shall tell your mother not to expect grandchildren from her youngest son in the near future.'

Roger ignored the gentle gibe. 'Nor shall I go into the church.'

Sir Hamon chuckled. 'Never in my wildest dreams could I think of you as a man of the cloth, my son.'

Roger chuckled, for he knew it to be as far away from his nature as the earth was to the moon. 'For now I am content to be in the King's army as long as he needs me.'

The smile left Sir Hamon. 'It would seem that at the moment the King does not need either of us.'

'But you are attending the council.'

'That's a fact. Though what good I do there, I don't know. No-one is interested in the views of a mere country squire.'

Roger raised an eyebrow. 'You are one of the most powerful men in Norfolk.'

Sir Hamon threw his head back and gave a shout of laughter, making everyone else in the room stare at him. When he sobered, he said: 'I think, my son, that you have an exaggerated idea of your father's importance in the county. There are men far more powerful than I.'

'But you were knighted by the King.'

'I was. And so was your brother. Both for services rendered.'

'And you have been at court.'

'I have.'

'And you own a large area of Norfolk.' This was indisputable, since Sir Hamon had inherited not only most of the north western corner of Norfolk, but also the village of Gressenhall near East Dereham as well.

'There are others with larger estates than ours.'

'And you were High Sheriff of Norfolk.'

'I was. And your brother is in the militia.' He meant Nicholas, of course.

Roger finished his stew and mopped up his dish with the last of the bread and popped it in his mouth. 'Then as I say, you are one of the most prominent men in Norfolk.'

Sir Hamon chuckled again and shook his head. 'Oh, my son, you have a lot to learn.' He too finished his bowl of stew and took a large pull at his tankard. 'If the King does as he should and sues for peace, you will not be able to join his army, for he will not have one.'

Roger took a breath. 'Perhaps I'll wait and see what his Majesty decides to do before I make a decision.'

THREE

Norfolk, End October, 1640

It was the home stretch. King's Lynn and Castle Rising lay behind them now and Dersingham with its heathland was just ahead. It had been a long ride from York, taking several days, for they had not wanted to push the horses. Around them the forest closed in, golden leaves carpeting the springy leaf mould beneath the trees and the bracken was beginning to turn that colour of russet that heralded winter. Yet this day the sun shone almost warmly.

The road was not busy. It was not Tuesday which was market day in Lynn, and few people had need to leave their villages to tramp the road. They had seen only a few travellers since Lynn: a man with a wagon loaded with hay, to be sold for fodder no doubt, two women walking to the next village, the younger of which was a pretty little thing to whom Roger doffed his hat, and a man moving a herd of cows from one field to another. But now the road was empty as it meandered lazily through the Norfolk countryside. As they approached Dersingham the heather still had a flush of purple covering the heath. Red squirrels darted across in front of them and alongside the road deer fled from their approach in panic.

'So 'tis done then,' Roger said.

''Twould appear so,' Sir Hamon agreed. 'It fair chokes me that the damned Scots should occupy Northumbria and Durham and be paid eight hundred and fifty pounds a day for the privilege! Eight hundred and fifty pounds—a *day*! And they to be reimbursed for declaring war on England!' He referred to the treaty with the Scots signed at Ripon a week previously. Roger had heard it before, and no doubt he would hear it again. With the treaty came the end of hostilities and any opportunity for Roger to continue in the King's army. The army had been disbanded.

'Damn their eyes!' Roger agreed. 'Why did the commissioners agree to it?'

'What choice did they have? *To the victor belong the spoils*. Even if they are damned rebel invaders.'

'Which they are!'

They had reached Dersingham village now. In the turning on their right was West Hall Manor, the home of one of the Cobbe sons. The prolific Cobbe family seemed to occupy half of Norfolk all by themselves, but they were not proper gentry, having made their fortune in the Icelandic fishing grounds. A tangle of old cottages snaked up the road from West Hall to the Old Hall, the home of the Pell family, the Puritan representatives in the area.

The road, the scenery, the village were so familiar. How many times had they travelled this road between Hunstanton and Lynn? It meant they were only ten miles or so from home.

As the horses plodded rhythmically on through the village, Roger felt himself dozing comfortably in the unusually warm October sun. Sir Hamon's head too had nodded forward.

Roger saw the dog too late. In a blur of motion it shot past the corner cottage and straight out in front of both horses.

Sir Hamon's horse sidestepped, but Roger's Achilles reared up suddenly with a shriek of fright, pawing the air, jerking Roger fully awake, but too late to stop himself sliding out of the saddle. He landed with a thud on the ground as a woman screamed, the dog squealed and Sir Hamon yelled.

It wasn't the first time he had fallen from a horse, of course, but he hit his head and had the breath knocked out of him and he lay there momentarily stunned.

Everything went quiet. He was not unconscious but he lay still for a few moments trying to work out if anything hurt enough to be broken. He decided that he was probably still in once piece. *Idiot!* If he not been dozing he would have spotted the dog sooner and been prepared for Achilles' reaction.

A wet nose nudged his ear, a long tongue slurped in his face and he opened his eyes to find the offending dog standing over him. A second later it was gone replaced by a vision of womanhood, mesmeric dark brown eyes looking down at him wide with horror. 'Oh, sir! Are you all right?'

For a long moment he could only stare at her, taking in her perfectly formed face, watching the raspberry-coloured lips forming the words. Then the woman was replaced by his father. 'What the devil are you doing down there, boy?'

Reminded of the ignominy of being found sprawling in the dirt by a vision of womanhood, his dignity in a thousand fragments, Roger growled: 'Whose damn dog was that anyway?' He struggled to sit up. A crowd had gathered around him, blocking out most of the daylight, a sea of concerned faces all peering down at him.

'It is my dog,' the young woman replied hotly, standing back, those hypnotic dark eyes flashing. 'And I'll thank you to mind your language, sir!'

Now that he could focus properly, even his hurt pride did not prevent him readjusting his first opinion. This was no common wench, but a maid of perhaps nineteen or twenty. Her clothes, although Puritan plain, proclaimed her to be gentry. The way they fitted snugly over full breasts and a small waist was not lost on him. 'I beg your pardon, mistress!' he retorted, not sounding in the least bit sorry. 'May I suggest that the animal be kept on the end of a rope?'

'And would it not have been better if you had a care when riding at crossroads? Barney could have been killed by your horse!'

'Barney . . ! What about me? And what about my horse?'

'The horse is safe,' Sir Hamon's calm voice cut in. 'Are you hurt, boy?'

Boy! He must remember to object to that when he next had the opportunity. He glowered at his father's amused face, much affronted. 'I don't think so.' At least someone was concerned about him.

'Well and I am pleased to hear it,' the woman said haughtily, brushing her skirt down. 'Barney's all right, you are all right and the horse is all right. So then everything is all right! Just fine!' It didn't sound just fine.

Roger stood up also and dusted off his clothes. 'What are you getting all upset about?' he demanded of her, ready to do battle, but even as he said it, the fight went out of him. This had to be the most beautiful woman he had ever set eyes on. He found himself staring at perfect smooth skin, wide dark eyes framed by long black lashes, full lips, to say nothing of the alluring curves the plain grey of her dress seemed to accentuate rather than hide. Her hair was partly hidden by a white starched bonnet and an escaped dark brown curl graced her peachy cheek.

'What am I getting upset about?' she replied, unaware of the shift in his perspective and bringing him back to the present. 'Well I will tell you, sir, that you nearly caused serious injury to my dog and to your own poor horse, as well as to yourself all because you were not paying attention!'

For a long moment Roger did not speak, while he continued to study this vision. Under his scrutiny the colour came into her cheeks and she looked away, licking her lips with the tip of a deliciously pink tongue which set the blood racing in his veins, and then looking back at him. The fight went right out of him.

'Seems t'me,' one of the local men offered, 'Tweren't nobody's fault.'

A woman added: 'Course it be the dog! Should've been on a rope.'

As a debate broke out among the onlookers, Roger bowed to the young woman. 'Forgive me, madam. I was indeed negligent.' He eyed the dog, a white and brown spaniel now on a rope which was in the hands of a much older man, possibly a servant. This was a lady, not some local farm girl; her speech was crisp and clear, untainted with the Norfolk burr.

Her eyes widened in surprise. 'So easily bested, sir?' she remarked.

Roger grinned, then looked around for his hat, saw it a few paces off lying on some grass and went to retrieve it, the assembled company parting to let him through. At the same time he put his hand to his head which was stinging at the back. It came away with blood on it.

'Oh, you are bleeding!' she cried, suddenly concerned and guilt-ridden.

''Tis nothing,' he assured her.

'Let me see.'

He looked at the circle of interested faces. 'It is nothing,' he repeated with more emphasis.

'Please, sir, do sit down.'

Roger hesitated, and Sir Hamon, grinning advised: 'Better do as the lady says, boy.'

So he sat on a lump of rock outside someone's front door and she moved behind him to examine the wound. So did everyone else, the onlookers craning their necks to get a better view. Sir Hamon tutted in exaggerated fashion and Roger flashed another glare at him, by no means displeased by this female attention. He was acutely aware of the proximity of her legs behind him, even if they were hidden in a skirt and who knows how many petticoats.

The maid searched in the inner pocked in her skirt, found a folded handkerchief and, just as it was, pressed it to the wound, her other hand on Roger's forehead, as if she were clamping it together. Her hand was cool, her touch sending shivers through him. 'Has anyone got some vinegar?'

The lady of the cottage where Roger was sitting, disappeared inside and came out with an earthenware jar.

He glanced at his father who was still grinning like he found the whole episode highly amusing. 'I see you have no concern for me, sir!' Roger remarked sourly.

Sir Hamon continued to grin. 'You forget, I've seen you unseated too many times to worry about you! But this must be quite a new experience for Mistress . . ?'

'Pell,' the woman supplied. 'Ruth Pell.'

Sir Hamon's blue eyes widened. 'Then your father is—'

'Sir Valentine Pell, yes, sir, and no, sir, this is not a new experience for me. Not only do I ride myself, but I also have brothers.'

Sir Hamon inclined his head. 'Sir Hamon L'Estrange at your service, madam, and this errant cub is my son, Roger.'

'Oh!' Her tone suggested surprise and even a little awe. But she inclined her head in return. Then to her patient she added: 'If you would just turn around, Mr. L'Estrange, so that I can see. I am afraid this will sting, sir.' The astringent smell of vinegar filled the air, as she gently dabbed at his scalp. She was right, it did sting, but he refused to flinch. His male pride had taken enough knocks in the last few minutes to add complaining to it. All his senses were on the maid, who stood so close to him, and the touch of her fingers.

'It's stopped bleeding,' she announced. 'Only a small cut. You'll live.'

'I did not think I would not!' Somehow Roger felt irked that his father took the girl's attention, and that he insisted on belittling him to her. *Boy* and *errant cub* indeed!

She was done, and reluctantly he came to his feet and turned towards her. He bowed. 'I thank you Mistress Pell.' He smiled at her and she blushed again and smiled back, lowering her eyes and dropping a curtsey. He was fascinated by the way she blushed so easily, the coy way she looked away. One minute she was angry, the next business-like as she tended to his wound, and now the shy maid which betrayed her youth. And that shy smile as she looked back at him through those long lashes set his heart racing.

'Sir.'

Sir Hamon also thanked her, 'Mistress Pell.' He bowed, took hold of Roger's arm, jerking him back to reality and marched him to the horses now being held by a boy hoping to earn a penny. He was not disappointed as Sir Hamon tossed him a coin. 'Come, boy,' he called to Roger, 'I want to be home before nightfall. I want to surprise your mother!' Sir Hamon put his foot in the stirrup.

She bobbed a curtsey to Sir Hamon in acknowledgement.

For the sake of his wound, Roger did not put on his hat, but looped the reins over his horse's head and jumped nimbly into the saddle. He winced inwardly as he landed and rubbed his shoulder surreptitiously. He seemed to be developing aches in all sorts of expected and unexpected places, but he had no intention of telling the world! He used his hat to brush Achilles' flank, which caused the animal to jolt forward.

Then he looked back at Ruth Pell and grinned, again waving his hat in the air.

Now that the entertainment was over, the small gathering drifted away.

Sir Hamon swung his horse's head in the direction of Hunstanton and Achilles automatically followed, but Roger kept looking back at the girl even as he moved off. She fussed the dog. She spoke to a villager. She spoke to the servant. But she looked back at him, and their eyes met, sending a shiver of excitement through him.

'You know who she is, don't you,' Sir Hamon interrupted his thoughts.

Roger brought his horse beside Sit Hamon's. 'Ruth Pell. She told us.'

'Of Dersingham Hall.'

'Yes.'

'You have heard of Sir Valentine Pell? A great Puritan if ever there was one.'

Roger sighed with resignation. 'Yes. And he's her father. I heard her say.'

'It would not do to tangle with that young lady,' Sir Hamon warned severely.

Roger looked at him in wide-eyed innocence. 'Trust me, Father, I have not the slightest intention of tangling with that or any other young lady.'

'No?' Sir Hamon raised his orange brows in disbelief. 'Not even one so pretty that she deserves to be in a painting? I must say you seemed taken with her.'

'No. Tavern girls are more in my line.'

'Yes and that is a subject I wanted to speak to you about.'

Roger urged his horse forward at a trot, leaving Sir Hamon behind.

FOUR

Ruth Pell marched smartly home, her skirts kicking up with each stride, the old servant Sam Tyler following behind with Barney the spaniel pulling hard against the unaccustomed restraint of the rope.

She was unsettled by the whole episode. In the first place the dog should not have run off the minute Sam let him off the rope. Another dog on the other side of the road had attracted him. In the second place, the horseman—Mr. Roger L'Estrange—should have been watching. Surely he knew the basics of looking out for anything else on the road? And wasn't the junction wide enough to see?

But what had really made her cross was that he had lain so still for several moments so that she feared he had been rendered unconscious or even killed. The panic that her dog might have been responsible and the resultant summoning to court which must surely take place after a fatality had made her defensive. If the gentleman had wanted to he could have accused her of deliberately causing the accident. The thought made her shudder and although her father's consequence would have helped, Sir Hamon's consequence was greater. After all he had once been Sheriff of Norfolk.

She turned around to Sam who was trying to keep up with her. 'That dog needs to be trained,' she said severely.

The old servant apologised: 'He be young yet, mistress. Give him time and 'e'll learn.'

She stopped walking long enough for the servant and Barney to catch up. The dog sat in front of her and looked up at her with appealing amber eyes. 'If he lives long enough!' she said severely, but her anger had gone. She crouched down coming to the dog's level and ruffled his long shaggy ears. 'Look at the accident you caused! You will have to learn to come when called!'

She stood up again and slowed her pace to allow Sam Tyler to walk beside her. 'You do know who the gentlemen be, mistress?' he asked.

Ruth looked at this strange bent little man with the big nose and small black eyes who had been with the family since she was a child. 'Yes, they told me.'

He stopped walking and turned to fix her with keen grey eyes. 'That be Sir 'Ammon L'Estrange and one of his sons. Of 'Unstanton.'

She stopped walking again and turned to look at the servant. 'And so?' She did not need the servant to tell her that Sir Hamon L'Estrange was the head of the most important family in the whole area surrounding King's Lynn. She considered the implications. 'Well no doubt he will complain to my father. Much I should care!' Yet a flutter of consternation in her stomach belied her words. Her father was the only person she actually feared.

'Oi doubt they be on speaking terms, mistress,' the servant reassured her, 'the L'Estranges being King's men an' all.'

They continued walking. 'Then perhaps we can keep this incident to ourselves.'

'That be Master Roger L'Estrange, mistress,' the servant persisted, 'the youngest son of Sir 'Ammon and Dame Alice, since the older sons be much older. Oi did hair that Sir 'Ammon and Master Roger did fight fer the King in Scotland.'

She nodded, digesting this. So, he was just back from the Bishops' war as it had come to be called. They walked on in silence, allowing her time to go over the incident again. In her mind's eye she could see the handsome young cavalier with vivid blue eyes and long fiery curls. There was no mistaking the way he looked at her, his eyes the colour of summer sky locking with her own, making her cheeks grow hot, her heart flutter in her chest. The hands that had tended him had trembled, and she had hidden that beneath a matter-of-fact manner, hoping she had not given herself away.

She took a steadying breath. It was of no consequence, she told herself. He was a King's man, and her loyalties had to lie with her father's loyalties.

§

Roger and Sir Hamon plodded on, past Gelham Manor on the left, near the edge of the sea, another property of the Cobbes, and out onto the open heathland again towards Ingoldisthorpe, the next village, although it was so small perhaps the word *hamlet* would have better described it.

'I had a letter from your lady mother,' Sir Hamon said presently. 'It seems she has been visited by Mistress Paston of Appleton.'

Roger compressed his lips, immediately suspicious. Appleton Hall was just outside Sandringham and the Pastons were part of another illustrious Norfolk Royalist family from nearer Norwich. It had been mentioned to him in the past that he could do worse than make an offer for young Margaret Paston, although how he was to decide to make her his life's partner when he had had not seen the girl since childhood was still a mystery to him. Besides, the Pastons were Catholic. However, he knew his mother was friendly with Frances Paston, wife of Edward Paston. Furthermore the L'Estranges and the Pastons had intermarried on one or two occasions in the distant past, which almost made them relatives.

'And so?' Roger prompted his father, thinking to draw his fire.

Sir Hamon shot him a sideways glance. 'If you are thinking about the Paston girl, let me tell you that she married Henry Bedingfeld of Oxborough some time ago and is already the mother of a hopeful brood.'

Roger looked at him. 'Margaret Paston married?'

'Your mother did not tell you? Ah, there has been an omission here.'

'I'll say!'

'I don't know why you are surprised. Is she not four-and-twenty, the same age as you? 'Tis more than time that she were married. Besides, the Bedingfelds are pious Catholics as are the Pastons, and is none more pious than Margaret Paston, let me tell you. She would not have done for you, for all your mother's wishes.'

'Faith, no!'

They laughed together, Roger in relief, and his thoughts swung back to the Pell girl.

The relief was short lived. 'And it is high time you were wed,' Sir Hamon added.

'Whom did you have in mind, sir?' Roger asked with a hint of asperity.

Sir Hamon wrinkled his nose. 'I leave that kind of thing to your mother!'

'So does she have anyone in mind?'

'I think all the eligible females in the district are spoken for. At least that was the lament of your mother when last we spoke of the subject.'

Roger's lips twitched. 'Good! I have no intention of marrying. I prefer to be single. Besides, I have nothing to offer a young woman. Except for my charming person, of course!' He laughed at his own joke. 'I have no intention of becoming a landowner, and I have yet to make my mark in the world.'

'What mark may that be?'

'That depends on whether we have more war or not. We shall see.'

'You are not without prospects, of course. You have a small inheritance coming your way.'

'*Coming* being the operative word!'

'I give you a generous allowance.'

'For which I am truly grateful, but it is not enough to keep a wife and a home. And I do not ask for more, for I am not getting married.'

Subject closed.

'However, if I am old enough to be married, surely I am old enough not to be considered a *boy*!'

Sir Hamon cast him a sideways glance, and Roger saw his lips twitch. 'Especially in front of comely wenches, I suppose.'

In spite of himself a laugh erupted from Roger. 'Indeed!'

They passed a few cottages at Ingoldisthorpe, could not see the Manor House at the top of the hill and hidden in the trees on their right, and plodded on through farmland to Snettisham.

Snettisham was a larger village than Ingoldisthorpe and had a farrier, a tanner, chandler, saddler, slaughterhouse, countless bakers and all the necessary trades, and a market on Thursdays. The land the market stood on and other surrounding land was part of the L'Estrange estate. Snettisham also boasted three manor houses, one, which they passed on the corner of the road which led to the church, belonged again to the Cobbes.

Heacham was next and the road meandered past the church and Heacham Hall where John Rolfe had brought his wife Pocahontas some twenty-three years previously. The story was well known to Roger, for her arrival at Heacham Hall had caused quite a stir in the area at the time and was still talked about, and Sir Hamon, who had never actually met the Indian princess, never tired of re-telling the story. It whiled away the time as they plodded on towards Hunstanton.

It was dusk by the time Roger saw the chimneys of Hunstanton Hall through the trees and they took a detour from the road, speeding up to canter across the grass towards the front gates. It was his first sight of home in some time and Roger checked his horse at the outer gates, open as usual to the large green sward leading to the bridge over the moat and the house itself, all enclosed by the perimeter castellated wall. The moat was actually the river Hun a little stream hardly warranting the word 'river' and which had been diverted around the front of the house before wandering off towards the sea. Behind the house, the spoil from the moat was piled up like a huge barrier wall, making an enclosed garden.

The bridge led them to the archway of the red brick fifteenth century gatehouse with the solar on the upper floor. Sir Hamon himself had added splendid new wings either side of the gatehouse, the walls a Checkerboard design unashamedly copied from the fourteenth century Trinity Guildhall in King's Lynn, complete with modern mullioned windows, and lead downpipes to take the water off the roof, proudly bearing the date 1623. Beyond the gatehouse, across the quadrangle was the old timber-framed hall, which had stood there for centuries, and which was now connected to the new wings.

The dogs spotted them as they stopped outside the gatehouse on the green sward, and two spaniels came running across the bridge excitedly, while the older yellow dog lumbered along behind. Someone shouted an order at them and the dogs halted in their headlong rush which was just as well for the horses sidestepped and fidgeted in their anxiety.

Sir Hamon dismounted stiffly while Roger struggled out of his saddle, thinking that the fall had taken a bigger toll on him than he cared to admit. A groom came to the head of Sir Hamon's horse and another ran to take care of Achilles.

Sir Hamon and Roger straightened their weary bodies and crossed the rest of the grass sward and trudged over the bridge. The heavy oak doors of the gatehouse always stood open and Roger smiled as he noticed the remembered Tudor roses carved on them. A moment later the family poured out of the hall opposite the gatehouse, brother Nick's children first, Hamon aged nine and Nicholas eight. They shrieked in noisy welcome as Sir Hamon picked up Nicholas.

'Hey there! Have you missed me?'

'Grandfather!'

Little Hamon, who at nine felt he ought to stand on some dignity, stood shyly by waiting to be noticed and Roger tousled his red head. 'Hello there, young'un.'

Little Hamon smiled quietly. 'Welcome home, sir,' he said formally. Roger knew he was eager to hear the tales of the battles, of the King, of the lords who went to the assembly, of the Scots, of the strange lands in the north. He made a mental note to spend time telling them of the adventures in the north at the first opportunity. He liked his nephews, although he knew they caused their mother and grandmother some headaches. They would be off to a tutor shortly and that time would then be lost.

His mother Alice emerged next. She was as pretty as ever, her dark hair tied up beneath a crisp linen cap. Despite her fifty-five years, she had little in the way of grey streaks to her hair and her face was unlined. She could have been ten years younger. She had become a little portly of late, but it had filled out her face and it suited her.

Lady Alice walked straight up to Sir Hamon and without embarrassment threw her arms around his neck as he encircled her in his embrace and they kissed and hugged, unashamedly pleased to see each other. Then, as Sir Hamon released her, she turned her attention to her son. Reaching up, she took his face in her hands and studied him with her penetrating gaze before planting a quick kiss on his lips.

Roger hugged her, pleased to see her, pleased to be back in the comforting embrace of his family.

'Well I am glad to see you both in one piece,' she announced, as Roger let her go.

Sir Nicholas, Roger's oldest brother greeted them next. He was thirty-six, a knight in his own right, and as Sir Hamon's heir lived with his family at the Hall.

'Well come, sir,' he said warmly to Sir Hamon and they shook hands, and he took Roger's hand and pulled him into a brotherly embrace. 'Good to see you back, cub.'

Alice ushered them inside. 'It is cold out here,' she told them, and it was, now that the sun had almost set.

Lady Anne L'Estrange, Sir Nicholas's pretty young wife, met them inside and she curtseyed to them as they came in.

The large old hall was home, the welcome space, the banqueting space, the gathering space. This was the original part of the house and it met up with the two new wings Sir Hamon had added on to the Gatehouse to make a quadrangle with an enclosed courtyard. A large log burned in the grate recently built into one of the long walls, but the heat it threw into the room drifted upwards and appeared to hang in the space of the lofty eaves.

'So, how did it go?' Sir Nicholas asked as they made their way through the hall and to the cosier winter sitting room, where the fire in the carved dark oak fireplace blazed welcomingly.

Sir Hamon gravitated to the fire to warm his chilled body. 'You've probably heard we have made a treaty with the Scots. And it's cost us a damned fortune.'

Sir Nicholas nodded. 'I've heard.'

Sir Hamon sank into a soft chair in front of the fire as his beloved wife brought him and Roger mugs of hot spiced ale. Sitting down gratefully on the settle at the side of the fire, Roger warmed cold hands on the cup. He had aches in his thighs, buttocks and his lower back, a result of the accident and the time spent in the saddle. He assumed his father felt the same, for as he looked at him he realised that his father's eyes seemed to have sunk into his head and he had developed lines around his eyes.

'Ah! The Scots will bleed us dry, if they have the chance.'

Roger said: 'They dare challenge the right of the King. Then they go to war. Then charge the King for it!'

Sir Hamon leaned his head back against the back of the chair. 'The victor sets the conditions of the treaty. 'Tis ever so. The King had to sue for peace and so he has to abide by the terms. And the Scots will never be kind where money is concerned.'

Lady Alice ushered the children from the room into the care of the nurse. But when she came back she came to her husband's chair. Sir Hamon caught her hand and she bent to kiss the top of his head. Roger smiled and glanced at his brother. They were used to the signs of affection between their parents.

'What's that in your hair, cub?' Nicholas demanded.

Roger put his hand to his scalp. 'Nothing.'

''Tis blood,' Sir Hamon said. 'He fell off his horse!'

Nicholas threw back his head in a guffaw. 'Fell of his horse? Faith, I wish I'd seen it! What did you do, fall asleep in the saddle?'

Roger flushed. 'If you must know it was a dog caused Achilles to rear up.'

'Didn't I teach you how to stay in the saddle when a horse rears?'

Roger frowned at him, but it was Sir Hamon who came to his defence. 'We were in Dersingham and it's been a long journey. We're both shot to pieces. Besides,' he added with a wink at Roger, 'the owner of the dog was the prettiest maid you ever laid eyes on! More than compensation for the hurt caused.'

Roger grinned then. 'Wasn't she just!'

'Belongs in a painting,' Sir Hamon said again, 'a vision of perfection. And a Puritan.'

'Puritan?' Lady Alice raised her brows. She moved to the rear of the settle peered at Roger's head. 'This needs washing.'

'The young lady washed it with vinegar, Roger said.'

'I thought as much! I can smell it. But it will bear washing again.'

Roger groaned inwardly, but he knew his mother would never admit that anyone else could care for her family as well as she did.

At that moment the servant came in. 'Supper is ready, my lady.'

Lady Alice nodded. 'Thank you. Half an hour if you please.'

'Very good, m'lady.'

'Half an hour?' Roger protested as the servant bowed and departed. 'I'm so hungry I could eat a vat of grasshoppers!'

Sir Hamon grinned affectionately at his son. 'I confess so could I.'

'Oh no you don't! Not before you've washed some of that travel grime off. I am not having the pair of you sitting down and putting dust and mud all over the table covers! And I will be up to your chamber in just a short while to look at that wound,' she added to Roger.

FIVE

May, 1641

Lady Alice picked up one of the dead rabbits from the basket and slapped it down on the rough wooden table. It was still warm and not yet stiff having been brought by a servant from the hawking expedition on the sea cliffs of Hunstanton not a quarter of an hour since. She and her daughter-in-law worked quickly. It would be difficult to remove the skin once the animal had grown cold and stiff. And if the hunting were successful she expected the men to turn up with more rabbits or hares which the cook needed for the stew. He was already preparing the vegetables and broth in the kitchen adjoining the room where Alice and Anne worked. With a careful movement, she slit the belly and unhooked the internal organs and carefully pulled them out.

As Anne cut the paws off her rabbit and turned it around so she could cut off the head, Alice said to her: 'You will be mistress of this household one day Anne.'

Anne paused and took a breath. 'I hope that will be many days into the future, Mother.'

Alice nodded. 'It is kind of you to say so.' And she meant it. Because for Anne to become mistress of Hunstanton Hall, Sir Nicholas, Alice's son, would have to inherit from his father.

She had grown fond of Anne since she had arrived as a girl of no more than eighteen summers at Hunstanton ten years previously. That she was in love with Nicholas Alice saw from the moment he brought her over the moat bridge and that won her favour in Alice's book. No mother wanted more than to see her children happily settled with husbands or wives who made them happy. Anne's personality was so different to Nicholas's that Alice had wondered at the attraction at first. Nicholas, roistering, loud, large seemed opposite to little Anne's quiet, mild, studious temperament. Yet they complemented each other. This girl had lost two sons in infancy, one earlier this year, yet she hardly uttered a murmur, keeping her grief hidden away. Thankfully she had three living sons, although the older two, Hamon and Nicholas, had been sent away after Christmas and were now living with Alice's own brother in nearby Sedgeford while being schooled by Mr. Loades who lodged there and who had taught Alice's own sons until they went to Cambridge. Two-year-old William was still in the nursery. Perhaps the good Lord would bless her with more.

Both Anne and Alice cut off the rabbits' heads at the same time and began the process of taking the skin off as if they were undressing them just as the door crashed open letting in sunlight and a cool draught. Alice turned to see Sir Hamon come in and toss two large hares on the table.

'Not a bad day's hunting,' He announced, his face flushed with the ride home. But he didn't grin. 'Two and a half brace of rabbits, and a brace of hares.'

As her other sons followed him in, Alice sized up the hares. Each had the skin slit behind the rear leg tendon with the other rear foot drawn through ready for hanging and she said: 'On the hook, if you please, sir! A good day's hawking, I see.'

Sir Hamon gave the first hare to Nicholas who did indeed hang the hare from a hook in the beam, quickly followed by the second. Roger held some rabbits.

'In the bucket with them, please.' She commanded, and he dropped them in.

Alice continued working putting the skinned rabbit in one bucket and the skin in another and washed her hands in a third. A few moment later Anne did the same.

Wiping her hands on her apron, Alice looked up at Sir Hamon and her sons. 'What are all of you doing in here, pray?' she demanded. Then, looking more closely at her husband's grim face, and her sons' fierce looks, she added: 'What's the matter? What has happened?'

'There is news,' Sir Hamon said gravely.

Her eyes widened and her insides contracted. 'Not Hamon.' Her middle son and his family lived in Pakenham, in Suffolk as did her daughter Elizabeth and her husband. It worried Alice when they were not near, for news took so long to travel. She had lost too many children and even though the rest were full grown, she still feared for them.

He hastened to reassure her. 'No, I have not had word of our second son, madam, nor our daughter. You may be easy on that. Rather, we have had a message from your cousin Yelverton who has heard from London.'

His face was so grim that Alice felt her heart stop within her. 'What news, Sir Hamon?'

'Not here.'

This was obviously of some moment, something not for the ears of the servants bustling about their own work in the kitchen next to the work room. 'Very well. Let us go into the house.'

As they crossed the quadrangle in the unseasonably cold wind, Sir Hamon could not wait. 'I tell you, madam, the news is grim.' The men walked fast, their long strides crossing the ground quickly, forgetting that both she and Anne were small women with much shorter strides and hampered by skirts. They both had to run to keep up.

'Wait until we get inside, Sir Hamon,' she begged, for she was behind him and unable to hear very well in the wind.

They gained the hall and into the winter sitting room for warmth. A welcoming fire glowed in the large grate, but Alice's discomfort in the cold was forgotten in her curiosity. Roger, the last one in, closed the door behind him with a definite snap.

Alice went to the fire, took the poker and prodded it into flame. Then, setting the iron aside, she stood facing her husband, her hands clasped to her apron. 'What is your news, Sir Hamon?'

Sir Hamon took a breath. His glance took in all of them. 'Wentworth has been beheaded on Tower Hill.'

Alice was so shocked her mouth dropped open. 'Wentworth? Thomas Wentworth? The Earl of Strafford? How can that be?'

Anne went to the huge fireplace and sat on one of the settles arranged perpendicularly to it. 'Forgive me, sir, but I thought the Earl of Strafford was the King's friend.'

'And so he is—was,' Sir Nicholas answered her. 'Not only his friend, but his advisor.'

'But surely—they cannot execute someone without the King's signature?' Alice paused. 'The King would not have betrayed his friend, would he?'

Sir Hamon began to pace the room restlessly. She sat down herself on the settle opposite Anne, perching on the edge of the seat, her hands gripping each other in her lap. Her question had bothered him, she knew, for it bothered her. The King must necessarily be above reproach. Yet his friend Strafford had been beheaded. Finally he stopped. Raising his head he said carefully: 'Many thought that Strafford was the power behind the throne. His opposers said it was Strafford who advised the disastrous war with the Scots, costing the King dearly not only in pay for the troops, but also in fines from the peace treaty. Now the King has had to ask Parliament for money, which of course, they won't give him.'

Nicholas added from his position near the table: 'The Bill of

Attainder condemned Strafford as a traitor for severing the ancient harmony between the King and Parliament. In short, Strafford had far too much say in the King's affairs.'

It was Anne's turn and she turned large brown eyes on her husband. 'But does not the King have to sign the death warrant? Surely they can't just execute him?'

'The King did sign the death warrant.' Sir Hamon's tone was dull with sorrow. He took a deep breath and then let it go. 'They must have forced him to do so.'

Alice digested this piece of information. So, the King had disowned his own trusted friend, sending him to the block. It was unthinkable that their King could have acted with such disloyalty. She began to see the King in a different light.

Sir Nicholas tried to make sense of it. 'He was a threat to them.' By *them* he meant Parliament.

Sir Hamon had sat in Parliament himself. 'Aye. Strafford had too much to say for himself. But it was in the wind when they passed the Bill of Impeachment back in March.'

'Bill of Impeachment? I haven't heard of that.'

Sir Hamon looked suitably guilty. 'I had not wanted to worry you, my dear.'

'You mean you *knew*?' The trouble with being a woman, Alice thought, was that no-one ever considered it worth their while to tell you anything!

'I don't understand,' Anne complained. 'What is a Bill of Impeachment?'

'It is the accusation entered against Strafford that he is a traitor,' Nicholas informed her.

'It accused Strafford of causing a rift between the King and Parliament, Sir Hamon added.

'And was he a traitor?'

'That depends on whether you are on the side of Parliament or on the side of the King! Each side calls the other *traitor*. Not having all the facts at our disposal, it is difficult to make a judgement. The word is, though, that the King immediately regretted it, but it could not be undone.'

Alice was deeply disturbed. 'Dear God in heaven! Poor man. Beheaded!' she had a mental vision of a man on his knees, his head on the block, the axeman raising the blade. She shuddered. 'Is no-one safe?

You said you had it from Yelverton? How does he know?'

Roger who had been sitting on the corner of the table all this time observing the conversation now spoke. 'A sheet came into his possession. There are plenty of them circulating in Lynn.'

Sir Hamon rubbed his face wearily. 'You know this means war, don't you?'

Alice and Anne exchanged glances, appalled. The men might view it in a grim light, but she knew that inwardly they made their plans to join in what would be carnage. And Alice and Anne could lose their menfolk, husbands and sons.

'That's unthinkable,' Anne said horrified. 'Civil war will put Englishman against Englishman.'

'Aye.' Nicholas's gaze fixed on her. 'It will mean sacrifice.'

'God have mercy!' Alice shook her head. She felt sickened to the deepest part of her and her heart had turned to lead. She glanced at Roger who looked down at the flagstone floor, trying to hide the glee in his face from her. Oh yes, this son of trouble would be so pleased to go to war, to fight for the King, to win fame and glory if it be the will of Providence. She was angry with him, with them all. Why did men so like to make war? 'So it will be—what? The King against Parliament? The Puritans against everyone else? Is it to be a war of religion?'

''Twould seem that way,' Sir Hamon said. 'But 'tis more complex than that.'

Roger looked up, his face fierce, his blue eyes blazing. 'Each side calls the other traitor. But how can the King possibly be a traitor? He is King of England, Scotland and France.'

'By Divine right,' Nicholas added.

Sir Hamon said: 'They've got the King tied up in knots. According to Yelverton, they put much pressure to bear on him to sign the Bill of Attainder.'

Anne again asked: 'What is a Bill of Attainder?'

'The death sentence,' her husband explained. 'The Bill of Impeachment is the accusation of treason, the Bill of Attainder is the condemnation to death.'

'There was much outrage against Strafford in London,' Roger said as if she had not spoken. 'To do with episcopacy. There have been riots against it there and people have been crying "No Bishops!" They say fifteen thousand have signed the "root and branch" petition against it.'

'That many?' Sir Nicholas asked.

'Where did you come by that information?' Sir Hamon demanded suspiciously.

'Lynn,' Roger said shortly, pleased to be the source of information for once. 'It's the talk of the taverns. It would seem that many people in London are looking for an opportunity to reform the Church.'

Sir Hamon took a breath and Alice knew his inward struggle, for he had expressed it in private conversation with her many times. His own faith and that of his family was Anglican but with Calvinistic ideas. And Calvinism did not agree with rule by bishops either. That put him in opposition to the King. Yet how could he oppose a king he viewed as put in his place by God? Besides, the King was England—wasn't he? Furthermore, he was head of the Anglican Church.

Unaware of Sir Hamon's inner conflict, Roger continued: 'Anyway, the King is still anxious to settle the treaty with the Scots. By all accounts he has agreed to the banishment of episcopacy from the Scottish church—here I have a tract on the subject.' He pulled out a dog-eared dirty piece of paper and unfolded it, handing it to his father who eyed it with disgust and raised a questioning eyebrow at his youngest. 'Where did you find this? In the gutter?'

'It was in the street,' Roger agreed affably. It had the mark of the best part of a horseshoe on it.

Sir Hamon raised his brows. 'And you didn't think to give it to me earlier?'

'I forgot about it,' Roger said, which was true. He had been drunk when he picked it up, had tucked it away in his doublet and completely forgot about it.

Sir Hamon, holding it gingerly in his fingertips lest some of the dirt transfer to himself read it quickly. The King, it seemed had made a number of concessions.

It wasn't good. Alice could see he was uneasy. He passed the paper to Sir Nicholas who also read.

'So where do *we* stand?' Sir Nicholas asked.

'On the side of the King,' Sir Hamon answered firmly. 'There is nowhere else to stand. His Majesty is known to me personally. And to you sir. How can it be otherwise? To stand in opposition to the King must be treason.'

''Tis the King who rules, not Parliament.' Roger put in. 'I'm for the King.' He wasn't much interested in the politics of religion. His faith was an easy-going one, rumbling on in the background, part of his upbringing. He didn't care much whether bishops ruled the church or not. In fact there was something to be said for the old established order of the Church. It gave stability.

'And I'm for the King, too,' Sir Nicholas announced.

'Pray God we do not have to fight,' Sir Hamon said.

SIX

King's Lynn, Summer 1641

The Tuesday Market Place in King's Lynn, so named because of a charter granted by Henry VIII allowing a market to be held each Tuesday in the town, was a noisy, heaving mass. Cattle, sheep and pigs competed for space with stall-holders around the Market Cross and stocks. For those who lived in Lynn, it was a commonplace occurrence, where those who could afford it could buy essential items. For those outside the town, it was an outing they enjoyed.

While his mother and sister-in-law visited the market, Roger wandered to the medieval inn called the Griffin, on the edge of the Tuesday Market Place, for some company and food.

The Griffin was packed. Outside the weather was overcast and cool for late June, with a threat of rain. Inside the gloom added to the oppressive atmosphere, as did the crush of so many sweating bodies.

Roger bought a mug of beer and then spotted Sir Charles Mordaunt with three men Roger recognised but could not name sitting in one of the leaded window bays to take advantage of what light there was.

Sir Charles beckoned Roger to join them.

'L'Estrange, dear boy! Allow me to introduce West, Levant, and James Goode. Gentlemen, this is Mr. Roger L'Estrange of Hunstanton.'

Roger bowed slightly to the introduced gentlemen, and shook Sir Charles's hand.

'Find a seat, dear boy!' Charles invited.

Pinching a stool from a man who stood up either to leave or to get another drink, Roger brought it over to sit down next to Charles.

'You have heard about Strafford, I suppose?' Charles asked.

Roger nodded grimly and took a swig of beer from his mug. 'Fed to the wolves.'

'Aye. Got too big for his boots,' one of the others, the man named Levant, put in.

Roger again swallowed some of his beer. 'It don't do to be in court these days.'

'The King fought for Strafford, tried his best to get him off. Even sent the Prince of Wales to Parliament to plead for clemency.'

'And they didn't listen?'

'There was a demonstration at Westminster against Strafford.

Archbishop Laud, too, has been arrested.'

Levant said: 'The King even sent Captain Billingsley with a troop of soldiers with an order to free Strafford, but they were repelled.'

'He did his best then. But why did he sign Strafford's execution?'

'No choice, dear boy, no choice. You must know that Parliament has the King under their control. Why he even agreed that he could not dissolve Parliament without their consent! The very idea! Just who rules this country, eh? That's what I'd like to know. Well, dear boy, they're after Digby's blood now.' Charles conveyed a lump of meat to his mouth with a fork.

Roger frowned. 'Digby? You mean George Digby?' Digby was another of the King's friends. 'They are obviously separating the King from his close supporters, trying to isolate him.'

'It's his own fault,' Levant put in. 'Digby's speech against the Bill of Attainder against Strafford was published in an attempt to rally people to the King's cause. Upset Parliament no end.'

'Not surprising, really,' West mumbled. 'Don't think I'd have stood up to them. Value my neck too much.'

'Makes you wonder what it's like to be beheaded,' Goode added. 'Do you think you feel it?'

Roger nodded. 'I can't think how you wouldn't. Must hurt like hell!'

Levant disagreed. 'No. If a man breaks his neck, he's dead, ain't he? I mean, stands to reason. Knew a fellow once, did that. He were up a tree and fell out, straight on his head. Neck snapped. Instantly dead. Didn't know a thing.'

'Got to be better than hanging,' West mumbled. 'Dangling for the Lord knows how long while the breath is slowly choked out of one. Ugh!'

'And that's got to be better than being hung drawn and quartered,' Goode said. 'Can you imagine?'

'I've seen that,' Levant said. 'When I was in London some years ago—'

Sir Charles hastily interrupted him: 'The King has given Digby a baronetcy to get him out of the Commons and into the Lords where the King thinks he will be safer. I do not think he will betray *him*—' Sir Charles stopped short of adding: *like he betrayed Strafford,* but the unsaid words hung in the air like a widow's veil. An uncomfortable silence settled on the men around the table as they all thought of

Strafford's end and the King's part in it.

Levant stood up. 'Well, I got things to do, gentlemen, if you will excuse me.'

'Me too,' West announced.

Goode said nothing, but he stood with the others, and Roger also had to stand to make room for them to escape. Everyone nodded their heads at each other. Deftly, Roger slid the stool away from him with his foot and claimed one of the newly-vacated chairs. The other two chairs were whipped away by others. 'Left a bit suddenly didn't they?' Charles remarked, surprised.

Roger smiled inwardly. Charles Mordaunt certainly had a way of saying the wrong thing! But then tact had never been his forte. 'Sensitive,' he said.

Roger had known Sir Charles a long time, for they were of an age. Charles lived not far from Lynn at Massingham where he had inherited his estates three years previously. He was a fine enough looking fellow, Roger supposed, which had won him the fair Catherine Tollemarche as was, widow of Drake William Playters, which union had saddled him with Playters' six children. Nicholas, Roger's brother, had joked that it had been the marriage which had seen Sir Charles Mordaunt senior off, and he thought it might do for the younger Charles too, having to deal with all those brats which were not his. On top of that, his wife had borne him a son and heir (another Charles) shortly after their marriage (giving rise to further gossip with all his acquaintances doing mental arithmetic as to timing) and a daughter just last year. So in effect he had eight children at the age of twenty-six. The thought was enough to make Roger feel decidedly queasy!

'A bit sensitive about Strafford,' Roger added.

Charles sighed dramatically. 'Well, yes, and Digby might go the same way yet, dear boy. The Scottish Committee of Estates have also ordered the arrest of the Earl of Montrose, and others loyal to the King because of what they called slander against the Earl of Argyll.'

'I thought Montrose was a Covenanter. Yes, indeed, he was on the Scots side at Newburn, as I recall.'

'Well, he upset Argyll and others. He's being held in Edinburgh Castle, demanding an open trial.'

'Sweet Jesus! No-one is safe.' He took a swig from his beer and ordered a mutton dinner from the serving girl Mary. All the Griffin's serving girls were buxom and comely, but Mary was Roger's favourite, a plump girl with ample bosom and round pink cheeks.

'Ah, Mr. Strange! 'Tis many days since you bin hair, sir!'

Roger grinned. 'Give me a kiss, Mary, for old time's sake!'

'What? And you'll lose me my job! I should think not!' But she allowed him to slip his arm about her waist and give her a quick squeeze. 'Now enough of that, Mr. Strange!'

'You still living in the same place, Mary?' he asked.

'No! And if I was I wouldn't tell the likes of you, Mr. Strange.'

Roger grinned as she wiggled away.

'I suppose it ain't my lucky day!' Roger said.

Charles, from the vantage point of having left the bachelor's lifestyle far behind him, strongly disapproved of what he assumed to be Roger's dissolute lifestyle. Roger smiled to himself. Let Charles think what he liked. It would do his reputation no harm at all!

'Do you think it will be war, Charles?' Roger asked when Mary left them.

Mordaunt nodded. 'Inevitable, dear boy. I think the King has dug his heels in and rightly so, but Parliament intends to have the upper hand. Each side calls the other traitor!'

§

When Roger left the Griffin later, he reflected that everything Charles had—a wife, children, a title, historic estates—was not what Roger wanted for himself. He shook his head, laughing inwardly. He just couldn't see himself as the country squire, with a doting wife and eight children.

King's Lynn was not a particularly large town. A person could walk from one end of it to the other in a quarter of an hour. It was surrounded by a wall and a moat, filled from one of the tributaries from the river, for it stood at the mouth of the river Great Ouse as it emptied into the Wash. Some wag must have named the river for the amount of oozing mud on each bank.

Intending to purchase some new leather gloves in Briggate, Roger walked from the Tuesday Market Place into Cook Row, keeping beneath the overhanging jetties of the timber-framed buildings in an effort to avoid the disgusting pungent mess left by horses, cows and sheep on their way to the Tuesday Market Place. The street sweepers, paid a full penny by the borough for their efforts, seemed to be taking their time today, and the thought irritated him. Cook Row became Mercer Row at the cross roads with Grassmarket, and since Grassmarket was the road that led (eventually) to the East Gate and was, therefore the main route for traffic coming into town, Mercer Row, with less traffic, was a good deal cleaner. He passed the plumber and the saddler, and a number of other trades, and came to the stone bridge over the Purfleet. Briggate was beyond. The names referred to different sections of the same road.

At low tide Purfleet was a muddy, stinking tributary of the Ouse, with a road running parallel to it on the left bank called Fincham Street, and another on the right hand bank which was Sedgeford Lane, both lined with higgledy-piggledy timber-framed houses, shacks and tenements backing onto the fleet and sinking slowly into the oozing, stinking mud. The less well-off lived here, mostly screened from view by houses actually built on the bridge.

From the corner, Roger could see down to the fleet. Small children played in the mud, heedless of the possibility of being sucked into it. As he watched, a woman lowered a bucket from an upper window into the trickle of water running down the centre—he hoped it was not for drinking, because the stench coming up from the mud made his eyes water. They must use it as a latrine, he thought. Boats anchored in the Purfleet sat drunkenly on the mud, stranded, until the tide came in again.

About to restart walking, Roger paused as a lady dressed in the drab Puritan style of dress, cloaked in black, strode purposefully towards him, and he raised his hat and bowed his head, indicating that she should pass ahead of him. She looked at him and hesitated as her eyes widened in recognition.

For Roger, everything else seemed to disappear, except for her face and intense dark brown eyes.

She halted abruptly and one of the Purfleet urchins, who chose that moment to run across the road, careered into her.

Automatically, Roger reached out to stop her falling into him, and found himself with an armful of woman who smelled of rosewater. At the same time she grabbed the child, whether because instinct made her clutch at anything in an attempt to save herself, or to deliberately restrain the boy, Roger could not tell. Whatever the case, Roger steadied her and immediately released her, well aware of the impropriety of the situation.

'Madam!'

'Le'me go!' the boy yelled. He lashed out with his bare muddy foot and caught her shin and she let him go, letting out a small cry of surprise.

Roger, just beside her, moved quickly and reached out to grab the boy's arm as he made to flee.

'Le'me go!' The boy's yell had become a shriek. People were stopping and looking.

'If, brat, you do not stop squealing I shall be obliged to give you a sound thrashing,' Roger told him severely.

Cowed by this threat, the boy stopped and looked up at Roger with large fearful eyes. 'Oi hin't squealing,' he said, sticking out his lower lip.

'Then what do you think that noise was? Or is there a pig here?' Roger looked around dramatically and at the same time caught Ruth's eye, to find her stifling a laugh.

'Oi hin't seen no pig hair,' the boy announced also looking around him.

'No? I think I am holding one! Certainly your manners mimic one.'

'Wha'?'

'You act like a pig,' Roger clarified for him. 'You have no manners. I believe you should apologise to the lady.'

'Wha' fer?'

'For running into her and knocking her off her feet and for kicking her.'

'Well, the missus hold me.'

'Like I am doing,' Roger added. 'That is no way to treat a lady. You should apologise.'

The boy looked down at his feet and Roger noticed that he had no shoes, his feet were caked in mud and now he looked, Ruth's black dress was streaked with mud too.

'I said 'apologise',' Roger ordered.

The boy looked up at him again. 'Wha's apologise?'

Roger took a restraining breath. 'Say you are sorry.'

'But Oi hin't!'

'Well you ought to be. No gentleman should treat a lady thus.'

'Oi hin't no ge'man.'

'While that may be true, nevertheless, you ought to apologise—say sorry—to the lady. It is manners.'

'Oi hin't got no manners,' the boy said sullenly.

'That is patently obvious! Nevertheless, I shall not release you until you apologise. And I warn you my patience is coming to an end.'

The boy fixed Roger with a proud, defiant stare to be met with an equally determined glare and then his eyes fell in defeat. A moment later he looked up at the lady, bowed from the waist and mumbled: 'Oi be sorry moi lady.'

As Roger looked up again, her amused eyes met his squarely for a few heartbeats and then, as the boy wriggled in Roger's grasp she looked down at him.

She nodded. 'Thank you, young man. Apology accepted.'

She again looked at Roger. 'I think that is a fair enough apology, sir, do not you?'

'Very well, madam.' Roger released the boy. 'And mind your manners where gentlewomen are in future, young man.'

The boy compressed his lips, once more mutinous.

Ruth produced a penny. 'There.' She pushed it into the boy's hand. 'Give it to your mother.'

His eyes grew round as he looked at it. 'Thank ye lady!' And he took off after the other boys, lost almost immediately in the tumble of shacks and houses lining the Purfleet.

'Do you think his mother will get it?' Roger asked as they watched him go.

'I doubt it. But it might help. I thank you Mr. L'Estrange for your intervention. I would have fallen had you not caught me.'

Roger removed his hat and swept an extravagant bow. 'At your service, Mistress Pell. If ever you need rescuing from urchins again, please send for me.'

Her eyes twinkled with amusement as she dipped a brief curtsey in answer to his bow, bending her head in acknowledgement.

She began to walk in the direction of the Saturday Market Place.

He took it as a tacit invitation to fall into step beside her.

She said with a quick smile at him then averting her gaze: 'I was unaware of the need to be rescued, Mr. L'Estrange. I think I can handle one small boy.' There, she looked at him again with those hypnotic dark eyes and he felt the breath catch in his throat. This girl was flirting with him.

He smiled too. 'It did not look that way to me, madam. But I see my intervention was not required. And if that is the case, how can you be thankful for it?'

She opened her mouth in a disbelieving laugh displaying impossibly white even teeth, but she came back quickly: 'It was the mannerly thing to say when someone has rendered one a service, however unnecessary. Of course, you must know that *I* am not in want of manners, sir.'

'Unlike the urchin?'

'Unlike the urchin,' she agreed solemnly, but her eyes danced with amusement. Faith! She was beautiful!

He found himself grinning at her.

'I trust you came to no hurt over your fall, sir?' she asked.

He smiled ruefully. Would he ever be allowed to forget the ignominy of tumbling from his horse? 'The cut healed in a few days. So did the aches and pains.' He could not resist teasing her. 'Dare I hope you were anxious over me!'

She pursed her delicious red lips thoughtfully. 'I am sure if ought had happened to you we would have heard about it in Dersingham. So no, I was not anxious. I was being mannerly again!'

He laughed. 'I deserved that!'

She chuckled too. 'Perhaps it will teach you to have a care when out riding in future!'

'If I had not been half asleep I would have seen your dog in time,' he agreed affably. 'My father and I were at the end of a long journey from the north. Just the same, the dog should have been tied up.'

'Since when have dogs been tied up, Mr. L'Estrange? In my experience they roam all over the place all day and come home for their supper!'

'True. Leaving chaos in their wake. Perhaps they ought to be confined more.'

'Well I suppose I cannot argue with that.'

They walked the length of Briggate and came to the Saturday Market Place where the great minster of St. Margaret rose majestically in front of them, a vision of intricately carved pale stone spoiled by the blood and guts of the shambles, the covered meat market, leaning drunkenly against its wall.

Ruth stopped walking at the corner opposite the church in the shadow of the jetty of a large ornate timber-framed medieval building known as Walter Coney's house. She turned to Roger. 'I am going into the church, Mr. L'Estrange. Is that where you are going?'

He had not been going anywhere in particular, having passed the glove makers in Briggate. He had merely taken the opportunity to walk with her, reluctant to leave her. He inclined his head to someone whom he vaguely recognised but who knew him enough to tug his forelock. 'No, Mistress Pell. Not today. Sunday I shall go to church. Today I have other business.'

'What business, Mr. L'Estrange? What could be more important than worshipping God?'

He thought at first she was serious and he began searching his brain for a suitable answer when he saw that mischievous light in her eyes. Bewitching!

He grinned. 'You have me there, Mistress. What indeed?'

'So you will join me?'

'No,' he said bluntly, offering no further explanation.

Her lips twitched and then she bit her bottom lip in an effort not to laugh. 'Of course, it is none of my business what you do with your time, sir. You should scold me for my impertinence.'

'Indeed, madam,' he agreed with mock seriousness.

She did laugh then, but quickly covered her face with her hand. It would not do to laugh out loud in public. 'H-how ungentlemanly of you!'

He chuckled. 'I hope you are not going to give *me* a lesson in manners, Mistress Pell.'

'Not that you do not deserve it, of course!'

'You mean, I am a great rogue?'

'Are you?'

'What do you think?'

She stood looking at him her expression growing more thoughtful and then warmth came into her smile. 'I think you and I shall be friends, Mr. L'Estrange.' As she said it, she looked down at her hands and her cheeks flashed crimson, then she ventured to look up at him again uncertainly. She took his breath away.

For an innocent Puritan maiden it was a forward statement. She had embarrassed herself, he could see and he immediately wanted to put her at her ease. He looked away from those dark earnest eyes, first at the church behind her and then at the cobbles beneath his feet, trying to decide how best to answer her. When he finally met her eyes again, he was deadly serious but he knew he could not yet say what had come into his mind. 'Mistress Pell,' he paused and his voice was soft and low, 'I too think that we shall be—friends.'

The blush which had started to fade now suffused her cheeks anew. She did not mistake his hesitation, or his meaning.

There was a long pause before she said awkwardly: ‘Sir, I thank you for your company.’

Oh, but she was an adorable mix of shy Puritan, playful child and flirtatious woman! At one time childlike, at another all woman. But he had been dismissed. Removing his hat, he reached out and took her slender hand in his and bowed to lightly kiss her knuckles. Straightening up again, he gave her fingers a gentle reassuring squeeze before releasing them.

‘Mistress Pell,’ he said formally, replacing his hat. ‘It has been my pleasure.’

Then he turned and walked away from her.

SEVEN

Sir Hamon met them in the great hall, welcoming his wife by taking her in his arms and kissing her soundly on the lips which left her a little embarrassed and struggling to pin her cap back on her dark hair before giving it up as useless.

'We've only been gone since this morning,' she remonstrated.

'A whole day without you, my sweet!'

Roger raised his eyes heavenward, shook his head and gave his hat to the footman. A moment later Nicholas appeared and greeted his wife with a quick kiss.

'I have news,' Roger began, but he went unheeded.

'Well what did you buy, my love?' Sir Hamon asked his wife, giving consideration to the number of parcels that James Oldham, the coachman, struggled in with before returning to the coach for more. 'Were there any goods left in Lynn?'

Lady Alice cast him an arch look. 'If you must know, sir, it is several months, if not half a year since we last set foot in Lynn and we were in great need—'

'Of woollen cloth, I see,' Sir Hamon finished for her as the parcels were placed on the large table.

'And linen,' she added. There was a great quantity of linen judging by the size of the parcel, and she gave him a full list of all the items she had bought.

Roger waited patiently, leaning his broad shoulders against the ancient door frame and crossing his arms across his chest, knowing that they must pass by him to go into the winter sitting room. Sure enough, Sir Hamon, becoming aware of his continued presence as he began to guide his lady from the hall, raised his brows in query. 'Are you still here, sir?'

'I have news,' Roger said again, pleased to have claimed his father's and everyone else's attention finally.

Sir Hamon guided his wife into the winter sitting room and Roger, Nicholas and Anne followed. 'What news?'

Lady Alice sat down by the fire with Anne, but the men continued standing in the centre of the room beside the table.

'I had dinner at the Griffin,' Roger told them, leaning his bottom on the edge of the table, folding his arms again, and crossing one long leg over the other at the ankles in a negligent attitude which he knew would irritate his brother. 'With Charles Mordaunt. He spoke of Strafford's execution. But he also said that Parliament is seeking to impeach George Digby.'

Both Sir Hamon and Nicholas were visibly shocked. 'Digby?' Sir Hamon exclaimed. 'They want to execute Digby as well? 'Sblood, is no-one safe?'

Pleased to have their full attention, Roger went on: 'Digby published a speech he made against the Bill of Attainder for Strafford, trying to gather support for the King and to save Strafford's life. It was not a popular move. So now they are out for his blood.'

Nicholas swore, then apologised to the women. 'So if you dare to speak against Parliament, you are viewed as a traitor, it would seem.'

'So it would seem. They haven't arrested him yet, and the King has made Digby a baron.'

Sir Hamon was ahead of him. 'To get him out of the Commons and into the Lords, I suppose. Out of harm's way.'

'That's not all. Archbishop Laud has also been arrested.'

'No!' Nicholas was further shocked. 'The Archbishop! They go too far arresting a man of God.'

'Not from their point of view, obviously,' Sir Hamon said acidly.

Roger added: 'He's not been tried yet. Also the Earl of Montrose is being held in Edinburgh Castle. It seems he dared to question the Marquis of Argyll's motives, and for that he has been viewed as a King's man. Other Royalists in Scotland have also been imprisoned.'

'But Montrose is a Covenanter.'

'Yes he is. But because he spoke against Argyll they think he's switched sides.'

Sir Hamon frowned, and Nicholas shook his head. 'Absolutely no-one is safe. We live in perilous times.'

'The talk is all of war,' Roger went on.

'What chance do we have when even Covenanters are arrested?' Nicholas demanded.

'Oh yes, and I found out that the King fought hard for Strafford. First sending soldiers to free him from the tower, and even after the Bill of Attainder, sending Prince Charles to the House of Commons to beg mercy for Strafford. Of course those Puritan dogs didn't listen.'

'So Strafford was not betrayed by the King.' Lady Alice, who had been listening, spoke in relief.

Nicholas said: 'It must come to war. Parliament have just snatched control. There is no room for an Englishman's conscience anymore. We have to fight for the King.'

Sir Hamon became thoughtful. 'Yes, we have to fight this tyranny. We will see what the King will do.'

§

The summer of 1641 wore on in an uneasy normality, while rumours of events in London filtered through to Norfolk.

Digby's speech was publicly burnt by the hangman in London; the King spent most of the summer in Scotland trying to make peace with them; and the King made the Earl of Essex, a staunch Puritan, lord chamberlain, and then commander of all his forces south of the Trent in an effort to get him on side.

None of which affected Norfolk people directly, although Sir Hamon and others refused to pay the ship money demanded by Parliament.

With little else to do, Roger helped his father on the estate, rounded up sheep and cattle, helped with the horses and generally made himself useful. He was good with the horses, but the work with the sheep, pigs and cattle he found distasteful. Particularly the pigs which he viewed as smelly dirty animals. When he fell flat on his face in the stinking mud of the pig-sty, he declared to his laughing father that there was nothing on God's earth that would make him deal with a pig again!

In high dudgeon he bathed and changed his clothes, consigning the smock and leggings he had been wearing to the rubbish pile and took his own horse Achilles, intending to ride to Lynn.

Much as he wanted to urge Achilles into a gallop across the Ringstead Downs, he reined him in, for the heat was chokingly oppressive, and he wanted to keep him fresh for the whole journey. He had ridden off his anger by the time he reached Dersingham and the crossroads where he had fallen from his horse, and his thoughts turned to Ruth Pell.

It had been six weeks since their encounter in Lynn. During that six weeks he had thought about her often as snatches of their conversation returned to him at odd moments fuelling a desire to see her again. In vain he kept dismissing the desire from his mind. After all, as the animosity grew between Puritans and king's men, the chances of his being received with any degree of friendliness at Dersingham Hall became ever more remote. Besides, did he really want to further a friendship with a damned Puritan?

What was it that drew him then? Why did his thoughts keep going back to her? Her dancing, intense dark eyes? She certainly had the looks to tempt any man, and a body to match. With an effort he dragged his thoughts from her body. Was it the child-woman he saw which intrigued him so much? It was all of it, and none of it. All he could say with any degree of certainty was that in her eyes he found a connection he had never felt with any other person. He could not explain it. He just knew he had to see her again, and he had resisted that urge long enough.

On sudden impulse he turned Achilles' head up the road towards Dersingham Hall and the church, doffing his hat to a matron he was acquainted with, one of the Cobbes, as he did so. On a trotting horse, it took only a few minutes to cover the distance and then he was outside the church of St. Nicholas, near the old dilapidated tithe barn opposite the Old Hall.

So what now? He surveyed the high perimeter carrstone wall, the wooden frame and wattle-and-daub building and the ranks of leaded-light windows in the upper jetties. Was she behind one of those windows? Could she see him from the house, sitting on his magnificent black stallion? He smiled at the thought. Should he just go up to the front door and knock? He pictured in his mind how he would be received. The same way Sir Valentine Pell would be received at Hunstanton Hall, he assumed. With distinct coolness and a refusal to let him speak to her anyway. Besides, it wasn't done just to turn up on a lady's doorstep without an invite from her guardian, at least not in Norfolk.

Faith! What was he doing here anyway?

On the thought and rattled, he urged Achilles onward along the same road turning down the road to West Hall Manor which belonged to the Cobbes, the new place they had built with carrstone, and then back out onto the Lynn road.

He rode on at quite a fast pace, allowing Achilles a short canter through the fields by Onion Corner, (so named for the wild garlic and bluebells that flowered there in the late spring) and finally turned into Lynn.

Sir Richard Hovell was in the Griffin, enjoying a tankard of ale with Sir Charles Mordaunt and Roger bought himself a tankard and sat down with them.

'What ails you, L'Estrange?' Hovell asked.

Roger stared at him. Hovell was older than Mordaunt and himself who were about the same age, but he spent a good deal of his time in Lynn and in the Griffin in particular.

'Pigs!' Roger said in disgust.

They stared at him for a moment and then Hovell started laughing, throwing his head back so that his light goatee beard pointed straight at Roger almost accusingly. 'Don't tell me Sir Hamon has had you minding the pigs!'

Roger took a large pull at his ale. But it did little to calm his ruffled feathers. 'Something about saving money on hired help,' he said with feeling. 'I don't mind helping out, but *pigs!*'

Mordaunt chuckled also. 'Seems to me like your father is trying to teach you a lesson, dear boy.'

'And what lesson might that be? Because if it is designed to make me want to be a country squire and manage estates, then I am afraid he is very much mistaken! Nothing could further confirm my intention.'

Mordaunt chucked again. 'At least you were not born to inherit title and estates.'

'But I do have an inheritance,' Roger told them. 'If I wished, I could buy a modest holding. Only I can think of much better things to spend my money on.'

'Like what?'

'Like having a good time.'

Sir Charles Mordaunt shook his head. 'All very well, dear boy, until your money runs out. Then what? You need to make your inheritance work for you.'

'And when you meet the right lady, you will change your mind,' Hovell put in.

'I am not getting shackled to a lady, thank you,' Roger retorted. 'I have too much to do.'

'Like what?' Hovell demanded.

'Like fighting for the King.'

'He doesn't need an army right now.'

'No, but he will.'

'You reckon?' Hovell asked.

Roger nodded and Sir Charles Mordaunt became serious. 'Yes, he will. It will come to war, Sir Richard.'

Sir Richard Hovell sighed and rubbed his hand over his face in a weary gesture. 'Dear God, I hope not.'

Roger took a long swallow of ale. 'My father and brother think it will. And we hear rumblings from London.'

They talked on for some time about a possible war, complained about the Puritans who had closed the theatre in Lynn and stopped all the street entertainment. 'That's Toll and Percival,' Roger grumbled. Thomas Toll and William Percival were the Puritan members for Parliament for the borough, 'A pair of miserable poker-faced bats if ever I saw any!'

Hovell started to laugh again. 'Bats?'

'Well don't you think so in their ill-fitting black clothes? They look like harbingers of doom!'

Mary, the pretty little plump waitress came into the taproom then and came over to the table. 'Mr. L'Estrange! Well come, sir.'

Usually Roger would have put his arm about her waist, pulled her onto his lap and given her a sound kiss. As it was he said: 'Hello, Mary.'

She looked at him, astonished. 'Hello Mary?' she repeated. 'Is that it?'

He looked up at her, as if seeing her for the first time. She was pretty, but she had aged. Debauched living had aged her. She had lines around her eyes and her lips were unnaturally dark. Her breasts spilled out from her low décolletage and her fair hair was a mass of curls. She looked a mess, he decided, a bawdy mess, so much at odds with the quiet understated chasteness of Ruth Pell that he suddenly had a disgust of her.

'Sorry, Mary,' he said. 'Not myself today.'

She stared at him for another moment or two and then turned away from him to find another gentleman who was not so particular.

Mordaunt too was surprised. His eyes narrowed as he looked at Roger speculatively. 'Are you ailing, L'Estrange!'

Hovell laughed again and Roger was beginning to find it tiresome. 'I know what it is, he has found a lady,' Sir Richard Hovell announced.

Roger glared at him and hoped he did not blush. 'I have not.'

'No? I did hear tell of a certain Mistress Pell.'

Roger's surprise was written right across his face; it did not improve his temper. He said tightly: 'Mistress Pell and I have not met above twice.'

As if he had not spoken Mordaunt said seriously: 'Won't do, dear boy. Puritan. Staunch Puritans all the Pells. Well known fact.'

'I am aware of that. I can assure you the lady and I are barely acquainted.'

'*"The lady doth protest too much, methinks,"*' Hovell quoted and laughed.

Roger stood up abruptly, his chair legs scraping on the flagstone floor.

'I'll bid you good day, gentleman' he said stiffly and left the inn. Richard Hovell and Sir Charles Mordaunt exchanged meaningful glances and then they both laughed.

Outside in the Tuesday Market Place, the cobble-stoned square was empty, save for a few pedestrians, it not being a Tuesday.

Roger was furious. He hated being teased and his temper had been put under too much strain already that day.

He decided to walk down to Common Staithe and strode across the market place keeping close to the Woolpack Inn on his left to avoid the mess horses had left and collided with a woman coming into the square from Stockfishrow.

'Oh!' She let out a cry and he just had the presence of mind to grab her arms before she fell backwards.

'Madam, I beg your pardon. I trust you are unhurt—' He let her go and raised his hat, as she turned her face up to him. His pulse stalled, then raced on. 'Why, Mistress Pell!'

'I am unhurt, Mr. L'Estrange,' she assured him a little breathlessly and blushing furiously. 'I am sure it was as much my fault as yours. I was in such a hurry on an errand for my aunt—but you do not want to hear my woes.' She paused, trying to calm herself. 'And I must thank you again for saving me from falling.'

He did want to hear it. He wanted to hear anything she had to say. 'I told you I would rescue you if you needed me,' he told her with a grin, and her face lit up in an answering grin. 'I trust you are well, Mistress?' He raised his hat and bowed.

She bobbed a curtsey. 'Very well, sir. And you?'

'Yes indeed!'

Well that was the formal bit over with, now what? 'Where does your aunt live?' he asked aiming for an air of polite enquiry.

'She has a house in Wingate. I am staying there for a few weeks. My aunt likes my company, whereas my mother—well never mind.'

'I was about to take a walk by the river,' he explained desperately searching for some way of keeping her with him, and hoping his voice sounded like an invite.

She nodded, her eyes searching his face. She seemed reluctant to continue on her way, despite her previous hurry. ''Tis a nice day for a walk.'

'Indeed. It has been busy in Hunst'on. I have been helping out with the jobs on the estate.' And talking of jobs, he hoped she could not smell the pigs on him! Despite bathing, washing his hair, and changing his clothes, he fancied he could still smell it!

'What kind of jobs?'

'Well—' he hesitated. They could not stand on the street corner chatting for long. He decided to take the bull by the horns. 'Would you care to accompany me to the river and I shall tell you?'

She rewarded him with a dazzling smile which lit up her face. 'I should like to see the river.' So together they turned towards Ferry Street which was no more than a passageway just wide enough to take a wagon between the buildings, towards the river. 'So tell me, sir, what did you help with on the estate?'

'Well, there were sheep to round up for shearing . . .'

He talked as they walked out onto the grassy river bank. It was fairly quiet at this spot, for the tide was out, exposing the mud, and above it a small sandy beach. The fishermen were out at sea until the tide came in again. To the right was the Common Staithe, with tall naked-masted ships tethered to the wharf, and leading inland the Fisher Fleet, the outlet for the Gaywood river, rather like Purfleet, along the banks of which the fisher folk lived in tumbling wooden-framed cottages. Across the river the village of Old Lynn (or West Lynn as it was sometimes known) lined the river bank.

'It is so peaceful here,' she said and sat down on the sand in the late afternoon sun.

He watched her for a moment, admiring the soft peachiness of her skin, and the long lashes resting on her cheek. She sat upright with her legs to one side, her grey woollen skirt billowing out around her. She looked up at him. 'Do you not sit, sir?' How did those eyes reach right into his soul?

He sat near her, on the side her legs were not, drawing up his knees and hooking his arms around them, looking out towards the houses on the opposite bank, yet acutely aware of the lady sitting with him. He had an odd excited feeling in the pit of his abdomen, and for that reason he dared not look at her just yet. He might give himself away! So he sat and looked at the river. To their right the river meandered away until it widened and flowed into the Wash. Several ships were tied up there around Fisher Fleet, another tributary of the Ouse. It was a reminder of the importance of Lynn as a port.

He became aware that she was looking at him and he turned his head towards her, whereupon her cheeks became a fiery red and she looked away at the river. It occurred to him that she blushed a great deal. Perhaps it was because she was young and shy. Or perhaps because she had been kept close. Or perhaps the same feelings raced through her as they did him. The thought made his breath catch.

They had been silent too long. For something to say, he managed: 'I am surprised to find you walking alone, Mistress Pell.'

'I escaped my maid,' she confided with a small grin. 'My aunt does not have enough people to accompany me anyway. So I sent the maid on an errand and slipped out. My aunt Mary wanted me to deliver a message to the carpenter, but she would not be pleased to discover I went alone.'

'Will you get wrong for that?' *Get wrong!* Now that was a Norfolk expression! He sounded like a yokel!

'No. Oh, perhaps a little. My aunt is more liberal than my mother or father, although she is Father's sister, you understand. Aunt Mary says that there is no harm in Lynn as long as one is home before nightfall.'

She fell silent, the smile vanishing from her face. When she next spoke, her voice was fearful, and she plucked at her skirt. 'Do you think there will be war, Mr. L'Estrange?'

He frowned. 'I do. I do not think we can avoid it now.'

'Will you go to war?'

He looked at her straightly. 'Yes.'

She nodded as though she had known his answer already. 'You will fight for the King.' When he nodded, she added: 'My father will, too, I think, but on the side of Parliament. He is hardly ever home now, so I don't suppose it will be very different if he goes to war. But not my brothers. Neither of them is skilled in fighting. My father did not teach them.' She sighed and picked up some sand, letting it trickle through her slender fingers. 'What is this great quarrel about Mr. L'Estrange?'

He stared at her. 'I cannot believe that you do not know.'

Her brows drew together crossly. 'I am a woman, sir. Perhaps the women in your family are not treated as idiots as they are in my family! Such things as talk of war are not fit for my ears. But I can see by what people say that it will come to it. I cannot see that the differences in how the church is run, or how people believe could result in war.'

He also frowned, trying to gather his disordered thoughts to put it as simply as he could. He looked out at the river again, for she was too much of a distraction.

He said carefully: 'It's all to do with the Scots first of all, breaking away from the Church of England.'

'But that happened years ago, didn't it? Why should it come to war now?'

'The King wanted them to come back into the fold, I suppose.'

'So why did the Scots leave then?'

'Because they felt that the church should be governed by elders, not bishops. Anyway, it came to war with the Scots over that, but the King was not victorious.'

'You were there, in Scotland?'

'Not quite. Northumbria. Newburn to be exact, almost next door to Newcastle. Well, a few miles away. The King made a truce with the Scots who imposed heavy fines on him. But he could not pay, so he summoned Parliament to give him funds.'

'So far I understand.'

He grinned. 'But Parliament refused to give him the money.'

'Why?'

'I've no idea. Perhaps because they were Puritan, they too objected to the idea that bishops should run the church. I wonder if they had it in mind even then to oust the King from Power. Or at least curtail his power. Parliament knew that without money the King would find it almost impossible to raise an army to turn on themselves, unless men volunteered for nothing, of course.'

'So you and your family volunteered themselves. Is that because you support rule by bishops then?'

'No. My family is Calvinistic in faith. So no. But we feel that the King rules by Divine right which should not be opposed.'

She digested this. 'My father thinks all Royalists are recusants.'

'We are not Catholic,' he said simply. 'Your father is either misinformed, or just puts everyone into the same barrel. True, most Catholics are Royalist but that is because Parliament opposes their religion too.'

'It sounds like a tangled mess to me. May I ask: How is it that you as Calvinists wear bright colours?'

'May I ask why you do not?' he countered. 'Or where does the Bible forbid singing, dancing, or other entertainment if it be free from sinful inclinations?'

'I do not know. But my father says that some clothes that Royalist ladies wear are—less than decorous.'

Roger smiled at that, thinking that the low *décolletés* he had been privileged to see in the not too distant past were indeed indecorous. Actually, they were indecent!

'He also says that the plays and entertainment have been sinful.'

Roger had to acknowledge that Sir Valentine Pell had a point. He remembered the riotous performances he had thoroughly enjoyed at the St. George's Guildhall in Stockfishrow.

He agreed: 'Indeed, I would not have wanted my sister to have sat through some performances. In itself, a play is not unwholesome if its content is good. But, as ever, people misuse their freedoms, until they are taken away. Then it spoils it for the rest of mankind. I have seen some good plays, but I have seen some very bad ones too. The same is true of dancing or singing. The behaviour of some spoils it for others and there are always those who will banish the whole entertainment for that.'

'Well I should certainly never frequent the theatre,' she declared primly and he wanted to laugh at her, but hid it. She was young and had been carefully brought up and she had much to learn. He nodded and said solemnly: 'That is your privilege.'

There was a short silence, then she said: 'I think we are not really that different after all, Mr. L'Estrange.'

She was right, he thought. The difference was political, not religious.

He nodded and stared at the river for a short while. 'It will come to war, Mistress.' He turned his head to look at her. 'And we shall be on opposite sides.'

His words acted like a catalyst, for she stood up abruptly and brushed the sand from her plain grey dress. He too stood, admiring the trim delicate figure, her beautiful face, somehow all the more beautiful for lacking adornment.

He said on impulse: 'Madam, may I call on you at Dersingham Hall?'

She looked up from her dress, her eyes widening in alarm. 'No!'

Taken aback, he frowned at her. 'I have honourable intentions, I assure you.'

'It does not matter what your intentions are,' she said forthrightly. 'If you call, my father will think I have encouraged you to come to our house. He will see you as an enemy. You will not be welcome and I—I will be punished. Please, sir, you must not! Promise me you will not come to the Hall.'

He had the unwelcome feeling that she was slipping out of his grasp. 'But I must see you again.'

'No, no that cannot be.' She was becoming distressed, and her eyes moistened as if she wanted to cry. Was her father such a harsh man that she should be afraid of him? 'I am sorry, I should not have come with you here this afternoon. I did not intend to—I don't know what I was thinking! Forgive me.'

Dismayed that he had blunderingly caused her such anxiety, he was at pains to reassure her. He reached out and caught her arm to stay her a moment longer. 'Mistress, please do not distress yourself. I shall do nothing that will cause you hurt.'

She dashed her hand across her eyes. 'Oh, sir, you do not understand.'

He said seriously: 'If you do not wish it, I shall not come to Dersingham Hall.'

Her watery gaze searched his face and in her eyes he saw real fear and at the same time regret. 'Thank you. Now please let me go, for I have tarried long enough.'

He released her arm and then she was gone, running back up Ferry Street to the Tuesday Market Place.

He stood looking after her, disappointed and hurt. He had rushed her and she had bolted.

'Damnation!' he swore. 'Damn it all to hell!'

EIGHT

Edgehill, Warwickshire, 23 October 1642

Roger shivered. It was a cool day, the iron-grey clouds thick with promised rain. Beneath his feet the ground was spongy with moisture, the grass soaking his new leather boots. Roger looked down at them and thought how much he had paid for them. An inconsequential thought.

They were on top of the escarpment and below them the Parliamentarian army were arranged in units. Since he was on the extreme right of the King's army, the Parliamentarians were diagonally to his left, all arranged in nice neat rectangles of men.

'You afraid, L'Estrange?' William Masters was the other side of Achilles, beside a smaller bay mare. A fair horse, Roger thought, but not a patch on the black magnificence of Achilles.

Roger stroked Achilles' neck with his black-gloved hand. 'Afraid? Faith! No!' Although in fact he did feel the crawl of fear in his belly at this the first major battle since the King had raised his standard in Nottingham in August. He stifled a shiver. 'You?'

'Lord no!' Masters too, was lying, Roger thought.

The waiting seemed everlasting. He thought of his mother. She had not been there to see him off. He knew why. She had not wanted him to go. She would never say so, of course, but he knew. What mother wanted to send her son to war?

'Who's that?' Roger asked, looking to his right where a man sat on a beautiful white stallion on the top of the hill.

'Haven't you seen Prince Rupert before?' Masters replied.

'No.' Roger squinted into the distance. He had heard about Prince Rupert of the Rhine. There had been much talk among the troops about him. He was the King's nephew, a foreign fellow, but a clever man, a strategist. He was the commander of the cavalry and dragoons who loved and respected him as a leader of men. Beside him was a fluffy white dog.

'Is that a dog with him?' Roger asked.

'Oh that's Boye, and he goes everywhere with him. They are never separated. The enemy views him as a devil-dog, a witch's familiar and attributes all kinds of amazing feats to him.'

Roger raised a disbelieving brow. 'Superstitious lot! He doesn't go into battle too, does he?'

'No. He'll be tied up in the camp in a minute. The Prince won't want him hurt. But they say he sleeps in Prince Rupert's bed, and they do say that whenever he hears John Pym's name, he cocks his leg!' Roger laughed. John Pym was the leader of the Parliamentarian forces.

Along the line of cavalry men began jumping into the saddle. With nerves twitching and a swoop of his insides, Roger did the same. So did William Masters. Achilles fidgeted beneath Roger but he had firm hand, and he held him in check. Under his dun tabard, the heavy iron plate that was his armor dug into his ribs, despite the padded gambeson he wore beneath his shirt. He tried to shift it to ease the pressure with little effect.

He looked uneasily along the line and adjusted his hat. Unlike the infantry who wore iron helmets, the cavalry wore large black felt hats some with a feather decoration.

Faith, he was nervous! Anyone would think he had never seen action before. Well, if you could count that fiasco at Newburn action, that is. Perhaps you couldn't. Such a humiliating defeat that had been. He looked at the massed ranks of the Roundheads carrying all manner of death-dealing weapons. Well, if it were them or him, he would definitely make sure it was him. No room for sentimentality here!

'You married?' William Masters asked.

'No.'

'Betrothed?'

'No.'

'A young lady waiting at home?'

'No.' His mind flitted to Ruth. He had seen her just once since the time beside the river. She had been in company with her aunt and he had almost bumped into them in the Tuesday Market Place and thus been forced to apologise. He had raised his hat, and Ruth acknowledged him, even introducing him to her aunt. It had been all very polite, but Mistress Mary Lead, Ruth's aunt, had ushered her party away from him with all speed. But not before Roger had looked into Ruth's eyes and seen misery where there had once been smiles and laughter. What could have upset her so much? It had disturbed him ever since.

He shook his head. There was no point in thinking about her. She was a prisoner of her family, and now that it had come to war, she was on the side of the enemy, a cursed Puritan.

'No,' he said again, 'there is no-one.'

Everyone else in the cavalry set their faces in a determined line. Anyone of them, or even all of them, could be dead by the end of the day. He, Roger L'Estrange, was not going to be one of them. He was as determined as any of them, if not more so, to take as many of the sanctimonious what's-names down before they got him!

Further along the ranks to his left cheering broke out as the King rode in front of them with a hefty entourage, encouraging his army. Roger shifted in the saddle to try to see him. He'd never seen the King before. This was the man who sat on the throne of England, Scotland and France, who ruled by Divine right. The King of England.

Roger waited, impatient. To see the King was what the ranks needed, to be reminded of what they fought for. From the Parliamentarians emboldened by the sight of the King and no doubt growing impatient, there was some musket fire, and to Roger's intense disappointment, the King retreated to safety.

Achilles sidled and bumped into Masters' horse. Damn he was skittish! Then he realised it was he who was jumpy and Achilles sensed it.

'We'll go soon,' Masters said, not taking his eyes off the enemy across the valley.

Prince Rupert, taking over from the King, rode along the line in front of them, shouting words of encouragement in his guttural English. He was near enough for Roger to see his face clearly, a handsome young man with strong unsmiling dark features. Roger didn't catch what he said, but it didn't matter. The encouragement was enough. He cheered with them all, his heart lifted. Oh, he knew they would be victorious!

It was after midday when the order was given to descend. The Parliamentarians had not moved.

'For the King!' cried the commanders. 'For the King and Jesus Christ!'

The ranks took up the cry, Roger too: 'For the King! For Jesus Christ!' He felt a sudden swoop in his belly and he shouted with the best of them. 'God save the King!' The chant echoed across the hills.

Emboldened, again the King rode up and down the lines of his men, and again Roger waited hopefully, but once more the Parliamentarian musketeers opened fire, a volley of popping coming from their ranks and smoke billowing out in clouds from their weapons. From a distance the sound seemed inconsequential, as if the guns were ineffective, but immediately, the King's bodyguards surrounded him and pulled him back from the front line. Absolutely nothing must happen to the King. If he died, all would be over. Roger tried not to be disappointed that the King had not made it as far as his troop.

The Royalists gave back fire and then the Roundhead canons boomed. Holes appeared in the ground, killing Royalist men, sending plumes of dirt and divots of grass into the air.

The noise terrified the horses who were unused to it and they broke ranks and had to be reassembled. Roger, already fighting to keep Achilles under control, managed to keep him relatively still, but one man's horse fully bolted and they all had to wait until he brought it under control and headed back to his place in the line.

The Royalist guns were ineffective, Roger could see immediately. They were firing down the hill and the shot dropped to the earth with no effect. However, the dragoons advanced on each flank at a trot.

From his vantage point, Roger could see them dropping from their horses to fight. Swords, pistols, muskets. And the pikemen waded in too. It was the pikes that most fascinated him. The weapons were about fifteen to twenty feet long, with a pointed iron blade at the tip. They advanced steadily, the pikes held out in front, as they engaged pikemen from the other side. The two sides locked in knot of pushing heaving wounded and dying men. The Parliamentarians gave way.

Now it was time. Prince Rupert, still yelling in his guttural English, gave the order. '*Charge!*'

Roger's heart smashed against his ribs as, with sword raised, he kicked his horse gently in the flanks and they went off at a trot together with the others. As they came down the hill, they gathered pace. Just as they broke into a canter, Roger saw the Parliamentarian horses fidget. The canter gave way to a full gallop and they thundered across the ground in what seemed like seconds. Leaning low over the front of the saddle, guiding Achilles with his left hand while his right held the sword out in front, Roger bellowed with the rest of them, the killing urge now surging in his veins.

This was too much for part of the Parliamentarian horse (under Faithful Fortescue) and they abruptly turned tail and fled. The rest of them fired at the advancing Royalist cavalry with pistols and muskets, just as Roger urged his horse over one of the canons, to chase after the fleeing Parliamentarians, jubilant at this small victory, whooping and crying out 'God save the King!' as the others did. And at that moment he felt a thud in his thigh.

Achilles reeled from the force of it, but stayed on his feet whirling around as Roger clung on desperately. Looking down at his thigh he saw a dark red stain spreading with alarming speed over his buff-coloured breeches.

The pain bit at that moment, a hot searing agony that shot right through his being and then, mercifully subsided a little. Gritting his teeth, he reined in, fished with shaking hands for a kerchief in his pocket and tied it as tightly as he could around his leg and above the wound in an effort to stop the blood pumping out. The rush of battle excitement completely evaporated.

William Masters turned back from the chase, looking for him.

'What's the matter L'Estrange?' He had to shout above the din.

'Been hit,' Roger shouted through his teeth and to his mind unnecessarily, for surely Masters could see. 'In the leg,' he added for Masters evidently could not see.

Faith! He felt faint! Must be the shock. The world, the field, the men of both sides, the smoke, seemed to spin in a sickening way, while the noise faded. *I must not lose my senses!*

Masters shook his arm. A good man, Masters. Not one Roger was particularly friendly with, but a good man nevertheless. He was from Yorkshire, Roger remembered inconsequentially.

'L'Estrange, don't pass out on me! Come, we must get you to the surgeon.'

Surgeon? Oh, dear God, not the knife!

Roger struggled out of the descending mists and looked groggily at Masters. 'Did we win?'

'Well we drove the cavalry off, if that's a win,' Masters said. He had hold of Roger's rein and was leading him off the field. 'For the rest, it is still going on. Come now, let's get you to the surgeon.'

§

Roger lay quietly on the pallet that acted as his bed, looking up at the white canvas roof, a mere tent offering little protection from the cold northerly wind whistling over the fields. He shivered violently. It was the shock, he told himself. The shock of being hit and the shock of the surgeon's knife later. His relief when the surgeon showed him the small lead ball covered in blood—his blood!—and the small piece of material which had been torn from his breeches had been equal to the fear he felt when the knife came to him. Men had held him down, but he had made himself not struggle. No point in making the surgeon work harder, and therefore take longer, and perhaps cause more damage.

Now it was over. It hurt like hell, but it was over. If he did not get a fever, he had a good chance of recovery.

He was not alone. This tent of the wounded contained many of the injured. Some of them cried, others screamed, others just moaned, but it was an awful lot of noise and he would have liked to sleep. Not much chance of that, it seemed.

Roger became aware of the surgeon nearby. His voice would be forever imprinted in his memory, the substance of his nightmares no doubt in time to come, and he could hear him now. Turning his head towards the sound, Roger saw him with another man. Pushing himself up on his elbow with a huge effort, he realised that the man with him was Prince Rupert.

No sooner had he thought it than Prince Rupert stood over him.

'This is Mr. Roger L'Estrange, your highness,' the surgeon said. 'He had a ball in his thigh. Missed the bone . . .'

The prince wasn't listening. Instead he focused on Roger. 'Thank you, Mr. L'Estrange for your efforts in behalf of the King.' His speech was heavily accented, and he did not smile.

Roger wanted to stand up and bow, but since that was impossible, he could only say: 'It was an honour, your highness.'

'We will be moving on, soon. Return to your home, and join us when you are well.'

And he moved on, leaving Roger immensely gratified at being singled out by no less than the King's nephew.

NINE

Hunstanton, November 1642

It was November when Roger finally turned off the coast road and through the perimeter gates of Hunstanton Hall. The air had the promise of winter in it, a cold biting wind that rattled the skeletons of already nude trees. His leg ached still where the wound was barely held together with a few coarse stitches and it oozed. He was more tired than a man had a right to be even when he had spent the last three (or was it four?) days travelling a hundred miles or more. He knew he had a fever, too, for his teeth chattered in his head despite the thick woollen travelling cloak wrapped tightly about him.

He paused to summon the strength to lean down to unloop the rope which held the gate closed to the paddock and then, when through, he had to lean again to close and reloop it lest the bull in the field escaped. He dared not dismount, fearing not being able to mount again, but the effort strained at the wound. He had no strength left. Even leaving the inn this morning he had suffered the ignominy of needing a mounting block to get back on his horse. Now he was done for. Every bone in his body ached. He felt chills and even his stomach and back ached. To say nothing of his head. It would have been better if he could have stayed in the camp, or perhaps taken up residence in an inn, but the camp moved on with the army, and the inns were full of other wounded. Besides, when he left Edgehill he felt quite well, if sore. The travelling had opened up the wound again and he was sure an infection had taken hold.

He had taken the short route to Hunstanton for the official route, the road that led in a large circle following the coast and past the church, would take nearly another hour. The old bull in the field eyed him and his horse balefully, but let them pass unmolested. He was on home ground and his heart surged with relief. He had missed home in the crash and thunder of guns. He ached for the comforting reassurance of his family and he knew he needed his mother's care.

The landscape had that strange bareness that comes with the onset of winter. A few gold leaves clung doggedly to otherwise bare branches and the long dry grass had fallen over. It made weird images in his fevered brain.

Achilles knew the way home and turned through the wrought iron gates of the hall as he had done countless times before. Now that he was home and safe, Roger let his head droop to his chest, not even acknowledging the L'Estrange crest atop the iron gates. Achilles took him on into the compound. Here the horse stopped of his own accord just as a boy came running from the direction of the stables to take the animal's bridle.

Roger sat where he was, unable to move, his head bent over his chest, the last of his strength spent.

He heard his father's voice. 'Roger! 'Pon my soul, Roger!'

He struggled to focus on his father's concerned face. He knew he needed to dismount and tried to stand up in the stirrup, but instead he felt himself sliding.

Someone, he supposed it was the boy, unhooked his boot from the right stirrup and Sir Hamon himself unhooked the left boot and he felt himself slithering into waiting arms. In the distance he heard his mother cry out his name and then he was out of it, allowing himself to drift into comfortable blackness.

§

When he awoke he was in his own bed. The winter sun streamed through the window and through the crack in the bed hangings. He looked at it for a while, noticing for the first time the intricate embroidery of peacocks and pheasants and flowers worked in gold and blue and red on a gold background.

He had been dreaming of summer woods and flowers and love. Ruth had been there and he had held her and kissed her and then she had gone and he ached for her, searched for her, but she was not in any place he looked.

He tried to move and immediately a stab of pain shot through his thigh making him cry out. Ah yes, now he remembered.

His mother pulled back the hanging. 'Ah, you are awake then.'

'Hello Mother.' Had she been there all night? He wouldn't put it past her.

'So you decided to pay us a visit!' she said, putting a hand on his forehead. She must have been pleased with the result because her lips curved into a satisfied smile.

'No choice in the matter,' he told her, lifting a hand to his eyes and finding he had the strength of a dry lettuce leaf, his hand shaking with the effort.

'You have been insensible for the last two days,' she told him. 'I won't ask what happened. You can tell your father when he comes in. All this heroic stuff will get you killed! In fact it nearly did. If it had not been for Dr. Harvey I hate to think what the outcome may have been.'

'He let my blood?' Roger asked.

'A full half pint.'

Roger groaned. 'I already lost a good deal of blood. I cannot afford to lose more of it. No wonder I feel like living death!'

'Do not exaggerate dear. You are much more like yourself. I can see it.' She looked at him sternly the way she always did when he was a child. He thought how pretty she was, her dark hair only lightly streaked with silver.

She pulled all the bed hangings back and tied them at the posts, to let the winter sun cheer him. A fire burned brightly in the grate. From this angle all he could see out of the window was pale blue sky dotted with pretty white clouds. His eyes followed her as she went to the dresser and poured liquid into a cup.

The door opened and Roger looked towards it. Sir Hamon stood there a moment, his shock of faded red hair sticking out at all angles from his head like a halo, which, Roger thought idly, he probably deserved.

He came further into the room, closing the door behind him to keep the warmth in the room. 'So, you are back with us then?'

'As you see, sir.'

'Sir Hamon, would you please lift him so he may drink?' Lady Alice asked.

Sir Hamon sat on the bed beside Roger and raised him up with his arm beneath him, while Lady Alice put two more pillows behind him. Then with the cup to his lips he drank thirstily.

Satisfied, she replaced the cup on the dresser and went to the door. 'Do not tire him out sir,' she said to her husband and she let herself out, closing the door behind her.

Sir Hamon shifted his position so that he could see his son, perching on the edge of the bed near his legs.

'What happened?'

Roger took a breath. 'Edgehill,' he said simply, resting his head back on the pillows. 'I took a ball to the leg. The surgeon cut it out. That is all.'

'Edgehill,' Sir Hamon repeated. 'What happened there?'

'We did well. We saw off their cavalry. And we could claim some small victory. But Byron's cavalry were for plundering the routed enemy and left the battlefield. We could have won if they had stayed to fight.'

'Damn their eyes! Discipline is necessary for an army. You know the enemy claim victory too.'

'Aye, I suspected as much.'

'A draw then.'

Roger's eyes closed for a moment. He was so tired. 'Essex withdrew his troops the following morning. He withdrew. So that leaves us the victors. Where is the King now?'

'Last I heard he was on his way to London. I expect he's there now.'

'Ah, good. Prince Rupert urged him to go to London.'

'That was sound judgement by the prince. 'Tis a great pity the King hesitated.'

'Did he?'

'So they say.'

'Rupert threatened to go without the King if necessary.'

Sir Hamon frowned, but tiredness, an incredible exhaustion was overtaking Roger and he closed his eyes.

'What did you think of the King's army?' Sir Hamon asked.

Jerked out of his nearly-sleep, Roger struggled to think. 'We are untrained. Raw recruits. But the officers seem to know what they are about.' It was an effort to talk.

'And their officers?'

Struggling now, Roger did his best to answer. 'I think they have good officers too from what I saw. But their men are also raw recruits.' He paused, trying to gather some strength. 'God—that England should come to this!' He closed his eyes again and Sir Hamon put his hand on his son's hand. Roger found the gesture comforting.

'Get some rest.'

He smiled weakly. 'That's all I seem to do these days! But I would like something to eat.' But he could not keep his eyes open.

'I'll send someone up with something.'

Roger heard the door snap closed and he allowed his mind to drift off away from the problems of war.

TEN

It was another two days before Roger had recovered enough to be allowed out of bed and another day before the doctor pronounced that as long as he did not overtire himself he could go downstairs.

This was a relief, because he had the feeling that everything was going on without him. He could hear his brother Sir Nicholas and his father talking somewhere in the bowels of the house, but on strict instructions from Lady Alice they did not share anything with him.

It was on the afternoon of the fifth day since his dramatic arrival that he emerged from the bedchamber having bathed and put on a freshly laundered shirt, under his black doublet. It was cold outside his room and he was careful to close the door behind him to keep the heat in from the fire.

He heard voices from the winter sitting room and he limped in.

Sir Hamon and Sir Nicholas were entertaining a guest and his other brother Hamon was present too. The guest, Sir John Spelman, rose to greet him.

'Ah, young L'Estrange. How are you?' He peered at him from beneath bushy black eyebrows.

Roger took the proffered hand and shook it. 'Sir John! Well come, sir.'

Sir John lived at Holme most of the time, with his wife Anne, although he was actively busy in the King's service. His father, Sir Henry Spelman has been one of Sir Hamon's guardians after his own parents had died and although he was younger than Sir Hamon by eleven years the two were firm friends.

'Good to see you up and about, Cub,' Nicholas greeted him, standing aside to let the wounded soldier have the chair he had been using.

Roger acknowledged the greeting with a nod. His leg hurt and the effort required to get himself down the stairs had left him weak and winded. He needed to sit down, so he eased himself into the upholstered armed chair, wincing with pain as his leg bent. 'Thank you, brother.' He ignored being called 'Cub' at the age of six and twenty. Today he had not the strength and he was far more interested in the conversation at hand.

Sir Hamon and his namesake son remained sitting and Nicholas found himself another seat, a most uncomfortable hard wooden dowel-backed chair. Sir John was pleased to continue the conversation Roger's entrance had interrupted. ''Tis a rum do,' he said, falling into the Norfolk vernacular.

Roger studied his brother's set face. Something was amiss.

'What has happened?' Roger asked.

Nicholas filled him in. 'That traitor Thomas Toll arrived from London not many days since and gave orders that Lynn was to be put into a state of readiness.'

'You mean they are preparing for attack?'

'They must think that an attack from the King's army is imminent' Sir Hamon said with a small smile.

'But the King's on his way to London. Who would raise an army for the King here?'

There was a moment's silence. Then Sir Hamon said pointedly: 'We could. We could take Lynn.'

Sir John Spelman's black bushy eyebrows snapped together above his bulbous nose. 'We do not have an army,' he pointed out.

'No, but there are enough ordinary men here who would fight for the right of the King.'

'You think so?' Nicholas asked.

Roger fired up immediately. 'Yes! They must see that the King has the right of it! He is King by divine right. How can they even think that Parliament can take that away from the King? We would not need much of an army. How many would actually oppose us?'

'Do you think Parliament will not come to recapture Lynn?' Nicholas asked his elders, ignoring Roger.

'Then we would need another string to our bow,' Sir Hamon put in thoughtfully. 'An army could come from the north across the Wash right into Lynn.'

'Yes!' Roger could see it all. A strategically placed town, a busy port, in the King's hands would give them the opportunity to import firearms and even men. It could be crucial to the King's winning the war.

'We'll have to be careful,' Sir John said. 'Toll gave specific orders that no *vagrant soldiers* were to be admitted to Lynn without the express permission of Parliament.

Sir Hamon let out an oath. 'Just who do they think they are?'

'They think they run the country,' Sir John said wryly.

'A plague on them all!' Roger fumed. 'What right . . ?'

'They have been elected.' Sir John reminded him calmly.

'Remember Toll and Percival are duly elected members of Parliament for Lynn.

'A pox on them all!' Sir Hamon fumed.

'I'll agree to that!' Sir John shifted in his chair, evidently getting scorched by the huge fire. 'You know what the answer is here, don't you, Sir Hamon?'

'I don't see—'

'We need you to be made governor of Lynn.'

'How can that happen? They know I'm a Royalist. They won't let me be governor.'

'That depends on the committee.' He meant the committee of burgesses who were responsible for King's Lynn. 'We can manoeuvre matters. But we will need to think this through and plan carefully.'

Roger's eyes shone. This could get interesting.

Hamon the younger now said: 'Did you know there is to be a special meeting in Norwich on Saturday?

They all looked at him. Hamon was eighteen months younger than Nicholas and although he also had the long nose of the L'Estranges, his features were less lean than those of his brothers and his eyes were brown, the only one in the family with eyes that colour, aside from their mother. 'I intend to go to this meeting.'

'Do you think it will be of any benefit?' Sir Hamon asked.

'Of some benefit, I think. Those dogs should not be allowed to take control of our county. They give themselves airs and reject the rightful King. And who is to speak for his Majesty if we do not? Besides, I may learn something to our benefit.'

'Mind they don't send you to prison.'

'They shall not do that,' Hamon replied with a grin.

'I'll go with you,' Roger put in quickly.

'Not in your state, brother!' Nicholas said laughing. 'This is Tuesday. You will not be well enough to ride by Saturday! I'll go with you Hamon.'

Hamon shook his head. 'No. I go alone. I'll not take you from your lady wife. Me, I'm between wives!' And he laughed, but not happily. For his wife Dorothy had died two months previously as had the child she did not deliver. 'If I go to prison, or lose my head, I have no-one to mourn me.'

'Except two brothers, a sister and parents,' Nicholas put in scathingly.

'And I'm not the heir.'

The fire finally having become far too hot for him, Sir John rose to his feet and moved away from it. 'All of which is immaterial. I am a magistrate. I deal with affairs of law. I shall go to the meeting with you, Hamon.'

Nicholas was alarmed. 'I will go with my brother, sir,' he said.

'I do not go to oversee your brother, sir,' Sir John told him. 'I go to put forward my own view. I believe Sir William D'Oyly and others loyal to the King will be present and we intend to give these Parliamentarian dogs a run for their money.'

Nicholas was displeased, but Sir Hamon said: 'Anyway, Nick, I have things to talk over with you. I need you here.'

Lady Alice came in then. 'Supper is ready, Sir Hamon,' she announced.

Sir Hamon stood up. 'Well then, let us go in, for in faith, my lady, I am in a great hunger!'

ELEVEN

Norwich, 5 November 1642

When Hamon the younger and Sir John Spelman entered the meeting at Norwich they found themselves in a large mixed company. The room used for the occasion, a rather grand affair with a lofty beautifully oak-beamed ceiling and carved oak panelling on the walls, could not be termed small, but it was full to overflowing with both King's men and Parliamentarians. The Puritans wore black with plain white collars; by contrast the King's men made a point of wearing any colour but black and their collars were lavishly decorated with lace. Everyone wore black hats.

The King's Lynn Parliamentary member, thin, miserable, bearded Thomas Toll, was there, of course and as he looked at Hamon contempt and dislike settled on his face. Hamon nodded an insincere greeting, enjoying hugely the other man's discomfiture at seeing him there. He seemed angry. Good.

Hamon also recognised the other Parliamentary member for Lynn, John Percival. He had expected to see him too, for where Thomas Toll went, John Percival was not far away. The Lynn Parliamentary representatives were like twins, glued to each other, Hamon thought derisively, dressed in plain, sombre black.

Hatred for these men whom he viewed as the enemy soured Hamon's gut. He was here as his father's representative, here to find out what the other side was about and here to oppose them if he could. He smiled wryly. He may well find himself in prison ere the meeting was finished, which is why he had come and Nicholas had not.

A chairman cried out: 'Order! Order gentlemen please!' but no-one paid him the slightest heed, although Hamon could see him from where he was standing and did indeed give him a cursory glance. 'Why are all these for Parliament sad-faced?' he asked Sir John Spelman rhetorically.

Sir John gave a small mirthless laugh. 'Wouldn't you be if you had to put up with their religion! Ah. I see Sir William D'Oyly.' But although he would have gone to speak to Sir William, Thomas Toll arrived in front of them.

Toll looked at Hamon narrowly. 'Look like your father,' he observed as though it were a misfortune to carry the L'Estrange characteristics.

Hamon looked him up and down. 'Indeed.' His tone was at its most dismissive.

The chairman was still trying to gain control and Toll disappeared as he and everyone else made their way to the benches which had been made available for them to sit on. Hamon eyed them with disfavour and 'Sir John said in his ear: 'Could they not get decent chairs with backs in?'

Casting him a sympathetic look Hamon sat down. 'I see Parlett and Leek over to the left.'

Sir John stretched upwards to see and caught Sir William D'Oyly's eye and managed a quick nod in acknowledgement.

Eventually the chairman was the only man standing and he took up a scroll to read in as grand a manner as a thin sad man could. 'Gentlemen, you have been invited here to discuss how best to secure our county of Norfolk from being invaded by foreign forces.'

'What foreign forces?' Sir William D'Oyly called from the audience. D'Oyly was a young man of eight-and-twenty and full of the hot-headedness of young men, Hamon thought, from the full complement of his thirty-seven years.

Thomas Toll groaned audibly. He sat just two men along from Hamon, but in the next row.

The speaker, apparently, did not hear the interruption for he continued without pause: 'Namely those enemies of the county who have allied themselves to the court of Queen Henrietta in Holland and awaiting their opportunity to invade our Norfolk coastline.'

Hamon came to his feet at once. 'If they are Royalist, then we must welcome them as friends!'

The chairman nervously peered at him over the scroll, but before he could speak Thomas Toll stood also and turned straight to Hamon. 'Can it be, sir, that you want Hollanders here?'

'Hollanders? Can it be that you are unaware that the Queen's court is made up of Englishmen?'

'Royalists! Traitors!' Toll spat out. 'They might as well be Dutch for they are traitors to England and her government!'

Sir John Spelman now rose. 'Forgive me, sir,' he said in his calm way, 'but I thought you said they were in the court of the Queen of England. Is that not so?'

'It is.' Toll 's eyes narrowed, his eyebrows knitting above his large, ugly nose.

'Then by definition, sir, they cannot be traitors. Surely the traitors would be those who oppose the King and Queen of England.'

Toll's thin face reddened. 'You are calling us traitors? If the King and Queen act treacherously, they must be the traitors!' A roar from the assembly spurred him on. 'And the King has acted with treason towards this Parliament which forms the government of England!'

Seeing that the meeting was rapidly degenerating into something resembling a bear pit, Sir John Potts came to his feet. A Puritan, he was a thin anxious-looking man with hair to his shoulders. The others all sat down again.

'I do not remember the honourable Mr. L'Estrange being invited to a meeting of the governors of this county, Mr. Chairman, especially as the business in hand is to arrange for the defence of the county against men such as he!' His voice rose over thunderous applause from Parliamentary supporters.

Sir John Holland, another Puritan also rose and turned to Hamon. 'Your papist army will not cross to take this county, sir and the Queen is as much a traitor and a papist as you are! As traitors, you will hang, sir, you and your friends.'

The meeting had become a mere exchange of insults. Everyone was angry. Sir John Spelman was once again on his feet. 'Traitors! Villains! It is those who take their stand against the Divinely constituted King and take up arms against him who are traitors!'

Sir John Holland tried to address the assembly again, but he could not be heard above the general din. Hamon and other Royalists hurled insults from their seats. Sir William D'Oyly clapped and cried his approval of Sir John Spelman's words; Toll also spoke up but he too could not make himself heard. Everyone seemed to have something to add to the cacophony, a point of view which must be aired whether there was an audience to appreciate it or not. It was mayhem. And these, Hamon thought disgustedly, were the cream of Norfolk governance.

Sir John Holland yelled for order, taking the mallet from the chairman and banging it down hard on a table top until the noise ceased and for a moment there was an expectant hush. He glared at the company from a darkened face and then fixed his smouldering eyes on the major culprits—Hamon and Sir John Spelman.

'This meeting,' he said awfully, 'is convened to see how best to protect our county, and these persons—' he pointed straight at the miscreants '—have seen fit to call those foreign invaders "friends". They have declared from the start of these proceedings their affiliation and I therefore recommend that they have no part in this discussion.'

A murmur of assent.

He went on: 'It is deplorable that those who are trying with God's will and help to guide the people of England through these troublous times should have to put up with nothing more than riotous behaviour and blasphemous insults—yes I say blasphemous insults—at what is, after all, a meeting to which they were *not* invited is shameful. And I would, therefore, ask Mr. Hamon L'Estrange, Sir John Spellman and Sir William D'Oyly and all those of their persuasion to leave immediately.'

Furious, Hamon stood up. 'We were not invited because you knew we would show you up for what you are, sir. You and your like have brought England to civil war and you will tear apart our nation because of your own desire for prestige and power. Our King allowed freedom of worship in this country and, sirs, I can only conclude it was a mistake, for had he exterminated you Puritan hypocrites from England, we should not have had this war to force your religion on everyone else. I know full well, sir, that it is not in the Puritan heart to grant a man freedom to worship where his conscience dictates unless he be a Puritan himself. Will Parliament allow those of us allied to the Anglican faith to worship as we wish? Or Catholics? Or Jews, perhaps? Nay. There is no Christian love and mercy in the Puritan heart, only hatred and plunder and the desire to dictate to everyone else what they can or cannot do and fix law accordingly. We who love our God and King will fight you, sir, for the right to our own freedom and the freedom of the people of England. We will fight you to the death!'

With that he turned and marched smartly from the hall with Sir John Spellman and the other Royalists closely behind him.

§

He was still furious two days later when he entered the gates of Hunstanton Hall, having left Sir John to go to his own home in Holme-next-the-Sea.

Lady Alice greeted him as he strode over the moat bridge and through the open ancient oak doors of the gatehouse. She had been expecting to ask solicitously after his journey, but one look at his thunderous face and she said to a servant: 'Ask Sir Hamon to come.'

As the servant scurried off, her son greeted her. 'My lady.'

'What happened?'

'Thrown out!'

He strode past her and into the hall itself. Alice followed him. She had that sinking feeling in the pit of her stomach which told her that things had not gone well.

Sir Hamon himself entered the great hall at the same time as his son and Roger and Sir Nicholas arrived shortly afterwards.

Lady Alice sat down on one of the chairs beside a blazing fire, while Hamon the younger paced back and forth. 'We were thrown out!' he repeated for the benefit of his father and brothers. 'Me and sir John and Sir William D'Oyly and all of us loyal to the King. They had the effrontery—the effrontery—' he hit the table with his fist so that the apples in the basket jumped out and sped over the table and down to the flagstone floor '—to suggest that action should be taken to secure the county from foreign forces. The Queen's foreign forces, no less!'

'How can they be foreign? They are the Queen's cavaliers!' Roger put in.

'Of course we declared that the Queen's cavaliers were English, were friends of ours and welcome. Holland and Potts and of course that traitor Toll, took exception and ordered us out!'

Sir Hamon shook his shaggy head, frowning. 'But that tells us something. They intend to defend the town against foreign invasion. I wonder how that will translate in Lynn.'

He did not have to wait long to find out. Almost immediately Parliament issued orders for the arrest of Mr. Hamon L'Estrange, Sir John Spelman and Sir William D'Oyly, for '*delinquency and affronting the Committees when they are met upon the service of the public; and thereby, as much as in them lay, obstructing and prejudicing the service of the Commonwealth.*'

Sir Hamon had been tipped off and so he sought out Hamon the younger in his room. 'I think it would be prudent if you absented yourself,' he said. 'Go back to your home in Pakenham.'

Hamon nodded. 'I do not like to leave you to it. For depend upon it, Toll and Percival will oppose us.

Sir Hamon put his hand on Hamon's shoulder. 'We have right on our side. God will help us.'

A devout man himself Hamon nodded. 'And I mislike going back to a house that is empty.'

Sir Hamon compressed his lips. It had not been many months

since his son's wife had died and he knew the wound was raw. 'Then I daresay it could do with some attention after all this time. But you must go. You will be safe there. But if they get hold of you here, well it could be the hangman. Or worse. You know they show no mercy and it will go ill with us too.'

'You are not safe here either.'

'I have a job to do. I have been sheriff of this county and I have a responsibility to the people here. They are reliant on me for justice.'

'Be careful Father.'

Sir Hamon laughed grimly. 'Oh, I do not intend to dangle at the end of a rope, my son. But you must go. By staying, you will endanger all of us.'

Hamon nodded and left that same day.

TWELVE

Dersingham, January 1643

From her chamber window Ruth had a clear view of the Shernborne Road. At present it was covered in virgin snow perhaps two inches deep and a few flakes were still floating down from a pale blue sky laced with cloud while bushes and trees resembled white spiky skeletons with frosted twigs and branches draped in white. The road took little traffic, the village of Shernborne being no more than a hamlet, but a few marks marred the snow as wild animals and birds left their prints. There had been no human traffic though. All the cart wheels and horse prints followed the bend by the church; no-one bothered with Shernborne today.

She sighed. How she hated winter! It seemed so long, so dark, so absolutely boring! The past storms had kept her confined to the house. The cold threatened to do the same.

There had been no festival for Christmas. Puritans did not have a feast for that time. Pagan, they called it, handed down from the Roman Saturnalia, nothing to do with Christ. And the debauchery of the feasting was straight from the Romans, the garlanding of houses from the superstitious pagans. Christmas was for the Catholics, the Anglicans, the Royalists, not for those who were true Christians.

No doubt Roger celebrated Christmas, wherever he was. She had tried to follow the King's travels whenever there was news of the war, having heard that Roger was with his army, but there had been no news recently. She listened eagerly also to the local gossip, because if a scion of the house of the powerful L'Estranges had been killed, it would have been all over the neighbourhood. So no news was good news.

Not that it mattered, she thought dismally. It had been so long since she had seen Roger, he had probably forgotten all about her. She had not forgotten him. She smiled when she remembered how he had met her and Aunt Mary in King's Lynn quite by accident, and how he had so gallantly lifted his hat and swept a beautiful bow, those blue eyes twinkling at her as she had no option but to introduce Aunt Mary to him. Even her aunt's detailed questioning later had not diminished the pleasure of seeing him again, or the understanding that had passed between them as their eyes met.

Her mother entered her chamber without knocking, as she had a habit of doing, jerking Ruth out of her thoughts.

'There you are, Ruth!' Lady Barbara Pell bustled over to the window beside Ruth, wiped the softly frozen condensation from three or four lights, and look out. 'Hmm, a pretty picture I'll agree, but bitterly cold out.'

It wasn't that warm inside either, despite the fire roaring up the chimney. The heat from it did not reach the window. 'I shall go out later,' Ruth said.

'What, in this?' Lady Barbara looked at her daughter suspiciously.

'It is only a little snow. I have boots.'

'You know those boots are not going to stop the wet coming in and soaking your feet! You will catch your death!'

Ruth took a steadying breath. At twenty-one and therefore what might be deemed an old maid, she did not feel that her mother needed to tell her how to look after herself. Girls several years younger than she managed large houses all by themselves. But it was useless to argue with her mother. Lady Barbara would not listen. Instead Ruth said: 'Still, I intend to go out. Barney has not had a walk in weeks and neither have I with all the rain we have had. I think I shall go mad if I do not get out soon.'

'Well, I am sure you do not need my permission for that. Your father raised you to be quite independent.' She came away from the window. 'I came to tell you some news. Your cousin, Mr. Charles Calthorpe has sent a letter to tell us that he is coming to stay with us tomorrow.'

Ruth's heart dropped. She met her mother's eyes steadily. 'I do not wish to meet him.'

'Nonsense! He is a very personable young man. What could you possibly object to in him?'

'I do not want to marry him!' Her mother had been a Calthorpe before her marriage, and now Ruth was to marry a distant cousin. At least, that is what they had planned for her.

'I do not think that to be an issue, do you? I think, more pointedly, would Charles wish to marry a lady whose name has been bandied about all over the neighbourhood in connection with a certain gentleman?'

Ruth felt her cheeks grow hot. 'Any gossip is unjust and untrue.'

'Untrue or not, for some reason the gossips have their say, and Mr. Calthorpe will have heard. Yes, you may blush, my woman,' her mother went on awfully, 'but you have no-one but yourself to blame. Walking alone with *that man* to the river with no chaperone! It is enough to put every possible suitor off. Whatever were you thinking of? I can only think that Mr. Calthorpe must be besotted with you to even consider overlooking it.'

Ruth had a mental picture of sitting on the sand and grass looking out at the river, and beside her a handsome young man. Her friend. It had been a beautiful day, one she had relived almost every night since, and her mother's words could not dispel the glow of that summer day.

'So you can be thankful, my girl, that Mr. Calthorpe may still consider you. He is a man of good character with a good living. You will be quite comfortable at his house.'

Seeing herself as the pious wife of a country divine, like her sister, Ruth shuddered. 'I do not want to marry him.'

'Squit!' Sometimes her mother's quick anger expressed itself in coarse language. She took a moment before adding: 'If you wait much longer you will be on the shelf. I tell you Mr. Calthorpe will make you a very good husband. He is a devout man. Your father thinks he is most suitable.'

'Yes, I know. I have been told. And I am sure you and Papa are both right. But I do not love him.'

'Love! Huh! What's love got to do with it, pray? Anyway, he is coming and he will be here for a week.' She paused and softened her voice. 'You'll see. He is a very nice young man, and you will like him.'

Ruth groaned inwardly. What man could match up to Roger L'Estrange?

Glancing out of the window again, Ruth saw a rider astride a black stallion, a white plume in his wide-brimmed hat, his cloak pulled around him, gauntlets on his hands coming half way to his elbows. He paused momentarily, glancing up at the windows of the house, then trotted on up the road towards Shernborne to disappear among the trees.

Her heart leapt up into her throat. She knew him immediately, and her insides began to tie themselves into knots. Well, Barney needed a walk. She would go now. Who knows, perhaps she might just come across him. In her excitement it did not enter her head that it might be unbecomingly forward to meet a man on her own.

Anxious to keep her mother away from the window, she came across the room to the fireplace where the log's flame had settled into a red glow, and while her mother protested, opened the chest in the corner and pulled out a woollen shawl which she wrapped around herself and tucked into the skirt band at her waist. Her cloak followed.

'You are mad to go out in this!' Her mother told her.

Ruth smiled, suddenly feeling radiant, and she turned away to hide it from her mother lest she guess. She said: 'I shall not be gone long.' She knew that her boots were kept in a drawer. As she pulled them out she looked at them wryly. Her mother was right. They were not able to keep water out. Well, it would be worth the sacrifice.

Ten minutes later and with her mother's protests ringing in her ears, Ruth left the Hall with the spaniel Barney prancing ahead of her in the snow and turned up the Shernborne Road.

Her mother had been right. Despite a bright winter sun making the snow crystals sparkle like diamonds, the air was numbingly cold. Even in early afternoon she could see her breath, and her hands beneath her cloak ached. Her toes in the ineffectual boots ached too. The dog seemed unaffected, but in a short while the long hair on his belly and legs became full of icy balls.

She followed the tracks made by Roger's horse and turned off the road into the wood, just as he had done. Even so, she was not prepared for it when he said almost in her ear:

'I feared you would not come.'

Her heart crashed as she jumped and spun round to see him standing beside his horse. He was even more handsome than she remembered, and she allowed herself a moment to take in the twinkling blue eyes, the aquiline nose, the teasing grin and the chestnut hair draped on his grey cloak. 'How ungentlemanly of you to creep up on me that way!' she protested.

'Don't pretend you did not know I was here,' he teased.

She suppressed a grin. 'Barney needed a walk. We have been confined because of the wet weather of late.'

'I saw you at the window.'

'I know you did.'

An ecstatic Barney danced around Roger's feet so that he crouched down to make a fuss of him. A moment later, the dog saw a male pheasant pecking at some bare earth further into the woods and he found it more entertaining to give chase.

'He hasn't a hope of catching it,' she laughed, watching the dog for a moment. 'Too much enthusiasm and not enough science, I think.'

'He's turned into a splendid dog.'

She turned back to Roger. 'Even if he did unseat you?'

Roger chuckled. 'That is more than two years ago. All is forgiven if not forgotten.'

She laughed at the memory. 'Just as well.' She allowed her eyes to follow the dog until he disappeared from sight. She said, still speaking of the dog: 'We are very pleased with him. He is a fine gun dog, but a better pet. He'll be back in a minute.'

She ventured to look up into his eyes and saw a warm arrested look there. It made her insides flutter and she looked away quickly. She found her hands were shaking. She should not be here, she thought belatedly. Her father would beat her if he found out. She ought to go.

'Come, let us walk, or we'll freeze to death standing still,' He began to lead his horse out of the wood back onto the road.

Alarmed, she whispered: 'Sir, if I am seen . . .'

'Ruth, your face is covered by your hood, and no-one has been along this road since the snow fell last night. Besides, in a short while we shall take the Ingoldisthorpe Road.'

'I don't like it,' she insisted, but her mind focused on his use of her forename.

'Then we will keep to the trees.'

Reassured, she stayed with him, her heart dancing. To make conversation she said: 'I thought you were in the King's army.'

'I was. I was injured and sent home.'

Her gaze flew to his face in alarm. 'Injured? Not seriously, I hope?'

'Serious enough. A musket ball in my thigh. It laid me low for a week or two. The army had no provision to take along wounded men, so I came home.'

She noticed, now that she looked, that he walked with a limp. She was horrified. 'You could have been killed!'

'I wasn't though. I'm much improved,' he told her conversationally.

'You do not go back to war?'

'Not yet.'

She met his eyes. 'Oh, I am so glad.'

'Why are you glad? Could it be that you are concerned for me?' His voice was light, but his eyes searched her face.

'I think you are teasing me, sir. Of course I am concerned—for my friend. Barney! Oh, where is that dog?'

She looked around in the snowy undergrowth, but her thoughts were not on the dog who she knew would not be far away. But she could not look at Roger, for she would give herself away if she did.

Even as she considered it, he touched her cheek with a warm finger. 'Ruth.' His voice was soft and she became rigid from the shock of his touch. Oh no, he was going to say something to her. Her pulse raced. She ought to go. Now.

'Where is that dog?' she said again to hide her confusion, and this time really did look for the animal, stomping off through the snowy undergrowth. 'Barney!'

'Ruth!' he said again and he was beside her. He put his hand out and cupped her face, turning her to look at him.

His hand was unexpectedly warm, but then he had been wearing gloves. She closed her eyes momentarily in the sheer ecstasy of his touch and when she opened them again he was in front of her, his face very close to hers. She could feel his warm breath as his lips came nearer to hers.

She ought to turn away. She ought to protest. She ought to go home. Instead she watched him coming closer, mesmerised, waiting until his lips brushed hers.

The touch was soft, brief, but his warm lips on hers sent a quiver through her whole body. He pulled back to look at her and the felt the heat shoot through her face.

She was shocked not only at him, but at her own reaction. 'Please, sir, do not do that!' she whispered, when every fibre of her body wanted him to do it again.

He took a step away from her, removing his hand from her chin. 'Madam, forgive me. I have misjudged the matter.'

Frightened by her own reaction, confused because he was offended, and sorry for it at the same time, she could not make sense of it. She should be the offended one, surely? Only ladies of ill repute or low birth allowed themselves to be kissed. God-fearing ladies of good breeding and manners did not give themselves to a young man in embrace or in a kiss. Not until they were married, at least. That's what her mother had told her—repeatedly. Had he not just treated her as a common taproom maid?

She said: 'You have misjudged *me*, sir. I apologise if I have given you the wrong impression. I am not—not that sort of woman that you should treat me dishonourably.'

His face reddened now. 'That was not my intention, madam, I

assure you.'

'Then what was your intention, sir?'

He couldn't answer her, so he too shook his head, letting his breath go in a rush.

She did not understand his exasperation.

'I should not have come,' she said, giving voice to her earlier self-reprimand.

'Why did you?'

His question hit home like an arrow-shaft. Just why had she come? Because she wanted to see him? Because he was exciting? Amusing? Because being in his company made her feel special. Now all the warnings she had been given about being chaperoned at all times, about not being alone with a gentleman made sense. Yet even now she was reluctant to leave.

Belatedly, Barney bounded up to her as though he had just found her after a long absence, tongue hanging out expectantly.

In as off-hand a manner as she could muster, she replied to Roger: 'I took Barney for a walk, as I often do, that is all.'

His eyes studied hers and he frowned. Was he angry? He shook his head and bowed formally. 'I apologise again, madam for the offence,' he said stiffly and put his hat back on his head.

She nodded, acknowledging the apology. For several moments she hesitated, feeling that she had been dismissed, and not wanting to go. The forbidding look to his face though, did not encourage her to stay. Reluctantly she turned away to walk back home, this time going out onto the snow-covered road, calling Barney as she did so.

She heard Roger mount up, and then the horse following her. A moment later he passed her at a canter, not acknowledging her or looking back.

She stood and watched him as he rounded the bend, and she felt tears stinging her eyes. Why was he so angry? Surely he would not have wanted his sister to be treated in such a way? He was being unreasonable in his expectations, wasn't he? Or was he? She shook her head. She did not know. She had never been permitted to read anything other than religious books. Nor had she ever been to the theatre to see a play, not even Master Shakespeare's plays which had been so popular at the St. George's Guildhall a short time ago, before the Puritans took control of Lynn. All her training told her that only a common woman kissed a gentleman to whom she was not betrothed. Yet it had stirred her like she had not expected, and she craved more.

Whatever the case, it was too late now, he was gone, and he would not be back.

THIRTEEN

January, 1643

By the time Roger arrived home at Hunstanton Hall it was nearly seven o'clock and supper was long gone.

'You cannot expect cook to keep supper waiting on the possibility that you might deign to join us,' his mother remonstrated when he cursed beneath his breath. 'I'll have cook provide you with cold meat if there is any to be had. Where have you been today?'

'Out.' He was a man grown and should not have to answer to his parents for his whereabouts. He hoped that the curt answer would brook no further inquiry.

She cast him an arch look, and he thought she was going to ring a peal over his head. He gritted his teeth, ready to bolt for his chamber, but she merely nodded and turned away. Immediately he regretted his sharp tongue. It wasn't his mother he was angry with.

Strangely, it wasn't Ruth either, well not after he reached Snettisham half way home. He was angry at himself. He should have known she would not understand his intent. *Hell*! He didn't understand his intent. He had acted on gut instinct. And he had taken things too fast. On the other hand, he thought angrily, if he took things any slower, nothing would ever happen between them.

But they lived in divisive times. The Puritans were a strange breed. They did not seem to be red-blooded Englishmen, mealy-mouthed preachers all. *Thou shalt not commit fornication* they chanted. Well, fornication was not what he had in mind. Well, yes, it had crossed his mind, but he wanted more than that.

Roger went to the fire in the winter sitting room, and found Nicholas sitting on the settle, peering in the light of a branch of candles at a book open on his knee. Nicholas looked up at his entrance and watched Roger for a moment. 'Been to see the Pell woman?'

Roger said nothing. He did not need interrogation by his older brother! He turned abruptly, intending to go to his own chamber and some privacy.

Nicholas shook his head. 'You'll never learn, Cub. Keep out of the Puritan nest.'

Roger paused with his hand on the door, glared at him and snapped: 'I do not know what you mean, brother.'

Nicholas arched thick sandy brows. 'Don't you? Well the whole of west Norfolk is alive with tales about you and the Pell maid.' His face clouded. 'And don't forget the woman's father took the troop from my command.'

Damn Nick! He just could not resist poking his long L'Estrange nose into Roger's affairs. 'Mind your own business,' Roger snarled.

Again Nicholas's brows shot skywards and a slow maddening smile slid across his lips, but he took pity on him. 'Not going so well?'

Roger turned back from the door and went towards the welcoming fire again where a half-burnt log smouldered, a full half a tree by the looks of it. 'If you must know,' he told him through clenched teeth, 'there is absolutely nothing between Mistress Pell and myself. She has made that perfectly plain.'

There was a short silence, then Nicholas said unexpectedly: 'I'm sorry for it, Roger. But we did warn you.'

Roger shook his head, the sympathy causing hurt to well up inside him. They had warned him. They had told him that her father would object, that she was an enemy. He knew that. But his hatred for the Puritans did not extend to Ruth. That was an entirely different matter! What they had not told him, though, was that she had been too rigidly brought up. Were all Puritans the same? So worried about the 'sins of the flesh' that they imposed a mental chastity belt on their daughters? So that when he wanted to show her he loved her, she would think him some kind of predator and accuse him of—of—of what? Lechery?

He was furious, and hurt. Love. *Damn it all!* He realised he did love her. Yes, he desired her with a deep aching longing, but he also loved her on a level above that, to the extent that he would never take her innocence away, no matter what that cost him in denial. To be accused, in effect, of doing so was a gross injustice, he felt. It hurt his pride.

Now, her misunderstanding of his intentions had cost him his 'friendship' with her.

'Are they all so straight-laced?' Roger asked Nicholas rhetorically. 'Puritans, I mean.'

Daylight gradually dawned on Nicholas. 'Are not we careful with our daughters and sisters? If you tried to bed her . . .'

'I most certainly did not!' Roger protested hotly, his colour rising. 'She's a maid! What do you take me for?'

Nicholas raised his brows. 'Oh, I see.'

'What do you see?'

Nicholas did not answer him directly. 'They won't let her wed you, if that's what you have in mind. You know that, don't you?'

'There are other ways.'

'Elopement? Lord, you have to get a special licence from the Archbishop of Canterbury.'

'I can do that!'

'No you can't. Archbishop Laud has been imprisoned by Parliament, remember?'

'There must be other ways.'

'Probably, but I've never had need of them! Besides, your gently-reared maid may not agree to something so scandalous as elopement.'

'Her name is Ruth.'

Nicholas frowned. 'Now is not a good time.'

'She is twenty. They will marry her off before long. It is a wonder they have not done so already. I cannot afford to wait.'

'You have no other choice, I think.'

Lady Anne came in then with the youngest member of the family, three year old William. Nicholas's expression brightened as he saw his son and Anne said: Go to greet your papa, William.'

William came running forward, stopped short and bowed quickly and then ran up to his father who picked him up and held him in his arms. 'Now isn't that astonishing?' Nicholas asked, transformed into the doting parent.

Well, possibly it was. Roger watched solemnly as Nicholas planted a kiss on his son's downy cheek. This child was precious. Anne and Nicholas had lost two tiny sons, victims of the marsh fever that plagued this coast. It was a sad fact of life that no-one expected all their children to live. Roger himself was one of four surviving offspring of Sir Hamon and Lady Alice. The other four all died. Even now, all the family suffered from the ague occasionally and sickly children did not survive it.

'He may look angelic,' Anne said, 'But he has led nurse quite a dance today.'

'Oh?'

'He hid from her in a chest and the lid shut down on him. Fortunately she heard him screaming and rescued him.'

Looking at the child Nicholas said: 'Not the best of things to do my son. Stay away from chests. What else have you been doing?'

While Sir Nicholas conversed with his three-year-old, Roger

focused on Sir Hamon who came into the library with Lady Alice.

'Ah, so we are to be blessed with your presence, sir,' Sir Hamon remarked acidly as he caught sight of his youngest.

Roger pursed his lips, not immune to Sir Hamon's displeasure, yet he met his eyes squarely. 'As you see, sir.'

'Well I won't ask where you've been, since the whole of Norfolk seems to be acquainted with your movements!'

Roger was vexed. It was one thing for Nicholas to question him—he was only a brother. But his father, who he revered and looked up to, well his criticism was another matter.

Sir Hamon came closer to Roger while the women and Nick focused on the child.

'You have been seen at Dersingham Hall.'

Roger took a deep breath and clenched his fists. But he clamped his mouth shut. He knew better than to give vent to his anger where his father was concerned. Sir Hamon was a man of iron strength and was more than capable of putting Roger in his place. However, he could not trust himself to speak and found it suddenly irksome to pay court to the youngest L'Estrange, so he nodded a curt response to his father and would have left the room.

Sir Hamon stopped him, by grabbing his arm. 'You and I shall speak about this later,' he said quietly so that only Roger could hear. 'But for now, stay, for I have some news.'

Temporarily, Roger's woes were forgotten. 'What news?'

Sir Nicholas dismissed master William and his nurse, picking up on Sir Hamon's words. 'What have you heard sir?'

Sir Hamon waited only until the door closed on the nurse and the child. 'The news is not good. The counties in East Anglia have formed something called the Eastern Association.'

Roger settled on the corner of the table, his interest piqued. News was hard come by and any information was precious. 'You mean for Parliament.'

Sir Hamon nodded. 'They are now calling it "the Commonwealth". But yes for Parliament. It has been ordained by Parliament that the counties of Suffolk, Essex, Cambridgeshire, the Isle of Ely and Norfolk should be united into the Eastern Association. You know what this means, don't you?'

Sir Nicholas let his breath go in a whistle. 'Yes. It means the whole of East Anglia is under the control of Parliament. They are united against the King!'

Lady Alice clutched her mouth in shock. 'Oh, dear God!'

'Was there no opposition to this?' Roger asked. 'Surely not everyone in East Anglia favours Parliament.'

''Twould seem our brethren are in the minority while Parliament flexes their muscles. In effect the counties have promised to defend themselves against the King. They've effectually isolated us by putting troops as a barrier. By keeping us isolated in groups, we cannot now unite and fight them.'

'And the people go along with this?' Lady Anne asked.

Lady Alice had the answer. 'They will do. They don't think for themselves, only what they are told to think.'

'So where does that leave Lynn?' Roger wanted to know.

Sir Hamon frowned. 'Lynn has not declared itself one way or the other.'

'Can the town remain neutral?' Sir Nicholas asked.

'No. We need to declare for the King. And we could do that. We have enough people on the side of the King in Lynn.' Sir Hamon began to pace the tiled floor, his finger to his lips in thought. 'If we can hold Lynn for the King, it would give him a foothold in East Anglia. An important one. Through Lynn he can bring in ammunition and troops from abroad. Not only that, it is a straight run to London down the Great Cambridge Road. If the King has Lynn, London will be next.'

'Can it be done?'

'Yes it can. I've been thinking about this. I've already got ammunition stored in various places.'

Nicholas pursed his lips. 'The cottage in Sedgeford.' It was on the Sedgeford to Docking road, looking for all the world like a chapel. Roger knew of it too and had wondered why his father had build such a place. Now he saw the logic behind it.

Sir Hamon nodded acknowledgement. 'And there are other places. And the plate is with your brother Hamon.' A nobleman's wealth was stored in his 'plate' literally plates and other articles made of gold or silver. It was disposable wealth which could be used to help the King. It would also be used by Parliament too, if they could get their hands on it, and they had passed a law to confiscate as much of it as they could from Royalist sympathisers.

'Is it safe there?' Alice spoke, and Roger knew she thought of his brother's safety, not the plate.

'It is not in his house, of course. He has stored it elsewhere. I will not keep anything here that could be seized and used.'

'You think they will come here to search?' Lady Alice's voice quavered.

'They will.'

The implications sank into Roger's brain. 'You intend to take Lynn by force?' He tried to visualise peaceful King's Lynn in the grip a revolt.

'No. I think with some gentle persuasion, the good people of Lynn will readily declare for the King. But this Alliance means that Parliament will not leave it at that. We must be prepared to defend Lynn against all comers.'

'A siege,' Nicholas said and shook his head.

'Oh, dear God!' Lady Anne spoke quietly but she summed up the feelings of all of them.

'Very likely,' Sir Hamon agreed.

'How can we win in that situation?' Roger asked.

'There is more than one way into Lynn,' Sir Hamon reminded them. 'Two main roads, two gates—the East Gate and the South Gate.'

'Surely the enemy will be watching those?'

'Naturally. But there is another way in.'

'Across the water,' Roger said, stating the obvious.

'That's where our relief will come from. From across the Wash, from Lincolnshire, or possibly Yorkshire. If Lord Newcastle will agree to come to our aid, and I am sure he will see that it would be of the utmost importance to do so, then we can beat the damned Puritans and once we have secured Lynn, Newcastle and his army can then march on London. If the King gains London, that will end the war. We are in the best place to facilitate that.'

Nicholas let his breath go in a whistle, but excitement filled Roger. 'So when are we going to do it?'

'When the time is right. When Newcastle is in the best place to come to our aid. We need not rush things. We must keep out of sight and make preparations. Food and weapons must be smuggled into Lynn. And at some point in the not too distant future I shall become governor of Lynn in readiness.'

Lady Alice said: 'How can you do that, with that dreadful man Toll and his friend Percival in control of the council?'

Sir Hamon smiled. 'You will see, my love.'

Roger grinned. He did not doubt for one moment that his father could do it. Or that he would be successful. And the more he thought about it, the more he was certain that they would succeed. 'The war could be over by this time next year.'

'Even sooner, my son, God willing,' Sir Hamon said.

§

When Roger retired sometime later, Sir Hamon sought him out, entering his chamber just as Roger had settled in a chair by the fire in the light of a single candle. Outside the wind had risen and squealed through the cracks in the window. He had a book in his hand, but the light was not enough to read by.

'You know what your mother will say if she catches you reading by candlelight,' Sir Hamon said, snapping the door shut behind him. 'You'll need spectacles by the time you are my age just to see the print!'

'Like you do!'

'Like both your mother and myself,' Sir Hamon agreed.

'So you both read by candlelight, then?'

'I did not come here to discuss reading by candlelight,' Sir Hamon scolded.

Roger nodded, marked his place in the book with a thread and then shut it. 'No, I did not think you did.'

Exasperated, Sir Hamon pulled another chair towards the fire and also sat down. 'I came to talk about the Pell woman.'

'I think you mean Ruth Pell, sir,' Roger corrected gently.

'I do. What are your intentions there?'

'Intentions?'

'You know perfectly well what I mean! Is it a dalliance you are after? Because if it is, then I can assure you that Sir Valentine will be after your blood. And I do not need that. I do not need you to draw attention to us at this stage. I need hardly remind you that the Pells are not on our side in this. They are our enemy. You could jeopardise the whole plan by your actions.'

'I am not after a dalliance with Mistress Pell.'

Sir Hamon frowned. 'Then what is it? Do not tell me you are just friends.'

For a moment Roger studied his father, meeting his eyes. Then he came to a decision. 'I am in love with Ruth Pell,' he admitted.

For a stunned moment Sir Hamon was bereft of speech. 'In love with her? How the hell can you love a damned Puritan?'

'It's got nothing to do with her being a *damned Puritan.*'

'I did not imagine it had!'

Roger paused. He did not want to alienate his father. 'I want to marry her,' he said quietly, momentarily forgetting the morning's argument.

Sir Hamon stared at him. 'Do you know,' he said at length, shaking his head, 'you never cease to astound me. You must know that this is a marriage that cannot be.'

'Father, I will have her.'

'You cannot have her. I heard that her father has someone very different in mind for her.'

Roger shot a look at him as jealousy squirmed in his gut. He swallowed. 'I shall speak to him.'

Sir Hamon set his face into stern determination. 'I do not approve of this, alliance, Roger. I forbid you to pursue it.'

'You cannot forbid me, sir. I am of age.'

'I can cut you out of my will.'

Roger knew it to be an idle threat, for nothing would prevail upon Sir Hamon to treat any of his sons in such a fashion, but he did not challenge his father on it. Instead he said: 'You are in love with Mother. You have made a good and happy marriage, despite her father being only a country squire. You could have married into any of the highest families in Norfolk, but you chose Mother.'

He knew he had hit the right note when his father said with a wry smile: 'It was an arrange marriage. And that, my son, I may tell you, is the best sort. Parents—or in my case my guardians—are the best judges of these things.'

'But you have not arranged a marriage for me. You have made it plain that I am free to choose where I marry.'

Sir Hamon interrupted him: 'Not for want of trying, but you would not co-operate. There was Margaret Paston for example.'

'Wouldn't have done for me at all! As you said, too religious—too Catholic! I am surprised she did not go into a nunnery! However, she accepted Henry Bedingfeld, another good Catholic! Anyway, I was still at Cambridge when she married.'

'Yes, well there have been others.'

'Who, exactly?'

'I don't remember right now. But you showed yourself unwilling.

So we had no choice but to leave you to find your own bride. Mind you, your mother despairs of you ever marrying.'

'I own I had no intention of marrying. I am not sure that a country squire's life is for me. But I have found Ruth. And I love her. And I will marry her. And if a country squire I should be, then that's what I will do.' He paused, trying to imagine Ruth in London. He wasn't actually sure that she would fit into London ways. No, they would likely have to stay in Norfolk. But he said: 'I intend to speak to her father soon.'

Sir Hamon raised a sceptical eyebrow. 'Sir Valentine will throw you out of his house,' he said standing up.

'Then I will steal her away. But we will marry.'

Sir Hamon raised his eyes to the ceiling. 'Faith! I hope it will not come to that! We do not need a war with the Pells as well!'

He left Roger to it and Roger opened the book again. But he did not read. Instead he thought of what had happened that afternoon. He had pushed Ruth too fast. He knew it. He had allowed his feelings for her to overcome his good judgement. Although in mitigation, she had encouraged him. Why had she done that if she did not care for him?

His father's words came back to him. '*We do not need a war with the Pells as well.*' That was putting it mildly. To upset the Pells while Sir Hamon was working out his plans could well lead to disaster.

Roger groaned. Very well. He would have to bide his time. But he would have to speak with Ruth, convince her that he was no rake, that he had honourable intentions. Because at any moment she could agree to marry someone her parents considered suitable. He needed to be sure of her.

Damn this war.

FOURTEEN

For two weeks Roger went daily to the Shernborne Road woods and waited all afternoon in the freezing weather in the hope that Ruth would meet him again in the woods, but there was no sign of her.

Reluctantly he admitted to himself that she was not coming. Yet the urge to see her was so strong that he took a different course, and decided to go one Sunday to the church service at St. Nicholas's in Dersingham, the church opposite Dersingham Hall, in an effort to see her.

However, she did not attend church that day, although he recognised Sir Valentine, and he assumed the black-clad lady on his arm was his wife. At the end of the service, he overheard a woman asking Lady Pell where her daughter was, to be told that she was staying with relatives.

At that moment, Sir Valentine Pell, dressed in Puritan black with a Bible tucked under his arm, caught Roger's eye and strode purposefully towards him.

Roger stood his ground, there in the church, clutching his own Bible and looked Sir Valentine straight in the eye.

'Mr. L'Estrange, I presume?'

Roger bowed. 'Sir Valentine. Lady Pell,' he added to Sir Valentine's wife as she turned curious eyes upon him. He could see where Ruth had inherited her good looks.

Lady Pell nodded in response, but Sir Valentine refused to acknowledge the salute. 'If you are looking for my daughter, L'Estrange, I can tell you, you will not find her here.'

'I saw that to be the case, sir,' Roger replied stiffly, wishing that he could not feel his cheeks reddening. Had Ruth told them of their last encounter? he wondered. Certainly they seemed to know about him. Probably hearsay, he decided, for if Ruth had let slip that he had kissed her, no doubt he would not be standing right now, but be lying flat on his back between the benches, nursing a black eye, or broken nose, or broken jaw.

Instead Sir Valentine smirked at him. 'You have had a wasted journey, sir.'

'Not at all, sir. I have enjoyed a good sermon.'

'I am surprised you approved of it.'

In truth, Roger had not heard much of the sermon but had spent his time studying those of the congregation who happened to be in front of him. Sir Valentine and Lady Pell, the extensive Cobbe clan, and a few other lesser gentry. 'I thought the vicar expounded on St. James very well.'

Sir Valentine eyed him suspiciously and then looked him up and down disapprovingly, but he said nothing about Roger's black embroidered doublet and lace collar and cuffs which proclaimed him Royalist. 'Good day to you, sir.'

Roger nodded acknowledgement. 'Good day to you too, Sir Valentine. Lady Pell,' he added as that lady studied him with interest.

He turned and left the church.

He had found out what he wanted to know. Ruth was not in Dersingham. No sense, then, in waiting in the Shernborne Road. Perhaps Lynn might be a better bet.

He waited until Tuesday and then, early in the morning, set off for Lynn on his horse. The weather was still icily cold and his first stop was the Griffin where he ordered a cup of mulled ale, allowing its spicy warmth to defrost his chilled bones, as he sat in the window and watched the market in the square outside for any sign of Ruth.

Edward Paston found him there a few minutes later.

'L'Estrange!' Paston boomed. 'By my life, young Roger L'Estrange if I am not mistaken! Not that I could be mistaken. Look too much like your father!'

Roger stood and took Paston's proffered hand to find his taken in a firm grasp and shaken warmly. 'Mr. Paston, how are you? Will you join me?' It was only polite to invite him.

'Indeed, sir I will. Landlord! Mulled ale for me and for my friend . . ?'

'I am fine at the moment,' Roger told him indicating his own mug still steaming on the small table.

Paston sat down. 'Not much going on in the market today,' he said conversationally.

'Hardly surprising. 'Tis cold enough to freeze the nose off a man!'

'Soon be spring.'

'Hmph!'

Paston smiled. He was a much older man than Roger, of his father's generation, and a staunch Royalist. He lowered his voice. 'Bad thing, this business,' he said seriously by which Roger assumed he meant the impending war.

'Indeed.'

'You have heard what Toll has done?' The steaming spice ale having arrived, he sipped at it.

Roger frowned as he also drank. He often heard rumours about the Parliamentary member for the borough of Lynn, so he wondered what Paston was going to tell him. 'What?'

'Ever since the meeting in Norwich, Thomas Toll and John Percival, have been working to put the town into a state of readiness against attack.'

Roger already knew this was in the wind, but in case there was more he prompted: 'What attack?'

'Presumably from the King's men.'

'I didn't know there would be an attack.'

'No. But they assume it will come across the sea. So they have ordered gunpowder and stored it at the Market Cross, St. Ann's Fort, Trinity Hall and Red Mount.'

'Good grief!'

'Just so! Furthermore, every citizen has been encouraged to buy two or three pounds of gunpowder in case he needs to defend the town. And at fourteen pence a pound, that will make Toll a tidy profit, I can assure you!'

'I wonder how many people will do that! Can he do this without authority from Parliament?'

'Toll went to London himself to get it. And he came back with further orders that Lynn should muster and train men for war, fortify the town and arrest anyone who tried to send plate or money to the King.'

'I thought something was in the wind as I rode in.' He had noticed a shift in the atmosphere in Lynn, a sort of suppressed expectation.

'Not only that, but he has sent a hundred pounds of Lynn's money to Parliament to help their war. But Mordaunt tells me that he was able at the same time to send a similar amount in plate and money to the King in Oxford.'

'I bet that pleased Toll.'

Paston's face grew serious, earnest. 'He went into a passion. He suspects your father to be behind it.'

Roger frowned. 'My father has not been to Lynn lately that I know of.'

'That don't signify. Toll views your family as the biggest threat to the security of the Commonwealth in East Anglia.'

'Does he indeed?'

'Well, think about it. You are not one man, but four if you count your brother Hamon. Together with the rest of us, you make formidable foes. All you L'Estranges are intelligent, capable, brave, trained in warfare and well-loved by the people.'

'Thank you for the accolade!'

'I am serious! Toll has much to worry about. Not only that, but King's Lynn has not yet declared itself either for Parliament or for the King. There are too many opposers in the council, not just your family, but also Spelman, Mordaunt, Hovell, Yelverton, me and others. Toll knows your father will be planning something, but he doesn't know what. Warn your father that Toll is up to no good. If he can get any of you, he will.'

'Thank you for the warning.'

'Least I can do, sir. If there is anything else I can do, remember, you have an ally in me. If you need a place to stay, I can hide you at my house. Don't be afraid to call on me. Any of you.'

Roger took another swig of his rapidly cooling ale. 'Thank you sir. We all appreciate that.'

'Do you intend to join the King's army?'

Roger considered his answer. He could not leave just now when his father needed him to help with his plans, but he could not tell Paston that. Instead, he said: 'Getting over an injury gained at Edgehill.'

'You were at Edgehill?' Paston cried, momentarily forgetting himself. 'What happened there?'

So Roger was obliged to tell him what he knew.

He had intended to stay the night at the Griffin, but with Paston's information ringing in his ears, he decided to return to Hunstanton, arriving home at what he knew his father considered to be bed time.

Indeed, Sir Hamon was in the process of putting on his nightshirt, his lady already snuggled up in bed, when Roger knocked on the door and at the invite, went in.

Sir Hamon reached for a robe and slipped it on. 'You are back? I thought you were staying in Lynn tonight,' Sir Hamon remarked on seeing his youngest son.

'I had intended to stay for a night or two, but I heard something that may be of interest and I thought it best to come home.'

'I appreciate your sacrifice, my son,' Sir Hamon said seriously, but his lips twitched beneath his greying moustache.

'Well it was a sacrifice, I call tell you!' Roger retorted, thinking of his mission to seek Ruth out. 'Anyway, I met Edward Paston in the Griffin.'

'Edward Paston frequents the Griffin? By my life, I would not have thought it!'

'No. I own I was a trifle surprised. Perhaps he followed me in.'

Sir Hamon sat on the chair by the fire and invited Roger to sit down while Lady Alice sat up in bed, clutching a shawl around her shoulders.

'What did he say?' Sir Hamon invited.

Roger found a stool and drew it to the fire so that he could hold out his frozen fingers to warm them. 'Well, since the Norwich meeting Toll and Percival have put Lynn into readiness for an attack from Royalists which they think will come from the sea. We knew this. What we didn't know is that they've ordered gunpowder which is stored at Market Cross, St. Ann's Fort, Trinity Hall and Red Mount. Furthermore, Toll has authority from Parliament to whit: every householder is encouraged to buy two or three pounds of gunpowder in case he needs to defend the town.'

'They have to buy it from Toll? How much does he charge?'

'Fourteen pence a pound!'

'If Toll wants the town defended, he can pay for the gunpowder himself!' Sir Hamon laughed. 'Ho! I cannot see many taking up that one! So Toll hopes to make a profit as well as defend the town!'

'That's not all. They are training men for war, strengthening the town's defences and they will arrest any who try to send money or plate to the King.'

'Strengthening the town's defences could well help us. Perhaps we should not act too quickly, let them do the work for us!'

Roger laughed. 'Toll's sent a hundred pounds of Lynn money to Parliament.'

'The Devil!'

'But Mordaunt has sent the same amount to the King. Toll knows about it and thinks you are involved, sir.'

'Does he indeed! Well done Mordaunt. A man we can trust.'

'And Toll thinks you, sir, are his biggest threat to the security of the Commonwealth in East Anglia. He suspects you are planning something. Master Paston thinks Toll will try to find an excuse to arrest us.'

'I think Paston is right,' Sir Hamon replied thoughtfully. 'I will make sure that what the constables find will be only what can be expected to be in a house of this size. The plate and arms are safe.

Lady Alice said from the bed: 'What if they arrest you, my love?'

'They will arrest all of us if they can,' Roger said, but he meant the men, not the women and she knew it, for women were commonly not held responsible for the actions of their menfolk.

'Would you that we should go into hiding, woman?' Sir Hamon demanded with asperity.

'No, my love,' Alice replied almost as sharply. 'I hope you know I did not mean that.'

'Good, because I cannot bring my plans to fruition if I am not here. Even if I am in Lynn in jail, I can still manage things.' He looked at Roger. 'You look dead on your feet, son. Go to your bed.'

'I'll have a serving woman warm the bed for you,' Alice offered, throwing the covers back ready to get out of bed.

'Do not worry yourself, Mother. I do not mind the cold. Don't make a maid leave her bed just for that.'

'But there is not even a fire alight in your room for you were to be away!'

'I am sure I can strike tinder and set it ablaze in no time.'

In the event, he did not bother, but went to bed in an ice-cold room, finding two extra blankets to throw on the bed from the cupboard on the landing. He didn't want to make the effort to light the fire, or to rouse a servant from their own beds. However, when he got in it, the bed was like ice. Well he'd had worse and no doubt would again, but it was a long time before the bed warmed up and while it did his thoughts were mixed. On the one hand he had not seen Ruth and that was becoming a nagging ache. And on the other he, his brother and father and indeed he himself could be arrested at any time. He wondered how they would fare then.

FIFTEEN

Thomas Toll the Lynn Parliamentary member, scratched his sparse grey beard thoughtfully. Something was going on, that much he knew. And the L'Estranges had much to do with it. They were brewing something. They had to be, for they were too quiet. Sir Hamon was a wily old goat, too loyal to the King to be sitting quietly at home in Hunstanton and twiddling his thumbs.

'I mislike it,' he said to his friend and fellow Parliamentary member John Percival as another meeting of the council broke up. 'We haven't seen L'Estrange in weeks.'

William Percival blew out his fat cheeks thoughtfully. 'No, I agree. Not like Sir Hamon to keep quiet.'

'I wonder what he's up to.'

Percival wrinkled his snub nose. 'No idea. But I tell you what I think. You have authority from London to arrest him and his brood.'

'I do have that authority.'

'Then do it.'

Toll compressed thin lips. 'The people won't like it.'

'The people of Lynn have no loyalties. Whatever their betters say, they do.'

Toll pulled a thoughtful face. 'Will we get away with it?'

'As long as you don't let Gurlin know.' Thomas Gurlin was the town mayor.

Accordingly Toll took it upon himself to summon and instruct the chief constables of the Smithdon Hundred in which Hunstanton lay.

'You are to disarm Sir Hamon L'Estrange and all the L'Estranges,' he told them. 'You are to confiscate his arms, his powder, his plate, indeed anything that he may use against us. And I want him and his sons arrested and brought here.'

The constables, Toby Peddar and Peter Belton, exchanged bewildered glances. They had both known Sir Hamon since they were children and they did not want this charge on them. 'Sir Hamon L'Estrange?' Toby Peddar repeated, his black brows raised.

Thomas Toll clucked impatiently. 'Did I not say so? Here is the warrant. You will find it completely in order.'

Peddar took the roll of paper, and unrolled it to peer at its contents. 'What if he oppose us?'

'Then you must deal with him by force.' Thomas Toll turned on his heel and left the men perusing the document.

The two constables again exchanged glances. ‘Use force on Sir ’Ammon? The man’s gorn soft in th’ead.’ Peddar said.

‘Better do as he say,’ Belton replied.

‘Lord, Oi don’t loike it,’ Peddar announced, removing his hat and scratching his almost bald head. ‘An’ Oi don’t loike ’im neither,’ he added, nodding in the retreating Toll’s direction.

‘Hin’t nuffen to do with it,’ Belton told him. ‘He got a warrant. That be good enough.’

§

Having been tipped off by a watchful servant, Sir Hamon waited in the courtyard to meet them as they arrived. They were accompanied by a dozen men on foot.

‘May I help you, gentlemen?’ he enquired as he stroked the face of Belton’s huge horse ‘Begging yer pardon, sir, but we be ordered to arrest you Sir ’Ammon and remove from these premises ammunition and plate,’ Belton announced apologetically.

Sir Hamon nodded his understanding. ‘May I see?’

He held out his hand and the man handed him a sheet of paper. Quickly Sir Hamon read it. Then he called his servant. ‘How long have I known you men, Peter Belton, Toby Peddar?’

‘’Tis a rummun, Sir ’Ammon,’ Peddar acknowledged. ‘But ’tis orders.’

‘Did Master Toll send you to do this?’

‘Yes, sir, that he do.’

Sir Hamon nodded saying to his servant: ‘See to it that these men be given what they wish.’

As Sir Nicholas came into the courtyard, Sir Hamon handed him the document which he read thoroughly, exchanged glances with his father and handed it back to Belton.

The men dismounted and went with the servant into the house.

Sir Hamon and Sir Nicholas followed and met Roger on the threshold. ‘What are these men doing?’ he demanded.

Sir Hamon told him.

‘Do they have orders to arrest us?’ Roger asked in a low voice.

‘Yes,’ Nicholas answered him, equally low.

‘Only if they find what they are looking for. But they won’t,’ Sir Hamon added also keeping his voice low. ‘They won’t find much. Only what we allow them to find. Oh, they can sequester what they like, or steal it, if you have a mind to put it that way. It ain't here. Before they got as far as putting guards on the roads and bridges, it was already gone! Horse furniture as well.' He meant bridles, saddles, and the like.

Two men came past them into the library where Lady Alice and Lady Anne sat with their stitchery. Lady Alice looked up. 'What do you think you are doing Toby Peddar?' she demanded.

'They are stealing our plate and ammunition,' Sir Hamon informed her. 'They call it "sequestration".'

'Just following orders, moi lady,' one of the men said.

They found nothing and left the room.

'How dare they invade my home!' Lady Alice hissed suddenly, with suppressed heat. 'Devil take them!'

But the men found only a musket used for hunting and a small amount of gunpowder to fire it. As for plate, they found none whatsoever.

'Where be your plate, Sir 'Ammon?' Belton asked.

'I do not have any,' Sir Hamon replied perfectly truthfully. At that moment his son had it in Pakenham, waiting to send some of it to the King the moment they could do so.

Belton studied him, not really believing him, but ready to let it pass. 'Well, we found nothing, so we'll be on our way. Sorry to disturb you and your good lady, Sir 'Ammon.'

Sir Hamon shook hands with his would be arrestors and watched with his sons as the two men rode out of the gate.

'Even our neighbours Toll turns against us,' Sir Nicholas observed.

Roger acknowledged it with: 'It will be every man against his neighbour 'ere this conflict is over.'

His father slapped him on the shoulder. 'Sadly, I feel you are right, my son.'

§

Thomas Toll was furious that the constables had found nothing and even more furious that they had not arrested the L'Estranges.

'Well where are they?' he demanded.

Peter Belton shrugged. 'Couldn't find them,' he said. 'couldn't find no plate, neither, nor arms. Oi reckon they be innocent.'

'Innocent? The L'Estranges? Don't make me laugh. If they are innocent, then I am commander of the King's Cavalry!'

Both constables shrugged.

'Ah, I see how it is,' Toll said suddenly. 'You've known the L'Estranges all your lives. You would no more denounce them than sell your own wives.'

Toby Peddar coloured at the accusation, puffing out his great chest. 'Oi hope, sir, that Oi always be doing my dooty, as Oi be paid for.'

As Toll walked away from them, Peddar said to Belton: 'He don't know, but if it be legal Oi'd be selling moi wife! Lord Oi don't know how Oi do put up with her . . .'

SIXTEEN

King's Lynn, February, 1643

There should have been a Mart in the Tuesday Market Place beginning on the fourteenth day of February as there had been since King Henry VIII had given permission for it well over a hundred years ago. There should have been jugglers, tumblers, dancers, singers, musicians, side shows, Punch and Judy and the hiring of servants and farm labourers. The Tuesday Market Place should have been full to the brim with people.

However, with the joyless Puritans in control of the town all entertainment had been banned. Of course there was still the hiring of servants and the buying and selling of goods and animals, but the entertainments were gone. Particularly noticeable was the absence of the musicians, singers, dancers and acrobats. Instead the Mart had become a glorified market, not much different to other markets and not as interesting as in past years. As Lynners had always said, the day the Mart came to town was the day that winter returned in all its ferocity. Today ran true to form with snow flurries dancing in the air.

To Roger Lynn was as bleak and uninviting as cold, congealed pottage. He had gone, as usual, to glean any information that might be had. In recent weeks he had become Sir Hamon's ears, dressing more modestly than he was used to in his trusty dun-coloured leather doublet, and thick grey cloak and without a hint of lace at throat or wrists. It seemed prudent to draw as little attention to himself as possible. He sported a neat little beard and moustache these days too, and his red hair was covered by his large black hat, though he had taken the ostentatious (and expensive) white ostrich feather out of his hatband.

He met his cousin Sir William Yelverton along with Sir Charles Mordaunt in the Griffin and had dinner there. The news from the war was of cities and towns far away, of victories and defeats. The King and Parliament were having peace talks but no-one held out any hope for success. For Lynn and East Anglia life went on normally and, save for the continued fortifications Toll made to the town, one could almost forget there was a war on. Yelverton did, however, give Roger a copy of *Mercurius Aulicus* a new Royalist news booklet, but it did not contain anything that Roger thought would be useful to Sir Hamon at this time. Nevertheless, Roger folded it and tucked it inside his doublet.

It must have been two o'clock when he finally emerged from the warmth of the Griffin's taproom into the frigid February air of the Tuesday Market Place. Some snow had settled in the joints of the icy cobbles making walking a treacherous affair, for shoes had either wooden or leather soles and no grip. He took heed that others were slipping and sliding, and one woman slid over onto her fat backside whereupon she let out a string of expletives which, had the constable heard, would have landed her in the gaol.

The market seemed to be over for the day, shivering stall-holders packed up their wares, and only a few late shoppers braved the weather. Belatedly, Roger remembered that his mother had charged him with obtaining some red thread. Cursing under his breath he made his careful way to the haberdashery stall.

'You be in luck, sir,' the thin female stall-holder beamed at him. 'Oi hev it roight hair! Which one do you loike?'

She held out two colours, different shades of red. Roger had no idea and, as the thread was only a few pence, he bought them both. No doubt the wrong one would come in handy.

'I never thought to find you at a haberdashery stall, sir.' A woman's voice beside him made him look up quickly to find Ruth smiling shyly at him, a pink tinge to her cheeks.

For several thudding heartbeats he could only stare at her. How long had he looked for her, waited outside Dersingham Hall in all weathers, hoping for a glimpse of her, searching the crowds in Lynn with no success? And now when he had all but given up hope, here she was!

Remembering his manners, he raised his hat and quickly bowed. 'Madam!' as she bobbed a quick curtsey. 'I buy for my mother.' A moment's silence. 'I trust you are well?'

Ruth glanced at the stall-holder who was watching them with blatant curiosity. 'I am well, sir, I thank you.' To the stall-holder she added: 'Three yards of white tape, if you please.' To Roger: 'I too am on an errand for my aunt.'

'Your aunt is well?'

She nodded. 'Yes indeed, as are my parents, my sister, my brothers and every other member of my family.' She peeked up at him through her lashes, her eyes dancing.

He pursed his lips. Relief flooded through him. They had last parted not on the best of terms, and she had every right to ignore him. He said: 'I am pleased to hear it. Permit me to escort you home, Madam.'

The formality was for the stall-holder's benefit.

Receiving her purchase which was small enough to conceal in her pocket, Ruth thanked the woman, and then nodded to Roger. 'Thank you. That is most kind, if it does not put you out of your way, sir.'

Roger inclined his head again. 'The cobbles are treacherous. Perhaps, madam, it would be wise for you to take hold of my arm?'

'Thank you, sir.'

He freed an arm from his cloak and she slipped her gloved hand into the crook of his elbow. Even through his doublet and shirt, her touch seemed to burn through to his skin. Together they left the stall-holder to draw her own conclusions.

'I have looked for you, Mistress,' he told her when they were out of earshot. 'I wanted to apologise for my behaviour.'

He felt her sigh, the light pressure of her hand on his arm. 'You were not entirely to blame. I have wished for the opportunity to apologise to you too. I was not altogether blameless.'

They walked on in silence for a moment, and he felt shy and awkward, unsure of himself. He ventured: 'I waited for you outside of Dersingham Hall.'

'I was not there. They sent me to my aunt here in Lynn. And I dared not write to you. I am dependent on others to get a letter to you, and there is no-one I can trust.'

They had come to the corner by the Woolpack Inn, and they turned now into Stockfishrow. The snow flurries began again, and her foot slipped on the ice. She grabbed Roger tightly, and he turned to steady her. 'Careful there! If you fall, so will I!'

She laughed, and he felt stiffness between them evaporate. When she looked up at him with those big dark eyes, his heart seemed to stop within him. *Oh, woman, if only you knew what you do to me!*

'Where am I taking you to?' he asked.

'Wingate Street. At the end here. But you must not come to the door. Indeed, if they knew I was with you—apparently there has been talk about us.'

'I heard it. So did my father.'

'My father too,' she admitted.

He gave voice to his inner torment. 'They have not—that is you are not married, are you?'

'No. So far I have avoided that. They have a distant cousin in mind for me, though.'

Unfamiliar jealousy twisted in his guts like a burning hot poker. He could not answer her for a few paces. Eventually he asked: 'What is he like?'

'Why do you want to know?'

'I want to know about the competition.'

She smiled, amused. 'Really? Well, he is good-looking, and kind, and dependable, and a man of our own religious persuasion.'

'Everything I am not.'

She said quietly: 'True. But I do not love *him!*'

He stopped walking and searched her face. Did she mean that she loved *him*?

A man came past them, knocking Roger's arm, and he remembered that they were not private here. Gently, with one hand on her back and the other holding hers he guided her into a lane on the right which led to the river. At the top of this lane on the right was the brewery, at present silent. Perhaps they had closed the doors because of the cold. He took her past the brewery thankful for the shelter from the northerly wind between an eight foot high wall on the left hand side and cottages and a storehouse on the right. The river lapped at the stone steps at the end of the lane, the wind sending salt spray into the air.

He turned her to face him as his heart thudded painfully in his chest. He loved this woman with everything in him. He loved the way she blushed so readily. He loved her youth, her sparkle, her laugh. He loved her entrancing eyes, her pretty little mouth, her even white teeth. He loved the way her eyes danced when she smiled. She was his life, his love, his happiness. Nothing mattered to him as much as she did, not the war, not riches, not religion, not even his family. And now he dared to think she felt the same way.

Still holding her hand, he pulled her into his arms, folding his cloak around her as if to protect her not only from the biting wind and snow flurries, but also from prying eyes, from sorrow, from the world. She came to him willingly, slipping her arms around him, resting her face against his cheek. 'Oh Roger, I have missed you so much,' she whispered in his ear, making his heart race.

Tightening his hold on her, he kissed the side of her face, her temple, her cheek. 'I searched for you.' He murmured. 'I even went to the church.'

'I know, my father told me.'

He pulled back to study her face, concerned. 'I hope you did not get wrong on my account.'

She shook her head. 'I don't care.'

He hesitated, a fleeting memory of the hurt pride of their last meeting making him unsure. She had not been ready then. She was now. He brushed her lips with his, and he felt her respond immediately. He pulled back just in case, but she was waiting for more, her lips slightly parted, her sweet breath coming in small gasps, her eyes on his face. He needed no further invitation. As his lips closed on hers, she opened up to him, and he lost himself in his love for her.

SEVENTEEN

March, 1643

'Kirby and Parlett have declared Lynn for the King. Cromwell and his troops are on their way to Lynn right now from Norwich,' Roger announced before he had even removed his cloak.

'You know this?' Nicholas asked, his brows knitting together over his nose.

'I've been in the Griffin.' Roger gave his thick travelling cloak to the servant and followed his father into the winter sitting room where a huge log fire roared up the chimney.

Sir Hamon uttered an oath which, in the circumstances, his wife chose to ignore. 'What does Francis Parlett think he is doing?' he demanded. His family had no answer to offer him. Instead they watched him pace up and down the room. 'Why could they not have waited? In the name of all that is righteous, did they not know that it is necessary to pick their moment? And when that bear Oliver Cromwell is in Norfolk, it is asking for trouble.'

'They are impatient,' Roger offered, handing cloak and hat to the servant. 'They've been talking about it for weeks.'

'Fools! Lord above, save me from fools! Don't they know that it requires meticulous planning to do this thing successfully. What do they think will happen now, pray? Cromwell is on his way. Now isn't that a surprise?'

Sir Nicholas put his foot on the fender: 'If Cromwell is coming, we ought to go to Lynn. Did you hear when Cromwell is expected, Roger?'

'The informer said Monday. Oh and I think you will want to know that Gurlin has offered him hospitality.'

The look Sir Hamon cast Roger on this information left him no doubt of his father's opinion of Lynn's Mayor. 'Gurlin! Why am I not surprised?'

Thomas Gurlin, a small anxious man, unsteady in his loyalties, neither a Royalist nor a Parliamentarian had become Mayor in the autumn. In fact Gurlin, as head of the council, was an ineffectual little man who annoyed Sir Hamon every time he opened his mouth, but whose very ineffectiveness could be useful if handled right. For that reason Sir Hamon tolerated him.

'Is it common knowledge?' Sir Nicholas asked.

'I don't think so. Yelverton found me in the Griffin—having dinner,' he added seeing his mother's widening eyes, 'and bade me bring you the news.'

'I am surprised your cousin joins you there,' Lady Alice said disapprovingly.

Roger thought it prudent not to answer.

'I have to go to Lynn,' Sir Hamon announced. 'I have to be there when Cromwell arrives.'

'And get yourself arrested, I've no doubt!' Lady Alice snapped.

'I will go with you,' Nicholas added.

Roger agreed: 'Me too.'

Sir Hamon nodded at his sons, touched by their loyalty. 'Too late to go now,' he said, 'but we will go as soon as it is light.'

It was sensible. Better than travelling on horseback in the dark and besides Roger was hungry and tired.

Sir Hamon turned to Alice. 'I know I can rely on you to take care of the estates while I am gone.'

'Do I not look after them anyway?' she retorted, but she smiled. Then, as her sons left them she turned to him. 'Please take care of yourself Mr. Strange,' she pleaded. In private she often called him Mr. Strange.

He held her close to him. 'I will.'

She nodded against his chest. 'That Cromwell is a dangerous man.'

Sir Hamon smiled into her cap. 'Your concern is a boon to me, my love.'

§

'Of course, you know why Gurlin's giving hospitality to Cromwell, don't you?' Sir Nicholas remarked as they rode into Lynn through the East Gates. There was no sign of Cromwell yet, so it looked like they had beaten him to it.

'What is your theory, then Nick? Do give us your views,' Roger goaded him.

Nicholas ignored him and said instead to his father: 'He is afraid.'

'Of course he's afraid.' Roger scoffed.

'I know it,' Sir Hamon answered Nicholas. 'I know that if he denies admittance to Cromwell there will be an attack. Probably offering hospitality will appease Cromwell. For now.'

They rode to the Griffin, leaving the horses to the ostler there and then split up. Sir Hamon to go to the council rooms in the Trinity Guildhall in the Saturday Market Place, Nicholas to find them a house to rent and, just in case he could not find one, Roger sought to procure rooms for the night at the Griffin in the Tuesday Market Place, before the incoming army could take them all. He could only get one room and the three of them would be sharing a bed, or rather one of them would be sleeping on the floor, and he knew who that would be! Either way, it was not something any of them would relish. He hoped Nicholas had more success in finding a house.

Roger then turned to the demands of a rumbling stomach. He had eaten before he left Hunstanton, but that was well over three hours ago, nay, nearly four in fact and he needed something substantial. So he ordered a plate of eggs and ham and ale and sat down at a table to wait for it. Later on, he hoped to see Ruth. They had an open arrangement to meet by the river behind her aunt's house later in the afternoons, where they could walk on the river bank almost unnoticed. He would stand just in sight of where her window looked out onto the river, shielded from most of the house by a high wall, and she would join him if she could get away. It was an arrangement that had worked well for them in the last weeks.

It wasn't long before he was joined by Nick. 'I've got us a house, just around the corner,' Nick announced. 'Not big, but decent enough. Comes with servants.'

Roger nodded. 'Good, because I could only get one room for the three of us here and I didn't fancy putting up with your snoring all night.'

'My snoring? You should hear yourself, little brother!'

They were joined at that moment by their cousin Sir William Yelverton. 'Cromwell is without the East Gate demanding admittance,' he said and Nicholas jumped to his feet. 'I must warn father.'

Hardly had the words left his lips when a boy came running in and shouted to everyone: 'General Cromwell and his troops be here! They be coming in the East Gate!'

Roger left his ale and his promised food and followed Nicholas and Yelverton out into the Tuesday Market Place. He could hear the noise of the horses, the clatter of iron hooves on cobbles, the jangle of harness, the occasional snort or whinny as many horses came down

Grassmarket, as yet unseen.

'Father!' Sir Nicholas cried and alarm was in his voice.

'Council chambers,' Roger supplied and Nicholas was gone immediately, running out of the market square towards Cook Row, just as the man himself, Oliver Cromwell, mounted on a bay stallion and at the head of his troop, turned into view at the corner of Grassmarket and Cook Row and brought his cavalry into the Tuesday Market Place. Roger, watching at the Griffin, saw Nicholas flatten himself into a doorway as the horses came by.

Immediately Roger and Yelverton shot back into the Griffin's doorway to watch lest they be trampled by this jangling, sweating, snorting army.

Roger had to admit that the cavalry were a magnificent sight mounted on horses, the riders dressed identically in buff coats, red sashes and iron helmets, sitting ram-rod straight in the saddle. Proud men, warriors, Roger thought, mentally comparing them to the half-disciplined rabble which made up the King's army. They piled into the Tuesday Market Place. He assumed this was not the sum total of Cromwell's troops. Probably a good deal more were outside the East Gate on the grass land there. It didn't look much like there would be a market tomorrow, either, if they were staying there. The acrid stench of sweating horses and the accumulating piles of dung, of damp leather, the jangle of horse furniture and clatter of iron shoes, the shouted orders brought the local people out to stare at such a spectacle.

Yelverton said abruptly in Roger's ear: 'Leave it to Nick, he'll warn your father, although I should think that by now he's heard them himself. If we don't want to be carted off to jail the best thing for us is to keep out of sight.'

Roger uttered an explosive sound in his throat. 'Look there! That's Gurlin! Damn me if he ain't greeting Cromwell! Lord, that man's an ass!'

Out in the square, Gurlin did indeed bow, then he went to the head of Cromwell's horse and stroked it's long nose and stood looking up at the great man himself.

Cromwell slowly dismounted.

He had the erect air of a leader. Unsmiling he looked around him at the market square and allowed Gurlin to escort him back along Cook Row, towards the Saturday Market Place, the location of the Trinity Guildhall. A squad of men went with him. Meantime Gurlin ran along beside him, forever turning to talk to him, bent obsequiously.

'Just look at him!' Roger said in disgust, coming out of the Griffin.

'Time to move, Coz,' Yelverton announced.

Well aware that their dress gave them away as Royalists, Roger and Yelverton sauntered out of the inn and, keeping to the edge of the market place, followed Cromwell, Gurlin and the guards as they walked back into Cook Row. No-one accosted them.

It was a walk of about five minutes at the pace Cromwell walked, his men in step behind him, all their ironmongery clanking in unison. At the Saturday Market Place they turned right and halted before the doors of the Checker-board walls of the Trinity Guildhall. Then, and Roger could hardly believe his eyes, Gurlin opened the doors to the Trinity Guildhall and invited—actually invited!—Cromwell in.

Cromwell was average height, not a handsome man, having rugged features, a large bulbous nose and two large warts. But this was a man who knew how to command respect.

'I'm going in as well,' Roger said to Yelverton.

Yelverton hung back. He had a family and could not afford to be arrested. 'Have a care,' he urged.

Leaving him behind, Roger followed the men into the Guildhall and up the stairs to the council chambers, where quite a few of the council members were waiting for them. As they went into the hall, Roger slipped in behind them and tucked himself into a corner behind a pillar, in the shadows and out of sight.

Cromwell's gaze ran over the men seated at the tables in the chamber. For a moment no-one spoke.

Parlett and Kirby, who had declared for the King, came forward. Gurlin made haste to introduce them. 'This, general, is Mr. Frances Parlett and this is Mr. Kirby.' Their clothes proclaimed them Royalist, and their names were known to Cromwell.

Parlett said stiffly: 'I have to say, sir, that you are intruding on council business.'

'And I am here to remove you from office, Mr. Parlett.' Cromwell announced smoothly. 'Arrest these two!' His way of speaking was quite matter-of-fact.

The other members stood up, perhaps to prevent the arrests, but Cromwell's men drew pistols and four soldiers grabbed Parlett and Kirby and roughly escorted them from the council chamber.

Cromwell surveyed the others coolly. His eyes rested on Sir Hamon standing beside Sir Nicholas. He looked like he was about to ask his name, but at that moment Thomas Toll came forward, eager to make a good impression on a great man and bowed. 'Thomas Toll at your service, sir. And this is Mr. John Percival. We are Parliamentary members. And this is . . .'

Cromwell cut him off and said coldly: 'I am pleased to meet an ally of England.' He sounded bored and the comment infuriated the Royalists who viewed themselves as England's allies. Roger saw Sir Hamon bristle.

Cromwell drew one gauntlet from his right hand and beckoned to a man behind him. The man came forward and ushered all the Royalists to the right hand side. They were easily distinguishable from the Puritans by their richly embroidered doublets and lace collars and cuffs.

Roger, standing back in the shadows watching, had his hand on his sword hilt, ready to act if his father or brother were threatened.

Immediately, the soldiers surrounded the Royalists. 'Your weapons, gentlemen, please.' With pistols levelled, he relieved them of swords and daggers and pistols.

Sir Hamon said nothing, accepting it as inevitable, but Roger understood the warning he shot in his direction.

Young Sir Charles Mordaunt, though, was furious. 'I say—that sword belonged to my father's father.'

'Then 'tis outmoded,' Cromwell said dismissively, adding curtly: 'We shall be securing the town, gentlemen. This town is for Parliament.'

Sir Hamon said nothing. It was not the time to disclose his hand. He did not seem too worried about the loss of his sword either. Perhaps he reckoned that Gurlin would keep the weapons and they could retrieve them later.

Turning his back on all the council members as if they were of no further interest, Cromwell asked: 'Mr. Gurlin, where may we be staying?'

Since Gurlin had offered hospitality at his own house for Cromwell, he offered to show him, and Cromwell and his men left the council chamber.

Roger remained undiscovered in the corner niche until they had gone, then he came forward.

'What are you doing here, sir?' Sir Hamon demanded privately when he saw him. 'You could have been arrested and for what?'

He was right, of course. It had been stupid and impetuous to follow Cromwell. He said: 'I wanted to be sure you were safe, sir.'

Sir Hamon shook his head. 'Sometimes I wonder about you!' he said under his breath, and Roger felt the colour flood his cheeks. If anyone but his father had said that, they would have been flat on the floor—Nick included!

Behind them, Thomas Toll was loudly triumphant. 'You Royalists think you can do what you like. Well, you can't! Parliament is the law here.'

With admirable self-control, Sir Hamon made no answer. He was not going to disclose his hand either to Toll or Percival. Ignoring the gibe he left the council chambers with his sons, followed by the other Royalists. It was too much to hear Toll crowing.

Because Cromwell's men surrounded the town on the landward side and also seized a small barque containing arms from Dunquerque which was riding at anchor in the harbour, no-one could leave or come into Lynn. The L'Estranges stayed in the hired house in Stockfishrow and Sir Hamon took the opportunity to discuss his plans with Yelverton, Mordaunt, Paston, Hovell and the others who were all similarly trapped in the sitting room.

'So what do you intend to do, Sir Hamon?' Sir Charles Mordaunt asked, sitting down on the floorboards beside Roger for all the chairs were taken by the older men.

Sir Hamon paced the room and Sir Charles ran his fingers through his long brown hair. It was obvious to Roger and probably to everyone else in the room that Sir Hamon was not a happy man.

Neither was Sir Charles. 'They took my father's sword,' he said, repeating his protest of earlier. 'And a fine sword it is.'

'The man's a jumped up little slug,' Sir Hamon's suppressed anger forced its way through his teeth. 'Comes here and acts like Norfolk is his alone.' From which Roger collected that he was not talking about Gurlin, but about Cromwell.

'Just so.' Edward Paston of Appleton Hall nodded. 'But what can we do about it?'

Sir Nicholas's brows drew together above his long nose as he watched his father's agitated pacing. He sat on the corner of the table. 'You have something in mind, sir?'

Sir Hamon stopped pacing and looked at him, but as though not seeing him. Then he focused on them all. 'Despite Mr. Parlett and Mr.

Kirby's assertions, this town has not declared itself, either for the King or for Parliament—yet.'

The assembled members of the council exchanged glances. Richard Hovell's eyes shone. 'You think we could get the town to declare for the King? How?'

'If we make Sir Hamon governor,' Paston supplied dourly. 'That should do it.'

'But what about Toll and Percival?'

'Oh, they'll oppose it. But we only need a majority vote,' Paston said. 'We need to make sure everyone is at the council meeting. All except the Parliamentary members, of course.'

'They have four. If they all turn up. How many can we muster?'

'Well there's us in this room. Excepting Roger of course,' Sir Nicholas said, staring thoughtfully at his seething little brother. Because he was not a landowner, Roger was not on the council, although Sir Charles Mordaunt at the same age was. It was galling. But now was not the time to put himself forward, so Roger just waited and listened. 'Sir John Spelman. Possibly the Cobbes.'

'It should be enough,' Sir Hamon said.

'We will need armaments,' Sir Charles Mordaunt stated.

'I have an arsenal stored in Sedgeford,' Sir Hamon said quietly. 'All we need to do is get it into Lynn. Also Toll has cannon he brought in from Norwich and London and a stash of gunpowder. We can make use of that.' He laughed. 'He will be furious when he knows we have taken possession of what he intended to use against us! When we are ready we will declare for the King. Never again must our town be in the hands of those traitors to the crown.'

'What will happen when we declare for the King?' Roger asked. 'Will not Cromwell come back and try to take the town again for Parliament?'

Sir Hamon nodded. 'So we will need reinforcements. If we could persuade the King's army to cross the Wash from Lincolnshire to come to our relief, it might be done. I will write to Lord Newcastle. He is currently on campaigns in Lincolnshire and Warwickshire. Lynn is a strategically placed port, valuable to His Majesty. We just have to hold out long enough for Newcastle to get here.'

'A siege, you mean?' Edward Paston was horrified. 'People will get killed.'

'Needs must in a dire situation like this,' Richard Hovell

announced.

'So what say you all?' Sir Hamon asked.

'I'm for it,' Mordaunt said.

'Me too.'

'Aye and me!'

They all joined in with their agreement, and Sir Hamon smiled. 'Pray God we are successful, gentlemen.'

§

Oliver Cromwell left Lynn on 24th March 1643, under the happy illusion that Lynn was secure. The Royalists departed for their own homes. Sir Hamon stayed because he had business with Gurlin and Roger remained in Lynn for another two days to see if any further news might be forthcoming. With ships coming in and out of Lynn's port, news came with them and was best picked up in the inns and taverns. The White Hart in St. James Street, the Three Crowns on the river behind Wingate and others, besides the Griffin, of course, were sources of information and he sought them out avidly. While he was thus engaged, he also managed to see Ruth, meeting her by the church of St. Margaret and then walking with her to the Guannock Gate.

A small insignificant structure without even a room for a gatekeeper, Guannock Gate lay on the town boundary wall between the South Gates and the East Gates. It was easy enough to get to from St. Margaret's church: straight up St. James Street, past the infirmary and on to open grassland. It was an open space within the town boundary, popular as a recreation area, where they could find a little privacy. The town wall here had large semi-circular alcoves with a stone ledge which allowed for seating, and in the spring sunshine with daffodils dancing in the slight breeze, it made for a pretty place to sit and talk.

They spoke of anything and everything. Of the war, of religion, of farming. As they talked, the better acquainted they became, and as he came to know her better, he found that the initial attraction he felt for her was turning to love.

As a Puritan she had definite ideas about church governance. 'There should not be priests and bishops,' she told Roger. 'Where in the Christian scriptures do you find the word priest?'

Roger smiled. He knew his Bible too. 'When the Lord is speaking to the Pharisees and priests; in the letters of St. Paul when he argues against the old Law; and of the Lord Jesus as high priest.'

‘But he does not use it, nor does anyone else, with regard to church governance. Does he not use the word ‘presbyters’ or ‘elders’ instead?’

‘He does indeed.’

‘And where does the word ‘bishop’ come from?’

Roger, who was a Greek scholar said: ‘From “*episkopos*”, “*epi*” meaning “over” and “*skopos*” meaning “looking” so over-looking or overseeing. We might say, an “overseer”. So a bishop is an overseer.’

He had the feeling she already knew this, for she said next: ‘In Titus the context is the apostle Paul telling Titus to make elders in every city, and goes on to give the characteristics of an elder, adding that a ‘bishop’ or ‘overseer’ must be blameless, and so on. So elders and overseers are the same thing.’

Roger nodded slowly, trying to think of a way to refute her argument, eventually admitting: ‘So it would seem.’

‘So why does the King insist on inflicting rule by bishops on everyone?’

Roger paused. She had summed it all up perfectly. Was it the King inflicting bishops on ‘everyone’ or was it the bishops fighting for their own power?

‘That is not what the war is about,’ he said.

‘Then what is it about?’

‘It is about the King being ruler of this realm without interference from Parliament.’

She digested this. ‘But Parliament stops the King being an autocrat, does it not?’

Roger, by no means pleased by the route the conversation was taking, said: ‘There is more to it than that.’

‘Well, I hope so,’ she said tartly, ‘because it seems a petty quarrel for people to die over otherwise.’

§

Sir Hamon took the opportunity to present himself at mayor Gurlin’s house and he arrived early the morning after Cromwell’s departure before the mayor had breakfasted. In fact Gurlin was still in the act of dressing and the servant ushered Sir Hamon into a small room to await his presence.

Kicking his heels in the room, Sir Hamon looked about him with interest. He had time to study the few artifacts in the room. A few pictures, a small silver bowl, a few plain pewter candlesticks. Obviously Thomas Gurlin was not a rich man. Worse, he appeared to have no taste and little refinement. His furniture was plain, with little comfort. It was sombre, dark and uninviting. Sir Hamon thought that a few wall hangings, tapestries, pictures that kind of thing, would liven the place up a bit with some vibrant colour quite forgetting that such things cost a good deal of money. He had come by his own at Hunstanton Hall by inheritance.

Of course, there was no fire in the grate since Gurlin probably did not anticipate using the room at that unreasonable hour of the day. Indeed, the grate still had ash in it, the maid, or whoever, not having cleaned it and set it yet and it gave off an ashy smell. Evidently Thomas Gurlin could not govern his servants. Lady Alice would send such a tardy wench packing if she were in the L'Estrange household!

Thomas Gurlin came in, not properly dressed, his light hair unbrushed and he seemed to Sir Hamon to be nervous. Well and so he had a right to be, Sir Hamon thought as he stood glowering as Gurlin hastily tucked his shirt in his breeches.

Gurlin smiled. 'Sir Hamon, well come sir. Forgive my appearance.'

Both men executed punctilious bows. 'I doubt you will think so, Mr. Gurlin,' Sir Hamon growled. He was still furious with the man. 'I expect you know why I am here.'

'Well yes. That is no.' He stopped, struggling with himself. 'Do go on sir.'

Having not been invited to sit down, Sir Hamon stood facing Gurlin. 'How came it, sir, that you thought it meet to entertain that—that—Parliament hound?'

'S-sir I must protest!'

'Inviting that snake Cromwell *here*!' he pointed to the floor to show that he meant to the house.

Gurlin shook visibly. He was much smaller than Sir Hamon who appeared taller because of the halo of red hair. 'But you must see the p-position I w-was in, sir. You well know that General Cromwell would have attacked the town if I had not welcomed him.'

Sir Hamon dismissed what he considered to be a feeble excuse. 'You, sir, are a ditherer! Yes, sir, a vacillator. You do not know on which side to post your colours, do you?'

'Yes, yes, Sir Hamon. But you do not understand.' Gurlin ran his hands through his unruly hair.

'You mistake, sir, I understand all too well. Are you, or are you not, for the King?'

'Well yes.'

'Then don't play the traitor!'

'I-I have to do what the good people of Lynn would want me to do as their representative. I have to think about them. Let the people choose.'

'The people have not chosen,' Sir Hamon snapped. 'Yet. So, Mr. Gurlin, you must decide. You have to think for them. For the good people of Lynn probably have no views either way—much like yourself I think. But when they learn, as they will, that Parliament has imposed another levy to finance this war—one thousand two hundred and fifty pounds a week to be paid by Norwich and Norfolk, Mr. Gurlin—which must come out of the pockets of the good people of Lynn, in part—how do you think they will view the Parliamentary cause then, eh?'

'I-I don't suppose they will like it.'

'No, I don't suppose they will. It is high time you made a decision. For Parliament or for the King. Then we know where we will all stand.'

Gurlin licked his lips nervously. 'Perhaps it would be wisest if—'

Sir Hamon ground his teeth in his impatience. 'This is no time for prevarication, Mr. Gurlin. It is time for action.'

'What—what do you suggest, Sir Hamon?'

Sir Hamon's grey eyes studied Gurlin for a moment. 'Make me governor,' he said.

Gurlin stared at him. 'You? Governor? Can it be done?'

'It can. With your support it can.

'How? I mean, Master Percival and Master Toll would never agree.'

'I am pleased to tell you that our Parliamentary members will be in London at the time of the next meeting of the council. There will be no hindrance, I think.'

'We have not yet set the date for the next council meeting.'

'No, but you will, won't you?'

Gurlin was thoughtful. 'There would be enough support for you, then,' he admitted.

Well satisfied, Sir Hamon nodded. 'But there will be no declaration for the king, yet. Do you understand? We do not want Cromwell's troops back here infesting us until we are ready.'

Gurlin looked aggrieved. 'Cromwell coming here again? What trouble do you bring on us, Sir Hamon?'

'If it be a quiet life that you wish for Mr. Gurlin, you should never have become mayor. Now, where is my sword and my pistol? And Sir Nicholas would like his too.'

'At the Trinity Guildhall, in the vault. I will write a note to allow you to collect them.'

Sir Hamon picked up the plumed hat which he had left on the low table and waited while Gurlin found a sheet of paper. Gurlin dipped the pen in the ink to write. When he had done, Sir Hamon retrieved his spectacles from his doublet, perched them on his nose and read the letter.

Satisfied, he bowed again. 'Good morning, Mr. Gurlin.'

Gurlin sat back on the chair, rifled through his breeches for a handkerchief and mopped his brow in relief.

EIGHTEEN

30th March 1643

Lady Alice watched from the window as Sir Hamon dismounted from his horse in the courtyard and strode into the Hall, closely followed by Sir Nicholas. Of Roger there was no sign.

'Roger did not return with you?' she asked as he planted a quick kiss on her forehead.

'Couldn't find him,' Nicholas answered. So we left without him. He is capable to seeing himself home.'

'No doubt on't,' she replied, 'but what if he is in trouble?'

'If Roger gets himself into a scrape, then he can get himself out of it,' Sir Hamon snapped, indicating the end of his patience towards his youngest and most annoying son. He gravitated to the fire in the oak-panelled winter sitting room.

Consternation creased Alice's face.

Nicholas threw himself onto the settle in the fire recess, where Lady Alice herself had been sitting not a few moments before. She did not protest, however, for at that moment Lady Anne appeared in the doorway, dropped a quick curtsey to her father-in-law and then, in obedience to Sir Nicholas's outstretched hand, came towards her husband to sit beside him. He pulled her into his arms and planted a kiss on her lips. 'How are you, pretty one?' he murmured.

She blushed at such an outward display, never having become used to the L'Estrange ways, but Sir Hamon and Lady Alice smiled indulgently.

Ketwood, the old butler came in dressed in his green livery and Anne pulled away from her husband's embrace, straightening her cap, a flush burning her pretty cheeks. The butler appeared not to notice. 'Beer for me.' Sir Hamon ordered as he sat down on the settle opposite his son and nearest the roaring fire.

'And for me,' added Sir Nicholas. 'And something to eat.'

The butler coughed. 'Cook begs me to tell you, sir, that he has set aside bread and cold meat for your return.'

'Just bring it on a platter!' Sir Nicholas ordered. 'I don't want fuss.'

'And for me,' Sir Hamon said. 'Faith! I'm half starved!'

The servant bowed and withdrew.

Lady Alice sat down on the down-filled cushion beside her husband, cosy in the fireplace alcove, watching the fire as it roared up the brick chimney. This was their winter parlour, their cosy room, the one where they could relax. It was the room they all liked best. 'So what happened?'

She knew it was good news from the way Sir Hamon's grin lit up his face, glittering in his grey eyes. 'My love, you are looking at the new governor of King's Lynn!'

Sir Nicholas also grinned.

But Lady Alice felt her spirits plummet.

Anne leaned forward to Sir Hamon to say: 'I congratulate you sir.'

'So you will be away more,' Lady Alice stated. 'And where exactly will this lead? Are you to declare King's Lynn for the King?'

'Not yet, my love,' he told her. 'We must pick our time carefully. There is much to do before then. Besides,' he added taking her hand in his, 'the good people of Lynn have to decide that.'

Nicholas nodded. 'We just have to persuade them that that's what they want.'

'Do the good people of Lynn have an opinion?'

'Probably not. But they know where their loyalties lie.'

She took a deep breath to steady her heart. They were entering the most dangerous time of their lives. 'Surely you were not without opposition? What about Thomas Toll and John Percival? Did they not oppose you?'

'Nope,' Sir Hamon's grin grew even wider. 'They were not there!'

'Not there? Where were they then?'

'London.'

She considered this information. 'Oh. What will they say when they find out?'

'Plenty I should think. But there is nothing they can do about it!'

Ketwood returned with the bread and cold meat and some cheese for good measure, and Sir Hamon took a swig from his beer pot before setting it on the flagstone floor, and his manchet bread and cold meat on a pottery plate on his lap.

Nicholas tore a chunk of his bread with his teeth, took a swig of beer and chewed heartily. The manchet bread was the white bread, the best the house could offer, the cheese had come from Hunstanton Hall's own dairy, the meat from their own herd, and the beer Lady Alice and Lady Anne had brewed it themselves. It was simple fare, but it filled empty bellies.

'We're on the winning side,' Sir Hamon announced chewing heartily. 'And I am not entirely without influence where Gurlin is concerned.'

'That rat Gurlin!' Sir Nicholas growled the words. 'Treacherous dog.'

Sir Hamon nodded. 'A weak man, I give you. He's no idea what side to be on.'

'He is as weak and vacillating as a leaf blown in the wind. A mere woman.' Then catching his mother's eye at the same time as his wife dug him in the ribs, he added with a twitch to his lips: 'Begging your pardon, ladies.'

Lady Alice pursed her lips. 'So I should think. I would remind you, my son, that when you men are away, it is we women who run the estate!' She thought for a moment. 'Did General Cromwell come to Lynn?'

'He did.' And Sir Hamon told her all the events of the last few days.

§

Roger stayed in Lynn, lurking in the Saturday Market Place by the church in hopes of seeing Ruth, for their previous arrangement of him loitering on the quay had proved inadequate. However, Ruth found it more and more difficult to get away to meet him, her aunt having become suspicious and days went by without his seeing her at all.

Meanwhile, Roger frequented the taverns. Although the Griffin was a favourite haunt of his close friends and fellow Royalists, and the food there was far superior, the White Hart and the Three Crowns had the advantage of being a favoured watering hole of sailors and lower class travellers, thus more likely to bring fruitful information. The White Hart's other advantage was that it was in St. James Street, just along from the Saturday Market Place, and Wingate where Ruth's Aunt lived, ran into the market place on the other side of the church. He could sit in a window and watch for Ruth, although he did not ever see her by those means, but it was handy to be able to walk down Wingate legitimately in order to go 'home' to Sir Hamon's hired house in Stockfishrow.

In the White Hart and the Three Crowns he listened to the gossip and came to the same conclusion as his father. One or two voiced opinions on the side of the King, matched by some who were for

Parliament, but for the most part, the common people did not understand what the war was all about and were convinced it was none of their business anyway. Deciding for one side or the other was very much a matter of emotion, or persuasion by their betters who were considered to be more knowledgeable about these things.

Both the White Hart and the Griffin had nubile serving wenches who always hoped to find themselves generous lovers. In days gone by he had been tempted. Now, no-one, not even Mary in the Griffin, could coax Roger. He could not be diverted by another woman when his soul ached for Ruth.

On the third day he heard news. William Yelverton came into the Griffin where Roger was enjoying a hearty breakfast of ham and eggs. He sat down with Roger after ordering the same for himself. 'Hello coz! Well met!'

'So, Yelverton, what's afoot?'

Yelverton leaned forward, so that only Roger could hear. 'Sir Thomas Richardson is dead.'

Roger was shocked. All the Royalists in Norfolk were acquainted and Sir Thomas Richardson was known as a great orator and hot for the King's cause. He was also the brother of Yelverton's wife, Ursula. 'Dead? How?'

'Some of the King's men were holding a secret meeting in the house of a man called Holl, just outside Norwich when the traitors invaded and arrested them all. Among them was Richardson and Sir William Denny. Everyone was arrested and Denny and Richardson were taken into custody in the castle prison.'

'Why them?' Roger asked.

'Because they had not openly declared themselves,' Yelverton said. 'Richardson hid his sympathies, always hoping that the war may come to nothing. Denny too.'

'So they wore Puritan clothes?'

'Very likely. And you know what that means. They were viewed as traitors to Parliament because they were at a meeting for Royalists but their clothes portrayed them with other loyalties. That's why they were arrested. If they had always worn Royalist clothes they might have been spared this. Richardson died in custody. They mistreated him so badly that he died. I don't know any more of Denny.'

Roger felt sick. For some inexplicable reason he had felt that each side would treat the other with respect. After all, were they not all

Englishmen? The Parliamentary Puritans, though, were showing an iron fist. No Christian love there, then.

Yelverton's breakfast turned up and after giving thanks, he tucked in with relish. 'Dreadful the way they treat loyal Englishmen.'

'Did they torture him for information?' Roger asked.

'Aye. And they are evil beggars, these henchmen of Parliament. Better not fall into their hands.'

Roger had a mental picture of a man broken and bleeding, and he shuddered. He finished his breakfast and slid his plate aside to replace it with his half-full flagon of beer. He took a long pull. 'There has to be a better way of getting information out of a man than to break his body,' he said. 'Did Richardson give away any information?'

'Doubt if he knew anything. Thing is, some of these people are sadistic bastards. Rabble who take great delight in bringing down their betters.' He chewed for a while, swallowed, took a swig of beer, then said: 'How goes it with the Pell wench?'

Roger stiffened, disliking that his private life was the talk of Lynn. 'The Devil! There's nothing in it.'

'No?' Yelverton shrugged. 'Won't do, coz. It makes people wonder where your loyalties lie.'

Roger glared at him, but Yelverton, confident in their kinship and his greater age (ten years) was completely unmoved. He continued to eat using the new-fangled two-pronged fork which the Griffin boasted and concentrated on his dinner, not even looking up to meet Roger's eye. 'You know,' he said between mouthfuls of food, 'we can't always have what we want. Sometimes, we must marry where it is more—' he searched for the word '—politic.'

Roger felt anger boiling in his belly. 'You mean a marriage of convenience.'

Sir William wagged his head thoughtfully. 'Well—yes. And these things, they usually turn out alright. But if you make sport with the Pell girl—'

'I am *not* making sport with her or with anyone!'

'Just so. But if you did, you would bring the war right to Hunstanton. I tell you, you are courting trouble.'

Now furious at this cousinly intervention, Roger stood up. 'Well, I thank you, sir, for your advice!' he snapped and left the Griffin, striding out into the Tuesday Market Place.

Struggling to bring his temper under control, he stood looking at the people wandering about on their business and considered his next move. Another day spent waiting in the Saturday Market Place for a glimpse of Ruth, or should he go home to Hunstanton and take the news about Sir Thomas Richardson to his father?

§

Roger arrived at Hunstanton to find that his brother Hamon had arrived from Pakenham while they were in Lynn, eager to be in the thick of things.

Roger had never been close to Hamon. He was as tall as all the L'Estranges and had the family nose, but the similarity ended there. For Hamon had put on weight and sported an overlarge belly. And where Roger was a born optimist, with a devil-may-care attitude and Nicholas had a turn for gossip and jesting, Hamon was the serious brother, the Godly brother, the one who was interested in religion. In fact he had already published his work '*God's Sabbath before and under the Law and under thee Gospel, briefly vindicated from novell and heterodox assertions*,' which, while a scholarly work, his mother had complained that she did not even understand the title! And that, Roger thought, was what came of being educated in the law.

The end result was that Hamon felt largely excluded from the family to which he belonged. It did not help that he lived near his sister in the same village in Suffolk, but hardly ever saw her.

He greeted Roger with a bear-hug. 'Well, little brother and where have you been these last three days?'

'Finding out things,' Roger said.

'Well, you are just in time for supper,' Lady Alice told him, bustling through to usher everyone into the splendid modern family dining room.

'What things?' Nicholas wanted to know, as Roger made for the dining room. He was ravenous and he needed no further encouragement to take his place at the oak dining table. Hamon pulled out a chair and sat down beside him.

Roger waited only until everyone was seated before addressing himself to all of them. 'Sir Thomas Richardson is dead.'

Sir Hamon's eyes were on his youngest son. 'Richardson? What happened?'

So Roger explained what Yelverton had told him. 'They caught Richardson and Sir William Denny at a secret meeting near Norwich and beat Richardson so badly that he died.'

'The Devil!' Nicholas exploded.

Everyone else sat in silence around the table, supper forgotten while the servants hovered in anticipation. With a wave of his hand Sir Hamon dismissed them. He was sure of all his staff, certain of their loyalty, but it was the course of wisdom not to let them in on their plans. Just in case. Besides, all the food was on the table, they could serve themselves.

'Why?' Sir Hamon asked at last.

Roger took a breath and shook his head. 'Twould seem neither had openly declared themselves as Royalist and they were in plain Puritan clothes.'

'So they viewed them as spies.'

'So it would seem. Or traitors. There is no news of Sir William Denny. He could be dead as well.'

It was a blow, for the stakes had suddenly risen immeasurably.

Sir Hamon said: 'You know what this means?'

Nicholas said: 'We live in dangerous times when men can be killed for staying loyal to their divinely appointed king.'

Sir Hamon nodded. 'If any of you would prefer not to be involved—'

His words met a chorus of protest. Not one of them would want to be viewed as a coward, or disloyal to the cause.

Nicholas said: 'We knew none of this would be easy. And we are aware of the danger.'

Anne's fine dark eyes flashed. 'Is it worth the danger? Is it worth the risk?'

'We have right on our side,' Sir Hamon answered tartly. 'We are fighting for our King's right to sit on his legal throne. We may even be fighting for his very life.'

'But at what risk?' she fired back. She stood up from the table. 'Excuse me, Sir Hamon, gentlemen, but I have a headache.'

'My lady.' But before she reached the door Sir Hamon added: 'There is no-one else. We are the ones who can retain Lynn for the King. No-one else can do it.'

Lady Anne paused. 'There will be no mercy from Parliament. They will view us as traitors.'

'When they are the traitors,' Roger put in.

Sir Hamon took bread from the plate on the table. 'There is

something else.'

Roger paused in the act of taking some meat from the dish.

'Newcastle is on his way here with an army, coming from the South.'

'What will that mean?' Alice asked.

'It's obvious, Mother!' Nicholas answered before his father could speak. 'If Lord Newcastle comes to Lynn, then we can secure Lynn for the King.'

The door snapped shut behind Lady Anne.

NINETEEN

King's Lynn, April, 1643

Whether the Earl of Newcastle's Royalist troops were intent on Lynn or not was also a matter of intense speculation for Parliament who felt that King's Lynn was vulnerable. Their euphoria at Cromwell's securing the town had lasted less than a fortnight before word came that the Royalist, Sir Hamon L'Estrange had become governor. Now they watched Lynn with an anxious eye, viewing it as a hotbed of rebellion.

Accordingly they sent orders to Norwich that a certain sergeant major by the name of Livewell Sherwood should be dispatched with two hundred dragoons to march on Lynn. Sir Hamon, who had repaired to the house in Lynn with his sons, viewed these Parliamentarian efforts as laughable. 'What in the name of all that is holy do they think a band of two hundred dragoons will do against Newcastle's army?' he demanded of his sons. 'Sherwood will be hopelessly outnumbered!'

Nevertheless, Sherwood arrived in Lynn on Monday 3rd April 1643.

And Newcastle was nowhere to be seen.

Having had word of his coming, Sir Hamon, as governor of Lynn, issued orders to Mayor Gurlin: 'No-one—*no-one*—is to be allowed into Lynn, least of all Sherwood.'

Gurlin all but collapsed in an agony of indecision. 'Yes, but Sir Hamon, he has two hundred dragoons!'

'Do you think we cannot defend ourselves against two hundred men?' Sir Hamon demanded.

Gurlin shook visibly. 'B-but, Sir Hamon—' he protested weakly.

'Mr. Gurlin, I have given my orders.'

Gurlin bowed and took himself out of Sir Hamon's house.

However, knowing Gurlin as he did, Sir Hamon thought it prudent to be present himself when Sherwood and his troops arrived. As he strode towards the East Gates with Gurlin trotting along behind like a reluctant spaniel, he surveyed the ancient wall.

His orders had been obeyed; men were stationed on the wall, behind the battlements, arms at the ready. Beneath them in the arches, others waited, huddled away from the wind.

As he entered the East Gates Sir Hamon ordered the gate keeper: 'Raise the drawbridge and lock the gates.' The gate keeper hastened to obey and Sir Hamon ran up the spiral stone stairs to the upper chamber. 'Come on Mr. Gurlin.'

From here he had a commanding view of the fields the other side of the smelly deep water-and-rubbish filled ditch which acted as a moat, in reality a tributary of the Gaywood River, and in the distance the small village of Gaywood and beyond.

His eyes scanned the road in front of him.

'No sign of him,' Gurlin announced and turned to descend the stairs again.

Sir Hamon grabbed him by the collar. 'Oh no you don't sir!'

'But 'tis time for my dinner! And he's not coming.'

'Oh, he's coming. You can eat this evening when this is all over.'

So Gurlin stood nervously at the window in the cheerless room reluctantly watching with Sir Hamon as the time moved on with agonising slowness. Just as Gurlin was going to make another break for freedom, Sir Hamon saw what he had been expecting. A troop of men on horseback, one of the leaders carrying a standard, emerged from the village of Gaywood and took the road towards the East Gate. 'There he is.'

Gurlin hopped from one foot to the other. 'Oh no!'

'Calm yourself, sir,' Sir Hamon said bracingly. 'I'll tell you what to say.'

Sherwood's troop of dragoons came to a halt the on other side of the ditch, outside the East Gate. No doubt he expected a welcome from Mayor Gurlin just as Oliver Cromwell had done. If so he was in for a nasty surprise.

He instructed his sergeant. 'Demand entrance,' and the sergeant urged his horse forward.

Watching from the upper room of the gate, Sir Hamon prompted the gatekeeper who obediently yelled: 'Who goes there?'

'Sergeant-Major Sherwood and two hundred troops. By order of Parliament, we demand to be admitted.'

'Please wait,' the gatekeeper responded. He was reluctant to take the blame for this himself. 'I must get permission.'

'Permission?' Sir Hamon heard Sherwood repeat in astonishment. 'What does he mean by permission?'

His sergeant could not enlighten him.

'Are they denying us entrance? This town belongs to Parliament, don't they know?'

The sergeant merely shrugged. He had no answer.

'Let me speak to them,' Sherwood decided and he urged his horse forward.

'I am Livewell Sherwood, the troop commander,' he cried grandly to the gatekeeper who deliberately kept them waiting. 'I demand admittance. I have orders from Parliament.'

'My orders, sir, are not to let you in,' the gatekeeper replied obstinately. 'Mr. Gurlin the mayor will be here presently. You can talk to him.'

'This is ridiculous,' Sherwood fumed.

'Orders be orders, sir,' the gatekeeper replied and disappeared from view as though there were no more to be said.

Sherwood could not believe his ears, nor his eyes, but all calls to the gatekeeper were not productive of the man's appearance and he was forced to return to his waiting troops who were still mounted.

By this time Sir Nicholas, young Hamon, Roger, Yelverton and Hovell had all heard that Sherwood was outside the East Gate and they came up the stairs into the small upper room.

Gurlin's eyes were wide with anxiety, but Sir Hamon was determined there would be no repetition of the farce of two weeks ago when Oliver Cromwell was welcomed with open arms. Not while he was Governor!

'Tell the gatekeeper to hail them again,' Sir Hamon hissed at Gurlin who shook visibly. 'Oh, Sir Hamon, I beg of you, don't make me do this!'

'Faith, Gurlin, you look like you'll wet yourself like a babe!' Sir Nicholas chided.

'Get on with it,' Sir Hamon growled.

So Gurlin nodded to the gatekeeper who hailed Sherwood again.

Trembling, Gurlin took his place at the window. There was only room for one person to be seen at a time and Sir Hamon stood right behind him.

'Keep him out!' Sir Hamon said from the room behind him. 'You are the mayor. You have the authority.'

Gurlin looked behind him like a trapped rabbit.

'Deny them admittance,' Sir Hamon said again.

Sherwood arrived before the gate. 'Who are you?' he demanded.

'I—' his voice squeaked and he coughed and tried again. 'I am Thomas Gurlin, the mayor of King's Lynn.'

'Master Gurlin,' Sherwood repeated through clenched teeth, 'I have orders from Parliament to enter this town and secure it for Parliament.'

Sir Hamon prodded Gurlin in the back. 'You may not enter,' Gurlin announced.

'*What?*' Sherwood thundered. 'What nonsense is this? Who says so?'

'By the authority of the Committee and the Governor of this town,' Sir Hamon prompted.

'By the authority of the Committee and the Governor of this town,' Gurlin repeated.

Sherwood let out an unchristian expletive. 'This is preposterous! Let down the drawbridge. Open the gates!'

'No! I c-cannot do that!'

'Mr. Gurlin, do not be a fool!' Sherwood bellowed.

Gurlin looked round at Sir Hamon. 'Permission denied.' Sir Hamon prompted.

'Permission denied!' Gurlin called dutifully.

Sherwood uttered another expletive and retired to discuss this with his sergeant.

Gurlin came away from the window, shaking visibly. 'This will bring us trouble, Sir Hamon,' he whined, wringing his hands. 'I am sure of it.'

Sir Hamon laughed quietly. 'No doubt, Master Gurlin, no doubt.'

Captain Livewell Sherwood exchanged heated words with his sergeant, unaware that their voices carried to the burgesses in the East Gate. 'We shall storm the town,' he announced. 'I'll make them pay.'

His sergeant was forced to bring certain facts to his attention.

'I don't think we can, sir. We are only two hundred men and there is a moat to cross and walls to scale and we have no heavy artillery.'

He was only telling Sherwood what he already knew. 'Damn their eyes!' he swore, fury and helplessness vying for top place in his emotions. He decided to try again, and he turned his horse back to the gates.

'Gurlin! Let us in. We have orders.'

'I cannot do that, sir,' Gurlin said, again showing himself. 'The Governor refuses you permission.'

'Who is your governor?'

'Sir Hamon L'Estrange.'

Evidently Sir Hamon was known to Sherwood, for he swore again. 'I have orders,' he repeated, for he could find nothing else to say in persuasion.

Gurlin said nothing, and came away from the window.

A stream of invectives now burst out of the Christian gentleman's mouth as he cursed them all. 'I will report you!' he roared. 'All of you. You Gurlin! And you L'Estrange! And all the people of this pestilential town! You have not heard the last of this! I will report you all to the Association. Daring to disobey the orders of the Government. You will pay for this.'

Gurlin came away from the window. His legs were shaking so much he had to sit down on the single wooden chair in the room.

Sir Hamon grinned. 'Well done, Master Gurlin. I am proud of you. It really was not so difficult, was it?'

'I hope we don't live to regret this day's work,' Gurlin whispered pathetically and turned and left them, descending the spiral stairs and striding away as quickly as he could before Sir Hamon involved him in some other outrage.

In impotent fury, Livewell Sherwood turned his troop around to march back to Norwich and Sir Hamon watched them go with a good deal of satisfaction.

Nicholas laughed as Sir Hamon closed the window. 'Wait 'till London hears about this.'

Sir Hamon gritted his teeth. 'Whatever the consequences, no Puritan scoundrel shall again be welcome in this town while I am Governor!' He laughed suddenly. 'Faith! Sherwood must have been surprised!'

§

'You have heard about that Captain Sherwood?' Roger asked as he reined his horse in before his father and brothers on the cliff top at Hunstanton, and slid out of the saddle to join them.

'He who tried to gain entry into Lynn?' Nicholas put the hood on the peregrine falcon which stood quietly on his outstretched and gauntleted hand, stroked the feathers on its back and then carefully handed it down to Christopher Townshend, the falconer, who stood ready to receive it. He removed the gauntlet.

Roger's eyes rested on a serene and unusually blue sea. It was low tide, and the sandbanks stood out like islands rising from the water. In the channel, two ships bearing full sail made their sedate way into Lynn. The cliffs were his favourite place, wild heathland, untouched by human hand, save for the ruins of St. Edmund's Chapel a few hundred yards away. His attention snapped back to Nicholas. 'Aye, the same. He's been pretty busy. The talk in Lynn is that he put down a counter-association drummed up by a Mr. Pettus and a Mr. Barker on behalf of the King.'

Sir Hamon frowned, removing his own gauntlet, and flexing his hand. 'Where was this? Norwich?'

'No, Lowestoft, Yelverton said.'

'I don't like it. They are strong, the Parliamentarians.'

Roger went on: 'The King's men near Norwich captured Oliver Cromwell himself.'

Sir Hamon began to walk back towards their horses, and all his sons fell into step with him. 'Arrogant peasant! I hope they gave him what he deserves.' He looked back at Roger. 'Did they?'

Roger shook his head. 'Well, it seems the Parliament men of Norwich rescued him before they could. But the upshot is that the Committee in Norwich thinks it a good idea to strengthen the garrison at Wisbech. And in Lynn, Palgrave and Hobart have been given two brass cannons and two dozen balls by the Parliamentary Committee,'

'Is that a fact?' Hamon the younger thought about it. 'They think there is going to be trouble here then. Could they know about our plans?'

Sir Hamon smiled mirthlessly. 'I cannot think how.'

'Very likely it is because you are governor,' Hamon the younger told them. 'They obviously see you—us—as a threat.'

Nicholas laughed. ''Tis no wonder when we have a Royalist as governor of Lynn. Of course they are getting twitchy. I reckon I would be from their point of view.'

'I don't know what you mean,' Sir Hamon retorted, his blue eyes wide with mock innocence. 'I have neither said nor done anything that could mean trouble for the Association.'

'Except deny Sherwood admittance,' Nicholas added.

'Well the cannon and shot will be very welcome when the time comes to declare for the King,' Sir Hamon laughed.

Roger now said: 'The Association won't like it.'

Sir Hamon's laughter arrested, and his bushy eyebrows met over his long nose. 'They will try to take Lynn by force, we know that. Lynn is of peculiar importance to both sides.'

'We can muster about five thousand men,' Nicholas said.

'It should be enough,' Hamon the younger put in.

'Depends on what the Association do. That peasant Cromwell will likely come back with his troops. And Manchester.' Sir Hamon nodded to his falconer Christopher Townshend, waiting by the cart on the track. The morning's kills had been loaded on the cart and the falcons were hooded and tied by the jesses to posts. He and another man brought the horses to them before turning to take birds and rabbits back to the Hall. Sir Hamon and his sons mounted and also turned their horses for Hunstanton Hall, cutting across the heath at a trot.

Sir Nicholas guided his large grey around a clump of heather. 'We'll deny them entry of course and then they will besiege us.'

'Just like that!' Hamon the younger snapped his fingers in the air.

Roger felt his insides lurch with excitement. Not that he had not known it, for it was an obvious move on the part of the Association and they had discussed it before, but now that Sir Hamon was actually governor, it had come closer as a reality. He would find action again, an opportunity to fight for his king and country and to put to good use all the battle training he had received.

Sir Hamon said: 'I have thought about that and we must make preparations. I have it on good authority that the King will send Newcastle to our relief. He is in the North at present.' He said nothing about his disappointment that Newcastle had not diverted to Lynn on his way from the south. 'We must make sure he can come to us from across the Wash. We need to arm ships in the harbour. It is of utmost importance. We also need to get arms into Lynn. And food.' He looked around at his sons, a big grin spreading across his thin features. 'So how do you feel like dressing up, gentlemen?'

§

Fully aware of the threat the L'Estrange family posed to the Eastern Association, Thomas Toll finally managed to secure a warrant for the arrest of Sir Hamon and all three of his sons and again Toby Peddar and Peter Belton the constables turned up at Hunstanton Hall.

'I could not say where my husband or sons are,' Lady Alice told them mendaciously. 'What do you want them for?'

'We have a warrant for their arrest,' Peddar announced and handed it to Lady Alice to read. 'We're just following orders, moi lady.'

'I know it.' She took a long time over reading the paper, for she knew that every moment's delay allowed her husband and sons to escape by the secret underground passage which led to an outlet behind the church. When the horses of the constables became fidgety and Lady Alice could pretend to read no longer, she folded the paper and gave it back. 'Are you going to search my home again?' she asked.

Peter Belton shook his head. 'No, moi lady. We will take your word for it.'

Her lips twitched and her eyes danced in response. As they rode away again with their small troop of horse, she said to Lady Anne: 'They did not even search. They have no stomach for arresting them.'

TWENTY

June, 1643

The sun beat down out of a hot blue sky, scorching the unripe wheat in the fields and the faces of the various tradesmen. It was Tuesday, the day for the market and everyone wanted to get a pitch on the Tuesday Market Place. The queue to get into Lynn was at a standstill and stretched for over a mile. People and animals alike waited with growing impatience.

'Wassup wi 'em?' someone demanded.

'They be occard,' Someone else responded. 'Suffen about keeping out Royalists.'

Roger stiffened beside Sir Hamon, who put a quieting hand on his forearm.

'Hin't no King's men hair,' Sir Hamon joined in the conversation. 'Yew c'n see fer yourself.'

Roger felt a laugh bubble up inside him. Of course Sir Hamon had been around Norfolk people all his life, so it was easy to get the dialect. But it did sound strange on him.

He glanced at his father. If Sir Hamon's speech was odd, his appearance was more so. He wore a grey wig that straggled down to his shoulders, topped by an old black hat and he sported a shaggy beard, the result of two weeks of neglect so that his usual goatee was lost in a mass of white hair. His usually pale skin was stained a dark tan colour with a good smattering of plain dirt, and he wore an old simple woollen doublet over an old plain shirt. He looked like a carrier. Roger too was in disguise, also with two weeks' worth of beard, stained black where ordinarily it would have been red and his long red hair, which always stood out in a crowd, was hidden beneath a black wig and a hat. He was dressed similarly to his father, while behind them on another cart, even Lady Anne would not have recognised Sir Nicholas. He was on his own, for Hamon the younger had gone home to Pakenham. His new wife was about to give birth and he was anxious to be there.

Roger grinned to himself. He thrived on danger, and this was dangerous work. Discovery could mean the death penalty, not only on account of the hidden ammunition, but also on account of their disguises, for they looked not like Royalists but like common men. That would condemn them as Royalist spies.

They had an open wagon and on it barrels, some containing flour, some with peas and other dried food stuffs in the top quarter of the barrel while beneath a leather cloth the other three-quarters hid gunpowder. Beneath a false bottom in the cart were muskets.

The queue moved up two carts, surprising them all. The sun baked down on them and the sweat trickled down Roger's back. He had wanted to chew a length of straw, but Sir Hamon said that was going a bit far. Besides, it wasn't the season yet for straw.

'I wonder what the time is?' Roger said in a low voice.

In a much louder voice Sir Hamon said: 'The toime? Wha' d'you want t' know the toime fer? When we get there be when we get there!'

Entering into the spirit of the thing Roger countered: 'Be toime t'be a-gorn, then.'

The queue moved on again.

'Oi do wish them bors would get a-movin',' the man from behind said.

'Wassup wi' you?' his wife replied. 'You hint nowhere else t'be. Stop yur barneying. Yur getting on moi wick!'

'Well, now and tha's a rummun!'

Roger struggled not to laugh beside Sir Hamon. ''Tis like another language! Are they really speaking English?' he whispered.

'I think there may be some doubt,' Sir Hamon whispered back.

The cart moved forward again, Sir Hamon moving the heavy horses further forward.

'You know what all this be about, don't you?' the man from behind said knowingly.

Sir Hamon looked around at him. 'No?'

'They be after the gov'nor and his sons. There be a warrant out for them. And them other Royalists.'

'Oi did hair that. Do they think Sir 'Ammon be a fool?'

'Oi reckon not. Sir 'Ammon do what Sir 'Ammon do, Oi reckon. He be a crafty one, Sir 'Ammon.'

'You mislike Sir 'Ammon?' Sir Hamon asked.

'Ooh no! Sir 'Ammon always be koind to his people, Oi hair. But he be clever loike. Whoy he could be hair now and we wouldn't know!'

Roger choked and hastily coughed.

'Oi reckon so,' Sir Hamon acknowledged.

They were approaching the gates at last and the guards, set up by the Association through Mr. Toll, were becoming bored with their role and started waving people through the gate.

But the wagon, with its barrels stacked two high and lashed with ropes, was stopped.

Roger and Sir Hamon waited, hearts thudding, as the guards asked who they were.

'John Dix,' Sir Hamon said, still with the Norfolk accent. 'Oi got foine flour.'

Roger felt for the dagger beneath his tunic and behind the seat, concealed, was his sword. He could get it quickly if need be.

Sir Hamon had done this run on more than one occasion and his shaggy appearance was known to the guards. One of them knocked a barrel. Roger held his breath, trying not to give away that his whole body tensed ready for action. Then the guard opened the lid of one of the barrels, hitting it with his musket stock to free it. He peered inside the barrel.

Roger held his breath.

'Hin't nuffen there but peas and flour,' Sir Hamon told the man.

'Where be you from?' the guard asked.

'Setchey,' Sir Hamon replied.

'An' who be this hair?' the guard asked next pointing at Roger.

'Oh this be Robert Drew,' Sir Hamon replied. He do 'elp me sometoimes.'

At last, evidently satisfied, the guard at the back replaced the barrel lid and they waved them on. Sir Hamon slapped the reins on the backs of the horses and they lumbered through the gate.

A short time later they were in the Tuesday Market Place and stopped outside the Griffin.

Immediately the landlord appeared, summoned someone from within and a man helped rolled the barrels down the ramp and into the cellar beneath the inn.

The guns followed. They were more difficult to conceal, but when Nicholas' cart drew up he positioned it so that it gave them the perfect cover to pull out the planks for the false bottom and slide them down the ramp as well.

The market place was busy, with stalls still in the process of being set up, but buyers were there, wandering among the stalls. Roger heaved the last barrel off the cart and rolled it down the wooden ramp into the cellar, looked up and his eyes met and locked with those of Ruth.

His heart almost jumped out of his chest with shock, for he saw her blink in recognition.

She was with two women and a young gentleman. He wondered who he was. An ordinary looking man, of less than average height. In fact, he was smaller than Ruth.

They finished unloading the cart and the other cart waited behind.

'Don't let it get damp, John,' Sir Hamon said to the landlord. 'It'll be no good to us damp.'

'You can rely on me,' John replied.

Roger joined them in the cellar and now as his eyes grew accustomed to the gloom he asked: 'Where are the other muskets? I don't see them.'

'Ed Barlow has 'em,' John said. 'They be safe. When will you act, Sir 'Ammon?'

'When the time is right,' Sir Hamon replied evasively.

'Can you rely on Newcastle? He din't come afore when we thought he would.'

'He has promised. When the time is right we will act and he will come to our aid. We need to be patient.'

The landlord was a worried man. He had much to lose. 'These are dangerous times and they still search for you, Sir 'Ammon. And your sons,' he added, casting a glance in Roger's direction. 'And if they catch you—'

Sir Hamon stopped him. 'They won't, my friend. Ah Nick, move the cart up.'

As soon as he could and before Sir Hamon had finished his business at the Griffin, Roger wandered off to find Ruth somewhere in the bustling Tuesday Market Place. It was impossible to see anyone, for the wealthy and the not-so-wealthy jostled for space between the packed-in stalls and barrows laden with all the goods a well-stocked market was known for, to say nothing of the cattle, sheep, pigs and goats, bleating, and lowing and squealing their protests. A pie man with his tray of pies balanced on his head called out his wares: 'A pie for a penny!' and Roger paid his penny and bought one. It was either still hot, or had been warmed by the sun—more likely the latter—and he ate it with relish for it had still been dark when he had forced some breakfast into his reluctant belly.

'My good man, be so good as to move out of the way.' The male voice beside him made him jump and Roger turned around, insulted. Never in his life had he been addressed as anyone's good man, much less asked to move, unless by a member of his family. He glared at the gentleman, outraged, but then his eyes rested on Ruth beside him and her aunt next to her.

Her eyes fluttered in recognition, then widened, warning him to play his part. He touched his forelock and bowed and said in slow broad Norfolk: 'Beggin' your pardon, ladies, sir. Din't see you there!' He stepped aside.

Ruth bit her lip and her dark eyes twinkled. 'Thank you,' and she moved forward to examine the woollen cloth on the stall.

Roger stayed quite close at the other end of the stall, waiting and noticing that Ruth fingered the grey woollen material which he supposed would make another dreary dress. How he ached to see her in strong vibrant reds, greens or blues, better suited to her dark colouring than the interminable greys and browns and blacks.

Uninterested in the cloth, Ruth's aunt began talking in earnest to the gentleman and Ruth moved along a little further towards Roger.

'What are you doing here?' She hissed without turning to look at him.

'Trying not to get caught,' he whispered back. 'Where have you been? I've waited for you.'

'They won't let me out on my own.'

'. . . don't you think so Ruth?' The aunt claimed Ruth's attention.

Conscious of the eyes of the gentleman upon him and not wanting to draw attention to himself, Roger did not dare meet the man's eyes as he might usually have done, but looked down subserviently in an attitude he had seen in the lower classes who knew their place.

'What are you doing here still?' the gentleman demanded roughly.

Roger grumbled slowly: 'Oi hin't hurtin' nuffen.' He hoped he sounded suitably dim-witted.

'If you do not move along, I'll have you whipped.'

Roger gripped his bottom lip and at his sides his hands balled into fists. He knew what he would like to do with this jumped-up little Puritan with his pleasant fat face and dark brown eyes. He could not resist the urge to say insolently: 'Only lookin' at the bootiful lady.'

Ruth choked. The man's rather large eyes bulged even more. 'Why you insolent scoundrel!' He raised his stick.

Roger couldn't take the risk of being caught. He tugged his forelock again to Ruth and dodged away as the gentleman took several bold steps towards him, waving his stick threateningly.

'He didn't mean anything by it,' Roger heard Ruth plead behind him. 'Leave him be, please Mr. Calthorpe. He's nothing but a poor man.'

'Then he should know his place,' Calthorpe responded, but already he had brought the stick down again and he seemed to have calmed.

Roger dodged swiftly, and turned into Stockfishrow where he waited, leaning against the wall of yet another inn, the Woolpack, hoping Ruth would follow.

It was some time later when Ruth found him just he had all but given up hope.

'I couldn't see where you had gone,' she complained.

'I didn't know if you would want to,' he responded roughly, taking her hand in his and leading her down towards the brewery lane. 'I thought perhaps you preferred the company of the Puritan gentleman with you. He is obviously a rich man, for all his plain clothes, such a fine gentlemen.'

Her eyes widened in what he thought was alarm. His heart flipped. She was so prim, but so beautiful. Had he been right? Did she indeed prefer the rich gentleman's company?

'That is Mr. Charles Calthorpe,' she told him after a long silence. 'My cousin. My father thinks he would be a suitable match for me, and he has come a-courting.'

Jealousy sliced through Roger like a physical pain. Tight-lipped, he pulled her roughly into the lane but instead of stopping by the brewery he led her down to the river's edge. He turned to face her. She looked at him anxiously, her eyes big and round in her beautiful face. Did she not realise how much he loved her?

'You cannot marry him!' he said, suddenly at a loss, his heart hammering in his ribs.

'He is a very nice Christian man, good and kind.'

'Who beats lesser mortals?'

'Well, you were not keeping to your place.'

'My place is beside you,' he murmured.

She looked down and her white cap hid her face from him. 'That cannot be. You know it, and I know it.'

He took a breath in through his teeth. 'What is this all about Ruth? Have we not been courting these last months?'

'Is that what it is? Courting?'

'What he hell—I mean what on earth did you think it was?'

'I don't know. You have never said. I thought perhaps it was an *affaire* that we had.'

Despite his panic, he could not hide a smile. 'My dear girl, trust me, we have not had an *affaire*.'

'Then what?' she snapped. 'You have made love to me, and yet you never speak of the future for us. What am I supposed to think? You make sport with me.'

Anger flashed up in him. 'Make sport with you? Damn it all, Ruth, I want to marry you!'

Her dark met his straightly. 'Do you? But you must know we cannot marry when we are on different sides.'

She doubted him! After all that had passed between them, she doubted him! 'You are surprised that I want you for my wife?'

She nodded. 'Yes, I am.'

He frowned. 'Why?'

She hesitated and he had a foreboding that she would say something he would not like. 'There is talk about you,' she said at last. 'Why you are not yet wed. They say . . .'

His heart missed a beat as he realised that they had turned her against him. 'Go on,' he encouraged, dangerously. 'What, pray, do they say about me?'

Fearful, now, she tried to back down. 'It doesn't matter what they say.'

'Oh you cannot back out now, Ruth. What do they say?'

'I ought to go. They will be looking for me.'

'No doubt about it. What do they say, Ruth?'

She swallowed, peeped up at him, and then looked away guiltily.

'Ruth?'

She was near to tears, but it did not move him. She swallowed again. 'They say—they say you are a drunkard and a gambler and that you have many women.' She flushed again, and ventured to glance up at him. Something in his face must have alarmed her, for she said: 'You are angry!'

'You are surprised? My character has been destroyed in your eyes by lies, and I am not supposed to be angry?' he studied her face. 'You believe, them, don't you?'

'No,' she replied quickly, but she could not meet his eyes.

She had believed them, he thought, and they had turned her against him. Anger rose into his throat like bitter bile. He had lost her because of their lies.

'Well, they were right,' he snapped. He turned away from her and stood on the edge of the river looking down into its muddy depths and the pain in his heart clawed at him. 'You will never want to finish up with a scoundrel like me.'

'Roger, don't!'

He spun round. 'Well, that's right, isn't it, madam? What am I? A mere third son, with a small inheritance which I have not yet collected, no land, no prospects. And remember, I am a confirmed drunkard, I gamble away what money I have, and I could never remain faithful to you. But worst of all, I am a king's man. Why on earth would you or anyone else want to marry me?'

She winced at the sarcasm in his voice, the violence of his anger, but she raised her head erect, her own anger sparking in her eyes. 'I think I ought to go.'

'I think you should.'

He went back to staring at the river as it lapped against the quay, furious and hurt. She might just as well marry the distant cousin, he thought viciously. Because it was clear he would never come up to their standards.

He heard the rustle of her clothes as she turned away and left him.

Damn it! Damn the war! Damn the sanctimonious Puritans! And Damn Valentine Pell!

TWENTY-ONE

The morning had fulfilled its promise for by two o'clock the heat was searingly oppressive and the air rose from the dried mud track road in wavering mirages. The wagon bumped along the road in a lazy fashion, the horses lumbering and occasionally snorting in protest. Sir Hamon, having received little response from Roger to his efforts at conversation had given up and was half dozing in the heat.

Roger sat beside him tight-lipped, angry and deeply hurt, going over again the conversation with Ruth an hour previously.

'So where did you get to?' Sir Hamon asked suddenly. 'We waited over an hour for you.'

Roger scratched at his whiskers. 'I went to the market.'

'I saw you disappear up Stockfishrow,' Sir Hamon accused. 'And then I saw a young Puritan woman follow you. Would that have been Mistress Pell by any chance?'

Roger did not want to talk about it, but he would not lie to his father. 'Perhaps.'

After a short pause Sir Hamon continued: 'She's a striking wench, I own that. Any man would be captivated by her. Faith! *I* am captivated by her! She must have many admirers.'

'Charles Calthorpe is among her admirers. She is going to marry him.' His words were clipped with suppressed hurt anger.

Sir Hamon looked at his son, his brows raised. 'Oh?'

'Evidently he's a good Puritan. Meanwhile, did you know that your son is a drunkard, a gambler, mixes with all the wrong sort, and is also a womaniser? No? Well I have to say it came as something of a surprise to me too! Besides being only a *third* son, with a paltry inheritance, and a *Royalist!*'

Sir Hamon cast a sideways glance at his son. 'Is that what she said?'

'It's what they have told her.'

'Is it true?'

Roger cast smouldering eyes on him.

'Well,' Sir Hamon excused this lapse, 'I am only your father. I do not get to hear everything my sons do. Though I do know you have a way with women.'

'In the past.' Roger spoke through his teeth. 'And I have never—*never!*—made sport of any gently-reared female in my life!'

'Oh! I see.'

Roger glowered at the road ahead. 'As for gambling,' he went on after a few moments, 'I view that as for fools. I do not have enough money of my own to risk. And I do not drink to excess and I never have.'

'But that is what they have told the lady.' Sir Hamon considered it. 'She believed them, it seems.'

'I think I have been painted as black as possible, and that she now thinks I am the most reprehensible rogue unhung! She will have Calthorpe.'

Sir Hamon thought it over. 'A L'Estrange is as good a match as any woman could expect to make,' he said. 'But it seems to me that the lady has no faith in you.'

'Well, you have no need to be anxious over my intentions in her behalf any longer. It is ended.'

Nicholas hailed them from the cart behind and Sir Hamon and Roger both looked around. 'Father, we are not alone!'

'Are you sure?' Sir Hamon asked.

'Riders. Several of them. I caught a glimpse of their dust.' He pointed through the trees, which were sparse enough to allow them a view across the field to the road. The dust cloud kicked up by galloping horses was unmistakable.

Sir Hamon swore profanely. 'How many?'

'Four that I could see and they ride hard.'

They could not outrun them with the carts.

'I mislike it,' Roger said. 'If they are after us it would be better if they found me, rather than you. Pull up the wagon.'

Sir Hamon met his son's eyes, but he did pull the wagon up and Nicholas stopped behind them. 'What if they discover who you are? There's a warrant out for you as well.'

'Then I rely on you and Nick to get me out of trouble. Go with Nick and take the trail into the woods. I'll continue on the road until they overtake me.'

Nicholas, who had pulled up his own wagon overheard the last bit. 'He's right, Father. If they arrest you that will stop all our plans. Come.'

Reluctantly Sir Hamon dismounted from his wagon and quickly climbed up beside Sir Nicholas.

Roger slid along the board to the driving seat, whipping up the reins and the heavy horses trundled onward, keeping to the road.

Nicholas took his cart off the road to the right where the forest was denser and was soon lost to sight in the dense bracken and foliage.

Not a moment too soon, for less than a minute later four pounding, sweating horses galloped by them, too intent on catching the cart to glance to the right or to the left.

Roger found himself surrounded and pulled up the cart.

'Do you want me?' he asked, adopting the slow thick Norfolk accent and looking from one to the other of them.

'What you got on the cart there?' one of them, he supposed their captain or leader asked. Seated on his horse, the man was on a level with Roger.

'Nuffen. Oi jest deliver flour to the Griffin in Lynn. They be empty kegs.'

The captain nodded to another man who dismounted, climbed up onto the cart and removed the lid of the first barrel. He nodded back confirmation.

'Who are you?' The captain demanded.

'No-lyen Samuels,' Roger replied dishonouring this assumed name, and wishing the man on the cart behind him would get off. He could feel it jolting as the man's weight shifted during his search. Roger knew that it would not be long before he found something of interest.

'And where be the other man with you?'

'What other man?'

'I saw another man with you.'

'Can't hev. Hin't nobbut me.'

The captain was not convinced and he looked around him as if expecting to see another man pop out of the undergrowth at any moment. 'Know what I think?'

'No, sir.'

'I think you be one of them fugitives.'

'What be a fugi—'

'Fugitive. Runaway.'

'Me? I hin't run away from nobody.'

'Look what I've found!'

The triumphant voice from behind him made Roger look round to see his own sword being waved in the air. His heart sank. The game was up and he knew it. He just hoped he had given Nick and his father enough time to get away.

'Get down from there,' the captain commanded, aiming a pistol at

Roger's abdomen. Seeing no point in refusing, he wrapped the reins around the brake and clambered down to the road, where he stood facing the captain.

At a gesture from the captain the man with the sword jumped off the wagon and came to Roger's side and another man dismounted to guard Roger on his left while he stood quite calmly watching them. He held himself straight. He was no country yokel now, but a proud cavalier, no matter what his clothes said, and he looked the captain straight in the eyes.

The captain and the fourth man dismounted and stood in front of him. The captain was quite a small man and he had to look up to Roger.

'Know what I think?' the captain said, enjoying this moment of victory.

'What do you think?'

'I think you are one of them L'Estranges.'

'Do you?'

'Not sir Hamon. You be too young for that. No I reckon you be one of his sons.'

Roger didn't answer him. Let the man wonder. Why provide him with information?

'And I am putting you under arrest.'

'Is that what you think?' They were not going to take him, Roger decided, eyeing the pistol. Pistols were notoriously inaccurate and, unless by accident, no-one could hit a moving target. Roger took a calculated gamble that, even though the distance between him and the captain was just a few yards, the matchlock pistol would take a heartbeat to fire.

In one swift movement he grabbed his own sword out of the hand of the man on his right, shoving him so that he overbalanced, and took off into the forest.

The captain fired the pistol, but it missed as Roger had expected. There was no time to reload. Instead they abandoned their horses and charged after him, yelling, as he hurtled through the bracken and into the dense summer undergrowth. He had the advantage of longer legs and he did not stop until he saw a pair of legs dangling from a tree branch just ahead of him. In that instant he spun round, sword raised, to face his pursuers as Sir Nicholas swung down from the tree to land on Roger's right side, as light on his feet as a butterfly. The pursuers crashed out of the bracken into the clearing and stopped dead, confronted now by two men, not one.

For a long moment, no-one moved. The hammering in Roger's heart had become the fizz of excitement at the coming fight. His sharpened senses focused on the men, on his brother, on the bumps and dips in the ground, the drift of sunlight through the tree canopy, all useful information to a swordsman. Roger and Nicholas in unison began moving in a circle, Nicholas to the right, Roger to the left, circling the soldiers who stood still watching them, their own swords held out in challenge. The pursuers separated into two pairs, turning to face Roger and Nicholas as they moved.

'Two to one,' Nicholas murmured. 'Should be interesting.'

Both Nicholas and Roger had height which gave them the advantage of a longer reach, but smaller opponents, although more easily overpowered, could slip under their guard, aiming for long undefended legs. Roger studied the two opposite him. They were a good deal shorter than he was. Less skilled. One man was stiff, tense, his body too upright, his sword held out defensively in front of him; the other was more confident, but he was much smaller than his partner. Stiff held back, letting Shorty come forward.

'Fancy your chances, do you?' Roger asked, a sardonic lift to his brow.

'Oi can take you any day,' Shorty growled. Roger smiled. The man's speech declared him a member of the lower orders and therefore his training in the sword was recent. He did not have the advantage of being taught from infancy as the L'Estranges had, so he would lack the necessary skill. And very likely that went for the other soldiers too. No-one could learn swordsmanship in a few hasty lessons. Their technique would be cut and thrust.

On his right, Nicholas engaged the first of his opponents, skillfully putting one attacker in the way of the other, so that he only had one at a time to deal with. Quickly he slashed the first man in the sword arm which took him out of the fight.

At the same moment, Shorty attacked towards Roger's legs, but he'd expected it and blocked. Shorty brought his blade beneath Roger's and heaved it upward, but Roger was too quick for him, again blocking. They were now in close to each other. Sour breath from the other man's panting made Roger want to gag, but of greater concern was Stiff who still hung back in an agony of indecision. With half an eye on Stiff, Roger brought his leg around Shorty's legs. The man was no expert. He did not keep his feet planted firmly on the ground and that made it easy for him to lose his balance. A moment later a bodily shove finished the job so that he fell backward over a fallen branch.

Roger could have followed up this advantage and killed the man. Instead he cried: 'Have done! Yield and I will spare you!'

Shorty was having none of it. Furious, he glared at Roger and scrambled to his feet in the most ungainly fashion, backing off to regain his posture.

Still Stiff hung back.

'Do you not know when someone has the mastery over you?' Roger demanded.

As he recovered, Shorty made the fatal mistake of being goaded into raising his sword, both hands on the pommel, in an attempt to cleave Roger's head in two. In a flash Roger's sword deliberately slashed the flesh against the man's ribs. Not a fatal blow but enough in this instance to cause the man to stop, drop his sword and clutch his side, doubling over.

'I could have killed you,' Roger told him as blood crept over the man's doublet. He sank to his knees, but Roger knew it was only a flesh wound.

But there was no time to dwell on what had happened. With a yell, Stiff seemed to have found his courage and he now rushed at Roger, his sword arm outstretched to full limit, an inexpert move if ever there was one. He left himself undefended. All Roger needed to do was sidestep and Stiff sailed straight past him at full speed.

Roger could also have killed him in that moment. Instead he stood and watched him as he hurtled forwards and crashed into the trunk of one of the mighty oaks of the forest, hitting his face on the tree and breaking his blade. He slid to the ground, blood pouring from his nose and mouth, evidently dazed.

Roger turned to see how his brother fared. He need not have worried. Sir Nicholas stood over a soldier who lay sprawled on the ground, the point of his sword at the man's throat, while the other sat propped against another tree clutching his sword arm.

'What shall I do with him?' Nicholas enquired of Roger, looking at the man in front of him. 'Shall I kill him?'

Roger came over to peer down at what turned out to be a mere boy, no more than fifteen or sixteen, his eyes wide open in terror. He didn't speak, but his brown eyes fixed on each of them in turn, awaiting his fate.

Roger knew Nicholas had no intention of killing anyone, especially not a fellow Norfolk man, a boy at that. But he said: 'We could hang him from a tree and use him as target practice.'

'Hmm. Let's string them all up then.'

The boy on the ground scrambled as if to get away, but Nicholas dug the sword point deeper into his throat until there was a little blood showing. 'Please! Please don't!'

They looked at each other as if to consider. 'What think you?' Nicholas asked. 'Shall we let them go?'

Roger said. 'Let this one go.'

'We won't tell,' the boy on the ground promised. It was an idle promise, Roger knew, but of no consequence. If they were believed, they could not prove who they were.

Sir Nicholas pulled his sword away. 'You live 'till another day, sir. On your feet!'

The boy scrambled up and stood bravely in front of them. His disarmed friends staggered to join him.

'Well go on then,' Sir Nicholas encouraged him.

A smile quivered about the boy's mouth. Then he took off for all the world like a pack of wolves were at his heels, his friends close behind.

'By the time they've walked all the way back to Lynn and given an accounting, we shall be long gone.'

Roger shook his head and sighed. As the fizz in his veins left him, he felt suddenly drained.

'Amateurs,' Nicholas derided. 'But it was foolish of you not to kill that Puritan when you had the chance. What if that had not stopped him? You'd be dead.'

'They don't know what they're doing. Are they trying to train raw recruits into swordsmen? They can't do it! 'Twould be murder to kill someone so incompetent.' He picked up their fallen hats and handed Nick's to him. 'Where's Father?' Nicholas paused in the act of gathering up the fallen weapons. 'I made him hide in the woods. Two more of those fools are looking for him.'

'There are more of them?'

'Yes.'

Nick put the weapons in the cart. Roger rounded up all the horses. 'Do we take the horses with us?'

'Why not? I think they owe us a half dozen at least, don't you?' Nicholas replied with a grin, referring to the time Hunstanton Hall had been raided and horses taken.

'Undoubtedly.' Roger tied two of them to the back of the hidden cart. 'Come,' Nicholas said. 'We need to find Father.'

Leaving carts and horses off the road and hidden in the forest, they each took a soldier's saddled horse and began their search for their father.

TWENTY-TWO

Thomas Thorowgood, the rector of Grimston and Little Massingham about five miles east of King's Lynn, pulled on a dressing robe and grumbled to himself. Taking hold of the night candle he shuffled out onto the landing and down the stairs as the knocker on the front door banged again. Several times in fact.

'Alright, alright,' he grumbled, more to himself than anyone else, because he doubted if anyone outside could hear him.

He hurried as much as he dared, for it was past midnight and the hall was as dark as a cave, save for the single candle he carried. It's light barely reached the stairs and Master Thorowgood had no intention of measuring his length at the bottom.

The urgent banging continued without letup. 'Alright, alright,' he muttered again as his bare feet finally found the cool floor tiles of the oak-panelled hallway.

'What is it, dear?' his wife enquired, leaning over the banister with her own candle, evidently confident in the rector's ability to discern the nature of a visit at the stroke of midnight before even the door was opened. Her dear bit back some suitable retort.

He reached the door, set the candle down on the table and turned the key in the lock. Even though he turned the handle, the door remained firmly shut. The bolt! Looking around to where he knew there was a chair, he padded over to it and dragged it across the hall tiles with a scraping and screeching of wood on tiles. Now he was able to clamber onto the chair and with an effort, pulled back the bolt.

Whoever was on the other side of the door tried to open it and Thorowgood only just about managed to get off the chair when the door was forced open, pushing the chair and the reverend, out of the way.

Thorowgood picked up the candle he had set down and raised it to the visitor's face. It took him several moments to recognise him, for the candle cast weird shadows on a face creased in agony all but covered with long grey hair and a wild beard. He struggled to stand. ''Pon my soul! Sir Hamon L'Estrange!'

'Sir Hamon L'Estrange?' Mistress Thorowgood ran down the stairs less carefully than her husband and arrived in the hall in her nightgown, a shawl wrapped around her in an effort to keep her modesty rather than to keep her warm, for it was mid summer.

Sir Hamon stood clutching the door and looked like he might fall on the floor at any moment. Thorowgood took his arm to support him and sat him down in the chair he had just used and after a quick look outside in the dark to make sure Sir Hamon was alone, he shut the door again and turned the key in the lock. One could not be too cautious in these difficult times.

'Sir Hamon, what are you doing here at this hour?' Mistress Thorowgood demanded.

'He's not well, I think,' the rector said, again raising the candle to Sir Hamon's agonised face glowing ghostly in the meagre light.

'Please—I need your help,' Sir Hamon gasped. He shivered violently.

Mistress Thorowgood put her hand on Sir Hamon's forehead. 'He's got a fever,' she announced. 'I'll fetch some ale from the buttery.'

'What happened to you sir?' The rector removed his dressing robe and draped it over Sir Hamon.

'I lost my horse around Castle Rising,' Sir Hamon managed with difficulty and not altogether untruthfully. 'Then I lost my way.'

The good reverend shivered as he stood in the vast hallway in his white nightshirt. 'Lost your way, sir?'

Sir Hamon was compelled to explain further which required a little embroidery. 'I was thrown from my horse in the woods.'

'Forgive me, sir, but that forest must be well-known to you.'

'It is not. The road is, of course, but I could not take that. There is a warrant out for my arrest, sir.'

'Well yes.'

'It has been two days. I've eaten nothing. I drank from a stream which made me throw up—'

'I'm not surprised! The water in the streams is toxic! All those rotting leaves and things. Ugh!'

'I'm asking for sanctuary. For the love of God, will you help me?'

Thorowgood did not hesitate. He was known to all as a friend, making no distinction between Parliamentarian and Cavalier. He knew where his Christian duty lay. 'Of course. You are welcome here.'

'Thank God!' Sir Hamon looked like he was about to burst into tears and Thorowgood eyed him with alarm.

'Do not upset yourself, my dear sir. You are safe now.'

'I know this is putting you in danger,' Sir Hamon managed with an effort. He passed a weary hand over his face. 'If word could be got to my wife in Hunstanton . . ?'

'Of course, Sir Hamon,' Thorowgood's wife said from behind him. 'Whatever are you doing, Thomas? Get Sir Hamon to bed before he collapses on the floor!'

§

Roger and Nicholas had spent the rest of the day searching the woods around Castle Rising for their father, but as night fell they had no option but to return to Hunstanton. The following day at three in the morning they left Hunstanton with some of their hired men, to search again, only to return after dark with failure weighing heavily on both of them.

The third day they widened their search.

'He's been captured, I'm sure,' Nicholas said, his eyes searching the undergrowth.

Roger was exhausted and demoralised. The thought of his father being incarcerated in Wisbech Castle made him feel sick to the pit of his stomach. 'Then why have we not heard? You'd think we'd hear Toll crowing all the way to Hunstanton!'

'True. The alternative is that he has been killed.'

'We'd have heard that too, if the soldiers had killed him. Perhaps he is sick.'

This was the most fearful of all the possibilities, the thought of their father lying sick or injured and in dire need of help and they could not find him.

It was gone ten o'clock when they arrived home, just about dark and their mother had waited up for them. Nicholas shook his head at her as he handed the reins of his horse to a servant. Coming into the house, he took her in his arms. She clung to him for a moment, but did not cry.

'He must be hiding somewhere,' she repeated. She would not have it that he had come to harm.

'We have found no sign of a fight,' Nicholas told her, 'so it could be that he has gone to ground.'

'But where?' she asked in despair.

A little later as Roger and Nicholas ate a late supper in the dining room alone, Nicholas asked yet again: 'How did the troopers know that we were in Lynn?'

The question plagued Roger day and night, because the answer that kept nagging him was the most unwelcome one.

She would not have betrayed him, surely? He thought he had her measure, that she would not give a man over to his death. Yet he could not be sure. She was on the side of the enemy. Her loyalties lay with her father, not with Roger. She was a Puritan. They had persuaded her against him. Had she denounced them?

His tired agonised brain tried to make sense of it. He thought of the loving way she had behaved towards him, allowing him to kiss her. He had not imagined her response, surely. That had been some weeks—months—ago. Two days ago she had changed, believing him to be a rogue, and very plainly pointed out that they were on different sides. Had she betrayed them to Toll?

In the heat of anxiety for his father, the hurt of rejection now turned to cold hard fury. If that were the case, he would kill her.

Four days after the attack from the troopers, Roger, beard neatly trimmed once more, but wearing ordinary clothes—his favourite leather doublet—left Hunstanton Hall for Lynn. Two hours later he left his horse in the care of the ostler at the Griffin and went in to find out if there was any news of his father. Finding nothing, he turned his attention to Ruth and walked the distance to Wingate. He was just in time to see her entering her aunt's house, and his heart made that annoying trip in his chest.

The sun had disappeared and an iron sky proclaimed rain. The light was beginning to fail as if it were dusk, not morning. Which was ideal, for he would not be so easily seen in his dark clothes. He studied the row of terraced houses and four houses along from College Lane, was the Leads' house.

Having worked out which house it was, he marched quickly down College Lane to the river bank. The bank was busy. Ships and boats lined the edge of the river, and dockers loaded and unloaded into the warehouses which were just behind the bank backing on to Wingate. Further along was the Three Crowns tavern. And at the side of that was a dark alley which would take him to the rear gardens of the houses in Wingate. It would serve.

As thunder rumbled out towards the Wash where the sky was darkest, he slipped into the alley, and at the end, with heart thumping, he scaled a wall landing behind the rose bushes in a garden. It was not the Leads' garden, and he had to scale two more carrstone walls until he was in the right one. Meantime the sunlight had gone altogether and an eerie darkness settled over Lynn.

The Leads' house was a large, wide timber-framed house as befitted a banker's house and a window was open on the ground floor, but he had to pass the kitchen window first. Just as he was about to duck beneath it, the door opened and a maid came out, carrying a bucket of kitchen waste which she put in a barrel next to the far wall. Roger stayed quite still in the opposite corner, tucked against the house and because she didn't glance his way, he remained undiscovered. He heard her mention something about the coming storm as she closed the door and he didn't wait for more. Ducking beneath the kitchen window and the door window, he came to the other end of the house where the window was open just a crack.

This was the point of no return, he thought, his heart still thumping. If he were caught it would be prison and probably the death sentence. And his father would likely disown him for being such an idiot! If his father were still alive. He shuddered at that thought and willed it from his mind, wiping sweat from his face on his sleeve. This is what he was here to find out. That and what part Ruth had played in it.

Cautiously he listened then opened the window wider to peer inside. It was some kind of sitting room, but there was no-one in it. Nimbly, he climbed inside, putting the stay back on the window so that it didn't slam shut and went silently and quickly to the door, listening.

Outside, all was quiet, so he let himself out and into a cool, dark, panelled passageway which would help to conceal him if need be.

Again he listened. He could hear the drone of conversation, but he had no way of knowing whether Ruth was involved, or whether servants spoke, but he went towards the sound anyway.

Footsteps clattered on the flagstone floor and he pressed himself beneath the staircase. A male servant carrying a salver with wine and goblets on it passed him without seeing him, but he followed the servant at a distance and saw him open a door and enter.

The sound of conversation grew louder through the opened door and as he recognised Ruth's voice his heart thudded harder.

'So you think there will be trouble, Father?'

'I most certainly do. We are one of only two families who are on the side of Parliament. All our neighbours are Royalist, as you are very well aware, from the Pastons at Appleton, the Cobbes at Sandringham and the L'Estranges,' he added with loathing.

Another male voice, possibly Ruth's uncle, said: 'The L'Estranges are the most dangerous. I don't think the Cobbes will ever do anything. But notice how the L'Estranges fought their way out of capture. They are ruthless men.'

Roger digested this. So they had not captured Sir Hamon then.

Sir Valentine said: 'I am convinced the L'Estranges intend to declare Lynn for the King.' Roger smirked in his dark hiding place. So they knew. However, what could Pell do about it?

'And what then?'

'Parliament will have to send Cromwell with his troops to stop L'Estrange. But that could put us right in the middle of a battle. I would wish that you Ruth, were not here then.' There was a short silence then Sir Valentine went on: 'If it were not for the L'Estrange boy, I would have you back in Dersingham.'

Again there was a silence, then: 'Well, have you nothing to say, girl? May the good Lord give me patience!'

Ruth said quite calmly, 'I will go wherever you wish me to go.'

'Then, if you have any sense, girl, you will marry Charles Calthorpe.'

'As far as I am aware he has not asked for my hand.'

Hope surged in Roger's breast.

'No. And it is no wonder. You and L'Estrange are the talk of Lynn! Your reputation is quite ruined.'

'I have done nothing for which you need to be ashamed, sir,' Ruth replied, just as calmly.

The voice of a woman, her aunt: ''Tis of no consequence, Ruth, you have associated with a known drunkard, a womaniser, and a Royalist. Your name has been besmirched, girl.'

Sir Valentine continued as if she had not spoken: 'Well Calthorpe, surprisingly, is still interested in you. Damned if I know why! The man must be besotted. If he offers, we will accept him. But you cannot carry on in this loose manner. And neither can I have you back in Dersingham. Your mother and I shall be away and besides it is too near to Hunstanton. You are better off here with your aunt and uncle. But I absolutely forbid you to go out on your own. Mary, I will hold you responsible. That devil L'Estrange is capable of anything.'

Mary murmured something.

Roger compressed his lips in a smirk. If only he knew!

He heard Ruth say: 'Father, I am twenty years old and am I not even to go out?'

Her father's voice raised in anger: 'Gently-bred females do not go walking in town on their own like common harlots! And if you have it mind to carry on a liaison with that man I shall disown you, do you hear me?'

Roger winced at the harsh words, and he heard Ruth answer, but he did not catch what she said.

'Get you gone, woman, go to your room.'

The door opened and Roger retreated quickly into the shadows. He caught a glimpse of Ruth as she came out of the room and ran up the stairs, her hand to her face. The door slammed shut as if someone had kicked it. Roger frowned. So this is what Ruth had to endure on his behalf. He'd had no idea. He wondered then at her betrayal. Because she must have betrayed them. John at the Griffin was the only other person who knew who they were, and he would not talk.

With no-one around, Roger quickly followed Ruth up the wide staircase, making sure his feet made no sound on the oak stairs.

At the top he halted and he was just in time to see her disappear into a door at the end of the dark passageway. Silently he made his way to it. Without knocking he opened the door as quietly as he could and went in. It clicked shut behind him, and he turned the key in the lock.

The room too was dark for the thick clouds obscured what little light there might have been from the window. He stood a moment looking about him, for he could not see her. Then on the bed draped with dark green curtains in the centre of the room Ruth lay face down, weeping. His heart wrenched, the urge to comfort her momentarily diverting him from his purpose.

She had heard him. 'Go away! I did not send for anyone!'

Roger came closer and said softly: 'Ruth!'

Abruptly she turned half over so that she could see him and her eyes were wide with shock. '*Roger!* How on earth . . .?' Then she came to her feet. 'If someone comes in you'll be arrested, and I'll be ruined. What on *earth* are you doing here? If they catch you, they will hang you!'

'I have locked the door,' he told her, still keeping his voice low for fear of being heard, but there was a hard edge to his clipped words. Who else could have betrayed them? It had to be Ruth. 'You know why I am here,' he added roughly.

He could clearly see the concern in her dark eyes, but he took a step away from her, fighting the desire she always awoke in him. She blinked at him. 'Forgive me, sir, but I do not think I do.'

'Well, madam, let me inform you! My father, brother and I myself were followed as we left Lynn on Tuesday.'

She nodded. 'I heard you escaped the soldiers.'

'Fortuitous wasn't it?' he sneered. 'I wonder how they knew we were in Lynn?'

Her eyes grew round with fear. He saw it and he saw how she trembled. 'I—I don't know. I did not tell them if that's what you think!'

'If you did not tell them, madam, then who did? Only two people knew that we were in Lynn. One of them I know can be trusted. The other one was you. Now you tell me how it looks.'

She drew herself up to her full height and looked him straight in the eye with splendid pride. 'I did not betray you. I have no wish to see you or your father or anyone else hang. I do not agree with this war, I've already told you that. I don't know how they found out about you, but I do know that it was not from me!'

'You are a Puritan,' he insisted, goading her. 'We are on opposite sides in this war. And you have clearly told me your opinion of my character. So, madam, what sharing does a Puritan have with a Royalist, eh?'

Her eyes flashed with anger, her cheeks flushed deliciously red, and her voice, although low, vibrated with fury. 'You mistake the matter, sir. I am on no-one's side. My beliefs are my own affair. The men in my family may do with me as they wish but their politics are not my politics. And just so that you know, I do not agree with this war at all. People are going to be killed—are being killed. But I shall not add to it by denouncing anyone!'

He began to believe her, but his anxiety for his father kept him on the attack. 'You are not a fool, madam, you must have guessed what we were about.'

Her anger equalled his. 'Since I do not possess a mind as devious as your own evidently is, sir, I had not guessed at all. And do not inform me, since I do *not* wish to know. I will repeat to you that my faith is personal to me and has nothing to do with you, my family, or the King. I *will not* be drawn into a conflict I do not agree with. Neither you nor my family will make me into some kind of intolerant zealot, prejudiced against my fellow Englishmen. What you do is your own business and is absolutely nothing to do with me. How dare you think I would betray a friend! How dare you think I care so little for you that I would sell you and your father to the hangman! Just what kind of person do you think I am, pray?'

He stood with his hands on his hips watching her and he knew he had misjudged her. His anger began to evaporate while she continued to glare at him in outrage, a beautiful termagant. His respect for her grew in direct proportion to his relief. She had not done it. He had been wrong. Never in his entire life had he been so delighted to be found wrong.

He let his breath go in a sigh as the agonised worrying for his father reasserted itself. He was no nearer to finding out what had happened to him.

It had grown as dark as night outside, thick iron-grey thunderheads blotting out the sun. A flash followed almost immediately by a window-rattling crash and rain began to fall in huge droplets, clattering against the window.

Roger looked away from her, trying to give voice to his thoughts. 'My—my father is missing,' he said and to his humiliation he heard the crack in his voice.

As the rain gathered pace, coming down with all the force of a Noachian deluge, Ruth went to the window and closed it. He could not see her clearly any more. Another flash and crash which made her flinch away from the window. She licked her lips with the tip of her tongue. If only she knew what effect she had on him! 'What do you mean *missing*?'

He took a few moments to answer. 'We were attacked. We sent him off. Nicholas—my brother, that is—and I, and distracted them, so that he could get away safe. We haven't seen him since.'

'Where do you think he went?'

'I thought—that is I hoped—you might know.'

Her anger seemed to dampen, but her mouth was set in a firm line. 'They don't have Sir Hamon in Lynn, of that I'm certain. I would have heard.' Her voice was still tight showing that he was not yet forgiven for accusing her.

Someone tried the door and, finding it locked, called out: 'Mistress Ruth, are you alright?'

They exchanged alarmed glances and Roger moved to conceal himself behind the bed drape on the far side of the bed from the door.

Ruth called out in her best upset voice: 'Leave me alone! I did not call for anyone.'

'With the storm and all, Mistress, I thought . . .'

'I am fine, Abi.'

'I can bring you some warm milk, Mistress.'

'Abi, go away, I want to be alone. If I want milk I will ask for it.'

'Yes, mistress.'

Another long pause as the storm flashed and crashed again and they gave the servant time to go away.

Roger came out from behind the bed hanging.

'You must go,' Ruth whispered urgently, and she had to come quite close to him in order for him to hear.

'I misjudged you, Ruth,' he said, and, for what he thought must be the first time in his life, he said: 'I'm sorry.' This woman certainly had him! Acknowledging wrongdoing was not part of his character, and he never forgave someone who, in his view, had sinned against him. But Ruth was not just someone. He was in love with her, and so he wanted to believe her, wanted to forgive, wanted things back to normal between them.

She relaxed a little. 'You do not trust me,' she whispered sadly. 'I see that.'

'You believe the worst of me,' he countered.

'I do not.' She frowned, taking a step towards him, holding out her hand. 'I do not, Roger.'

'What is it you said? A womaniser, a drunkard, a gambler, a third son and a Royalist. I think that's the list isn't it?'

'What am I to think, sir, when you kiss me and do not make your intentions clear?'

Well, she had a point. 'I wanted to be sure of you, Ruth. And I needed to be sure of myself, that I was not just captivated by your beauty, but that I truly love you and want you for my wife. And I am sure.'

'Yet you thought I would betray you.'

He made an effort to explain. 'No, you don't understand, do you? Don't you know why I came here? If I had thought anyone else had betrayed us, what do you think I would have done to him?'

'Killed him, I expect.'

'Yes I would. I would have expected a soldier to betray us. But not you. I did not want to believe it of you. I could see no other answer, though. I had to find out.'

'Well now you know,' she snapped. 'There is no more to be said. Perhaps you should leave.'

He stifled an oath and it came out as a hiss of air. 'Woman, you would try the patience of a saint!'

'I don't believe in saints!' Her eyes danced, and he knew he had won her. He took hold of her chin, tilting her face upwards so that she was looking into his eyes. 'You are the most provoking female!' he whispered. 'And, in faith, madam, the most beautiful!' and before she could protest, he kissed her.

Time seemed to stop. Outside the thunder rumbled, but inside the room was quite still. They looked at each other. 'Not friends,' he whispered. 'Something more than that.'

He no longer held her chin, but her face was still tilted up towards him. The light of the lightning flash came through the curtains illuminating the side of her face as her eyes searched his and he knew he was lost. He slipped his hands around her slender waist and pulled her towards him. Her body pressing against his made his whole body react. This time, when his lips met hers, they lingered, caressing. She made his senses reel. Everything in his being ached for her and when he felt her hands stealing around his neck, pulling him gently down to her, his need for her surged through him, blotting out all reason.

Then she fluttered in his arms, bringing him back to the present, and he pulled away to look at her.

Her eyes opened slowly, a small frown on her brow, her lips parted, her breath ragged gasps. She searched his face. 'I think you ought to go,' she said in a shaken voice.

She was right. Another minute and he would not be able to stop.

'If you are found here . . .'

His passion had frightened her, he thought. He needed to explain. 'Ruth—'

'No, Roger. Do not say anything. You must go. If you are found here I shall be compromised and you will hang. Now go.'

'As you wish, sweeting.'

She closed her eyes as if in pain, and shook her head. 'No, my love, it is not as I wish,' she whispered. 'It is what must be.'

Outside the lightning flashed several times, a thunder clap following immediately. The storm was directly overhead. 'Oh, my love, go,' she whispered in his ear. 'Please go. I am so afraid for you.'

'I will go, sweeting, but only because you ask me to.'

She turned her head to look up at him, and he kissed her lips, quite chastely this time.

'Until we meet again, sweeting.' He kissed her again and released her. She did not turn around to watch him as he let himself out of the door.

TWENTY-THREE

July 1643

Breakfast was a sorry affair. Roger picked at the cold meat on his plate. It had been too long. Either his father was in Wisbech now or he was dead. With his natural optimism deserting him, he felt sick with worry, his insides churning. This anxiety cast everything else out. He thought of Ruth often, and when he dwelt on their last meeting, he could feel the excitement of loving and being loved in return. But this business with his father cast a pall on everything. He could not escape from the sickening dread.

When his mother entered the dining room she looked worse than Roger felt. She managed to wish him a good morning, but then fell silent, lost in her own misery. Her swollen eyes bore testimony to a night spent weeping and her face was gaunt and pale. He ached to put comforting arms around her, but he knew it would bring on a fresh bout of weeping. Nothing but his father's return could comfort her.

She sat down with a cup of tea and a piece of bread and butter, but he knew she would probably leave it. She had eaten so little in the last few days.

When Nicholas and Anne came in, Roger decided to give breakfast up altogether, swallowing the last of his tea. It was the lack of news that bothered them all so much. No-one, not even the mayor Gurlin, knew anything about Sir Hamon.

'I think we should send a messenger to Wisbech to see if he is there,' Nicholas announced suddenly. ''Tis the only way we'll find out.'

'Gurlin would have known,' Roger insisted. 'Toll would never be able to keep it to himself. He'd have been crowing it from the rooftops. It would be all over Lynn. But I was there yesterday and no-one knows anything.'

'He cannot be dead,' Lady Alice whispered through white lips. 'What will we do without him?'

Roger and Nicholas exchanged glances. Roger had begun to think that his father must be dead and he could see that Nicholas feared the same.

'We have searched every square inch of that forest,' Nicholas said. 'If he were lying there, we would have found him.'

'He must have hidden up,' Lady Anne suggested.

'Where?' Roger demanded. 'We've looked everywhere.'

Anne shrugged. She had no more idea than any of them.

He stood up to leave the room, his chair scraping on the tiled floor and as he did so he glanced out to the front of the house. The windows were fogged by the rays from the morning sun, but he saw a rider, the horse coming up to the bridge.

'Who on earth would be coming at this hour?'

Nicholas too came to look out of the window, but the newcomer was out of sight of the window. 'Visitors?'

'Perhaps it is news,' Alice suggested hopefully.

'I'll find out,' Roger said, but as he went to the door, it flew open, nearly knocking into him and Sir Hamon himself stood there.

There was a moment's stunned silence before Lady Alice gave a shriek, burst into tears and flew into his arms. Sir Hamon hugged her while Roger and Nicholas exchanged relieved glances and Roger uttered a prayer of thanks in his heart. Never in his life had he felt so pleased to see his father and he had a strange sensation of wanting to cry himself.

Sir Hamon was overcome by the welcome. Lady Alice bade him sit down. 'What will you have, sir?' she asked him, mopping her face on a handkerchief hastily retrieved from the folds of her dress.

'Not too late for breakfast, I see. Do we have beef? Cold beef, please my love.' His love did not have to serve him however, for old Ketwood, who had followed him in and who stood near the dresser, served the master of the house. 'Coffee too,' Sir Hamon added. Lady Alice sat down beside him and Roger and Nicholas and Anne all sat too. Sir Hamon began to eat. With relief giving rise to a new appetite, Roger too began to eat his cold meat and bread and butter.

'Forgive me, my love,' Alice said after a moment, 'but would it be too intrusive to ask where you have been?'

'I know you must have been worried about me,' Sir Hamon said through a mouthful of food. 'I am sorry to put you to such anxiety.'

'What happened to you?' she asked again.

Nicholas shook his head in relief. 'We thought you either in Wisbech Castle or dead,' he said bluntly.

Roger tore off a large piece of bread. 'We searched the wood for you and the surrounding countryside. It was as if you had vanished off the face of the earth.'

Sir Hamon sipped his coffee. 'Those rascals followed me,' he explained. 'I ran, I hid and I had to keep avoiding them. By the time they gave up, I was thoroughly lost. I had no idea where I was, I had no horse. I walked towards where I thought I had left you both, only to find myself somewhere I didn't recognise. For two days I wandered. I drank from a stream which made me ill and I had nothing to eat.

'Then I found myself in Grimston. I recognised the church there. It was midnight when I threw myself on the mercy of Mr. Thorowgood, the rector and by then I was in a pretty bad way.'

'I'm not surprised,' Nicholas put in. 'Grimston is miles away.'

'I was afraid to travel on the roads where I could be seen, for they were looking for me.' He paused to drink more coffee.

'We were looking for you too!' Roger said.

'Anyway, I woke the good rector at midnight and he took me in. By then I was running a fever and very ill, I can tell you. I wanted to send a message here, but Thorowgood could not spare anyone.'

'I'm surprised you felt you could trust Thorowgood,' Nicholas remarked. 'I thought rectors were all on the side of Parliament.'

'Not all. You forget, I've known him a long time. He is a man of God. He would not denounce me. Although he has some strange ideas. Do you know he actually thinks that the natives in America are descended from the lost tribes of Israel? I told him that he was wrong on that one. He said he will write a book about it!'

Lady Alice caught his hand. 'I think you should know, Sir Hamon, that your sons have been searching for you each day.'

Sir Hamon smiled. 'Well, I thank you both. And for your prayers, my lady.'

'But you are tired, sir. You must rest.'

'I awoke only this morning recovered from the fever. I confess I am still weak.'

'Yes, you will be sadly pulled down.'

'The rector will need his horse back,' he said looking at Nicholas.

'I'll do it,' Roger offered. 'I want to go into Lynn again.'

Sir Hamon cast him a reproachful look, but Sir Nicholas was blunter. 'If I were you I'd forget the Pell woman.'

Roger ignored him. 'I'll be back by nightfall.'

§

With the alarm about Sir Hamon over, he and his sons made final preparations for the surreptitious arming of Lynn, smuggling in the last of the muskets and gunpowder and hiding them in various locations about the town.

Sir Hamon waited only for the turn of events which would make a coup successful and kept out of sight, well aware that Parliament still had a warrant out for his and his sons' arrests. He was governor at the moment only in name. The members of the Committee, that is the Puritans, kept the authority with themselves and made their plans to defend the town while he bided his time, watching and waiting.

The Committee which included Thomas Toll, John Percival and the neutral Mayor Thomas Gurlin, sent the town's stock of slightly deteriorated gunpowder to London in exchange for new. Sir Hamon smiled when Roger on one of his Lynn jaunts brought the news back. 'That will come in very useful.'

Roger brought other news too. 'The Committee in Lynn has issued an order that no householder may entertain anyone without the permission of mayor Gurlin.'

Sir Hamon gave another wry laugh. 'You know why, don't you?'

Nicholas perched on the corner of the table. 'They don't want Royalists coming in. Yet they have a Royalist governor!'

Sir Hamon's laughter increased. 'They can't do anything about that. And I'll be bound that Gurlin doesn't enforce it.'

Roger did not laugh with them, but waited quietly until their mirth subsided. Becoming aware that his youngest son was standing quite still and waiting, a sombre expression on his face, Sir Hamon frowned in concern. 'What is it?'

Roger swallowed the lump that had formed in his throat. 'Bad news, I am afraid, sir. I have to tell you, sir, that Sir John Spellman is dead.'

All three men in the room were silent, Sir Hamon and Nicholas in shock, Roger in sorrow.

Sir Hamon's eyes filled. 'How? When?'

'On the twenty-fourth day of July. Brasenose College, Oxford. He was with the King's troops. He died of camp fever.' Camp fever was another name for typhus.

'Camp fever!' Sir Hamon digested this. 'What a waste! Damn, he was only forty-nine.'

'Camp fever is no respecter of age,' Nicholas observed. 'I heard the King's army has small rations and bad living conditions. A man is struck down and is too weak to recover when he has little food and no good shelter.'

Roger lapsed into silence, allowing his father time to assimilate the information. He thought of Sir John, his father's dear friend, son of his father's guardian and mentor. who had lived in Holme for a time, who had travelled with Hamon the younger to Norwich to infiltrate the Parliamentary meeting there, and who had been knighted in 1641 by the King. And only in December, Parliament had sent for him as a delinquent. Not that they found him. Since the meeting in Norwich he had served the King in Oxford.

'He was a fine man,' Sir Hamon said eventually. He smiled sadly, lost in his memories. 'He stood up for the King.'

Roger put a hand on his shoulder. 'I am so sorry, sir.'

Sir Hamon put his hand on Roger's acknowledging the sympathy. 'I must see his widow.'

TWENTY-FOUR

August 1643

The summer of 1643 was long, hot and dry, and August was unbearable.

It was also a month of activity, and not just on the harvest front. Sir Hamon advised Roger against going to town at all because of the risk of discovery. If anything, going in disguise put him at greater risk than if he went as himself. Yet the knowledge that Ruth was there prompted him to risk it, and occasionally he was rewarded when he caught a glimpse of her in company with her aunt. Yet, frustratingly, finding an opportunity to be alone with her eluded him. Her aunt kept her too closely confined. However, he continued for a while to be the main source of information for Hunstanton.

Until, that is, his father forbade him outright to go to Lynn until they were ready.

He did not protest. He knew what he risked each time he went, and his reward was small at best. He worried that Ruth was slipping away from him, for he could not even speak to her, and he cursed her father, as well as her aunt and uncle, viewing them as the barrier to winning her hand.

On the twelfth of August Royalists approached Norwich. Immediately, the Parliamentary holders of Norwich Castle invested it with more soldiers and sent a panic message to Oliver Cromwell, but the Royalists turned out to be just a few friends and Captain Poe for Parliament repulsed them easily.

With Sir Hamon unable to reveal his hand just yet, some Royalists in Lynn became impatient. William Leek leading a detachment of Royalists from Lynn, rode to Norwich and took three men prisoner. The Castle's defenders immediately arrested Leek, demanded the release of the prisoners. They compelled Leek to give the Parliamentarian sergeant at arms, John Hunt, five hundred pounds as a bond and released him, whereupon he returned to Lynn and sought out Sir Hamon in Hunstanton.

'They expect me back in two weeks,' he told Sir Hamon as they sat together in the shade on a bench in the garden at the rear of the Hall. 'If I do not go they will keep my five hundred pounds. Five hundred, mark you! 'Tis daylight robbery.'

'That is a strange thing to do.' Sir Hamon was puzzled. 'Why did they release you?'

Leek took a large swallow of ale from the flagon in his hand and wiped the sweat from his brow. 'I assume it is because they want my money to arm their men!'

'I take it you will not go back, then?'

'They made me swear an oath to do so. But if I do, they will no doubt try me and hang me and keep my money just the same. So no, 'twould be suicide to do so. I'd rather keep my head on my shoulders! And they know it. When this is all over I swear I shall have my revenge!'

'I would that you had not acted so hastily my friend,' Sir Hamon remonstrated gently. 'I know it is galling when our brother Royalists are in difficulties. But, I promise you, our time will come. We just need a little patience.'

'That may be so, Sir Hamon, but people are becoming uneasy. Rumours fly around Lynn. Forgive me for speaking frankly, sir, but people are saying that you are not interested in being governor, that you have been captured, or even that you have died.'

'Do they now?'

'Well you have not been seen in Lynn for some time.'

'Perhaps they have forgotten that I am a hunted man. As are my sons.'

'The fear is that the armies on both sides will come and fight it out in the meadows around Lynn and people are flocking into the town for safety.'

'Ha! And how does Gurlin cope with that?'

'You know Gurlin. He has been inundated with requests for people who wish to enter Lynn. He just agrees to them all! 'Tis easier for him! Not only that, but the Committee has decided that all the lanes leading to the water should be boarded up and the gates to be locked up all night, but open all day. They are expecting an attack, I think.'

'From whom, I wonder?' Sir Hamon was thoughtful. He could not afford to wait much longer.

More news filtered through to Hunstanton. The unease had grown into unrest. People became tense and protest gatherings took place in the Tuesday Market Place while fights broke out in the streets. When a rumour reached the Eastern Association that Lynn had decided for the King the Eastern Association panicked. They had no troops at that time to send to Lynn to put down any trouble there. The Earl of Manchester had been sent to intercept the Earl of Newcastle whose Royalist army was marching from the north towards London, while Oliver Cromwell was in Gainsborough in Lincolnshire securing that town after his victory there.

East Anglia had been drained of Parliamentary soldiers.

In an attempt to secure Lynn, Parliament issued new orders for the arrest of Sir Hamon, Sir Nicholas, Roger, Sir Charles Mordaunt, Lord Allington, Sir Robert de Grey, Robert Bacon and Anthony Hevingham, Captains Goodman, Naunton and Havers, together with 'strangers, lodgers and popish recusants'. They were to be sent to the castle of Wisbech, there to be kept until further notice.

Receiving the order to arrest the chief Royalists and any other sympathisers, Thomas Toll and John Percival went together to Mayor Gurlin.

Gurlin looked the written order over and his hands shook.

'You must implement this, Gurlin,' Toll ordered. ''Tis a direct order from Parliament.'

Gurlin assessed the situation. Never a brave man, the thought of confronting Sir Hamon L'Estrange with such an order was more than he could cope with.

'But gentlemen—Sir Hamon L'Estrange!'

'You have no option, Gurlin. If you don't, you will be arrested.'

'By whose order?'

'I can get a warrant.'

'Not without my say so, you cannot.'

'Don't be so sure!'

Still, Gurlin put it off. A day or two went by as he prevaricated, but with Toll constantly on his back, he caved in. He instructed the magistrates accordingly.

§

It had become a regular occurrence for Lady Alice to find the constables Toby Peddar and Peter Belton with armed men coming to search Hunstanton Hall. Sometimes the menfolk of the family would not be at home, in which case they carried out a quick search of the premises, carried off anything which might be useful and then politely departed. After all, they were local men and they were known to Lady Alice who had to deal with them.

She bore it with a sigh and tried not to complain to Sir Hamon about her home being ransacked on a weekly basis.

She found it more nerve-wracking when her husband and sons were at home, in which case a warning from the boy posted on lookout would send them hurrying down the tunnel before the troops had even entered the front gates.

It had become a game. The constables and troops put little effort into finding the L'Estranges. That is until Captain Slaney took control of the situation.

He planned his assault on Hunstanton with military precision. With his troops he entered the outer gates, did not stop in the quadrangle, despite several male servants emerging to intercept them, crossed the bridge over the moat, through the gatehouse gates and into the courtyard.

The double-doors to the hall were open and Steward Trench, Sir Hamon's Clerk, stood blocking the way, just in case Captain Slaney intended to ride his horse straight into the Hall. Well if he did, he would have to get through Steward Trench first! To Trench's relief, Captain Slaney and his troops dismounted. However, his relief was short-lived, for the captain did not feel it necessary to ask permission to enter; the warrant in his hand was permission enough. He brushed past Trench as if he were of no importance, pushed Lady Alice aside without so much as a by your leave and sent his men in all directions to search the house.

'I have a warrant for the arrest of Sir Hamon L'Estrange, Sir Nicholas L'Estrange and Master Roger L'Estrange,' he said not looking at her but looking about him. Then his cold grey eyes rested on her. 'By order of Parliament.'

Lady Alice drew herself up to her full five feet height and said coldly: 'They are not here.' And she hoped they had made good their escape.

His eyes searched her face, blatantly doubting her word.

Then Toby Peddar, the Chief Constable, came in also without Lady Alice's permission and said to Captain Slaney: 'They've been captured. Outside the church.'

Captain Slaney's scowl turned to a mean smile as he looked at her, then he left the house to take his prize.

Lady Alice squared up to the Chief Constable. 'What kind of treacherous dog are you, Toby Peddar?' she demanded in accents of deepest loathing.

This rugged man had received his office due to Sir Hamon's influence. In her opinion it had caused him to become full of his own importance. He had obviously forgotten where his loyalty ought to lie.

He shifted his gaze, as well he might. 'Just doing my job, my lady.'

If she'd a man's strength she would have knocked him down and as it was she was sorely tempted. Instead she brushed past him contemptuously and came into the courtyard to see her men mounted on horses, their hands tied in front of them.

She fought the instinct to cry out, especially as her husband shook his head ever so slightly when he saw her. She went to his horse.

'Send the servants to the house in Lynn,' he instructed her.

'Let us know what happens,' she whispered to him.

He nodded, for there was no time for more. Already the troops led the horses out through the gatehouse. Beside her Anne broke down into weeping.

'L'Estrange women do not weep,' Alice told her, despite her own eyes filling with tears. 'L'Estrange women hold their heads up high, daughter, and they are strong for their men.'

But her heart quailed as she watched her husband and sons being taken off to Lynn by the Parliamentary troops.

TWENTY-FIVE

August 1643, King's Lynn

Because the gaol was full of other miscreants, it had been decided that Sir Hamon and his sons would continue under house arrest in Sir Hamon's own town house, which is what he had hoped. As his men released them from the ropes that tied their hands, Captain Slaney could not resist one last dig.

'Tomorrow you will be in Wisbech Castle,' he said with immense satisfaction. 'Now *there* is a dungeon that has to be the epitome of all hell-holes.'

'I am governor of this town,' Sir Hamon fumed. 'How dare you do this!'

'I have a warrant from Parliament which says I can do this,' Slaney said with a maddening smile. 'Only doing my duty, Sir Hamon.'

'Your duty, sir, ought to be to your King,' Nicholas told him.

Roger, standing in front of the empty fireplace, struggled to contain his fury. The ignominy of being arrested, of being paraded through Lynn's Streets like common criminals, and the confiscation of their horses stoked the fires of injustice burning in his soul. Achilles, his beloved black stallion had been confiscated along with Sir Hamon's bay and Nicholas's piebald, which cut deeply. Horses had been confiscated more than once from Hunstanton, but somehow Achilles had escaped that. Not this time. Perhaps this coming to Lynn would be the last time he saw him.

He ground his teeth. Everything had come to nothing. All his father's plans were for nought. Instead they were to be sent to Wisbech, where they would not be treated gently (and he thought of Richardson's suffering here), and probably sent for trial for treason while Slaney and probably that traitor Toll and his friend Percival congratulated each other on ridding themselves of the pestilential L'Estranges. He knew a great desire to plant his fist squarely in the infuriating Captain Slaney's face. It would only serve, however, to put him straight into irons for his pains and thrown into the gaol cellars.

Slaney growled disparagingly in his throat and left without another word.

Once they were alone Sir Nicholas let out an oath. 'By all that is sacred . . .'

Sir Hamon put his hand up to silence him. It struck Roger that his father was not as despondent as circumstances would suggest. Indeed, the older man had a gleam in his grey eyes.

'This could be what we have been waiting for,' Sir Hamon whispered.

Roger exchanged glances with Nicholas and Sir Hamon went on: 'The game is not up. This will force the people of Lynn to take sides.'

'You intend to declare for the King, *now*?' Roger asked.

Sir Hamon smiled. 'Can you think of a better time? With Manchester and Cromwell busy elsewhere, Parliament cannot raise enough men to stop us. East Anglia has no Parliamentary troops at present. It is the best time of all. True, Toll has forced our hand sooner than I thought, but it will still serve. I need to get hold of Gurlin.'

§

As it happened Gurlin, in a state of nervous anxiety that he should have been put in the position of having the governor of Lynn himself arrested, decided to visit Sir Hamon with a view to making Sir Hamon see that he, Gurlin, had been forced into action by that pain in the nether regions Thomas Toll. Accordingly, he was shown into the panelled parlour by Sir Hamon's servant who had arrived from Hunstanton less than an hour after Sir Hamon himself.

Gurlin bowed quickly when he saw Sir Hamon. However, his nerves almost got the better of him when the two L'Estrange sons rose like veritable giants from the settle and came to stand with their father. The L'Estranges did not bow.

'Master Gurlin! I am pleased that you are here,' Sir Hamon said awfully, 'Perhaps you would like to explain yourself to me?'

Gurlin began to shake. 'W-well, S-sir Hamon, I-I—w-well—w-well, I c-came to explain it all to you. It was Master Toll that made me do it. I was under orders, see?'

Roger moved around him and towards the door, folded his arms across his broad chest and leaned against it, blocking the exit. Gurlin eyed him anxiously, then his gaze flitted back to Sir Hamon, Sir Nicholas and back again to Roger. His hand went nervously to his throat and he tugged at his collar.

'I do see,' Sir Hamon assured him with deceptive calmness. 'I see a man before me who cannot make a decision as to what side he ought to be on. Toll is merely an alderman.'

'Um, a Parliament member, sir.'

'As I said, merely an alderman. Whereas I am the duly elected governor.'

'Well yes.'

'How can you arrest me and my sons?'

Again Gurlin's gaze flitted to Roger and back again to Sir Hamon and then at the window, judging whether he could make his escape that way.

'I—uh—didn't want to do it Sir Hamon. Master Toll and Master Percival. They made me.'

'They made you do it?' The scornful look Sir Hamon cast in his direction was not lost on Gurlin.

'I am sorry, Sir Hamon,' he said miserably, clearly wishing he had not come.

There was a silence while Sir Hamon let him broil. Then Sir Hamon said: 'Whose side *are* you on, Master Gurlin?'

Gurlin felt as though he was about to burst into tears. 'I don't know,' he whispered.

'Are you really going to send us to stand trial as traitors, Gurlin?' Sir Nicholas demanded. 'Perhaps for us to be executed? Me and Sir Hamon and young Roger.'

Gurlin was appalled and his face mirrored his shock. 'There are others,' he admitted, once more tugging at his collar. 'There's a warrant also for the arrest of Sir Charles Mordaunt, Lord Allington and Sir Robert de Grey, Bacon and Hevingham and Captains Goodman, Naunton and Havers.'

'Gurlin!'

Gurlin stared at the floor. 'What can I do about it?'

Again there was a silence as Sir Hamon let him think about it a bit longer. Then he said: 'I will tell you what you can do, sir. You can put it to the people of Lynn. You are their mayor. Do what they tell you. Ask them. Which side do they want to be on? Do they want their governor to be sent to Wisbech to stand trial?'

Gurlin's gaze flew to Sir Hamon's, hope of redemption suddenly warming his soul. 'You think I should do that?'

'Oh yes,' Sir Hamon said seriously. 'I really think you should.'

Gurlin nodded, beginning to feel much better. His eyes took on a faraway look as he saw a beautiful picture of himself before all the people of Lynn, commanding their attention and of course respect, as he,

Gurlin, acted like Pontius Pilate in either releasing Sir Hamon or sending him to his death. What power!

Sir Hamon brought him back to reality. 'Well go on, then.'

With another bow and 'Servant sirs,' Gurlin left them through the door Roger obligingly opened for him.

As Roger closed the door again, he said: 'You think the people of Lynn will declare for the King?'

Sir Hamon frowned. 'I cannot say. I don't know that Lynners are all loyal subjects of the King. I don't think they understand much of the politics of this situation. But I do know that they have respect for us.'

'For you, you mean,' Nicholas said.

'Well I have had much to do with Lynn over the years and I have done much for them. And your lady mother too has fed them and nursed them and helped them when they were bereaved. If they won't do it for the King, they might do it for us.'

'It's a gamble,' Roger said.

'It is a gamble. We shall have to wait on Gurlin.'

§

Word had spread fast that Sir Hamon and his sons and the other Royalists were imprisoned in Lynn. Gurlin did as he was bid by spreading the word and, as they were used to doing whenever there was an event, the people of Lynn packed into the Tuesday Market Place. Here they waited patiently in the broiling sun for Gurlin to produce the prisoners.

A platform had been hastily erected and all the arrested Royalists, Sir Hamon and his sons among them, surrounded by soldiers, were marched on to it. There they stood, hands tied, with the soldiers guarding them as though they were common criminals.

Sir Hamon surveyed the crowd, picking out faces he knew. That one had come to him needing money for treatment for his son and had been given it. This one had been sick and asked that sir Hamon wait for the rent. The debt had been cancelled. Lady Alice had helped nurse that woman's child and brought a herb potion for her girl.

He hoped it was a favourable sign. Yet it had not escaped his notice that there was a sizeable Puritan contingent in the crowd discernible by their clothes.

Everything that Sir Hamon had done in the past few months, the scheming and plotting and the preparations had all led to this moment. It all hung on the decision the people of Lynn made today. Would it be prison and possibly death in the squalid conditions in Wisbech? Or would it be the King's rule for Lynn? Only the townspeople could decide.

If they decided for the King, it could change the whole course of the war and make a possible victory for the King. The future hung in the balance on this day. Sir Hamon's future, the town's future, the country's future. What would they decide?

Sir Robert de Grey, a man of middle age and white-streaked hair, whose loyalty to the King had only recently become apparent and who had until then continued to act as one of the deputy-lieutenants under the control of Parliament, shifted nervously. 'The game is up, L'Estrange. They are all Puritans. A devil's brew if ever I saw one.'

'All is not lost yet, sir,' Roger replied as he looked out over the crowd.

His heart crashed in his ribs. There was Ruth. She was at the edge of the market place dressed as always in the dark Puritan garb, with the white starched cap. She looked at him with wide horror-struck eyes, her hand over her mouth. Her aunt, beside her, spoke to her, and she closed her eyes as if in pain, shaking her head.

Thomas Gurlin in all his finery and with his badge of office dangling about his neck ascended the platform together with Thomas Toll and John Percival in their black robes and the crowd fell into tense silence.

Gurlin looked at Sir Hamon who glared back at him. Turning to the people, Gurlin began to shake visibly. *His nerve's gone,* Roger thought.

Sir Hamon thought the same. 'Get on with it, Gurlin,' he growled.

Gurlin cleared his throat and looked out onto a sea of expectant faces. 'Good people of Lynn!' he began and unfolded a piece of paper in order to read. 'Sir Hamon L'Estrange, Sir Nicholas L'Estrange, Mr. Roger L'Estrange, Sir Charles Mordaunt, Lord William Allington, Sir Robert de Grey, Mr. Robert Bacon, Anthony Hevingham, Esquire, Captain Goodman, Captain Naunton and Captain Havers stand before you. By order of Parliament these men have been arrested and they are to be detained in Wisbech Castle.'

William Toll, standing to the right of the platform together with John Percival, nodded approvingly and allowed himself a self-satisfied smile. Roger saw him and felt such anger that he would have hit him had he been free. As it was, he was obliged to stand and wait while Gurlin hesitated.

The crowd was restless. 'Surely you don't intend Sir 'Ammon to go to Wisbech Castle, Tom Gurlin?' Someone called.

''E be our governor,' A woman yelled. 'Tom Gurlin, yer wits hev gone a-begging!'

A ripple of laughter slid across the crowd.

Toll, who had been leaning against the Market Cross straightened, the smile drained from his face. He exchanged uneasy glances with Percival. This was not at all how it should be.

'No respect these days,' Gurlin muttered to himself. But he waved his hands in order to quieten them so he could speak. 'In this present struggle we must make a choice. As your mayor, I represent you, the people of this town. Yet this town has not decided whether for King or country. You, the people of Lynn, must decide. If you decide for the King, then these men shall be set free. If you decide for the country, they shall be taken forthwith to Wisbech Castle. Whatever you, the people of Lynn, decide, as your mayor, I shall faithfully carry out.'

The murmuring broke out again. A man cried out: 'What be you thinking, Tom Gurlin? Send Sir 'Ammon to Wisbech? Sir 'Ammon whose succoured us in distress, fed our children when we lacked bread?'

'We hin't that lacking in gratitude.'

'Whoever heard such ingratitude?'

'Our little'uns hin't going to blush with shame in remembrance of this day!'

A man in simple peasant clothes pushed his way to the platform, jumped up and faced the crowds. 'I want to say something.' The crowd fell silent. 'You've gorn sorft in the 'ead, Tom Gurlin. Sir 'Ammon he be our friend. When times be hard, where be there to go but to Sir 'Ammon and Lady Alice? We can't send them to that dungeon, do they'll die there. Who be left then to give us bread when our children be starvin'? We be able to go to them in all times of difficulty and strife. Can we be so ungrateful? Are we to blush for shame in mem'ry of this day's work?'

'No, no,' roared the crowd.

The man looked around at Sir Hamon who was staring at him, his eyes watering. Then he went on: 'Sir 'Ammon, he don't know who Oi be. Nay, for Oi be not one of his men. And Oi be a Nonconformist by faith and don't hold to the prayer book. But when Oi do come to Dame

Alice and begged something for moi fam'ly, he said to give it me. Oi hin't never forgot that, though Sir 'Ammon, 'e prob'ly hev. An' it seem t'me that it don't matter what religion we be, Sir 'Ammon, he hev done nuffen wrong and it'd be sinful to put him and his sons in that hell-pit when they hin't never hurt us. Oi say let 'em go! That be the roight thing to do.'

As the crowd broke into loud cheering he nodded at Sir Hamon in a sort of bow, ringing his felt cap between his hands and then, his head still humbly bent, got down and disappeared into the crowd.

Gurlin raised his hands in an effort to quieten the tumult. 'Good people of Lynn,' he began again, but he was interrupted yet again as people shouted out:

'Dame Alice cured our son of the fever.'

'Sir 'Ammon lent us ploughing oxen and . . .' but this last voice was lost as nearly everyone seemed to be anxious to tell of the good that the L'Estranges had done in their behalf and again the noise was deafening.

Sir Hamon raised his head and looked upon the people, tears spilling over from his eyes and coursing down his thin cheeks. It had never occurred to him that his beneficence might be remembered to this extent and be returned to him, and he was touched by their loyalty. He owed them his life.

Roger too wept openly, as did Sir Nicholas.

Gurlin made another attempt to address them, raised his voice until he was shouting: 'Then I ask you, good people of Lynn, will it be for King or for Country?'

They came back at him. '*For the King!*' Religion notwithstanding, loyalty to Sir Hamon and his family carried the day. They loved him and they showed it.

'*For the King! For the King!*' they chanted.

Thomas Gurlin turned and nodded to the guards who hastened forward with the keys to the manacles and in a moment Sir Hamon was free of his chains.

Furious, Toll and Percival left the platform.

'*For the King! For the King!*' The houses, the inns, the churches echoed to their voices and they shouted on and on until they were hoarse. '*For the King! For the King!*''

Sir Hamon's lower lip trembled as he came forward to the place where Thomas Gurlin had so recently stood, waiting for the moment to speak to them. Nicholas, standing just behind his left shoulder, put his hand upon his arm, while Roger stood on his other side, his heart full. It was a wonderful victorious moment.

'For the King!'

Sir Hamon held up his hands and gradually silence fell and they waited to hear what he had to say. He paused a moment, struggling for self-control.

'Good people of Lynn—my friends. Thank you all for this confidence in me. As your governor, I promise I will do all in my power to carry out your wishes and to protect you and your families from the enemy.'

His voice broke, but it didn't matter. Wild cheering had begun again. *'For the King! For the King!'*

Long after the crowd had dispersed, the Tuesday Market Place still seemed to echo: 'FOR THE KING!'

TWENTY-SIX

King's Lynn, August 1643

Sir Hamon's first task after his victory was to order the arrest of the magistrates who had been instrumental in his own arrest. Naturally, he could not ignore such enemies as the Parliamentary members for the town and so Thomas Toll and John Percival, to their intense chagrin, discovered armed guards outside their houses and themselves under house arrest.

In high dudgeon, Thomas Toll wrote a letter of bitter complaint to the major-general of the Parliamentary forces, the Earl of Manchester.

Sir Hamon then repaired to the Council Chambers in the Trinity Guildhall in the Saturday Market Place with Nicholas and the other Royalist councillors, or burgesses, to begin the task of making the town ready to withstand the Parliamentary forces.

As soon as he could, Roger went in search of Ruth, desperately hoping she had not returned to her aunt's house, and eventually found her in the hushed precincts of St Margaret's church in the Saturday Market Place. Thankfully, she was alone, kneeling and praying, and he sat down next to her on the pew.

'So, your father is victorious,' she whispered as she resumed her seat.

''Tis a small step.'

'And what will that mean for the town, then? Lord Manchester will not let this rest.'

'This is not the place to discuss it. Will you come with me to Guannock Gate?'

'Now?'

'Can you not come now?'

She hesitated and he was afraid she would not agree. His father was already in the council chambers beginning the job of governing the town as he should have been doing all along. Later, there would be celebrations and his father intended to hold a council of war. He had a short time to be with her and he did not want to lose it. He was impatient to be alone with her; it had been too long since he had last spoken to her, when he had broken into the house in Wingate.

She picked up her Bible and stood in an attitude of asking him to allow her to pass. As he stood to let her out of the pew she whispered:

'Yes now.' He sat down again briefly and bowed his head. It would not do to be seen leaving together. A short time later he followed her outside.

The heat of the day had not cooled when Roger met her in Stonegate, the lane beside the church. They had no privacy here to embrace, so he contented himself with taking her hand as they walked towards Mill Lane. The touch of her hand in his, hidden from prying eyes by the folds of her skirt, warm and intimate as she held his fingers, sent his heart beating wildly.

'It has been too long,' he told her.

'It has. I saw you waiting for me, but they would not allow me out on my own. Right now they think I am in church, praying for God's help in this war. My aunt thinks I am quite reformed now.'

'Reformed?'

'Obedient to their wishes. If only they knew!' She chuckled delightfully and he noticed a dimple appeared in her cheek when she laughed. The laughter died as she looked at him, an intense look in her eyes which did nothing to calm his thudding pulse. 'I've missed you,' she told him.

'In a short while, when this is over, we shall be wed,' he said.

She arched her brows playfully. 'I do not believe, sir, that I have agreed to wed you. In fact, you have not asked me. Can it be that you assume too much?'

He grinned. 'I was coming to that.'

'Were you?'

'I hoped you would agree.'

She turned her face away from him, troubled. 'And what about my father?'

'I shall ask him.'

She sighed. 'He will never agree. Especially after this declaration for the King. My father has no love for your father.'

'I am not my father.'

'I doubt that will weigh much with him.'

They had left the houses behind now, and were in a wooded glade which led to the grassland and Guannock Gate. Large oaks, horse chestnuts and sycamores arched overhead, their thick summer foliage surrounding them like a tent, keeping them from other eyes.

They stopped walking and he turned her to face him, holding her hand in front of him. 'Ruth, if you will have me, I will approach your father for your hand.' When she did not reply immediately he grew impatient. 'Answer me, maiden! Will you marry me?'

Looking up at him she searched his face, her eyes softening and filling with tears. A lump came into his throat as he tried to find the answer in her eyes, fearing refusal.

'Oh yes, I will, Roger L'Estrange.'

He had not realised he was holding his breath until he let it go in a sigh, happiness bubbling up in him like a spring. 'My darling, I promise you will want for nothing.' He was still holding her hand and he brought it now to his lips, kissing her fingers reverently. His own hand trembled. He wondered if she could sense it.

'I do not care if we live in a barn!' she told him, happily. 'As long as I am with you.'

'A barn was not quite what I had in mind!' He slipped his hand around her waist, feeling her body heat through the woollen material. She turned towards him instinctively with her face tilted upwards waiting. He drew her into his embrace and kissed her tenderly, letting his lips linger on hers as a great wave of desire washed over him. Time stood still. All he could think of was the woman in his arms, and his great love for her. She had just agreed to become his wife!

When he pulled back, she opened her eyes slowly to gaze up at him, her breath shallow gasps, her lips remaining slightly parted just as he had left them. He could not resist kissing her again, but this time with more urgency in keeping with his need.

A warning sounded in his head. He must not take this too far. Pulling back he struggled to calm the fire in him. After a moment he said: 'I think perhaps we should sit down.'

Finding a suitable place beside the little river, still in the shadow of the trees, he helped her to sit down on the sloping bank, before sitting right beside her. A late brood of fluffy brown ducklings paddled in the murky water with some adults. Leaning against him, she rested her head on his shoulder as his arm slid again around her. That scent of roses, clean and pure, mixed with her own scent would remain with him forever. She was so beautiful, so perfect, so trusting. Untouched by any man, she would be his wife. How could he even consider taking advantage of her, sullying that purity? Yet her body in his arms made him want to do just that!

She watched the ducks on the river and sighed deeply. 'I don't think I have ever been happier than at this moment,' she said. 'I was so miserable after—after I insulted your honour.' She covered the hand on her waist with her own, playing with his fingers. Her touch was delicate.

He kissed her temple, breathing in the wonderful scent of her. This morning he could have been on his way to Wisbech Castle and possibly death, and this afternoon he had won the hand of his lady and she now sat with him, in his arms. How wonderfully fickle life was!

'How are we going to do it, Roger?' she asked at length. 'My father will never agree.'

'I will find a way. When this is over, I will find a way.'

She took a deep breath. 'If not, then we will have to elope and I shall live with you,' she said quietly. 'Then my father would have to agree to our marriage, don't you think?'

'Ruth!' He was a good deal shocked and she immediately sat up and turned to look at him, her brows raised. Was this the same woman who had rung a peal over his head for daring to kiss her a few weeks ago? 'Do you know what you are saying?'

She frowned. 'I think I do. I have considered it carefully. It would force my father's hand. I've heard of it before. Lovers elope and then they can marry.'

His insides squeezed as he considered what she was prepared to sacrifice to be with him; her good name, her reputation, even her faith. He looked into her eyes and he thought how much he loved her and how much he wanted her. And what she suggested was no more than he had thought of himself. However, he said: 'No, Ruth.'

She pursed her lips. 'No,' she snapped. 'Just like that? No explanation. Do you not want to be with me after all? Do you toy with my affections?'

'There is no need to get on your high horse,' he retorted.

She made to get up, but he held her down. 'Stay, and hear me,' he ordered.

She bit her lip, and he saw that she was near to tears, but she stopped her attempts to rise. He drew a breath trying to make her understand. 'For a woman to live with a man to whom she is not married—well you know what people think of such a woman.'

'We could go where no-one knows us. No-one need know we are not married. And anyway, once my father agreed, we would be married.'

He shook his head. '*We* would know we are not married. Our families would know, and your family in particular would be very hurt and angry. But most of all, God would know. Ruth, I love you. What kind of man would I be if I took advantage of you in such a way?'

There was another long pause, as she frowned, playing with the grass, considering. She took a breath and looked up at him at last with those big dark eyes. 'Forgive me, I did not mean impugn your honour again,' she said. A thought occurred to her. 'You do not think me to be a—a—a fallen woman, do you?'

He was betrayed into a shout of laughter but stifled it quickly. 'Faith, no!' He continued smiling inwardly. She was too naïve to understand. The women in her family had been quite remiss in this part of her education. One day—when they were married—he would have to educate her. He could hardly wait!

'What have I said that is so funny?'

'Oh, you are absolutely adorable, my sweet innocent little love!' and he chuckled some more.

She frowned at him again, clearly not understanding and not a little hurt at his laughter. 'Only I cannot see any other way.'

He sobered at once. 'As God is my witness, I will find another way,' he told her seriously, pulling her back into his arms. 'When this war is over. Besides,' he added on a lighter note, 'some would say my honour is past redemption.'

It was her turn to laugh. 'I do not believe you!'

He did not smile now. Not that long ago she had believed him to be a man without honour, a rogue, and it stung him to remember. But he would not let the memory spoil this day. 'But believe my promise, Ruth. I will find a way.'

'I trust you,' she whispered looking up at him. He kissed her waiting lips, delighting in the taste of her, but it fuelled his desire for her again. It was too much, and he had his and her honour to consider!

He came to his feet. 'The sun is almost set. I do not think it meet that you should be out after dark. I will take you home.'

She also stood. 'If my aunt should see you with me—'

He pulled her into his arms again and his lips lingered on hers, fanning the flames once more. 'They will not,' he murmured. 'I will be waiting by the church again tomorrow if you can meet me, and every evening after that, even if you cannot I shall wait.'

'I will try,' she whispered before his lips closed again on hers.

TWENTY-SEVEN

August 1643

In Norwich, the right honourable Edward Lord Montagu, Baron of Kimbolton, Viscount Mandeville and Earl of Manchester and major general of the Parliamentary forces in the Associated Counties of Norfolk, Suffolk and Essex, the son-in-law of the Earl of Warwick the fleet's commander, held out his hand so that his manservant could tie his shirt sleeve.

'The buff coat,' he ordered quietly. Then, as someone knocked on the door, he called: 'Come!'

Another servant entered and bowed. 'Begging pardon, my lord, but there is a messenger for you.'

'What does he want?' his lordship demanded, irritated by the intrusion.

'He won't say. Only that he must see you personally, my lord.'

His lordship rolled his eyes and sighed. Since he had been appointed by Parliament as major-general of the Associated Counties just a few days previously it seemed everyone had a message for him, usually requesting a favour. 'Send him in,' he said impatiently.

A small man, poorly dressed, came hesitantly into the room, cloth cap in hand which left his stringy, dirty and no doubt lice and flea-infested dark hair uncovered to his lordship's horrified view.

His lordship stared at this dirty unkempt individual with something akin to disgust, while the man's eyes grew round in awe at this august presence. His lordship said discouragingly: 'Well?'

'Begging yer pardon, sir—milud, Oi do hev a letter for you.'

His lordship held out his hand. 'Who is it from?'

'From Master Thomas Toll, sir. In King's Lynn, sir.'

The name meant nothing to his lordship, but the place did. As the letter had not arrived in his hand, he clicked his fingers twice and held out his hand imperiously. Meantime his servant continued dressing him, buttoning his waistcoat, seemingly oblivious of the interruption.

'Oh, yes!' The man remembered the letter, dragged it from a coat pocket, tried unsuccessfully to straighten it and then gave it into his lordship's hand.

For a brief moment his lordship and his servant exchanged speaking glances, then his lordship found a coin on the dressing table and tossed it to the messenger who caught it deftly. 'That will be all. Wait outside in case I want to send you back with a letter for Master Toll.'

'Very good, sir—milud!'

The door closed, his lordship sat and the servant set to buckling his master's shoes as his lordship broke the seal and spread the sheet.

Thomas Toll's letter told him of Lynn's defection and of his imprisonment in his own house.

His lordship uttered an unchristian expletive. 'King's Lynn,' he announced to no-one in particular, 'has declared for the King! Here—in Norfolk!'

His servant met this news with a surprised stare. It was not his place to comment.

'Where's that messenger?' Manchester bellowed.

Immediately the door opened and the messenger came in again, standing nervously near the door in case he needed to make a swift exit.

Manchester fixed the messenger with his brown eyes. 'Who is behind Lynn's defection?' he demanded, then seeing the blank uncomprehending stare of the man, repeated: 'Who is—ah, it says here. L'Estrange.'

The messenger, pleased to have understanding again, said: 'Tha's roight. 'Sir 'Ammon L'Estrange.' He said.

'That Royalist dog! He's been trouble in that town all along. He's supposed to be under arrest. Whatever does the mayor—ah! Thomas Gurlin—think he's about letting him roam at large?'

But it was no use talking to servants. He dismissed them both, but again told the messenger to wait.

Alone, he thought about it. 'I'll have L'Estrange's head for this,' he muttered to himself. 'As for the mayor . . .'

He sat down at the writing table, took a sheet of paper and dipped the pen in the ink standish and wrote to the hapless Gurlin demanding an explanation for this outrageous state of affairs.

§

Having dealt with the opposition within Lynn, Sir Hamon set about his preparations.

During the next few weeks he finished the fortification of the town, completing the defences which had been started by the enemies. He stored ammunition, so that besides the ships in the harbour mounted with culverins, he could boast forty pieces of ordnance, one thousand two hundred muskets and five hundred barrels of gunpowder, together with five thousand men to defend the town. Trees which would provide cover for the enemy were cut down and the alms houses in Old Lynn across the river were blown up for the same reason.

Sir Hamon entrusted his youngest son with this task and with a few men and gunpowder Roger crossed the Ouse on the ferry. He had been waiting for the opportunity to make himself useful to the cause and he had dressed for the part with a red sash across his body and a white fluffy ostrich feather in his hat. It did little to impress the inhabitants of the alms houses, however. They were ordered out, together with their belongings.

''Old you 'ard! That be our 'ome!' one over-endowed woman with at least six dirty children clinging to her equally dirty skirts protested.

'I'm sorry, but we cannot have these houses shielding the enemy,' Roger said briskly, nodding to his men to take out of the houses anything that appeared to belong to the woman. 'There are houses for you all in Lynn.'

'What make you think we want t'go to Lynn?'

Roger took a breath and put his hands on his hips in an long-suffering attitude. 'You will be safe there.'

'Safe from what?' She scratched her armpit.

'From the roundheads.'

'What Round'eads?' She looked around her in exaggerated fashion. 'Oi don't see no Round'eads.' She laughed, not humorously, revealing a single badly discoloured tooth in the front of her top jaw and sending a blast of fetid air in his direction.

He coughed, but recovered his dignity. 'They will be here,' he told her and wondered how on earth any man managed to father six children with her. He closed his mind to that thought.

Immediately she was joined by an old man who could hardly walk. 'Wha' be the trouble, moi woman?'

'This nob 'ere think he can tek our 'ouses. Fer the Round'eads be comin'.'

The old man glared at Roger through milky eyes. 'You can't do that.'

Despite his repulsion, Roger felt sorry for them. 'These houses are to be demolished,' he said. 'You will be safer in Lynn. And the governor will rebuild them once this conflict is over.'

'Safer be damned! Oi be safe in me own 'ouse.'

'Wha'd 'e say?' the old man asked.

''E say they rebuild them.'

'Better to leave be, then.'

Realising that there was nothing to be gained from further dialogue with the inhabitants, Roger turned away and nodded to his men. They forcibly removed the villagers from the almshouses and placed the barrels of gunpowder where they would be most effective.

With protests still ringing in his ears, he ordered their meagre belongings and anything useful to be put in the cart, now empty of gunpowder, and his men marched the dispossessed to the ferry to be taken, still noisily complaining, back to Lynn. The alms houses which had stood in the town for at least two centuries were made ready.

Roger ordered the rest of the villagers back, away from flying debris, and he stood back with them. Taking a glowing match he bent down and touched it to the single fuse which after a yard's length divided into six, one for each house.

In silent fascination the people watched the gunpowder spark and fizz across the ground with surprising speed until it disappeared into the buildings.

A few seconds later the first explosion shook the ground and rent the air, quickly followed by others. The houses disintegrated into a million pieces which took to flight seemingly suspended in time, until they fell gradually to earth.

The people were awed, but thought it a very good show, some even clapping, and it effectively silenced the fat woman and the old man waiting on the ferry. The children screamed in delight.

Roger ordered his men back across the river and most of the villagers decamped and went with them into Lynn for protection, the ferry having to make several trips.

Thomas Toll was so angry at what he called the 'wanton destruction' of the alms houses that he wrote to Sir Hamon threatening that he would make him pay for the damage. The letter arrived at the council chambers before Roger did.

'Looks like he's unhappy about it,' Nicholas said with classic English understatement when he had read the letter. 'Anyone would think he owned the houses!'

Unperturbed, Sir Hamon grinned.

§

Receiving Lord Manchester's letter, Gurlin immediately brought it to Sir Hamon.

'Well, Master Gurlin,' Sir Hamon said, his lips twitching ever so slightly as he handed the letter to Nicholas, 'what are you going to tell his lordship?'

'What can I tell him?' Gurlin asked miserably, feeling that since Sir Hamon was the cause of his present discomfort, he might at least be a little more helpful in the matter. 'What is there to say?'

Sir Hamon removed his spectacles and stared at Gurlin. 'Prevaricate, Gurlin. You have had much practice at that! Or better still, don't reply at all!'

Gurlin stared at him. ''Not reply?' Gurlin could hardly believe his ears. 'Not reply to the Earl of Manchester?'

'Well, you cannot exactly defend your position now, can you?'

'No and whose fault is that? That's what I'd like to know.'

'Cut it, Gurlin,' Nicholas warned.

Gurlin cast him an aggravated look, but persisted. 'I mislike this, Sir Hamon. You have put me in a difficult position.'

'The way I see it, you had little choice. Remember it was the people's decision which you promised to uphold.' He looked at the papers spread out in front of him, clicked his tongue in annoyance and again reached for his spectacles. Gurlin took his letter back from Sir Nicholas and as he folded it, Sir Hamon looked up again over the rim of his spectacles at his son. 'Are the defences complete?'

'They are. And Master Toll is demanding to see you.'

'Is he indeed? Making a lot of noise is he? He is certainly safer where he is. What about the others?' He took the spectacles off again. *Confounded things!* He needed them to read, but when he looked up he could hardly make out the face of his own son!

'Huggins and Coke and the rest are all in the bridewell.'

Sir Hamon stood up, well pleased. 'Good, then we are nearly ready. Ah Roger!' he added as his youngest son entered the room. 'How did it go?'

'You must have heard the explosions,' Roger replied. 'It was straightforward enough, no-one gainsaying us, except a toothless crone and an old man. The townspeople were so excited, for it was quite spectacular. We had to keep them at bay or they would have been blown up themselves! I don't think they were too happy about the alms houses, but I told them they would be replaced when the current troubles were over.'

Sir Hamon nodded. He expected his son to make beneficent promises on his behalf.

'Good afternoon, Master Roger,' Thomas Gurlin said pointedly.

'Ah, Gurlin! Are you here? How are you?'

'Not in a very good frame of mind,' Sir Nicholas informed him with a sideways grin. Roger knew he would hear the news later and did not ask questions now.

Gurlin left, grumbling, and wrote a reply to Lord Manchester and it was as evasive as only Thomas Gurlin knew how to be. It would please Sir Hamon, but it would infuriate his lordship.

Thomas Toll continued to write angry letters to Sir Hamon, but it did not interfere with the preparations, which Sir Hamon organised with military precision. Sir Hamon also sent a letter to the Earl of Newcastle commanding the King's men on the other side of the Wash in Lincolnshire requesting his help. At the same time Captain Poe on the Parliamentary side wrote to his masters in London warning that Newcastle might try to reach Lynn by sea and to take preventative action.

Nicholas had the news first and brought it to his father in the Governor's office in the Guildhall. 'It seems that the Earl of Warwick together with Parliament's fleet is on its way to Lynn.'

Sir Hamon took his spectacles off his nose and looked at his son. 'Damn!' He tapped a front tooth thoughtfully with the end of his spectacles, then he put them on again and peered at the piece of paper in front of him. 'I have here Lord Newcastle's promise to come to our relief from across the Wash.'

'How are they going to get into Lynn if the sea is blocked?'

'Exactly my thoughts.' The spectacles came off again. 'Newcastle is a seasoned warrior. He will know what to do. Besides, Parliament is only doing what I would have done if I'd had the ships. It's a blow, but not unexpected. No, Newcastle will find a way around it. By land, I expect.'

'He'd better be quick, before Manchester gets here.'

'I have his promise. He will come.'

'I hope you are right, Father, because if he doesn't, we cannot win this. 'Twould be better to go no further, than to risk lives for no cause.'

'I know it. And if I thought we could not win, I would surrender Lynn now. But Newcastle has promised. With God and right on our side, he will come.'

It was a pity, he thought, that he did not have ships under his own control, but the fleet was under the control of Parliament, not the King. He could raise a small army, but he could not raise ships. Anyone with any sense could see that the sea was worth having in one's control. To be blockaded by sea would be a blow, but not insurmountable. He doubted the enemy would mount an attack from the sea in any case. Too much of a bottle-neck here at Lynn where the Wash narrowed into the Ouse.

How are the preparations coming along?'

'St. Anne's Fort is ready,' Nicholas assured him. This structure, standing outside the walls of the town towards the East, had been given a number of guns from the Tower of London by the previous Puritan council.

'How many men do we have all together?' Sir Hamon asked.

'Eight troop of horse, eight of foot-soldiers and many zealous volunteers. About five thousand men in all.'

Sir Hamon smiled and looked at his two sons. 'Good!'

§

Thomas Gurlin's letter may have won him favour with Sir Hamon, but it did not please the Earl of Manchester. If anything could tell him that the defection was total, this was it. Even the mayor was taken in by those Royalists. 'Gurlin!' he spat with loathing. 'I'll have his head!'

The servant had seen his master's rages before. 'Very good my lord,' he said impassively.

'Bring me pen and paper!'

'Yes my lord.'

His lordship sat down to write a second missive to the town, this time addressing the members, Toll and Percival, but the letter did not reach its destination. The messenger was intercepted and arrested and the letter came into Sir Hamon's hands.

When it became clear that a reply was not forthcoming, Lord Manchester immediately set his plans into motion. Norwich Castle had two old brass falconets and two brass demiculverins and he ordered these massive weapons to be dragged the fifty miles or so to Lynn.

Captain Sotherton, in charge of this mission was not the happiest of men and his labourers less so. The demiculverins weighed three thousand four hundred pounds each and the falconets six hundred pounds. They were not easy to move and to add to their discomfort the weather had turned even hotter. Men and horses sweated and strained for every yard of the fifty miles or so to Setchey, some five miles south of Lynn. His lordship ordered two other cannons weighing seven hundred pounds each to be brought from Wisbech and Captain Sotherton brought them all with powder, shot, sponges and ladles to Setchey

Lord Manchester wrote to Oliver Cromwell, ordering him back from Gainsborough with his men.

Preparations on both sides were complete.

TWENTY-EIGHT

August 1643, King's Lynn

'That'll be getting out again,' the young man prophesied as he rubbed the cloth over the muzzle of his flintlock, his eyes fixed on the distance.

Roger smiled to himself. He knew that the man was referring to the sun which was not yet up. It was a typical Norfolk observation on the weather, the unrelenting heat of the last weeks, which showed no sign of abating.

Like the young man, Roger had his eye fixed on the skyline, looking for movement. 'You'll wear that barrel away if you keep rubbing it like that.'

The young man shifted uneasily and the man next to him looked up at Roger. 'Will they be a-coming today, Mr. Strange?'

Word had come to his father that the enemy was approaching. 'Looks like it.' They were on the town's defensive wall near the East Gate which opened onto the Gaywood Road. 'But wait for the order before shooting. Don't waste shot on men who are too far away.' He looked across at St. Anne's Fort just to his right sited on a mound. Sir Hamon had repaired it and now there were men there also. It wasn't a good place to be, Roger thought, right in the middle of what might come to be enemy territory.

The men were anxious and tension rippled through the ranks. They had never been in this situation before. They were a mixture of a few soldiers with little experience, raw recruits, and enthusiastic volunteers. Although they had been tutored in the art of firing a musket by Captains Goodman, Naunton and Havers, they had no idea what to expect. Roger had at least been to Newburn and Edgehill and seen some action. Not that it counted for much as experience went.

'Remember, gentlemen, we are defending the good people of Lynn, our wives and children, mothers and fathers. They are relying on us.' Roger patted the first young man on the shoulder and then walked on along the wall, checking on them, repeating the order not to fire until they heard the order.

Expectation hung in the air like a foul smell. The men on the wall were mostly silent, watching, waiting, talking in whispers as if an ordinary voice would alert the enemy. Young boys, acting as powder monkeys sat by firkins of gunpowder, several primed muskets beside them, for any man that might need them.

Roger came to Captain Wharton under whose command this troop had been placed by the governor. 'No sign of them yet,' Roger said unnecessarily.

'It don't do to be too hasty in these matters,' Captain Wharton said.

Roger turned and began to walk back along the wall. He wished they would get on with it. He hated the tense restlessness which kept his nerves jumping.

Word spread along the wall that Lord Manchester's troops were just the other side of the rise and a profound silence fell on the defenders as everyone strained their ears to listen for any sound.

They all heard it, a faint rumble on the early morning air. Straining his ears, Roger tried to work out what the sound might be and at that moment a large shadow appeared on the rise. Men. Looking from that distance far more in number than the four and a half thousand they had been told to expect.

Yet again the command to hold their fire echoed down the wall as Lord Manchester's Parliamentary army advanced towards King's Lynn across the fields outside Lynn. At the order, given first by Captain Wharton and then by Roger, those with flintlock muskets pulled back the hammers with loud clicks and those with the old matchlocks made sure their tapers were alight.

They waited.

Slowly Manchester's men advanced, cast into silhouette by the rising sun. Three quarters of them were infantry and about one and a half thousand were cavalry and in their midst Roger could see their battle standard. As they watched, cannon appeared on the flanks and set to face the town.

With the sun in their eyes, the defenders watched the advancement. Roger's mouth had gone dry and his stomach squirmed, partly through fear and partly through excitement. A man could get drunk on the excitement, he thought.

And then, just out of musket-range, the army halted, the voices of command as they cried the order echoing across the silent fields to the waiting cavaliers. The accompanying rhythmic rumble of an army on the move ceased abruptly and an eerie silence fell over the whole area within and without the town. Not even a bird could be heard. It was as if the whole world held its breath.

A lone voice called out an order which echoed across the fields to the defenders, and the troops rustled in obedience, although they were too far away for Roger to see what they did.

After several minutes, two men on horses, one carrying the battle standard, advanced at a trot towards the East Gate. Again the reminder to hold fire passed along the lines of waiting defenders on the ramparts. They halted outside the East Gate on the other side of the moat in front of the raised drawbridge.

'People of Lynn,' the foremost rider, the one without the standard, cried in a strong carrying voice, addressing the gatehouse. 'You are advised to yield this town to the army under Lord Manchester.'

Sir Hamon's voice rang out from the gatehouse. 'We keep this town for his Majesty King Charles and with God's help will keep it so. Manchester may as well raise his father from the dead as force his entrance into Lynn. He has as much hope of entering Heaven's gate as forcing his way in here!'

His voice could be heard by many of the defenders and a large cheer confirmed everyone's agreement.

'If that be your answer, then you must suffer the consequences,' cried the horseman and, turning, both of them broke into a gallop as they made their way back to the safety of their own lines.

Later that day, a written message was sent to the Earl of Manchester confirming the stand the people of Lynn had taken and signed with twenty-five names, taunting that Manchester should now know whom to plunder when he had taken the town.

This was productive of some merriment by the burgesses meeting in the council chambers in the Guildhall.

'We are too well-defended for the likes of Manchester's mere four-and-a-half-thousand men,' Sir Robert de Grey said with satisfaction. 'They'll never storm this town.'

Sir Hamon was more cautious. 'For all our might, we must put our trust in God. He did, after all, decree Charles to be our King. Furthermore, I have no doubts that before long the four-and-a-half-thousand could be double that number or more. It is rumoured that Oliver Cromwell and Captain Poe with their forces are on their way to Manchester's assistance.'

Young Sir Charles Mordaunt was thoughtful. 'They have control of all the bridges from here southwards. We cannot get help from anywhere except across the Wash.'

'We have Lord Newcastle's promise,' Sir Hamon reminded them.

Gurlin said nervously: 'Well he'd better come soon. We will exhaust our food. If Newcastle does not come, I mean.'

Every eye in the room turned upon him. No-one needed a pessimist at this moment. Gurlin looked at them all and then looked down sheepishly. 'Well, we have to think of these things,' he said.

'All in hand, Mr. Gurlin,' Sir Hamon informed him.

The burgesses rode high on a tide of optimism. Things were progressing just as they had expected and now it was time to consider their next move.

Sir Hamon said: 'We could do with putting some obstacles in the way of Manchester's armies. The longer we can keep their troops from joining them, the more chance we give Lord Newcastle of coming to our aid.'

Sir Nicholas was thoughtful. 'There is a bridge on the Cambridge Road, not far from here, which if we were to—dismantle—would cause problems for Manchester's supplies.'

Sir Hamon nodded. 'You're thinking of the bridge at Setchey over the Nar.'

Nicholas smiled. 'Just so. Manchester has made his headquarters there, as I understand it. It's destruction would make life pretty difficult for him and any other advancing armies to cross the Nar.' The river was a modest affair, no more than twelve feet across.

''Tis a stone bridge, as I recall,' Sir Hamon mused. ''Twould take a lot of gunpowder to destroy it.'

'I'll do it for you,' Roger said immediately and the eyes of everyone in the room turned towards him.

'Do you think you could?' Sir Robert de Grey asked. 'What experience have you of explosives?'

Roger frowned. 'I commanded the detail which blew up the alms houses,' he said.

Sir Hamon spoke up for him. 'He is capable, Sir Robert. He has experience and he knows how to get the job done. I have every confidence in my son's ability, having fought beside him in Scotland.'

Momentarily Roger thought of the debacle at Newburn. He had not shown any outstanding tendency to heroism at that time, and again at Edgehill he had been wounded too early to engage in anything. But as a youth which was not really that long ago, he had been famous in the family for his ability to climb trees, and walls, and even shin up Sir

Hamon's prized new downpipes when he had come home late and could not wake the servants.

Sir Charles Mordaunt said: 'I'll go with you, Roger, if you will.'

Roger smiled at his old friend. 'You will be most welcome.'

But Sir Hamon did not like it. 'Sir Charles has a wife and children, Roger, and, I think I am right in saying, Sir Charles, that you have no experience of explosives?'

Mordaunt shook his head regretfully.

'Well then, I am sorry, sir, but I will not let you go. This needs someone who has experience. I will send Captain Havers with you, Roger. And if he thinks more men would be necessary, then he will know who to choose.'

It was useless to protest, so Roger contented himself with the knowledge that his father trusted him with the task and Sir Charles acquiesced.

Later when the other burgesses had gone, Sir Hamon, Sir Nicholas and Roger sat together in the Governor's sitting room. It was cooler in here, for the small casement window was open on the catch, and a gentle breeze wafted around them. He could hear some noise from outside, but there was almost no traffic, just a few pedestrians going about their daily lives. Despite an army sitting down outside the town gates, people were trying to carry on as normal. He wondered if he would see Ruth this evening.

Sir Hamon looked at Roger in the gloom. 'This is dangerous work,' he said quietly. 'You do not have to go.'

Having stated his intention to go, Roger could not back out now and have everyone think him a coward. 'I appreciate that, sir. But I have no intention of being captured.'

At that moment the door opened and captain Havers himself entered the room before the servant could announce him. Roger had met Havers briefly and had formed a good opinion of him as a man of good sense and ability. He was a man of medium height and a strong muscled body. This man knew what he was doing.

He inclined his head in a bow, acknowledged by all, and shook Sir Hamon's hand. Quickly Sir Hamon explained what was required. Havers looked at Roger, sizing him up, evidently reluctant to work with him.

'You have experience, sir?' he demanded.

'I led the detail which blew up the alms houses in Old Lynn,' Roger said evenly.

Havers nodded pursing his lips, his bushy moustache quivering.

'You know about gunpowder?'

'I do. I am sure that where I have gaps in my education you will fill them, sir.'

'Hmph!' Havers turned his attention to the plan. 'We will need to get behind the enemy lines, sir,' he said to Sir Hamon.

'How do you think you could do that?' Sir Hamon asked.

'The roads are guarded, of course,' Havers observed. 'And although it would be possible to go out the Guannock Gate without being observed, we would spend much time trying to avoid the enemy.'

'By boat then?' Roger suggested and he thought Havers looked at him with surprise. Well he, Roger, had a brain after all!

Sir Nicholas unrolled a chart and spread it across the table but it was too dark to see it. Roger began the task of striking the flint to fire the tinder in order to light some candles which he then brought across as Nicholas reached across the table and closed the window lest the draught should blow them out again.

Now they could all stand and peer at the chart. Sir Nicholas pointed with his finger. 'The enemy lies between here and Gaywood, taking in the South Gate as well, just about down to the river. There is no way through that way.'

'Oh, it could be done,' Havers said, also pointing to the map. 'There is cover here, in these trees, and a gap in enemy lines just outside Guannock Gate. But I think that the best way is what Mr. L'Estrange suggested, by the river. We would not need horses for that and we could carry everything we need with us. Horses are noisy,' he added by way of further explanation. 'Also, we could use the incoming tide to take us most of the way up the river until the tidal reach ran out. I think a man or two who has local knowledge of the river would be useful to us.'

Sir Hamon nodded thoughtfully. 'A boat could be almost silent.'

Not wishing to be left out of this conversation, Roger added: 'With rags in the rowlocks and careful rowing, it could.'

'So boat it is.' Reluctant respect began to grow in Havers' eyes.

Roger pointed to the map. 'It should be easy to coast along the Ouse until we come to the Boal. Then turn left into the river Nar.'

'Make sure you don't take that creek.' Sir Nicholas pointed to a little offshoot on the right. ''Twould be easy to make a mistake in the dark.'

Roger nodded. 'Understood. If the tide is coming in, it will take us with it.'

Havers put in: 'Aye, but there will be eddies and currents to deal with. That's why a local river man would be useful.'

'Agreed.'

They discussed this at length.

Sir Hamon brought them back to their plans. 'You will need to take gunpowder with you. Enough to blow up the bridge.'

Havers agreed. 'Two barrels ought to do it with a long enough fuse for us to get clear.'

Havers and Roger discussed how they would achieve their aim. It was not difficult for Roger to acknowledge Havers' superiority in such matters and as they talked his respect for this man grew. At the same time he sensed that Havers was thawing towards him. A good thing if they were to work together.

TWENTY-NINE

The following evening, Roger met Ruth briefly in the lane to explain that he could not stay. The sun was going down and the small arms fire which had rattled on all day had become sporadic as the light began to fail.

'You are up to something,' she told him.

He frowned. 'Up to something?'

'I can see it in your eyes. You are excited.'

He could not deny it, for the excitement boiled in his insides. 'I have a job to do.' He could say no more.

She studied him disapprovingly for several moments. 'Be careful,' she said at last, before giving him a quick kiss and then turning to go back to her aunt's house.

He could not detain her. He had preparations to make. He hoped Havers thought he had gone to the privy.

Obligingly the tide was well on its way in at half past eight and Roger and Havers were ready. Dressed only in dark breeches and without shoes, they clambered into the boat at Purfleet with two rugged and taciturn river men Havers had found, and they allowed the tide to take them southwards as they hugged the edge of the Ouse all the way.

It was not yet dark, the sky still glowing in the west from the sun which was already below the horizon and they hoped to make it to the Nar turn off before the light was gone completely. Using the oars to guide and keep them where they wanted to be they let the tide take them past Boal Fleet (which was also known as Millfleet further upstream), rounded The Boal (a spit of land jutting into the Ouse) and then took an offshoot of the Ouse, known locally as Friars Fleet, in reality the outflow of the River Nar. They made good progress, but the currents were treacherous, and at times they had to fight to keep the little boat from spinning around on them. They passed the creek Nicholas had pointed out and then they could just see the turn in the river where two rivers met—the Esk, which was little more than a glorified stream flowing eastwards, and the river Nar, their target which was straight on towards the south. The South Gates were on the edge of the Esk just a few yards from the junction which flowed outside the curtain wall to make a defensive moat around the town. At present the South Gates drawbridge over the Esk was up, the portcullis down and the gates closed, for Cromwell's troops had arrived and they were camped in the fields from the junction of the two rivers all the way around the town to the East Gates.

As they made silent progress along the Nar, Roger could hear the sounds from the camp, of some men snoring, others talking and they could see the campfires, smell the smoke and cooking food mixed with the usual odour of horses, of dung and urine and unwashed humanity. Their proximity reminded him of the danger of being discovered and excitement chased through him. It made him feel alive. There was no moon as yet, but they dipped their oars into the unrippled water with hardly any noise, grateful to have taken the precaution of oiling and ragging the rowlocks in advance. Well aware that the slightest noise, the creak of wood, the splash in the water, could arouse someone's curiosity, they kept well into the shoreline and rowed carefully, knowing the overgrown vegetation of high thistles and nettles and reeds would keep them out of sight.

At length they left the enemy camp behind and they could relax a little more. The Nar narrowed gradually the further upstream they rowed, but the current as the water raced towards the sea flowed quickly. It made heavy work of the rowing. The need for silence added to the difficulty. Even in open country sound travelled. The river men cursed in low whispers, but kept the boat into the edge as best they could where the current was less forceful. They all sweated and panted in the heat of a muggy late summer night, but at last Setchey came into view. Or more accurately the small single arched bridge over the Nar at Setchey came into view. Together Roger and Havers looked at the stone structure, looming black in shadow. It was the first bridge on the Nar after Lynn.

The village of Setchey spread out on their left, dark shadows against the midnight sky. The stars were out, but no moon. While it suited them for cover, it certainly did not help in seeing where they were going. The river men, though, seemed to have a sixth sense which guided them effortlessly around irregularities in the bank and clumps of reed.

With some manoeuvring they turned the boat around so that the prow faced downstream, ready for their getaway, and brought it into the bank tying it off between two other moored boats just downstream from the bridge.

'One guard,' Havers whispered. 'On the right.'

'I see him.' The man seemed to be leaning on the bridge parapet, dozing. Roger turned to look at the barrels of gunpowder stored at each end of the boat covered with leather sheets to protect it from accidental splashes. 'We'll come back for them, let's deal with the guard first.'

'I'll deal with the guard. You get the gunpowder onto the shore.'

Havers climbed the river bank on the northern side of the bridge, and came up to the road. Roger watched him for a moment, as Havers started to cross the bridge, approaching the guard. He had an uneasy feeling about Havers' alacrity to deal with the guard. He did not know Havers at all, but he had detected a ruthlessness about him that bothered him.

However, the river men were already unloading the barrels. Someone else had loaded them into the boat, and now as Roger came to help, he realised just how heavy a barrel of gunpowder was. They could not let it down onto the ground, for in his bare feet Roger was paddling in water up to his shins. The river, it turned out, was only about eighteen inches deep in the centre! Still, it would be enough to render gunpowder useless.

As he and one of the river men heaved the first barrel onto dry ground Havers' voice reached them from the bridge. 'Hello friend.'

The guard raised the lantern and for a moment Havers stood in its glow. 'Who be there?' the guard demanded.

'A friend. A weary traveller. Tell me, where may I find a bed for the night?'

Roger watched the bridge.

'Ah, tha' be the Dray an' Horses in Tottenhill just down yonder.' As the man looked to the south in the direction of the inn, he saw Havers strike. The man fell where he stood, and Havers bundled him out of the way. Silently he ran back to the men by the boat.

'He won't cause any trouble,' Havers whispered and he could not hide the note of satisfaction in his voice.

Roger studied him more with his senses than his sight in the darkness. 'You didn't kill him?' The guard was probably a local man, drafted by the Parliamentarian army. There was no sense in killing him when it was unnecessary.

'No. Knocked him out.' Seeing that Roger was still not satisfied, he added: 'A stone on the side of his head.'

Unsure whether he believed him, Roger could do nothing about it anyway.

All four men worked quickly and quietly to bring the barrels onto the bridge. Four barrels, carried rather than rolled, for the sound of them on gravel might alert someone. Several times Roger stood on stones on the bridge, which cut into feet unused to going unshod, but he gritted his teeth.

They positioned the barrels either side of the bridge on each side of the keystone in the single arch, lying them down against the parapet. They set the fuses, twisted rope coated with gunpowder, twisting them all together. They knew that the fuses would burn at the rate of one inch per second. The river was only ten or twelve feet across, the bridge a little more, the barrels near the centre. Although they snaked the fuse, they could reckon on no more than three minutes to get clear.

Roger carried the lighted match, a smouldering length of rope, in a perforated tin hanging from his waist. As the boatmen ran back to the boat, and Havers stood at the edge of the bridge waiting for him, Roger retrieved it, gently blew on it to make it glow and then touched it to the end of the fuse. Immediately it burst into life with sparks and he watched it burn for a second or two.

'Jim, Jim, where are you?' The male voice from the other end of the bridge carried across the night. 'Jim? J—who's there? Stop or I'll shoot!'

Roger and Havers needed no further warning. Running like bolting horses, they left the bridge, Havers in front, leaping and running across the grass and down the bank.

A musket did indeed fire, and suddenly the place was in uproar.

They'll see the fuse and pull it out! Roger thought. The others were in the boat, and when Roger reached it he pushed it out from the edge as they let the tethering ropes go. As soon as the boat was clear of the undergrowth and he felt the tug of the current, he leapt in, Havers heaving at him as the river men used the oars.

Now there was a string of musket-fire. A hot wisp of air brushed Roger's cheek as he righted himself in the boat and grabbed the last pair of oars.

They were travelling with the flow of the river now, and making good speed, as what seemed to be the whole of Lord Manchester's army gave chase along the river banks.

'They'll have found the fuses and pulled them out by now,' Roger remarked as they gained the bend in the river which would hide them from view.

'So, we've given the enemy a store of gunpowder. Your papa is not going to be happy with that!'

At that moment a mighty explosion like the end of the world tore the very air as one of the powder kegs exploded. The others quickly followed. The blast hit the men in the boat full in the face, tearing at their hair, for they rowed English-fashion facing backwards. Brick and stone hurtled heavenwards to land with thuds on the earth and mighty splashes in the water, narrowly missing the boat. The saboteurs all ducked down, hoping to be shielded by the banks, but were still showered by small debris.

As shocked silence fell over the river, they paused just before the bend to look at the damage. Lights moved about at each end of the bridge, but the middle was completely gone. It was as Sir Hamon had thought. Without the keystone the arch had no strength and the whole thing collapsed. There was nothing left!

'Sir 'Ammon be 'appy with that, Oi do think,' one of the river men ventured. 'But you better get rowin' do we be caught by them as chase us!'

Roger grinned in the darkness, the excitement still rushing through his veins. 'Yes!'

Havers too grinned, his teeth glowing white in the scant light. 'I think we might have overdone it with the gunpowder,' he remarked, and laughed.

And with that they rowed downstream for Lynn.

THIRTY

The Earl of Manchester, safely ensconced in a house in Setchey, was not a happy man. He ran his fingers through his long dark hair in a gesture of despair. 'Well, what have you to say?' he demanded.

Captain William Poe stroked his moustache, uncomfortably aware that his had been the responsibility for guarding the bridges between Lynn and Downham, (about fifteen miles south of Lynn) and now one of them was little more than rubble while a dirty great gap in the road marked its passing. 'I say, my lord, that I do not have enough men to guard the bridges and those I do have are local men, who have little heart for the war.'

Manchester put his head in his hands. The commission he had received to impress twenty-thousand men looked fine on paper, but in fact it did not translate into much of an army. Furthermore, the people in the countryside were sympathetic to Sir Hamon L'Estrange's Royalist cause and they refused to supply provisions to the besiegers, while the locally trained bands also refused point blank to participate in the siege.

Captain Poe's troops sitting down outside Lynn were much smaller in number than the Royalists supposed. Worse, they were poorly disciplined, with little in the way of equipment. Their lack of co-operation cost Manchester many sleepless nights. 'Our own troops are far more dreadful to me than any enemy,' he groaned.

'I don't reckon the enemy can hold out more than five days,' Poe said optimistically.

Manchester laughed mirthlessly. 'You think so? We thought we were dealing with country squires who don't know on which end to put their hat, yet they have just blown up the bridge here! Here! On my doorstep! Five days? I tell you they can hold out weeks. And if Newcastle comes down from the north to relieve them, it will be the finish of us! He'll be in London before the summer's out! We could lose the war over this.'

Poe offered: 'The regiment was raised in Suffolk. That county should pay us what we need.'

'Well it ain't forthcoming!' Manchester told him bluntly. 'If you want supplies, you'll have to requisition them from the local people. You've been requisitioning horses in Suffolk, despite the complaints, so I reckon you can manage to find food for your troops!' He stood up and went to the window where he could see men trying to clear the rubble.

'How long before the bridge is passable?'

'A few days, but it will have to be makeshift, if we can find the wood.'

'Then cut some trees down!'

'*Seasoned* wood!'

'God give me patience!' However, fortunately for his lordship, he was billeted on the north side of the river and therefore unaffected personally, but getting supplies and troops in from the south was going to be a nightmare until the bridge was again in commission.

At that moment a servant entered, bowed and said: 'Lieutenant-General Cromwell, my lord.'

And before Manchester had a chance to reply Cromwell strode into the room.

Manchester and Cromwell harboured a mutual dislike, but since Cromwell was Manchester's second-in-command they had to work together. Manchester viewed Cromwell as overbearing. Cromwell viewed Manchester as too soft.

'What happened to the bridge?' Cromwell demanded abruptly without so much as a greeting.

Lord Manchester had to take a deep breath. 'Saboteurs,' he said simply. 'Last night. How did you get through?'

'News travels fast hereabouts. We went towards Swaffham from Downham Market and crossed the river at Narborough. Thankfully we had a man who knows the way to guide us. How did they do it? You put men to guard it, I assume?'

'Naturally.' His lordship's irritation grew and he said: 'Where are your troops?'

'They've joined Poe's outside King's Lynn.

'So have mine!' Sir Miles Hobart joined them through the still-open door, but he at least had the good grace to bow.

'Good, for we are desperately short of men.'

Cromwell nodded. The man was insufferably proud, which further irritated his lordship. 'They will be forthcoming if the Lord wills,' Cromwell said.

However, Captain Poe thought better than to rely totally on the Lord. His troops were the first ones to have arrived and therefore it was his troops that came under constant attack from the town's defenders. With no relief he was becoming quite desperate. 'I'll send letters to the Association for help,' he said.

Manchester nodded. 'Very well.'

§

On Sunday afternoon, a hundred and twenty Royalist musketeers set an ambush for the invaders.

Sir Nicholas and Captain Wharton had planned it meticulously.

'We'll need two troops of horse and two bodies of foot as well as muskets,' Sir Nicholas told his father eagerly. 'We'll cut them down to size!'

Sir Hamon studied him thoughtfully. 'Better take Roger. Since the Setchey bridge he has not been able to keep still.' His laughing dark eyes rested on his youngest son and Roger grinned back. He found the excitement of the bridge success to be addictive.

Captain Wharton nodded. 'Well by me,' he said.

So Roger found himself mounted, armed, armoured and beside his brother as they sallied forth from Lynn's East Gate. The danger did not worry him, but the excitement of battle, of contest and conquest made his insides jump nervously. He had something to do, something worthwhile, fighting for his King.

The troop crossed the rough ground outside Lynn's wall quickly, keeping together. Captain Poe and his troop rose to the challenge and came forward to meet them on foot.

At that moment and without waiting for the command, Royalist musketeers hidden in the undergrowth fired upon them.

No! It was too early. Roger swore and he heard Nicholas swear too. Poe had not come far enough forward so that the muskets could cut them down. Instead he gave the command and his troops fell to the ground, giving fire upon the Royalist cavalry.

Nicholas swore profanely and whirled his horse around. They had become easy targets. 'Retreat!' he yelled, for it was the only thing they could do.

The musketeers did their best in keeping the rebels' heads down, but they could not work miracles.

Roger swore again and caught Captain Wharton's eye. If they did not quickly get out of harm's way they would be cut down by the muskets. He and Captain Wharton both took up the cry of 'Retreat!'

Some men from Lynn brought a cannon out of the East Gate and brought it around ready to fire on the rebels. Roger watched in disbelief. Were they going to be killed by their own cannon? Even as he watched he saw the disaster as if in slow motion. The cannon turned over. Now it was unusable, because the barrel would be full of earth, even if they managed to right it.

He shook his head in dismay as Sir Nicholas called the troops off.

Sir Nicholas was livid. He stormed into Sir Hamon's study to give an account of the proceedings, almost inarticulate with fury, with the luckless Captain Wharton and the dismayed Roger in his wake.

'It was a d-damned f-farce!' he cried, falling over his words in his anger. 'An absolute damned farce! Who gave the order for those muskets to open fire? That's what I would like to know!'

Sir Hamon who had been discussing the blockade from the sea with Sir Charles Mordaunt and Sir Robert de Grey looked up at him in surprise at this outburst. 'Am I to understand that the operation was not a success?' he enquired, his calm voice in stark contrast to Sir Nicholas's heat.

'Not a success? *Not a success*? I can imagine what Poe will make of it when he reports to his superiors. Damn me, *I* have never seen such a farce! It was a comedy! And we ran back with our tails between our legs like whipped dogs!'

There was a short embarrassed silence.

Roger, whose success with the bridge took some of the ignominy out of the situation for him, said with less vehemence than his brother: 'The muskets fired too early, warning Poe of what we were about rather than trapping him, and he dug in, giving fire on us.'

'And the cannon?' Sir Hamon dared to enquire.

'Turned over!' Sir Nicholas answered promptly through clenched teeth. '*Turned over!* I tell you, Father, these men here are useless!'

'Filled with dirt, so could not be fired,' Roger corroborated.

Captain Wharton coughed. 'Excuse me, sir, but it be fair to mention that the men are eager and have not had much experience.'

'They have had some training,' Sir Hamon observed.

'And if they were to obey orders—' Sir Nicholas cut in, but he was too angry to find words to finish his sentence. Instead he turned away.

Captain Wharton's moustache bristled. His was the responsibility to deal with the troops, to train them, yet how to discipline in a siege situation was a question he had evidently not addressed.

Sir Hamon, as governor, had the final responsibility. He knew the men were eager, anxious, ready for a fight. He knew that tensions ran high. While Sir Nicholas, who had been a Lieutenant in the army before the war and Roger who had fought in Scotland and Edgehill and Captain Wharton and other commanders had experience, their troops did not. Furthermore, it seemed to him that the other side had better trained troops. Not blessed with knowing about Lord Manchester's despair, Sir Hamon assumed the defenders were less prepared for battle than the attackers.

However, Sir Hamon had been aware of this problem all along and his reliance had not been on his army, but rather on the relief army from across the Wash under Lord Newcastle's command. He expected him daily, for the prize of Lynn and what lay beyond—London—must surely be of prime importance to his lordship. He knew it was to Lord Manchester.

§

William Cavendish, the second Earl of Newcastle looked out over his straggling army and sighed. 'So what would you have me do then?' he asked of Sir William Saville.

Sir William looked at the letter. 'Sir Hamon L'Estrange wants us to come to their aid at King's Lynn. Manchester's army is scant. If we secure King's Lynn, we could press on to London.'

The Earl of Newcastle frowned and shook his head. 'Which is more important to the King? King's Lynn or Hull?'

'They are both important.'

'So which should I go to?'

'My thoughts are for King's Lynn. We have more chance of success there. If we go to Hull, we will have to lay siege to the city. If we rout the Puritans in Lynn, we can press on to London.' Sir William studied his commander. He knew that Lord Newcastle did not want to go to Lynn. He had to cross the Wash, or go around it, to come to the relief of the town. And pressing on to London was not what he wanted to do. That would incur more engagements, more battles. And, Saville suspected, his lordship was not a courageous man. However, Sir William Saville was sure that if they seized this advantage they could win the war.

The Earl huffed. 'Perhaps we should go on to Hull.'

Unseen by his lordship, Sir William Saville rolled his eyes heavenward. He knew also that Hull would be a long drawn out siege and that there would be little hope of success. He said: 'If Manchester is successful in King's Lynn, he will press on northwards and will defeat us at Hull.'

Lord Newcastle compressed his lips. 'I will think about it,' he said at last.

Sir William knew he could say no more and that he had been effectively dismissed. He bowed his head and left.

The Earl's secretary asked: 'Do you wish to write to Sir Hamon L'Estrange to inform him of your decision, my lord?'

The Earl frowned. 'Not just now.' He said.

THIRTY-ONE

Conditions in the town deteriorated. Usually the 'night soil' would be taken away from privies by what the people, with typical English irony, called the 'honey cart' to somewhere outside the town and dumped. With the town blockaded, the night soil was left where it was, and in the overbearing heat of the hottest summer anyone could remember, the stench rose heavenward in a miasma of offence. Added to that, they had brought animals into the town for food, cattle and sheep, and of course, the horses, and their dung and urine added to the problem.

'There will be a plague,' Ruth told Roger when they met one evening just inside the Guannock Gate. 'All this bad air is sure to breed sickness.'

He frowned, concerned. 'I will speak to my father about it.'

Ruth followed up her advantage. 'And speak to him about the food situation, too, if you please. It is becoming harder to get meat of any kind. I think the herd must be greatly reduced.'

From outside the gate the sound of sporadic popping of muskets filled the air. The noise worried Ruth, but she would not have missed this opportunity to be with Roger, if it were just for a few minutes. She needed to see him and not only to reassure herself that he remained unhurt.

The men on the wall gave back fire.

'They are out of range, save your shot!' Roger called to them, but no-one paid him any heed.

He shook his head, and turned his attention back to Ruth, managing a small smile. He had changed, she thought. Subtly. He had grown with the responsibility his father put on him. Some of the devil-may-care attitude had gone, replaced with a new maturity. She liked it.

The cattle and horses had been moved to the other side of the Purfleet for the pasture had been over-grazed. They wandered hand in hand on grass no more than half an inch long and brown because of the lack of rain. Feed had been brought in and stored for this eventuality. Beside the Millfleet, the grass was greener, but that too was grazed down to the bare earth.

'I will mention about the food to my father,' he said. 'It is handy that we have water coming into the town.' Millfleet, Purfleet and Fisherfleet all took their water from the Gaywood River, the lower reach of which was called the river Esk, and all of them flowed through the town and down to the sea. The upper reaches, at least, were uncontaminated by human waste, unlike the lower end of Purfleet.

The men on the wall stepped up their firing. 'Wasting shot,' Roger grumbled, as he took Ruth by the arm and led her away from the wall towards the chestnut trees. It was a protective gesture. He made her feel safe.

A sudden cry behind them caused them both to turn to see a man fall off the wall a distance of perhaps six or seven feet, to land with a thud on the hard dry earth where he lay still.

Both Roger and Ruth ran to him, reaching him before others did.

The man had been shot in the shoulder, blood seeping into his clothes. He moaned, which Ruth viewed as a good sign.

'You should have kept low,' Roger reprimanded him, producing a kerchief which Ruth pressed over the man's wound.

'Think I've broken me damned arm!' the man complained. Opening one eye and spotting Ruth, he added: 'Begging your pardon, ma'am.'

Well, at least he was conscious, Ruth thought, relieved.

Roger felt down the length of both arms, but it was the left forearm which caused him to cry out. 'Yes, indeed,' Roger announced. 'You need to see the surgeon.'

The captain of the detail approached. 'I cannot spare men to take him to the infirmary,' he said gruffly.

Roger's face told Ruth what he thought of the captain's lack of humanity. After all, the infirmary was no more than a couple of hundred yards away across the grass in St. James' Chapel. 'We'll take him,' Roger said with a raised brow at Ruth. 'I'll do it if you wish to go home, madam.'

She shook her head.

'I'll come with you. Can we get a cart?'

Roger looked around him but there was no cart in sight.

'No.' The captain answered for him. 'Ain't got none.'

Roger asked the man: 'Can you walk?'

'Oi can.'

'We need to splint the arm,' Ruth told Roger. 'Before we move him, that is.'

Someone produced a straightish stick, and someone else a light rope. It would serve, and Ruth bound the man's arm to the stick. She also wedged Roger's handkerchief into the wound in the man's shoulder. He was bleeding alarmingly, and she hoped it would staunch it a little.

Men lifted the casualty onto his feet and he all but swooned with the effort.

'We can carry 'im,' someone volunteered.

'I can't spare any of you,' the captain said.

Ruth rolled her eyes heavenward and said: 'It is such a short distance, and he can walk. Being pulled about will not do him any good.'

Roger put his arm around him to steady him, and Ruth did her best to keep the pressure on the wound in the man's shoulder, the opposite shoulder to the fracture.

The infirmary may have been just a short distance, but the man was winded, and in pain, and their progress was necessarily slow.

'Where did you learn to do that?' Roger asked Ruth as they walked.

'What? The splint? 'Tis common enough practice. Besides, I've two brothers, and I saw it done when one of them fell off his horse and broke his arm.'

The man began to stumble, probably through blood loss weakness, and Ruth saw that Roger did his best to hold the man upright. She wondered how many noblemen would actually do this for someone they not only did not know but who was also not of their class. He soared in her estimation.

At last they came to the infirmary which was housed in the old chapel of St. James.

As Ruth opened the door the stench hit them. Roger paused and exchanged glances with Ruth, then he staggered in with the man who was now barely conscious. With Ruth's help he let him down to the floor, propping him against a once white-washed wall. They were in what was the main body of the chapel. Wounded men were lying or sitting everywhere with barely room to walk between them, and only a privileged few had a straw mattress. The smell was appalling. Not only of unwashed humanity, but also the odours of the privy. Blue-bottles buzzed and landed on open wounds and filthy bandages. It took a second or two for Ruth to realise that the patients, the most of whom appeared to be in the throes of a fever, had not been tended to by anyone, that they had nowhere to relieve themselves except where they lay, too ill to move. There was no evidence that they had been fed, either, and bandages were filthy with dirt and caked blood. Her heart wrenched at the sight of them, pitiful, sick, unclean people, even as her stomach heaved. She fought it with an effort. 'Dear God! Is there no-one to care for them?'

Roger too looked around him, appalled. His eyes met hers. He was as shocked as she was. 'I will find someone,' Ruth decided, and she left Roger with the casualty.

Something seemed to be happening in a room at the side of the chapel, and so she lifted her skirts clear of the wet stone floor and picked her way carefully through the moaning bodies towards it

The fly-infested room turned out to be the place where the surgeon operated. He had someone on a blood-soaked table, and was digging at a hole in the man's abdomen. Mercifully, the patient was unconscious. Another man was at the patient's head, and a third came in an outside door carrying a bucket of water. As Ruth stood there, the surgeon glanced at her.

'What are you doing here? Get out! This is no place for a woman!'

Ruth was inclined to agree.

The surgeon swatted at a fly with his spare hand and then, dived with his fingers into the wound. Victoriously, he produced a lead ball from the man's insides soaked in blood and tissue. The orderly at his head announced: 'He's dead!' and the surgeon sighed, dropping the lead ball into a metal dish with a clank which suggested it stuck to the bottom. 'Get rid of him!'

The orderly and the other man removed the body.

The surgeon again looked at Ruth who was regarding the scene with horrified eyes. 'You still here? What do you want?'

Ruth swallowed, and tried not to let her eyes linger on a bucket that contained a bloody hand attached to part of a forearm. 'My—friend—and I have brought a casualty from the wall. He is shot in the shoulder and has broken the bone in his arm.'

The surgeon sighed again wearily. 'Bring him in.'

Ruth nodded and exchanged the scene of butchery for the loathsome mess of the general ward, once more picking her way through the bodies.

Roger looked at her and raised his brows. She thought he looked as sick as she felt.

'He said to bring him through.'

Roger nodded, and tried to raise the man on his own, but Ruth had to help. Together they managed to get the man to the side room. This time she had no hands to delicately raise her skirts, and she knew they dragged in the filth. The orderlies came back in from removing the body and now helped the man onto the table.

One of them cut off the man's clothing from the upper part of his body, exposing a skinny frame covered with grey white skin topped with chest hair. She saw Roger glance in her direction out of the corner of her eye, but she could not look at him. In other circumstances the sight of a man's bare torso would have embarrassed her. She was not embarrassed now.

The surgeon looked from Roger to Ruth. 'Who did this?' he demanded roughly, pointing at the splint.

'The lady,' Roger replied.

The surgeon's brows raised and Ruth thought he was impressed. 'Well you can leave now.'

'You're not going to cut his arm off, are you?' Ruth asked alarmed, and casting another glance at the arm in the bucket.

'Young woman, I am going to remove the ball from his shoulder first, then, if he survives that, I shall set the bone in his arm. But this is no place for a lady.'

Ruth put her head up. 'I think it is.'

She heard Roger splutter beside her, but she ignored him. Instead she went to the patient's head. He had dirt across his face from his fall, and a graze on his cheek, and she looked around for some fresh water. Seeing the bucket in the corner and finding a metal bowl on a ledge behind her, she fetched some water to the patient. Taking her handkerchief she dipped it in the water, and while the surgeon worked, she soothed the patient by wiping the dirt off his face with the damp cloth, and talking soothingly to him. Although the patient cried out, she continued unabated.

Roger said nothing. She knew he watched her, could feel his eyes upon her. He also stood by, watching the operation. The surgeon was quick, dropping the lead ball into the metal dish, cleaning the wound, tying a clean pad over it with a bandage. He washed his hands in the bucket and dried them and then assessed the broken arm. A moment later he pulled on the wrist and the bone clicked into line. Re-using the splint Ruth had used, he bound it.

'Are you leaving him here?' the surgeon asked.

Roger came nearer to the man on the table. 'Where do you live?'

'Mill Lane,' the man replied weakly.

'You have a wife?'

'Oi do.'

'In that case we will take you home.'

The orderlies helped the man up.

'The ball chipped the bone in his shoulder, but it must have been almost spent, for it did not do the damage I've sometimes seen. If he doesn't get a fever, he'll do.'

Ruth thanked him.

The surgeon looked at her. 'I expected to be picking you up from the floor, mistress.'

'I cannot desert anyone in need, sir,' she replied. She saw the respect for her grow in the man's eyes. It was there in Roger's also.

Glancing through the window she saw a cart and a single horse. 'May we borrow your cart? We will, of course, return it.'

'What for?'

'So that we can take this man home. His wife can take care of him.'

''T-has bodies on it, one of the orderlies pointed out.

'They can be removed,' Ruth said practically. 'This man cannot walk now.'

'My men do not have time to off-load and re-load bodies,' the surgeon complained.

'Rubbish! Of course they do. How long does it take? A minute? Less than that? Now, if you please . . .'

Roger grinned, appreciatively she thought.

The surgeon's dark eyes flashed, but Ruth refused to be cowed. 'If you please,' she repeated at her most haughty.

The surgeon sighed loudly and nodded to the waiting, grinning orderlies, and in short order the man was on the cart.

Roger climbed up to drive, and Ruth, with a glance over her shoulder at the patient, climbed up to sit beside him. As he slapped the reins, she said: 'I have never been so appalled by anything in my life. The condition of those poor wretches in there! Your father has been remiss in not thinking of the casualties of this war and making proper provision for them. They need care, and food, and—and help!'

'My father is unaware of the problem, I think. I will speak to him about this also.'

'Would you? It might help if there were wages for the helpers.'

Roger managed a small smile. 'I promised I would speak to him.' The horse and cart trundled on, across the remnants of grass towards the

Millfleet. It jogged the patient, who groaned, but it was the shortest route. Mill Lane ran alongside the fleet. 'I thought you might faint,' Roger observed. 'I am pleased you did not.'

'I am made of stronger stuff than that!'

'So I see! And I thought you a delicately bred female!'

'I was brought up on a farm,' she said. 'And we all know what happens at slaughtering time. I do not think this is much different.' She paused. 'However, the stench in there is appalling. Those people need care. They will die without it.'

'There is not much you can do about that,' Roger said.

Ruth looked at him thoughtfully. 'Isn't there?' she asked.

Roger turned to look at her and their eyes met. 'What is going on in your pretty head, mistress?' he demanded.

'Nothing you need to worry about,' she told him, folding her hands in her lap and staring at the horse's ears.

§

'You are doing *what*?' her uncle demanded.

'I am going to help at the infirmary,' Ruth repeated.

It had been a day since her visit to the infirmary, and she had spent a sleepless night thinking of all the poor wretches who had endured injury lying on the wet stone floor of the infirmary in their own filth. She could not close her mind to the intense suffering, the pain, the fevers, she saw there. The surgeon could not cope with the volume, the orderlies were only two men, and there was no-one else.

'No niece of mine is going to work at the infirmary! Absolutely not! Over my dead body!'

'Oh, the shame of it!' Aunt Mary put in.

Ruth did not answer, but she put her chin up. She had already been to see the injured man in his home in Mill Lane, and he seemed to be making good progress—so far. His wife had shown immense gratitude.

'They need help at the infirmary,' Ruth had told her. 'If you know anyone who would be willing to show some Christian charity, it would be very welcome.'

She had gone on to the infirmary herself. She had cleaned and washed people and utensils, she had re-bandaged wounds, she had bathed feverish faces, she had called the orderlies to remove bodies. And she had come home stinking of the place. And during the day four other young women, had arrived and followed her example. Word had got around. Furthermore, the surgeon had been told by none other than the mayor himself that all the carers would be paid and that he could hire as many as he needed. She blessed Roger, for he had obviously mentioned it to his father. Furthermore, Mr. Gurlin promised tents to relieve the overcrowding in the chapel.

Ruth said now to her uncle: 'I have been brought up a Christian by my parents. Did not Christ say we should show charity to one another? And if a person is suffering, should we not do our best to alleviate that suffering, if it is within our power?'

He studied her. 'You, girl, are bred for better things. Only lower class females care for the sick.'

'I cared for my brothers when they were sick.'

'It is not the same thing at all.'

'Why not?'

He looked helplessly at his wife who shook her head. 'Ruth, we forbid you to go.'

Ruth smiled, her hands folded primly in her lap. 'Very well.'

They exchanged glances, and Ruth knew that they knew she would not obey them.

THIRTY-TWO

Blithely unaware of Lord Newcastle's decision to go to Hull instead of Lynn, Sir Hamon daily looked for the promised help from across the Wash. Meantime, not only Roger, but also Gurlin informed him of the problems within the town.

'We need fresh meat,' Gurlin announced as he came into Sir Hamon's office in the council chambers.

Sir Hamon came to his feet and inclined his head politely. 'Good morning Mr. Gurlin.'

'Oh yes. Good morning, Sir Hamon. Gentlemen.' To make up for his lapse, Gurlin swept a magnificent bow, and the other men in the vaulted room variously nodded or bowed.

'So where do you think we will get fresh meat from?' Sir Hamon asked him. He had already been informed of the food situation in the town by his youngest son, but he allowed Gurlin to offer suggestions.

Gurlin shook his head, obviously at a loss.

'There's a market at Setchey,' Sir Robert de Grey offered, sitting down again, stretching out his long thin legs and crossing them at the ankles on the corner of Sir Hamon's desk. It was a slovenly habit Sir Hamon deplored, and besides he had dirty shoes on *his* desk. He glared pointedly at the feet, and then at their owner, and, taking the hint, Sir Robert removed them.

'Would that be on the other side of the bridge?' Roger asked his eyes twinkling.

Sir Charles Mordaunt pursed his lips and then laughed. 'No, dear boy. I think this side. Still, I expect they've repaired that by now.'

'No doubt they have jury-rigged something.' Sir Hamon was practical. 'So how can we relieve Lord Manchester of his beef?'

Sir Robert grinned.. 'We could send the good captain Goodman out with some men to capture it.'

'I'll go,' Roger said immediately.

Sir Hamon smiled to himself. *Oh! To be young and enthusiastic!* 'I've no doubt you will.'

This sortie was to be on horseback, surprising the attackers and forcing a way through the enemy lines.

Roger was one of fifty men under the command of Captain Goodman and they left Lynn by the little used Doucehill Gate at the north end of the town before the sun was up at the ungodly hour of five o'clock in the morning.

Captain Poe either did not know about the Doucehill Gate or he did not have enough men to surround it, probably thinking that no-one in their right mind would try to cross the marshy ground here. The Roundhead camp was further towards the East Gate. The marsh, although wet and soft underfoot, had the advantage of muffling the sound of horses and riders as they moved stealthily away from the town until they reached the trees. Skirting the Roundhead camp, they took the long route around the back of Gaywood, and then straight across country towards Hardwick, urging the horses into an easy canter. The sun began to rise in the sky in the north-east casting rays upon an undulating landscape. At Hardwick they took the road for West Winch and then Setchey, speeding up again to a canter in the fields alongside the Setchey Road. Here the land flattened, the beginning of the fens.

The plan was to ride in, threaten the herders and ride off with about four hundred head of cattle, but as they neared Setchey they had to leave the cover of the trees for a hundred yards, heading for the market and the herds they could see in the near distance.

Roger looked about him uneasily. He felt that there should have been more stealth, and less bravado. However, he was not in command of the troop, and Captain Goodman, a seemingly capable soldier, though, it had to be said, not such a capable horseman, and certainly no cavalry officer, had little time to listen to the likes of Roger whom he viewed (wrongly in Roger's opinion) as inexperienced. It would have been better if Nicholas had been in command. He, at least, had more understanding of cavalry.

Captain Goodman's idea appeared to be that speed would be better than stealth. So he led his troop at a canter along the road.

Roger saw them first, a glint of silver in the bushes ahead, and his insides jolted. He pulled Achilles up sharply as Captain Poe's foot soldiers, perhaps fifty men in buff coats and metal helmets, appeared out of the bushes at the side of the road to confront them with pikes, bills and muskets. Horsemen also emerged from the bushes and came to a standstill in front of them. The Royalists came to a halt, some turning away in momentary panic, but turning again to remain with their fellows. Roger made his horse Achilles stand and he and his fellows all drew their swords, the sound of metal ringing in the air. At the same time Roger sized up the opposition. The Royalists were badly outnumbered by at least four to one.

It was difficult to see how many men the enemy were. Fifty perhaps, and a large number on horseback. Some were still hidden by the bushes. All were armed. All were ready to attack. However, not all were trained. He could see that by the way some of them held their drawn swords.

Roger looked about, taking note of terrain for advantage and also for an escape route. No sense in getting killed for a herd of beef! However, he would never desert his fellows. Yet his heart pumped forcefully in his chest, and his nerves tensed, while he focused on the enemy, watching every movement, every shift. The men on the horses would be their biggest worry.

The Roundhead lieutenant came towards them on a dun-coloured horse, his sword in his hand. He stopped in front of Captain Goodman.

'What do you want, traitor?' he yelled.

Captain Goodman glared at him, one hand arrogantly on his thigh, the other holding the reins, but he stood his ground. 'Rebel!' he spat.

Angered, the lieutenant spurred his horse forward and aimed a slashing blow at Goodman with his sword, but he deftly turned his horse and slashed back.

Roger saw no more, for at that moment the other horsemen surrounded them with a clash of metal on metal, shrieking horses, stamping hooves and cursing men.

Roger singled out a man who was staring directly at him. 'Come on then rebel!' Roger hissed.

As if he heard him the man spurred his horse towards him, sword raised, ready to hack at Roger's left arm. He put his whole weight behind it, yelling: 'For God and Christ!'

Roger parried awkwardly, saving himself, and hit back twice, striking nothing but jarring metal. He cursed through his teeth: 'Sanctimonious bastard!'

In too close to strike a proper blow, the man launched himself out of the saddle at Roger, hitting him on the shoulder with his body weight and unseating him. Roger fell to earth with a thud, the attacker landing on top of him, knocking the breath from his lungs and pinning him to the earth. Stunned, and having lost his weapon, Roger struggled with his bare hands to free himself of the weight but the attacker followed up his advantage by grabbing Roger's throat and squeezing.

Gagging and fighting for breath, Roger struggled desperately, trying to push the man off. He forced his hand against the man's chin, trying to push him off, but the attacker had all his weight behind the grip. Roger's lungs began pumping, screaming for air that was denied him. The world began to slip away and his arms stretching upward to his attacker drained of strength. With sudden momentary clarity, he knew if he did not act now he would die. Self preservation kicked in and in one last desperate effort he brought his knee up sharply between the man's legs.

With a shriek of pain, the Roundhead was gone from off him to land somewhere beyond Roger's head. Roger did not have the luxury of time to recover. Painfully heaving air past his injured throat into his lungs, he struggled to his feet, grabbing his sword on the way, but the enemy was also standing, albeit clutching his crotch with one hand, sword in the other, his helmet, like Roger's hat, gone, his short-cropped hair sticking up comically from his head.

The man did not wait, but came forward with an inexpert lunge, which Roger deftly parried and followed up with an attack to the man's leg. The man was no swordsman, Roger saw immediately, although he defended the attack, more by luck than any expertise. He had murderous hatred in his eyes, desperation, and Roger, the expert, knew how to deal with him. A moment later he slipped under his guard and caught the man a cut to his thigh.

A crimson stain seeped through the slash in the buff breeches and the man cried out and threw down his sword not only in surrender, but to clutch his leg in a worthless attempt to stop the blood pouring out.

Roger brought his sword to the man's throat while he tried to massage the pain away in his own, tempted to end the man's life the way he had tried to end his. However, seeing the anguished look in his prisoner's eyes, and realising that he could bleed to death in a few minutes, Roger felt the killing madness leave him, and pity take over.

'Over there!' he said, but no voice came out, so he indicated with his head.

Taking a belt from his hips and trying to tie it around his thigh above the cut, the man paused. Roger allowed him this time, but he was aware that the fight around them had ended. His company had valiantly forced back the Roundheads while he was engaged, and they were already in the saddle to go. He had no time to waste and he urged his prisoner onward.

'L'Estrange,' Captain Goodman growled, 'stop tarrying and bring that man here! Watts! Take the prisoner.'

Roger jerked his head and wanted to say: 'You heard! Move!' He managed a croak.

The man walked with difficulty the two or three paces to a waiting horse, as blood dribbled down his hose and into his shoe, to where Watts waited, holding both their horses. Already the others had left and the Roundheads were on their way.

'Get up! On your horse!'

The man hesitated.

Watts pulled a pistol. 'Do it now or you are a dead man!'

The man clambered into the saddle and Watts took the reins and, dragging the captive's horse, sprang his horse into a gallop.

Roger, climbing into the saddle and urging Achilles to his full potential, was the last to leave. He left the cover of the trees and followed the others. Behind him the Roundheads were almost upon him. A pistol ball whistled past his ear, but he could not stop to look around. *Faith! L'Estrange, you are going to die now if you don't get moving!*

With his heart pounding, he leaned low in the saddle, uncomfortably aware that they were now no more than two horse-lengths behind him, while his friends were some distance ahead of him.

He knew the area well and, gambling that the enemy were not locals, he turned away from the road and headed across the fields, Achilles taking a dyke, then a hedge with ease and making for a small wood in the distance. His thoroughbred was built for speed. The enemy had farm animals and dainty riding ponies, so he had the advantage.

Daring to glance behind he found that they had fallen back a little. He didn't let up the pace, but kept Achilles at it, even though it increased his breathing rate causing pain in his throat. He saw his friends coming from his right to join him, the Roundheads hard on their heels. They must have followed the road.

Roger merged into the group, as they hurtled through Gaywood, terrifying the women and children who rushed to get out of the way and then sped through the enemy camped in the fields outside Lynn, over camp-fires, through tents, leaving stacked muskets, pots and linen strewn over the grass. Taken by surprise, the encamped Roundheads scrambled to recover their weapons as the men on the walls of Lynn gave covering fire.

Ducking low to avoid the enemy or their own side taking their heads off, they tore across the grassland between Lynn and the Roundhead camp.

Thank God! Nicholas had seen them coming and ordered the East Gate opened, portcullis up and the drawbridge over the river Esk down.

Relief flooded through Roger as, with the others, he flew through the gate and into the safety of Lynn. The portcullis slammed down behind them and the drawbridge raised again.

Sweating, gasping horses stood in the space behind the gates, recovering, and their equally sweating, gasping riders slid out of the saddles. Roger's legs buckled and Someone caught hold of him. He held his throat. It felt bruised and swollen.

'Roger! What the hell happened?' Nick had hold of him.

Roger swallowed with difficulty and looked about him, surprised. They had four prisoners, three men including the one who had tried to kill him, and the Roundhead Lieutenant. But they were five men missing. Was that five men dead? Or prisoners.

Roger looked for his prisoner. 'Get your leg seen to,' he recommended hoarsely. His throat hurt like hell, and breathing, swallowing and talking were a real effort.

The man glowered at him, but he said nothing as someone else came to take the prisoners away.

Nicholas slipped a steadying arm around his shoulders. 'Cutting it a bit fine, Cub,' he said. 'Where's the beef?'

Roger shook his head, giving his brother an outraged glare. 'Beef?' he rasped with difficulty. 'You want beef? Then you damned well get it!'

THIRTY-THREE

Ruth was so shocked when she saw Roger later that day that, just as Nicholas, his father, and umpteen other people had done earlier, she demanded: 'What on earth happened to you?'

Roger shrugged non-committally. 'You should see the enemy,' he croaked in an miserable attempt at a joke.

'Well, you look awful.'

He did not need her to tell him that. He had studied himself in a mirror. Near strangulation had badly affected him. Blood vessels had burst in his eyes, giving him a maniacal appearance, like some ghoul, dark red stains had appeared beneath his eyes, and red dots peppered his cheeks beneath them. His throat was swollen, the skin red and blue, and a large blue thumb print glowed vividly on the side of his throat. His breathing had improved a little, although it still rasped, but in addition to the hoarseness in his voice, talking was painful.

She touched his cheek in a gut-wrenchingly tender gesture. 'What happened?' she asked again, softly.

'We went to bring back some beef, but we were ambushed.'

'But what happened to *you*?' she repeated insistently.

'A fight.'

She became impatient and put her hands on her hips. 'Alright, I will tell you what I think. You look like someone tried to strangle you.'

'They did,' Roger admitted ruefully. 'He nearly succeeded too, for he had the advantage. But I—threw him off.'

She shook her head in exaggerated disbelief. 'What is it about men?' she asked rhetorically.

Roger swallowed with an effort in an attempt to clear his voice. He did not dare to cough. She looked at him and her tone changed and her face softened. 'It looks like you could do with some nursing,' she added, touching his throat. 'Does it hurt?'

'Like the devil! Begging your pardon, madam.'

''Tis a wonder you did not get yourself killed.'

She reached up and put her arms around his neck, kissing him tenderly but briefly on his lips. Her body against his awakened his desire for her, like it always did, and his arms tightened around her. 'Please keep safe, Roger,' she whispered.

§

For Roger, the days were filled with activity. As the hot August sun continued to scorch the earth unabated, the people of Lynn choked in the smoke-clogged air. Day after day Roger took his position on the wall near the East Gate and gave musket-fire to the attackers when they came within range. Others manned the artillery, sending cannonballs into the midst of the Roundheads. Not only did the weapons themselves produce smoke, but the fires kept burning for the matches added to it.

The constant bombardment from both sides deafened those nearby and irritated those further away. They had never known anything like it. Ordinary folk were terrified.

The terror increased when Captain Poe, under the command of Oliver Cromwell took up a position across the river at Old Lynn, the better able to fire on the town.

Roger was actually in the Tuesday Market Place when the first cannonball whistled through the air and landed not far from the Market Cross, sending cobbles heavenwards and creating a hole in the ground. The earth shook with the force of it and Roger turned to see what had happened as women screamed in fright and debris clattered to the ground.

An eerie silence settled on the square. People stared at the hole in the ground in disbelief. It lasted no longer than it took to re-arm a cannon then another two shots landed in the square simultaneously. A house suddenly collapsed, hit by another ball, sending shards of wood and more debris into the air. Gathering their scattered wits, people ran in all directions seeking some kind of shelter from the bombardment.

A man was hit by flying masonry and he fell to the ground dead, a bloody shard of wood protruding from his eye.

Some people began tearing at the remains of the fallen house with their bare hands.

'Somebody's copped it!' Roger heard someone say beside him.

He was with them, shoving aside wood and debris in an attempt to reach the people inside, choking on the dust from the lime plaster and what was called 'daub', a mixture which included dung used to spread on 'wattle' the woven wooden structure which made up the walls. But the only person, a woman servant, was dead by the time they got to her, crushed by a fallen beam.

Cromwell was not done. He kept up the bombardment of the town from across the river all day and well into the night, terrifying the people. In his view, it would make short work of Lynn, either causing the burgesses to yield, or flattening the town.

Along with others, Roger stopped frequenting the Griffin; it was far too dangerous to enter the Tuesday Market Place and he took to frequenting the White Hart in James Street instead. The clientele were different there and the food quite basic, but it wasn't long before he had wormed his way into the confidences of the sailors and others who replaced his noble friends.

Cromwell may have wanted a swift end to Lynn, but Lord Manchester was in no hurry. He could wait. He set about the task of cutting the town off completely, blockading from the land side, while his father-in-law the Earl of Warwick, in charge of the Parliamentary fleet, successfully blockaded from the sea. Only one ship outwitted Warwick's fleet by flying false colours, making it safely into Lynn with much needed supplies.

Supplies were still a pressing problem. Once again Roger went out with Captain Goodman's troop, using more stealth than they had previously, and succeeded in liberating five hundred cattle which they were able to bring into Lynn through the East Gate under covering fire from the town's defenders.

At the very moment that they made the East Gates, the man beside Roger, Watts, fell off his horse with a cry.

Pulling up his horse, Roger looked down to see him clutching his shoulder. He did not hesitate but slid off his horse to help him, sending both horses on their way into the town with a smart slap to their rumps.

Watts was by no means a dead man, but he was winded and on the ground. Left out here by himself he would die. Roger had not thought it through, but it did not matter. The man needed help. He had been helped in a fight on numerous occasions, now it was his turn. With all the rest of the troop inside the gates, he felt exposed and naked to the enemy's fire as he bent down to Harry Watts. Musket balls whistled past his head and pinged into the wall and he expected to feel the burning agony of a ball anywhere on his body at any moment. He hoped the musketeers were too far away to have any sort of accuracy, that the defenders would keep them from coming closer, that he could get Watts into the gates before a stray musket ball found him or Watts. Yet he felt no fear, only the desperation of the situation.

Alternately praying and cursing under his breath, he grabbed Watts by his good arm and hauled him with an effort to his feet.

Watts seemed dozy, stunned perhaps from the fall from the horse.

'Come on, man, you can do this! Move, or we'll both be killed!' Wrapping Watts good arm around his neck and with his arm around his waist, he heaved him towards the gates.

Watts did his best, his feet scrabbling at the bare earth outside the gates. Aware that as a pair they presented a much larger target, Roger had a feeling of impending disaster. 'Move, damn ye!' he bellowed at Watts. Finally Watts' feet made proper contact with the earth and they moved towards the gate, but it was agonising moments before they finally entered the safety of the town and heard the portcullis go down, the gates close and the drawbridge go up behind them.

'I'll take him to the infirmary,' Roger told Captain Goodman. Someone had taken care of the horses and Roger knew where to find Achilles when he needed to. So now he put a kerchief over Watts' wound and took him to the infirmary.

The casualties had been mounting and the sight which met his eyes made him want to leave immediately. Yet conditions had improved. The stone floor was dry; men and women and even some children were mixed together lying on straw-stuffed mattresses instead of on the floor; a pot on a fire on the end wall contained food; clean bandages covered wounds, and the dreadful stench of the privy had abated considerably. They were tended by whoever could be prevailed upon to attend to them, among them Mary the barmaid from the Griffin, wearing a blood-stained apron over her low-cut dress, a 'lady of the night' he recognised also, and a coarse low-life female with an over-large bosom.

Amid this noble company was Ruth, kneeling on the flagstones and bent over someone who cried out dementedly in pain. Seeing the mayhem, and seeing her in the midst of it, outrage flared inside Roger. What on earth did she think she was doing?

As if sensing his eyes on her she looked up and straight at him, defiant.

'I would speak with you, madam,' he snapped.

She put aside a blood-stained cloth, rinsed her hands in a bucket, dried them and finally came to her feet to walk towards him. 'Outside!' she ordered him.

She went ahead of him and he had no alternative but to stride along angrily behind her. As soon as they were outside in the old monastery cloisters, she turned to him, her eyes sparkling dangerously. 'How *dare* you talk to me like that! Just who do you think you are, *Mr. L'Estrange*?'

He ignored the question. 'I do not wish for my betrothed to be nursing—men!'

'I have brothers, sir. I doubt there is much that would shock me!'

'Well it shocks me!' he retorted, appalled that his future wife should be assisting other men in the most intimate of situations.

'And if you were wounded, would you not wish for kind, gentle hands to help you in your time of need?'

'But you are *nursing!'*

Her eyes widened in mock surprise. 'Why, so I am! Isn't that strange for a Christian woman to care for others less fortunate than themselves!'

'You, madam, are a gently-bred maid.'

'You mistake the case, sir. The Pells are not at all high ranking.'

'Your father is a knight.'

'And I am merely a daughter. Now, if you do not mind, I have work to do.'

She turned to leave him, but he gripped her arm. She looked back at him, her eyes burning with anger and he glared at her.

She raised her chin. 'Let go of me, Mr. L'Estrange. I have work to do.'

He released her arm and she picked up her skirts and went back inside, shutting the door firmly behind her.

She was furious. How dared he assume the right to tell her what she could or could not do? That was the trouble with men. They all wanted to control their women! But she was *not* his woman, she reminded herself. Yet. It had been bad enough fighting her uncle and aunt to be allowed to help here and it had not been until they had realised that they were powerless to stop her that they had given up trying.

She glanced about her, becoming more accustomed to the lack of light and met the eyes of the man Roger had brought in. He was staring at her with interest, yet his face was so pale as to be almost transparent, suntan notwithstanding. He swayed as she looked at him and she went to him immediately.

'Sit down here!' she commanded. She had stopped being Mistress Polite some days ago when she needed to organise her patients. In fact her aunt complained she had become an army captain.

Harry Watts sat down on a stool. He looked ready to pass out at any moment.

'You and Strange—?' he ventured.

'That, sir, is none of your business!' she snapped. 'And you need not grin like that. Now take your doublet and shirt off, let us have a look at that wound before we get the surgeon.'

She continued to work through the rest of the day, with the backdrop of groans and cries and the roar of cannon and musket fire outside. It was hot work, the flies tried to find open wounds and she was intent on not letting them do so. She fetched and carried buckets of urine and worse and tended to those with fevers.

As the night came on she was exhausted and hungry.

'Go home, Mistress Pell,' the surgeon, a surprisingly small man, told her. 'Mistress Withers is here now. Go home before you drop!' Thankfully, she obeyed to get some much-needed rest.

She knew he would be outside waiting for her.

She acknowledged him with a glance, but continued briskly on her way as he fell into step beside her. She did not want to discuss this right now. She was far too tired. She did not want the questions, or the pull he had on her emotions.

'Ruth, this cannot go on.'

She stood still and glared at him with the little energy she had left. 'I work at the infirmary, sir. To clear up the mess you L'Estranges have created. Look at it! *Look at it!* The town is in ruins, there is hardly any sleep for anyone because of all the cannons and muskets and no-one knows if their house is to be destroyed next! People are starving, they are hurt, they are sick. And for what? For your precious King, that's what.'

'You knew how it would be. I warned you, lady, to get out of town.'

'And leave these poor wretches to fend for themselves, I suppose. Your precious father cares not one jot for what he has put them through.'

'He cares a great deal. He—'

'Well he has a strange way of caring then,' she told him roundly, her voice rising in pitch and power. 'You too. When are you L'Estranges going to come down from your lofty perches? When are you going to see it for what it is? Needless slaughter. And you won't win. Manchester has eighteen thousand troops outside Lynn now. How can you beat that? And where is your precious Lord Newcastle, eh? Riding to your assistance? I think not. No, he's gone elsewhere. You have lost, you Royalists. You cannot win this one. And it's about time your high and mighty father realised it. God is not on your side!'

'No, he's on yours, I suppose,' he retorted. 'Your men are

obviously more God-fearing than ours! That is why they torture men in Wisbech Castle and hang, draw and quarter them at Tyburn and cut off their heads at the Tower of London, I suppose. So Christ-like. So obviously Christian. So full of mercy and pity. And what do you suppose they will do to the good people of Lynn if they come in here?'

'*When* they come in here, they will treat the people with Christian dignity.'

'Is that after or before they slaughter them?'

She picked up her skirts and walked off from him striding out as fast as any man in her fury.

He let her go, too angry himself to forgive. She had questioned his father's authority, his rule, his integrity even. It was unforgivable and he was convinced in that moment that he never wanted to see her again.

No, he told himself, he would never forgive this. Never.

§

Ruth arrived in Wingate still furious and quite out of breath from striding so fast.

Her aunt greeted her as she entered the front door. She knew she must be submissive, so she dropped a curtsey.

'You look flustered,' Aunt Mary said, peering at her in the candlelight.

'It has been a busy day and I walked home quickly,' Ruth explained. 'If you do not mind, Aunt, I would like to go to my chamber and if supper could be sent to me on a tray . . ?'

She did not wait for a reply, but picked up her skirts and ran up the narrow staircase.

In her room she paced the floor like a caged animal as wild, furious thoughts flew through her brain. What on earth had come over her that she fancied herself in love with that man? She must be addled in the brain! And he must be stupid to think that he, a Cavalier, could actually wed a Puritan. It was unthinkable! Hard on that thought came the remembrance of his kisses. Her cheeks grew crimson as she thought of it. How could she have succumbed to that? What kind of wanton hussy was she?

She made up her mind suddenly. She had kept John Calthorpe dangling long enough. A God-fearing man, a worthy man, she would accept him. He may not be as exciting—or infuriating—as Roger L'Estrange but he would look after her and he loved her in his way. She would grow to love him, she knew.

By the time the maid had come with her supper, she had written to John Calthorpe accepting his offer of marriage, sealed it and when her aunt came in later she gave it to her.

'What is this?' her aunt asked suspiciously.

Ruth smiled a tight little smile. 'I have decided to accept John Calthorpe,' she said simply.

Aunt Mary's eyes grew round. 'You are sure?'

'If I were not sure, Aunt Mary, I would not have written to accept him,' Ruth snapped.

'And Mr. L'Estrange?'

'What has Mr. L'Estrange to do with me?' Ruth retorted dangerously.

Aunt Mary raised her brows. 'But I thought . . .'

'Mr. L'Estrange can go and hang himself for all I care,' Ruth declared.

As the door closed behind her aunt and the maid, Ruth stood looking at it mutinously. Then her lip began to quiver and the tears came into her eyes and trickled silently down her cheeks. She wiped them away angrily with her hand.

'Damn the man!' she swore and found some comfort in the word. 'Damn, damn, damn him!'

THIRTY-FOUR

Setchey, September 1643

Lord Manchester stared the letter in his hand. It was from that overbearing pain in the nether regions Oliver Cromwell.

'So,' he said at length to Captain Poe, 'Cromwell's gone to Hull to fight Lord Newcastle, has he?'

'As you see,' Captain Poe said shortly.

Manchester raised an eyebrow at him. 'Well, at least we know where Newcastle is. Certainly he is not coming across the Wash in the foreseeable future.'

Captain Poe remained impassive.

'Four weeks we've been kicking our heels in this God-forsaken county. As if I haven't other pressing things to do.' He scratched at a large red spot on his cheek. '*And* I've been bitten half to death! These damned fens are breeding grounds for the ague!' He took a deep angry breath. 'For the love of God, how long does it take to starve a town into submission?' he demanded.

'Can't rightly say, my lord,' Poe answered impassively, quite forgetting that he had once suggested the town would fall in a week.

'Well, enough is enough. It is time we sorted out this shambles once and for all.'

Poe's dark eyes followed his lordship as he paced the room, but he knew now was not the time to interrupt his commanding officer's thoughts.

'We'll storm the town,' his lordship decided.

Captain Poe blinked. 'Very good my lord.'

Manchester looked at his charts spread out on the table. 'The easiest way into Lynn is by the river. It is far too difficult to defend such a vast stretch of water when there is no wall,' he decided. 'So make ready boats for an assault.'

'The cannon bombardment from the town is constant, my lord, keeping our men pinned down.'

'I do not want to learn that it cannot be done, Captain Poe. Just do it. We will also take Old Lynn and intensify the cannon fire into Lynn.'

'Very good my lord.'

'And we will need ladders to climb the walls. How long do you think? Twenty feet? Make them ready.'

Poe inclined his head in agreement.

'They have fresh water also,' Manchester said. 'We need to stop up the sweet water sources.'

Poe smiled mirthlessly. 'With no water it will be just a few days.'

Manchester's expression was sceptical. 'Good! I want this over with. We have dallied here long enough. See to it.'

'My lord.' Poe bowed and left him.

§

Sir Hamon prayed and struggled with his conscience as the death toll mounted. He had sworn to do his utmost to hold the town for the King, yet the loss of life had become a nightmare on his conscience, a charge against him, an indictment of his governorship.

'There are so many innocents in the town,' he confided to his sons, 'women and children and old people. I do not want them to lose their lives on my say so.'

'Newcastle will come,' Nicholas repeated. 'He must come.' It was unthinkable that Newcastle could have abandoned them. For if he had, they could not hope to win.

But as September dragged slowly by and there was no sign of the Earl of Newcastle, it became obvious that for some reason his lordship was not going to honour his promise. For some few more days Sir Hamon was reluctant to abandon all hope. The raiding parties now went out at night to bring cattle into the town to feed the people, but it was not enough.

Almost daily Roger rode out on some sortie or another, finding himself in the thick of the action, riding with others out on the cattle rustling expeditions or to stop the transportation of ladders and the preparations of boats for the final assault.

It had ceased to be an excitement, but a drain on his energy and spirits. All of them lived on the edge of their nerves, wondering if the next casualty would be themselves. Roger found he lost his appetite, was drinking more and sleeping badly when he did get the chance to sleep. Men died at his side. Cannon and musket fire and sword play cost more than eighty lives on both sides. He knew now that they could not succeed. Dimly in the recesses of his brain, he realised that Ruth had been right.

He had not seen her since the argument about the infirmary, although he thought of her often. In his mind's eye he could see her toiling like a slave in that cursed infirmary, dealing with things no self-respecting lady should ever have to deal with. He was still furious with her, but he had a great deal of respect for her too. This was a different side to her, one he had not seen, a woman of courage and strength, of determination and pity. She did not agree with the cause, yet she helped save the lives of his men, of his friends, of people who were desperate and she soothed the dying. He was appalled and full of admiration at the same time.

However, until his father, the governor, gave the order to surrender, they kept on.

The town's defenders, with so much practice, had become so skilled at cannon that they could put a ball through the same hole three times, one man in a boat on the besiegers' side losing an arm in the process.

Again Roger went out, this time to release water into the town, for the besiegers had cut off the fresh river from Kettle Mills and the pipes that brought water into the town. Under heavy fire, they dug at the banks to release water, while Roger and others defended them with sword, musket, pistol and fists. They were successful, but they lost many men.

The people of Lynn stored as much water as they could before the besiegers repaired the damage. They too were becoming depressed, exhausted with the effort of just staying alive.

'There be too many of them,' someone said as Roger's band readied themselves for yet another sortie.

Roger sighed. He was weary and sick to the pit of his stomach. He needed to find out what was happening. He stood up.

'Where be you going then?' the same man asked.

'I am going to see the governor,' Roger said and glared at them all, waiting for someone to dare to challenge him.

'Going to papa eh?'

Roger's fists clenched. 'You go, then. Find out what is going on. See if he will tell you!'

Captain Naunton intervened. 'Go, L'Estrange. Find out if we are to go out again today. Find out what is happening.'

Roger left the barracks and strode angrily across the Tuesday Market Place.

He knew he would find his father in the Town Hall. He knew also all the burgesses would be there, including his brother, so he was not surprised to find that he had interrupted yet another meeting, when he entered the Guildhall and climbed the stairs to the upper chamber.

They looked at him, but straight away got back to business as Roger took an empty chair beside his father.

'Well it seems to me that Newcastle's not coming,' Sir Robert de Grey stated the obvious.

Sir Hamon wiped his hand over his face in a weary gesture. The strain was showing. His gaunt face had become even thinner, the little beard jutted out from his chin and his eyes sank into his head, for he was neither eating nor sleeping well. Roger was shocked. Never had he seen his father look so—so what? Exhausted? Depressed? Actually the word was *defeated.*

Where the devil was Newcastle? But he had to acknowledge that Newcastle and his army should have been here weeks ago. He could not understand why Newcastle, with Lynn being handed to him on a plate and the way to London opened up, did not follow up this advantage. The whole war could have been over by now.

Sir Hamon looked at the men seated around the large table. 'I think you are right, sir. Besides, if he did show up, Manchester now has eighteen thousand troops sat down outside the East Gate. Victory would by no means be certain. It is too late.'

This was met with silence as the reality of their situation sank in and Roger felt the full weight of defeat.

De Grey said: 'We are running out of food. We have precious little water. We cannot hold out.'

Sir Charles Mordaunt pointed out: 'The town is filthy, the stench unbearable. There is little water, no food and no rain to clean anything. People are sick and they suffer.' Sir Hamon groaned audibly, his head in his hands. Although he knew he did not rule alone, the weight of responsibility was still his. And it was becoming too much to bear.

Sir Hamon said gruffly: 'They stripped our dead and set them up naked against the gate. We cannot get to them to bring them in for a Christian burial.'

They had all seen this gross disrespect for their dead. The whole town knew. Roger swore. It was painfully demoralising, a constant reminder that they could not win. In an effort to divert attention away from this atrocity, he said: 'They've erected a bretash at St. Agnes's gate, at the Doucehill bridge.' A bretash was a small fort-like structure made of wood.

'It's a diversionary tactic,' Sir Hamon acknowledged. 'While

Manchester's men pound Lynn from the sea end of the town, he intends to bring his men round towards the East Gate.' He paused. 'They are getting ready to come in.'

There was a long silence as they all contemplated what defeat meant. Roger watched them as their plight sank in. These men, the burgesses, including his father and brother, stood to lose everything. Even their lives. Viewed as traitors by the victors, they could expect execution, their estates forfeit. Yet the price for trying to keep Lynn was just too high, too terrible to contemplate. And it was a lost cause. If these men surrendered it would be a matter of sacrificing themselves to save the people in the town.

For Roger, it was a bitter defeat. Not only did he stand to lose his father and brother, but he felt keenly the lost opportunity. The soldier in him wanted to fight to the death, but the man in him wanted to protect the innocents.

And Ruth was in the town.

§

He lay in wait for her in the lee of St. James' chapel. It was close to half past six o'clock, and the evening was going on apace, but he was sure that she would be coming home shortly, so he waited patiently as the cannons continued to fire from the wall ramparts, the muskets popped and the more distant firing of the guns from across the Ouse made continuous noise. They would stop when the light died.

It was unsettling. No longer did he feel the excitement of impending battle, of victory almost theirs, but he felt the dread of defeat. It made him sick and bitter and he was afraid not just for himself but for his father and brother and the other burgesses. He was afraid, too, for the people of the town. He hoped that the besiegers were actually decent Christian Englishmen, as Ruth believed, that they would behave with mercy, but he knew nothing of the character of Lord Manchester, whether he was a merciful man or one set on vengeance. The corpses at the gate did not suggest a man of compassion. Of Oliver Cromwell he had heard ill, that he was merciless, but that was mere hearsay and anyway, Cromwell and his troops had gone.

It was almost too dark to see by the time Ruth came by on her way home from the infirmary, wrapped in a cloak against the evening chill, but he knew her by the way she walked and the way his heart skipped. He cursed the attraction he felt for her, the all-consuming love which overrode reason, for he had not forgotten their last meeting, the slights she cast on his Father and thinking of it, his anger burned again. He did not easily forget a slight. He still loathed the Scots for the defeat at Newburn and the heavy taxes imposed on the King, and he was not about to forgive Ruth. At least he did not think he was.

If only the sight of her would not cause his heart to hammer in his chest! He reminded himself of the reason why he had come.

As she came nearer, he stepped out from the shelter of the chapel and spoke immediately so that she would not be startled and do something that females did when startled—scream. 'Mistress Pell! Well met!' And he bowed.

He heard her gasp and she stopped walking. It was impossible to gauge her expression in the fading light, but he felt the tension between them. 'Mr. L'Estrange.' Her voice did not invite further conversation, but he persisted doggedly.

'I particularly wish to speak with you.'

'Oh do you? Well I have nothing to say to you.' She tried to move on, but he caught her arm. She stopped and looked into his face and in that split second he knew she still loved him. She covered it well. 'Mr. L'Estrange, I am tired and hungry and I wish to go home. If you do not let me go immediately, I shall scream.'

He couldn't take the risk, so he let her go. 'Stay and hear me, Mistress.'

'I cannot think that you have anything to say which would interest me in the slightest.'

He said quietly: 'Ruth, Lord Manchester is making ready to come in.'

It stalled her and her eyes searched his face for clues. 'Dear God!'

'They are getting ready. If there is a chance for you to leave, you must take it.'

She took a deep breath and began walking towards St. James' Street. He fell into step beside her, thinking to escort her home. 'They are gentlemen. They will not harm us,' she repeated, but he could hear she was uncertain.

'Do not think that because they are Puritan they will treat you with respect, madam.'

'I will take my chances.'

He stopped walking, and spun her round to face him, putting his hands on her shoulders so that she had to look at him. 'Ruth, if there is a chance to leave, you must go. If Manchester is the man they say he is, he may give the women and children a chance.'

'I cannot leave. I work at the infirmary, remember.'

'Ruth, you have to. Promise me.'

She shook her head, troubled. 'You and your Father, and the other burgesses, they could have surrendered by now and saved a great many lives.'

He struggled to ignore the criticism and to keep his temper even. 'Why will you not go?'

'Why do you want me to?'

'Because I could not live with myself if ought happened to you.'

He meant it sincerely, but she retorted: 'You might not have to, if you hang!'

'Ruth! Stop it and listen to me!'

'I told you, I have my work in the infirmary.'

He suppressed an oath. 'If they give an amnesty, we will send the wounded and sick out as well. There will not be anyone in the infirmary! Ruth, you must go. Promise me.'

She relented then, and bowed her head. 'If the sick go, so will I go.'

He sighed with relief.

'Have they offered an amnesty then, for the women and children?'

'Not yet. But I believe it to be usual in these situations.'

'And what about you?'

He shrugged. 'In truth I know not. Whatever the case, I have no choice in the matter.'

Pulling her cloak around her she continued walking quickly past the

White Hart and into the Saturday Market Place.

He stayed with her, as they passed by the shambles outside the Church. 'Ruth,' he said quietly and as he'd hoped she stopped again and turned towards him. 'Ruth, I do not know what tomorrow will bring, or the next day. For me, I mean. Or for any of us.'

The moon had come up now and it illuminated the street, the houses with the overhanging jetties, and her eyes were wide as she stared at him. 'They will take you to Wisbech Castle, will they not?' She stopped to consider. 'They would not—they will not—hang you?'

Despite himself, despite the anger he had felt, despite vowing never to forgive her, her concern for him sent a rush of love through him, making his insides contract. They had reached the beginning of Wingate and he pulled her into the lane beside the college for some privacy. They could not stand arguing in the middle of the road.

'I do not know what they will do to us,' he said frankly as they stood facing each other in the lee of the college wall. 'But we must expect many months, if not years in prison.' He frowned struggling to say what he knew he must say. 'I know you cannot wait for me. If we had eloped—but probably in light of this, it's best we did not.' No, he thought as the reality of the situation swamped him. No, it would have been cruel for her husband to be captured, taken, imprisoned for the rest of his life, or perhaps hanged. He considered his own possible fate dispassionately. He had known all along that defeat could lead to his death as a traitor. But to leave her, perhaps with a child, unable to marry if he continued to live in prison, well he had no right to inflict that on her.

He could see the outline of her beautiful face in the glow of the moonlight, could see her eyes as they looked into his, the glistening of not-yet-shed tears and a lump lodged in his throat as he realised he might never set eyes on her again. He added: 'But if by some miracle we are free, I will come for you.'

'Roger—Roger—' She shook her head, no longer hiding her anguish from him.

He understood what she wanted to say. She wanted to tell him that it would not happen, that he would get away safely, but her honesty stopped her. For she knew just as he did what they did to traitors. This was greater than a silly argument over her working at the infirmary. Why had he let days elapse without seeing her? Why had he been so angry with her? Why had he allowed stupid prejudice to come between them. This woman loved him truly. How could he have doubted it?

He pulled her into the folds of his cloak, holding her against him, burying his face in her neck, smelling the sweet rose fragrance of her. His love for this woman washed over him in gut-twisting intensity, and he clung on to her. He could not let her go. She was the only woman he wanted to marry. Yet he knew that once Manchester came into the town, she would be back under her father's control.

Yet what could he offer her? If he did not hang, he would be imprisoned. He had to lose her. He could not keep her. Her destiny lay with another man, not with him. He knew it and he thought now that he had always known it. And it pierced him as thoroughly as a sword-thrust.

He became aware that she was weeping. 'I will always love you, Roger L'Estrange,' she whispered.

Desperately, in the darkness of a September night, in a small lane leading to the sea, with the moon casting soft light around them and with the water lapping against the quay, they clung to each other.

THIRTY-FIVE

15 September 1643, King's Lynn

Sir Hamon stared at the man before him for several unblinking moments as though he had not understood what had been said to him. In the stretching silence Roger watched his father, his brows drawn together. He had that lurch in the pit of his stomach which warned him of imminent disaster. A glance at his brother told him he felt it too.

'I have a message for the governor of this town,' the messenger repeated with the air of one who had a job to do and would be pleased to get it over with. His voice echoed in the cavernous room.

Sir Hamon took a deep breath. He knew what it was, just as Roger and Nicholas knew what it was. They had all observed Manchester's preparations to end the siege for days now and they had been expecting it, but Sir Hamon asked: 'Where is the message?'

'Are you the governor, sir? My message is only for the governor.'

Sir Hamon's eyes did not waver from the messenger's face. He looked weary, his eyes had dark rings around them and the lines on his face seemed deeper, his skin sallow. The worry had caused sleepless nights and Roger knew he was not eating. 'I am he,' he answered with his quiet dignity.

The messenger came further forward, his hand reaching inside his dirty grey doublet and immediately Roger's hand flew to the sword at his hip.

Catching the movement, Sir Hamon put his hand up to still any violence Roger had in mind and held out the other hand to receive the document just extracted from the doublet. 'This man has safe passage,' he reminded him quietly.

Safe passage or not, if the man threatened his father, Roger would stop him without hesitation and his hand stayed on the pommel, even though the sword remained in the scabbard.

Sir Hamon picked up his eye glasses from the desk and fixed them on his nose, then broke the seal on the letter and quickly made himself master of its contents. He looked up at the messenger, his face inscrutable. 'Wait outside if you please. Roger, please ask the other burgesses to come in' he said quietly.

Roger escorted the messenger from the vaulted hall and came back in with the burgesses who had gathered on the landing on the news that a messenger had come from the enemy. He closed the heavy oak door behind him with a large bang that reverberated around the hall. Sir Hamon, who had stood politely at their entrance, now sat down to look at the message again, but he peered at his youngest son over the top of his eye glasses reprovingly. He said nothing, however, returning to the letter in his long slender fingers.

As the burgesses sat down around the table in silence, waiting patiently, they occasionally exchanged nervous glances. It was as if no-one wanted to hear what they knew they must hear, putting off the moment.

Sir Hamon frowned, perplexed, his lips pressed together, his whole body slumped as he stared at the letter he replaced on the table in front of him. He clearly struggled to break the news to the burgesses and Roger felt the anxiety rising still further inside him. He met Nicholas's eyes and his disquiet was mirrored there.

Removing his spectacles, Sir Hamon looked up at last at the silent, expectant men and took a steadying breath. 'Gentleman—you might as well know that Lord Manchester has again demanded our surrender. He says that if we do not yield by nine o'clock tomorrow morning he will take the town by storm. He suggests, therefore, that we send out all the women and children before then.'

His words echoed in the hush like the tolling of a funeral bell. It wasn't as if they had not been expecting it, but the letter was the confirmation of that expectation.

No-one spoke and Sir Hamon looked away from them, unable to meet their eyes. Roger knew what he must be thinking. All that he had promised them had come to nothing. He had let them down. But it wasn't Sir Hamon who had let them down, Roger thought fiercely. It was Lord Newcastle who had not kept his promise.

Feeling suddenly limp, Roger sat down on a vacant chair. Nicholas closed his eyes and shook his head. It was the end of all their hopes, their plans. The disappointment was tangible. All those people dead, on both sides and for what had they died?

Sir Charles Mordaunt was the first to break the long silence, stroking his moustache and small beard in one nervous gesture. 'The way I see it,' he ventured, 'we have no water, no food and Newcastle is not coming. If we succeeded in repelling Manchester, which I think must be in serious doubt for we are heavily outnumbered, how much longer can we expect to hold out?'

Sir Nicholas said: 'I do not think we should give this town to the enemy. That is not what the good people of Lynn decided five weeks ago!'

'The good people of Lynn, want only to have a peaceful life,' Sir Hamon reminded him wearily. 'They care not who rules them as long as they can go about their lives.'

'We all want a peaceful life,' Sir Robert de Grey put in. He just wanted to go home to his family.

Lord Hevingham coughed. 'Sir Charles is right. We cannot win and I think we all know it. We are lost.'

Mordaunt picked up the letter and read it for himself. 'We have to yield before anyone else is killed. When he says we are to send the women and children out first, Lord Manchester expects there to be slaughter.' He shuddered. And Roger felt a chill slither up his back. He thought of Ruth, and deliberately dismissed her from his mind. He needed to have a clear head to comprehend this.

Sir Nicholas looked directly at his father, grey eyes meeting grey eyes. 'What do you think we should do, sir?' he asked quietly.

Sir Hamon stood up, turning away from them to the latticed mullioned window and looked down into the Saturday Market Place, defeated. Roger's heart went out to him. He had so desperately wanted to keep Lynn for the King, had wanted victory so badly, had talked of nothing else. They could have been victorious if Newcastle had come, perhaps won the war in a few weeks. But no, Newcastle was not coming. *Damn the man!* The disappointment overwhelmed Roger and he felt tears starting into his eyes as he thought of all that was lost. He felt his father's pain as if it were his own.

Finally Sir Hamon spoke without turning around to face them. 'I think it is time to yield, gentlemen,' he said quietly.

Roger swallowed the lump that had come into his throat, trying to clear the ache there. He ached for his father, for them all, of course, but for his father principally. For Sir Hamon's dream was over and he would pay dearly for his defiance of Parliament.

Gurlin was the only one not cast into total dejection. His tenure as mayor was almost over. He would hand the office and the problems on to someone else. The little weasel rubbed his hands together in business-like fashion. 'Well then,' he said matter-of-factly, 'do we all agree to yield?'

No-one answered.

Gurlin frowned. 'Well, does anyone disagree?'

Still no-one answered.

Roger shook his head in disbelief. Gurlin, on neither one side nor the other, seemed not to understand that no-one wanted to agree to surrender, despite knowing they must.

Sir Hamon said: 'I will write to Lord Manchester informing him of our decision.'

'Tell him we want pardons for all of us,' Sir Robert de Grey suggested. 'I've no wish to end up in Wisbech Castle. Or worse. Make it part of the agreement.'

Sir Hamon nodded, but de Grey's reminder that they could all face the hangman appalled them all. Sir Hamon looked at his sons. Roger wanted to tell his father not to worry about him. He and Nicholas would survive somehow, but he felt his father's fear. Thank God his other brother Hamon, was away in Suffolk.

Sir Hamon shook his head, struggling to battle the fog of bitter disappointment which swept through him. This was no time for weakness or fear. He needed a clear negotiating head.

Roger nodded to him almost imperceptibly, a gesture of encouragement and his father gave him a small smile. 'I shall write to Lord Manchester informing him that we wish to negotiate a peace treaty,' Sir Hamon said. 'I will ask for mercy and appeal to Lord Manchester's better self. I understand he is a God-fearing man and a merciful man.'

''Tis to be hoped you are right,' Anthony Hevingham put in sourly.

'And whilst we do not object to their demolishing our fortifications,' Sir Charles Mordaunt further recommended, 'we still want Lynn to retain local government.'

'Yes, yes, yes.' Sir Hamon wanted them gone and one by one they filed out, leaving Sir Hamon with his sons.

As soon as the door closed, both Roger and Nicholas turned and hugged their father who kissed them both.

'I am proud of you both,' he said in a voice hardly above a whisper. 'Young Roger, you have fought valiantly and you too Nick. You have supported me in this difficult situation.'

'I wish it had turned out differently,' Nicholas said. 'You have done your best for them.'

'My best wasn't good enough.'

'Lord Newcastle deserted us,' Roger put in. 'You were not to know that.'

'Without Newcastle's promise I would not have gone ahead with this,' his father said. 'I would not have risked so many lives for a lost cause.'

'Damn Newcastle,' Sir Nicholas cursed.

§

As the Earl of Manchester studied Sir Hamon's letter his face broke into a broad grin. 'They have surrendered, gentlemen,' he said addressing his officers.

Captain Poe allowed himself an uncustomary self-satisfied smile and he met his lordship's eyes squarely.

'You said it would be over in a week,' Manchester accused. 'Well they held out for five. I'll give them that, they made a valiant effort. But in the end good sense prevailed.'

His lordship's other officers congratulated him and thanked God and said all that was proper.

'We can go in, then?' Sir Miles Hobart asked.

'Not yet,' Manchester replied. 'They have asked for terms. There will need to be a discussion of those terms.'

'Damn their impudent eyes! Don't they know they are beaten?'

'They do. But they also know that we are keen to save further bloodshed. I think we can afford to be magnanimous—to a point.'

'So you'll let them get away with it!' Hobart was furious.

Manchester frowned at him. He was the general here, not Miles Hobart. He said: 'Not at all, sir. Delighted I may be to be able to put an end to the trouble in that pestilential town and be on my way north where I have other business calling me, but I'll be damned if I am going to let them call the terms.'

Mollified Miles Hobart retreated with Poe and the others.

His lordship stood in his empty room tapping his front teeth with the folded paper thoughtfully. So, Sir Hamon L'Estrange wanted amnesty for all of them, did he? Understandable, of course. Furthermore, his lordship wasn't anxious to hang men just for the sake of it. Nevertheless, he knew he could also drive a hard bargain and he wanted Lynn sewn up right and tight and out of the way. The best way to hurt Sir Hamon would be to ruin him financially. He smiled. Probably more painful than hanging. He sat down at his desk, dipped his pen in the ink and began to write a reply.

§

When it came later that day, Lord Manchester's reply to the burgesses' demands was not conciliatory. He told Sir Hamon that he could not give them amnesty, since it was not in his power to do so, only Parliament itself having that power, and he reminded them of the criminality of their behaviour: sheltering Royalists, imprisoning Puritans—including the Lynn members of Parliament Toll and Percival—and misappropriating the funds and armaments that Parliament had collected for its own war effort.

To which Sir Hamon raised the ghost of a smile. 'I wonder what else Manchester expected me to do in the circumstances? Indeed, it is only what Manchester himself would and did in fact do when it was necessary to advance Parliamentarian interests.'

All that was left was to discuss the terms. But until those terms were thrashed out, there could be no real truce and the gates remained firmly closed.

At seven o'clock on that Friday evening 15th September, 1643, eight commissioners from each side including Sir Hamon L'Estrange, Sir Richard Hovell of Hillington, Francis Parlett, Edmund Hudson the new mayor elect (at last the weaselly Gurlin was on his way out!), William Leek (who had once given five hundred pounds as a pledge to secure his release from Norwich), Walter Kirby, Robert Clench and Mr. Dereham for the Lynn burgesses and Sir John Palgrave, Colonel Valentine Walton (a kinsman of Oliver Cromwell), John Spelman (a kinsman of the dead Royalist Sir John Spelman, Sir Hamon's friend) and others for the Parliamentarians met in Gaywood to discuss the treaty.

And while the men talked, the guns at last fell silent and an unaccustomed quiet fell over the town for the first time in six weeks, broken only by spasmodic fire from some of the Royalist defenders who were reluctant to surrender.

A sense of relief filtered through the town and the Puritans were euphoric.

Lord Manchester, though, was not one to count his chickens and he marshalled all his forces in the meadows around Lynn in a formidable display of strength while awaiting the outcome of the parley.

With the other defenders on the wall ramparts Roger could only watch as eighteen thousand men assembled outside the walls to the accompaniment of shouted commands and drum rolls which drifted on the hot September air across the fields. They filled all the available space. His father had been right to surrender. Lynn's five thousand defenders would not have stood against such a force. Probably they would all have been killed. The despair at the loss of the town though, had become a deep ache in the pit of his belly. As for his King, he began to think that his cause too might be lost.

He reflected on the five short weeks since the town had so joyously declared 'For the King', the pain and the anguish, the heroics, the patient endurance of the people in the face of hardship, near starvation and the destruction of so many buildings, not a heavy price to pay for victory, but a terrible price for defeat.

He thought too of his father, that proud man who had done his best. The thought of his disgrace caused tears to prick his eyes. He knew Nicholas felt it too. Nicholas was not here on the walls, but was in the Guildhall, awaiting news. Perhaps Roger should go there too. Not yet. Soon, though.

Time wore tediously on with no news from the commissioners who were talking over the treaty terms. The defending soldiers were restless. Not understanding the situation completely, they felt they had been betrayed by their leaders and dissensions started, arguments and bickering.

Roger went to find his brother in the Guildhall and found it strangely quiet, with Nicholas, Sir Charles Mordaunt and other burgesses sitting quietly, just waiting. The tension hung in the air like thick fog. It was worse here than it was on the ramparts. No-one had slept.

Roger said: 'The men are restless.'

'We are all restless, L'Estrange,' Sir Charles snapped.

'What the devil are they doing?' This was Sir Robert de Grey whose patience was clearly wearing thin.

Roger exchanged glances with Nicholas, who stood up to come to his brother. 'What do you think?' Roger asked him steadily.

Nicholas placed a comforting hand on Roger's shoulder. 'I think they have arrested them and taken them into custody,' he said quietly.

Roger's heart seemed to fly up into his throat and he caught his breath. The thought of his father in custody made the colour drain from his face. If Sir Hamon could not make a deal with Manchester's side, if he were indeed in custody, they were all dead men. 'Surely Manchester would not still be waiting if that were the case?'

Nicholas nodded. ‘I hope you are right. But they are in the heart of the enemy.’ He took a deep steadying breath and Roger knew his brother felt it as keenly as he did himself. ‘I mislike the delay,’ Nicholas added. ‘Not knowing is the worst.’

Roger nodded. It was bad, not knowing, but knowing something had gone wrong would have been far worse. As it was, with Manchester still outside Lynn’s walls, there was hope of some deal, hope for their lives.

Harry Watts, his shoulder now healed, came into the Guildhall. ‘The men be barneying. You must talk to them,’ he appealed to Roger. ‘Things be getting ugly. They might listen to you.’

Roger was reluctant and glanced at Nicholas. Who was he to stop the men from bickering? ‘I don’t know,’ Roger said. At any moment the governor and the others could appear with the treaty agreed.

‘There be a riot if something hin’t done to stop it. You must stop it. Sir Nicholas, sir, please come and talk to them.’

‘I shall speak to them,’ Nicholas said.

§

Out in the meadows, Lord Manchester too was restless. He decided he could wait no longer. He gave the order and the troops in the meadows began to march, with drums beating and trumpets blowing and with Colonel Russell at the head they advanced towards the East Gates.

Roger and Nicholas heard it as they strode through the streets towards the East Gate in the dark with Harry Watts. A man came running towards them, saw them and said: ‘They be coming in!’

As they arrived at the gate, they could also hear the men on the ramparts arguing among themselves.

‘We should yield!’

‘We must not yield!’

‘Let’s shoot them!’

In the absence of his father Nicholas took it upon himself to climb the wall parapet and address them and Roger was right beside him.

‘What are you fighting about?’ Nicholas demanded.

‘We hin’t surrendering,’ someone yelled. ‘Nor should we!’

A roar of mixed opinions reached him and he waved his hands for quiet. ‘It is not in our hands to do anything else,’ he told them. ‘You know that we must yield. No-one wants to, but how can we fight eighteen thousand of them? The town has surrendered.’

He was immediately drowned out.

'No surrender! No surrender!'

'We must yield!'

Then above the noise a voice won out loud and clear: 'Here they come. Shoot them! Shoot! Give fire! Give fire!'

The voice carried across to the soldiers just outside the gates and immediately all the troops in the vicinity fell flat to the ground, some into the ditches, while those on horseback dropped on top of their companions in the ditches.

Roger and Nicholas watched in amazement at this panic in the attackers' ranks, and yelled together into the din: 'Hold your fire!' After several tense minutes, when it became obvious that no-one was going to obey the call to fire, the attackers all scrambled up again and took up their positions.

Roger shook his head in dismay.

Colonel Russell, Manchester's second-in-command, now approached the East Gate himself and the mob inside grew quieter to hear what he had to say.

'In the name of God we demand to be admitted to this town!' he called.

The soldier in charge of the gate showed himself. 'Oh no! Can't do that, not at this toime o'night!' And he sounded like a half-wit.

'This is ridiculous!' Colonel Russell fumed. 'You cannot deny us admittance! You have surrendered!'

'Well Oi don't roightly know,' the garrison soldier replied dimly, ''Oi hin't got the authority to let you in.'

'You stupid little man!' Colonel Russell raged. 'Let us in.'

But the gate man liked the sudden authority that he had. 'You can come in,' he told the astounded Colonel Russell, 'one at a time. Through the wicket gate, if you loike.'

Roger's eyes widened at the gate man in surprise. *Wicket gate? One at a time? Eighteen thousand men? It will take for ever!*

Colonel Russell uttered something that was extremely unchristian. Evidently he did not like. The obvious drawbacks of a whole army marching one by one through a small gate into an enemy town were not lost on him. 'No!' he bellowed. 'I demand that you let us in! Your town has surrendered. Open the gates!'

Some began speaking of setting an ambush for them when they came in. Nicholas shook his head in despair. 'No!'

Enjoying himself hugely the gate man waved his arm expansively. 'Then you'll hev to go to St. Catherine's gate.'

Furious, Colonel Russell made an explosive sound in his throat.

'This *is* St. Catherine's Gate!'

'Is that roight?'

'Let them in,' Sir Nicholas said to him, weary with it all. 'The town has surrendered.'

So they lowered the drawbridge, raised the portcullis and opened the gates.

Finally victorious, with drums beating, the invaders marched through the East Gate, along Damgate and Grassmarket and right into the Tuesday Market Place.

Standing on the wall, Roger watched them come in, all in their buff coats, torches in their hands, the light reflected in iron helmets, strangers in the town, his town. He wept, but he was not the only one. The defenders on the wall had fallen silent as they watched them come in and some sobbed openly.

If Colonel Russell had expected a good reception he was sadly disappointed. The few women and children who were in the streets were largely silent. Only the occasional cry of 'God bless us!' punctuated the beating of drums and marching of feet. Did they mean it as an expression of thankfulness or dismay that the Parliamentarians had come in?

The men of the town who were on the walls melted away.

The siege was over.

THIRTY-SIX

King's Lynn, 17th September 1643

If it were a victory, it did not feel much like it to Colonel Russell. Still he was not swayed by public opinion and he set to work in businesslike fashion. He secured the South Gate for the Parliamentarians, set watches at other gates and strategic points and quartered a force of infantry and cavalry in the Tuesday Market Place.

Early on Sunday morning the Earl of Manchester himself, with his own bodyguard, rode in stately splendour into the town and then attended divine service at St. Margaret's church where the reverend Simeon Ashe, an army chaplain, preached a thanksgiving service.

Sir Valentine Pell, Ruth's father, also entered the town with Lord Manchester and, after the church service, went straight to his sister's house.

'Where is my daughter?' he demanded of the footman as he stood in the hallway and stripped off his gloves.

His sister appeared at the top of the staircase, peering past the balustrade and down the stairs. 'Brother! An unexpected honour.' She glided down the stairs in a waft of lavender, an affectation Sir Valentine deplored. 'Jane—tell cook an extra one for dinner.'

'I doubt we shall be staying for dinner,' Sir Valentine said curtly as the maid took herself off. 'Madam, I shall ask again, *where is my daughter*? Why was she not at church?'

Mary, having now reached the bottom of the stairs, wrung her hands in her agitation. She was not yet dressed properly; her hair was still tied in rags, with a dressing robe over her night shift.

'Now, Valentine, do not get yourself in a pet.'

Sir Valentine glared at her. 'Am I to understand my daughter is not here?'

Shooting him an alarmed glance, Mary struggled to find the right words. 'Well, no. That is to say, yes, she is in Lynn, but no, she is not here at—at present. She—she felt it to be her Christian duty.'

'Madam, if you do not stop prevaricating and tell me where she is—'

'Ah, Sir Valentine. You are well come, sir!' John Lead appeared from a room behind the stairs and inclined his head graciously to his brother-in-law. His calm tone was at strong variance to Sir Valentine's anger, and had the effect of pouring oil on troubled water.

Sir Valentine disliked this little man but he knew his measure. Little John Lead might be, but he had a will to be reckoned with. He could not be as blunt with him as he could with his sister. 'Sir. Your most obedient,' and he managed a bow. 'I am looking for my daughter.'

'Of course you are,' John said soothingly. 'Come into the parlour.'

Thus dismissed, Mary, thankfully, departed and Sir Valentine allowed himself to be ushered into the stylish front parlour.

'I am afraid Ruth is not here at present,' John said as he closed the door.

'So my sister told me. But she is in Lynn?'

'Oh yes. You see she decided to do some charitable work.'

'Yes?'

'At the infirmary.'

Sir Valentine was silent for a long moment as he digested this. 'You mean she is *nursing*?'

'Indeed, I regret to inform you, sir, she is.'

Sir Valentine could only stare at his brother-in-law, bereft of speech for several moments. Then: 'You, sir, allowed my daughter to nurse at the infirmary?'

'No I did not allow it. And neither did my wife. But, sir, your daughter did not listen to either of us. We are as horrified as you are.'

'Only *common* women work in infirmaries.'

'That is what I told her when I remonstrated with her. I have to tell you, sir, that she dismissed my concerns. She said that as a lady in the house, her job was to nurse the sick. And if she could nurse the sick in her own or her father's house, why not elsewhere? She said it was her Christian duty and nothing anyone said could stop her.'

'You could have locked her in her room!' Sir Valentine said.

'I did. But she had a key of her own.'

'How on earth did she get that?'

'She had one cut by the locksmith, I should think. When my wife looked in on her later, she was gone. Believe me, sir, we tried, but she outwitted us in all directions.'

Sir Valentine snorted in derision.

Mr. Lead shook his head and sighed. 'You know yourself, sir, how it is with the girl.'

'And that's why I sent her here. Perhaps I should have sent her to her sister instead.' He only just stopped himself accusing the Leads of severe neglect in his daughter's case. The deed was done, it would not do to argue with John Lead, especially as he was his banker.

'I thought her sister refused to have her,' John Lead said mildly.

Sir Valentine glared at him. This was true. He compressed his lips in a thoughtful moment. 'Has that L'Estrange been sniffing around her?'

'We saw him once or twice over by the church, but we were able to keep her from knowing about it. That was before the siege started. After that we did not see him at all. I heard he has been busy with the fighting. And with her busy with the sick and injured, I do not think they can have met.'

'I told you to keep an eye out for him. He is trouble that one. If he so much as lays a finger on her, I will cut off that carrot head of his! L'Estrange or not.'

'Well I think you may be easy on that score. Besides, the way I understand it, all the L'Estranges are in a good deal of difficulty at the moment.'

Sir Valentine nodded. 'Where is the infirmary?' Sir Valentine demanded abruptly.

'St. James' chapel.'

'Where's that?'

'Straight on from the church. Where the road branches in two directions, take the left. You will see it.'

Sir Valentine stood up. 'I've just come from the church! I did not see you or your family there, Mr. Lead.'

'We will be attending evensong,' Mr. Lead told him.

Sir Valentine allowed himself to growl in his throat. 'Well I bid you good day, sir.' He strode from the house, opening the front door himself before the footman could get there.

§

The first Ruth knew about her father's arrival was when she looked up from tending a wounded man's foot to see him standing in the open doorway, his feet planted apart, hands on hips, surveying the scene before him, every inch the wrathful parent. A woman, a helper, automatically crossed herself, publicly declaring her religious allegiance, but he was not interested in her. Instead his eyes fixed on Ruth kneeling down beside her patient.

Fear clutched at her insides. She knew what he would think of her ministering to a man who was neither husband, brother nor father and what he would think of a room that resembled the battlefield: blood, bandages, groans and shrieks, of men, mostly, but women and children too, injured by the continual bombardment. The stench of humanity with little in the way of the necessary conveniences, would not go unnoticed by him, she knew. To say it was no fit place for a delicately bred female was an understatement and he bore down on her with steely determination.

With her heart hammering against her ribs, she stood up, her task half done and tried to assume a poise and dignity she was far from feeling. She bobbed a curtsey.

'What do you think you are doing?' he demanded, unconsciously echoing Roger's words of a few days ago.

Ruth took a breath and said as calmly as she could: 'Helping the wounded. My Christian duty as I see it.'

'Not any more! You are coming home with me.'

A man with a stick tucked under his arm to help him cope with a broken leg, asked Ruth: 'Do you need help, mistress?'

She smiled at him kindly. 'No, thank you, sir. This is, in fact, my father.'

It added to Sir Valentine's fury. He thundered: 'Get your things, woman!'

She did not hesitate to obey. She had been on the receiving end of too many beatings to argue with him. Quickly she ran off to find her cloak, paid a quick visit to the surgeon in his operating room to offer an apology and not waiting for a reply, she presented herself back in front of her father in less than a minute.

Without waiting for her to throw her cloak around her, he thrust her before him out of the infirmary doors, his hand gripping her upper arm. He marched her through the streets towards her aunt's house, at the same time taking the opportunity to sound forth on the shortcomings of his youngest daughter, unheeding of who would hear.

'Whatever do you think you were doing there?' he demanded.

Ruth, running to keep up with his fast long strides, tried to give an explanation: 'People were hurt, Father. There were not enough people to help them.' She wished it did not sound so much like an apology.

He paused momentarily in the headlong rush to spin her round so that he could see her face to face. His eyes bulged with anger, his cheeks were dark red and his breath came in short gasps. His voice shook with fury. 'No daughter of mine shall be dealing with the sick and wounded. *And* helping the enemy at that! There are enough common women to do that. For God's sake, cover your apron! You are covered in blood!'

She was also splashed with other even less savoury things, but she thought better of mentioning it. However, she took the opportunity to throw her cloak over her shoulders, and pull it closed in front of her to cover her apron. Once more, he grabbed her, this time on her wrist and again dragged her along.

'Your cousin Charles shall hear of this! He won't want you after this! As for your aunt . . .'

Alarmed, Ruth tried to forestall him: 'Do not be harsh on aunt Mary, sir,' she gasped, hardly able to breathe by this time. 'She tried to stop me.'

'Like she tried to stop you seeing L'Estrange, I suppose?'

She could not speak and now she panicked that he knew about her friendship with Roger. It was no good talking to him. He dragged her down past the church. People were staring at her humiliation.

Even as she struggled to keep up with her father's furious paces she dimly registered the Parliamentarian men in uniforms and armour littering the town, swaggering in victory, grinning at the spectacle. When she did not answer, he spun her around again to face him and she cowered in the face of his rage. He terrified her. 'Do not pretend you do not know what I am talking about, woman! Your aunt told me how you have been seen with him in public! And not even betrothed.'

But I was betrothed, she wanted to tell him, but did not dare. The reminder brought fresh tears. What had happened to Roger in all of this? Where was he? Was he in custody?

'I told you to have nothing to do with him.'

Again he whipped her round viciously and she was yanked after him. Her cap had come off, lost somewhere on the road and her hair slipped out from its pins, flying out behind her. People were staring. Soldiers laughed and jeered. Women called out. Her arm hurt, she could hardly breathe, her face must have been scarlet, for she was so hot and she thought she would die of the shame. Her father did not seem to care that he had made her a spectacle.

By the time they reached Wingate, she was shaking in terror. She had experienced his rages in the past. He threw her in the door of Aunt Mary's house and she only just kept her feet, falling into the baluster and clinging to it.

She turned to dash upstairs to the protection of her room, but he grabbed her hair, stopping her.

She was sobbing and she turned away from him hiding her face from the blow she knew would follow.

'Sir! I must protest!' John Lead's voice interrupted him.

'You, sir would do well to keep out of this!' Her father thundered.

'Sir, I must ask you to leave my house.'

'We will be leaving. Immediately.'

Aunt Mary and all the servants had by now arrived in the hall, as if to back up their master. Aunt Mary came to Ruth and took her in gentle arms and Ruth allowed her to cradle her as she struggled to control her tears and her fear. She shook with sheer terror.

Aunt Mary nodded to a maid who ran upstairs.

'You can send her things on later,' Her father ordered. 'We leave now. I have horses ready. We do not wait for a carriage,' he announced. 'I will not have my daughter another minute in this pestilential town.'

'You must allow her to change, sir,' Mary Lead pleaded.

'You, sister, should keep your peace and mind your business!' Sir Valentine bellowed at her.

'I protest!' John Lead cried. 'Do not speak to my wife like that! You are nothing but a bully, sir!'

Sir Valentine turned on him, his voice low in pitch and vibrating in his wrath. 'How *dare* you, sir! How dare you intervene between father and daughter!'

'Get out of my house!' John Lead ordered.

Sir Valentine turned his back on him just as the horses appeared outside the front door.

Aunt Mary was trying to tie Ruth's streaming hair into a plait, and a maid brought a new cap for her. At the same time Ruth rid herself of the blood-stained apron, but Sir Valentine interrupted them by grabbing his daughter and pulling her roughly from the house.

'Get on it!' he ordered as she hesitated. 'Get on!' he ordered again, and lifted her bodily and threw her into the saddle. She had no way of adjusting her skirts, and the groom ran to help her arrange her foot and her knee over the pommel in the time it took for her father to mount his own horse. With her horse's rein in his hands and without looking back he urged both horses into a brisk trot and led her away.

§

Lord Manchester's troops had come into Lynn last night and Manchester himself had been accommodated by the ever-hospitable Gurlin. It was time enough for the erstwhile governor to be back.

If he were coming back.

In an agony of anxiety and under house-arrest, Roger and Nicholas waited for the return of their father and the other burgesses. They had been gone two agonising days.

'They must have been taken into custody,' Nicholas said as he paced the parlour's flagstone floor, the worry making his voice tight.

Roger swallowed, the solid ball of fear in his stomach a physical pain. He had not slept for two nights, and his head seemed not to be his own. It was as though he watched the world through a fog of misery. In the first place, he had given Ruth her freedom, certain that his own imprisonment was not far away. Their parting had been painful, and he ached for her. But at least he knew she was safe. Whereas his father could even now be in the dungeon at Wisbech Castle, and he and Nicholas could be following soon.

His father was a courageous man, loyal to the King and certainly no traitor. When he thought of him he could see again his quiet dignity, the love he showed his wife and family. He hero-worshipped his father. The thought of him being held at Wisbech Castle, perhaps in chains, or being subject to that treatment which had killed Sir Thomas Richardson, which was a very real possibility, brought a lump to his throat and tears to his eyes. Men had been executed for lesser crimes than Sir Hamon's.

'We must help them all,' he said to Nicholas, although in truth he cared not so much about the others as he did about his father.

Nick shook his head, momentarily pausing in his pacing. 'We cannot storm Wisbech Castle.' He said it through his teeth, impatient with Roger as though he found his suggestion ridiculous. 'And once they send them to London, we have lost them.'

'We need to find out first.' Determination lit up Roger's eyes. They would not hang his father while he lived! 'If they send them to London there might be a way of freeing them on the road.'

Nick met his eyes squarely, a sardonic eyebrow raised. 'You think you and I can rescue him out of their hands, boy? They will be hundreds strong and there's only two of us!'

Roger bristled. He was nearly seven-and-twenty, no longer a boy. However he let it go. He was too intent on pressing his point. 'Subterfuge.'

'Oh. So we sneak up and magically his chains drop off without a sound and then we spirit him away. Besides, you are forgetting that we, too, are under arrest.'

'Do you have a better idea?'

'No, I do not. Because it ain't possible,' he repeated. He took a breath and let it go in an impatient sigh, his brows drawing together. He came over to Roger and put his hands on his shoulders. The gesture and the pressure of his fingers brought the tears to Roger's eyes.

'I won't let him die,' Roger said with simple determination.

'Well I don't intend to die,' Sir Hamon announced from the doorway, making them both jump.

Roger and Nicholas turned disbelieving eyes towards the door where their father stood in his black embroidered doublet.

Nicholas crossed the room in two strides, taking his father's hand, relief written across his face. 'Thank God you are safe, sir!' He embraced Sir Hamon while Roger hung back, knowing that he was not the heir, not the firstborn, just a lowly third son, awaiting his turn. Catching his eye, Sir Hamon held out his spare hand towards him in invitation. Roger went to his father then and hugged him tightly, grateful to feel his affectionate embrace, the slap on his back. 'We thought they had you in Wisbech,' he said gruffly and his gratitude spilled over in a rush of emotion which filled his eyes anew.

'They did imprison us,' Sir Hamon confirmed affably. 'Comfortably so. Until the terms were met, namely that the town with the ordnance, arms and ammunition should be given to the Earl of Manchester when he comes into the town.'

'That has been done, sir,' Nicholas confirmed. 'As you see.'

In the pause Roger had the chance to study his father. Clearly he had had no sleep for the last twenty-four hours. His face was grey beneath the tan of the summer, large pouches had developed beneath his grey eyes and the lids drooped with weariness. He was sixty years old, but he looked at least ten years older, his once-red hair now snow white. He had lost his vitality in the exhaustion of defeat, the spark that made him such a vibrant, commanding man.

Sir Hamon went on: 'They were anxious to finish with Lynn and not to have to fight their way in, so we had some force to our demands. Most importantly, we, all of us, have been given our freedom.'

Roger shook his head in amazement. 'They have? We are free to go?'

Sir Hamon nodded, not displeased. 'We are. Our horses will be ready shortly. It was not easy. Often we argued. And we had to insist on our liberties. But we can depart with horse, pistols and sword. And our estates are not to be molested.'

''Tis more than we expected,' Nicholas observed.

''Tis more than they wanted to give us,' Sir Hamon agreed, pulling his hand down his face in a weary gesture. 'We must go to retrieve our weapons from the vault at the Guildhall.'

'There is something I must do first,' Roger said.

Sir Hamon stared at him. 'You will go to the infirmary.'

'I shall bring her home with us, Father.' He was not asking permission.

Sir Hamon's clenched fist came down so heavily on the table that both Nicholas and Roger jumped. 'No you shall not! I will not have Pell declaring war on us in Hunstanton! We barely got away with our necks in tact this time. It won't happen again! If you want that girl so badly you will have to find somewhere else to take her. And if you do that, I'll have done with you!'

Roger's temper came to the surface. 'Very well. I shall do just that!' He wrenched the door open so that it flew back and struck a chair placed behind it and marched the distance to St. James' chapel. Someone slammed the door behind him. The defeat had taken its toll on all their tempers.

He knew immediately Ruth was not at the infirmary for there was more chaos than usual as though no-one had any direction. Tellingly, the odour of the privy once more permeated the air.

'If you be looking for Mistress Pell, she hin't hair,' a man said. He had sticks under his arms as an aid to walking.

Roger turned to go, thinking to go directly to Wingate and blow the consequences, when the man added: 'Her father took her away.'

Roger turned back. 'Her father? Sir Valentine Pell?'

'If that be his name. Foine Puritan, he be.' The man said it derisively.

Roger touched his hat and gave the man a coin. Then he turned and left. There was nothing to be gained by staying.

Sir Valentine Pell had taken her. He would take her to Dersingham. *Then I shall wait for her in the Shernborne Road, or see her at church.* He turned towards the Saturday Market Place and the Guildhall where he met his father and brother, and other burgesses all intent on reclaiming their swords and pistols.

'And so?' Nicholas asked.

'She's gone,' Roger said shortly. 'Her father took her home.'

He did not miss the upward flick of Sir Hamon's eyes. 'Thank God for that!'

Roger bit his tongue. He had more hope of seeing Ruth now that she was in Dersingham, than he would have had with her in Lynn. For Lynn would be barred to them from now on.

As soon as they had their own weapons, they left immediately on their own horses, riding out of the East Gate and out on the Gaywood road away from Lynn at an easy canter. Unknown to Roger, they were just an hour behind Ruth and her father.

Neither Nicholas nor Roger asked any questions and it was not until they had parted company from Sir Richard Hovell and Sir Charles Mordaunt and were near South Wootton that anyone spoke.

Sir Hamon reined in his horse and looked back across the marsh towards the town. One or two sparse trees on Gaywood Common interrupted the view, but there was Lynn, sitting on the river.

'King's Lynn,' Sir Hamon whispered and his eyes filled with tears.

'*King's* Lynn,' Roger repeated.

Both Sir Hamon and Sir Nicholas looked at him for a long moment. 'Not any more!' Nicholas said, and turned his horse's head for Hunstanton.

THIRTY-SEVEN

Hunstanton, Autumn 1643

Despite assurances that their estates would be safe, Sir Hamon discovered on his return to Hunstanton that the enemy had taken all the L'Estrange sheep as well as all their wheat, barley and hay, the harvesting of which Lady Alice had overseen during the absence of her men, to feed the large Parliamentarian army. They had also taken their horses and cattle, leaving them nothing. It was a blow for Sir Hamon and also for Sir Nicholas who would inherit the estates one day. They discovered too, that not only had they lost the town for the King, and all the harvest and animals, but they also had to make reparation for the damage supposedly sustained by the town and Parliamentary officers. It was contrary to the terms of the surrender, the agreement which Sir Hamon had personally worked to secure.

They had to pay heavy levies for Sir Thomas Fairfax, for the Eastern Association, to 'the rate for all garrisons' as Lady Alice noted in her accounts. This was in effect a tax to help towards the Parliamentarian cause and to his fury, Sir Hamon had to pay not only for Hunstanton, but for his estates at Heacham, Ringstead and Sedgeford as well. The worthy magistrates of Lynn also laid claims and Toll and Percival put in special damages for themselves and their wives for their imprisonment in their own homes during the siege although they did not yet know the amount of compensation.

The L'Estranges, those who worked for them, and all who relied on them, faced famine during a desperate winter. Financial ruin stared them in the face.

Sir Hamon was a broken man. Even so, it could have been much worse. They thanked God daily that they had not been incarcerated in Wisbech Castle—or worse. But that thought did not ease the financial pressures Sir Hamon now found himself struggling with.

It was Lady Alice as his capable wife who, with the responsibility of balancing the books, bore the brunt of these results of her husband's courageous efforts. It did not for a moment occur to her to blame him, for her loyalty would always be to uphold her husband's decisions, whether good or bad, but she had much to say on the conduct of Thomas Toll, reputedly such a God-fearing man who sought to extort money from his neighbours. And Parliament which allowed him free rein.

Roger did his best to help, working wherever Sir Hamon or Sir Nicholas asked, uncomplaining, making himself useful, saving them the cost of paying a labourer as they tried to salvage what they could. Each day also, he made the trip to Dersingham to wait on the corner outside Dersingham Hall, and then to wait in the Shernborne Road, hoping that Ruth would join him. As the days turned into weeks, hope faded. He went to the church opposite the Hall, but none of the Pell family attended. He realised that they either had her under lock and key, or she was not there.

Just as his family were cast into deep gloom, his own spirits joined them.

In a way, much as Roger loved his family and hated to see them suffering, it was not his problem, just as it was not his brother Hamon's problem either. For neither Hamon, nor Roger would inherit the estates. That was for Nick and his sons and grandsons after him. However, he lived at Hunstanton Hall rent free and neither did he have to find his food. Furthermore, he had an allowance which was generous by any standards, plus he had the expectation of an inheritance from his father which would be large enough to care for his needs—if he invested it in, say, property, or a holding as his brother Hamon had done. That is, if Sir Hamon had any money left after this. Sir Hamon had made it clear that he would provide for his other children besides the heir. And Roger was not unappreciative. They were a close family and it was unthinkable that he should leave them to cope with their problems alone.

However, for Roger the loss of Ruth pushed all other concerns aside.

Without her, he felt as though all the colour had been drained from his life. She consumed his every waking moment, invading his sleep, for he knew his chances of reclaiming her were slipping away.

'What is it, Cub?' Nicholas asked him when he found him staring at the ranked spines of books lining the walls in the library instead of reading the tome open on his knees. One of the spaniels was asleep by his side.

Jerked out of his reverie, Roger forced a smile. 'Nothing, why?'

Nicholas pulled a face. 'Nothing, eh? For the last three weeks you have been like the walking dead! And don't say it is worry for Father or for the Hall. 'Tain't like you to be all doom and gloom. What ails you, little brother? Is it the Puritan wench?'

Roger let his breath go. The urge to confide in Nicholas was strong. He said: 'I've been to Dersingham every day I could since we left Lynn, and there is no sign of her.'

'So that's where you disappear to! But I'm not surprised. Pell would have sent her away as soon as he got her here. I heard her father came into Lynn with Manchester, caught her in the infirmary. By all accounts he was so angry with her that he dragged her through the streets shouting his head off, and then rode off with her. 'Twas a right spectacle, they do say.'

Roger had not known that. 'Hell fire and brimstone!'

'Aye. And he'll do anything to keep her from you.'

Roger felt sick. No doubt by now she was married to the odious Calthorpe. The thought of her in another man's arms, in his bed, turned his stomach.

Nicholas continued easily: 'No wonder Pell was angry. I would be too. I would not want a daughter of mine working in the infirmary!'

Roger only half heard him. Jealousy as sharp as a knife had torn open his soul. His thoughts became enmeshed in a fog of desperate fear and raging anger. He had lost her. He could think of nothing else.

Watching him with growing alarm, Nicholas continued speaking for something to fill the sudden silence: 'Aye, no place for a woman. She would see things that a maid ought not to see 'til she's wed!'

I've lost her! She has gone! Roger came out of his thoughts as Nicholas's words filtered through. He felt the need to defend her. 'She was helping the King's cause. Her father would not have liked that either.'

Nick shrugged. 'I daresay you are right there.'

With sudden clarity, Roger said: 'He's sent her to her sister to keep her out of my reach.'

'Where is the sister?'

'I've no idea.'

'Christopher Anguish's brother works in the Pell house. I wonder if he can find out for us.'

Roger thanked him, touched that he would try to find out even though he disapproved of the match.

Nicholas put his hand on Roger's shoulder. 'I'm sorry, Cub.'

Two hours later, as they were going into supper, he pulled Roger aside. 'The Calthorpes, your lady's sister and her husband, live at Hickling, in the rectory.'

Roger's heart swooped. 'Where is Hickling?'

'On an area of wetland called the Broads. 'T'other side of Norwich. Two days' ride, I'd say. Best go through Cromer.'

Roger took a breath. 'Thank you, Nick.'

Nicholas grinned. 'The brother had told Anguish some time ago. It just took him time to recall it!'

§

The following day, Roger took Achilles and followed the coast road which would lead him through Cromer where he stopped for the night at an inn, and then on to Hickling.

He found himself a room in an old inn in the centre of the village, and went into the taproom to find something to eat and drink.

'Oi'll be with ye directly sir,' the landlord said as Roger sat down at the table on a stool. It wasn't the most comfortable of inns, he reflected, but that was of no consequence to him. The taproom was warm with a roaring fire up the chimney. It mattered little that it needed a good scrub.

'What'll it be, sir?' the Landlord asked.

'Beer,' Roger said. 'And supper.'

The landlord disappeared and Roger sat staring into space, brooding that he was already too late.

No-one else was in the room, and he turned around and stretched his boots towards the fire. It had been an impulse to come, stupid really. How could he even see her if she were here?

Someone, a woman, put a flagon of beer down on the table in front of him. 'Sorry, sir, we got no lamb tonight. But there be pottage that Oi cooked for me and the family. It got beef in it. You're welcome to some of that and some bread.'

Roger looked up to see a middle-aged overweight woman, whom he presumed was the landlord's wife.

'The pottage would be fine, thank you,' he said without much enthusiasm.

'Very good, sir.' She seemed disinclined to go. Curious, Roger assumed. 'Don't mind my asking, sir, but what're ye doing in these parts?'

'I'm looking for some friends. The reverend Calthorpe and his wife. Do you know them?'

'Oh, yes, the reverend. He live at the Rectory, he do. A pity you di'n't come last week. Could've gone to the wedding.'

Roger shivered, and his heart began to thud uncomfortably. 'Wedding?'

'Ay. The reverend's sister-in-law married the reverend's brother. 'Twere a rum do, that were. Sisters marrying brothers. Mark my words, no good'll come of that. Bad luck that be.'

Roger had stopped listening. He felt sick, and his heart pummelled in his ears. He'd missed her by a week. He was too late, and she was wed. She belonged to another man. All his hopes and desires had come to nought. He had indeed lost her.

Trying to sound casual, he asked: 'Are the new Mr. and Mistress Calthorpe living here?'

'Lord luv yer, sir. No indeed. They go away soon after. Next day.'

'Do you know where?'

Her eyes narrowed suspiciously. 'No, sir, and that be the God honest truth. Oi'll get that pottage for you, sir.'

Roger groaned. 'Forget the pottage, Mistress. I'm not hungry. Bring me more beer, if you please,' and he tossed some coins on the table.

'Are you all roight, sir?' she asked peering at him with motherly concern.

'I feel a little unwell.'

'You hin't got the ague, Oi do hope.'

He managed a smile. 'No.' *Go away! Leave me alone!*

'Oi get your bed ready, sir.'

Roger nodded, only just hearing her. All he could think of was Ruth. She must have been forced into this. He could hear her whispered words of love, feel her in his arms, taste her kiss. Yet she was on the edge of his vision, just out of reach. She was no longer his.

Damn Pell! Damn the war! Damn the Puritans in general!

And damn Charles Calthorpe!

In any case he had no idea where she was now. She was not here in Hickling, and there was no point in staying.

However, he could not leave tonight. Achilles had gone far enough for one day, and it was dark and cold outside. So he drank to the point of dulling the pain, and then took himself to bed where he slipped into a troubled sleep. He returned to Hunstanton the following day.

§

As the days grew shorter and the weather turned colder, Roger became more morose and bad tempered.

His father caught up with him one morning before he had dragged himself out of bed.

'This has got to stop,' Sir Hamon announced angrily, tearing back the bed hangings and letting a ridiculous amount of white light into his son's aching eyes.

Shielding his eyes with his hand, Roger groaned. 'What has got to stop?'

'This.' Sir Hamon waved his hand in the general direction of Roger's face. 'Look at you! You are drinking yourself to death, boy.'

'I am not a boy!' Roger snarled. He had a stinking headache and someone was pricking his eyeballs with a darning needle.

'Then stop acting like one! You look like you're about to quit this world, you are hardly eating and you drink yourself insensible. Nick put you to bed last night. You frightened your mother. What has got into you?'

Roger said nothing, but his lip trembled like a small child and he wanted to cry. Faith! What had happened to him? He was torn to shreds.

His father saw and said more kindly: 'Is it the Pell girl?'

Struggling for some kind of self control Roger said roughly: 'You need not worry any more about her. She has married Charles Calthorpe.'

'I see.'

Roger raised sorrowful, bloodshot eyes to his father. 'Do you?'

Seeing that more was required of him, Sir Hamon probed a little. 'What happened?'

'She worked in the infirmary.'

'Yes. She worked hard and did a good job. But 'tis no place for a maid.'

Roger ignored the last comment. 'The night before Manchester came in, we all knew the game was up. I thought we would be arrested. You, Nick, me and the others. I was afraid for her. Her father . . .' He went on to relate the bare facts.

Sir Hamon sat down on the bed and Roger moved his foot just in time. 'Well, it cannot be undone, if she's married Calthorpe.'

'I know. It's been too long.'

'What's done is done. Drinking yourself into oblivion will not alter things. You have to accept what has happened. Sir Valentine Pell had no intention of allowing you to marry his daughter. He put every obstacle in your way.'

'I would have eloped with her if—if—'

'If it had not been for the siege.' Sir Hamon took a breath. 'It wasn't meant to be, son. You have to let her go. Here—' he thumped his own chest '—in your heart.'

Roger nodded, too sick both physically and emotionally to argue. He knew it. He had known it for the last three months or more. He just did not want to know it.

'How do you think I feel?' Sir Hamon went on. 'When I came into my inheritance there was hardly anything left. I have worked to build up this estate and I have brought it to a financially successful situation, only to have those thieving bastards steal it from me. I cannot build it up again to the same degree, not a second time. That will be for Nick to do. But life goes on. We all have to go on, despite the disappointments, the tragedies. You have a whole life ahead of you. There will be other women and a wife for you.' As Roger started to speak he silenced him by talking over him. 'I know. You loved her. There will never be another like her. You don't want anyone else. But you will find someone one day. This is not the end of your life. So get up, get dressed and come hunting boar with us.'

He left him then and Roger thought about what he had said. He was right. Ruth had indeed married Calthorpe and he could do nothing about it. He had to forget her, to get on with his life. There was work to be done on the home farm and he applied himself to it in an effort to lift the black mood that had settled on him.

§

On the ninth day of December 1643 the order of the House regarding the payments of damages stated that the claimants and enemies of the King should be the ones to assess the amount of damages:

'That such Persons as did take any of the Goods of the well-affected by themselves or such as they appointed, or did any Damage to their Houses or Mills or any other Ways, shall make restitution to all such well-affected Persons as have been damnified according to the Greatness of their Losses and that Colonel Walton (otherwise Wauton) Governor of King's Lynn, Mr. Percival and Mr. Toll, members of the House of Commons shall examine what Damage hath been done to the well-affected and appoint such as have done them Injury to make them Reparation accordingly. And if any of them shall refuse to make such Reparation, That the said Governour, mr. Percival and Mr. Toll shall

have power to Sequester so much of the Estates of such malignants, as will make them Reparation and Assign it to those that have been damnified.'

On the committee of four men was Robert Thorowgood, brother to the Reverend Thomas Thorowgood who had once assisted Sir Hamon.

Thomas Toll, along with the new governor of Lynn, Valentine Walton, thus were able to impose extreme fines and damages on Sir Hamon. Having suffered house arrest, Toll felt that no price was too high to recompense him for the loss of his dignity and the affront to his person. Furthermore, the flattened almshouses in Gaywood and Old Lynn had to be rebuilt and Sir Hamon had to pay for them too. The fines were extortionate and far in excess of the actual cost of rebuilding.

Lady Alice later wrote in her household accounts book:

'May 1644—paid to Toll and wife for imprisonment £50 0 0.

'May 1644— paid to May, Wormwell &c. for their pretended losses £225 11 0.

'April 1645—(1) To the town of Lynn for the Town Houses that were pulled down and the governors took away all the materials, yet by his order we pay £95 13 10. (2) to Mr May, Mayor of Lynn, upon an unjust order made by Mr Miles Corbet, Mr Valentine Walton, Governor of Lynn, for the pretended loss sustained as they falsely suggest by the command of Sir Hamon himself £47 13 4.'

(This last entry was for damages caused by Manchester's own artillery, the total sum of £267 1s. 6d. to be divided between Mayor Gurlin, Sir Hamon and Robert Clench, of which the £47 13s. 4d. was Sir Hamon's share.)

The charges and levies impoverished the family.

Roger saw the effect it had on his family. He saw his father's health all but destroyed by the stress of it and Nicholas was not much better. He ached for them all. Worse, in 1644 Lady Anne gave birth to a son, Edward, who died soon afterwards.

With the child's death a torrent of emotion was suddenly unleashed. He saw his father cry, his mother at a loss as to how to comfort her husband. He saw his brother in despair and heard the desperate crying of his wife.

Hunstanton Hall became a dismal and depressing place to be.

By the time the summer ended he knew he could not spend the rest of his life in rural pursuits. It was time to move on.

'I have decided to join Major Cartwright's troops in Newark,' he announced to his family.

Sir Nicholas nodded. 'I thought you'd go soon. You've been restless, kicking your heels here for too long.'

Sir Hamon stroked his beard. 'Is that what you intend to do with your life? Is it the army for you?'

'In faith I've no definite plans,' Roger admitted. 'But for now it will do. What is it they say about a younger son? The army or the church? Well I'd as lief not join the church in the present turmoil, if you don't mind.'

'Well the King needs able-bodied men and you're handy with a sword. But the war will not last for ever and your inheritance will not now be what it might have been. You need to look to the future.'

'I'll think about it,' Roger promised without much enthusiasm.

THIRTY-EIGHT

September 1644

On the day Roger left to join the King's army at Newark the weather turned from warm summer to the chill of autumn. The sky became that colour of pewter heralding yet more rain and the ground squelched beneath his horse's hooves. A biting raw wind stung his cheeks and permeated his thick travelling cloak and clothes, like finding chinks in armour, right through to his bones.

As he left Hunstanton Hall he paused just outside the iron gates. This was where he had been born, this was where he had been brought up. This was home, but it would be home no more, for he would never return here, he was sure. The thought cost him a pang, for all the people he loved—save one—were within those walls, his family. And he loved them dearly. His brother Nicholas, who lorded it over him, yet who looked out for his youngest brother; Hamon, of course, was in Pakenham in Suffolk; but there was also his dear mother who cared for him so much and who wept now as she watched him from the solar window. And of course his father, that giant of a man, brought low for his loyalty to the King, growing old now with more than just age.

This was Hunstanton Hall, the most of which his father had built when Roger was still a child. But it would never be his. Nicholas was the heir and his sons after him. He turned Achilles' head. A life of adventure beckoned, and his insides rolled with excitement.

He started off at a trot then eased Achilles into a canter, to put distance between himself and home before he changed his mind. Out of the perimeter gates, turning right following the road past what had once been the chapel of St. Andrew's at Ringstead Barret. The chapel had been turned into a barn and the village had long since vanished, a victim of plague, Downs Farm on his left all that remained. After that he turned right towards Heacham, past Heacham Hall, through the village and on towards Snettisham, the home of the Cobbes, Ingoldisthorpe the home of the Cremers. Dersingham held memories, memories causing him to pause. She still haunted his heart. Perhaps she always would.

He shook his head to clear the memory and urged his horse into a canter to get through Dersingham as quickly as possible and put Ruth behind him.

As he approached Lynn, he had a decision to make. Either he

could carry on south, cross the Setchey River and on to Wiggenhall St. Germans to cross the river Ouse there, which was a day's journey out of his way, or he could take the ferry across the Ouse at Lynn.

The ferry at Lynn was the most direct route, but it meant going into the town he had been barred from entering. If they caught him, it would be his life, so he chose the longer route down to Setchey and across the bridge that he had once helped to blow up, and then turned right towards Watlington.

As the evening came on the weather worsened, the wind rose and rain lashed down. The road turned to squelching slippery mud and either side of the road were the dykes that drained the land. Much good it did. Most of the land was still fen, or marsh, and treacherous to those who did not know it.

As the light began to fade, Roger dismounted to lead his horse, the better to see the road in what light there was and at last, with a prayer of thanks, found himself at an inn in what he assumed was Watlington.

The following morning the weather started fair and he left Watlington behind, but by mid afternoon it took a turn for the worst, raining hard, and blowing a gale. The road to cross the river Ouse took him up to Wiggenhall St German's and across the bridge. The Ouse was much smaller here, making a bridge crossing possible. The road was by no means a straight one, and several times he had to ask the way, and he found himself following the road alongside the River Ouse which took him up to Tilney All Saints, and then on to Clenchwarton. It was a long convoluted way to cross the river without going through Lynn.

By the time the light had all but gone, he had to lead Achilles again because of the treacherous dykes. It was time to stop for the night and when he saw the board and lights of an inn he thanked God. He was cold through to his bones, soaked to the skin and dog-weary and he and Achilles had had enough for one day. Giving the horse into the care of an ostler, he entered a wonderfully warm taproom with a roaring log fire. A few customers sat around the table which his travel-weary brain registered as Roundhead soldiers. Immediately, his senses quickened and he took proper stock of the room.

It was fairly typical of an inn, plain dirty whitewashed walls, flagstone floor, one long table with benches and two smaller ones by the fire. The long table had the four Roundheads seated at one end, eating, drinking, rowdy. Two sailors occupied one of the tables. They studied him in silence before returning to their engrossing occupation of a game of dice. The only other occupant was a fat man who must have been the landlord for he wore a dirty homespun apron and he poured ale from a jug into a tankard for one of the rebels.

Roger squelched to the other table by the fire and sat down on the settle which was perpendicular to it with a table in front of him. He removed his sodden hat and put it on the settle beside him then the cloak draping it over the arm of the settle where it dripped onto the greasy flagstone floor, not so that it would dry but because it would hide the sword which he now also removed, draping the baldric strap over the edge of the seat corner so that the grip of the sword and scabbard were hidden from view behind the cloak.

'Welcome, sir,' the landlord said. 'Dreadful evening.'

'Dreadful,' Roger agreed. 'Where is this place?'

'This be the Black Horse.'

'What village?'

'Clenchwarton.'

Ah, so he was now back on the right road. 'Do you have a room?'

'Yes, sir. And boiled mutton for supper with caper sauce and potatoes.'

Roger raised a surprised eyebrow. 'Excellent! A pot of beer too, if you please.'

One of the Roundheads cut in on the landlord. 'You harbour Royalists, now, publican?'

Roger paid them no heed, but he wondered what had given him away.

'A king's man! A caballero!'

One of the Roundheads came to his feet with much scraping of a chair. With exaggerated gestures the man pretended to remove a non-existent hat and to execute a very regal bow amid much clapping and calling from his friends. Then the performer began to trip around the room in a very dainty manner. This was productive of much mirth.

Roger sat still, all his senses alert to danger although he adopted a deliberately relaxed appearance, with his arm draped over the wet cloak and his eyes seemingly on the fire. He was turned away from them, his left side towards them, his right arm across his belly and his hand resting on his sword hilt beside him. Already he had loosened it from the scabbard under cover of the cloak.

The landlord came back with Roger's steaming ale. 'Please, gentleman, I want no trouble,' he said nervously, eyeing the prancing man. He put the tankard down on the table in front of Roger, who reached forward with his left hand to take a large warming mouthful.

As the landlord moved away, the performing Roundhead became braver and came over to Roger where he stood, swaying slightly, in front of him.

Roger put down his tankard and looked up unsmilingly. 'You have something to say to me, sir?'

'Yes, sir, I do. Damn traitor, I say sir! A coward and a papist!'

'I see.' Roger held the man's attention but on the edge of his vision he saw the hand of another of the Roundheads move towards his sword. His grip tightened on his sword hilt. He said evenly: 'How can a man be a traitor when he upholds the sovereignty of his divinely anointed King?'

'Divinely anointed? Huh! Inherited more like. The King's nothing but a mere woman!'

Before the man had time to blink Roger was on his feet, his sword drawn and the blade at the man's throat. 'Apologise!' he demanded.

The man backed away, but Roger followed, the deadly sharp point of his sword digging into the flesh at the man's Adam's apple. Continuing to back away, the Roundhead failed to see the stool behind him. He fell backwards with a cry and lay spread-eagle on the flagstones, the deadly blade still at his throat.

'Apologise!'

'Never!'

Roger's eyes burned with the hatred he felt for these Puritan dogs who had brought his family to near ruin. For a few moments no-one dared to move lest the cavalier thrust the point into the man's windpipe. Then quite deliberately and almost with sauntering steps, one of the other rebels came up to Roger and drew his sword.

In a flash Roger turned to meet him, blocking the intended blow and coming in under the man's guard to slash at his leg, a move he favoured most.

Blood spurted in time with his pulse from the wound and he retired begging for a rope to act as tourniquet.

His friend, now up on his feet, also drew his sword. He was an amateur, Roger saw at a glance from his stiff stance and by the way he lunged forward without any forethought. Roger was kinder on him. With a flick of his wrist he disarmed the man, the sword sailing across the room and landing with a clatter on the flagstones in the corner.

That left one man.

This man was a different matter. His stance, the way he sized Roger up, the way he held his sword told Roger that he was well-trained and therefore, a more deadly opponent than either of the other two.

The man attacked and Roger sidestepped, following up his advantage by slipping his sword under the man's outstretched arm. But his opponent had seen it coming and also sidestepped.

Now they battled in earnest. Lunge, block, slip under guard, block, sidestep. The deadly dance travelled quickly back and forth over the flagstone floor. They were evenly matched and it meant that Roger could not quickly dispatch this opponent. Roger was the better swordsman and he pressed forward, forcing the man back. His right arm screamed in protest and his breath came in gasps, but he was not finished. His opponent, however, was done for. His sword kept dropping as his arm tired and his efforts no longer had the force of a minute ago. Roger pushed him towards the wall and saw his way and took it. In a flash of steel and using just his wrist, he gathered the other's blade and sent it too flying through the air where it embedded in the taproom wall to his right. His point was now at the man's throat as he pressed him against the wall.

He felt he was within his rights to kill this Puritan, but he had no intention of killing people for no real reason. So he said through gritted teeth: 'Yield!'

Panting heavily the man glared up at him, but he had no option. He had nowhere to go. 'I yield.'

Then, as Roger stepped backward, releasing the man, the second Roundhead put his own sword to Roger's jaw. 'You yield, Royalist!'

For a tense moment no-one moved. And then, unexpectedly one of the seamen pulled the hammer back on a pistol with an audible click and the match glowed in the dimly-lit room. Still seated he aimed it at the Roundhead. 'Drop it, or I'll drop you!' he growled.

Roger and the two Roundheads turned their heads to look at him. Then the Roundhead dropped his sword and so did Roger, backing off from them, but keeping them in his line of sight.

'Seems to me that the cavalier here has won this one,' the sailor said. 'A fair fight as can be, four to one. No-one killed.' He smiled through rotting teeth. 'You Puritan, see to your friend.' He jerked the pistol in the direction of the wounded Roundhead who now had a tourniquet on his blood-soaked leg and sat holding it. 'Better get him to a doctor,' he advised.

The Roundheads gathered themselves together, picked up hats and cloaks and with directions from the landlord helped their wounded friend into the wet night.

Roger turned to the sailor. 'Thank you, friend.'

THIRTY-NINE

'Leman's the name, seaman's the occupation. Thomas Leman. Of Lynn.'

'L'Estrange. Roger L'Estrange. I would buy you a drink, sir.'

'You can buy me and my friend some of that there mutton supper if yer like!'

Roger laughed and took the man's hand. 'Well, Leman the seaman, supper it shall be. Landlord!'

Roger looked at the other man who nodded sombrely and invited both of them to take the settle opposite his by the fire. Strangely, the other man excused himself. 'I'm agorn for my bed,' he said and left them. Roger was puzzled. He didn't know any man who would turn down a free supper, and it was not as if the man appeared to have much money.

Thomas Leman sat down opposite Roger. He was of medium height, stocky build and of a rough cut. He needed a shave and, by the smell of him, a wash too. But it was his eyes that made Roger look at him twice; one, the left, looked straight at Roger, while the other seemed to be looking past Roger's left ear. He found it distracting and unnerving, and he made a conscious effort to look at Leman's good left eye.

'I've heard of you, Mr. L'Estrange,' Leman said as Roger sat down again. 'I be in Lynn last year.'

'Then you are no stranger to the facts, sir. Are you for the King?'

'That I be, sir, that I be.'

'Then you will join me in a toast. His most excellent Majesty. Health to him.'

It seemed to Roger that Leman hesitated just fractionally, but he could not be sure. Then Leman took his newly-acquired tankard and raised it too. 'A pox on them that be opposing him.'

'Your friend is not of the same opinion?' Roger asked.

Leman pointed a grimy finger at his own temple and made circular movements and then with a flick of his hand, dismissed the other seaman. 'Don't know him well. I only met him in this tavern.'

'A sailor also, I collect.'

'That be he. There be many seamen around these parts.'

For some reason, Roger felt a nag of disquiet, but now that he was warm from the exertion, although his clothes were still damp, he was in a mellow mood and dismissed his misgivings as nothing more than chasing shadows.

The suppers arrived and without preamble Roger tucked in. Leman, however, hesitated, seemed to fumble and hung his head. Surprised, Roger watched him. It was as if the man were praying over his meal. It was common enough practice and one carried out at home in Hunstanton and Roger felt vaguely ashamed that he had not done the same.

Then Leman picked up his knife and carved a piece of meat from the bone and with the point of his knife conveyed it to his mouth.

'You hear about Marston Moor?'

'Everyone's heard about it.' The two-hour battle of Marston Moor had taken place a few months earlier at the beginning of July and the King's nephew Prince Rupert's defeat at the hands of Lords Manchester and Fairfax had been a major topic of conversation throughout the land.

'Terrible thing. Many dead. There be fighting suffen savage and the King's men chased all the way to the very gates of York. They say more'n four thousand King's men were lost and fifteen hundred taken prisoner, while the—the Roundheads lost just 300 men.'

Roger did not miss the slight hesitation before Leman used the derogatory term for the Parliamentarians that the Royalists used. 'You were there?' he asked.

'Me? No. But I heard tell.'

'I heard Prince Rupert was out-manoeuvred.'

Leman had a habit of chewing with his mouth open, slurping noisily in the process, a sight Roger would rather avoid, so he concentrated on his plate. 'If Newcastle had done as he were bid and be at the place Rupert told him at the right time, he would have won. But no. Newcastle takes some crotchet into his head and he don't show.'

Roger chewed thoughtfully. He wondered what sort of man Lord Newcastle really was, for this same man had not come to Sir Hamon's aid either. Two opportunities lost and defeats for the King, all because of one man's decisions. He wondered what else Newcastle had managed to cost the King and he was momentarily angry at the sheer arrogance of the man.

However, Roger did not fully understand the extent of the defeat at Marston Moor, nor what it meant in real terms to the Royalists. News was sketchy and hard come by at times and assessing a situation was difficult. However, he knew that until Marston Moor, the Royalists had been riding high on a wave of victories, (King's Lynn notwithstanding) largely due to the redoubtable commander Prince Rupert who was a brilliant strategist. However, Marston Moor had changed things. With so many dead and taken prisoner, no-one but the most optimistic of Royalists could hope for an all-out victory now. They could only aggravate the Parliamentary leaders, nothing more.

'Newcastle di'n't come to Lynn's aid either,' Leman said matter-of-factly, as if reading Roger's thoughts.

'No.' Roger eyed his plate dolefully. 'He turned instead to Hull to assist the Hothams who were holding the town against Fairfax. Much good it did.'

Leman studied Roger with his one good eye. ''Tis a pity. Lynn be a seaport, see?' A fact of which Roger was very well aware, of course, but he did not interrupt. 'Important to both sides. If the King had Lynn, he would have at least one seaport and he could land men from 'Olland and France and Spain and—well, if Newcastle had turned up sweet, the whole of the war would be diff'rent.'

'Yes,' Roger agreed and really wished the man would finish eating before he began speaking.

'Oh aye. Why else would Manchester come hotfoot from Norwich when he be on his way somewhere else? Aye and Cromwell too. Oh yes, Lynn be very important.'

Roger paused in the act of conveying mutton to his mouth. 'Parliament controls three quarters of the country and the whole of East Anglia, Norfolk included.'

'Not if Lynn were again for the King,' Leman said his voice low so that only Roger could hear.

Roger leaned forward. He stared keenly at Leman's right eye, before remembering and switching his gaze to his left eye. Leman had touched a sore place in Roger's heart. 'What, sir, are you saying?'

'Lynn could be retaken, I reckon.'

Unsure what the man intended, Roger said carefully: 'It could, perhaps.'

'Need an army, o' course.'

'Indeed.' Were they talking hypothetically? 'And where would a man raise an army like that, I wonder?'

Leman waved his dagger, his eating implement, in the air. 'Seems t'me that there be plenty of men to fight for the King when I be in Lynn.'

'You know these men?'

'Maybe.'

Roger, his supper now finished, digested this information.

'Who would lead this army?'

'The right man could do it.' He paused to chew and finally swallow. A knowing smile spread across his ugly face. 'Like yourself, p'raps.'

Roger blinked at him, his mind working quickly. 'Me?'

'Well, sir, an army cove like you got the 'sperience, like. *And* you know other King's men. Got connections, like. Seems t'me that you be just the cove to do it.'

'I couldn't do it alone.'

'No, course not. But I got connections too. I ken help yer. You ken find me in Lynn and I'll help you get men. I know men.' He handed Roger a slip of paper which Roger glanced at and recognised an address in Fisher's End in Lynn. He slipped into the pocket inside his leather doublet. Could it be done? He would need help, of course. And subtlety. Not brute force. And money. His family had paid dearly for the siege, so Sir Hamon could not spare anything towards such a scheme now. Besides, Roger could not embroil his family in it. If discovered they would lose everything including their lives.

Leman was not done. 'The best thing would be to see the King, of course.'

Roger said nothing, but Leman grinned, again showing his rotting teeth. He stood up and patted his bulging stomach. 'Well, I thank you, sir, for supper. I hin't had such a supper in a long while. I'm nowa gorn to my bed.'

And he took himself off.

Roger wasn't long behind him and had the luxury of a tiny room all to himself in the eaves. He looked at the bed. Not only did it have lumps and bumps in the straw-filled mattress, but the sheets did not look too clean either. Well, it would have to do and he climbed in, almost fully clothed, his loaded pistol on one side of his head and his sword and dagger beside it. He was learning to be more wary.

He slept badly, not only because he felt that he was being eaten alive by bedbugs or whatever it was that inhabited the bed, but also because the scheme kept running through his head. He looked at it from every angle, peering into the darkness and listening to the rain dripping through the thatched roof and onto the floorboards not far from his head. He could find no fault with the plan. Yet there was a nagging in his insides that he could not place.

Thomas Leman. Roger thought him an odd man. It seemed strange to Roger that a King's man had not immediately come to his aid at the beginning of the fight with the Roundheads to defend the King's honour. At least, that is what Roger would have done. Had he imagined the fractional hesitation before drinking the King's health? Yet Leman *had* helped him and he *had* drunk the King's health. So, he brushed these thoughts from his mind and attempted to sleep. Immediately, he was wide awake again and he could see King's Lynn in his mind's eye, the Tuesday Market Place with the Market Cross and the stocks, and St. Margaret's church in the Saturday Market Place.

Would it really be possible to re-take the town? He lay on his back, his hands behind his head, staring at the damp-stained lime-plastered walls flickering in the candle-light, turning the matter over in his mind. He saw himself at the head of an army of five thousand or so men, marching towards Lynn. He would lay siege to Lynn this time, to get the cursed Roundheads out. However, he must be assured of help. Not like his father who had hoped for help and been let down badly by Lord Newcastle. He certainly would not ask for help from that quarter! Furthermore, he could not ask for help from his family who were still reeling from Lynn's disastrous siege.

For his own neck he had no qualms. With the optimism of youth he assumed that he would be successful and if not, he could talk or fight his way out of trouble, but his family were too old and broken to take such a risk.

The candle guttered and went out and he drifted off to sleep, but a few hours later he woke up again as the blankets had slipped off him and he was cold. Getting up to use the chamber pot and then pulling them back on again, it was the end of sleep. He wondered what the time was, but had no means of knowing whether it was near to dawn or midnight.

His mind was on Leman's words again. He wanted so much to have a meaningful place in the war, which was why he was travelling to Newark in the first place. Newark was in Royalist hands, under Major Cartwright, and had suffered a siege of its own earlier in the year. It was a safe place for a Royalist to be at the moment, an easy berth. But what if he could do more? Certainly, no-one else was going to reclaim Lynn for the King. More than all else, he wanted to see his king victorious and it might be that he, Roger L'Estrange, could be the one to turn the tide of the war. He believed it was still possible for the King to win the war.

With a sigh of relief he saw the first lightening of the dark and knew that dawn was near, and by that time his mind was made up. He would go to Oxford and obtain a commission from the King.

He, Roger L'Estrange, would make his king victorious.

FORTY

Oxford, October 1644

Arriving in Oxford, cold, wet and tired, Roger found himself longing for some decent creature comforts. His first task must be to find lodgings, to wash and shave and to change his clothes, before seeking out the King.

This proved more difficult than he had anticipated. Since the King had decided to use the city as his headquarters, setting up court in the buildings belonging to the university, just about every available space in every available room had been taken. Even all the colleges had been used as barracks.

As the evening came on and the light began to fade he came upon an apology for an inn, a dilapidated building with the daub coming off the wattle walls beneath a blackened leaking thatched roof. A stream of smoke poured out of the chimney, however, indicating a welcoming fire and there were lamps or candles flickering inside. He would be able to get a meal here and something to drink and perhaps somewhere to lay down his head.

He left Achilles with the ostler and made his way inside.

The tiny single room was packed with men, kindred spirits, Royalists, eating, drinking, telling jokes and eyeing the buxom women servers, of which there were plenty. In a corner half a dozen or more men sat together singing and when they finished they raised their tankards and yelled together.

The inn-keeper could offer him a bowl of pottage and some bread, as well as ale, for which he was heartily grateful, but there was no room available to sleep.

'Every room in the city is taken,' the landlord confirmed. 'Oxford is full to bursting and that's a fact.'

'If you could spare me a corner somewhere for tonight, I can pay.'

'What and have you drinking all my ale while I'm abed?'

Roger's heart sank. 'I see.'

He found himself a seat on the end of a bench and a corner of a table to rest his bowl of pottage. A Royalist soldier slid along a little to make room for him.

'Where are you from, friend?' he asked, as Roger thanked him and sat down.

'Norfolk,' Roger said.

'Thought they were all Puritans there,' another man who sat across from Roger remarked. Roger looked at him. He was thick-set with dark skin and black hair to his shoulders. Dark brooding eyes studied Roger from under thick black brows which met over his nose in a frown.

Roger added: 'I'm lately from Lynn—King's Lynn.'

'Weren't there a siege there last year?' the first man asked. Since he sat next to Roger he had to turn his head and his upper body to see him properly. His collar came up too high and hampered his movements, Roger thought with an inward smile. This man liked his high fashion.

'There was. Lynn was lost.'

'I heard that. 'Tis a pity.'

'If Manchester had been beaten at King's Lynn, we would have won the war by now,' the second man put in morosely and took a long hard pull on his ale, slammed his tankard down and glared meaningfully at the landlord.

Heartily sick of the oft–repeated words, Roger felt the need to justify his father's actions. 'My father was expecting help to come from across the Wash,' he said carefully. He did not want to mention Newcastle by name, for he had no wish to bring that name into disrepute.

'Your father?' The first man raised his brows and stared at Roger with interest through cool light eyes. 'Who are you, then, sir?'

Roger chewed through a particularly gristly lump of meat which he hoped was beef and swallowed while it was still almost whole, following it quickly with a large swallow of beer to dislodge it from his throat. 'Roger L'Estrange,' he confirmed eventually, 'and my father is Sir Hamon L'Estrange of Hunstanton, the governor of King's Lynn during the siege.'

'Roger L'Estrange?' He clapped Roger between the shoulder blades just as Roger was conveying more stew to his mouth and he dropped stew and spoon back into the bowl, splashing himself and the table liberally. ''Pon my soul! A L'Estrange. We have heard of you, sir. Or more correctly, your father. You are famous!'

The second man peered at the sleeve of his jacket which may have received a speck of gravy and brushed it delicately with a hand the size of a spade. 'Well, it seems we have no need to doubt you sir,' he said and studied Roger unsmilingly. He downed another tankard of ale and again that glare at the landlord which brought him another tankard. 'What do you do here in Oxford?'

'I've come to see the King,' Roger said and immediately wished he had not, for the man searched his face intently.

'Why?'

Roger was suddenly cautious. He did not wish to reveal all his business to someone who was a complete stranger to him. So he met the man's dark eyes stare for stare. 'That, sir, is between the King and myself.'

The man's eyes narrowed, but his lips twitched ever so slightly. Roger noticed it.

'You'll be lucky if you get an audience with His Majesty,' he said. 'Everyone wants to see the King.' He took yet another swig from the ale and Roger knew he must be fairly drunk by now. The man showed no signs of it, however. 'If you go looking like that,' he added dourly, 'you will give His Majesty a disgust of you. You had better clean up first.'

Roger felt his hackles rise. He could not quite take this man's measure. He had a brooding sense of menace about him. He was older than Roger by anything up to ten years and it was clear he viewed Roger as some kind of greenhorn and Roger resented it. 'I am aware of that, sir,' he said evenly. 'And when I find lodging, I shall attend to it.'

'Won't find lodging here,' the first man told him brightly. 'Oxford is full. All the rooms taken.'

'So I gathered.'

'You can share our room for tonight,' the second man said unexpectedly.

Roger did not answer immediately as his brain worked its way around this unexpected turn of events. He studied the man, unsure of his motives.

The first man agreed with a grin: 'Everyone doubles up here, else we'd all be sleeping in the streets. We have a room at the baker's. Mind, it would be the floor for you.'

'I can sleep on the floor,' Roger said, realising that he had no option. He needed shelter from the cold and wet and he could not quibble.

'Well, L'Estrange, my name is Harold Wells.'

'And my name is Oliver Bates.' The brooding man said.

§

It was around midnight, after an enjoyable evening of drinking and singing and tale-telling that Roger with his two new friends staggered through the narrow cobbled streets of Oxford to find their lodging which happened to be in a garret room above a baker's. The baker himself had to be roused to let them in.

'What hour of the clock do you call this to get me up?' he demanded crossly. Roger, in his inebriated state, thought he looked comical, with a long pointed white bed cap on his greying hair and his nightshirt half way up his legs exposing hairy shins and bony feet. He started giggling and so did Wells. To be fair they tried to stifle their mirth, but it exploded from both of them in great guffaws. Bates continued morose and unhappy.

'Who is this?' The baker demanded, sorely affronted.

'This is L'Estrange,' Bates explained groggily and waving his hand in the air. 'New fellow. Lately come from Norfolk. He can share with us.'

The baker held out his hand. 'That will be a shilling a night.'

It was extortionate, but Roger, in his inebriated state, fumbled in his innermost pocked and pulled out some coins, fished among them and finally found a shilling piece, which he gave to the man.

The baker grinned and let them in.

Together they staggered and stumbled up two flights of stairs until they came to the attic which was accessed through a ladder and trap door. Having fallen off the ladder twice, Wells launched himself into the room and sprawled across one bare straw mattress and Bates across the other. Roger took the floor and laid his cloak down so that he could lie on one corner and pull the other over him. His saddle roll was his pillow and he fell into an exhausted dreamy sleep.

He awoke to the smell of fresh bread as the sun streamed in through a tiny window in the gable wall. He blinked at it, trying to remember where he was. His head throbbed sickeningly and it felt like someone was poking him in both eyes, they hurt so much. His throat and mouth were sand-dry, which was wonderful considering how much liquid he had downed the night before. He'd lost count at eight tankards and he reckoned he had spent half the night filling one of four chamber pots provided by the landlord who evidently thought it well to provide more than was usual where young drinking men were concerned.

He could hear snoring and looked up to see Wells fast asleep on sacking stuffed with straw. Bates was up, though, sitting in an upright chair and reading.

Roger ran his hand through his hair. Even his scalp was sore. 'What are you reading?'

'The Bible.'

Roger frowned, surprised. 'Why?'

Bates studied him unhurriedly. 'Because that's what I do every morning.'

Realising that it was all the answer he was likely to get, Roger pulled his unwilling body into a sitting position. 'What time is it?'

'Getting on for noon, I think, judging by the sun outside. Now, if you do not mind?' He went back to his reading.

Roger did mind. He once again emptied his bladder into a pot. 'Is there water for washing?'

Without looking up from the book Bates pointed roughly and Roger now saw a washstand and basin. Beside it was a large pitcher with ice cold water in it.

Bates looked up at him. 'I would not drink the water if I were you,' he recommended mildly. 'You don't know where it has come from. There is sickness in the city.'

With his thoughts darting to the late Sir John Spelman, Roger got up and started to undress. It was icily cold in the room, but he stripped down to his shirt and then removed it.

Bates shuddered as Roger poured the icy water into the bowl and plunged his hands in and sloshed it over his face, before asking: 'Do you have any soap?'

'Soap? I can't afford soap,' Bates replied as if he were talking to a stupid child.

Roger frowned. He had some but that was in his saddle bags somewhere else in Oxford, along with his clothing.

He washed as best he could without soap, scraped away at his chin without soap, using a razor which probably belonged to Wells and then washed his torso without soap. It was a pretty poor job and it made him shiver, even as it made Bates shudder, but as he finished off with a towel (which clearly needed laundering) he felt fresher. He put his shirt back on and his doublet, hose and breeches, stockings, garters and boots, put on the red sash around his middle, borrowed the sleeping Henry Wells' comb which he tugged brutally through his long red locks and plonked his hat on.

'So where are you going?' Bates asked.

'Me? I told you. I am going to see the King,' Roger replied with a jaunty grin which belied the marching drums behind his eyes. 'But I need you to tell me where we supped last night, for my horse is there and

I need you to tell me where I can find the King.'

'The King is in Christ Church College, the Queen in Merton. Take your pick.'

'It is definitely the King I wish to see. Where is the Inn?'

Bates glanced at the still slumbering Harold Wells. 'I will take you there.'

'Thank you, sir. That is kind of you.'

Bates snapped the Bible shut and stood up, all business-like as Roger took the bowl of water he had washed in to the window and tossed the contents out into the street. It was illegal to do so, but no-one enforced the law. The contents of the chamber pot followed.

'Right then,' Bates said briskly, 'Come with me.'

It had taken them half an hour to stagger home last night, now it took them five minutes at a brisk walk to get to the inn.

'I'll show you where you can stable your horse,' Bates said.

With the horse stabled, Roger took his saddle bags up to the garret room where Harold Wells still slumbered, and changed his clothes for something more presentable. It was now time to find Christ Church college.

'Do you come with me?' Roger asked Bates.

Bates shrugged. 'No. I can see the King another time. I have other business. But I will take you there. I doubt you will see His Majesty today anyway. So many people are demanding an audience with him.'

So Roger found himself walking briskly with Bates once more.

The college of Christ Church was built around the Tom quadrangle. The King held court in the Deanery. Bates left him at the outer doors where he spoke to the guard on Roger's behalf and Roger was directed across the square. Never in his life had he seen anything so grand. He had thought Hunstanton Hall to be a marvellous building and had taken Cambridge for granted while he was there, but the sheer size of the college buildings, with their ornate castellated walls, and arches, pediments and towers, oriel windows and even a clock in a spire, were outside of his experience or dreams. Never had he seen such magnificence and all for a seat of learning! It occurred to him that Hunstanton Hall had also been built in a square, but that is where the similarity ended. This was more like a church or cathedral in design. Part of it was the cathedral.

He was admitted and directed towards a grand staircase. He looked up to find a ceiling decorated with fan-shaped plasterwork.

His King had chosen well, for this was as good as any palace, Roger thought. If he had seen Whitehall palace he may have changed his mind, but as it was Roger was well satisfied.

The King, though, had a set time for speaking with anyone who wished to seek his presence and many were the courtiers who were ahead of him in the queue and seemed to be able to have that audience which he so much desired but which proved so elusive.

He waited patiently in the ante room, a splendid place with a lofty intricately beamed roof space and tall windows. He compared Christ Church to the college at Cambridge he had attended himself. There were similarities and dissimilarities. Cambridge, he decided was not so large, not so sprawling.

He inclined his head to other, better dressed, courtiers, but they ignored him. One man looked him over disdainfully, which caused Roger to look down at his own clothes and wish he had attended to them better. They were crumpled from being in his saddle bags. He could see he would have to purchase better clothing if he were to be fit to see the King. So it was just as well that just when he thought he might have a chance of an audience with the King, the time for it was gone and he and the other hopefuls were dismissed.

He returned to the garret room dispirited, but happy to have the opportunity to make good his sartorial deficit.

By then Wells was up from his bed, evidently none the worse for last night's drunkenness. In fact, he looked to Roger as though he had never had a day's illness in his life, whereas Roger still had a nagging headache and Oliver Bates' hang dog expression had changed little.

'Have you eaten, L'Estrange?' Wells asked brightly.

'I bought some bread as I came through the shop,' Roger told him. And in fact he had eaten half a small round loaf, swilling it down with small beer.

'No, I meant have you *eaten*? As in had supper?'

'No.'

'Then it's back to the *Magpie*.'

Roger was wary. He had no desire to drink the night away again. He said: 'I've very little money.'

'That's probably more than the rest of us have.'

'Well I am not spending it on drink for you and your friends,' Roger announced.

Bates gave a tight mirthless smile. 'Of course not. So I collect you did not see the King?'

'I did not. I was too late and in any case I was not well-enough dressed.'

'Who can be? We all of us only have the clothes we can carry on a horse! And some of that is taken up with armour.'

'Do you have armour?' Wells asked.

'No.'

'You'll need armour,' Bates put in, 'if you're to fight with us.'

'Perhaps I can buy some.'

'You have enough money for armour?' Bates asked the question, but it was for both of them and they studied him intently.'

'Well—no.'

Wells roared with laughter. 'Then how are you going to buy it?'

He frowned at them. 'I hadn't thought.' And that was the trouble, he had not thought. Worse, these two men, more experienced on the field of battle than he was made him feel so young, even inferior, when he was the son of one of the best families in the country. He needed to recover some of his dignity. 'Anyway, I am not here to join the army.'

They both stopped laughing and stared at him. It was Wells who spoke first. 'Not here to fight? Then, In the name of all that is sacred, why are you here?'

'I told you, to see the King.'

Bates almost pushed Wells out of the way, coming close as an interrogator, his face serious, his dark eyes penetrating. 'Why do you so want to see the King?' he demanded.

'I told you, that is between the King and me,' Roger replied and turned away from him. He was beginning to feel uncomfortable around Bates.

He heard the scrape of metal and an instant later he found himself spun around and pushed against one of the upright beams supporting the roof so violently that he had no time to react. He felt the sharp point of cold steel pricking his throat. 'Perhaps you are a spy,' Bates growled, so close to him that Roger could feel his warm breath and smell the beer he had recently drunk.

Roger met his eyes. He felt quite calm, even though he was an inch from death and Bates had him pinned against the beam. He said evenly: 'I am no spy. I am a King's man, I fought for the King at Edgehill and I was with my father at Newburn, in the cavalry each time. If you think I would change sides, your wits have gone begging.'

'Then why are you here.'

'I keep telling you. To see the King. I want a commission from him. To raise an army. In Norfolk.'

Bates continued to search his face, then he let him go, turning away from him and putting the dirk away again.

'If I thought you were in any way a danger to His Majesty, I would kill you,' he said over his shoulder, almost casually.

'I am not a danger to His Majesty. I want to help him.'

Wells looked nervously from one to the other of them. 'I've heard of what happened in King's Lynn,' he told Bates. 'He's a King's man.'

Bates turned to Roger then, and smiled briefly as though nothing at all had happened. 'Well now, let's get some food.'

FORTY-ONE

Oxford, November 1644

It was frustrating trying to see the King. Day after day Roger presented himself in the ante-chamber, doing his best to make himself presentable with the limited resources at his disposal. He and other hopefuls waited for hours.

If it had not been for the intervention of the King's nephew, he might never have achieved his ambition.

Roger had seen Prince Rupert at Edgehill. The dashing son of the King's sister Elizabeth and her husband King Frederick of Bohemia, he was lieutenant-general of all of the King's armies. He was famed for his military genius and although he was known to be young, Roger was quite unprepared to discover that he was younger than himself by almost three years. At just twenty-five, Prince Rupert had subjugated Newark for his majesty and relieved York in an amazing strategic manoeuvre which surprised everyone, even those who knew him well. And if Lord Newcastle's army had met him outside that city at the appointed time instead of delaying, the battle of Marston Moor might well have had a different outcome.

All this flashed through Roger's brain as the prince came into the ante-room to the King's chamber on his way through to the King and Wells who, had accompanied Roger and was unaware that he had already met the Prince at Edgehill, whispered unnecessarily in his ear: 'Prince Rupert.'

Catching Wells in the act of whispering, the prince stopped and looked at them both sternly for several seconds. 'Do I know you, sir?' he demanded roughly, fixing his eye on Roger and he had a strange guttural accent.

Roger bowed politely. 'I am Roger L'Estrange, your highness, of Hunstanton in Norfolk.'

'Hunstanton?'

'It is near the town of King's Lynn, sir.'

'Ah. There was a siege.'

'There was, sir.'

'Were you at Edgehill?'

'Indeed I was, sir.'

'That is where I have seen you. I never forget a face. You were wounded, I think. Did you join in the fighting in King's Lynn?'

'I did, sir. My father, Sir Hamon L'Estrange was governor of the town during the siege.'

'Ah! And now?'

'That is what I would discuss with His Majesty.'

Prince Rupert nodded. He had a handsome face, but a severe expression that seemed to be perpetual.

Without another word, he continued on his way into the King's chamber and Roger bowed politely after him, wondering what it was that had just occurred.

Wells was impressed. 'Prince Rupert recognised you,' he said excitedly. 'Just wait until I tell Bates!'

At that moment a cleric in his black robes and strange collar came up to Roger and took hold of his arm, drawing him away from Wells. 'You do know who that was, don't you, sir?' he said.

'Prince Rupert.'

'Aye, and he has the King's ear. I doubt not that you will be seeing His Majesty next.'

Roger's heart jumped into his mouth. He had, of course, rehearsed what he was going to say, but he had grown lax in his preparation as hope of ever saying it waned. Seeing the look on his face, the cleric chuckled.

'The King won't eat you, you know.'

Prince Rupert emerged from the King's chamber a full half hour later and once more stopped to talk with Roger. 'His Majesty is ready to see you now, Mr. L'Estrange. May God be with you in your plans and if I can help in some way, I will be happy to do so.'

Overcome by this blessing, Roger thanked him. 'And may God go with you too, sir.' He bowed.

Then Rupert was gone. Probably by the time he left the building he had forgotten Roger's very existence. It didn't matter. What mattered to Roger was that a footman now called him to see the King.

The King's chamber was smaller than Roger had expected, panelled in oak and hung with various works of art, portraits mostly, but also hunting and battle scenes. The King himself was standing at the table by the window and Roger only knew who he was because those around him were more stiffly formal.

The King himself, a slight man, delicate, with dark brown eyes, shoulder-length hair, moustache and small beard had a regal bearing. He had to look up at Roger, who executed his most flourishing bow and tried not to let his excitement at being in such august company befuddle his wits.

'Mr. L'Estrange. You are the brother of Sir Nicholas L'Estrange, perhaps? You are like him.'

Roger was again impressed. It had been some years previously that Nicholas had received his knighthood from the King. And no doubt hundreds of people had received honours. For him not only to remember him, but also to see the likeness between them was more than Roger had expected.

'Your Majesty remembers well. The likeness to my brother has been remarked upon.'

'It is the colour of the hair, no doubt.' King Charles smiled vaguely. He had much on his mind, Roger thought, much worry, with the war going badly and he had a young family whose safety had to be causing him anxiety.

'Have you been waiting long?' King Charles asked.

'It has seemed like just a moment, sire.'

The King's lips twitched and a light danced in his eyes. 'So, Mr. L'Estrange, you play the courtier, when we are sure you have been waiting a very long time. What is it that you would request of us?'

Roger knew he must get to the point. 'As your Majesty's most humble and obedient servant, I request, sire, a commission to subjugate the town of King's Lynn in Norfolk to your Majesty's control.'

The King was thoughtful. 'Did not your father hold King's Lynn for us last year?'

'Yes, sire.'

'Aha! Indeed we cannot forget such loyalty. We are grateful to your father. But King's Lynn was lost to us. Indeed a great pity.'

Roger reflected again for a moment that a little help from the King in the form of Lord Newcastle's army might not have gone amiss, but he prudently forbore to say so.

King Charles was thoughtful. 'If we could again have the port for ourselves, it would be a foothold once more in East Anglia and could be the turning point for the war.'

Roger said: 'It could be effected again, sire.'

'And how, Mr. L'Estrange, do you propose to do that?'

'Your Majesty has many loyal servants in King's Lynn and the surrounding districts. It would be a small matter to muster an army.'

King Charles studied him. 'Who do you think should lead this army, Mr. L'Estrange?'

'If your Majesty would commission me, your Majesty's most humble and obedient servant, I know I could do it.'

'And what would you want as a pension, sir?'

'If it please your Majesty, five thousand pounds in support of your Majesty's army and the aid of another of your Majesty's armies to relieve the garrison once the town is subdued.'

'And the governorship of King's Lynn for yourself, I've no doubt.' The King smiled. 'Digby—'

A man, came forward from out of the shadows and inclined his head. 'Yes, sire?'

There was something about George Digby and Roger tried to remember. Ah yes, wasn't he the man who had opposed Strafford's execution? And had not the King given him a baronetcy or something to get him out of the Commons and into the House of Lords where he would be safer? Roger looked at him with interest. Such a small dark man to have raised the ire of Parliament!

King Charles said: 'Provide Mr. L'Estrange with a commission to that effect.'

Realising that the short interview had ended and that he had indeed acquired his commission, Roger bowed again. 'Thank you, your Majesty.'

The King smiled. 'And may God go with you, Mr. L'Estrange.'

'Thank you, your Majesty,' Roger said again, 'And may God grant victory to your Majesty.' And he bowed himself out of the room.

Back in the ante-room waiting for Digby to finish writing the commission, Roger had time to think on what had passed. Wells wanted to know the details.

'Well? What was he like?'

'It seemed very quick. Not at all what I expected.'

'What do you mean?'

Roger considered. The King was smaller than Roger had thought he would be, almost frail, although not old. His dark eyes were kind and caring and he had a ready smile, not at all intimidating. Already an ardent Royalist, Roger had fallen under his spell and was now confirmed in his loyalty. But then the King's quiet dignity and general disposition captivated all those who were fortunate enough to come in contact with him—Oliver Cromwell notwithstanding—and he drew men to him like a magnet draws iron.

'I meant it was over too quickly.'

Walking back through the back streets of Oxford to the bakery, the commission safely tucked away in his doublet, Roger could hardly believe that he had at last achieved his goal, that he had actually been in the presence of King Charles himself, had spoken to him—and been spoken to—and that he had also been noticed by Prince Rupert, that hero of heroes. It was heady stuff and it encouraged him to tackle the next task, namely to ride back to Lynn and raise his army. He would prove himself equal to the task, equal to the faith his King had placed in him. He knew what he must do. He must raise an army to oust the small number of Parliamentarians holding Lynn at the moment and he was sure he could muster enough men for his purpose. After all, there had been five thousand prepared to defend Lynn under his father, many of whom were against surrender and now that he was assured of assistance from the nearest Royalist army when the time came, he was certain that he could be successful.

Perhaps King's Lynn would once again be worthy of its name.

Wells walked beside him chattering away, but Roger was lost in his own thoughts. It was only when they met Bates, also on his way back to the *Magpie*, that he remembered where he was.

'He saw the King,' Wells told Bates.

'So, did you get it?' Bates asked Roger.

'I did.' He patted his chest where the commission lay next to his heart.

Bates was impressed.

'Prince Rupert spoke to him in the ante-room,' Wells added. 'He *recognised* him! The Prince!'

'The King knew my brother, too,' Roger informed them.

Bates compressed his lips and nodded. 'So do you think you can raise this army?'

'I can. I have contacts. Do you want to join me?'

They both shook their heads. 'No,' Bates informed him. 'We are under orders to stay here. When will you leave?'

'In the morning.'

'Then tonight we celebrate.'

Roger shook his head. 'I want an early start. Some supper is all I require.'

'Then we dine.'

Roger laughed. He knew that Bates and Wells were the sons of aristocrats, men of his own rank. They had become friends and he was sorry to leave them. However, he did leave them early to go to his bed.

In the garret room, by the light of two candles, he pulled out the commission and read it again:

'Charles Rex

'We having received from out trusty and well beloved Roger L'Estrange, declarations of the good affections of divers of our well affected subjects of our counties of Norfolk and Suffolk and particularly of our town of Lynn, we have thought fit forthwith to return our royal thanks unto our said well affected subjects; and particularly to give our said trusty and well beloved Roger L'Estrange these encouragements to proceed in our service, principally in the work of reducing the said town of Lynn.'

There followed the terms:

'That in the case that attempt should be gone through withal, he, the said Roger L'Estrange, shall have the government of the place.

'That what engagement shall be made unto the inhabitants of the said place or any other person capable of contributing effectually to that service, by way of reward, either in employment in His Majesty's Navy or Forts, or money not exceeding the sum of £5,000 the service being performed shall be punctually made good unto them.

'That they shall in this work receive what assistance may be given them from any of our nearest garrisons.

'That when our said Town shall be reduced unto our Obedience we shall further send thither a considerable Power as shall be sufficient to relieve and preserve them, we being present, (even without this) fully resolved to send a considerable power to encourage our faithful Subjects in those Parts and to regain our Rights and Interests therein.

'Given at our Court at Oxford, this 28th of November 1644

'By his Majesty's command, George Digby.'

With his heart soaring, Roger put it away again in his doublet. He had changed from his fine blue coat into his ordinary leather doublet and now he packed up his belongings. Before the other two came back he had gone, leaving enough money to pay for his bed.

FORTY-TWO

Norfolk, December 1644

Leaving the misty spires of Oxford behind Roger had a journey of several days ahead. It allowed him time to think without the constant chatter of Wells, or the dark brooding of Bates to goad him. Yet they had taken care of him, found him a bed and showed him how to come to the King. He could have added that they had cost him a lot of money in drink, as well as getting him blind drunk on two or three occasions. He liked them and they had become friends; Wells with his joy-of-life thinking, Bates with his sombre life-is-a-place-in-hell approach. He doubted, though, that he would ever set eyes on them again.

As he crossed mile after freezing mile, he clarified his plans. He would seek out Leman the seaman and get his help to recruit men for his army. Leman could do it, for he could go in and out of Lynn unhindered. Roger, on the other hand, could not.

He would not go home to Hunstanton either, no matter that he wanted to see his parents and brother, for his plans were too dangerous to embroil them in and if ought should go awry he could not bear to bring his father to the scaffold. For there would be no escaping a second time and he knew it. He loved them too much, so he intended to keep away.

So where could he stay? As a member of the nobility, he could invite himself to stay at the house of any other members of the nobility. It happened often. It would be a good idea to stay with someone he was known to and could trust. At the first inn he stayed at, therefore, he dashed a letter off to the Pastons at Appleton Hall.

Appleton Hall had several advantages. It was tucked nicely out of the way something like eight miles from Lynn, and not far from Dersingham—far more convenient than Hunstanton which was fifteen miles from Lynn.

He had considered applying to the Cobbes at Sandringham House, not far from Appleton, but he was not well-enough acquainted with them, whereas he had known the Pastons since he was a child. He had grown up with Margaret Paston, their only child and her mother, Frances, had become like a second mother to him, for their mothers were friends and had visited each other often. Margaret had been his schoolboy's infatuation, but at about the time he went to Cambridge,

Margaret had wed Henry Bedingfeld of Oxborough Hall, near Stoke Ferry. He chuckled to himself. The Pastons were staunchly Catholic and Margaret was as pious as it was possible to be without taking holy orders. Not only would all her piety have driven him to the edge of madness, but his easy Calvinism would have driven her away. No, she was better off with Bedingfeld, a fellow staunch Catholic.

As Catholics, or recusants as the Puritans called them, the Pastons were firmly Royalist. Roger had no doubt of their loyalty to the King, for there would be no freedom of worship for them under Puritan rule. He knew he could trust them.

He had last seen Appleton Hall before he went to Cambridge and as a child he had just accepted it with its grounds and farms and dairy, just like any large manor house. But Appleton was grander than Hunstanton, an impressive seat for a scion of the Catholic Paston family.

Mistress Paston, a lady of ample girth with a smiling motherly round face framed by a lacy white cap, met him at the door as he dismounted, saddle-weary and cold.

He would have bowed politely, but she would have none of it, instead pulling him into her ample bosom and kissing him soundly on is unshaven cheek, leaving a wet impression. 'Roger L'Estrange, you are well come, sir. And mighty pleased I am to see you.' Evidently she still viewed him as the son she never had, his Protestantism notwithstanding.

She ushered him into the house, pushing him before her into the spacious, dark, oak-wainscotted hall. 'Let me look at you!' she spun him around on the words, held him at arms' length and looked him up and down critically. 'Are you well?'

'Well enough, madam,' he assured her.

'You do not look it to me!' Of course, he had been travelling all day and he needed a wash and a shave and to sort out his unruly hair, so he did not expect to be a thing of beauty. 'You're so thin!' she went on and then squeezed his upper arm. 'No meat on you at all! You've been drinking too much I expect with those young fellows at Oxford. And not eating enough, I'll wager. Well, you'll get good food here. How long do you stay?'

'A few days, if I may,' he told her, 'before I go on to Hunstanton. I have business in Lynn.' It would be impolitic to tell her the real reason why he was there, to let her think he was using her home for his own convenience.

She was delighted. 'And pleased for the company I shall be.

Supper is almost ready. I will tell cook immediately.'

'If I may wash and also change my clothes before dining?'

'Oh yes! Of course!' She turned to the footman. 'Take Mr. L'Estrange to his room,' she said.

Roger found himself in a very well-appointed room with windows overlooking the fields and woods. Unlike the hardships of Oxford, this room had a large four-poster bed, all for himself, with clean sheets and rose-patterned counterpane matching the hangings. The bed looked good, but the promise of supper looked better.

A male servant had provided hot water in a ewer on the stand, together with the necessary things to wash and shave, and he poured it into the bowl. It was his first decent wash since leaving Hunstanton which seemed like months ago. He gave himself a shave, leaving just his treasured moustache and small beard, then put on the fresh clothes provided by the servant.

Frances Paston waited for him alone in the dining room, smiling when she saw him. 'That's better! Do sit down, sir.' As he did so, she added: 'I shall say grace.' He was uneasy with this Catholic way, but she was his hostess. She said what she wanted, while he prayed in his own head, asking for success on this venture.

Supper was a more informal meal than midday dinner. A selection of meats and vegetables, soup and pies, loaded down the table and the eaters helped themselves to whatever they wanted.

Helping himself to some cold pork, he asked: 'Is Mr. Paston not at home, madam?'

'Alas, sir, do you not know? My husband is away at present.'

'Away?' Roger, pausing in the act of conveying the meat to his mouth on a pretty two-pronged fork, only just prevented himself from crying out with vexation. He had been banking on Edward Paston's help in his venture.

'On business.'

'I see.' He was on his own then. 'Do you expect him home soon?'

'He thinks several weeks.'

They continued eating for a short while in a silence which became oppressive. Clearly Frances Paston was not happy to have been left behind at Appleton while her husband was goodness-knew-where. 'I have just come from the King at Oxford,' Roger told her in an attempt to lighten the mood.

'The King? You saw the King? And how did you find him?'

'Well enough and in good calm spirits, I think. But the talk is not good. Many are saying that the King cannot win.'

Her eyes widened. 'Do you believe them?'

'No!' he grinned suddenly. 'If I believed them, madam, I should not be here now. I have business in Lynn, but obviously I cannot enter there at the moment. I would be grateful to stay here for a few days.'

'Of course you must stay here. Hunstanton is too far away.'

'In truth, madam, I came to visit you and your husband.'

The lie brightened her. 'You are always welcome, Roger L'Estrange. You know that. It is a pleasure to have you here.'

'And how is Mistress Margaret?' he enquired.

Her eyes glowed. 'She is well. And her husband. And her children.' Roger nodded. 'But I worry. Bedingfeld is known to be a King's man and he gets involved in politics. Parliament will have him if they can. We live in troublous times but she is happy with Bedingfeld. I could not wish for more. Of course, at one stage I hoped that you and she might make a match of it.'

'But I am a younger son,' he finished for her. 'I could not give her what Bedingfeld can give her. And I am not Catholic.' She flushed with embarrassment, but he laughed. 'Do not fear, madam, I had no attachment to your daughter other than as a friend.'

They chatted well into the evening still sitting at the dining table, where both seemed quite comfortable. She asked about Sir Hamon and Dame Alice, and Sir Nicholas and his wife, so sorry to hear about the dead babe. Roger asked about the neighbours, the Cobbes in particular and the Pells.

Frances Paston was derisive of the Pells. 'I don't like that man, never did,' she told Roger and he concluded she meant Sir Valentine Pell. 'A great sombre Puritan if ever there was one.'

'Do you know anything about the daughter.'

'Catherine? Lives in Hickling, I think. Her husband is a rector.'

'The other daughter. Ruth.'

'Oh, the youngest. Married another of their mother's family, a Calthorpe. No idea where she is, though. I daresay in Norfolk somewhere.'

Roger ignored the pang clutching at his insides. 'Norfolk is a large county,' he said.

'It is.' She studied him. 'You were sweet on her, were you not?'

He did not answer, lost for a moment in his own thoughts.

'It was common knowledge about you and Ruth Pell,' she went on almost by apology. 'Not that I listen to gossip, you understand.'

He stood up. 'Well, if you will excuse me, madam, I have been travelling most of the day and I am tired.

She stood up too. 'Forgive me. My tongue runs on wheels!'

'I am sure, madam, that there is nothing to forgive,' he said magnanimously, and smiled at her.

She beamed at him. 'Well goodnight Roger. I hope you sleep well. I have asked Jack Taylor to wait on you. Be so good as to tell him when you wish to rise on the morrow.'

He bowed over her hand. 'You are too good, Mistress Paston.' He brushed the back of her hand with his lips and left her blushing as he climbed the stairs.

§

The next day Roger dispatched Jack Taylor to Lynn to find Leman the seaman and bid him to attend him at Appleton Hall. He had spent a strange night, punctuated by periods of sleeplessness. His first thoughts were of Ruth and it still hurt like a knife wound that she belonged now to another man who had the rights he had once coveted for himself. However, he acknowledged that if he had married her as he had hoped, he would not now be set on this course.

He used the time to go over his plan. He was here, back in Norfolk and Leman the seaman was in Lynn. He was within an inch of putting this plan into action. He had the coveted commission from the King, now safely tucked away in the canopy of the bed, and he would have the men to raise an army. His stomach swooped in excitement. He, Roger L'Estrange, would be a hero. He would be governor of Lynn at the ripe old age of eight-and-twenty and Lynn would belong to the King.

He looked forward to seeing Leman. He could not wait to tell him how he had actually seen the King and been given a commission to reduce Lynn to his Majesty. After all, it was Leman's idea.

''Tis a great pity you could not have come with me,' he told Thomas Leman when that worthy finally entered Roger's bedchamber later that day.

'Me? They wouldn't let me in to see the King now, would they?'

Roger studied Leman in his dirty cheap clothes, his long dank hair, his bristly cheeks and his misaligned eyes and thought that no-one in their right mind would think him suitable to come into the King's presence.

'Prince Rupert actually recognised me,' he told him, his eyes shining with excitement. 'He it was that got me the interview with his Majesty.'

'What be he like, the King I mean?' Leman asked, sitting on a hard chair near the window and fixing Roger with his good eye.

'He is kind. And mild. And likeable. Not big. And not at all grand like you would think. He said he thought I looked like my brother, Sir Nicholas, for of course, the King gave my brother a knighthood some years ago.'

'Were he in a palace?'

'No. In the University. Not so grand as a palace, I believe. But he gave me the commission, Mr. Leman.'

Leman smiled then, displaying a mouth full of rotting and missing teeth, and Roger thought it was the first time he had seen him smile. 'Can I see?'

Roger felt about in the bed canopy where he had hidden the precious document and brought it out to give to Leman, who read it thoroughly. Then he re-folded it and gave it back to Roger.

'Are you with me in this?' Roger asked him, not expecting anything other than a 'yes'.

'Course. It can be done.'

'If we are successful, there's a thousand pounds in your pocket. And a promotion.'

Leman nodded, pursing his lips. 'A thousand pounds, you do say?' he said thoughtfully. 'That be a deal of money. More'n I ever seen.'

'Will you help me to form a party within the town?'

Leman grinned broadly and stood up. 'Aye. And I know just the man to help. I bring him with me tomorra.'

'Good!' Roger shook the seaman's hand. 'Until tomorrow then.'

§

Thomas Leman rode back to Lynn through frosty lanes. Once inside Lynn's gates, however, he went straight to the governor's house and demanded to see Colonel Valentine Walton.

Since Colonel Walton had been appointed governor of Lynn, he had moved with his wife Margaret who was Oliver Cromwell's sister, into a house in the town. His wife, however, had died earlier that year and his son also called Valentine had been killed at Marston Moor in

July.

His grief had been absolute. The letter he had received from his brother-in-law Cromwell had begun with the words: '*Sir, God hath taken away your son by a connonshot . . .*' Margaret's grief had been such that she had died of a broken heart.

His brother-in-law, Cromwell, viewed him as a close friend, an ally in God's camp and clearly felt that Walton should view the sacrifice of his family as a worthy contribution to the efforts of Parliament. He struggled with it, but knew that the fight was for his God.

All day he had been interrupted by visitors, despite wishing to be quietly by the fire in his sitting room and now Rabye, his servant told him that a sailor, a sea-captain, wished to speak with him urgently.

Walton frowned. 'Send him away.'

Rabye stood his ground. 'Sir, I must inform you that Captain Leman has intelligence of an uprising that you would want to hear.'

Walton rubbed his face and groaned. 'Very well, show him in.'

He seated himself behind the large desk as Leman, cap in hand, came into the room.

To Walton Leman was the most insignificant of the rabble. He doubted he was a sea-captain. He looked more like a common sailor and his clothes needed—well he needed new clothes. He studied Leman's unlovely features, tried to decide which eye to look at and said: 'Well?'

Leman bowed slightly. 'I've just come from Appleton Hall, sir,' Leman began tentatively.'

Walton was becoming impatient. 'Yes? What of it?'

'I bin talking with a man—L'Estrange.'

Walton stared at him. L'Estrange! What was the old dog up to now?

'Not Sir 'Ammon,' Leman went on. 'Master Roger. 'E plan to raise an army and take King's Lynn for the King. Again.'

Walton's mind was racing. 'How does he plan to do that?'

''E ask my help,' Leman said. 'I told 'im I could find a man who could help. He said he give me a thousand pound if I do 'elp 'm like.'

Walton felt his heart lurch. Here at last was the opportunity to make the L'Estranges truly pay for their part in the siege. It had galled him that the treaty of surrender prevented him from touching them. Now, though they were playing right into his hands. All he had to do was allow Leman to reel them in.

He listened to all that Leman had to say and formed his plan. He asked Leman to wait. Sending Rabye off with a message to the garrison, he soon had his plan in action.

'You, sir,' he said to Leman later, 'are to be commended for your loyalty to God and the country.'

Leman managed a toothless smile and bowed his head in humble acceptance of this accolade. 'I took the Covenant some time ago, sir.'

'What I want you to do is to keep your appointment with Mr. L'Estrange and take with you as your companion Corporal Hagger.'

Leman nodded.

The following day, Leman and Hagger presented themselves at Appleton Hall.

'This be 'Agger,' Leman announced by way of introduction.

So this was the accomplice Leman had spoken about. Roger looked him over quickly. Another poor seaman from the look of him. Otherwise he was unremarkable, although he would have been much improved for a shave and the application of a little soap and water. Hagger returned his gaze stolidly.

'Where are you from Mr. Hagger?' Roger enquired.

'Oi be from Fishers' End in Lynn. And Oi run an alehouse,' Hagger replied expansively.' He had a thick Norfolk twang.

'And are you for the King?'

'Well Oi hin't for them Roundheads. Forty pound the worse Oi be for them.'

Roger was silent for a moment, but Leman filled the gap. 'He know people, he do.'

'He does?'

'He do.'

Roger felt uneasy. For some reason he was not convinced, but he was unsure why. 'Can we trust you, Mr. Hagger?'

Hagger bristled immediately. 'Oi told you hin't Oi? Do you keep asking me? Oi ask you, Mr. L'Estrange, sir, can Oi trust you?'

'Why should you not trust me?' Roger asked, puzzled.

Hagger shrugged non-committally.

'In any case, I have a commission from the King. Mr. Leman has told you that, I expect.'

'He have.' Hagger put his head on one side. 'Let's be seeing it, then.'

Roger, anxious to get on with his plans, silenced his misgivings, for which, after all, he had no real basis and reached for the Commission which he had hidden in the bed canopy. He unfolded it and showed it briefly to Hagger, certain that this man could not read, so he read it out loud, slowly and deliberately and when he had finished he refolded the paper and put it in his pocket.

'I don't have to tell you both, that what is said in this room is to stay between ourselves. This is a matter of utmost secrecy.'

'I swear on m' mother's grave not to breath a word. Not a titty-totty word,' Leman promised.

'Nobody shall hear it from moi lips,' Hagger averred.

They seemed sincere and Roger was satisfied.

'Well then, Mr. Hagger, should we meet with success, a hundred pounds will be yours and you shall be appointed cannoneer in the town.'

'Well, Mr. Strange, sir, you be needing two hundred friends.'

Roger nodded. He knew he needed men to help in the enterprise. 'I know not where to get the men, Mr. Hagger, but I reckon you do.'

At that moment a rap on the door and Mistress Paston entered. 'Begging your pardon, Mr. L'Estrange,' she said, 'But there are six or seven poor old sailors in the courtyard begging for alms and I cannot get them to leave.'

Roger clicked his tongue with annoyance, felt in his pocked and produced twelve pence which was all he could lay his hands to quickly. 'And send them away, madam,' he added as she hurried off.

He turned his attention once more to his companions.

Suddenly he heard Mistress Paston cry out amid the protests of her servant and the sound of several pairs of feet on the stairs.

Concerned for the safety of his hostess, Roger began go to the door. Hagger grabbed Roger's arm, stopping him dead and spinning him round to face him.

'What the devil . . ?' And in a moment Roger's fist came out and connected with Hagger's jaw, sending him reeling backwards across the room where he crashed into the cupboard. Realisation dawned as he watched Hagger lying sprawled on the floor. The men were on their way up to the room and they were not poor sailors at all. He had been betrayed! And Hagger must have been the Judas.

He knew that at all costs he must not be found with the commission on him and he quickly and quietly slipped it into Leman's pocket, just as the six 'sailors' burst into the room.

He was hopelessly outnumbered, but that did not prevent him from slinging a punch in someone's direction before he was subdued with a man on each of his arms and another behind him held him by the throat. It was time to stop struggling and regain some of his dignity. They also subdued Leman, although he had not struggled at all and Hagger too.

'I am Lieutenant Stubbings, from the garrison in Lynn,' one them, a short man with a large black moustache, announced. He looked at Hagger. 'Let him go, he's one of us.' Then back to Roger: 'You, I collect, sir, are Mr. Roger L'Estrange.'

Roger did not answer. His brain raced as he desperately tried to think of a way out of the situation and his heart beat hard in his chest with outrage as much as fear. He knew what they would do with him. He was under no illusions. Betrayed! Anger welled up in him against Hagger, who he was certain was responsible for this betrayal, but mostly against himself for being so gullible. Fool! It had been such a simple trap and he had walked straight into it. And poor Leman too!

Lieutenant Stubbings repeated his question and when Roger still did not answer, struck him hard across his face, snapping Roger's head to the right and cutting his lip. 'You, sir, are my prisoner. Do you make me no answer? What is your name?'

Roger glared unblinkingly at the man, licking at his cut lip and tasting blood. 'This is still England, sir. Do you treat your prisoners with scant respect?'

'Scant respect?' Stubbing threw his head back and laughed. 'There is little enough respect where you are going Mr. L'Estrange.' He studied Leman. 'Your accomplice, I see. What is your name?'

Leman opened his mouth and shut it again.

'He is Thomas Leman,' Hagger said meaningfully and his Norfolk accent had disappeared.

Stubbings turned back again to Roger. 'You are in the home of a known Papist, a delinquent and a traitor. You were going to betray the town of King's Lynn to the enemy.'

'You, sir, are the enemy.'

Stubbings grinned, mightily pleased with the way things had turned out. 'Mr. Roger L'Estrange and Mr. Thomas Leman, I am arresting you both for treason.'

He nodded to one of his men and Roger and Leman were both searched. They found nothing on Roger, of course, but the commission in Leman's pocked was handed to Stubbings who unfolded the sheet and read it with much satisfaction, then folded it and put it in his own pocket.

'Take them.' Stubbings commanded curtly.

FORTY-THREE

King's Lynn, December 1644

Alone in the tiny cell beneath the Town Hall opposite St. Margaret's Church, Roger sat bleakly staring down at the flagstone floor as he contemplated what had befallen him.

Of Thomas Leman there was no sign. At first Roger could not work out why he too was not confined. Perhaps they were interrogating him. But when he asked the gaoler he was shocked at the reply:

'Never heard of 'm.'

'He was arrested with me,' Roger insisted.

The gaoler shrugged. 'Oh—him! Oi 'eard tell that they let 'im go.'

Roger pulled the old black blanket around him. It smelled of something awful and it crawled with vermin, but he had no choice. The weather was bitingly cold, there was no fire and no straw either. He shivered miserably and digested the gaoler's words. So, not only was Hagger a corporal in the Parliamentary army, but Leman had betrayed him as well. The more he turned it over in his mind, the more he realised that Leman had set him up from the time he had met him in the inn. Leman had taken the Covenant, Roger was sure of it, and lured him into a trap. He remembered Leman suggesting that Lynn could be retaken for the King. And he, Roger had fallen for it. *Fool! Stupid fool!* Now he realised also that Leman must have gone straight to Colonel Walton to inform him of Roger's plans.

The heavy metal door of the gaol creaked open and Roger assumed they had come to take him to London

Instead, when he looked up his heart smashed against his ribs in dismay. *Dear God in heaven, not my father!*

Sir Hamon looked at his youngest son with accusing eyes.

'You'll have to share,' the gaoler told them as he shoved Sir Hamon in. 'Hin't no more room.' He slammed the door and turned the key in the lock.

Father and son stood facing each other. Roger was the first the speak. 'Why are you here, sir?' He knew the answer.

'Why do you think?' Sir Hamon demanded wrathfully, glaring at his youngest.

'They arrested you?'

'They did!' He had never seen his father so angry. 'I could knock you through to kingdom come, you damned idiot!' He growled through his teeth. 'You damned, stupid fool!' he repeated, his voice rising in pitch and power. 'What, in the name of all that is sacred do you think you were doing?'

Roger hung his head wretchedly, unable to think of a suitable reply.

Sir Hamon went on: 'Did I not tell you to have done with Lynn? Did I not say? You stupid blasted half-wit! I *told* you not to do anything like this! Do you know what you have done?'

Roger did know, but he knew his father was going to tell him anyway. He felt tears sting his eyes. He swallowed and said: 'I'm sorry, sir.'

'They do not need an excuse against us!' Sir Hamon raged. 'I will stand trial for treason, and so will Nick. We could hang, all because of your stupidity!'

Tears spilled out of Roger's eyes and trickled down his ashen cheeks. 'So will I.' He struggled not to break down completely. 'Have they got Nick?'

'No. I thank God he's away at present. Went to visit Hamon and your sister, and just in time!'

Sir Hamon sat down heavily on the bench which served also as the only bed and turned his head to look at his son accusingly. Roger sat down beside him, so that he did not have to look at his father's face. He wiped his face on his sleeve and whispered miserably: 'I deliberately did not go to Hunstanton, but to the Pastons at Appleton Hall. I did not tell you what I was going to do. I kept you out of it.'

Sir Hamon took a deep breath and let it go in a sigh, and his rage seemed to calm a little. 'So, what happened?'

Roger decided to tell him the whole. 'At an inn on the road to Newark I met a sailor called Leman. He helped me best four Roundheads in swordplay. He knew about what happened here, knew about us, and he suggested I could re-take Lynn for the King.'

Sir Hamon groaned. 'And you fell for it! Don't tell me. He betrayed you.'

'Yes, it turns out he did!'

Sir Hamon shook his head in disbelief. 'Did you not think how difficult it would be to raise an army. And without the King's say so?'

'Leman said he could help me with that, that he knew people. Anyway, I went to Oxford and I saw the King. I received a commission from him.'

'A commission! Don't tell me—they found it?'

Roger nodded wretchedly.

'You've got more bravado than sense. Dear God, Roger, you will hang for this!'

'I know.'

After a long pause Sir Hamon continued: 'They think I am in league with you in your harebrained scheme. And how am I supposed to convince them otherwise, eh? I told you not to bring problems to our door. Your mother and I are too old for this. I suppose they are sending you to London?'

'They are.'

'Well I hope I do not see you there, or we will both hang. Hell's teeth, Roger, what were you thinking of, so soon after the last year's events? Don't you know we only just about got away with our lives? To get involved in such dangerous dealings is inviting trouble.' He paused, overcome by the sheer stupidity of the whole situation. 'I *told* you not to do it! How many times do you need to be told? Are you still a child needing scolding, nagging, being kept in the schoolroom for your own and others' safety? Don't you know the King is lost? Why then all this posturing?' He paused again but just when Roger would have spoken he said: 'I brought you up to be well-educated, clever, accomplished. Sadly, I obviously neglected the common sense!'

Under the tirade and acutely aware of the danger he had put his family in, Roger again felt the tears trickle down his cheeks. He wiped them away impatiently. 'I am so sorry, sir,' he whispered. He could think of nothing else to say, no excuse for his conduct, no logic for his actions. Of course, if he had been successful it would have been different. He would have been the conquering hero. 'I go to London soon,' he added. 'Today.' He paused, trying to regain some composure. 'I wanted to help the King.'

'I know what you wanted,' Sir Hamon replied and as he looked at his son, his eyes softened. 'You damned hothead!' But the anger was less in his voice. 'No-one can doubt your loyalty to the King. But this wasn't the way, Roger.'

'I was betrayed. If I had not been and if the attempt had been successful—'

'It would have been the siege all over again.'

'No. The King promised relief from the nearest garrison.'

'He cannot promise, Roger,' Sir Hamon said almost gently. 'He has no idea where his troops are. There are none in East Anglia. We had a promise from Newcastle, remember? But he went to Hull instead. No-one would have come to your aid. And the people of Lynn would suffer again. You couldn't do it, Roger. Not a second time. They would not have been behind you.'

Roger put his head in his hands, utterly defeated. When he had thought to be the conquering hero, he was now in a fight not only for his own life, but for his father also and perhaps his brother. Of course they would think Sir Hamon was behind this plot. It was obvious. Why had that not occurred to him? 'I'm so sorry, Father.'

They heard footsteps and the clink of the gaoler's keys.

'They come for me,' Roger said with certainty.

'I'll probably see you in Newgate, then.' Sir Hamon stood up and so did Roger. Then, unexpectedly after the tirade he had just endured, Roger found himself crushed in his father's embrace. Something inside him snapped and he clung to him, begging his forgiveness.

'Fight your case, Roger,' Sir Hamon said in his ear and there was a catch in his voice. 'Don't let them hang you. Do anything necessary, but don't let them hang you. Keep your dignity. May God go with you, my son.' He kissed his cheek.

'And with you, Father.' Roger replied. There was no time for more.

The gaoler opened the heavy iron door. 'Come now, Mr. L'Estrange, sir.'

Father and son separated and Roger summoned all his dignity. He held his head high as he left the cell. He looked back at his father, and his last impression was of him standing proudly, which characterised him. To his dying day, though, Roger would never forget the sorrow in his father's eyes.

FORTY-FOUR

Newgate Prison, London, December 1644

Even to one experienced in the inconveniences of King's Lynn gaol, Newgate prison came as a nasty shock.

The prison had been built around one of the ancient entrance gates into the city of London, the New Gate, which for centuries had served as a holding for criminals, but which in time had grown and spread to include the area called the Old Bailey (old wall) as well. Entrance to the prison was still through the gate itself which had a permanently raised portcullis. Roger had an impression of dirty faded grandeur, of sculptured stonework embellishing windows and walls, and stone figures in niches above the gate itself. There was even the figure of a man in medieval garb with a cat, which he later learned was a statue of Richard Whittington, Lord Mayor of London, who had rebuilt the old prison into the 'new' one. Hence, it was also referred to as 'The Whit'. The ornamentation surprised Roger who had formed an entirely different idea of the notorious prison, the mere mention of which struck terror into the soul of any man. His spirits lifted a little. Perhaps it would not be as bad as he had expected.

The guards gave him little time to admire the view, for the clerk admitted Roger immediately and had him taken to the Lodge, the general clearing house for new inmates. Here, the first hint of what awaited him assailed his nostrils, a stench of something between the noxious fumes of the privy mingled with vomit, human sweat, mouldy straw and filth.

His stomach heaved and he controlled it with an effort.

The lowest forms of human life England could produce occupied the Lodge. The inmates consisted of a number of men, most of them young men, but one or two older ones and three women, sitting or standing according to their desire. It turned out that they had been appointed gaolers, although felons themselves, earning money and a postponement of the day of their execution. All of them eyed the newcomer with the same baleful and, Roger thought, greedy stare. He knew his clothes, no matter that they had seen him through months on the road and he had slept in them for several nights, betrayed that he was a man of means. In Newgate, money meant one could buy privileges denied lesser mortals.

'This cull's worth a shillin' or two,' one man said to another in a loud broad London accent.

'A mighty fine gent, I do think,' the other man responded. He had a different accent, not one Roger could place. He came and stood in front of Roger, staring him in the face, although he was shorter and had to look up at him. He lifted a bony hand and with a long grimy finger reached out and touched Roger's hair. 'And mighty fine hair too.'

Roger only just stopped himself recoiling. He glared at the man and stood his ground. 'Who is to take care of me?' he demanded.

No-one answered him and silence fell as they watched him.

'Who is to see to me?' he asked again.

A woman, an ill-favoured creature with numerous chins, greasy dark hair falling out of a simple knot and a massive bosom over-spilling a filthy dress grinned showing him a mouthful of rotting teeth. 'And who are you, my fine gent?' she demanded.

'I am Roger L'Estrange,' Roger said, trying not to flinch at the added stench coming from the woman's mouth. 'Who are you?'

The woman threw her head back and laughed and Roger had to take a step backwards. His stomach threatened to shed its contents all over again and he fought it valiantly. He wondered what he had said to provide such mirth, but gradually the laughter which had been joined in by her companions died down. 'I'm Mary. But first a drink to your 'ealth, sir.'

Without moving his head Roger's eyes shifted from one to the other of the room's occupants. All the men were standing now and were edging towards him. Thinking quickly, it dawned on him that *he* had to provide the money to pay for the drink. He had heard that extortion was rife in Newgate and had heard also of the practice of 'chummage' whereby newcomers would be stripped of their clothing and their money stolen if they did not prove to be generous with their acquaintances.

He managed to smile and bowed grandly which pleased them no end. 'But of course, madam.' Fishing in a pocked he found a few coins.

The gaoler in Lynn had warned him about pickpockets and he had listened to his advice to have various hiding places about his person for his money, for if one place were found and his pocket picked, he would still have enough to survive on. And here, money was survival.

Roger grinned at them all in as friendly a manner as he could manage, bowed to the woman again as he handed the coins over and received some of the 'strong drink' his money had bought.

'Your 'ealth sir,' they chorused and drank.

Roger watched them, his face impassive, wondering what fate was to befall him. He hoped he would not have to share quarters with any of these feeble excuses for humanity and the thought prompted him to ask again: 'Who will take me to my room?'

'Room?' They all laughed riotously. 'There'll be time for that by and by.'

They grabbed him, then and he feared the worst and tried to struggle. 'Stop fighting,' someone recommended in his ear. 'We got to put leg irons on yer. 'Tis our job.'

Horrified to find himself shackled, ankles and wrists joined by a chain, Roger had to fight to keep from breaking down. The shackles so absolutely impressed upon him that he had lost his freedom.

From the Lodge he was taken, clanking and with slow small steps, to the Condemned Hold. If he had thought the Lodge bad, this was worse. The terrible stench grew stronger here and once again he gagged, and he put up his forearm as far as the chains let him to cover his mouth and nose.

He found himself in a deeply dark room with just one small glassless window letting in little light or air. As his eyes grew accustomed to the gloom he could make out thirty or more men and women lying, sitting, or standing against wet moss-covered stone walls. The furniture consisted of wooden boards which served as beds, seats, tables, or whatever seemed to be required. The wet stone floor had staples cemented into it and one man was chained to one. This man could not walk about, and he threw himself around in a frenzy and cried out dementedly, no doubt the reason for his being chained. The poor man was out of his mind. And it was no wonder, Roger thought. It was enough to break the strongest mind. A drain serving as a privy, ran through the centre of the floor and discharged somewhere else and no doubt this accounted for much of the smell. No privacy for necessary bodily functions, then. There was a grate, but no fire, despite it being December with a damp, penetrating cold.

Unlike the gaolers in the Lodge, these prisoners took little notice of him; they had their own despair to deal with. Some coughed and moaned feebly as they lay on the board beds, obviously sick. The man stapled to the floor continued to scream and swear, the obscenities hurting Roger's ears. He hadn't realised he had led such a sheltered life in Norfolk! One other seemed completely out of his mind and babbled unintelligibly, while not a few appeared completely broken in spirit, staring into space.

Roger turned in panic and cried out to the turnkey who came at his calling. 'There must be some mistake. I should be in private apartments.' He would have paid any price to get out of that gruesome, fearful place.

'See the Governor in the morning.' The man shut the grille on the door and went away again.

One man approached him. 'You don't look like you belong 'ere.'

Roger took a shuddering breath and choked, coughing until he heaved. 'I don't,' he managed at length.

'What did you do?'

'Prisoner of war.' He thought of his father and hoped they didn't send him here. He would not survive it. In fact Roger doubted if *he* would survive it. 'What is this place?'

'Condemned Hold.'

'I haven't been tried yet.'

'Some 'ave and some ain't. This is the holding place for them as'll hang, but also for the new ones.'

'Which are you?'

'I 'ang tomorrow.' He seemed cheerful enough about it, but Roger looked at him horrified. 'What did you do?'

'I killed a man. 'Twere self defence, but I didn't get to tell 'em that. No chance to defend meself, see?'

Roger shuddered. This would be his lot, no doubt about it. 'You don't seem upset.'

'Where I'm going's got to be better than where I bin living. I said my prayers, I made my peace with God. I be alright.'

Roger could think of nothing to say to him and turned away. Shackled and utterly defeated, Roger stood still with shock and despair. He could not think of the past, nor of the future. Only here and now filled his senses. He thought of the condemned man and glanced in his direction and met coal black eyes. He was right. Death would be better than this.

He dreaded the night even more, dreaded the dark, for he feared the rats, but he feared the people even more. However, as night fell, he found that he could purchase a candle for an extortionate price and when he found no board bed for himself, he purchased some damp and mouldy straw to protect himself from the worst of the excruciating damp cold of the stone floor.

The rats took the candle the moment he had stuck it with great difficulty to the floor, pitching him again into dense darkness. Everyone else, he realised, had already learned this lesson and had not wasted their blunt on a candle which would not last two minutes. So, with the demise of the candle went the demise of all light and the only thing to do was what everyone else did—try and settle down to sleep, the demented ones included.

But sleep did not come. His stomach alternately threatened to throw up the drink he'd had earlier, and at the same time ached with hunger, for no food had been offered to him, either for mercy or for money. The rats ran over him continually and nibbled at him. They would have had the clothes off his back if he had not been lying on them. The cold penetrated through the damp straw and into his bones until they ached and he was past shivering, and the rusty irons on his wrists and ankles had rubbed great sores and blisters which bled. He curled up miserably and did his best, but just as the effect of the strong drink began to soothe him, someone cried out and made him jump. The sound also triggered the chained man's hysterical sobbing and someone else groaned pitifully. Some, evidently inured to the rigours of prison life, slept soundly and snored loudly, while he was sure he could hear the sounds of a couple in the throes of lovemaking. *Here!* His every sensibility revolted.

Listening to the various noises with growing desperation Roger wept quietly to himself. Misery clawed at his soul. If there were such a place as hell tormenting souls everlastingly, it must have been modelled on Newgate. The misery in the Condemned Hold had to be without equal.

FORTY-FIVE

Newgate, London, December 1644

The grating of a key turning in the lock and the metallic slide of bolts being drawn announcing morning long before the winter sun could cast its grey light on the scene made him sit up. A man, dressed rather better than any Roger had so far met in this God-forsaken place, entered the room smiling and bowing slightly to Roger. The other inmates backed away and Roger, blinking in the unaccustomed light of the man's flaring torch, left his straw bed and came unsteadily to his feet.

'Mr. Strange? I must apologise, sir, for such terrible treatment and I tell you, sir, that those who brought you here shall be dealt with when I find them. Please come with me.'

Roger ran his fingers through his hair in a futile gesture to ease the pounding in his head. 'Who are you?' he asked.

'Skeet is my name,' the man said. 'I've come from the Governor. A terrible oversight, Mr. Strange, sir. A terrible oversight. As a gentleman, you would, of course, desire separate apartments.'

He paused, looking at Roger expectantly, but it was a moment before he realised what the man required and, with resignation, he fished in his necessarily bottomless pocket for some coins and dropped them into his hand.

Skeet bowed again and led the way out of the Condemned Hold as Roger bent to pick up his chains in order to avoid tripping over them and, rattling and clanking he followed Skeet into the now seemingly salubrious Lodge.

Roger sat down at the dirty roughly-sawn table and pulled the fine lace frills of his shirt sleeves through the iron between skin and shackle to try and protect his wrists from the irons. His ankles suffered too, for the rusty rough iron had rubbed holes in his hose and the bleeding sores made him wince with pain.

The Lodge, it seemed, was the drinking place and once again Roger funded everyone else to whatever their pleasure might be, even at this unearthly hour. He drank small-beer himself, but then discovered that he might have some bread and mouldy cheese, for which he paid and for which he was grateful, having had nothing to eat since the previous morning when he and his escort had left the inn which had been their stopover.

Skeet, sitting opposite Roger at the table, rattled on and on and Roger let him.

'I'm so sorry Mr. Strange, so very, very sorry. The Condemned Hold is not for the likes of you Mr. Strange and no mistake. I don't know how it could have happened. I am so sorry for it. If I hadn't been absent myself when you was brought in yesterday, Mr. Strange, sir, then I would have seen to it that you would have been looked after like a gentleman should be.'

Roger knew it was a ploy to get more money out of him, but it suited him to let Skeet think he believed him and he listened in silence, while eating the bread and cheese with ravenous zeal.

'No, sir,' Skeet continued unstoppably, 'The Condemned Hold ain't for the likes of you, Mr. Strange, sir.'

'No,' Roger agreed only half listening. Never had bread and dried-out mouldy cheese tasted so good!

'No, sir. 'Tis the Press Yard you should be in.'

Roger almost dropped his bread. 'The Press Yard?' *Surely not*! He had heard, as everyone had, that prisoners who refused to plead guilty or not guilty would be pressed to death, weights being applied to their chests until they expired. Common knowledge said that a prisoner who pleaded and then was found guilty forfeited all his goods to the King, (or more accurately these days, to Parliament) leaving his widow and children destitute. But if a prisoner refused to plead he could not be found guilty.

Skeet, seeing the look of horror on Roger's face, hastened to reassure him. 'No, sir, not the Press *Room.* The Press *Yard.* It is also called the Governor's House. Where the better apartments are.'

Roger's heart, which had temporarily suspended activity, now resumed beating with a rush.

Skeet smiled, showing a row of stained teeth.

Now becoming quite familiar with Newgate ways, Roger said: 'How much?'

'Twenty guineas,' Skeet said. 'And eleven shillings per week.'

Oh yes, he would have to pay to get out of the Condemned Hold and no mistake! Roger thought bitterly that everything so far had been designed to make sure he paid up. Skeet knew that he would do anything rather than go back to that dreadful place. He wondered how others who were less well-off than himself fared.

It was extortionate, but then what could he expect from people who were probably professional thieves? He knew he had no choice if he were not to die in the Condemned Hold before even coming to trial, so he paid up, grateful for once that his position and relative wealth which he had always taken for granted, could now afford him some form of civilisation, even in this hell-hole.

Skeet led Roger through Phoenix Court to the Governor's House, or Press yard, stopping at some point for the irons to be removed. At first Skeet conducted him to a cell which slept three, but his complaint and a further donation, secured him a private cell much more to his taste as it afforded him the necessary solitude to work out his defence. He had just a few days to his trial which was set for the twenty-sixth of December. He did not need the distractions of other inmates.

The cell was cheerless enough, with bare stone walls liberally decorated with the graffiti of countless other visitors and a small barred and glazed window high up in the wall, but it did have a fireplace for which he could buy fuel, a table and stool, a bowl for him to wash in and a board bed with a flock mattress and even *clean* sheets. Luxury indeed, compared to the nightmare which had just passed.

As soon as the door closed Roger took off his shoes and stretched out on the bed, pulling the blankets over him and discovered that the mattress stuffing was so inadequate that he could feel the wooden slats through it. Nevertheless in moments he fell into a deep sleep.

He woke when someone shook him and then the man stood by his bed saying in a rich baritone: 'Come now, sir, 'tis time you were paying your entrance fee.'

Blinking in the light of the candle the stranger held aloft, Roger slowly remembered where he was and recognised that this was a fellow cavalier, a man older than himself, but with a genial smile.

'What is the entrance fee?' Roger managed thickly, sitting up now and trying to gather his disordered wits. The sleep had done much to restore him and repaired the pounding headache which travelling and the previous night's experiences had caused.

The stranger sat on his bed. 'Six bottles of wine,' he replied carelessly.

Roger nodded. 'I see. And where do I buy this wine?'

'The taproom.'

'There is a taproom here?' Was there no end to the surprises in Newgate?

The stranger laughed. 'Oh yes. 'Tis where we eat and drink until bedtime.'

'What time is it now?'

'About seven o'clock.'

'In the morning?'

'In the evening, of course! No-one drinks wine in the morning, do they!'

Roger shook his head. He had slept for most of the day. 'In this place, nothing would surprise me. And besides, I had to fund for some rum this morning, even before it was light!'

The stranger laughed and held out his hand. 'Welcome to Newgate, lad. Henry Dryden.'

Roger took it. 'Roger L'Estrange of Hunstanton in Norfolk. Sir Hamon L'Estrange is my father.'

'Never heard of it, sir.'

Roger smiled. 'Hun-stan-ton. 'Tis near King's Lynn.'

'Ah. Now did I read that King's Lynn declared for the King?'

'You did.'

'There was a siege?'

Roger got out of bed straightening the sheets and blankets. 'There was.'

Henry Dryden nodded. 'Well I'm from Hull. We had a couple of sieges ourselves.'

Roger went over to the fireplace, and started to lay the fire. The room was cold. 'Hull, you say?'

'Aye.'

'What was that with Sir John Hotham and his son?'

Henry Dryden rubbed his small beard ruefully as Roger abandoned his attempts to get the fire going again and sat down on the bed. 'Sir John was governor of Hull. He held it for Parliament and twice he refused the King admittance. Then all of a sudden, he and his son, also John by the way, declared for the King.'

'Really?' Roger sat down to pull on his shoes, but paused to study Henry Dryden. Perhaps fifteen years older than Roger, of average height and larger than average girth, Henry Dryden seemed a jovial fellow, the eternal optimist. His clothes proclaimed him wealthy, for the lace on his collar and cuffs was of the finest. Roger shook his head. 'So they were turncoats.'

'Aye. Well me, I were always for the King, but somehow Fairfax thought I was doing the same as they were. When he eventually took

Hull, I got arrested and here I am.'

Roger stood up, buttoning his doublet. 'Are the Hothams here?'

'No. They're in the Tower.'

Roger's eyes grew round. 'There's no getting out of the Tower.'

'No, there isn't. But then they were indeed turncoats. They changed sides. Worse, the son denounced the father in an effort to save his own skin. At least, I heard that Sir John blamed his son for his predicament.' He stroked his small beard.

An uncomfortable feeling wormed its way into Roger's belly as he thought of his own father. Had they sent him to the Tower? Or would he turn up here in Newgate? Roger knew that the blame for Sir Hamon's fate lay squarely with himself. He shivered. *Oh God! What have I done?*

He blocked the thought and said to Dryden: 'But you have always been for the King?'

'Aye.'

'So they cannot accuse you of treason.'

'Doesn't seem to have stopped them doing so, though.'

In the taproom, Roger found that almost all the prisoners on this side of Newgate prison were political prisoners like himself and Henry Dryden, minor Royalists sent for trial as traitors by Parliament. Henry Dryden led Roger to a table and they both sat down on a bench.

Dryden introduced him to the others, naming so many people that for now they seemed to be a mass of faces and a blur of names.

Henry Dryden smiled a lot, jested a lot and drank a lot. Roger, not yet as genial, studied everyone and everything, his eyes flitting from face to face. He tried to take in everything, in case it came in useful.

Dryden took the money Roger offered and bought some wine and sat down with Roger again, pouring into earthen cups.

'So when's your trial?' Dryden asked.

'Twenty-sixth,' Roger told him.

'I'm the next day.'

'Have you prepared your defence?'

Dryden grimaced. 'What defence? I have no defence, sir. No, they will have me hanged, drawn and quartered.'

He said it cheerfully enough, but Roger saw that he was troubled and he shuddered involuntarily. Of course, no-one knew what fate awaited them until their trial was over and sentence passed. All the men crowded into this room awaited trial, cavaliers all, some with rich clothes, some less so, but all of them King's men. What fate awaited them? What fate awaited him?

Roger had never dared think beyond the sentence of death and to be hanged was bad enough. To be beheaded seemed somehow worse. But to be hanged until half dead, taken down and disembowelled while still alive and then cut up into pieces, one's head boiled in saltpetre and put on a spike on Temple Bar or one of the other gates was more than he could comprehend. It made him shudder to think of it.

Dryden's voice had carried and a thick silence hung in the taproom. Roger realised that Dryden had spoken the unthinkable and that there was not a man present that did not live in fear of that terrible sentence. Once sentence was passed, the best one could hope for would be for the hangman to leave the victim hanging longer than he should so that he would be dead at the time of 'drawing' and 'quartering'.

Henry Dryden himself broke the silence. 'Well then, sirs, there is no need for this! Come now, "let us eat, drink and be merry, for tomorrow we are to die"!' Immediately, more wine appeared and the company broke into jesting and laughter.

Sitting on the end of the bench, Roger could not join in. He had a churning in the pit of his stomach, which refused to go away and he found he had begun framing some kind of defence in his brain. In a short while he left them to go back to his room, to begin work on his defence.

FORTY-SIX

London, 26th December, 1644

Roger spent the following days preparing for the trial. If he were going down, it would not be without a fight, he decided. His life was worth fighting for. The time passed quickly and all too soon, before he felt he was ready, Thursday the twenty-sixth of December dawned, a gloomy dismal day in keeping with the proceedings. He was taken from Newgate Prison in a covered wagon to the London Guildhall which had been divided into individual courts. Even so, he had a view of a lofty interior so ornate that his first impression was of a cathedral, complete with stained glass windows, which the Puritans had not yet destroyed or replaced.

Every available seat in the court had been taken, row upon row of men dressed in black, with unadorned white collars and black hats. So many black hats! Like rooks on a tree branch. No wonder the collective word for a gathering of rooks was a 'parliament'!

Evidently Roger's notoriety had spread and he was unsure whether to be gratified or uneasy. In the middle of the room at a table sat the judge-advocate, fifty-year old clean-shaven and slightly portly Sir John Corbett, also in black, who studied Roger dourly.

The trial was supposed to take the form of a court martial. However, the normal rules of court martial were dispensed with in cases like Roger's in an effort to rid Parliament of annoying Royalists.

Despite the churning in his insides, Roger stood quietly, his head held high, his hands clasped in front of him. He was not afraid to look Sir John Corbett in the eye, or to face those in attendance, whether members of the court or onlookers. He stood straight and defiant.

Sir John Corbett read out the charge.

'Are you Master Roger L'Estrange of Hunstanton Hall near King's Lynn in the county of Norfolk, son of Sir Hamon L'Estrange, born the seventeenth day of December in the year of our Lord sixteen hundred and sixteen?'

'I am, sir,' Roger replied clearly and he was pleased his voice did not wobble.

Again Sir John Corbett studied Roger. 'Be seated, sir, if you please.'

Roger did so on the stool provided.

Sir John turned his attention to the papers on the table in front of him.

'Mr. L'Estrange, you are charged with obtaining a commission from his Majesty the King to reduce the town of King's Lynn to his Majesty's pleasure. Further, you obtained this commission under the false pretense of having abundant interest in the town where there was none and furthermore you were given or promised five thousand pounds to effect this treachery. You stand, therefore, accused of spying and treachery. How do you plead?'

Roger stood up again. 'Not guilty, sir.'

The judge-advocate studied him with interest. 'But I have here a copy of your commission, Mr. L'Estrange.' He made it sound as though that were evidence enough. He continued: 'Your commission, Mr. L'Estrange, was not the commission of a soldier, but a commission of bribery and corruption, to make a party in the town by clandestine ways with promises of money and preferment. For is it not true that you could not think of any other way to do it than to send for Captain Thomas Leman of King's Lynn and promise him one thousand pounds if he would betray the town? And as the court should be aware, Captain Leman is zealous for Parliament, having taken the Covenant and so the effort to corrupt such a one is therefore treasonable.'

Roger came to his feet again. 'I did not know that Captain Leman had taken the Covenant. He presented himself to me as a man loyal to the King!'

His words, spoken in heat, echoed around the court.

'Sit down, Mr. L'Estrange,' Sir John Corbett said evenly, peering over the top of his spectacles at him and as Roger reluctantly did so he continued: 'On arriving in King's Lynn, you did not go into the town, but instead went to the home of Mr. and Mistress Edward Paston at Appleton Hall, although Mr. Paston was in fact away from home at the time. I put it to you, sir, that had you been not a spy, you would not have come skulking in such a manner.'

Roger jumped up again. 'I am no spy, sir,' he cried out. 'If I had been a spy I would have worn clothes befitting such. I am well-known in Lynn and known for all that as a Royalist and faithful to the cause of the King. I have never ever pretended to be anything else. My mistake was in believing Thomas Leman to be a Royalist like myself when he was not and he betrayed me.'

'But you did offer him a thousand pounds and promotion if he helped you?'

'I did. I do not see that I have done anything untoward in that, sir.'

'But Mr. L'Estrange, you tried to bribe Captain Leman.'

'It occurred to me that Captain Leman might be reluctant to assist me in what was going to be—and did indeed prove to be—a very dangerous scheme without some remuneration. Yet, I had no reason to doubt his loyalty to the King. I did not know that he was a Covenanter.'

'Sit down Mr. L'Estrange.'

Roger did so.

'After you had bribed Captain Leman, he brought with him to Appleton Hall the following day, one Corporal Hagger of the garrison of Lynn, to whom you also frankly showed your commission and offered remuneration. I put it to you, sir, that that is the works of a spy.'

Roger was off the stool again.

'The man introduced to me as Hagger presented himself as a poor sailor who lived in Fisher's End in Lynn and who kept an alehouse. When I questioned him as to his loyalties he told me that he disliked the Roundheads because he was forty pounds the worse for them! He was dressed as a seaman and I did not doubt his story. Thomas Leman I did not doubt at all. I had met him some weeks previously when on my way to Newark and it had been his suggestion that Lynn might be retaken for the King. I did not doubt his loyalty at all. And since it was he that introduced Hagger to me, I did not doubt him either.'

'Very well, Mr. L'Estrange. Please sit down!' Sir John Corbett shuffled papers again. 'While you were in discussion with Captain Leman and Corporal Hagger, you were interrupted by six men from the garrison in Lynn, soldiers dressed like poor seamen who came begging for alms, whereupon you sent them a shilling and told them to be gone. Is that not so?'

'It is.'

'Lieutenant Stubbings and his men then forced their way into the chamber you were using and arrested you and Captain Leman. Evidently Lieutenant Stubbings was unaware that Captain Leman was a Covenanter at this juncture.'

'That is so.'

'Is it not so, then, Mr. L'Estrange, that having come without drum, trumpet or pass to the quarters of Parliament that you must indeed have been a spy?'

'I did not go to the quarters of Lynn. I went, as you yourself are saying, sir, to Appleton Hall. That is outside the garrison of Lynn. Eight miles outside it, I think you will find.'

He knew this to be a good argument, for Parliament had clearly stated that '*whatsoever persons shall come from Oxford or any part of the King's Army to London of the parts adjacent, or to any part of the army under the command of the Earl of Essex, etc., without the warrant of both Houses of Parliament, shall be apprehended as spies and intelligencers and proceeded against according to the rules of war.*'

He went on: 'I did not enter the garrison, nor speak to any I knew to be Covenanters. I did not come as a spy, sir, for I have never pretended to be anything other than a Royalist and I did not enlist the help of anyone I knew to be a member of the garrison. Leman was not a member of the garrison, as you yourself, sir, are well aware. I came as an open enemy, with no treacherous ends. It cannot be treason to take a town according to the rules of war. I was apprehended by the rules and customs of war, a just enemy and a prisoner of war. My commission was that of a soldier enabling me to raise and conduct an army as should attempt a surprisal of the town. That is not the work of a spy, nor is it the work of a traitor. For surely a traitor is one who was once on one side and then changed sides to betray his friends? I have never been anything other than what you see; I have never pretended to be, or ever wanted to be, a Covenanter. I am a Royalist, as is my father and my brothers. I fought for the King at the siege of King's Lynn. No-one could ever say that I am a traitor to any cause and I am certainly no traitor to the King!' He paused, his eyes blazing at the injustice. 'If you wish to treat me as a prisoner of war under the rules of war, then so be it. But I am no spy and I am no traitor. I demand to be treated as a prisoner of war!'

A murmur rolled around the court and Sir John Corbett scratched his head. The young L'Estrange was certainly a brave young man. Foolhardy, some might think. In the right of it, others may think.

Yet Sir John had been given the task of finding Roger L'Estrange guilty and of sentencing him to death. Parliament wanted rid of people like him; Sir Alexander Carew who had conspired to deliver the fortress island of St. Nicholas in Plymouth Sound had been beheaded. The Hothams were on trial this very day for a similar offence. Parliament was determined to put an end to such treachery and espionage behind their lines, although the young L'Estrange could scarcely be put in the same league as either of the other two cases.

Indeed, Sir John Corbett did not want to sentence the prisoner to die. He had taken a liking to him, to his arrogance and his naïveté which had caused him to put his trust in the betrayer, Leman. He thought he had argued well and that his defence carried weight. But at the same time, he knew what it would mean for himself if he did not bring in a guilty verdict and sentence accordingly. He wavered. He looked at the clock. He yawned. It was early yet, but he said: 'this court will adjourn until Saturday the twenty-eighth of December. Court dismissed.'

And that was that.

Roger was furious. He knew he had made a good defence and he knew also that it would be wasted, for it would not now carry the same weight on Saturday as it did today. With insight he knew too that Parliament would not, could not, allow him to go free.

Even so, there was a measure of hope. He had seen the respect he had won in Sir John Corbett's eyes. There might still be a chance that he would be treated as a prisoner of war, not a spy and a traitor.

He had a day to kick his heels in Newgate, a day during which he prayed and went over his defence again and prayed some more. He knew his life now hung in the balance, but he also recognised that Sir John Corbett was favourable towards him. If he could be swayed just that little bit more, Roger would keep his life.

He tried to keep positive. He had hope and he refused to be anything other than optimistic. For that reason he shut himself in his cell and spoke to no-one. He could not afford any negative influences to bring him down to hopelessness. He ate and drank little and did not see even Henry Dryden who had his trial the next day.

Saturday the twenty-eighth was bitterly cold and Roger had a long wait for the court. It was well after dark before they admitted his case and he entered the court then, as before, tall and proud—and suffered a profound shock. For seated in the judge-advocate's chair was not Sir John Corbett but someone he did not recognise. The new judge-advocate turned out to be Doctor John Mills.

Why change the judge-advocate? He wondered. This was not according to law, surely? He would have to go through the whole trial again, wouldn't he?

Not so. Doctor Mills who was older than Sir John Corbett, greying and balding and with cold distant eyes, looked at Roger and began as Sir John had done:

'Are you Roger L'Estrange of Hunstanton Hall . . ?'

Roger confirmed that he was.

'You are charged, sir, with coming into the jurisdiction of Parliament, namely the town of King's Lynn, with a commission to betray the town to the enemy. You stand condemned, sir, as a traitor and a spy.'

Roger came forward his notes for his defence in his hand. 'You will hear me, sir?'

'The way I understand it, Mr. L'Estrange, you have already submitted your defence.'

'I have, sir. But you and those of you who sit as my judges have not heard it.'

'That is a pleasure we will have to forego, sir.'

'If I may be permitted to speak . . .'

'You may not!' Doctor Mills cried. 'Silence I say, sir. You have been tried.'

'But I have not spoken before you.'

'Silence!'

Indeed there was silence as Roger stood in front of the table, his eyes blazing with injustice. 'I demand to be heard.' His voice vibrated with suppressed anger.

'You will be silent!'

There was nothing he could do. If they refused him permission to speak, he could not do so. But in a final futile gesture he marched over to the row of judges sitting like crows at a feast and threw the papers into their midst. 'That, sirs, is my defence. And if you have any justice in your souls, I suggest you read it!'

A murmur from everyone in the room and two guards came and took an arm each to conduct him back to his seat in the dock. He shook them off defiantly and walked back proudly himself.

He glared at Doctor Mills. He would carry a hatred for this man to his grave, a time period that appeared to be of short duration.

'Roger L'Estrange,' Mills read from a paper on his desk, 'you have been found guilty of espionage and treason and in accord with the law on the second day of January in the year of our Lord sixteen hundred and forty-five, you will be taken to a place of execution at Smithfield where you will be hanged by the neck until you are dead. May God have mercy on your soul. That is all. Court dismissed.'

The noise of general conversation immediately filled the room, but Roger refused to be cowed. His gaze took them all in. 'No!' he yelled, outraged, 'this is not a fair trial! I demand a fair trial!' The conversation stopped immediately. 'I have been tried by one committee and sentenced by another!'

'Mr. L'Estrange,' Doctor Mills spoke with authority. 'One more word from you and I will have you drawn and quartered as well!'

This threat effectively silenced the prisoner, but he stood glaring at the now-retreating form of Doctor Mills, outraged at the injustice. It was illegal and blatantly unjust. But then what did legality and justice matter to Parliament whose sole aim was to rid itself of opposition behind its lines. It was obvious now why Sir John Corbett had been replaced as judge-advocate. He had been won over by Roger's defence. Yet there had never been any intention that Roger should receive a fair trial. Doctor Mills, though, behaved just as Parliament required.

They would make an example of Roger L'Estrange and he would pay the ultimate price.

FORTY-SEVEN

Newgate, London, 29th December 1644

Back in his cell Roger paced the floor. It was midnight now, the verdict having been reached at eleven o'clock, but he could not sleep. For the time being his anger superseded all other emotion, even fear. Bitter rage filled his entire being. *Puritans! Huh! Men of God, eh?* Well in his opinion, they neither knew God nor followed his precepts of justice and mercy. Such good Christians!

After a while he calmed down enough to begin thinking. It was no good sitting in his cell waiting until the second of January—when was that? Thursday. It was already Saturday now. No—it was already Sunday morning. He had no time to lose. He must fight for a reprieve.

He first petitioned the House of Lords for a reprieve. '*I have never claimed to be anything other than a Royalist,*' he told them.

A second letter went to the Earl of Essex, the Commander-in-Chief of the Parliamentary army. He stated again that he could not be a traitor since he had never been of the Parliamentarian party. He enclosed a printed copy of his commission from the King, a copy of his defence—the same paper he had thrown among the judges when they would not hear him—and this included legal precedents pertaining to his case.

The King received a similar letter, as did Prince Rupert.

He would try every avenue possible.

As his blood cooled, his letters written, he set to pacing the room again, for now it began to sink in that this was the end of his life. In four days he was to die. He could not comprehend it. He was only eight-and-twenty, full of youthful vitality and had so much in life that he still wanted to do. He was not an old man having lived his life, ready to let others take his place. Neither was he ill or in pain so that life had become a laborious burden. Neither was he in the heat of battle to be struck down by an enemy sword.

No, he was a young man and there was still so much living to do, so much to fulfill. He had no offspring, for he had not married. And suddenly Ruth came to him in full clarity, and his heart lurched. He had wanted to marry Ruth. She was all that was good and kind and pure. He ached for her very calmness, her good sense and most of all her love. Ruth, if she were here, would comfort him. In his heart he could hear her laugh, see her dark eyes, the smoothness of her white-and-pink cheek.

She was there, on the edge of his consciousness, yet when he tried to capture the image and hold on to her he felt he was trying to grasp a cloud.

He wondered where she was now. Married to Charles Calthorpe, of course, but where? Did she have children? The thought of her bearing another man's child sent a sharp pain through him and it was the first time he had thought of it.

Now he realised that unless a miracle happened, there would be no wife, no children, no happy ever after for him.

Oh God, will there be no mercy for me?

He had done all there was to be done. He could only wait as time rolled on relentlessly. He spent much time in prayer and read the Bible. He wrote to his family. He could not face the other prisoners. Not even Henry Dryden, who had been spared the death penalty, but was to stay in Newgate. So he stayed in his cell. For nothing could assuage the deep restless fear inside him.

He was angry at Thomas Leman and at himself at the same time. He had been a naïve fool to trust such a man. How he had not seen the trap he could not answer. Leman had set him up, offering friendship and help and a great scheme. Deliberately set him up. Even now, it astonished Roger to think of the duplicity of the man. Why did he do it? Roger could have gone off quietly and joined Major Cartwright's troops in Newark and fought the war out on a battlefield. All this was unnecessary. Why did Leman bother to trap just one more Royalist soldier? Did he get paid for it? Or was it religious zeal?

As for the court that had tried him, his fury knew no bounds. The injustice burned in his brain. He liked anger. It was better than fear. Fear weakened a man; anger strengthened him.

However, the fear kept returning like a magnetic compass needle, always coming back to the same place.

The Hothams, father and son, had also been sentenced to die, this time by beheading. He wondered which would be worse, hanging or beheading. At least beheading was the death of the nobility. Hanging was for common criminals, an ignominious death, where the victims wet and soiled themselves. Would it hurt? He thought it probably would. He could not imagine it being a painless procedure. But if he were going to die for loyalty to the King, he would die bravely. True, it would be difficult to die with dignity when dangling over empty space while the life was slowly choked out of him. He hoped he would not disgrace himself.

Henry Dryden came to see him forcing his way in when Roger tried to prevent him.

'I heard you put up a good defence, L'Estrange,' he said.

'How did you hear that?'

'Oh, one has one's sources. I heard that Sir John Cobbett was swayed by your words. He was under orders to find you guilty, but your defence was so strong he could not. That's why they switched him to Dr. Mills.'

'Such God-fearing people,' Roger said bitterly. 'Hypocrites!' Then he looked at Dryden. 'You are not to hang?'

'No, but neither am I to be released. Sir John Corbett was my judge-advocate too. A good man, that.'

Roger nodded in some sort of agreement. 'Have you any news of my father?'

'None. He's not in here. And I can tell you he's not in the Tower, either.'

Roger let his breath go in a sigh. 'Perhaps they let him go. He was innocent, after all.'

'But then, so were you.'

'I am innocent of treason.' Roger wondered if his parents had received his letters yet, if they knew by now of his predicament. His poor dear mother. He ached now for her tender care. His beloved father. He needed his strength. His brothers and sister. He needed their jolly teasing as they looked upon him as the youngest. It was hard to leave them.

And as Dryden left him he sat down on his bed and wept.

A day later he decided also to write to Ruth. He would have it sent to Dersingham Hall in the hope that she would receive it.

He sat at the table pen poised above the paper while he tried to decide what to write. Memories flooded over him, sweet memories of happy days, though the storm clouds were gathering even then. Days of snatched kisses and romantic trysts. How he yearned for those days.

What could he write? What could he tell her? That he loved her and needed her? No, he could not tell her that. It had been a long time, a year and a half. He had not changed, but she had. She had married the Puritan idiot and such a letter might embarrass her and in any case would be wrong to write such to a married lady. Yet he had to say something to her, to let her know that while he was waiting to die, he thought of her.

He wrote, filled a page, read it and tore it up. No, it was too passionate, totally in keeping with his own emotions, but not at all in keeping with propriety. He smiled wryly. He wasn't even sure if she would ever read it. He tried again.

This time he carefully understated his feelings. The result when he read it over, was not what he had intended, but was almost one friend to another. Not really a letter to the woman he loved and wanted to marry. He told her that he was no turncoat, nor a spy and had been unfairly and illegally condemned, for he wanted her to believe the best about him. What he really wanted to tell her, but did not dare, was how much he still loved her and wanted her here with him now in his hour of need. *Oh Ruth!* He had wanted to marry her and live as quietly as his personality would allow, somewhere where they could bring up children. He regretted the potential children. Instead he wrote: *I take comfort in having known your friendship . . . As long as I have breath in my body I will always be your loyal and obedient friend.*

It wasn't much for nearly two hours' effort, but it was as close as he dared come to a declaration.

He sealed it and directed it and intended to give it to his keeper, a man called simply John. He opened his Bible then to the gospel of John which was a particular favourite and began reading, hoping for a more positive outlook.

The turnkey opened the door and Roger looked up. 'Visitors for you Mr. Strange.'

Two clergymen entered the cell, Puritan ministers. They were both known to him: John Arrowsmith, the very ordinary minister from King's Lynn and the very fat Thomas Thorowgood of Little Massingham who had assisted Sir Hamon when he had fled from the Roundhead troops.

He felt pleased to see them, for they were familiar faces, the first he had seen since coming to London. He got up from the stool and came forward, shaking their hands warmly and inviting them to sit down, which they did, Thorowgood on the bed and Arrowsmith on the stool. Roger perched on the corner of the table.

'My good sirs, you are well come. How came you to be in London?'

'The Assembly of Divines at Westminster,' Thorowgood explained. 'We heard about you. Indeed not only are you of much interest in Lynn, but all London is talking about you. So we decided to come and see you and offer what comfort we could.'

'You are kindness itself,' Roger said smiling, but he observed them closely. Thorowgood smiled, his usual genial self, and patted his overlarge belly. John Arrowsmith, though, seemed to be ill-at-ease. Perhaps he had not wanted to come. 'Do you have news of my father? He was arrested on my account by Colonel Walton.'

'They let him go,' Thorowgood replied. 'Had nothing on him. Couldn't prove anything. He is back in Hunstanton.'

Roger closed his eyes in relief and thanked God in his heart.

Arrowsmith said: 'A terrible thing, war, Mr. L'Estrange. I hear you are to be hanged.'

Roger looked at him in some surprise at the lack of tact. 'Thursday,' he confirmed.

Thorowgood was shocked. 'My God! 'Tis Tuesday today!' Indeed it was the last day of December. 'I hope you are in good standing with God.'

'I have done nothing wrong,' Roger replied. 'I acted in accord with the dictates of war.'

'Well indeed, it is a great pity you are to—er—um—that is that you are not to be freed.' Thorowgood had never been on one side or the other, but it did not do to make that known.

Arrowsmith glared at him and Thorowgood stumbled into silence.

'I fought for the King. There is no shame in that. But I hardly expected to be freed,' Roger told them.

'Well there is one way you could find yourself a free man, sir,' Arrowsmith said carefully.

Roger's eyes narrowed suspiciously. 'How?'

'By taking the Covenant.'

Roger's eyes widened. So that was it! He had to become a Puritan like those hypocrites who had sentenced him. 'No.' he said flatly.

Both men studied him. Thorowgood turned watery grey eyes on him. 'But just think, Mr. L'Estrange. You could live out your life peacefully on the Continent with other Royalists.'

Roger stood up from his perch on the table, a good deal grieved. 'Why on earth would I want to do that?' he demanded. 'That really would make me a traitor. If I were to take the Covenant, I would be betraying my King and my family and my faith. No.'

'But you must see how convenient it would be.'

'I thank you for your concern, gentlemen, but even if I changed my religion, it would not stop me serving my King. For I know he sits on his throne by Divine right. If I changed my religion to save my neck, do you think I should have changed what I really believed to be true? No, sir, I would be a liar and a hypocrite and I thank God, I am neither. I am a believer in the Anglican faith, gentlemen and, furthermore, I am prepared to fight—yes, I will die for my King.'

Arrowsmith stood up, irritated. 'Sir, you are a fool.'

'Perhaps,' Roger retorted, 'But I will deny neither my King nor my faith, though I die for them. And if I should be freed, I would not live my life in exile. I would return to fight for my King while there is still breath in my body.'

'Is that how you will feel when you are dangling at the end of a rope?' Arrowsmith demanded, angry.

'I will. For I will not give up my integrity.'

Thorowgood also stood, his disappointment showing in his face. 'Do you have letters to be conveyed to Norfolk when we return?'

Roger gave him the letters he had written to his family and also the one to Ruth.

Thorowgood tucked them in a concealed pocket. 'Would you like us to pray with you, sir?'

Roger's eyes met his. 'No, sir, but I thank you for your kind offer.'

'Then may God go with you, sir,' Arrowsmith said, but he was clearly rattled.

'And with you, gentlemen.'

As they left him, he seethed with anger.

FORTY-EIGHT

London, January 1645

On the same day, Roger sent another petition to the House of Lords. Surprisingly, it had effect, for immediately they sent for the judge-advocate Doctor John Mills to come to the House and present to their lordships the charge for which Roger had been sentenced.

Doctor Mills was unhappy. On the first day of January he made his appearance in the House of Lords dressed in customary black, his grey-white beard hanging down over his black robes. He did not have the requested charge. 'Forgive me, my lords, but I have not had the time to draw up the charge yet.'

The Earl of Northumberland, Algernon Percy, who came from a Catholic family and had once been King Charles's Lord High Admiral but had been one of the first to join the Parliamentarians, stared down at Mills with dark piercing eyes. 'Yet there has been a trial, Doctor Mills and I understand that Mr. L'Estrange is condemned.'

'That is correct, my lord.'

'Is Mr. L'Estrange, then, condemned and the charge not yet drawn up? Or perhaps you intend to execute him in the interim?'

'I shall have the charge ready in two days, my lord.'

'And when is he to be executed?'

'The warrant is out for his execution tomorrow, my lord. The authority of the court expires then.'

Henry Grey, the Earl of Stamford leaned forward, his eyes bulging with anger. 'How dare you to do this, sir?' he demanded. 'This House has reprieved him!'

Doctor Mills had not been aware of this, but he was not fazed. 'My lord, I have an order from the Commons that no reprieve shall be allowed without *both* houses agree.'

'This is preposterous!' Stamford fumed.

Northumberland agreed. 'Something ought to be done about this!'

'We must confer with the Commons,' Stamford declared.

But the House of Commons did not want to confer. They fully intended to make an example of Roger L'Estrange and they did not want those interfering busybodies in the House of Lords to change that. Messengers were sent back and forth between the two Houses in an effort to arrange a conference and at last the Commons reluctantly agreed.

On Roger's side were Northumberland and Stamford from the Lords, while in the Commons Sir Henry Cholmondely, Sir John Corbett, Sir Edward Baynton and Sir John Evelyn, the diarist, also supported Roger's application, while both Arrowsmith and Thorowgood, the two worthies who had visited him in prison added their weight on his side. Doctor Mills and Robert Tichborne who had condemned him in the first place fought vigorously for his execution.

Lord Stamford brought to the Commons' attention that the gentleman, Roger L'Estrange had been condemned to die the following day.

'I am afraid, Lord Stamford, that this House has this morning voted that no private business be moved for the next ten days, as is our custom at this time.'

Stamford's eyes blazed. 'But the gentleman is condemned to die without even a charge being drawn up! Surely that is not the way of English justice!'

Robert Tichborne said: 'This man was tried and found guilty. It does not matter that a charge has not been drawn up. He is a traitor and a spy and should suffer as such.'

'But it is illegal!' Stamford replied.

Lord Northumberland came to his feet. 'We have received a communication from Lord Essex enclosing a letter by the hand of Prince Rupert—' a groan from the assembled members and Northumberland raised his voice to be heard '—which Lord Essex says—and I quote—"*I would think we should heed.*" I shall read the letter:

' "*Prince Rupert to the Earl of Essex.*

' "*Oxon, 1st January 1644*

' "*My Lord,—the occasion of my sending unto you at this time is the Report of one Mr Roger L'Estrange, his being condemned to death at London upon a charge of having undertaken somewhat for the reducing of Lynn to his Majesty's obedience. If the person be found guilty of any treachery as having been engaged anywise on your side, I shall not interfere. But if not I should be very sorry that any bloody examples should be begun at this season contrary to that fair quarter which hath hitherto been observed on his Majesty's part in this unhappy war. For a particular conclusion of which no man prays more heartily than—Your Lordship's servant, Rupert." '*

'Clearly,' Northumberland went on, 'Prince Rupert threatens revenge if we proceed illegally in this matter. And as Lord Essex advises, perhaps we should heed that threat.'

'Idle words!' Doctor Mills cried jumping to his feet. 'The man is a traitor and a spy! And what revenge, pray, can the King have on us?'

Northumberland eyed this odious bloodthirsty little man with disdain. 'He can treat our prisoners in the same way,' he replied tartly.

'We should vote on it,' Sir Henry Cholmondely advised.

'We moved no further business,' Robert Tichborne reminded him.

There was a chorus of agreement from those against a reprieve.

Sir John Corbett came to his feet. 'I was judge-advocate at Mr. L'Estrange's court martial before Doctor Mills replaced me,' he told the Houses. 'And I found his defence well-argued and correct in points of law. In my opinion, he does not deserve to die.'

'In my opinion, he does,' Tichborne roared. There is too much of this kind of thing going on.'

'But this is war, sir!' Corbett retorted. 'You must expect 'this kind of thing' in war. The gentleman is a Royalist. He has never claimed to be anything else. His loyalties, rightly or wrongly, are with the King. He will, of course, act in accord with those loyalties, just as we act in accord with our own loyalties. It is a matter of conscience.'

'That is so,' the reverend Thorowgood put in unexpectedly and everyone turned their attention to him.

'Who are you, sir?' Lord Northumberland inquired.

'I am Thomas Thorowgood, rector of Little Massingham. The Reverend John Arrowsmith seated beside me here—' he waved his hand in Arrowsmith's face, '—and myself visited Mr. Roger L'Estrange in his cell and tried to persuade him to take the Covenant to save himself. But even if it would mean saving his life, he would not do so, for, says he "my loyalties are with the King and I should be a hypocrite if I changed my faith without believing in it." That, sirs, I think you will agree, is a man with a conscience before God.'

'He is an enemy and a traitor,' Doctor Mills insisted, his voice rising in anger almost to a squeak. 'He has been found guilty of treason. He should die. He has been sentenced.'

'That sentence is illegal,' Corbett retorted. 'You know it is. You did not even hear his defence!'

A general uproar broke out now and it was some time before they quietened enough for Sir Edward Baynton to say his piece. 'It occurs to me, gentlemen, that Mr. L'Estrange should be reprieved for the time being as their lordships suggest, until a charge has been drawn up.'

Northumberland hid a smile. This would not be to the liking of the opposers he knew, for a reprieve now would cost them their momentum and the condemned man may actually have his life after all.

Tichborne came to his feet instantly. 'No! I say to you gentlemen that the man is condemned as a traitor and a spy and as such he should not live to repeat the offence. Traitors should die. It is the law. There is no need for a reprieve.'

Thomas Toll of King's Lynn, Sir Hamon's sworn enemy, now entered the fray. 'I know the man in question,' he said, his little grey eyes taking in everyone at a single glance, 'And I know his father, as does my honourable colleague Mr. John Percival here. And I dislike Sir Hamon L'Estrange, the defendant's father for certain wrongs he has done me. He is no friend of mind. But this I say to you, gentlemen, Sir Hamon L'Estrange and all his sons, including the defendant, are known for their loyalty to the King. There has never been any suggestion that any of them have swerved in their allegiance, nor has there been any suggestion that Mr. Roger L'Estrange has been anything other than a king's man. He cannot be a traitor, by the definition of law, for he was never of the Parliamentarian party. I think that there should be further discussion on his case and I think, therefore, that he should be reprieved until this can be carried out.'

There was a short stunned silence, for quite a few, Northumberland included, were aware of Thomas Toll's anger at Sir Hamon L'Estrange for his treatment in Lynn. The gathering deteriorated into uproar as the opposing sides tried to shout each other down in a most uncivilised manner which had Lord Northumberland shaking his head sadly.

Finally Sir Edward Baynton made himself heard: 'I think we should put it to the vote,' he said. 'We have debated enough. Their Lordships have already voted for a reprieve. It is up to us to decide whether we are in agreement.'

So they voted.

§

All the while the two Houses debated, Roger paced the floor in his cell, unaware of the efforts being made for justice on his behalf. He had hoped his final appeal might save him. But time was slipping by. He had just a few short hours now until the execution.

The waiting, the hoping, the praying were agony. He felt so helpless, trapped in his small cell, cut off from the rest of the world. The churning in his insides would not let him rest, would not let him eat. He had no-one to turn to, no-one to vent his anger on. He paced restlessly, stopped, picked up the Bible, opened it and put it down again.

His life was almost finished.

It was late evening when the turnkey announced that Mr. Strange had a visitor and Roger turned to see Sir John Corbett standing at the door. His heart jumped into his mouth and for a long time Roger could only stare at him, searching Sir John's impassive face for any clue. Then he remembered his manners. 'Well come, sir.' His voice croaked and he could not manage more as he indicated with a wave of his hand that his visitor, the judge-advocate as he had been, should sit.

Corbett declined. 'Mr. L'Estrange, I have just come from the Commons.'

Roger could not speak. This was it, then.

'I have to tell you, sir, that you have been reprieved for fourteen days.'

Roger bit his lip to stop himself bursting into tears of gratitude. Instead he took a deep shuddering breath.

Sir John went on: 'You have Lord Northumberland and Lord Stamford to thank, primarily, I think for bringing it to the attention of the Lords, first and then by insisting on a conference with the Commons. The Reverends Thorowgood and Arrowsmith also spoke up for you. And so did a certain Thomas Toll. You know him, I think. It was a hard struggle, but the vote was for a reprieve.'

Roger could not take in all the words, all the names. All he could think of was that he had been reprieved. He took Sir John's hand and shook it. 'Thank you, Sir John.' His voice did not seem to be his own and it vibrated alarmingly.

Sir John turned to go and then turned back. 'I wanted to bring you the news myself, for, sir, I tell you this, I would not have condemned you to death. It was not lawful, as I think you know. It was this that gave you your reprieve. Your defence, sir, was well conducted and your efforts on your own behalf have helped you. A letter was received from Lord Essex containing Prince Rupert's letter concerning you which must have come by relay, the speed by which it came here and I daresay in due course you shall have a copy of that. Both his Majesty and the Prince speak well of you and threatened revenge if you were hanged. I think it helped.'

'Thank you, Sir John, for your efforts in my behalf,' Roger managed.

Sir John smiled then. 'I only pointed out the law,' he said self-effacingly, but Roger could tell that he had spoken up for him. 'But I am away now to my supper.'

Roger shook his hand and thanked him again and Sir John Corbett left him.

Alone now, as the daylight faded, Roger sat down on the bed, as he tried to assemble his thoughts and found he was shaking violently. He began to pray, to thank God and, quite suddenly, he wept.

FORTY-NINE

Norfolk, January 1645

Alice poked at the fire beside her. She sat at the end of the settle in the big fireplace, for it was warm there, but nothing was capable of dispersing the icy hand that gripped her heart.

She had lost children before. Little children. Little Jane had been the worst for she was nine years old when she died of fever. The other three had been babes and that had been bad, but Jane was her dear sweet little girl. However, they had all had natural deaths. Indeed, who expected all their children to live?

Roger, though, was a man grown and the grief she felt was on the same level as little Jane. And it was so unjust. Her dear handsome, brave son, taken by the hangman. It broke her heart.

Anne sat down beside her and put her arm around Alice's shoulders in a comforting gesture. 'He will have written to us,' Alice said to her, but not looking at her. 'He will have said goodbye to us.'

'I am sure he will, Mother,' Anne said soothingly. She was a good girl, Anne. The kind of daughter-in-law any woman could wish for. She had lost children herself, John and Edward, both babies, but she now had four surviving sons and another child due in a few months.

Alice nodded. 'Children bring you grief, Anne.'

'Roger did not intend to bring you grief, Mother.'

'No. But he has. And his folly could have cost us our dear Sir Hamon.'

'Colonel Walton is a just man, I am sure of it.'

'But not, it seems, those men in London.'

She heard Sir Hamon come into the room and as he sat down opposite her on the other settle, she raised her eyes to him. He had aged ten years in the last few weeks, she thought. His skin had lost the glow of the sun which had burnished him, and it now had a grey tinge. His blue eyes were faded, sad and red-rimmed.

'He was a brave boy, madam,' he said gently to her. 'He will have gone bravely.'

Alice swallowed. 'I know.' Tears again rolled down her cheeks in an unstoppable flood.

'A foolish boy, I know, but a brave boy. He gave his life for his King.'

'May we have a service for him in the church, Sir Hamon?' Anne asked.

'I see no reason why not. I will ask the rector. Would you like that, my love?' he asked Alice.

Alice nodded, unable to speak. And suddenly Sir Hamon stood up as if unable to keep still. He began to pace the room. 'If only he had listened to me! That brave, foolish, *stupid* boy! I *told* him not to do anything stupid. I told him. He said he would go to Newark and join Cartwright's troops there. That should have kept him out of trouble. What in the name of all that is sacred possessed him?'

Alice looked at him and managed a watery smile. 'He was your son, my love,' she said gently.

§

Two weeks later the reverend Thomas Thorowgood stood in the winter sitting room at Hunstanton Hall, warming his nether regions in front of the fire.

Sir Hamon met him warmly. He had affection for him and he remembered the help he had once given him. 'Sir you are well come.'

Thorowgood said: 'I bring letters for you from London. From your son.'

Sir Hamon's heart missed a beat. 'From Roger?'

'Yes, sir. Master Arrowsmith and myself took the opportunity to visit him after his trial.'

'We have suffered a great loss, Mr. Thorowgood.'

'A loss, sir?' Thorowgood frowned. 'Then you have not heard? My dear Sir Hamon! Your son was reprieved.'

Sir Hamon stared at him in disbelief. 'Reprieved? He did not hang?'

'No, sir. They reprieved him for fourteen days. And that means he may well not hang at all.'

Sir Hamon stood quite still, trying to take it in. He took a deep breath and released it slowly, looking up to the ornate ceiling, then closed his eyes and thanked God in his heart. Then after a long time he brought his focus back to Thorowgood who stood quietly waiting, a large grin across his face. Sir Hamon's lips quivered. He took Thorowgood's hand again, clasping it in both of his. 'Thank you, sir. How came this about?'

So Thomas Thorowgood related the events surrounding Roger's

trial, verdict and sentence, particularly emphasising his own part in the proceedings, but not forgetting all those who had made efforts to obtain a reprieve for him.

'I have a great deal to thank you for, sir,' Sir Hamon said when he had done. 'I am doubly in your debt.'

Thorowgood nodded in acknowledgement, but he said: 'Only doing what I think to be right, Sir Hamon.'

'And Thomas Toll! I can hardly believe it!'

'You and he may be on opposite sides in this war, sir, but that does not preclude him from doing what he thinks is right. None of us wanted to see the young man hang. But here, I have the letters.' He felt in the capacious pocket of his coat and held out a parcel of letters to Sir Hamon who took them carefully. He wanted to open them immediately, but good manners stopped him.

'I only wish others could have had the same outcome. The Hothams, father and son, were beheaded. And you no doubt heard about Archbishop Laud.'

'No?'

'He was beheaded on the tenth of this month, sir. Just before I left London.'

Sir Hamon shook his head in dismay.

Thorowgood stood up to leave, and Sir Hamon was jogged into remembering his manners. 'You will stay to sup, sir?'

'I will not, Sir Hamon, I thank you. I wish to be home this evening. So I'll bid you a good day, sir.'

As soon as he had gone, Sir Hamon went in search of his wife and found her in their bedchamber, sitting disconsolately by the fire, staring down into its depths.

'We have had a visitor, my love,' he told her.

'Oh?' She looked at him then, trying to be interested.

'It was the reverend Thorowgood. He is lately come from the Assembly of the Divines in London.'

'Oh.'

'He brings letters from Roger. Sweeting, Roger was reprieved.'

It took several seconds for the news to permeate Alice's distraught brain. She turned questioning brown eyes upon her husband and took a shuddering breath. 'Reprieved? You mean, he's alive?'

'He is.'

She closed her eyes, her hand coming to her mouth as she began fresh tears. She held out her other hand to Sir Hamon who dropped to his knees in front of her and took her hand in his. 'Oh, thank God!'

§

Dame Barbara Pell opened her eyes as she heard the imperious knocking somewhere else in the house. She had gone to bed early with a sick headache and had slept for most of the day but it was not dark yet. Indeed the sun, at the low angle of winter, poured into the chamber window and onto her ladyship's face. It hurt her eyes and she turned away from it, temporarily blinded.

The pain had gone, but she felt disorientated, muzzy headed and not quite in control of her thoughts. She was pleasantly warm, for although she was fully clothed, her maid must have covered her with a thick eider down quilt.

Her mind wandered. With Ruth married for more than a year with a son and baby on the way, Dame Barbara was satisfied. It would have been good for Ruth to have married into the aristocracy, she reflected, thinking momentarily of that rogue Roger L'Estrange with something almost akin to regret. That was something she did not quite agree with her husband about. However, Charles Calthorpe was a good and decent man, a God-fearing man and the Calthorpes were not nobodies in Norfolk. She was a Calthorpe herself and her son-in-law was a member of the extended family. Her other daughter Catherine had also married a Calthorpe, John, rector of Hickling. She wondered idly what relationship Charles Calthorpe had to Ruth, other than that of husband of course, and lost track at second or third cousins several times removed.

But little Charles was a beautiful child, dark hair and eyes like his mother. And already Ruth was pregnant again. Added to the other grandchildren, Barbara had become the matriarch to quite a brood.

On that happy thought she was drifting off towards sleep again when there was a scratching at the door and her maid entered.

The maid curtseyed. 'John the footman sent me, madam. The Reverend Thorowgood is here. He asked to see Sir Valentine, madam, but seeing as he hin't here, would madam care to see him?'

Sighing, Lady Barbara sat up and was obliged to wait while the room stopped spinning. '"*Is not*", Mary,' Lady Barbara corrected yet again. 'The Reverend Thorowgood?' He was always a welcome visitor. 'Very well. Help me up.'

The maid came forward and put shoes on Dame Barbara's feet,

straightened her dress and pinned her cap on her head. The maid supported her as she stood and then feeling more certain of herself, she dismissed the maid and went downstairs a little unsteadily.

She tried to smile when she saw him, for she liked Thorowgood. She bobbed a very small curtsey. 'Sir?'

'Madam. I trust you are well?'

'You find me a little under the weather, sir. Would you care to be seated?'

Thorowgood sat. 'I am sorry to hear it, madam. I asked to see Sir Valentine.'

'I believe he has gone out, sir.'

'Well then I shall not detain you, madam. Seeing that you are unwell.'

Barbara also sat before her legs gave way. 'I will ask the servant to bring some refreshment.'

'Not for me. I am passing through merely. I have letters for Mistress Ruth,' he said. 'From Mr. Roger L'Estrange. I did not know what to do with them, seeing that she is now Mistress Calthorpe. I thought it best to bring them here and let Sir Valentine deal with them. Perhaps I could give them into your keeping, madam?'

Barbara's eyes widened. 'Yes, of course, I will see to it,' she said and held out her hand.

Thorowgood placed two packets in her hand, both sealed with red wax and both addressed to Mistress Charles Calthorpe. She looked at them curiously. A strong cursive hand, she thought inconsequentially. She wondered what was inside them. 'I will give them to my husband,' she said and tucked them away in the pocket inside her skirts. 'Are you well Mr. Thorowgood?'

'I have been to London for the Assembly of the Divines, madam,' he told her. 'I did call in to see the unfortunate Mr. L'Estrange.'

'He is hanged, then.'

'No indeed, madam. He was reprieved. He did not deserve to hang, for he has not done anything to warrant it.'

She made no comment, for she was well aware that her husband did not agree.

He stood up, evidently satisfied that he had achieved what he had come for. 'I wish to be home in Grimston before it becomes dark.'

When he had gone, Dame Barbara took the letters over to the fire, intent on burning them but as she looked down at them in her hand, she hesitated, unsure.

Would she regret the day she burned the letters?

Her disorientated brain could not cope with the decision, so she slipped them into the pocket inside her petticoat and with a grateful sigh went back upstairs to her chamber.

FIFTY

Newgate Prison, London

'What are they saying in the taproom about me?' Roger demanded of Henry Dryden.

Dryden pulled a face, reluctant to say.

'If you do not tell me Dryden, by God I will knock your teeth down your throat!' The effort he put into the threat started him coughing and he coughed until he was exhausted.

'I doubt you have the strength, L'Estrange,' Dryden retorted drily, but he backed up to the door anyway.

'Damned prison,' Roger grumbled, pulling the blanket around his shoulders again. Despite the fire it was bone-chillingly cold and he shivered violently. Dryden's demur made him furious in his weakened state. Not that he had not heard whispers, but once it was out in the open he could set the matter straight. 'Tell me, damn you. I want to know.'

Henry Dryden sighed and ventured further into the cell again. 'They are saying—and you won't like this—they are saying that L'Estrange is false.'

Roger swore profanely and Henry Dryden skipped out of range again just in case he carried out his former threat. 'Don't they know I nearly hanged?'

'They think because you got reprieved that you have friends in high places.'

'I do. The King and Prince Rupert!'

'Well, they think Northumberland—hell L'Estrange, I don't know!'

'I hope you put them right.'

'They don't say anything to me, but whisper it. They know I'm your friend, see. They say the Hothams did not get a reprieve.'

John Hotham had been beheaded on the day Roger was to have been hanged and his father the following day. Roger shuddered at the mention of them and coughed again.

'Well they were guilty of treason. They switched sides. I was not. I've always been a King's man.' He coughed again, a harsh barking cough. He was weak and feverish.

'You are ill,' Dryden said.

'You know I am. 'Tis this accursed place. Everyone is ill here. If only I could get out!'

'You have your life.'

'Such a life! Imprisoned in Newgate! And if this goes on, I'll die here.'

Henry Dryden evidently thought him over dramatic, for all he said was: 'Well, I'm for my supper. You coming?'

Roger shook his head. He had no wish to mix in company with men who thought him a traitor. Besides, he was not hungry.

Henry Dryden left and Roger staggered over to the fireplace to put more wood on the fire and then went to sit down at the table, picked up his pen, dipped it into the ink bottle and squared his paper. Then he wrote a petition for liberty to the House of Lords. If he were not guilty of treason, of course, he should have been freed, not just reprieved. But he did not take that route. Instead he implored mercy, saying that he had '*an indisposition of health upon him and much strengthened in prison.*'

He folded the paper, sealed and addressed it and set about writing to his father. The King, before all the troubles, had set up a postal service of sorts and it met with some success, although not wholly reliable. If an acquaintance was going to the same place as the letter, that would be a surer carrier. He hoped the letter would reach Hunstanton, but he was by no means certain of that.

Then he wrote to Ruth yet again at her father's house. She had not replied to his other letters, but perhaps she had not received them. Or perhaps she did not want to remember a romance so long ago now. Perhaps as a married lady she would not think it proper to receive letters from a past suitor. But he persisted. He could not let go of her in his heart.

A few days later the reply came back from the Lords with an order for '*such accommodation as may stand with the security of his person.*'

They were not going to release him.

He sank into deepest depression. His life stretched before him empty and short. Empty because there was nothing in Newgate of any worth. Short, because he could not hope to live a long life in such a place, deprived of sunlight, fresh air, decent food, exercise and most of all, companionship. He missed his family with surprising acuteness. And Ruth was a continual ache.

Even worse, outside the war raged on and he was no part of it.

He received letters from his family. His father told him again what an idiot he was and he hoped he had learned his lesson, but he was glad he still lived.

Roger was beginning to regret that he still lived. Perhaps he should have let them hang him and put an end to his miserable existence.

His mother was more encouraging. She gave him news of home, of the way the seasons progressed, whether the new sheep had produced lambs this year, the horses. The wheat and barley fields ploughed, harrowed and ready for sowing when the weather permitted.. The beer making, bread making. She told him that his nephews were well and turning into fine strapping lads. She told him that Ann was pregnant again and that she would like a girl to go with her sons. A woman liked to have a daughter, his mother said.

It was small-talk and it was painful, because it reminded him of what he had lost and it made him ache for home, but at the same time he needed it.

He had the occasional visitor. Sir Charles Mordaunt visited him one day.

Roger was pleased to see him. 'Charles! What on earth are you doing in London?'

'You haven't heard then?'

'Heard what?'

'I lost all my estates.'

Roger frowned. 'All your estates in Massingham? Why, what did you do?'

'They thought I was in league with you and your scheme for re-taking Lynn.'

'They know that is not the case. I made it clear in my trial.'

'Your trial details have not reached Lynn. They only know you were found guilty and reprieved. It pleased Colonel Walton to think I was part of your scheme.'

Yet another thing to lay at his door. Was there no end to the reverberations of his folly? 'I'm so sorry, Charles.'

Mordaunt shrugged. 'They are thieving bastards. If you had been successful I would have been with you, so in a way they were right. Perhaps when the war is over, the estates will be returned to me.'

He stayed the afternoon with Roger, engaging in talk about the war, and when he left Roger was sorry to see him go. Charles had been a good friend. Even now, with the loss of his estates he had no rancour. Roger was humbled and at the same time felt guilty that others should suffer for his actions.

The Reverend Thorowgood also visited him with Arrowsmith each year when they came to London for the Assembly of the Divines at Westminster and he always brought letters from home for which Roger was particularly grateful.

To stop himself going mad with the conditions in Newgate, Roger turned to his pen and began writing.

Writing kept him sane. He wrote letters of thanks to those who had helped him. He wrote to his family and received replies. He wrote to Ruth and heard nothing from her. He wrote over a hundred appeals to be released, including copies of his commission from the King and John Corbett's comments about him.

He also wrote more creatively, particularly a poem, a cavalier song, with the title *Loyalty Confined* and beginning: *Beat on, proud billows; Boreas blow.* It was a proud defiance of his prison bonds which he expressed as:

That which the world miscalls a jail,
A private closet is to me;
Whilst a good conscience is my bail,
And innocence my liberty:
Locks, bars and solitude together met,
Make me no prisoner, but an anchoret.

He kept his devotion to the King uppermost in his mind:

What though I cannot see my King,
Neither in prison or in coin;
Yet contemplation is a thing
That renders what I have not mine:
My King from me what adamant can part,
Whom I do wear engraven on my heart?

He even tried to think of his confinement as something of a protection.

Here sin for want of food must starve,
Where tempting objects are not seen;
And these strong walls do only serve
To keep vice out and keep me in:
Malice of late's grown charitable sure
I'm not committed, but kept secure.

They could imprison his body, but they could not change what was in his heart.

My soul is free as ambient air,
Although my baser parts immew'd
Whilst loyal thoughts do still repair
T'accompany my solitude;
Although rebellion do my body binde,
My King alone can captivate my minde.

Finally satisfied with it, he called his jailer, his 'keeper' as he called him, the man John.

'Can you have this taken to the printer's?' he asked and of course rewarded him well.

John grinned. He had taken other bits and pieces to the printer for Roger and it was always worth his while.

While *Loyalty Confined* expressed the proud defiant cavalier spirit, the reality was a good deal different. He chafed against confinement which, to one of Roger's temperament, was excruciating. There was nothing he could do about it. As a condemned man, still technically under the sentence of death, his cell was all but solitary confinement. He was no longer allowed in the taproom which was for prisoners awaiting trial, although some of them, like Henry Dryden, did visit him.

He was thirty-one now and his youth was being wasted in inactivity. He did occasionally reflect that he might actually have been dead by now, like the Hothams, beheaded on Tower Hill, but at times even his natural optimism deserted him and he wondered if he would indeed live his life out in this place.

He had as much comfort as money could buy him, yet conditions were basic. No matter what the weather outside might be, his cell had just two temperatures: cold and freezing and the small fire he was allowed only just about took the chill off, but did little to dispel the damp for water ran down the walls constantly. It was a miserable existence, at best and at worst life-threatening as one sickness followed another, giving him fevers, stomach cramps and chest-rattling coughs. His general health was fading fast and he knew that not much longer and he would be dead anyway.

He struggled to keep positive, yet every thought brought him into depression. If he thought of home, of Norfolk, he missed his family with a physical ache he would never have thought possible when he was with them.

Then there was Ruth. He knew she was married with a brood of children, but the fancies that near-isolation in desperate conditions bred made him focus on her. He had truly loved her, loved her still, but she remained out of reach on the edge of his memory. Sometimes he would remember a snatched conversation, hear her laugh and she was there with him, but as he tried mentally to grasp the image, it fled, like clutching at a cloud. His heart ached for all that he had lost, his freedom, which was his life, his love. In despair he would sink into the blackness that Newgate nurtured.

Dear God, I must get out of this place before I die of consumption or I go totally insane!

FIFTY-ONE

Dersingham, Norfolk, February 1648

The last time Ruth had been in her mother's bedchamber had been the night her father brought her home from Lynn in disgrace five years ago. Little had changed. The chair was still by the fireplace where her mother sat that night as her father dragged Ruth into her presence. She could see now her mother's shocked face as Sir Valentine Pell informed her of Ruth's sins.

'Nursing?' her mother had cried in horror. 'Nursing *men*?'

Unrepentant, Ruth met her mother's eyes and repeated the same thing she had said to her aunt and uncle, to Roger and to her father. 'Should I not help those in distress? Is it not my Christian duty?'

'You see,' Sir Valentine said, not without a certain perverse satisfaction. 'There is no reasoning with her. But that is not the sum of her wrongdoing. She has been seen with that cavalier.'

'L'Estrange? Is this true Ruth?'

Ruth was spared the necessity of answering as her father thundered on: 'Aye. She's the talk of Lynn. If Calthorpe hears of this, he will not marry her. *No-one* will marry her!'

'I have done nothing wrong,' Ruth said quietly. She tried to sound confident, but frightened tears threatened her composure.

'You have been alone with a man with whom you are neither betrothed, nor married, Ruth,' her mother remonstrated. 'You know the reputation females have when they do not have a chaperone. Sir, I told you we could not rely on your sister and that *banker* of a husband to take proper care of her!'

'My sister Lead has no blame in all this. She and her husband locked this lady in her room, and she still escaped. She had another key cut! The duplicity of it!' He glared at Ruth.

Ruth said nothing. She had enjoyed six weeks or more of comparative freedom, a freedom she did not regret. And never, no matter what happened to her, could she regret knowing Roger.

Oh, dear God, what has become of him? Where is he?

Her father shook his head, fixing Ruth with a sorrowful stare. 'After all I have taught you, lady, you treat me like this. I am a laughingstock! Me! I am known for my beliefs, and you, my daughter, are out of control, consorting with a cavalier. A L'Estrange at that!' He shook his head. 'My enemies and even some of my friends, will be enjoying this!'

If you had not dragged me through the streets, shouting at me, perhaps they would not have known anything about it. Wisely, Ruth forbore to say what she was thinking, but stood mutely in front of them both.

'We will send her to Catherine at Hickling,' her father said.

'She is nearer to Charles Calthorpe there,' Lady Pell said. 'Perhaps he may decide on her anyway, and perhaps these doings in Lynn might not come to his ears.'

'I do not wish to marry Charles Calthorpe,' Ruth told them.

'Nonsense!' her mother snapped. 'Calthorpe is a very good match for you. And at your age, you cannot afford to be choosy.

Her father added: 'If you are hoping that rogue L'Estrange will come asking for your hand, you are much mistaken, lady. L'Estrange and all the other Royalists are at this moment on their way to Wisbech Castle where they will stand trial for their crimes against God and man.' He added for good measure: 'Besides which nothing on this earth would prevail upon me to give you to that traitor's brood!'

Bit by bit they had worn her down. They sent her to Hickling, to her sister, and even then she hoped that Roger had somehow escaped and would come for her. When he did not she sank into depression, convinced he had been condemned. No-one she asked could tell her anything. She was too far from Lynn for news to reach Hickling. Eventually, defeated, she had let them do what they wanted.

Charles Calthorpe had been willing to forgive all Ruth's past misdemeanours because he was in love with her. With Roger imprisoned she knew she had no choice. She was twenty-one and therefore securely on the shelf at a time when her sister and their contemporaries were married at seventeen. Pretty she may be, but what good were looks when one was grown old and haggard and *single?* Catherine pointed out. It wasn't that Ruth disliked Charles; on the contrary, she liked him very much for his kindness and mildness and courtesy, not least his calmness and good looks, all of which won her respect. But her heart belonged firmly to Roger.

'I do not love you,' she told Charles more than once.

'It doesn't matter. I shall win your love,' he had always replied. And in time she had indeed grown to love him. Not the all consuming once-in-a-lifetime love she felt for Roger, but a quiet love which brought her contentment, and they had settled in Great Massingham.

Roger's arrest at Appleton Hall, relayed to her by her maid, caused her to seek out her husband. 'I do not understand,' she said carefully. 'I thought the L'Estranges had been arrested after the siege and sent to Wisbech Castle. Were they released? Was that the outcome of the trial?'

He frowned, mystified. 'No. Did you not hear that the treaty of surrender gave them their freedom?'

No, she had not heard that. Her brother John, sister Catherine and her parents had deliberately kept that from her. At the time she had been angry with them, but she was married to Charles, with a son Charles, and another little one, her eldest daughter Joanna, on the way.

She took a deep breath and looked around her mother's bedchamber, surprised that so little had changed in the years since she had married. A deep sadness had settled over her as the memories came flooding back, a sadness that had become part of her being since she learned that Roger had been condemned to death as a traitor and a spy.

That was nearly four years ago. She drew in another breath. This would not do. She had come here for a reason, namely to search for the Bible she knew her mother kept, the one authorised by King James, for there was a scripture she particularly wished to look up. After all, she had not much else to do, since her mother had gone to Lynn, and her father was out too. Of all the times for them to be out! She had come to visit her parents, a journey of a few hours in the carriage. It was frustrating to find them gone to Lynn with her brother and his wife.

She clicked her tongue in annoyance as she cast her eyes about the familiar room. She could see no Bible, no book of any kind. It was the only book she knew to be in the house which was accessible to her, every other book being locked away in her father's library.

The room was very sparse. An old bed sagged noticeably in the centre. Probably the ropes beneath the mattress had stretched and needed tightening. Plain ancient bed hangings of an indiscriminate colour draped against blackened posts and kept out draughts. The chair, a bedside cabinet which contained the chamber pot, a table with an inkstand and paper, a chest of drawers which was taller than Ruth herself, and a large ornately carved oak chest. Despite Sir Valentine's protest at the ornamentation on the chest, Mama had insisted on keeping it, for it had been her mother's and her mother's before her. It probably dated to the time of the old queen. No doubt her sister Catherine, as the eldest daughter, would inherit it one day.

Perhaps the Bible was in the chest.

She went over to it and knelt down to it. With difficulty she pulled up the heavy lid, pushing it back until it rested against the whitewashed wall. Some clean linen—shifts, night-dresses, and night-caps, petticoats—seemed to fill the chest. It did not look as though the Bible were here.

Just in case, she pulled up the corner of the stack of neatly-folded garments and there, beneath them were letters at the bottom of the trunk. Intrigued, she put the garments aside and pulled out some of the letters in bundles tied up with ribbon or string. They were in her father's hand addressed to her mother, which meant they must have been from their courtship days. Ruth looked at them, curious, wondering if it would be too intrusive to read any of them, decided it would and put them back, stifling the intense curiosity that they had awakened. There were other letters. She recognised her own handwriting and smiled. Dutiful letters she had written from her now-home in Great Massingham. There were letters from various aunts and uncles. Her mother had kept everything.

And then, a letter addressed to herself in a hand she did not recognise. It was still sealed.

Puzzled, she stared at it, turned it over, in her hand. Why had Mama not given it to her? Who would write to her here? Unless . . ?

Her heart thudded suddenly and her insides lurched. With trembling fingers she broke the seal which bore no impression and spread out the sheet. The date was the thirty-first of December 1644, the address Newgate prison.

Her heart stopped inside her and then lurched on. Her eyes flew to the bottom of the page where he had signed it with a flourish: *Roger L'Estrange*.

Her heart thudded in her chest and her fingers trembled. They had kept this from her! He had written to her before he died, and they had kept it from her. She would never forgive them. Never!

Impatiently, she dashed tears away with the back of her hand, and began to read:

Dear Lady, I hope my letter finds you in better health than I am. By the time you read this I shall probably be already with the Lord, if he allows, for I am sentenced to hang on 2nd January. A fitting end, no doubt, although I have been unfairly and illegally condemned. But I assure you, whatever you may have heard, that I am no spy, nor turncoat and no traitor to my King, as I am sure you are aware. I acted, as I always have, in loyalty to my King and I have betrayed no-one.

I take comfort in having known your friendship, brief though that was. Perhaps at times in your life you will remember me kindly. As long as I have breath in my body I will always be your loyal and obedient friend, Roger L'Estrange.

It was so like him and yet not like him. She guessed how he must have laboured long over that letter and that he had not said what he wanted to say, perhaps for fear of compromising her good name if the letter fell into the wrong hands. She pictured him sitting in his cell, writing to her, perhaps his final thoughts being of her. Tears rolled down her cheeks. Her mother had not even given her this, his last letter. She should hate her for it, but she did not. As a mother herself now, she pictured her own little daughter in fifteen years' time. Would she have given the letter of an unsuitable suitor to her daughter? No, she would not.

Eventually she folded the letter and put it in the pocket inside her under-skirt. Then she looked to see if there were others. Yes, indeed. Stifling her tears, she found a handkerchief to blow her nose and wipe her eyes. Picking one of the other letters up, she opened that too.

This one was dated the 15th July 1647, Newgate. She looked at the date again. Sixteen-hundred-and-forty-seven. Her brain cleared. That was just last year! The realisation hit her. He was alive? Again her eyes searched the bottom of the page for his signature and there it was. He had not been executed at all!

Her heart thudded with such force that she had to take deep breaths to try and still it. He was alive! They knew it. Her Father, her mother, her husband, they all knew it and they kept it from her. All of them. All this time they let her think he was dead! Well, Charles she could forgive, because he was probably jealous of her friendship with Roger, but her mother and Sir Valentine she could not forgive. All this time she had thought him dead! Even Aunt Mary Lead and her sister Catherine had not told her he was alive!

Charles! Faith! He must never find out that she knew. And he must never know what had happened between her and Roger. Let him think it a mere friendship.

Realising that someone could come in and catch her at any moment, she read the first line of the letter, scanned the rest, which seemed to be an account of prison life and re-folded it. She found more letters from him, collected them all up and stuffed them in the pockets of her inner petticoat to read later, as the questions galloped through her brain. How was he still alive when he was to be executed? Why was he still in prison? She needed to read to find out, but she dared not tarry any longer lest a servant caught her and told on her. If that happened, she would be forced to give the letters back. Her mother, too, would be back soon.

Realising that her mother would know she had been in the trunk if everything was not exactly as she found it, she carefully replaced everything except the letters and left the room. Only just in time as her mother's carriage came lumbering noisily into the courtyard.

She could not find the solitude to look at the letters properly until the next day and she spent a sleepless night, thinking over what she had discovered. All this time she had thought him dead, only to discover that she had been lied to. Again. He had not died after all. She needed to find out how and why.

Back at home in Great Massingham the following day, she found her husband had gone out to Lynn and she saw her opportunity. Telling her servants that she had a headache and that she would lie down for a while, she locked herself in her chamber and began, opening all the letters and arranging them in date order.

She read of the injustice he had suffered. She read of the trial. She read then of how he had fought for and won a reprieve, but that he was committed for life in Newgate.

In later letters she read of the appalling conditions he had to endure, which was nothing compared to the ordinary less affluent prisoners. *Men are driven to madness in these confines.'* He wrote. '*It is solitary confinement, for I am condemned, and is worse than it might have been in the wards; there at least among the filth and the squalor is companionship.*' And he added: *'I shall die, I think if I do not get out of this place soon.'*

And through it all he told her of his enduring love for her.

More than once she wept. ''Tis too late, Roger,' she whispered into a tear-drenched handkerchief, 'I'm a married woman with a husband who loves me and whom I love.' *Oh Roger!* How she missed his cheeky grin, his impulsiveness, his joy of life! He was exciting, handsome, impetuous.

She thought about him languishing in prison; a free spirit such as he would chafe at the confinement. It must be agony for him. And all this while, though she had not written to him, he kept his love for her alive.

Carefully she refolded the letters and put them in a place she had in the lining of her own travelling chest. Even if someone searched they would not find them. Even servants could not always be trusted.

Her first impulse was to write to him, but as Charles arrived home at that moment, she had to wait.

Charles was in jovial mood, and her heart warmed towards him. Roger still had a corner of her heart, and always would have, but she also loved warm, generous, calm Charles, and could not now contemplate life without him.

'I've been thinking,' he said through a mouthful of mutton, 'I need to go to London on business. I thought we could all go, for my stay will not be short.'

She stared at him, wondering if it were God, or fate that was sending her to London just now. It sent a shiver down her spine. 'London? But Charles, I've never been further afield than Hickling!'

He swallowed his food. 'I know. I thought you would like to see London. But if you do not like to go, I shall go alone.'

'What is it like?' she asked, even though she already knew she would go with him.

'There is so much to do there and to see. I think you will like it. We can hire a house for a few months and we can take the children.'

'What business?'

'Now you know I cannot tell you that, my love. Why should you worry your head about my affairs?' He conveyed another piece of mutton to his mouth with one of the new-fangled two-pronged forks he had found and bought for her in Lynn. 'Perhaps you would make arrangements to pack up the house?'

'I shall see to it directly. When are we to go?'

But even as she said it, a plan formed in her mind.

'Will a week give you enough time?' He asked.

FIFTY-TWO

Newgate, London, March 1648

Sitting on the stool in front of the paltry fire, Roger coughed again and pulled the blanket closer about his shoulders. Nothing could dispel the chill in this God-forsaken place. He felt tired and old before his years, dispirited. He had received a letter from his mother, telling him news of home and homesickness overwhelmed him anew. He wanted to be back there with his family, even if briefly, to enjoy their tender love. Or he wanted to be back in the war. Perhaps both.

Deep depression had settled on him, robbing him of his customary good humour and optimism. Four long years he had lingered here. He was thirty-two now and his life was slipping by.

The keys clanked in the outer lock, but Roger did not look up.

John the keeper would want something but Roger could hardly be bothered with him. He did not want to see anyone. 'Visitor for yer.'

Roger did not get many visitors. Some had come to gawp at him, for it was an upper class pastime to come and laugh at the prisoners, but they did not want more than a few words of conversation. Newgate charged people admission fees (of course!) to come and see the inmates. Roger hated them for what they were. Real visitors in the last four years he could count on the fingers of one hand and the Reverend Thorowgood was among them. Each year he came for the Assembly of the Divines and always visited Roger two or three times while he was here. Even Henry Dryden had finally been acquitted and released and he missed him dreadfully.

John the keeper turned the key in the lock of the inner door and ushered the visitor inside before locking the door again.

Roger looked up, wondering who should be admitted to his room and was surprised to see a lone woman cloaked in black with a hood covering her face standing just inside the door. Hurriedly he threw off the blanket and came to his feet, mindful of his manners and almost falling over the stool in his haste. He could not imagine what woman could possibly want to visit him here. A few possibilities flitted through his mind. His mother was the first possibility on the list, but the woman was too tall. Anne, his brother's wife? No, she would never darken Newgate's doors; Nicholas would not allow it.

As he peered into the gloom to try to see who she was his heart started a slow painful thudding in his chest, robbing him of his breath and turning his insides. For he knew her. 'Ruth?'

She removed the hood and he had a view of her beautiful face, her dark eyes regarding him sombrely. His insides seemed to somersault, and despite his wretched state, his whole body reacted to her presence. He had been four long years in Newgate, and although women could have been bought, he had refused the offers John Smith the turnkey brought to him. He did not want their pseudo love.

'Mr. L'Estrange.' Her voice was soft, almost a whisper.

He stood staring at her, bereft of speech, trying to work out if his eyes were playing tricks on him and struggling with the turmoil her presence caused.

The last time he had seen her was the night before the siege ended five years ago. She had changed little in appearance, although she had the bearing of a more mature woman. Her hair was hidden beneath a stark white matron's cap, which he thought quite becoming, and her dark eyes darted over his face and then his clothes. Dimly he remembered that he had not shaved for two days, or washed, come to that, or bothered to brush his hair—he ran his hands through his hair hurriedly—and his clothes were not his best, either. He must look a shambles. Come to think of it the meat market probably looked and smelled better than he did!

'I—forgive my appearance, madam. I was not expecting visitors.' He managed a belated bow.

'No. I can see that.' She continued to study him, her wonderful dark eyes soft and moist, as though she could not tear them away from him, but then she looked about her. 'May I sit down?'

Remembering his manners somewhat belatedly, he bowed and motioned to the stool in front of the table. She sat in a rustle of black silk. He perched on the edge of the bed, nervous and anxious. His hands had begun shaking and he clasped them together between his knees lest she should notice. His mouth had gone dry.

She was so perfect, her skin so flawless, her hands and nails spotlessly clean, everything about her neat, tidy and smelling of roses. By contrast, he felt filthy in her presence.

Feeling that one of them ought to speak, he asked: 'Why have you come, madam?'

She took a moment to answer, those lustrous eyes looking into his as if she could read his soul, and his insides swooped all over again. He looked away lest she saw the torment there, the naked desire her presence awakened in him. 'I was in London. My husband has business to attend and we have taken a house.'

'Your husband is Charles Calthorpe?'

'Yes.' She looked down at her own hands, her brows drawn together, and he realised she was not as confident as she appeared. 'He is a good man, Mr. L'Estrange. He is good to me.' She took a deep breath. 'We have three children—Charles, Joanna and Hannah.'

He swallowed. *They should have been my children.* He said: 'Your husband is a rich man?' A stupid question, for she wore silk.

'A merchant. I want for nothing.'

'And you are happy?'

'My husband loves me and treats me well. Yes, I am happy.'

Silence settled between them. After what seemed to be a long time she said awkwardly: 'I thought you were dead.' She looked at him with that candid direct gaze and her lip trembled. It made her seem so vulnerable and aroused in him a sharp need to take her in his arms. 'I thought you had hanged,' she said and tears came into her eyes. 'They let me think you had hanged.'

Oh, please, no tears. His poor emotional state would not let him deal with tears. 'I nearly did. They reprieved me.'

'So I discovered—later.'

'I wrote to you.'

'I received nothing. I thought they had arrested you after the siege.

'No. Under the terms of surrender, we were all allowed to go free.'

She shook her head, becoming quite distressed. 'Then why? Why did you not come for me? Why did you not rescue me? I thought you were lost.' Her voice broke. 'I looked for you every day. When you did not come, I could hold out against them no longer. I felt sure that if you were free you would come and take me away.' She covered her mouth with her hand and closed her eyes on a sob.

Shocked at her outburst, he tried to explain. 'I came every day to the woods in Shernborne Road. Ruth, I did not know where to look.'

She struggled to compose herself. 'They sent me to my sister, and they gave me no peace. I tried to resist them, but I could not. They made me believe you were condemned. They forced me to marry Charles. If you had been there, I could have been strong. You would have strengthened me.'

He reached across and put his hand on hers, wishing he had discovered her whereabouts sooner. 'As soon as I discovered where you were, I did go Hickling,' he told her earnestly. 'I was a week too late.' He let go of her hand and stood up to go to the grate. He stared miserably at the smouldering wood, remembering the devastation he had felt at knowing she now belonged to another man. He put another log on the fire. 'You should have waited, had faith in me.' He looked back at her, and it was her turn to look away, her hand hiding most of her lower face.

'I should have waited,' she agreed simply.

Roger turned to come back to his place on the bed, and hesitated as she fumbled for her handkerchief. He desperately wanted to take her in his arms, to hold her tightly against him, to reassure her of his continued love, but although he did not think she would spurn him, he remembered that she was another man's wife. He loved her too much to compromise her. So instead, he returned to the bed and sat down again on it.

After a while she seemed to recover her equilibrium. 'What happened to bring you to this place?'

'You did not hear? I was betrayed into the hands of my enemies and accused of being a traitor.' And he told her the story.

When he had finished she said: 'I heard nothing of this. Only what I read in your letters.'

'You received my letters?'

'No.' She drew a shuddering breath. 'My mother kept them safe, and I found them, not two weeks since. When—my husband—wanted to come to London, I determined to see you.' After a pause she added: 'I thought a traitor was one who changed sides.'

'So did I. How wrong can one be? It turns out that a traitor is determined by viewpoint.'

'I could not think that you had changed sides.' She managed a watery smile. 'You were always the King's man and always will be. So how did you get reprieved?'

He smiled wanly. 'Friends in high places and others who were interested in justice. But you know this. You read the letters I sent you.'

Her eyes filled again, and he was afraid of another outburst, but she struggled for self-control. 'How could you not have known?' he asked because the silence that fell on them unsettled him.

She shrugged sadly. 'I do not see many people. We live in Great Massingham now. My husband goes to Lynn, but I do not go to Lynn. I hear no gossip. No-one told me'

'I see.' And he did see. He sighed, exhausted and sunk back into wretchedness. 'I might as well have died, for this is worse than death. To think I fought so hard to escape the hangman—for this!'

''Tis a terrible place.'

'It is.' There was no point denying it.

'And I can see you are ill.'

He shook his head in answer, not trusting himself to speak. Her kindness, her gentle words, her very presence, were too much for him.

She stood up. 'I am sorry. I have distressed you. Perhaps I should not have come. I ought to go.' She turned away from him and went to the door and he heard the key grating in the lock. John turnkey had been listening, and waiting!

He stood up too, realising that he had to speak. 'I am glad you did,' he said and he heard the traitorous crack in his own voice.

She paused, her face away from him, and he waited, expecting her to go but she turned to look at him. 'I will come again,' she said. Then she left him alone.

He was grateful for it, for she had opened the dam and he needed solitude.

FIFTY-THREE

London, March 1648

Ruth lay in bed beside her husband and stared at the ceiling in the darkness. Never in her life had she imagined a place as terrible as Newgate. His letters had not told her the half of it. Roger had bought himself the best luxury Newgate could offer but all his money had really bought was solitary confinement, she thought with disgust. A room which, despite a fire, was still icily cold, a stained flagstone floor, dirty brick walls and a stench which could render a pig unconscious.

Far worse than the conditions, however, was the sickness. She had been shocked by Roger's appearance. Not because he had not shaved. That was inconsequential, except that he was too depressed or too weak to want to bother. No, it was the colour of his skin, pale as lime wash, almost transparent and eyes so sunken the skin around them seemed bruised. His cheeks had hardly any flesh on them. He sat shivering beneath a blanket when she first saw him, so she knew he had a fever. The strong muscular young man he had been was gone.

He worried her. His depression was agonisingly evident in the droop of his once grinning mouth and the tears he struggled to keep under control. She remembered the lively, vibrant, optimistic cavalier with the ready smile and the flashing eyes of five years ago. The change was horrifyingly dramatic. He had lost hope. His words '*It would have been better if I had died*' kept repeating in her brain.

She had to get him out of there.

By the time the morning came she had formed a plan, but she could not do anything about it as Charles stayed at home all day. So she returned to Newgate two days later to find Roger shaved and washed and dressed in clean clothes and struggling to look less defeated. It was an improvement, but his skin was still grey, his cheeks still sunken, his lips chalky. However, when he saw her, a light leapt into his eyes, reflecting that for him, things had not changed. Her heart wrenched again not only with pity at his skeletal condition but with love for the man she used to know.

She gave the keeper a small amount so that he would leave them alone. He was to return in an hour to let her out.

'I didn't know if you would come again,' he told her and his blue eyes searched hers. Mindful of her marriage vows, she kept a respectable distance between herself and Roger, fighting the urge to give him a comforting embrace. Thankfully, he did not come towards her for she knew her willpower might not be strong enough to resist.

She scrutinised his face. 'Have you eaten today?' she asked briskly in the manner of a woman concerned about her child.

'Some pottage. It was better than usual. I found a piece of meat. At least, I think it was a piece of meat. It might have been something else!'

She wrinkled her nose, acknowledging the more positive tone in like manner. Pottage was a term which meant any kind of boiled slop as long as it contained oats. It was what the lower classes ate and sometimes it might even contain a sliver of meat.

'Surely you can buy something better than that!'

'I'm a condemned man,' he reminded her. 'There is little in the way of choice. Besides, I do not have that much money left.'

'Well, I have brought some good fresh bread and some cheese and some cold meat, ale too,' and she pulled out a bottle with a ground glass stopper. 'There are also two apples I bought from a girl yesterday.'

'Apples! Fruit I haven't seen in four years!' He moved some paper and the ink pot so that she could put her basket onto the table.

She took an apple out of the basket and held it out to him. 'Well, eat up, then!'

'Madam, I thank you. But you are not my mother!'

Without being asked, she sat down on the stool, looking meaningfully at the offerings on the table. 'How are you today, sir? You look a little better I think.'

He tore a lump off the round loaf and broke off a piece of cheese, taking them and the apple to the bed, yet he seemed reluctant to eat. Perhaps his illness had curbed his appetite. 'Better for seeing you, lady,' he said with a cheeky grin, sitting back on the bed and resting his back and head against the damp wall for the effort to sit upright was too much. He bit into the cheese with little enthusiasm.

'You don't look it to me!'

'You know you are a managing female,' he told her and his eyes held the old spark of humour so that she could not be cross with him. He was the same Roger.

In that moment she knew she still loved him, with the all-consuming madness of passion she had felt five years ago. It welled up in her from the depths of her being. She took a deep, steadying breath trying not to betray her emotions. She smiled briefly. 'It's part of being a married woman,' she told him archly. 'I have to manage a husband and children and a household. I fear I've become very *managing*!'

The old grin came back to him. 'I've been wondering how sweet young maids turned into nagging wives!'

'Now you know!' She sobered and lowered her voice to a whisper. 'I've been thinking. Roger, you've got to get out of here.' How easy it was to slip back into the old familiarity.

He also whispered, aware that the keeper probably even now had his ear pressed to the iron door. 'I know it. But the place is heavily guarded, impossible to escape. Believe me, I've looked at all the chances.'

'I could help you.'

He managed a short, bitter laugh, and forgot to lower his voice. 'How could you help me?'

She continued to whisper. 'What if I brought in some women's clothes for you to dress up in? You could leave with me, then.'

He shook his head, and continued in a very low voice: 'I would never get past my keeper. John knows me too well. Besides, he sees you in and out again.' He chuckled. 'Not only that, but I am quite a bit taller than you are, just in case it escaped your notice.'

Annoyed that he did not seem to grasp the benefit of her plan she continued in an angry whisper: 'Then we must bribe him handsomely to turn a blind eye.'

For a moment he was bereft of speech. 'Bribe the turnkey?' Then he laughed, which made him cough. 'What with, pray? This place has bled me dry.'

'I have money. Make it worth his while.'

He continued to laugh. 'Bribe the turnkey! With your money? Now I have heard it all! Woman, you are incorrigible!'

She did not laugh. 'I have money. I pawned a ring. I got forty guineas for it!'

He stopped laughing. 'Forty? That's a fortune.'

'It would have been more some years ago, but now that rings are banned, the pawnbroker said it was not worth much, so that's all he gave me. How much do you think we need to buy the turnkey?'

'Twenty ought to do it. But Ruth, you cannot pawn your ring.'

'It's mine to do what I wish with it. Besides, it was a very old ring.' She stood up and fished for the pocket she kept in her petticoats. She held a purse out to him. 'Here, I give it all to you. Make sure the deed is done before I come tomorrow.'

He was appalled. 'Ruth, I cannot take this.' Never in his life had he taken money from anyone, let alone a woman and he had no intention of doing so now.

Her eyes widened expressively. 'You have no choice, sir. Either you stay here and rot, or you take it. And let me tell you that if you die of consumption in here, Roger L'Estrange, I will never forgive you!'

'Then, fair lady, I will endeavour not to die.'

She laughed despite herself. 'Marry, but you are enough to try the patience of Job!' To make sure, she reached out and took his hand in hers, pressed the leather purse into his long bony fingers and closed them over it. The touch was meant as a means of making him take the money, but his familiar long fingers beneath hers made her heart begin thudding in her chest again.

His eyes, appearing dark blue in this light, never left her face as he raised her hand to his lips and kissed her fingers.

For a moment she stayed thus, with his lips lingering on her fingers, and time seemed to stand still. She was back in Lynn, standing with him in the shadow of Walter Coney's house, as he kissed her fingers then, when it was just beginning.

She pulled her hand away, remembering that she was a married woman. He put the offending purse back in the basket which was on the table. 'You have not considered,' he whispered seriously. 'If we are caught I would hang and you would be up before the court for helping me.'

She took a breath. 'Well, it occurs to me, Roger L'Estrange, that if you do not get out of here soon, you will be dead within six months anyway.'

'And you?'

She looked into his eyes. 'I don't think anything will happen to me.'

He said straightly: 'They hang men they view as traitors, but they burn women traitors at the stake.'

Her eyes widened in shock. His words had made her realise what she risked.

'Surely not!'

'Oh yes indeed. I cannot let you take this risk. It is far too dangerous.'

There was a long silence while her brain visualised someone standing on bundles of sticks and tied to a pole. She forced the thought from her head. Such things occurred too often for comfort. She knew he was right.

'It will work, though,' she said at last. 'If you can bribe John turnkey, it will work. No-one else pays visitors more than a cursory attention. And if you are dressed as a woman, how will they know it was you? Now, for the love of God, take the money!' She took it out of the basket and put it on the table.

His eyes searched hers. 'I shall repay you, Ruth.'

She shook her head and put her hand again on his. His hand was cold beneath hers. 'No sir, you shall not. I do not wish to be repaid. I have no use for the ring, as it is forbidden to wear it anyway, and will only cause me embarrassment. In fact, this will be our secret. You must promise never to divulge my part to a living soul.'

'My lips are stuck together like a limpet to a rock.' It was an easy promise. He would do nothing to hurt her. 'You are taking a terrible risk. You have more to lose than I do.'

She looked into his eyes. 'You think I would not risk all to save you?'

He shook his head. 'I am not worthy—'

'Roger! I do not want to hear it! Now then,' she became business-like and rose to her feet abruptly. 'I will see you tomorrow and bring the clothes with me.'

He stood up too and called John. 'The lady is leaving,' he said.

He turned to her and raised her hand to lips which burned against her skin. Reluctantly Ruth let go of his hand. She noticed he hid the purse from view. Satisfied, she went to the iron door but turned back to look at him again.

He stood straight, watching her with his intense gaze.

'Goodbye sir.' And she dropped a small curtsey.

FIFTY-FOUR

Roger spent a wakeful night, alternately pacing the dimly-lit cell, or lying down, trying unsuccessfully to sleep. However, the fever had left him and as his head cleared of the fog of sickness, the difficulties of the plan worried him.

His first worry was turnkey John Smith. He had been with him the whole four years since the reprieve and they had become friendly. John Smith was a decent sort. He treated Roger with respect, cared for him when he was too ill to care for himself, found an extra blanket, extra wood for the fire, extra candles and, on occasion, extra food. Furthermore, when Roger wanted some writing of his printed, John obligingly took it to the printers. For all of which services Roger paid him handsomely. At the same time Roger had learnt that times were hard for John and his family of twenty-one children, all of them still living. True, only ten children were still at home, which was a small tenement in the city, the others having variously gone into service, to sea, or married, but a turnkey's pay could not have been large. The extra money must have come in handy.

Roger offered him a sum tempting enough for John to let him go, enough to set himself up in some business or another. He had mentioned becoming a publican. Certainly the man would lose his job after this day's work and would need some kind of income and he knew John wanted to leave Newgate where he was almost as much a prisoner as Roger was. He hoped it would buy the man's help, for without it, he would be finished. However, he was not sure he could trust the man even then. Past experience had made him suspicious. Yet what choice did he have?

The second worry was, of course, capture. If he could get past John, there were other turnkeys at various stages on the way out. If any one of them suspected, the game would be up. Not only would he be returned to custody and his reprieve revoked, meaning he would hang, but Ruth would be viewed as a traitor. When he told Ruth she could be burnt at the stake, he did not exaggerate. That is what they did to women found guilty of treason. His blood ran cold at the thought. How could he put her in so much danger? Dear, brave woman that she was, already she had risked so much for him just in coming to this dreadful place.

Added to these worries, once he had left Newgate, assuming he would get that far, he could not go home to Hunstanton, for that would be the first place anyone would look for him and it would endanger his family once again. Understandably, his father would not take kindly to it a second time. As for joining the King's army, he had a vague idea that there was some activity going on in Kent connected to the riots there over Parliament banning celebration of Christmas, but exactly where and what it was all about he had no idea. He wondered vaguely if it might be possible to make some kind of effort to rescue the King from Carisbrooke Castle on the Isle of Wight where he had been imprisoned in November. Time enough to worry about that later.

Right now he knew he had to take the risk. He could not spend the rest of his life in Newgate. Or if he did, that time would be excruciatingly short. There was a world outside, and a war being fought, all without him. Just the thought of being on the outside of Newgate sent the excitement racing through his body.

However, his chief anxiety had to be Ruth, and just thinking about her being in peril made his insides turn over. By the time she arrived, soon after the gates opened in the morning, he had decided that he would not involve her. He had set upon other way.

As the key turned in the lock Roger's heart jumped into his throat, and his hands began to tremble. *It's the excitement*, he told himself, but as she came into his cell, his insides slid. She was heart-stoppingly beautiful, and totally unconscious of that beauty, or the effect it had on him. Even reminding himself that she was another man's wife did not curtail the desire he had for her.

She bobbed a curtsey, and he bowed and said: 'Madam, you are well come,' and all he could think about for that moment was the deep hypnotic colour of her eyes, the way her breasts rose and fell in the confines of her bodice, of her trim waist, of hair the colour of polished oak, hidden now beneath her cap. How he longed to see it loose, flowing down her back! He ached to kiss her pretty red lips, to feel the heat of her body through her clothes, to hold her against him.

'You have spoken to the turnkey?' Her words brought him back to the present.

He sat down again on the bed and she put the basket down on the table and unfastened her cloak, a plain black woollen travelling one. 'This is yours,' she said. Beneath it she wore another. She draped the first over the end of the bed. When he did not answer she raised an eyebrow.

'I have, but I am going alone. Ruth, I cannot involve you in this.'

She paused in the act of draping her own cloak on top of his. ''Tis already done,' she replied with false lightness. 'You cannot get out of here without me.'

He shook his head. 'The risk is too great. I go alone.'

She stood still, glaring at him, just the way she had so many years ago when he did something she disapproved of. 'Do you know what a risk I have taken for you?' she demanded, sitting down on the stool and leaning towards him.

'I do. But I will not allow you to risk your own life for me. The danger is too great. Never could I put you in such danger. I would rather stay here and rot.'

She pursed her lips disapprovingly. 'Well, I cannot leave you here to die for want of my help.'

He took both her hands in his and looked earnestly into her eyes. 'I know what you have done for me, what you have already risked. I am so grateful to you, and one day I will repay you. But this is something I will do alone.'

She looked down at her hands still resting in his, and he could see she was unable to resist his determination. However, plucky as she was, she gave it another try: 'You think to pass as a woman on your own, do you?' Her questioning gaze came back to his face. 'You *are* getting out?'

'I am, but I go as a man.'

She shook her head and pulled away from him. 'What? After all we discussed? No! You will be found out!'

'I trust not. I am sure I make a much better man than I would a woman!' He grinned, trying for lightness, but she did not appreciate the joke.

'But I have brought everything you need!'

'And I am grateful. But I go alone and I shall be dressed as a man.'

'Then let me go with you. They will not suspect a man and his "wife".'

'No, my sweet. I go alone or not at all.'

She took a deep unhappy breath. 'If they catch you . . .'

'If they catch me, it will be me alone, not you.' She tried to protest further, but he silenced her by putting his finger to her lips. Her lowered eyes told him of her submission. He said: 'I want you to do something for me. Did you bring scissors with you?'

Puzzled, she frowned. 'I brought half my sewing things, because I thought I might have to make adjustments to the extra skirt I am wearing so that it will fit you! What a waste of effort!'

He eyed up her person and realised that she actually looked a good deal fatter around the hips. God bless her! She had brought clothes for him, and to get them in, she was wearing them. He said, however: 'Good girl! I want you to cut my hair.'

She blinked. 'Cut your hair?'

He touched his hair. It fell past his shoulders in long red curls, almost like a woman's ringlets, he thought disgustedly. He hadn't bothered much about it during his time in Newgate, but he knew now that his hair would denounce him quicker than any traitorous friend. 'I cannot go out with all this!'

'I'm hardly a barber,' she warned.

'Just do your best, make it as short as you can.' He stood up from the bed, and motioned for her to move so that he could sit down on the stool with his back to her.

'Very well.' She fished around in her basket until she found the scissors, and then came up behind him. 'If you are sure about this?'

She was so close to him that her scent made him hunger for her. Instantly he was transported back to the day they first met, when he had sat on the rock, and she had been behind him, tending the cut on his head. So much had happened since then. 'I'm sure,' he confirmed.

She took a lump of his hair and hacked her way through it close to the scalp. She showed it to him, a long red ringlet. 'Throw it in the fire,' he commanded.

She did so and it fizzed as the flames consumed it.

She worked quickly and, he knew, with little science. He hated to think what the result looked like! All the while the nearness of her made him ache for her. When she came to the front of him to work, it was all he could do not to reach out for her. He no longer had the right.

'That's as much as I can do,' she told him at length.

He put his hands to his head, and it felt quite strange, his hair now short and stubbly all over, and there were places where he was sure his scalp was quite bald. It felt cold too. Well, when he was safe, he could let it grow again.

He stood up. 'Madam, I thank you.'

She was staring at him. 'You don't look like you,' she said. 'You look—oh, I don't know—rugged!'

He grinned. 'Do I? Perhaps I'll keep it like this, then!' The grin vanished. 'Thank you. Now you must go.'

Her eyes clouded. 'You need me, Roger. I don't think you will get out alone.'

'I will take my chances. I'll keep the extra cloak, if you do not mind.'

'Keep it. I have brought you some bread and cheese. It is all I could get without arousing suspicion. And some ale.' She pulled a bottle and a parcel wrapped in a cloth from her basket and set them on the table.

'Go, sweet lady,' he said again, his voice gentle, and he picked up her cloak and put it on her shoulders.

Clutching its edges, she pulled it around her, and he worked at the fastening. She was so close, the temptation was too much.

'Go.' He commanded.

She nodded mutely, not looking at him, and turned towards the door. There she hesitated and then turned back to him. For a long moment she looked at him as tears flooded her eyes.

'Oh, Roger!' In two steps she was in his arms, hiding her face in his neck. 'Oh, Roger, please take care! If ought happened to you, I couldn't bear it!'

His arms closed around her, feeling her body against his, the warmth of her through her clothes. This woman, the love of his life, had risked everything for him. For the last time, he held her in his arms, and as he did so his heart broke, for he knew this would never happen again. In another moment she would be gone forever out of his life, back to her husband and children.

A moment later she looked up at him, her eyes still flooded with tears. 'May God go with you Roger L'Estrange,' she whispered.

He felt as if he had a lump the size of a canon ball had lodged in his throat. 'And with you lady.'

She stood back from him, resolve straightening her back and holding up her chin up. Then, without another word, she left him.

FIFTY-FIVE

Knowing that most visitors would be leaving just before the gates closed for the night, Roger waited for his chance, sitting alone in his cell, eating some of the bread and cheese Ruth had brought him, and thinking of her. He remembered all the plans they had once made, the laughter they had shared, the arguments. He remembered their first meeting when he had found her bending over him as he lay on the ground, and later sitting in the warm sun on the river beach, and their first kiss, and how angry she had been at their first kiss, there in the snow.

She had her life now, with her children and her husband, and he could not take it away from her, or let her sacrifice it for him. He loved her too much to allow it.

As he waited, he listened for the sounds which would tell him people were leaving the prison and watched as the day grew darker outside, watching the shadows on the wall. He could not actually look out of the window unless he stood on the table, for it was high up in the wall, but he had become adept at telling the time of day by the pattern of the shadows.

Directing his thoughts away from Ruth, he tried to think of the future, with little success. His first objective must be to get out of London, which meant going south towards the River Thames, and then East until he reached London Bridge. He had no idea how far it was, or even if it were possible to walk along the river bank. He assumed (wrongly) that it would be a little bit like Lynn's river Ouse. Still, as his mother was fond of telling him, he had a tongue in his head and he could ask!

At last he heard the sounds which told him that others were beginning to leave the prison, and his insides lurched. This was it. He put on the large travelling cloak which Ruth had brought him. He had little else to take. Some papers which he stuffed inside his brown leather doublet, and the remainder of the food. He might need that later, although right now he was far too jumpy to consider eating. Lastly he took up his hat, no longer sporting a feather, and jammed it tightly on his head and pulled the brim down. It hadn't seen light of day in four long years, and it was a little moth-eaten, but it would serve his purposes.

With his nerves jangling and his hands shaking he pushed the iron-and-wooden door of his cell. True to his word, John had left it unlocked and it swung open noiselessly. He blessed the man! With his heart hammering in his chest, Roger stepped over the imaginary threshold into the outer chamber where John spent his time, the first time he had been outside that small cell in years. John was nowhere to be seen. *Thank you, Lord!*

The second door too had been left unlocked, and silently Roger again thanked his jailer.

He was now in a narrow corridor with windows which opened onto the yard. It had filled with people emerging from the cells and he found himself in company with a middle-aged gentleman.

'Who have you been visiting, sir?' the gentleman asked. He wore the dark garb which everyone wore in London these days, but he was expensively dressed for all that, with the finest quality cloth, neat stitching, and bone buttons.

'I've been to see Mr. L'Estrange,' Roger said. 'And you?'

'Ah, the man who should have hanged! I've been to see Mr. Longfellow. Is Mr. L'Estrange an acquaintance of yours then?'

Roger inclined his head as two females joined them in the march along the corridor but his heart was running at breakneck speed and his body wanted to join it. The last thing he wanted was to be in conversation with anyone. He said however: 'No. Just curious. And a little Christian charity.'

One of the ladies turned to Roger. 'It does you credit, sir, to help these poor wretches. The Lord knows they have little creature comforts in here.'

'In the common wards they have even less,' Roger observed.

'True, sir. But the stench! It fair turns my stomach, although they are good sport.' She meant that the common criminals, the lower classes, were fine entertainment to watch.

Roger's disgust must have shown on his face, for the gentleman said: 'If it were not for the entertainment, we would not come, would we?'

Roger said nothing. They had reached a door which stood open, with a guard. Another turnkey, Roger thought. Poorly dressed, hardly sober, and giving only a cursory glance to the people leaving the Press Yard.

Yet he peered at Roger, his alcohol-laden breath enough to stop a raging bull. Roger's heart seemed to drop to his shoes. 'Name?' he demanded.

Roger thought quickly. 'Ralph Calthorpe,' he said, thinking that if

Ruth had given her name on the way in, and it had been written down, the word 'Ruth' could be mistaken for 'Ralph' in a slovenly hand by someone who was only semi-literate.

The man looked at something—perhaps a list—while Roger stood quietly, despite every nerve in his body telling him to run. The turnkey looked at him again and then, evidently satisfied, indicated with a toss of his head that he should go through.

On the other side of the door, Roger took a breath. His whole body seemed to be shaking. He steadied himself and followed the crowd around the corner and down another corridor and had another inspection from that guard at the end. However, he again went through without a hitch. Surprising, really, he thought. For his heart was crashing so hard in his ribs he was sure everyone else could hear it!

They now descended some stone steps, through another door, and Roger found himself outside for the first time in four years. He took a lung full of (comparatively) fresh air, air filled with the smell of horse-dung, which was new, for he had not been near a horse in all his confinement. The sun was shining too, thin and wan, but shining, and for a brief moment he closed his eyes, feeling it on his face. He wanted to cry because it was so wonderful to be outside.

However, he was not yet free, and his heart stalled as he looked at what lay before him. He stood in the yard surrounded by the walls of the prison, the cells and rooms, where people were held at the whim of the law. He looked up and wondered briefly which cell had been his, if any of them. Perhaps his was on the other side. At the end of the yard was the outer gate itself, the New Gate. He had to get through that gate before he could be free.

People occupied almost every square inch of the yard, talking and jostling and eager to get out through the gate before it was locked for the night, more people than Roger had been used to. Momentarily they seemed overwhelming, but also glorious, for his solitary life had driven his depression. Helpful, too, for as he well knew, the best place to lose a book was in a library. Thankfully, Roger had lost the garrulous gentleman in the melee and now he mingled with the rest, blending in. Other men wore a plain doublet like his, and some wore cloaks. Mingling with them, Roger managed to thread his way through them until he was almost at the front of the queue.

The guards here were more plentiful in the gate and they seemed to be questioning some people and looking at others. The gate itself was open and he could see the busy street beyond, thronged with people, horses, carriages and the acrid stench of horse-manure. Freedom beckoned just a few feet in front of him.

'Name?' the guard demanded.

Roger looked up, surprised to be at the front. Again he used his new alias. 'Ralph Calthorpe.'

The man studied him. 'I ain't seen you afore.'

'First time,' Roger told him truthfully, but he was taken aback that in all these people the guard expected to recognise everyone. He hoped the man would be satisfied.

'Seeing a friend?'

'Bringing gifts of mercy,' Roger replied steadily, but his senses searched for his exit. A well-placed blow to the man's jaw would likely knock him off his feet, and Roger would make a break for freedom. True other guards had weapons, pistols and muskets, but if he moved fast enough they would probably not hit him. Probably. Possibly. Perhaps.

To his intense relief, the man waved him through.

Quite suddenly Roger found himself outside of Newgate, standing in the spring sunshine, feeling a breeze on his face, but he knew better than to hesitate. Opposite, in the jetty shadow of a building, he noticed a cloaked woman speaking with a man. A pair of horses pulling a cart with barrels on it clattered past, and with it he turned to his left, and tacked himself onto the rear of a group of people walking towards the south, towards the river.

§

Ruth had not been able to resist coming back to Newgate. She stood across the road, waiting anxiously for Roger, wanting to see him safely away. She had been there most of the afternoon, just standing and waiting and praying. She had watched countless people coming and going, had been accosted by a costermonger, a female selling mouldy apples, and a boy wanting to sweep a crossing for her, had her skirts splashed with filth from the road, but her eyes had watched the whole time for sight of Roger. Only when she knew he was safely away would she be able to rest.

'Why, Mistress Calthorpe!'

Ruth jumped and turned to find herself looking into the small grey eyes of the kindly, and rotund, reverend Thomas Thorowgood. She bobbed a curtsey. 'Sir!'

'Are you waiting for someone? Or may I escort you to your destination?'

'I—I am waiting for someone,' she said with perfect veracity, and wished he would go. What on earth was he doing here in London anyway? 'I do not need assistance, sir, I thank you.'

'For whom do you wait?'

Curse the man! He was certainly nosey. 'A friend.'

Mr. Thorowgood's bushy brows drew together above his nose, and Ruth coloured. 'A friend?'

Curse him! It really was none of his business!

Thankfully she was spared having to make an answer because she saw Roger emerge from the gate. She knew instantly that it was he, for her heart gave the tell-tale thud in her chest. He was taller than most, his hat jammed tightly on his head, his cloak pulled up, and he looked down at the ground as though trying to be inconspicuous. Oh, how she loved that man! How she ached to cross the road, to join him on his travels, to be his companion wherever he went.

She watched him as he walked past on the other side of the road without recognising her, which is what she had intended. She watched him raise his head high, every inch the proud cavalier, which no amount of plain clothes could disguise, and stride out in the direction of the river behind a group of people. In a short while he was out of sight around a bend.

She became aware of Thorowgood still standing beside her and turned to him. 'Forgive me, sir, you were saying?'

Thorowgood had been following the direction of her gaze, but now he turned his attention back to her and searched her face intently, and she knew he had the answer to his question before he asked it. 'Who was that man?'

Ruth again looked at the spot where Roger had disappeared from view around the corner.

She smiled. He was free. He was gone, but he was free! Her heart soared. He would live!

'That, sir,' she said, 'was Roger L'Estrange.'

The End.

If you have enjoyed reading FOR THE KING, please tell your friends, and please leave a review on Amazon.

LOYALTY CONFINED
By Roger L'Estrange

Beat on, proud billows; Boreas blow;
Swell, curled waves, high as Jove's roof;
Your incivility doth show
That innocence is tempest proof;
Though, surly Nereus frown, my thoughts are calm:
Then, strike, affliction, for thy wounds are balm.

That which the world miscalls a jail,
A private closet is to me;
Whilst a good conscience is my bail,
And innocence my liberty:
Locks, bars and solitude together met,
Make me no prisoner, but an anchoret.

When once my Prince affliction hath
Prosperity doth treason seem;
And to make smooth so rough a path,
I can learn patience from him:
Now not to suffer shows no loyal heart,
When kings want ease subjects must bear a part.

What though I cannot see my King,
Neither in prison or in coin;
Yet contemplation is a thing
That renders what I have not mine:
My King from me what adamant can part,
Whom I do wear engraven on my heart?

I, whilst I wished to be retired,
Into this private room was turned;
As if their wisdoms had conspir'd,
The salamander should be burn'd;
Or like those sophists that would drown a fish,
I am constrained to suffer what I wish.

The cynick loves his poverty;
The pelican her wilderness;
And 'tis the Indian's pride to be
Naked on frozen Caucasus:
Contentment cannot smart, stoicks we see
Make torments ease to their apathy.

These manacles upon my arm,
I as mistress' favours wear;
And for to keep my ancles warm,
I have some iron shackles there:
These walls are but my garrison; this cell
Which men call jail, doth prove my citadel.

I'm in the cabinet lokt up,
Like some high-prized margarite;
Or like the great Mogul or Pope,
Am cloister'd up from publick sight:
Retiredness is a piece of majesty,
And thus, proud Sultan, I'm as great as thee.

Here sin for want of food must starve,
Where tempting objects are not seen;
And these strong walls do only serve
To keep vice out and keep me in:
Malice of late's grown charitable sure
I'm not committed, but kept secure.

So he that struck at Jason's life,
Thinking t'have made his purpose sure,
By a malicious friendly knife,
Did only wound him to a cure:
Malice, I see, wants wit, for what is meant
Mischief, ofttimes proves favour by the event.

Have you not seen the nightingale,
A prisoner like, coopt in a cage:
How doth she chaunt her wanted tale
In that her narrow hermitage?
Even then her charming melody doth prove,
That all her bars are trees, her cage a grove.

I am that bird, whom they combine
Thus to deprive of liberty;
But though they do my corpse confine,
Yet maugre hate, my soul is free:
And though immured, yet can I chirp and sing,
Disgrace to rebels, glory to my King.

My soul is free as ambient air,
Although my baser parts immew'd
Whilst loyal thoughts do still repair
T'accompany my solitude;
Although rebellion do my body binde,
My King alone can captivate my minde.

AUTHOR'S NOTE

Sir Roger L'Estrange was famous in his own lifetime as a prolific writer, pamphleteer and, it has even been suggested, as the first publisher of a newspaper in England. Many of the phrases he used have passed into the English language, such as '*Free as ambient air*', '*live and let live*' and '*good servants, but bad masters*'.

The siege of King's Lynn and the L'Estranges' part in it is all based on fact and although there are many details available, it has been necessary to invent at times. We have no record of Roger's involvement in the royalist war effort, apart from the Battle of Newburn, except to know that he and Sir Hamon were there, but he was at Edgehill, and very likely in the cavalry. Neither do we know exactly what action Roger took during the siege. The events I have mentioned during the siege are matters of historical record, but whether Roger was personally present at each one is my conjecture. History merely tells us that he 'fought at King's Lynn.'

All the members of the L'Estrange household came from history. The Pastons are historical, as were the Cobbes and the Pells. However, while Sir Valentine Pell and his wife Barbara (Calthorpe) were historical, Ruth is an invention, as is Charles Calthorpe. All other members of the Pell family are historical, including Aunt Mary Lead and her husband. There is no record of the names of the constables who tried to arrest Sir Hamon. The reverend Thomas Thorowgood did indeed shelter Sir Hamon, and did also visit Roger in Newgate with Arrowsmith, and the events surrounding Roger's trial and imprisonment are historically accurate, including much of the dialogue.

Roger did indeed attempt to re-take King's Lynn after securing a commission from the King and he was betrayed by Leman the seaman and captured at Appleton House (which house no longer exists, but the Victorian house Appleton Farm has been built on the site and is part of the Queen's estate of Sandringham). The account of his trial and subsequent reprieve are all detailed in the excellent biography of Roger L'Estrange by George Kitchin, the principle source of my information.

Part of Hunstanton Hall still stands, although one wing and the old medieval hall succumbed to a devastating fire in 1850. Sir Hamon lived until 1654 dying at the age of seventy-one. His wife survived him by two years. His heir, Sir Nicholas L'Estrange died in 1655, so he only had a year to enjoy his inheritance. The family never quite recovered from the sequestrations placed upon them after the failed attempt at keeping the town for the King.

Roger did indeed slip out of Newgate 'with the privity of my keeper'! It has been suggested that Parliament was tired of keeping political prisoners, and had decided unofficially to let them go.

There were two explanations as to exactly when Roger met Leman. One suggestion is that Roger joined Prince Rupert's army and was at the Relief of Newark, and that it was there that he met Thomas Leman. The other account is as I have described.

BY THE SAME AUTHOR

GENTLEMAN OF FORTUNE,
The Adventures of Bartholomew Roberts,
Pirate

In 1719 third mate on the *Princess* Bartholomew Roberts is loading slaves on the West African Coast when he is captured by pirates. He has at first no intention of joining them until Captain Davis's death catapults him into the office of captain in his stead. As Roberts takes the pirate company to adventure and fabulous treasure in the Caribbean, his love for the beautiful Lúcia jeopardises his career.

His daring exploits soon come to the attention of the Admiralty in London, who commission Captain Chaloner Ogle to hunt him down. Ogle's obsession with finding Roberts is matched by Roberts' determination to evade justice and continue his ruthless pursuit of fortune. In a cat-and-mouse game up and down the slave and gold coasts of West Africa they become locked in a battle for survival. Can Roberts escape Ogle? Can he be reunited with Lúcia?

GENTLEMAN OF FORTUNE is a swashbuckling adventure and is based on the true story of Bartholomew Roberts.

www.evelyntidmanauthor.com

ONE SMALL CANDLE,
The Story of William Bradford and the Pilgrim Fathers

William Bradford is just eighteen when he leaves England with the Separatist congregation for Holland. However, struggling to make a living in Leyden, the Separatists decide to move again, to America.

The voyage on the *Mayflower* is plagued with difficulties and terrible sickness. But the Pilgrims make it to Plymouth, New England, where they begin the struggle to build a colony. William Bradford, as the governor of that colony, is their strength. Can he protect them from Indians? Can he turn around failed harvests? As the colony grapples with the wilderness, Will's heart aches for a forbidden love.

ONE SMALL CANDLE is the story of the birth of a nation, and is based on the true story of William Bradford and the Pilgrim Fathers.

ABOUT EVELYN TIDMAN

I was born in London in the 1950s, the daughter of avid readers. From an early age, my father not only taught me to read but also instilled in me his own passion for reading and writing. Before long, while still a child, I was writing my own stories.

In my teens discovered historical fiction in the form of Jean Plaidy, Georgette Heyer and, much later, Wilbur Smith, each of whom had a profound influence on me. Fascination with the true stories behind the fiction, about real people and events, led to my historical interest. With Errol Flynn dashing across the television screen on the end of a rope in Captain Blood, or clashing swords with Basil Rathbone in some other swashbuckler, I began to wonder what it was really like to be an eighteenth century pirate. The eventual result was Gentleman of Fortune, the Adventures of Bartholomew Roberts, Pirate. One Small Candle about the Pilgrim Fathers followed. For the King is based on a local event.

I live quietly in Norfolk with my husband and two spaniels.

Look out for further adventures of Roger L'Estrange in a sequel to For the King.

www.evelyntidmanauthor.com